A COURSE IN MIRACLES FOR DUMMIES
Volume I
Text Chapters #1-15

Author: Thomas R. Wakechild

Published by Bay West Centre LLC

Table of Contents

PREFACE

ACIM For Dummies

What we did and why?

1)We have taken what is commonly referred to as the second edition of the text of **A COURSE IN MIRACLES** and replaced pronouns and unclear references with their antecedents or meanings. This was done in an effort to clarify the text by making it more readable to the student. These changes are **clearly noted** and **highlighted in bold print**. Students are encouraged to cross-reference the highlighted **bold print areas** with their favorite version of the text. We believe that the substitution of pronouns and unclear references with their antecedents or meanings will make the text more readable, yet, at times, it will appear rather redundant. We have attempted to err on the redundant side rather than leave an area unclear as to what the pronoun might be referencing.

2)We have added notes or commentaries below each ACIM paragraph to assist the reader in their own interpretation of the paragraph. As we move through the text, the notes will become more extensive. We have attempted not to expand the comments beyond what has previously been mentioned in the text. Often, due to the circular nature of the text, previous areas that interrelate may be mentioned although most notes will directly relate to the current passage. These notes are designed to foster discussion and clarity, not to limit ideas and prevent expansion. Each person is on their perfect path and will glean something out of their studies. By offering this paragraph-by-paragraph format, we believe that the student will be assisted toward a more rewarding and expansive learning experience.

3)We have often come in contact with people who have dismissed ACIM as unreadable and too complex to study on their own or even in a group setting. This formatted material will allow an individual to move through the text in a timely and comprehensive manner. Most group classes take years before even one reading of the entire text has been completed. Often they must rely upon second-hand resources and "experts". This text will aid both group and independent, private study. It provides enough information to foster discussion and meditation for the serious inquirer. Never blindly accept another's explanation but rather go within and follow your own inner guide's advice.

4)If you are already involved in a private or group study plan and would like more information or perhaps adopt ACIM for Dummies as your preferred core source material, please feel free to contact us at **acourseinmiraclesfordummies.com.** We offer online, local and private classes. You can also register your approved ACIM for Dummies class at on our website or contact us for classes in your area.

Comparative Sample - ACIM Chapter 17.I

Below is an illustrative sample that compares the second edition text to the annotated ACIM for Dummies version. Anytime <u>ACIM for Dummies</u> replaces a word with its antecedent, this change is **clearly noted** and **highlighted in bold print**. Following each paragraph of the annotated text is a detailed explanatory note about that paragraph.

Chapter 17.
FORGIVENESS AND THE HOLY RELATIONSHIP

I. Bringing Fantasy to Truth

Text as it appears in second edition of ACIM
T-17.I.1. The betrayal of the Son of God lies only in illusions, and all his "sins" are but his own imagining. 2 His reality is forever sinless. 3 He need not be forgiven but awakened. 4 In his dreams he has betrayed himself, his brothers and his God. 5 Yet what is done in dreams has not been really done. 6 It is impossible to convince the dreamer that this is so, for dreams are what they are <because> of their illusion of reality. 7 Only in waking is the full release from them, for only then does it become perfectly apparent that they had no effect upon reality at all, and did not change it. 8 Fantasies change reality. 9 That is their purpose. 10 They cannot do so in reality, but they <can> do so in the mind that would have reality be different.

Revised text with antecedents / references in bold highlights
T-17.I.1. The betrayal of the Son of God lies only in illusions, and all his "sins" are but **the Son of God's** own imagining. 2 **The Son of God's** reality is forever sinless. 3 **God's Son** need not be forgiven but awakened. 4 In **the Son of God's** dreams **the Son of God** has betrayed himself, his brothers and his God. 5 Yet what is done in dreams has not been really done. 6 It is impossible to convince the dreamer that **what is done in dreams has not been really done in reality**, for dreams are what **dreams** are <because> of **the dream's** illusion of reality. 7 Only in **the dreamer's** waking is the full release from **dreams**, for only then does it become perfectly apparent **to the dreamer** that **dreams** had no effect upon reality at all, and **the dreamer's dreams** did not change **reality**. 8 Fantasies change reality **temporarily within the sleeping mind of the dreamer**. 9 That is **the** purpose **of fantasy**. 10 **Fantasy** cannot do so in reality, but **fantasy** <can> do so in the **sleeping** mind that would have reality be different.

Commentary on above ACIM paragraph
Note #1: Dreams have no effect on the reality of truth. Yet, to the dreamer during the sleeping state, the dream appears to be true. As long as the dreamer believes that the dream is his current experience, it will appear real to him. Within the dream itself, illusions are as strong in their effect on the dreamer's mind as what would normally be viewed as the truth. Once fully awakened, the dreamer realizes that the dream was a fantasy and, therefore, had no effect on the truth. Yet, while he was dreaming, the dream did appear to be his reality. During this dreaming state, the dream becomes the dreamer's provisional reality. All that appears within the dreamer's mind is not real to anyone else. We all agree when wide awake that any imagined "action" which took place during a dream should not be punished or rewarded

since it has no impact or effect on the truth of reality.

Text as it appears in second edition of ACIM
T-17.I.2.It is, then, only your wish to change reality that is fearful, because by your wish you think you have accomplished what you wish. 2 This strange position, in a sense, acknowledges your power. 3 Yet by distorting it and devoting it to "evil," it also makes it unreal. 4 You cannot be faithful to two masters who ask conflicting things of you. 5 What you use in fantasy you deny to truth. 6 Yet what you give to truth to use for you is safe from fantasy.

Revised text with antecedents / references in bold highlights
T-17.I.2. It is, then, only your wish to change reality that is fearful, because by your wish you think you have accomplished what you wish, **which was to change your reality**. 2 This strange position, **which is to change the appearance of reality within your own mind**, in a sense, acknowledges your power **to be the cause and source of your own experience**. 3 Yet by distorting **your power to be the cause and source of your own experience** and devoting **this power to be the cause and source of your experience** to "evil," it also makes **your perceived experience** unreal. 4 You cannot be faithful to two masters who ask conflicting things of you. **These two "master" are the thought system of the ego and the Holy Spirit's.** 5 What you use in fantasy you deny to truth. 6 Yet what you give to truth to use for you is safe from fantasy. **The ego is the protector of fantasy and the Holy Spirit's thought system is the defender of truth**

Commentary on above ACIM paragraph

Note # 2: God's Will is only that His Son should be happy. What causes us to be fearful is our belief that we have changed God's Will. Therefore, by our past actions, we believe that we have or will lose our happiness because we have tampered with God's reality. We have gotten caught up in the belief that we could oppose God's Will. We believe that our action actually changes the Mind of God. This is impossible since God's Will is changeless. The "problem" with the dream of separation was not our wanting to watch or play in the dream game of separation. Rather the problem occurred when we forgot that we were making up the dream. When we forgot we were the dreamer, we started to believe that our dream was true. We forgot to laugh and took the dream seriously. Fear was birthed within the dreamer's mind.

ACIM states that our mind has the power to create or project its own internal movies. These movies appear to be real within the dreamer's mind. The world of perception, time and space act as the movie screen for our mind's thoughts and desires. Yet, when we realize that our thoughts are projected into an illusionary world, we realize that the dream can have no impact on the reality of our real world called Heaven. These dreams or movies do affect the dreamer or moviegoer. By watching the movie, the observer is either entertained, taught some lesson, or both. When this paragraph references "evil," evil is the false belief that the Sonship, which is an Effect of God, could somehow change God's Will. An effect was no power to change its cause. The ego is the protector and "movie projector" of false images and the belief in fantasy. The Holy Spirit's thought system is the defender of truth

Text as it appears in second edition of ACIM
T-17.I.3. When you maintain that there must be an order of difficulty in miracles, all you mean is that there are some things you would withhold from truth. 2 You believe truth cannot deal with them only because you would keep them from truth. 3 Very simply, your lack of faith in the power that heals all pain arises from your wish to retain some aspects of reality for fantasy. 4 If you but realized what this must do to your appreciation of the whole! 5 What you reserve for yourself, you take away from Him Who would release you. 6 Unless you give it back, it is inevitable that your perspective on reality be warped and uncorrected.

Revised text with antecedents / references in bold highlights

T-17.I.3. When you maintain that there must be an order of difficulty in miracles, all you mean is that there are some things you would withhold from truth. 2 You believe truth cannot deal with **some things that you wish to withhold from truth** only because you would keep **some things** from truth. 3 Very simply, your lack of faith in the power that heals all pain **(the power of truth)** arises from your wish to retain some aspects of reality for fantasy. 4 If you but realized what this **desire to withhold some parts from truth** must do to your appreciation of the whole! 5 What you reserve for yourself **are your fantasies that are under the guidance of the ego's thought system. What you reserve for yourself,** you take away from **the Holy Spirit,** Who would release you **from these fantasies.** 6 Unless you give **all your fantasies** back **to the Holy Spirit,** it is inevitable that your perspective on reality **will** be warped and uncorrected

Commentary on above ACIM paragraph

Note # 3: Since only the Holy Spirit is aware of both the truth and your perceived dream, only the Holy Spirit has the knowledge to show you that the dream is not true. The Holy Spirit can only do this if you ask for His guidance. The Holy Spirit does not force you to listen to the truth against your free will. However, if you choose to give up only selective parts of your dream to the Holy Spirit for His reinterpretation, you will still remain trapped within the dream itself. You cannot pick and choose which part in the illusion you will keep and expect to awaken from your insanity. If you wish to awaken from the dream, all illusion must be given to the Holy Spirit. Until you give up all illusion, you will maintain the false idea that you could be something other than what you truly are. It is the things that we value that we refuse to give over to the Holy Spirit. People are willing to give up the illusion of pain and suffering but wish to maintain the illusion of pleasure and specialness. You cannot be "totally committed" some of the time. Truth is not a "sometimes thing."

Text as it appears in second edition of ACIM

T-17.I.4. As long as you would have it so, so long will the illusion of an order of difficulty in miracles remain with you. 2 For you have established this order in reality by giving some of it to one teacher, and some to another. 3 And so you learn to deal with part of the truth in one way, and in another way the other part. 4 To fragment truth is to destroy it by rendering it meaningless. 5 Orders of reality is a perspective without understanding; a frame of reference for reality to which it cannot really be compared at all.

Revised text with antecedents / references in bold highlights

T-17.I.4. As long as you would have **some parts of fantasy withheld from truth,** so long will the illusion of an order of difficulty in miracles remain with you. 2 For you have established this order **of difficulty into your** reality by giving some of **your fantasies** to one teacher, **the ego,** and some **of your fantasies** to another **teacher, the Holy Spirit.** 3 And so you learn to deal with part of the truth in one way, and in another way the other part. 4 To fragment truth is to destroy **truth** by rendering **truth** meaningless. 5 Orders of reality is a perspective without understanding. **Orders of reality are** a frame of reference for reality to which **reality** cannot really be compared at all

Commentary on above ACIM paragraph

Note # 4: By trying to seek guidance from two different teachers, the ego and the Holy Spirit, we receive two different sets of answers to each question that we ask. Both responses are based on the teacher's own viewpoint of reality. The ego's response represents the false, while the Holy Spirit's represents the truth. By attempting to listen to two totally different teachers with opposite belief systems, our world becomes very unstable. Now, instead of just true and false, we have introduced the concept of conditional truth or the "sometimes". Sometimes something is true; sometimes it is false. Now, we have varying degrees of truth, which claim to represent reality. Rather than absolute truth, each person has his or her own version of the truth. This varies from person to person and, therefore, each individual develops their own viewpoint and perception, which in turn becomes their own provisional reality. Because we have changed truth from an absolute to a maybe, we have introduced the concept that reality is a "sometimes thing." "Sometimes" creates degrees of difficulty. Prior to the existence of "sometimes," there was only the true and the false. Now, change has an endless array of possibilities. Our dream world has now become very complex with the introduction of partial or half-truths. With orders of reality, the absoluteness of true or false also loses its reality in the shifting sands of "sometimes" and "maybes."

Text as it appears in second edition of ACIM
T-17.I.5. Think you that you can bring truth to fantasy, and learn what truth means from the perspective of illusions? 2 Truth <*has*> no meaning in illusion. 3 The frame of reference for its meaning must be itself. 4 When you try to bring truth to illusions, you are trying to make illusions real, and keep them by justifying your belief in them. p351 5 But to give illusions to truth is to enable truth to teach that the illusions are unreal, and thus enable you to escape from them. 6 Reserve not one idea aside from truth, or you establish orders of reality that must imprison you. 7 There is no order in reality, because everything there is true.

Revised text with antecedents / references in bold highlights
T-17.I.5. Think you that you can bring truth to fantasy, and learn what truth means from the perspective of illusions? 2 Truth <*has*> no meaning in illusion. 3 The frame of reference for **truth's** meaning must be **truth,** itself. 4 When you try to bring truth to illusions, you are trying to make illusions real, and keep **illusions** by justifying your belief in **the illusions**. 5 But to give illusions to truth is to enable truth to teach that the illusions are unreal, and thus enable you to escape from **the illusions**. 6 Reserve not one idea aside from truth, or you establish orders of reality that must imprison you. 7 There is no order in reality, because everything there is true

Commentary on above ACIM paragraph
Note # 5: Reality is always true. There is only one choice we are asked to make. This choice is always between the true and the false. Reality is always true and fantasy is always false. "Something" does not vacillate between true and false. It is always only one or the other. We either know the truth, which is the real world of Heaven, or we appear to live in an illusionary fantasy of perception, which becomes our provisional reality. There is no in between.

Text as it appears in second edition of ACIM
T-17.I.6. Be willing, then, to give all you have held outside the truth to Him Who knows the truth, and in Whom all is brought to truth. 2 Salvation from separation would be complete, or will not be at all. 3 Be not concerned with anything except your willingness to have this be accomplished. 4 He will accomplish it; not you. 5 But forget not this: When you become disturbed and lose your peace of mind because another is attempting to solve his problems through fantasy, you are refusing to forgive yourself for just this same attempt. 6 And you are holding both of you away from truth and from salvation. 7 As you forgive him, you restore to truth what was denied by both of you. 8 And you will see forgiveness where you have given it.

Revised text with antecedents / references in bold highlights
T-17.I.6. Be willing, then, to give all you have held outside the truth to Him, **the Holy Spirit,** Who knows the truth, and in Whom all **fantasy** is brought to truth. 2 Salvation from separation would be complete, or **salvation from separation** will not be at all. 3 Be not concerned with anything except your willingness to have **salvation from separation** be accomplished. 4 **The Holy Spirit** will accomplish

salvation from separation; not you. 5 But forget not this: When you become disturbed and lose your peace of mind because another is attempting to solve his problems through fantasy, you are refusing to forgive yourself for just this same attempt **to solve your problems through fantasy**. 6 And you are holding both you **and your brother** away from truth and from salvation. 7 As you forgive **your brother**, you restore to truth what was denied by both you **and your brother**. 8 And you will see forgiveness where you have given **forgiveness.**

Commentary on above ACIM paragraph

<u>Note # 6:</u> When you become disturbed and lose your peace of mind because your brother is attempting to solve his problems through fantasy, you are judging another and are falling into the same egoic belief system in which he is suffering. Both of you are now seeing yourselves as separate and with some power and will outside the Will of God. Rather than judge your brother, you need to turn the moment over to the Holy Spirit. Only by giving this moment over to the Holy Spirit can you avoid the pitfalls of the ego's thought system. When we judge, we are saying that something is unacceptable to us and that we are separate from our brother. If we wish to change our brother, we are also saying that our egoic self has the power to change our brother. By myself (the ego, or little "s" self), I can do nothing. Yet, through me, God can do everything. We need to turn our egoic judgments over to the Holy Spirit and get out of God's way.

Again, under the laws of God, "To give is to receive." When we grant forgiveness to a brother, we grant forgiveness to ourselves.

The Story Behind A Course In Miracles For Dummies

How It Came About

I was an unlikely candidate or transmission vehicle for writing <u>A Course In Miracles for Dummies</u>. This is because I would be looked upon as a relatively new student with no formal training in ACIM. I drew no information from second hand sources or previous publications about the course. People are often surprised to discover that prior to 2004 I had never even heard of <u>A Course In Miracles</u>. Being unfamiliar with the work, it is surprising that by 2007, <u>A Course in Miracles for Dummies</u> had been completed. This is why I would say that I was chosen and that ACIM for Dummies came through me and was not of me. It was something that I was chosen and guided to do through the Holy Spirit.

The reason that I was an unlikely candidate has nothing to do with my background. Instead, it was because I was no longer seeking to find anything new on the spiritual level. For me, my spiritual seeking years seemed to be over. I felt that I had already found what I had been looking for. For many years I had been on a mission of self-discovery with the goal of not having to return to this time-space continuum. I did not want to come back to earth. I had utilized the first 50 years of my life to move towards that goal. I felt that I had found what I was looking for and that the goal was within my reach. I knew I was the creator of my experiences. I thought I had already moved out of fear-based thinking and that I had found the inner peace that comes from trusting my Higher Self. Thus, I felt I had moved from being a seeker to someone who had found their path. It had been a convoluted path up the mountain but I was satisfied with my progress and felt that it was unnecessary to go off on some other path. Therefore, it is more appropriate to say that <u>A Course in Miracles</u> found me to be its instrument for I certainly was not looking for ACIM to enter my life at that time.

The path that I had chosen was a blend of the Eastern mystical traditions and the self-improvement concepts of Western thought. This strange combination had helped me become what I would call a practical mystic. Meditating daily, I was able to move quite successfully in the world of business and finance and yet maintain a high level of spirituality and inner peace. I was someone who was in the world but no longer attached to it. Hinduism has the concept of different stages of life that people should naturally pass through during their lifetime. According to Hinduism, around the age of 50, we should be looking at leaving the business world and focusing our attention on our spiritual growth on a full-time basis. This was my intent. I had already sold my business and was transitioning out of the business world. My wife longed to escape from the cold sunless, gray winters of Michigan and spend her winters in the sun. Unlike most Midwesterners, we felt that out destiny laid west of the Mississippi. We wished to explore the Southwest as a possible future home site.

Originally, we had just planned to visit the southwest and try to narrow down the list of possible communities that we might like to live in. Yet, upon this initial visit, we felt that we had found what we were looking for and we purchased a home in Arizona. This early purchase could allow my wife, Nancy, to spend her first winter out of the cold if she so desired. But unfortunately for me, I had a prior commitment that required my return to Michigan for the winter. Thus, if she where to stay, she would have to spend the winter alone. We decided to go for it. We set up housekeeping in our new winter home in the late fall. Nancy would remain throughout the winter while I would return to Michigan in early January to fulfill my commitment. Once completed, I was to rejoin my wife in Arizona. When the weather broke in the late spring, we would return to our Michigan home. Since she would be alone for about three months, I wanted her to develop a social support network of friends and neighbors that could help her pass her time while we were apart. It was during this initial stay in Arizona that Nancy decided to attend a weekly class that was beginning on <u>A Course in Miracles</u>. When I returned to Arizona that spring, I discovered that Nancy was still involved with ACIM.

In the spring of 2004, we returned to our Michigan home. Nancy would now have to be on her own if she were to continue studying the course. She continued her independent studies by reading the text, doing her workbook lessons and sometimes asking me questions about what she had read. When she referenced the text, it became apparent that the text was not the most clearly written document in the world. It was complex and mystifying. Each paragraph would often use pronouns that were difficult to determine what they originally referenced. You need to carefully go back to earlier paragraphs or sentences to be able to trace the antecedent for that unclear reference or pronoun. Once this was done however, the passage might become clearer but too often they seemed to remain nonsensical to the everyday reader. The text was not easy to decipher and often used terminology that had specific unique definitions that were different from common everyday usage. The text required a comprehensive systematic study plan since a casual reading of the material would not release ACIM's secrets for retraining the mind. This mind training entails the reprogramming of our own egoic fear-based thought system. If the reader is unwilling to examine the textual context outside of their own fear-based thinking, the reader will encounter a great deal of stress and the Course will seem insane and counter intuitive. This is because the ego always resists any attempt to change its old programming. This old programming supports the belief that you are the body. It tells you that you are a victim and not the creator of your world. It takes a great deal of fortitude and will power to change this mind set and go through this process of retraining your mind. This is why the workbook lessons have been provided. The workbook moves the intellectual concepts of the text from the head to the heart. Since many students fail to do the daily workbook lessons, the change they claim they seek is not forthcoming. ACIM requires effort, not just good intentions. Since most of us are entrenched in our fear-based programming, the peace of God that is our destiny remains an elusive mystery to our minds. The ego has no desire to change. As the course says, our tolerance for pain is great, but it is not unlimited and until you say, ' There must be a better way," you will continue to follow the advice of the fear-based thought system of the ego.

Since I wanted to encourage Nancy to continue her work with ACIM, I thought it would be helpful and most appropriate to actually read the text. I was fascinated by its claims of authorship. Since ACIM claimed to be a work dictated by Jesus to Helen Schucman, I was interested in seeing what it actually said. The book seemed to call to me. When I read the introduction, "Nothing real can be threatened. Nothing unreal exists." I knew that this was not a book of this world. Although the main ideas were not new to me, they were presented in a systematic way that included a complete philosophical argument that revelation had taught me, but that revelation could not explain. What was more fascinating was the idea that it was not just a theoretical text. It actually had a workbook that was included. This workbook could allow anyone to actively participate in the process of their own self-enlightenment without the need of some outside guru. If this was the case, this would be truly helpful and liberating for human consciousness. I tried ACIM out. I did the work. After one year I had completed the 365 workbook lessons. I realized that ACIM was a complete independent self-study class that was available to anyone who was really serious about their own spiritual growth. What had taken me years of study could be achieved inexpensively by thoroughly studying and practicing one book. It was self-contained. Not only that, if properly understood, ACIM could move the student beyond simply managing or coping with their fear. It could actually provide a new paradigm that would overcome fear. This new paradigm was based on forgiveness and love. I realized that over the course of my studies, I had become excellent at coping with fear but still had not completely removed fear from my life. Intellectually, I have never been able to fully reconcile the contradictory concepts of a God of unconditional love with free will. This apparent contradiction had always left a fear-based grain of doubt in my mind. I had always wanted to intellectually understand what revelation had taught me. That there is just the One Self and we are That One.

Both the Buddha and Jesus came from the mystical traditions. Both taught from their own insights which came from their personal revelation. They quieted their egoic mind and went within. Buddha's teachings came more from the seventh chakra, which is associated with the mind or the intellect. Jesus' teachings came from the fourth chakra which is associated with the heart. Two thousand years ago when Jesus walked the earth, mankind did not have the scientific knowledge or the language to explain the psychology behind his teachings. His teachings were to be understood through the heart, not the mind. After Jesus' death and the death of his direct disciples, the meaning of his esoteric message became even murkier than when he had originally pronounced them. Personal revelation has never been a practical means for the masses to obtain an understanding of someone else's teachings. If what was later to be called Christianity was to have a wide appeal to the masses, all its teachings needed to be codified. This codification would allow the new message to be taught in a uniform way rather than through individual personal revelation. Thus, the church leaders attempted to explain Jesus' teachings on the egoic level of the body-mind. Unfortunately, any attempt to explain Jesus' teachings like "I and the Father are One,' is difficult. It is impossible to explain this concept of Oneness at the egoic level that perceives the separation to be real. Some church leaders, believing themselves to be separate ego-bodies, could not help but interpret Jesus' message on a fear based level. Thus, Jesus, who claimed to be just like us, was made into God's only begotten Son and thus, different from you and I. This clearly implies that the separation is real. When you attempt to explain Jesus' esoteric teachings on the level of the egoic mind, they became shrouded in mystery because they are unexplainable on the egoic level.

ACIM is Jesus' attempt to bridge the gap between personal revelation and our ego's need to intellectually understand. Jesus is trying to correct the multiple mistakes about his teachings that continue to perpetuate the fear-based thought system that we see so prevalent in the western religions of Judaism, Christianity and Islam. Two thousand years ago, the concept of a Oneness Of All That Is could only be understood through the mystical tradition of personal revelation. By the 20th century, however, mankind had started to unlock the psychological secrets of our own mind's ability to project its internal beliefs upon the world that we perceive. Later in the 20th century, with the arrival of quantum physics and string theory, the idea that this world could be created through individuated consciousness is not the crazy idea that it would have been two thousand years ago. String theorists now tell us that whole galaxies exist merely because there is some astronomer, somewhere, that wants to observe them. If an astronomer's conscious desire can create a galaxy, the idea that we can create our own world of private individuated perception does not seem so far-fetched. In ACIM, Jesus utilizes the text to explain his teachings on the intellectual level to satisfy our need to understand things egoically. He couples the text with the workbook lessons that are aimed at transporting these ideas from the mind to the heart. Thus, in A Course in Miracles, Jesus has provided the reader a complete system of self-study that can achieve the desired results of reawakening our One Self to the truth of what we truly are. This can be done either through the mind or the heart. Coupled together, the workbook and text provide a student with the ability to move from the egoic fear-based thought system to a new paradigm based on forgiveness, love and the guidance of the Holy Spirit.

A mystic does not rely on the intellectual study of someone else's teachings. A mystic learns through personal revelation. Revelation is inspired through direct insight. Although a mystic may have difficulty explaining to another why and what he knows, the mystic will know that he knows.   The mystical experience, being personal, requires no explanation.   Revelation just is. Yogi Paramahansa Yogananda, founder of the Self Realization Fellowship, teaches that the best way to understand the written word is to read a few words, a sentence or passage. Next, you seek guidance and finally, you meditate on those words. Through this three-step process, one gains the wisdom that the passage seeks to inspire within you. This is what I did with the ACIM text material that became <u>ACIM for Dummies</u>. Because I was already free from most egoic fear-based thinking, my mind could act as a clearer channel for inspiration from the Holy Spirit. Yogananda's three step study method reduces the egoic mind chatter and quiets the mind, thus allowing the practitioner to hear the truth.

When I first began studying ACIM, I would make notes on what the passages said. I would sit at the dining room table for hours reading and studying the material. Most people would consider this a waste of time and not worth the effort. But I pressed on because that is what guidance told me I should do. Perhaps, more importantly, I pressed on because I was getting something out of it. It was all making sense. I realized that the material was synthesizing all the assorted parts of the puzzle that I had gleaned from my previous studies. Over the past years, I had found many pieces to the puzzle. Yet, no one system seemed to have the whole answer. Each system often was only a partial solution. But through the past amalgamation of these various programs, I had developed a working concept of the whole. Yet, there were still many missing parts or gaps that remained beyond the reach of my previous studies. Everything fit loosely together but the reasoning behind it still remained a mystery in my mind. The ACIM text was solving the whole puzzle on an intellectual, or should I be as bold to say, on the egoic level of understanding. The text did not move the information to the heart that, of course, was left to the workbook lessons. But the text did provide practical solutions to everyday problems. It was not just an esoteric document that sounded nice but was impossible or impractical to implement in your everyday world of individuated perception. After one year dedicated to the Course, I had a good working knowledge of what the Course taught and more importantly what it could do when you choose to silence the ego and listen to the guidance of the Holy Spirit.

Throughout this period, I had many serendipitous events that mysteriously moved me forward in this work. When we returned to Arizona the next fall, I attended Nancy's ACIM class which consisted of reading from the text and some discussion. When the class was having a difficult time understanding a paragraph, I would often read the paragraph out loud while replacing the pronouns with their antecedents. This simple exercise helped clarify the passage. One day someone gave me a complete electronic version of ACIM on a computer CD. Since I was computer illiterate, I was unable to access this CD. Yet, once again an unsolicited volunteer showed up at my home and got this CD functional and then proceeded to show me how to work the word-processing program on my computer. People kept showing up in my life to secretly assist me with this undisclosed mission. Numerous people arrived on my doorstep offering materials that they felt guided to give me. My guidance indicated that I should not read or study any material that was not directly channeled from Jesus. I was not to read any ACIM material that came from any secondhand sources. My study was to be limited to direct source content only. This was fine with me since I preferred to keep my mind clear from any second party observations.   Direct source material is always preferable over secondhand thinking that can contaminate the reception process.

The actual material for <u>A Course in Miracles for Dummies</u> was generated without the intent of it ever being made public. It was to be a private document that I was drawn to work on because that is what spirit advised me to do. No one was advised as to what I was doing and I had no idea why I was directed to do it. I just followed my inner guidance and trusted. In hindsight, I believe that I was given the task simply because I would do it. Each night at approximately 2:00 to 3:00 AM, I would be awakened by spirit to continue the writing process. I would normally cover one subsection a day. I would read the prior, current and next subsection of the text that I was working on. Next, I would meditate on it. Finally I was directed to go to the computer and transcribe what was forthcoming. I would ask for guidance then replace the text pronouns and references with their antecedents. I would then write the explanatory notes that came into my awareness for that ACIM paragraph. I completed one paragraph before moving to the next paragraph. After it was completed, I would normally go back to bed. That was the daily process.

The materials stayed on my computer with seemingly no other purpose other than for my own personal insight and as an exercise in following the guidance of the Holy Spirit. Eventually, this body of work caught up with the same chapter we were studying in our class. I showed the material to Nancy and asked what she thought. Since she found it helpful, I decide to take my annotated version of the material to the class so that I could use it as a reference tool. Some of the other students wanted their own copies since they found it helpful in their comprehension of the teachings. One of the class members suggested that I eventually publish the material. I told her that would be impossible since the material pivoted off of previously copyrighted materials. I thought that that would be the end of the matter. Instead, she informed me that the copyright that been broken and that she had been involved in the case. She also told me that she had received a letter to that effect and she would give me a copy. Within an hour she was at my doorstep with the letter. I still didn't see any likelihood of the material that I was working on extending beyond this class. It was too voluminous for any publisher to pick up for such a small niche market. So I just continued with the daily processes thankful that someone had found the information useful.

Later someone suggested since this was the computer age that I should get a website and he would help me develop it. He also suggested that I should create an e-book and make it available to the public. This ultimately led to the website **acourseinmiraclesfordummies.com.** When we got the website up and running, I felt that my tasks had been completed. To my surprise, people throughout the world discovered this website and found it aided them in their effort to rediscover who they truly are.

I trust that the Holy Spirit will continue to guide whomever this material is meant for.
All my life, I have felt like I was preparing myself for something. Preparing for what? I did not know but if and when it arose, I wanted to be ready. With <u>ACIM for Dummies</u> completed, I feel that I have fulfilled my life's purpose. Throughout this process I have felt guided and directed by spirit. I am grateful for all the help that I have received and continue to receive on this project from both people like you and the Holy Spirit.

Create a great day
Love and peace,

Tom Wakechild

The Quest

About the Author, Thomas R. Wakechild

The Recurring Nightmare

As a child, I cannot remember going to bed without a sense of fear and dread. I had a recurring dream or more accurately, a recurring nightmare. I was sitting on the basement steps of my home and there, I witness a horrible crime being committed. The perpetrator of the crime had not noticed my presence and as he continued his dastardly assault upon his victims, I had plenty of time to escape unnoticed by going up the steps, locking the door and returning to the safety of my home. But, unfortunately for me, I was unable to turn and move up the steps and so escape the attention of the criminal. I seemed paralyzed with fear. Finally the crime was over. My twin sisters were dead. The executions were completed and now the perpetrator, my father, turned to leave the crime scene so that he could be free to kill again. As he turned, my father spotted me sitting on the steps. I still had plenty of time to escape. All I needed to do was turn and run up the stairs and lock the basement door. Yet, I was paralyzed with fear. I tried to move but I remained frozen to the steps. I tried to scream for help, yet nothing came out. At first, his movements were slow, as if he thought that I had not noticed him spotting me. But as he saw me looking at him and attempting to scream, he picked up the pace. Finally, he reached the stairs and quickly accelerated up them. I, still frozen with fear, could do nothing to defend or save myself. My father was upon me and it was quickly over for me. I had been unable to even get out a whimper, let alone a scream. I had done nothing. Fear had immobilized me and rendered me incapable of responding to the situation. The escape from this recurring nightmare has been my quest ever since.

Perceiving this world to be a living hell, I was always terrorized by the thought that when I died, I would have to come back to this earth and do it all over again. Therefore, I lived in a constant state of fear. Fear of what? Fear of the idea that I was not good enough to ever escape the torment that seemed to be my lot in life. Being raised a Catholic, I believed that I had been born in original sin and that God would judge me and find me wanting. If I escaped this earth, it would only be to be damned eternally to a place that was worse. Yet, I found it hard to imagine anything worse than being on this earth. On earth, you were constantly being judged and found not worthy. Being not good enough meant that you were also incapable of earning love. The universe was a cruel and loveless place. I was a victim. Everybody was out to get me and my major objective was not to be caught. By my teenage years, if you had awakened me from a deep sleep and asked me what my purpose was, I would have blurted out, "Not to come back here."

The First Breakthrough

My first major breakthrough occurred in an unlikely place, my high school biology class. When discussing genetics, the teacher illustrated the probability of receiving a certain genotype. His example utilized the tossing of a coin and the likelihood that it would be heads. It seems that if a person were to flip a coin, each coin flip was independent of past results. The likelihood of each coin flip would always be 50% heads and 50% tails. No matter how many times you had flipped the coin in the past, with each new flip the odds remained 50-50. This meant that the past did not control the present or the future. This was a new concept to me. Prior to that, I had felt what had happened in the past must continue to happen in the present and the future. What I gleaned from probability theory was that the universe could be neutral. The past did not dictate the future. If someone had fourteen years of bad luck, that didn't mean that he was doomed to have "bad luck" for the rest of his life. It opened my mind up to the possibility that the universe could actually be a neutral place and that good or bad "luck" was a 50-50 proposition. I perceived the possibility that I could have a run of fourteen years of good luck coming just as easily as bad luck. I could live in a world where the past did not determine the present or the future. This was now a possibility for me. I was slowly beginning my ascent from victim consciousness into becoming a proactive and creative force in my life.

Still as a teenager, I had another breakthrough. I read Napoleon Hill's classic book <u>Think and Grow Rich</u>. That turned me on to the idea that thoughts are things and that "as a man thinketh, so he becomes." I began my search for self-improvement and self-empowerment. This search, however, continued to have its major focus on escaping the confines of earthly existence. Planet Earth was still a place from which to escape.

The New Goal

In my early 20s, I took a proactive stance in regards to my life. I no longer saw myself as a victim and realized that this earth provided a vast array of possibilities. I wanted to avoid what I perceived as the traps of world materiality and getting too involved with earthly matters. Rather than attempt to change the earth, I felt that the earth would benefit best if I became a better me. By becoming a better person, I felt that I would be more capable of responding to any situation that the future might bring. That the best example I could give to the world was to live a good life. I felt that spirituality and wealth were incompatible. I wanted to adopt the attitude of a young child. Most children in their early years are inquisitive and absorbed in learning. A young child enters life with a sense of awe, adventure and wonderment. They see their world as a play school. This innocence and desire for learning often is transformed by our environment into the need to conform and please our family and society. The inquisitive sense of learning and awe is replaced by the need to earn their parents, peers and society's approval. The need to get the right answer replaces the natural wonderment of the learning process and now life becomes drudgery. As we grow up, life becomes an attempt to earn someone's love and respect. Life is no longer fun but rather a competitive struggle. As we move from early childhood into our teen and adult years, we gradually exchange our desire to be happy for our need to be right. Constant judgment leads us to sacrifice our happiness so that we can claim we are right even when we are dead wrong. Rightness, not our happiness, becomes the major objective of our life.

As a tool to help maintain my focus on the spiritual goal of escaping earthly bounds, I decided to change my last name. I wanted to maintain a young child's attitude of wonderment while I learned to awaken from the nightmare of earthly limitations. I wanted to awaken to my true spiritual essence. In short, I desired enlightenment. Since I wanted to awaken from my childhood nightmare yet maintain the wonderment of the young child, I selected "Wake-Child" to be my new last name. By doing this, I would be constantly reminded of my spiritual goal. Anytime I heard, spoke or wrote my last name, I would be constantly reminded of my true life purpose.

The Journey

By my mid-20s, I was already an instructor for the School of Metaphysics. This is where I learned about manifestation or the creation process. Utilizing these tools of manifestation, I moved into the business world. I started a new lucrative and successful business consulting firm. What differentiated my firm from my competitors was that rather than just focus on the bottom line, we were equally concerned with the lifestyle of the owners and their employees. By moving into the competitive world of business, I was able to meld the esoteric with the material. I became a practical mystic. I learned to operate in the world but not necessarily be of the world. While operating this business, I continued to seek spiritual growth by delving into both Eastern religious practices and Western self-help programs. In the late 1990s, I was fortunate to work with Harry Palmer as an Avatar Wizard. Harry's work provided the key to unlocking the power of what I would call discreation. Now I seemed to have both sides of the equation. The School of Metaphysics had taught the principles of manifestation and Avatar taught how to discreate any beliefs that no longer served me. You would think that having the power to create and discreate would result in the elimination of fear. But this was not the case. Instead, what I had learned was how to manage and mitigate fear. Yet, the elimination of all fear remained an unrealized and elusive goal.

Moving the Rig

When looking for oil, people tend to place an oil rig in one location and continue to drill the hole wider and deeper with the hopes that if they go wide and deep enough, they may eventually hit a pocket of oil. Others play it safe and drill in the vicinity of an already proven field. This method tends to reduce the risk of total failure. Yet, the overall gain in new oil is rather minimal. The new well is merely siphoning off part of the proven reserves of the old well. Yet, if we look historically, we will find that most new oil fields are discovered not by drilling wider and deeper, but by pulling the rig and moving it to a totally different area.

If we are to escape fear, one must be willing to examine their fear-based belief system. If your belief system is based on fear, you can dig deeper and deeper into the field of fear and yet never escape from fear. Why? Because you remain digging in the domain of fear. Since you refuse to leave the field of fear, the mitigation and management of fear becomes the only favorable scenario that could possibly be achieved. In order to escape fear, one must be willing to explore a thought system that is not fear based. A Course In Miracles (ACIM) offers a new paradigm that allows the student to shift from a fear based thought system to one that is love based. ACIM offers the student a methodology to examine the beliefs that make up their current thought system. Once examined, if these beliefs are determined to be incapable of securing the prize that one seeks, it is insanity to expect different results by continuing to follow that same failed belief system. If one discovers that their beliefs about God, their world, and who they are consistently leaves them in fear, sanity would require that one look in another direction. You need to stop drilling in the field of fear and go somewhere else. You need to tell yourself that there must be a better way. ACIM offers an approach that not only allows you to minimize and mitigate your fears but offers a way out of fear itself.

In 2004, I first became aware of A Course in Miracles. Yet, when I first picked up the book, I realized that ACIM provided the missing link that had prevented me from achieving my goal of overcoming fear. It was a complete philosophical thought system that also contained a series of workbook lessons that if followed, would allow the ideas to move from the mind to the heart. The Holy

Spirit seemed to call to me and I was ready. Although the Eastern religions had talked about the world as being an illusion, this concept had never really made much sense to me. Experience had taught me that this so call world of illusion could not be the work of a loving God. ACIM instead clearly states that God did not create this world. We did. And with that one thought, all the pieces of the puzzle fit together. This world is not a world of physical reality. Instead, it is a world of individuated perception. Our perception makes our experiences which we perceive to be our reality. As <u>A Course in Miracles</u> states, "If God made this world, He indeed would be cruel." As long as I perceive my world to be created by God, I would always be able to the blame God for creating this world that blocked true happiness for myself and my loved ones. For any god that created this world could not be a God of unconditional love. As long as God's love was not unconditional, it would have to mean that love was conditional at best and more likely impossible. You could never escape fear for there would always be the implied threat that God could withdraw His love if you failed to make the grade. If God's love was conditional, it implied that God was constantly judging us to determine whether or not His love should be withdrawn. Love would have to be earned. If God did not create my world of individual perception, then God indeed could still be a loving God. This thought gave me the confidence to move the drilling rig from the field of fear to the field of love. ACIM says there are two emotions, fear and love. Each emotion has a thought system associated with it. Only in a love based thought system can fear be made to disappear into the nothingness from which it arose. Only love can bring us home.

The New Visionary Dream

I was walking through a deep forest. Suddenly I came to a clearing. I realized it was not just a clearing but the end of the forest. There, before me was a vast plain. There was a wall that divided the plain into two separate halves. On my side, the land was parched and dry. On the other side, green fields seemed to stretch into infinity. I approached the wall. It was thick, made of stone and too high for me to reach the top and pull myself over. I kept jumping but to no avail as the top remained just beyond my reach. I struggled to find a handhold that would give me the additional leverage that I needed if I was to reach the top. Finally, after many attempts, I was able to grab the top of the wall and I struggled to pull myself over the top. I succeeded. Exhausted, I laid resting on the top of the wall. The wall was about four feet thick so one could safely stand upon it As I laid on the wall, I heard a voice from the other side telling me to jump off the wall and claim my prize. I stood up on the wall and looked over the lush landscape and admired my prize. The other person at the base of the wall was there to help me. He was an angel. The angel exclaimed, "You've made it. Your home. Quickly jump and claim your prize." Yet, just before I jumped to the safety of the other side, I paused for a moment and looked back upon the land that I had traversed. In the distance, there seemed to be some movement. I strained my eyes and was able to determine that another person was attempting to escape from that same forest. I yelled at the top of my lungs and waved my arms. He saw me. He started running towards me. The angel once again implored me to jump and save myself. I paused, and calmly said. "No, someone is coming. Let me help him scale this wall. It will only take a minute." As the young man approached, I once again laid flat on the wall with my hand outstretched. The young man grasped my hand and I easily pulled him up. I then told him to jump down to save himself. He did not hesitate. He jumped down and he was home. Once again I stood on the top of the wall and prepared to jump down and join my comrade. But before I jumped, I heard someone else cry out from the distance. Another person had made their way out of the forest. Once again I hesitated, than decided to resume my post on top of the wall. Again, the angel told me to save myself. "Just one more," I said. I got down on that wall and pulled my brother over. Before I could even get up, I saw another and yet another. They were now coming fast out of the woods and I called back to the angel and said. "Just one more! Just one more!"

I got caught up in the enthusiasm of helping each one over the wall. I was straddling this wall and pulling people over the top, yet I had forgotten that my goal had always been to get to the other side. I had wanted to be home. Finally I felt a strong arm on my shoulder. It was the angel. He pulled me to my feet. I was now standing face to face with the angel on top of the wall. I told him, "Leave me alone. There are other people to help." Then the angel stepped back and physically turned me so that I could see down the length of the wall. And there on top of that wall that had been so empty were hundreds of people laying flat helping others over the wall. It seemed that some of the people that I had helped over the top had also stopped and joined in helping their brothers and sisters get home. Next, I saw a man who had been standing on top of the wall being handed a sledgehammer. He started pounding the top of the wall with that hammer. He pounded on the wall until finally a single stone gave way. Then another fell off. Then someone else grabbed a sledgehammer and started working next to the first man, enlarging the opening in the wall. Now the people at the base of the wall started clawing at the opening. They too began pulling the stones down. Finally, the opening had reached the ground and the people just started pouring through the wall. And then, the angel took my hand and together we jumped down. My work was over and I was home.

PROLOGUE

What I did and why?

1) I have taken what is commonly referred to as the second edition of the text of A COURSE IN MIRACLES and replaced pronouns and unclear references with their antecedents or meanings. This was done in an effort to clarify the text by making it more readable to the student. These changes are **clearly noted** and **highlighted in bold print**. Students are encouraged to cross-reference the highlighted **bold print areas** with their favorite version of the text. I believe that the substitution of pronouns and unclear references with their antecedents or meanings will make the text more readable, yet, at times, it will appear rather redundant. In some cases the reference is clarified in previous, current or following paragraphs. I have attempted to err on the redundant side rather than leave an area unclear as to what the pronoun might be referencing.

2) I have added notes or commentaries below each ACIM paragraph to assist the reader in their own interpretation of the paragraph. As we move through the text, the notes will become more extensive. I have attempted not to expand the comments beyond what has previously been mentioned in the text. Often, due to the circular nature of the text, previous areas that interrelate may be mentioned although most notes will directly relate to the current passage. These notes are designed to foster discussion and clarity, not to limit ideas and prevent expansion. Each person is on their own perfect and unique path. Each will benefit from their own independent or group studies. By offering this paragraph-by-paragraph format, we believe that the student will be assisted toward a more rewarding and expansive learning experience. Your choice of paths will always be the perfect path for you.

We have often come in contact with people who have dismissed ACIM as unreadable and too complex to study on their own or even in a group setting. This formatted material will allow an individual to move through the text in a timely and comprehensive manner. Most group classes take years before even one reading of the entire text has been completed. Often, they must rely upon second-hand resources and "experts". This text will aid both group and independent, private study. It provides enough information to foster discussion and meditation for the serious inquirer. Never blindly accept another's explanation but rather go within and follow your own inner guide's advice.

If you are already involved in a private or group study plan and would like more information or perhaps adopt ACIM for Dummies as your preferred core source material, please feel free to contact us at our website at: **acourseinmiraclesfordummies.com** or at **ACIMfordummies.com**. We offer online, local and private classes. You can also register your approved ACIM for Dummies class on our website or contact us for classes in your area.

INTRODUCTION

T-in.1.This is a course in miracles. 2 **The course in miracles** is a required course. 3 Only the time you take **the course** is voluntary. 4 Free will does not mean that you can establish the curriculum. 5 **Free will** means only that you can elect what you want to take at a given time. 6 The course does not aim at teaching the meaning of love, for that is beyond what can be taught. 7 **The Course** does aim, however, at removing the blocks to the awareness of love's presence, which is your natural inheritance. 8 The opposite of love is fear, but what is all-encompassing can have no opposite.

T-in.2.This course can therefore be summed up very simply in this way:

2 *Nothing real can be threatened.*
3 *Nothing unreal exists.*

4 Herein lies the peace of God.

Note # 1: Miracles reflect a change in your thinking. Thus, at some point in your awareness, you must change your thinking about how you perceive yourself and your surroundings. Free will only allows you the ability to decide the timing of when you will elect to reawaken to your spiritual magnificence, which is the truth about yourself. The miracle aims to remove the blocks to love. Although we perceive that there are two emotions, love and fear, fear is not a part of the Mind of God and is not real. Love is all encompassing and the truth of "All That Is." Free will allows us to deny the truth that only love exists, yet, our denial cannot change the truth. What is truth cannot be threatened by our deluded fantasies.

Chapter 1. THE MEANING OF MIRACLES

I. Principles of Miracles

Note # 2: This section, entitled "Principles of Miracles," forms the basis for the text. This being the case, we have not attempted to add detailed explanations after each paragraph since this will be done throughout the rest of the book. It is not necessary that you understand each point at this moment. The writing style of ACIM is circular and symphonic rather than linear. Each area will be introduced and interlaced over and over with additional details being added as we proceed. What is not immediately clear now may be clarified later in the reading. We encourage the student to study and reflect on what you are currently covering but do not get bogged down over a particular section. Continue to progress through the text remembering that with each reading, your understanding will become richer and more comprehensive. The notes will aid you on this journey. Remember, intellectual understanding is not the goal; rather incorporating the teaching into your life's experience is the quest that we intend to achieve.

T-1.I.1. There is no order of difficulty in miracles. 2 One **miracle** is not "harder" or "bigger" than another. 3. **Miracles** are all the same. 4 All **miracles are** expressions of love **and** are maximal.

T-1.I.2. Miracles as such do not matter. 2 The only thing that matters **about miracles** is their Source, which is **God, Who is** far beyond evaluation.

T-1.I.3. Miracles occur naturally as expressions of love. 2 The real miracle is the love that inspires **the miracle.** 3 In this sense everything that comes from love is a miracle.

T-1.I.4. All miracles mean life, and God is the Giver of life. 2 **God's** Voice will direct you very specifically. 3. You will be told **by God** all you need to know.

T-1.I.5. Miracles are habits, and should be involuntary. 2 **Miracles** should not be under conscious control. 3 Consciously selected miracles can be misguided.

T-1.I.6. Miracles are natural. 2 When **miracles** do not occur something has gone wrong.

T-1.I.7. Miracles are everyone's right, but purification is necessary first.

T-1.I.8. Miracles are healing because they supply a lack; **Miracles** are performed by those who temporarily have more for those who temporarily have less.

T-1.I.9. Miracles are a kind of exchange. 2 Like all expressions of love, which are always miraculous in the true sense, the exchange reverses the physical laws. 3 **Miracles** bring more love both to the giver <*and*> the receiver.

T-1.I.10. The use of miracles as spectacles to induce belief is a misunderstanding of their purpose.

Note # 3: Miracles are a change in perception within the mind of the individual involved. As such, there may be no observable change in the physical realm that someone outside the mind of the miracle worker might notice on the physical level.

T-1.I.11. Prayer is the medium of miracles. 2 **Prayer** is a means of communication of the created with the Creator. 3 Through prayer love is received, and through miracles love is expressed.

Note # 4: Prayer is defined by ACIM as a means of communication of the created with the Creator.

T-1.I.12. Miracles are thoughts. 2 Thoughts can represent the lower or bodily level of experience, or **thoughts can represent** the higher or spiritual level of experience. 3 One **(ego or body level)** makes the physical, and the other **(spiritual level)** creates the spiritual.

T-1.I.13. Miracles are both beginnings and endings, and so **miracles** alter the temporal order. 2 **Miracles** are always affirmations of rebirth, which seem to go back but really go forward. 3 **Miracles** undo the past in the present, and thus release the future.

Note # 5: Miracles take place in the realm of time.

T-1.I.14. Miracles bear witness to truth. 2 **Miracles** are convincing because they arise from conviction. 3 Without conviction **miracles would** deteriorate into magic, **this deterioration would make miracles into magic. Magic** is mindless and therefore destructive; or rather, **magic is** the uncreative use of mind.

Note # 6: Miracles and magic are not the same. On the physical realm of time and space, they both may appear to affect the physical realm of form and, thus, appear to give the same physically observable results. Miracles are based on the natural order of truth, while magic is based on limitation and belief in lack. The difference between miracles and magic will be cover in greater depth later in the text.

T-1.I.15. Each day should be devoted to miracles. 2 The purpose of time is to enable you to learn how to use time constructively. 3 **Time** is thus a teaching device and a means to an end. 4 Time will cease when **time** is no longer useful in facilitating learning.

T-1.I.16. Miracles are teaching devices for demonstrating it is as blessed to give as to receive. 2 **Miracles** simultaneously increase the strength of the giver and supply strength to the receiver.

T-1.I.17. Miracles transcend the body. **2 Miracles** are sudden shifts into invisibility, away from the bodily level. 3 That is why **miracles** heal.

Note # 7: Miracles take place at the level of mind. Mind is in the non-physical realm of spirit. All healing takes place at the level of mind. Miracles may or may not be readily observable at the bodily or physical level.

T-1.I.18.A miracle is a service. **2 A miracle** is the maximal service you can render to another. 3 **A**

miracle is a way of loving your neighbor as yourself. 4 **In a miracle,** you recognize your own and your neighbor's worth simultaneously.

T-1.I.19. Miracles make minds one in God. 2 **Miracles** depend on cooperation because the Sonship is the sum of all that God created. 3 Miracles therefore reflect the laws of eternity, not **the laws** of time.

<u>Note # 8:</u> ACIM defines the Sonship as the sum of all God created as God created it.

T-1.I.20. Miracles reawaken the awareness that the spirit, not the body, is the altar of truth. 2 This **reawakening of the awareness that the spirit is the altar of truth** is the recognition that leads to the healing power of the miracle.

T-1.I.21. Miracles are natural signs of forgiveness. 2 Through miracles you accept God's forgiveness by extending **God's forgiveness** to others.

T-1.I.22. Miracles are associated with fear only because of the belief that darkness can hide. 2 You believe that what your physical eyes cannot see does not exist. 3 This **belief that what your physical eyes cannot see does not exist** leads to a denial of spiritual sight.

<u>Note # 9:</u> Physical sight deals with physical form. ACIM makes a distinction between physical seeing and spiritual sight. ACIM will later refer to spiritual sight by the term vision.

T-1.I.23. Miracles rearrange perception and place all levels in true perspective. 2 This **placing of all levels in true perspective** is healing because sickness comes from confusing the levels. **Because of true perspective, the miracle does not confuse the spiritual level of experience with bodily level of experience.**

<u>Note # 10:</u> The miracle corrects errors in our perception. The miracle transforms an experience that we perceived through fearful eyes and realigns our understanding of that same experience with true perception. This transformation takes place at the level of the mind, which is where the error originally occurred.

T-1.I.24. Miracles enable you to heal the sick and raise the dead because you made sickness and death yourself, and **you** can therefore abolish both **sickness and death.** 2 You are a miracle, capable of creating in the likeness of your Creator. 3 Everything else **that is made by you not in the likeness of your Creator** is your own nightmare, and does not exist. 4 Only the creations of light are real.

<u>Note # 11:</u> God did not create sickness and death. We did. Because we made sickness and death, we must have the power to discreate them.

T-1.I.25. Miracles are part of an interlocking chain of forgiveness which, when completed, is the Atonement. 2 Atonement works all the time and in all the dimensions of time.

T-1.I.26. Miracles represent freedom from fear. 2 "Atoning" means "undoing." 3 The undoing of fear is an essential part of the Atonement value of miracles.

T-1.I.27.A miracle is a universal blessing from God through me, **who you historically have known by the name of Jesus, which represents** the **Christ consciousness,** to all my brothers. 2 **This universal blessing, which is the miracle,** is the privilege of the forgiven to forgive.

T-1.I.28. Miracles are a way of earning release from fear. 2 Revelation induces a state in which fear has already been abolished. 3 Miracles are thus a means and revelation is an end.

Note # 12: Miracles are thus a means to the earning of release from fear while revelation is an end to the abolishment of the state of fear.

T-1.I.29. Miracles praise God through you. 2 **Miracles** praise **God** by honoring **God's** creations, **thus** affirming **the** perfection **of God's creations**. 3 **Miracles** heal because **miracles** deny body-identification and affirm spirit-identification.

Note # 13: Miracles occur at the level of mind, not at the level of the physical. They are the recognition that we are spirit and not "the body".

T-1.I.30. By recognizing spirit, miracles adjust the levels of perception and show **the levels of perception** in proper alignment. 2 This places spirit at the center, where **spirit** can communicate directly.

Note # 14: The miracle transforms misperception into correct perception. We perceive our spiritual essence, not the body-form.

T-1.I.31. Miracles should inspire gratitude, not awe. 2 You should thank God for what you really are, **which is your spiritual essence as a child of God.** 3 The children of God are holy and the miracle honors their holiness. Your holiness as a child of God can be hidden **or forgotten by you,** but **your holiness can** never **be** lost.

NOTE # 15: We can forget who we are (God's children) but we will always be Sons of God. Our divine inheritance is never lost. We have just temporarily forgotten to claim it. Our divine inheritance as God's children is always available to us. God never takes our inheritance away since God only see us as God created us, always perfect, whole and complete.

T-1.I.32.: **I, who represent** the **Christ consciousness,** inspire all miracles, which are really intercessions. 2 **Miracles** intercede for your holiness and make your perceptions holy. 3 By placing you beyond the physical laws, **miracles** raise you into the sphere of celestial order. 4 In this **celestial** order **of unlimited spirit** you <are> perfect.

Note # 16: Miracles follow the Laws of God and not the laws of this physical world.

T-1.I.33. Miracles honor you because you are lovable. 2 **Miracles** dispel illusions about yourself and perceive the light in you. 3 **Miracles** thus atone for your errors by freeing you from your nightmares. 4 By releasing your mind from the imprisonment of your illusions, **miracles** restore your sanity.

Note # 17: Miracles allow you to look past the physical body, to the true spiritual nature of all that you perceive.

T-1.I.34. Miracles restore the mind to its fullness. 2 By atoning for lack, **miracles** establish perfect protection. 3 The spirit's strength leaves no room for intrusions.

NOTE # 18: Due to your current belief that you are a limited ego-body, your mind appears to have been split into two parts. Your higher self, your Big "S" Self or Christ consciousness, knows that you remain God's prefect and sinless Son. Your egoic mind, your small "s" self, is under the delusion that you are a separate, limited ego-body with a separate will that could oppose God's Will. The miracle brings you to the reality of what you really are, God's beloved Son. Although this truth that you are the sinless Oneness of the Mind of God appears to be only momentarily in your consciousness, it is the ultimate truth, which we all will someday recognize. When we accept Oneness for ourselves, this truth is the Atonement and the return to the shared One Self that is the Mind of God.

T-1.I.35. Miracles are expressions of love, but **miracles** may not always have observable effects.

Note # 19: Miracles take place within the mind of the miracle-maker, not on the level of physicality.

T-1.I.36. Miracles are examples of right thinking. **Through right thinking the miracle aligns** your perceptions with truth as God created **truth.**

Note # 20: Miracles correct misperceptions and allow for our experience to better align with what is the truth at the spiritual level.

T-1.I.37. A miracle is a correction introduced into false thinking by me, **who represents** the **Christ consciousness.** 2 **The miracle** acts as a catalyst **by** breaking up erroneous perception and reorganizing the **erroneous perception** properly. 3 This places you under the Atonement principle, where **the erroneous** perception is healed. 4 Until this **placing of yourself under the Atonement principle** has occurred, knowledge of the Divine Order is impossible.

Note # 21: As long as we follow the erroneous egoic thinking of our split mind, we will tend to misperceive all our experiences. The higher consciousness of Christ is needed to move beyond our fallacious egoic thinking and return us to right-mindedness.

T-1.I.38. The Holy Spirit is the mechanism of miracles. 2 **The Holy Spirit** recognizes both God's creations and your illusions. 3 **The Holy Spirit** separates the true from the false by **the Holy Spirit's** ability to perceive totally rather than selectively.

Note # 22: The Holy Spirit has both the ability to know the truth of what you are and, yet, is also aware that you believe yourself to be something separate from God. As such, the Holy Spirit is the only One, Who has the complete story. The Holy Spirit knows the "Big Picture." This unique perspective of the "Big Picture" allows the Holy Spirit to act as the mechanism for miracles.

T-1.I.39. The miracle dissolves error because the Holy Spirit identifies error as false or unreal. 2 This **dissolving of error** is the same as saying that by perceiving light, darkness automatically disappears.

Note # 23: Whenever we awaken from a dream, we realize that the dream had no affect upon the truth. As the dreamer, we need only recognize that we were dreaming and then the dream fades away.

T-1.I.40. The miracle acknowledges everyone as your brother and mine. 2 **The miracle** is a way of perceiving the universal mark of God.

Note # 24: The miracle sees the Christ consciousness in all. It looks past physical appearance and beholds the truth that when God created us, He extended all of Himself. God as Cause and we as His Effect are the totality of the perfect, the whole and the complete. The Sonship can only be like Its

Source, which is only Love.

T-1.I.41.Wholeness is the perceptual content of miracles. 2 **The miracles through wholeness** thus **correct** or atone for, the faulty perception of lack.

Note # 25: Although we can imagine that we lack something, we always remain part of the One Self. There can be no separation in a Oneness of "All That Is."

T-1.I.42.A major contribution of miracles is their strength in releasing you from your false sense of isolation, deprivation and lack.

T-1.I.43.Miracles arise from a miraculous state of mind, or a state of miracle-readiness.

T-1.I.44.The miracle is an expression of an inner awareness of Christ and the acceptance of His Atonement.

T-1.I.45.A miracle is never lost. 2 **A miracle** may touch many people you have not even met, and produce undreamed of changes in situations of which you are not even aware.

Note # 26: Since the miracle is a change in perception, we cannot always observe the total impact that a miracle has. The Holy Spirit insures that a miracle is never wasted but always provides maximal benefit.

T-1.I.46.The Holy Spirit is the highest communication medium. 2 Miracles do not involve this **highest** type of communication, because **miracles** are <temporary> communication devices. 3 When you return to your original form of communication with God by direct revelation, the need for miracles is over.

T-1.I.47.The miracle is a learning device that lessens the need for time. **2 The miracle** establishes an out-of-pattern time interval not under the usual laws of time. 3 In this sense **the miracle** is timeless.

Note # 27: Time is the measure of change in minds that perceive themselves to be separate from the Oneness of "All That Is." Miracles speed up change and thus, time. The miracle transcends the normal linear pattern that comprises the elements of time that we call the past, present and future.

T-1.I.48.The miracle is the only device at your immediate disposal for controlling time. 2 Only revelation transcends **time, since revelation has** nothing to do with time at all.

Note # 28: Since time is the measure of change, miracles allow for both the compression of time and the speeding up of change.

T-1.I.49.The miracle makes no distinction among degrees of misperception. 2 **The miracle** is a device for perception correction, effective quite apart from either the degree or the direction of the error. 3 This **lack of distinction among degrees of misperception** is **the miracles** true indiscriminateness.

Note # 29: There is no degree of difficulty in miracles since all miracles deal with the some fundamental principle. All bring the false before the truth. All forms of illusion are equally false. Once you identify a dream as a dream, you merely need to awaken and the dream disappears. The size or scope of the dream does not matter to the awakened mind.

T-1.I.50.The miracle compares what you have made with creation, accepting what is in accord with

creation as true, and rejecting what is out of accord **with creation** as false.

<u>**Note # 30:**</u> Creation is based on love and love's extension. Making is based on fear and exclusion and lack. Only loving thoughts align with creation. Both in **T-1.I. 24** and this paragraph, ACIM mentions creation and making. What is the difference? When the mind sees itself as a limited ego-body, the mind is unable to create like God. This mind is ruled by fear rather than love. When we allow our egoic self to identify and perceive itself to be "the body," we deny our spiritual nature. We no longer see ourselves as God's Son or God's Creation. Since God is only Love, creation is the extension of Love. Fear is the opposite of love. Fear is the mistaken belief that there could be something other than love. Since we are attempting to create out of fear, we believe that we lack something. We fail to claim our divine birthright as God's Son and, therefore, are unable to act as co-creators with our Father. Because of this belief that we are a limited ego-body, we believe that we are separate from our Source and are incomplete without our Father. We perceive that we lack the wholeness of the Mind of God. Thus, our "creations" are also limited and lack wholeness. Our failed attempts at creation are not real since what we "make" is not an extension of the wholeness that is the Mind of God. What the egoic mind "makes" is not perfect, whole, nor complete since it is attempting to create from the perspective of fear and lack. Making is the product of fear, limitation and lack. Making's purpose is to exclude.

God is only perfect love and thus, could know nothing that could be fearful, limited or lacking. When God created the Sonship, His creation was the perfect extension of God, Himself. An extension is part of, not separate from, its source. Love, which is both extension and inclusion, are not part of egoic thinking. Egoic making attempts to create an illusionary image that appears to confirm the erroneous belief that there is a separation between God and His Son. Making is the Sonship's attempt to take our mistaken perception about our imagined separation from the Oneness that we call God and make the separation appear real. Making appears to take place at the level of the physical body and is observable by the physical eyes. When we utilize our egoic mind to make something that is not the extension of Love, we have miscreated. Miscreation cannot be real and only appears real within the mind of the deluded dreamer. Within the dream of separation from the Oneness, our egoic mind can believe that we have created something unlike the Oneness of the Mind of God. Since creation is the extension of the Oneness that is the Mind of God, there could be nothing outside this One Self. The Sonship's belief that he is separate from his source is a false fantasy. A fantasy cannot change the truth and thus, this dream is not real. Truth is real and truth cannot change. This egoic "making" of an illusionary dream world that is "something apart from God" can exist only in the make-believe world of our egoic mind. Because we have been given free will, we are able to imagine a dream about anything we like, but our dream cannot change the truth of "All That Is." In the dream world of the egoic body-mind, we can pretend that anything, including limitation, separation and lack are real. Yet, a mistaken belief in the false cannot change the changeless truth that we are an indivisible part of the One Self that is the Mind of God.

<u>**Note # 31 - General Comment:**</u> These first fifty items describe the nature of a miracle. Miracles are a change in thinking that may or may not result in a physically observable change. Miracles take place at the level of mind, not necessarily at the physical bodily level. The Course uses the rest of the text to explain the why, how, what, where and when that make this curriculum about miracles a required course.

II. Revelation, Time and Miracles

T-1.II.1. Revelation induces complete but temporary suspension of doubt and fear. 2 **Revelation** reflects the original form of communication between God and His creations, involving the extremely personal sense of creation sometimes sought in physical relationships. 3 Physical closeness cannot achieve **revelation**. 4 Miracles, however, are genuinely interpersonal, and result in true closeness to others. 5 Revelation unites you directly with God. 6 Miracles unite you directly with your brother. 7 Neither **revelation nor miracles** emanates from consciousness, but **both revelation and miracles** are experienced **from consciousness**. 8 Consciousness is the state that induces action, though **consciousness** does not inspire **action**. 9 You are free to believe what you choose, and what you do **choose** attests to what you believe.

<u>Note # 32:</u> Free will allows us the opportunity to believe anything that we like, but our beliefs cannot change the truth of the Mind of God. What we choose to perceive is the direct result of what we chose to believe. If we wish to believe that fear exists, we will make a body of evidence that will appear to support our belief that fear is real. Revelation is based on the knowledge of truth. Perception is not based on knowledge, but rather on the false belief that you are separate from the Mind of God. If you believed correctly that you were a Oneness of "All That Is," there would be nothing outside yourself to perceive. A miracle deals with the illusion of separation and corrects a false misperception that is found within the egoic mind's dream that envisions fear to be real. The miracle corrects this mistake in thinking and you realize that the false cannot threaten the truth of what you are which is an extension of the one Mind of God.

T-1.II.2. Revelation is intensely personal and cannot be meaningfully translated. 2 That is why any attempt to describe **revelation** in words is impossible. 3 Revelation induces only experience. 4 Miracles, on the other hand, induce action. 5 **Miracles** are more useful now because of their interpersonal nature. 6 In this phase of learning, working miracles is important because freedom from fear cannot be thrust upon you. 7 Revelation is literally unspeakable because **revelation** is an experience of unspeakable love.

<u>Note # 32:</u> Miracles deal with the realm of perception. Perception requires our belief that there is both the observer and something to observe. Thus, it implies our belief in separation and a relationship between something that is perceived to be apart from itself. Perception involves thinking, which forms the basis for when and what we choose to perceive. Revelation does not involve thinking. It is the experiencing of that knowing.

T-1.II.3. Awe should be reserved for revelation, to which **awe** is perfectly and correctly applicable. 2 **Awe** is not appropriate for miracles because a state of awe is worshipful, implying that one of a lesser order stands before his Creator. 3 You are a perfect creation, and should experience awe only in the Presence of the Creator of perfection. 4 The miracle is therefore a sign of love among equals. 5 Equals should not be in awe of one another because awe implies inequality. 6 **Awe** is therefore an inappropriate reaction to me, **whom you historically have known by the name of Jesus.** 7 An elder brother is entitled to respect for his greater experience, and obedience for his greater wisdom. 8 **An elder brother** is also entitled to love because he is a brother, and to devotion if he is devoted. 9 It is only my devotion that entitles me to **your devotion**. 10 There is nothing about me that you cannot attain. 11 I have nothing that does not come from God. 12 The difference between us now is that I have nothing else **but what comes from God**. 13 This leaves me in a state which is only potential in you.

Note # 33: Jesus is stating that he is no different from you. The only current difference is that his experience as an older brother has led him to reawaken to the fact that he is not a limited ego-body. Instead, he understands the reality of himself as part of the Oneness that is an extension of the Mind of God. When we drop our belief in fear and separation, we too will remember the truth of what we are.

T-1.II.4."No man cometh unto the Father but by me" does not mean that I, **whom you call by the name of Jesus,** am in any way separate or different from you except in time, and time does not really exist. 2 The statement, **"No man cometh unto the Father but by me",** is more meaningful in terms of a vertical rather than a horizontal axis. 3 You stand below me and I stand below God. 4 In the process of "rising up," I am higher because without me the distance between God and man would be too great for you to encompass. 5 I bridge the distance as an elder brother to you on the one hand, and as a Son of God on the other. 6 My devotion to my brothers has placed me in charge of the Sonship, which I render complete because I share **in the Sonship.** 7 This may appear to contradict the statement "I and my Father are one," but there are two parts to the statement in recognition that the Father is greater.

Note # 34: Jesus states that the following two statements, "No man cometh unto the Father but by me" and "I and my Father are one," appear to be contradictory but are not. The first statement demonstrates that we need the help of our elder brother, Jesus, to clear our path back to the knowledge of God. The second statement indicates that creation is extension and thus, there can be no separation between God and His Creation. God is Cause and we are His Effect. As such, we are intertwined and inseparable. The only difference between God and the Sonship is that the Father is the first Cause. We, being an extension, have the same power to co-create with God.

T-1.II.5. Revelations are indirectly inspired by me because I am close to the Holy Spirit, and **I am** alert to the revelation-readiness of my brothers. 2 I can thus bring down to **my brothers** more than they can draw down to themselves. 3 The Holy Spirit mediates higher to lower communication **thus** keeping the direct channel from God to you open for revelation. 4 Revelation is not reciprocal. 5 **Revelation** proceeds from God to you, but **revelation does not proceed** from you to God.

Note # 35: Revelation is a one-way street. The flow is always from God to His Creations.

T-1.II.6. The miracle minimizes the need for time. 2 In the longitudinal or horizontal plane the recognition of the equality of the members of the Sonship appears to involve almost endless time. 3 However, the miracle entails a sudden shift from horizontal to vertical perception. 4 This **sudden shift from horizontal to vertical perception** introduces an interval from which the giver and receiver both emerge farther along in time than they would otherwise have been. 5 The miracle thus has the unique property of abolishing time to the extent that **the miracle** renders the interval of time it spans unnecessary. 6 There is no relationship between the time a miracle takes and the time **the miracle** covers. 7 The miracle substitutes for learning that might have taken thousands of years. 8 **The miracle** does so by the underlying recognition of perfect equality of giver and receiver on which the miracle rests. 9 The miracle shortens time by collapsing **time**, thus eliminating certain intervals within **time**. 10 **The miracle** does this, however, within the larger temporal sequence.

Note # 36: The miracle reduces the need for time by removing from the mind of the miracle worker the idea of separation. Instead, the concept of separation is replaced by the awareness of the truth of there is a spiritual oneness with each brother. It joins what was perceived as separate and thus, "speeds up time." In this joining, both the giver and the receiver benefit from this joint realization of their spiritual equality. When the "miracle giver" goes from the mindset of an ego-body, separate and apart, to the mindset of being the perfect, sinless and guiltless Son of God, he also sees his brother this same way.

Their shared equality is recognized. Thus, both advance toward the path to truth. Miracles are part of an interlocking chain of forgiveness which, when completed, is the Atonement. A miracle affects the entire Sonship and all seemingly separate parts benefit. This is why the entire Sonship benefited by Jesus' realization of what he truly was. The entire Sonship, which is all God created as God created it, are all joined as one mind.

III. Atonement and Miracles

T-1.III.1. I am in charge of the process of Atonement, which I undertook to begin. 2 When you offer a miracle to any of my brothers, you do it to <yourself> and me. 3 The reason you come before me is that I do not need miracles for my own Atonement, but I stand at the end in case you fail temporarily. 4 My part in the Atonement is the canceling out of all errors that you could not otherwise correct. 5 When you have been restored to the recognition of your original state **before the separation**, you naturally become part of the Atonement yourself. 6 As you share my unwillingness to accept error in yourself and others, you must join the great crusade to correct **errors in yourself and others**; listen to my voice, learn to undo error and act to correct **error**. 7 The power to work miracles belongs to you. 8 I will provide the opportunities to do **miracles**, but you must be ready and willing to do **the miracles**. 9 Doing **the miracles** will bring conviction in the ability **you process to do miracles**, because conviction comes through accomplishment. 10 **In regards to performing miracles**, the ability is the potential, the achievement is its expression, and the Atonement, which is the natural profession of the children of God, is the purpose **of miracles**.

<u>Note # 37:</u> Jesus is a symbol for the Holy Spirit and Christ consciousness. Jesus is like the older brother that has already made the journey back to the truth of what we are. He is capable of guiding us along this journey to our reawakening of our knowledge that we are part of the One Self that is the Mind of God. Jesus stands ready to assist us whenever we believe we cannot accomplish the task alone. This dream of separation gives us the opportunity to reclaim our ability to perform miracles and to relearn how to accomplish them. By expressing forgiveness and love, we play our part in the miracle and the Atonement process. Miracles are part of an interlocking chain of forgiveness which, when completed, is the Atonement.

T-1.III.2. "Heaven and earth shall pass away" means that **heaven and earth** will not continue to exist as separate states. 2 My word, which is the resurrection and the life, shall not pass away because life is eternal. 3 You are the work of God, and His work is wholly lovable and wholly loving. 4 This is how a man must think of himself in his heart, because this is what he is, **wholly lovable and wholly loving**.

<u>Note # 38:</u> Heaven and earth are not physical places but rather states of mind. When we reawaken to the truth, we will rediscover that only love is real and that we are an expression of that love.

T-1.III.3. The forgiven are the means of the Atonement. 2 Being filled with spirit, **the forgiven** forgive in return. 3 Those who are released **(the forgiven)** must join in releasing their brothers, for this is the plan of the Atonement. 4 Miracles are the way in which minds that serve the Holy Spirit unite with me for the salvation or release of all of God's creations.

<u>Note # 39:</u> We cannot be a part of the Atonement and accept it for ourselves unless we are willing to both give and receive forgiveness to all including ourselves.

T-1.III.4.I am the only one who can perform miracles indiscriminately, because I am the Atonement. 2 You have a role in the Atonement which I will dictate to you. 3 Ask me which miracles you should perform. 4 **By asking me what miracles you should perform**, this spares you needless effort, because you will be acting under direct communication. 5 The impersonal nature of the miracle is an essential ingredient, because **the impersonal nature of the miracle** enables me to direct **the miracle's** application, and under my guidance miracles lead to the highly personal experience of revelation. 6 A guide does not control but **the guide** does direct, leaving it up to you to follow. 7 "Lead us not into temptation" means "Recognize your errors and choose to abandon **your errors** by following my guidance."

<u>Note # 40:</u> We need guidance from someone who has both the road map and the ability to successfully read the map. Jesus or the Holy Spirit can provide this guidance. Our egoic mind lacks both the map and the ability to read it.

T-1.III.5. Error cannot really threaten truth, **for truth** can always withstand **error**. 2 Only the error, **not truth**, is actually vulnerable. 3 You are free to establish your kingdom where you see fit, but the right choice **for determining where you place your kingdom** is inevitable if you remember this:
4 Spirit is in a state of grace forever.
5 Your reality is only spirit.
6 Therefore you are in a state of grace forever.

7 Atonement undoes all errors in this respect **that you believe in the false** and thus uproots the source of fear. 8 Whenever you experience God's reassurances as threat, **this supposed threat** is always because you are defending misplaced or misdirected loyalty. 9 When you project **misplaced loyalty** to others you imprison them, but only to the extent to which you reinforce errors **the others** have already made. 10 This makes **the others** vulnerable to the distortions of other **ego bodies**, since their own perception of themselves is distorted. 11 The miracle worker can only bless them, and this undoes their distortions and frees them from prison.

<u>**NOTE # 41:**</u> The Atonement is the acceptance of the truth, which in turn corrects erroneous thinking. Erroneous thinking occurs whenever you perceive yourself to be something other than the unlimited spirit of the Son of God. We have accepted the belief that we are a limited ego-body. You will establish your kingdom based on what you perceive yourself to be. Are you an unlimited spiritual being or are you a limited ego-body? When you believe that you are an ego-body, your mind's loyalty has been misdirected. The miracle undoes this error and you now correctly view yourself and others as a Son of God, which is unlimited spirit. You cannot "imprison" others who view themselves as spirit. Only those who see themselves as a body can be imprisoned.

T-1.III.6. You respond to what you perceive, and as you perceive so shall you behave. 2 The Golden Rule asks you to do unto others as you would have them do unto you. 3 This means that the perception of both **you and the others** must be accurate. 4 The Golden Rule is the rule for appropriate behavior. 5 You cannot behave appropriately unless you perceive correctly 6 Since you and your neighbor are equal members of one family, as you perceive both **you and your neighbor** so you will do to both **you and your neighbor**. 7 You should look out from the perception of your own holiness to the holiness of others.

Note # 42: The golden rule does not work if you incorrectly perceive yourself to be a limited ego-body. Your belief that you are a body fosters separation, competition and conflict. With correct perception, you view yourself and others as Sons of God and unlimited spirit. We cannot love our brother if we do not perceive ourselves as loveable. We cannot give what we do not possess.

T-1.III.7. Miracles arise from a mind that is ready for **miracles**. 2 By being united this mind **that is ready for miracles** goes out to everyone, even without the awareness of the miracle worker himself. 3 The impersonal nature of miracles is because the Atonement itself is one, uniting all creations with their Creator. 4 As an expression of what you truly are **which is the Son of God,** the miracle places the mind in a state of grace 5 The mind then naturally welcomes the Host within and the stranger without. 6 When you bring in the stranger, he becomes your brother.

Note # 43: Ego-bodies cannot join; only mind (spirit) can be joined. Being not of body, we truly are of one mind, which is the shared Oneness of the Mind of God. Until we are ready to ask for guidance from the Holy Spirit or Jesus, our minds will not be receptive to miracle mindedness and the truth of our spiritual nature.

T-1.III.8. That the miracle may have effects on your brothers that you may not recognize is not your concern. 2 The miracle will always bless *<you>*. 3 Miracles you are not asked to perform have not lost their value. 4 **These miracles that you were not asked to perform** are still expressions of your own state of grace, but the action aspect of the miracle should be controlled by me because of my complete awareness of the whole plan. 5 The impersonal nature of miracle-mindedness ensures your grace, but only I am in a position to know where **the miracle** can be bestowed.

Note # 44: Jesus is a symbol for the Holy Spirit and Christ consciousness. Only the Holy Spirit is aware of all parts of God's plan for the return of God's Son to knowledge. Without the big picture, we lack the basic understanding of how each miracle fits together to become the Atonement. Thus, we need to follow the guidance of the Holy Spirit.

T-1.III.9. Miracles are selective only in the sense that the **miracles** are directed towards those who can use them for themselves. 2 Since this makes it inevitable that they **who can use the miracle on themselves** will extend **the miracle** to others, a strong chain of Atonement is welded. 3 However, this selectivity takes no account of the magnitude of the miracle itself, because the concept of size exists on a plane that is itself unreal. 4 Since the miracle aims at restoring the awareness of reality, **the miracle** would not be useful if **the miracle was** bound by laws that govern the error **the miracle** aims to correct.

NOTE # 47: Truth, which is reality, never changes. Miracles correct wrong thinking. Wrong thinking is always based on your egoic belief that you are separate and, therefore, a body. The miracle recognizes that you are unlimited spirit. Anything the ego makes based on its false belief in the illusion of separation, fear and limitation being true, cannot be real. It can only be a temporary mirage held by the misinformed party. It is only within the split-mind of the dreamer that the dream of separation appears to be real. Yet, an illusion or dream cannot change the eternal truth of your Oneness within the Mind of God. When the egoic split-mind is made whole again, your false belief that you are an ego-body will disappear. This correction is inevitable since it is God's Plan for the return of His Child to knowledge. Truth by definition never changes. Since this false belief that we are a separate ego-body will change and disappear, it cannot be real or the truth.

IV. The Escape from Darkness

T-1.IV.1. The escape from darkness involves two stages: First, the recognition that darkness cannot hide. 2 This step, **the recognition that darkness cannot hide**, usually entails fear. 3 Second, the recognition that there is nothing you want to hide even if you could. 4 This **second** step **that there is nothing you want to hide even if you could** brings escape from fear. 5 When you have become willing to hide nothing, you will not only be willing to enter into communion but will also understand peace and joy.

Note # 48: Darkness is associated with the belief that you are an ego-body. When you believe that you are an ego-body in competition with other ego-bodies, the world you perceive becomes a fearful place.

T-1.IV.2. Holiness can never be really hidden in darkness, but you can deceive yourself about **holiness' ability to be hidden by darkness**. 2 This deception about **your holiness** makes you fearful because you realize in your heart it <*is*> a deception, and you exert enormous efforts to establish **the** reality **that your holiness can be hidden by darkness**. 3 The miracle sets reality where it belongs **and confirms your holiness cannot be hidden by darkness**. 4 Reality belongs only to spirit, and the miracle acknowledges only truth. 5 **The miracle** thus dispels illusions about yourself, and puts you in communion with yourself and God. 6 The miracle joins in the Atonement by placing the mind in the service of the Holy Spirit. 7 This **placing the mind in the service of the Holy Spirit** establishes the proper function of the mind and corrects **the mind's** errors, which are merely lacks of love. 8 Your mind can be possessed by illusions, but spirit is eternally free. 9 If a mind perceives without love, **the mind** perceives an empty shell and is unaware of the spirit within. 10 But the Atonement restores spirit to **spirit's** proper place. 11 The mind that serves spirit <*is*> invulnerable.

Note # 49: Because you are the holy Son of God, you are an extension of God and cannot be limited by your misperception that you are a body. Your denial of the truth cannot change truth's reality. Eventually, your mind must awaken to the truth. As the extension of God, Himself, His Son must also be invulnerable.

T-1.IV.3. Darkness is lack of light as sin is lack of love. 2 **Darkness** has no unique properties of its own. 3 **Darkness** is an example of the "scarcity" belief, from which only error can proceed. 4 Truth is always abundant. 5 Those who perceive and acknowledge that they have everything have no needs of any kind. 6 The purpose of the Atonement is to restore everything to you; or rather, to restore **everything** to your awareness. 7 You were given everything when you were created, just as everyone was given **everything when God created everyone**.

Note # 50: When God creates, He extends Himself to all Creation. God being everything extends everything to His creations. Since there is no lack in God, His creations must also be created perfect, whole and complete.

T-1.IV.4. The emptiness engendered by fear must be replaced by forgiveness. 2 That is what the Bible means by "There is no death," and why I could demonstrate that death does not exist **by my crucifixion and resurrection**. 3 I came to fulfill the law by reinterpreting **the law**. 4 The law itself, if properly understood, offers only protection. 5 It is those who have not yet changed their minds **and thus are still engendered by fear**, who brought the "hell-fire" concept **into their interpretation of the law**. 6 I assure you that I will witness for anyone who lets me, and to whatever extent he permits **me to witness**. 7 Your witnessing **by replacing your fear with forgiveness** demonstrates your belief **in the**

reinterpretation of the law, and thus strengthens the law **by replacing fear with forgiveness**. 8 Those who witness for me are expressing, through their miracles, that they have abandoned the belief in deprivation in favor of the abundance they, **who witness for me** have learned belongs to them.

Note # 51: Jesus' death and resurrection proved that we are not a limited ego-body. When we replace fear with forgiveness, as Jesus did, we will awaken to the truth that we are unlimited spirit. Being an extension of the Mind of God, we have everything. As Spirit, we are in need of nothing for we are "All That Is." God being only Love and a Oneness could never condemn you to hell for to do so would be to condemn Himself. Hell is only in the insane mind of someone who believes that he could be separate from the Mind of God. Delusions about yourself can never change the truth about yourself. Yet, these false beliefs can appear to govern your current field of awareness and thus, "prevent" you from experiencing your oneness with your Source.

V. Wholeness and Spirit

T-1.V.1. The miracle is much like the body in that both are learning aids for facilitating a state in which both **the miracle and the body** become unnecessary. 2 When spirit's original state of direct communication is reached, neither the body nor the miracle serves any purpose. 3 While you believe you are in a body, however, you can choose between loveless and miraculous channels of expression. 4 You can make an empty shell **of lovelessness while you believe you are a body**, but you cannot express nothing at all. 5 You can wait, delay, paralyze yourself, or reduce your creativity almost to nothing. 6 But you cannot abolish **your creativity**. 7 You can destroy your medium of communication, but not your potential. 8 You did not create yourself. **God did.**

Note # 52: Although we can deny the truth, our denial does not change the truth. Eventually we must come to our senses and reawaken to the truth of our divine birthright. This birthright can be forgotten but it can never be lost. We, God's only Son, will eventually reclaim our divinity.

T-1.V.2. The basic decision of the miracle-minded is not to wait on time any longer than is necessary. 2 Time can waste as well as be wasted. 3 The miracle worker, therefore, accepts the time-control factor gladly. 4 **The miracle worker** recognizes that every collapse of time brings everyone closer to the ultimate release from time, in which the Son and the Father are One. 5 Equality does not imply equality <now>. 6 When everyone recognizes that he has everything, individual contributions to the Sonship will no longer be necessary.

NOTE # 52: When we refuse to make a decision, we waste time. Any decision, whether "right or wrong" moves us one step closer to making the right decision. If we are not at peace, we need to make a decision and choose differently. If we refuse to make a new choice, we remain stuck in victim consciousness and delay our progression to our reawakening into the truth of our holiness. This lack of a new decision on our part wastes time.

T-1.V.3. When the Atonement has been completed, all talents will be shared by all the Sons of God. 2 God is not partial. 3 All His children have His total Love, and all His gifts are freely given to everyone alike. 4 "Except ye become as little children" means that unless you fully recognize your complete dependence on God, you cannot know the real power of the Son in his true relationship with the Father. 5 The specialness of God's Sons does not stem from exclusion but from inclusion. 6 All my brothers are special. 7 If **my brothers** believe they are deprived of anything, **my brother's** perception becomes distorted. 8 When this occurs **and my brother's perception becomes distorted**, the whole family of God, or the Sonship, is impaired in its relationships.

<u>Note # 52:</u> We are special because we are extensions of God. Yet, each perceived part is not special from another since we are all the same. The Mind of God is holographic. Each part contains the whole and the whole contains each part. There is no separation within a Oneness of "All That Is." In our holiness, we are made whole.

T-1.V.4. Ultimately, every member of the family of God must return. 2 The miracle calls **a member of the family of God** to return because **the miracle** blesses and honors **the member**, even though **this member** may be absent in spirit. 3 "God is not mocked" is not a warning but a reassurance. 4 God <*would*> be mocked if any of His creations lacked holiness. 5 The creation is whole, and the mark of wholeness is holiness. 6 Miracles are affirmations of Sonship, which is a state of completion and abundance.

<u>NOTE # 53:</u> The miracle lifts the mind back to the truth about itself. A member of the Sonship is not an ego-body in completion with other ego bodies, but rather a Oneness of spirit. Spirit must be as God created it, perfect, whole and complete. God's creations are sinless and guiltless because God, their creator, created them eternally perfect. God's creations are and remain always as holy as He.

T-1.V.5. Whatever is true is eternal, and **whatever is true** cannot change or be changed. 2 Spirit is therefore unalterable because **spirit** is already perfect, but the mind can elect what **the mind** chooses to serve. 3 The only limit put on **the mind's** choice is that **the mind** cannot serve two masters. 4 If **the mind** elects to do so, the mind can become the medium by which spirit creates along the line of **spirit's** own creation. 5 If **the mind** does not freely elect to do so **and freely serve the spirit, the mind** retains **the mind's** creative potential but places itself under **the** tyrannous **control of the ego** rather than Authoritative control **of spirit, which is represented by the Holy Spirit**. 6 As a result **of the mind's decision to serve the ego, the mind** imprisons, because such are the dictates of tyrants, **which is the nature of the ego.** 7 To change your mind means to place **your mind** at the disposal of <true> Authority **which is represented by the thought system of the Holy Spirit.**

<u>NOTE # 54:</u> The mind can either serve spirit or the ego. If the mind believes that it is an ego body in competition with other ego bodies, its viewpoint or belief comes from separation and lack. If the mind attempts to "create" from this egoic viewpoint, the only thing that it can "make" is something that is fear based and lacks wholeness. Thus, making is based on exclusion and is not true creation. True creation can only extend what it really is. Creation is love based and inclusive. Since your true nature is spirit, made holy in God's image, your true ability to create is like God's ability, which comes from abundance. When God extends Himself, He gives all because He is all. Nothing is held back. If the mind believes that it is a spirit, the mind comes under the direction of its true nature and creates as the Son of God. Spirit's source is based upon our true reality and is changeless. As spirit, our true authority and power comes from God. Your ego's source comes from a false belief of who you are. Because your mind accepts your misperception that you are a separate ego-body, your mind believes it comes from lack. The ego is a tyrant because it believes in lack and its own vulnerability. The ego's authority is not based on truth. Instead, it is based on your false belief that you are a limited body. The ego tells you that you are not God's beloved Child and that you are different from what God created. The Holy Spirit will guide you to the truth that you can only be as God created you, an extension of God, Himself. You are

perfect, whole and complete. You must decide if you will follow the thought system of the ego or the Holy Spirit. Your mind cannot serve both. The Holy Spirit, Jesus and Christ consciousness all symbolize the voice for the truth of our spiritual nature as God's beloved Creation.

T-1.V.6.The miracle is a sign that the mind has chosen to be led by me in Christ's service. 2 The abundance of Christ is the natural result of choosing to follow **Christ**. 3 All shallow roots must be uprooted, because **shallow roots** are not deep enough to sustain you. 4 The illusion that shallow roots can be deepened, and thus made to hold, is one of the distortions on which the reverse of the Golden Rule rests. 5 As these false underpinnings are given up, the equilibrium is temporarily experienced as unstable. 6 However, nothing is less stable than an upside-down orientation. 7 Nor can anything that holds **the equilibrium** upside down be conducive to increased stability.

<u>NOTE # 55:</u> The reverse of the Golden Rule would be as follows: DO NOT do onto others as you would have them do onto you.
Since most people view themselves as ego bodies in competition with other ego bodies, the Golden Rule, as the ego understands it, is dangerous to our true spiritual nature. To base action on false beliefs of what our true nature is can only result in "wrong thinking". The thought system of the ego is based on the belief that you are a limited ego-body in competition with other ego-bodies. Egoic thinking is based on the belief in lack. Coming out of fear, the ego would have you attack your brother. If we realize that we are unlimited spirit, we would understand that there could be no lack and thus, nothing to fear. If a thought system's major premise is incorrect, logic tells us not to believe any of its conclusions. Each of the two thought systems results in opposite conclusions. If you believe that you are a body, you will follow the thought system of the ego. If you believe that you are unlimited Spirit, the thought system of the Holy Spirit will make sense to you and you will respond only with love. The choice is between separation or oneness, fear or love. Both thought systems cannot be right. Eventually you must and will freely choose the thought system of the Holy Spirit since only truth is real. Because you have free will, you will decide when you will make the decision to value only truth.

VI. The Illusion of Needs

T-1.VI.1.You who want peace can find **peace** only by complete forgiveness. 2 No learning is acquired by anyone unless he wants to learn it and believes in some way that he needs **to learn** it. 3 While lack does not exist in the creation of God, **lack** is very apparent in what you have made. 4 **Lack** is, in fact, the essential difference between **God's creations and what you have made**. 5 Lack implies that you would be better off in a state somehow different from the one you are in. 6 Until the "separation," which is the meaning of the "fall," nothing was lacking. 7 There were no needs at all **because you were one and therefore were everything**. 8 Needs arise only when you deprive yourself. 9 You act according to the particular order of needs you establish. 10 This, in turn, depends on your perception of what you are.

<u>Note # 56:</u> Are you an ego-body or a spiritual being? Only if you claim you are separate from the Oneness of "All That Is" could there be any lack. When God creates, He extends all, because He gives all. There can be no lack. There remains only the extension of the Whole. Lack only can arise in the deluded mind that believes it is separate from the Oneness that is the Mind of God.

T-1.VI.2.A sense of separation from God is the only lack you really need correct. 2 This sense of separation **from God** would never have arisen if you had not distorted your perception of truth, and had thus perceived yourself as lacking. 3 The idea of order of needs arose because, having made this fundamental error **of perceiving yourself as separate and, therefore, lacking**, you had already fragmented yourself into levels with different needs. 4 As you integrate you become one, and your needs become one accordingly. 5 Unified needs lead to unified action, because this produces a lack of conflict.

<u>Note # 57:</u> Correct the problem at it source and you automatically correct all errors that logically follow from the first error. All errors in egoic thinking can be traced back to the original error of the belief that we could be separated from the Mind of God. Once we correct this original error, there can be nothing that we could lack or fear. Love is all that remains.

T-1.VI.3. The idea of orders of need, which follows from the original error that one can be separated from God, requires correction at its own level before the error of perceiving levels at all can be corrected. 2 You cannot behave effectively while you function on different levels. 3 However, while you do **function on different levels**, correction must be introduced vertically from the bottom up. 4 This is because you think you live in space, where concepts such as "up" and "down" are meaningful. 5 Ultimately, space is as meaningless as time. 6 Both are merely beliefs.

<u>Note # 58:</u> We must correct the problem where it occurs. The problem will be corrected at the level of mind, which is where the error occurred. It cannot be corrected at the body level for the body is not real and is only an instrument of the mind's creative power. Its error in thinking will be corrected in time and space since that is the level we perceive our mind to be operating within.

T-1.VI.4. The real purpose of this world is to use **this world** to correct your unbelief **that you are one. You believe that you are separate**. 2 You can never control the effects of fear yourself, because you made fear **by believing that you were separate**, and you believe in what you made **which is your separateness.** 3 In attitude, then, though not in content, you resemble your Creator, Who has perfect faith in His creations <because> He created **His creations**. 4 Belief produces the acceptance of existence. 5 That is why you can believe what no one else thinks is true. 6 **What no one else thinks is true** is true for you because it was made by you.

<u>NOTE # 59:</u> Your beliefs make your world as you perceive your world to be. Beliefs do not have to be based on truth or reality. In our situation, we believe that we are separate ego-bodies and that we come from lack. Thus, we are unable to create like God because we have chosen to deny our birthright as Children of God. We believe that we are not made in God's own image. Since each ego-body comes from his or her own unique belief system, everyone has a slightly different perception of "the world". Since we believe we are separate, any attempt to create (technically "make") can only result in confirming our belief that we lack something. God creates by extending His true Self. Since God is everything, God creates by extending what He is. God's creations also must share God's Oneness and give everything if they are to create like their Father. Since we have free will, we can temporarily deny or forget what we are. It is this forgetfulness that allows us to falsely believe that we are limited ego-bodies. When we limit ourselves, we can only make false illusions in time. This incorrect belief in limitation cannot change the true reality that we are unlimited spirit. It can, however, allow us as to act as if we are separate and limited since this is what we choose to believe. It is our beliefs that make our perception and our perceptions determine what we choose to experience as our "reality."

T-1.VI.5. All aspects of fear are untrue because **all aspects of fear** do not exist at the creative level, and therefore do not exist at all. 2 To whatever extent you are willing to submit your beliefs to this test, to that extent are your perceptions corrected. 3 In sorting out the false from the true, the miracle proceeds along these lines:

4 Perfect love casts out fear.
5 If fear exists,
Then there is not perfect love.

6 But:

7 Only perfect love exists.
8 If there is fear,
fear produces a state that does not exist.

9 Believe this **about this relationship between perfect love and fear** and you will be free. 10 Only God can establish this solution, and this faith <*is*> His gift.

Note # 60: ACIM is black and white. There is no gray. God is only Love and nothing exists outside of the Mind of God. If we perceive anything that is not love, we are suffering from a false state of delusional thinking. Fear is false evidence appearing real. When delusion is brought before the light of truth, fear must disappear. There is only the Oneness of God's Love. God knows His Creations to be extensions of Himself. Thus, in the Mind of God, we cannot be anything other than as He created us to be. We are and must always remain perfect, whole and complete. This is God's Will and God's Will must not be mocked. Because of this, any belief that the separation is real is just a game that sleeping minds pretend is real. When we choose to reawaken to the truth, we will realize that nothing has changed at all. All our dreams of separation are forgotten. No punishment will be required since nothing really happened. The separation is a dream or illusion that never occurred within the Mind of God. As such, it has no reality.

VII. Distortions of Miracle Impulses

T-1.VII.1. Your distorted perceptions produce a dense cover over miracle impulses, making it hard for **miracle impulses** to reach your own awareness. 2 The confusion of miracle impulses with physical impulses is a major perceptual distortion. 3 Physical impulses are misdirected miracle impulses. 4 All real pleasure comes from doing God's Will. 5 This is because <not> doing **God's will** is a denial of **our true** Self, **which is your Big "S" Self.** 6 Denial of **our Big "S"** Self results in illusions, while correction of the error of denial of **our Big "S"** Self brings release from **illusion**. 7 Do not deceive yourself into believing that you can relate in peace to God or to your brothers with anything external.

Note # 61: Our true nature is our Oneness in the Mind of God. We are unlimited spirit, the perfect, whole and complete extension of the Mind of God. We cannot be happy to be less than what we are. To mistake our Big "S" Self for a limited ego-body, a small "s" self, is to deny our reality. This denial of truth can never make us happy. We are not a body. Instead, we are as God created us to be. Herein lies the Truth and the Peace of God.

T-1.VII.2. Child of God, you were created to create the good, the beautiful and the holy. 2 Do not forget this. 3 The Love of God, for a little while, must still be expressed through one body to another, because vision is still so dim. 4 You can use your body best to help you enlarge your perception so you can achieve real vision, of which the physical eye is incapable. 5 Learning to use **your body as a tool to help enlarge and correct your perception** is the body's only true usefulness.

Note # 62: We should use our body as a communication devise to be and teach only love and forgiveness. We should not use the body as a vehicle for attack upon another. To attack another only makes the dream of separation appear real. We can only attack what we believe to be separate from ourselves.

T-1.VII.3. Fantasy is a distorted form of vision. 2 Fantasies of any kind are distortions, because **fantasies** always involve twisting perception into unreality. 3 Actions that stem from distortions are literally the reactions of those who know not what they do. 4 Fantasy is an attempt to control reality according to false needs. 5 **When you** twist reality in any way and you are perceiving destructively. 6 Fantasies are a means of making false associations and attempting to obtain pleasure from **these false associations**. 7 But although you can perceive false associations, you can never make **false associations** real except to yourself. 8 You believe in what you make. 9 If you offer miracles, you will be equally strong in your belief in **miracles**. 10 The strength of your conviction **in the miracle** will then sustain the belief of the miracle receiver. 11 Fantasies become totally unnecessary as the wholly satisfying nature of reality becomes apparent to both giver and receiver. 12 Reality is "lost" through usurpation, which produces tyranny. 13 As long as a single "slave" remains to walk the earth, your release is not complete. 14 Complete restoration of the Sonship is the only goal of the miracle-minded.

NOTE 62: Our true Self has forgotten that it is God's Child and believes itself to be an ego-body and thus, separate and limited. This mistaken belief allows our now "split" mind to come under the control of the ego. When we believe that we do not know what we are, our ego is manufactured in our imagination and moved into our deluded mind to fill this void. When we chose to forget who we were, we also lost knowledge of the truth. The ego makes a world based of its belief in fear, limitation and separation. Fantasies are made up by the ego to give the illusion of separation the appearance of reality. The ego claims that it has the power to usurp or change, the Will of God. As long as any part of the Sonship is in denial of its Big "S" Self, the Sonship cannot be restored to knowledge.

T-1.VII.4. This is a course in mind training. 2 All learning involves attention and study at some level. 3 Some of the later parts of the course rest too heavily on these earlier sections not to require their careful study. 4 You will also need **the earlier section of the course** for preparation. 5 Without this **careful study of the early sections**, you may become much too fearful of what is to come to make constructive use of **the sections of the course that are to follow**. 6 However, as you study these earlier sections, you will begin to see some of the implications that will be amplified later on.

Note # 63: ACIM is written circularly. Ideas that are introduced in one chapter will be expanded throughout the text. Thus, it is helpful to comprehend the fundamentals of these early chapters. However, with that said, do not believe that you must understand everything in one chapter before you tackle the next passage. If you do this, you will never advance to the next chapter. It is in these future chapters that the explanations that you seek may be found. With patience and by doing the daily lesson in the workbook, your practice will gain the rewards that you seek.

T-1.VII.5.A solid foundation is necessary because of the confusion between fear and awe to which I have already referred, and which is often made. 2 I have said that awe is inappropriate in connection with the Sons of God, because you should not experience awe in the presence of your equals. 3 However, it was also emphasized that awe is proper in the Presence of your Creator. 4 I have been careful to clarify my role in the Atonement without either over or understating **my role**. 5 I am also trying to do the same with yours. 6 I have stressed that awe is not an appropriate reaction to me because of our inherent equality. 7 Some of the later steps in this course, however, involve a more direct approach to God Himself. 8 It would be unwise to start on these steps without careful preparation, or awe will be confused with fear, and the experience will be more traumatic than beatific. 9 Healing is of God in the end. 10 The means **for healing all fantasies** are being carefully explained to you. 11 Revelation may occasionally reveal the end to you, but to reach **the end**, the means are needed.

Note # 64: Jesus again mentions that he is no different from us. He should be respected as an elder brother but not held in awe. Jesus, like us, is part of the indivisible Sonship. The Sonship is all God created, as God created it. God is the first Cause and we, like Jesus, are God's Effect. It is from this causal relationship with our Creator that all our power derives. God will awaken His sleeping Son to his divine birthright and return the Sonship to knowledge. Only God, being first Cause deserves awe.

Chapter 2. THE SEPARATION AND THE ATONEMENT

I. The Origins of Separation

T-2.I.1. To extend is a fundamental aspect of God which **God** gave to His Son. 2 In the creation, God extended Himself to His creations and imbued **His creations** with the same loving Will to create. 3 You have not only been fully created, but have also been created perfect. 4 There is no emptiness in you. 5 Because of your likeness to your Creator you are creative. 6 No child of God can lose this ability **because his ability to create** is inherent in what he is, **but as a child of God** he can use **his ability to create** inappropriately by projecting. 7 The inappropriate use of extension, or projection, occurs when you believe that some emptiness or lack exists in you, and that you can fill **this lack** with your own ideas instead of truth. 8 This process **of inappropriate use of extension, or projection,** involves the following steps:

9 First, you believe that what God created can be changed by your own mind.
10 Second, you believe that what is perfect can be rendered imperfect or lacking.
11 Third, you believe that you can distort the creations of God, including yourself.
12 Fourth, you believe that you can create yourself, and that the direction of your own creation is up to you.

Note # 1: Because we are extensions of the mind of God, we have inherited the ability to create as God does. When we create like God, we give everything since we are unlimited, abundant and love. Nothing is held back and there is no lack in our creations or us. The Oneness of "All That Is" remains perfect, whole and complete. Due to free will, we also have the ability to pretend anything we want. If we choose to believe untruths, it has no impact on reality but it does affect our ability to create like God. When we choose to believe that we lack something, we extend or "make" based on that same belief of limitation and lack. Making is based on separation, fear and lack. Believing ourselves to not be perfect, whole and complete, we project that same lack upon our creation.
Sentences # 9 – 12 are the core beliefs that form the bedrock of the thought system of the ego. The egoic thought system is based on the belief in change, separation and lack.

T-2.I.2. These related distortions represent a picture of what actually occurred in the separation, or the "detour into fear." 2 None of **these related distortions** existed before the separation, nor does it actually exist now. 3 Everything God created is like Him. 4 Extension, as undertaken by God, is similar to the inner radiance that the children of the Father inherit from Him. 5 **This inner radiance's** real source is internal. 6 This **extension** is as true of the Son as of the Father. 7 In this sense the creation includes both the creation of the Son by God, and the Son's creations when his mind is healed. 8 This requires God's endowment of the Son with free will, because all loving creation is freely given in one continuous line, in which all aspects are of the same order.

Note # 2: The Sonship, which is all that God created, as he created it, has been given free will. Your free will does not give you the ability to change the truth. It only means that you can elect to temporarily deny the truth until some given time. This denial cannot change the truth for truth is changeless. Ultimately, everyone will freely choose to return to the truth of the Oneness of the Mind of God. Since the oneness of truth remains eternal, our will and the Will of God are the same. We will only be happy when we accept the reality that we, as an extension of the Oneness of everything, can lack nothing.

T-2.I.3. The Garden of Eden, or the pre-separation condition, was a state of mind in which nothing was needed. 2 When Adam listened to the "lies of the serpent," all **Adam** heard was untruth. 3 You do not have to continue to believe what is not true unless you choose to do so. 4 **All that is not true** can literally disappear in the twinkling of an eye because **this untruth** is merely a misperception. 5 What is seen in dreams seems to be very real. 6 Yet the Bible says that a deep sleep fell upon Adam, and nowhere is there reference to his waking up. 7 The world has not yet experienced any comprehensive reawakening or rebirth. 8 Such a rebirth is impossible as long as you continue to project or miscreate. 9 It still remains within you, however, to extend as God extended His Spirit to you. 10 In reality this **ability to extend as God extended His Spirit to you** is your only choice, because your free will was given you for your joy in creating the perfect.

Note # 3: The separation is not God's Will. The separation is the "mad idea" that led to projection instead of creation. Projection is based on lack. Creation is based on abundance. We, as Children of God, must be perfect since God only extends what He is, which is perfection. Due to the separation, we have forgotten who we are. Believing that we lack something, we abdicate our true creative ability and, thus, are unable to create as God's Sons. This loss of creative power has not actually left us but we have failed to recognize the truth about ourselves. Due to our belief that we lack something, we have forgotten how to use our full creative powers to create in God's image. In this "deep sleep" we have projected (made) a world, which exists only within an illusionary dream based on separation, fear and limitation. We, being the dreamer, perceive our "dream world" to be real because we have chosen to dream it. This dream world of our own projections becomes our "provisional reality." It is provisional since it only exists within the mind of the dreamer. Although this provisional world has no reality in God's creation, it does appear to exist to us, the dreamer. When we awake from the dream and once again realize our divine nature, our dream world will disappear just as darkness disappears when a light is turned on. This personal, private "provisional reality" that we experience as real is the basis for different levels. We have dreamed that there is something that exists or can oppose the truth. We have made up the "false" In this projected dream world of separation, we believe that we are limited ego-bodies rather than unlimited Sons of God. This result is level confusion. Are we spirit or are we a body? The aim of the course is to correct this type of level confusion. Are you a limited ego-body or are you an unlimited spirit?
Note: ACIM uses the terms spirit and mind interchangeably. Mind and the brain are not the same. The brain is a physical body part. Mind is your spiritual essence. Mind or spirit is real. The body is a false projection that the ego mistakenly perceives to be what you truly are.

T-2.I.4. All fear is ultimately reducible to the basic misperception that you have the ability to usurp the power of God. 2 Of course, you neither can nor have been able to usurp the power of God. 3 **The correction of this basic misperception that you have the ability to usurp the power of God** is the real basis for your escape from fear. 4 The escape is brought about by your acceptance of the

Atonement, which enables you to realize that your errors never really occurred. 5 Only after the deep sleep fell upon Adam could he experience nightmares. 6 If a light is suddenly turned on while someone is dreaming a fearful dream, he may initially interpret the light itself as part of his dream and be afraid of **the light**. 7 However, when he awakens, the light is correctly perceived as the release from the dream, which is then no longer accorded reality. 8 This release does not depend on illusions **but rather the truth that the light brings to your reality that the dream was not real.** 9 The knowledge that illuminates not only sets you free, but also shows you clearly that you <are> free.

<u>Note # 4:</u> Misperception can only occur in our dream world that has made the false seem possible. The false is anything that would bear false witness to the truth that there is only the Oneness of the Mind of God. God's reality is perfect and changeless because that is God's Will. Within our dream world of projected, provisional reality, we can pretend that the separation is real. Yet, once the sleeping child is awakened to the truth, all fear-based dreams of separation disappear.

T-2.I.5. Whatever lies you may believe are of no concern to the miracle, which can heal any of **the lies you believe** with equal ease. 2 **Miracles** makes no distinctions among misperceptions. 3 **The miracles** sole concern is to distinguish between truth on the one hand, and error on the other **hand.** 4 Some miracles may seem to be of greater magnitude than other **miracles.** 5 But remember the first principle in this course; there is no order of difficulty in miracles. 6 In reality you are perfectly unaffected by all expressions of lack of love. 7 These **expressions of lack of love** can be from yourself and others, from yourself to others, or from others to you. 8 Peace is an attribute <in> you. 9 You cannot find **peace** outside. 10 Illness is some form of external searching. 11 Health is inner peace. 12 **Inner peace** enables you to remain unshaken by lack of love from without and **inner peace enables you to remain** capable, through your acceptance of miracles, of correcting the conditions proceeding from lack of love in others.

<u>Note # 5:</u> There is no order of difficulty in miracles. Once we realize that all illusions are equally false, each is easily dissolved before the light of truth. The solution or miracle is always the same correction. An illusion cannot change the reality of truth. Any expression of lack of love is merely a cry for love. Love is the only proper response to a cry for love. Introduce love to the equation and the perceived problem disappears. Love is all that is real and fear's illusions crumble before love. When you know the truth of your divine inheritance nothing except yourself can rob you of your inner peace. Your inner peace can come only from you. No external force or thing can give you inner peace.

II. The Atonement as Defense

T-2.II.1. You can do anything I ask. 2 I have asked you to perform miracles, and have made it clear that miracles are natural, corrective, healing and universal. 3 There is nothing **miracles** cannot do, but **miracles** cannot be performed in the spirit of doubt or fear. 4 When you are afraid of anything, you are acknowledging **the item you fear has the** power to hurt you. 5 Remember that where your heart is, there is your treasure also. 6 You believe in what you value. 7 If you are afraid, you are valuing wrongly. 8 **Because you are afraid,** your understanding will then inevitably value wrongly, and by endowing all thoughts with equal power **you** will inevitably destroy peace. 9 That is why the Bible speaks of "the peace of God which passeth understanding." 10 This peace is totally incapable of being shaken by errors of any kind. 11 **This peace of God** denies the ability of anything not of God to affect you. 12 **The inability of anything not of God to robber you of the peace of God** is the proper use of denial. 13 **This peace of God** is not used to hide anything, but to correct error. 14 **Through the proper use of denial, the peace of God** brings all error into the light, and since error and darkness are the same, **the peace of God** corrects error automatically.

Note # 6: When we deny that the false can impact the truth, we are properly using denial. Unfortunately, we normally choose to follow the egoic thought system. The ego denies the truth and then attempts to substitute the false belief that we are a separate, limited ego-body in place of the truth. This is an improper use of denial.

T-2.II.2. True denial is a powerful protective device. 2 You can and should deny any belief that error can hurt you. 3 This kind of **true** denial is not a concealment but a correction. 4 Your right mind depends **on the belief that error cannot hurt you.** 5 Denial of error is a strong defense of truth, but denial of truth results in miscreation, the projections of the ego. 6 In the service of the right mind the denial of error frees the mind, and re-establishes the freedom of the will. 7 When the will is really free **the mind** cannot miscreate, because **the mind** recognizes only truth.

Note # 7: When you deny the truth, you claim that you are a separate, limited ego-body. This is a denial of the truth about yourself that you really are an unlimited spirit called the Son of God. When you come from fear and limitation, you cannot create in God's image. You have forgotten your birthright. This egoic belief in separation results in miscreation, which is the projection of egoic wrong-mindedness. The proper use of denial is the rejection of any belief that attempts to contradict the truth that you are a Oneness with God, your Creator. The proper use of denial confirms that you are not a body but rather the sinless Son of God who remains perfect, whole and complete as God created you.

T-2.II.3. You can defend truth as well as error. 2 The means are easier to understand after the value of the goal is firmly established. 3 It is a question of what **the means** is <*for.* > 4 Everyone defends his treasure, and will do so automatically. 5 The real questions are, what do you treasure, and how much do you treasure it? 6 Once you have learned to consider these questions **of what do you treasure, and how much do you treasure it?** and to bring **these same questions** into all your actions, you will have little difficulty in clarifying the means. 7 The means are available whenever you ask. 8 You can, however, save time if you do not protract this step **about questioning what you treasure** unduly. 9 The correct focus will shorten **the means** immeasurably.

Note # 8: We must decide which thought system to value. Would we prefer to claim that we are a limited ego-body in competition with other ego-bodies or would we rather claim that we are "only" the unlimited spirit of the Oneness that comprises the Mind of God? When we value the egoic thought system, we freely choose to claim to be a limited small "s" self. Although it seems strange that anyone would freely choose littleness over the Big "S" Self, the choice for littleness is also the claim that we are special. The ego would rather be special than know the truth that it is just like everything else in the Oneness of everything. Specialness claims that we could be something other than what God created us to be. Egoic specialness claims that we are not perfect, not whole and very incomplete. When we understand the choice is between being everything and being an illusion, we can see why ACIM would state that to follow the false logic of the ego is to be insane.

T-2.II.4. The Atonement is the only defense that cannot be used destructively because **the Atonement** is not a device you made. 2 The Atonement <*principle*> was in effect long before the Atonement began. 3 The principle was love and the Atonement was an <*act*> of love. 4 Acts were not necessary before the separation, because prior to the separation, belief in space and time did not exist. 5 It was only after the separation that the Atonement and the conditions necessary for **the Atonement's** fulfillment were planned. 6 Then a defense so splendid was needed that **the defense** could not be misused, although **the defense** could be refused. 7 Refusal to use the defense **(the Atonement)** could not, however, turn **the Atonement** into a weapon of attack, which is the inherent characteristic of other defenses. 8 The Atonement thus becomes the only defense that is not a two-edged sword. 9 **The atonement** can only heal.

Note # 9: Because the Atonement is an act of God's love, it cannot be misused by the ego. Atonement means "At - Onement" and it testifies only for the truth that the Sonship is like Its Father, perfect, whole and complete. The Atonement states that God's Son remains eternally sinless and guiltless in the Mind of God. Free will allows us the ability to deny this truth of the Oneness but it cannot change this truth.

T-2.II.5. The Atonement was built into the space-time belief to set a limit on the need for **the belief in space-time**, and ultimately to make learning complete. 2 The Atonement is the final lesson. 3 Learning itself, like the classrooms in which **learning** occurs, is temporary. 4 The ability to learn has no value when change is no longer necessary. 5 The eternally creative have nothing to learn. 6 You can learn to improve your perceptions, and can become a better and better learner. 7 This will bring you into closer and closer accord with the Sonship; but the Sonship itself is a perfect creation and perfection is not a matter of degree. 8 Only while there is a belief in differences is learning meaningful.

Note # 10: The belief of separation resulted in our belief in differences. Prior to the separation, there was only the perfect oneness. Since God's creations are eternal and thus, changeless, we can never lose our true identity as Sons of God. We have simply chosen to forget who we are. The belief in the separation and its resulting mistaken follow-up belief that we are an ego-body gave rise to the belief in time-space. The Atonement utilizes time-space as a learning device to reawaken our mind to who we really are. Time is the measurement of change. It is our egoic belief in differences that spawns the specialness of the separation. When our belief in differences is corrected through acceptance of the Atonement for ourselves, our Oneness will return and perceived differences will fade away.

T-2.II.6. Evolution is a process in which you seem to proceed from one degree to the next. 2 You correct your previous missteps by stepping forward. 3 This process **of evolution** is actually incomprehensible in temporal terms, because you return as you go forward. 4 The Atonement is the device by which you can free yourself from the past as you go ahead. 5 **The Atonement** undoes your past errors, thus making it unnecessary for you to keep retracing your steps without advancing to your return. 6 In this sense the Atonement saves time, but like the miracle **the Atonement** serves, **the Atonement** does not abolish **time**. 7 As long as there is need for Atonement, there is need for time. 8 But the Atonement as a completed plan has a unique relationship to time. 9 Until the Atonement is complete, **the Atonement's** various phases will proceed in time, but the whole Atonement stands at time's end. 10 **When the Atonement is complete** at that point the bridge of return **to knowledge and truth** has been built.

Note # 11: Normally, evolution is a change from old to new traits with the new traits being viewed as "better". In our evolutionary cycle, we are attempting to return to our previous condition of knowledge. We are reawakening to the realization that we were, are and always will be perfect. In this regard, we are attempting to get back to our original state of whole-mindedness, which occurred before the dream of separation. ACIM's goal is to remove all blocks to love so that only love remains. These blocks to love are the ego's belief that we are separate, limited ego-bodies. Once removed, we reawaken to the truth that we are only the expression of God's Love and that we are Love.

T-2.II.7. The Atonement is a total commitment. 2 You may still think **the Atonement** is associated with loss. **The belief that the Atonement is associated with loss** is a mistake all the separated Sons of God make in one way or another. 3 It is hard to believe a defense **like the Atonement** that cannot attack is the best defense. 4 This is what is meant by "the meek shall inherit the earth." 5 **The meek** will literally take **the earth** over because of **the meek's** strength. 6 A two-way defense is inherently weak precisely because **a two-way defense** has two edges, and can be turned against you very unexpectedly. 7 This possibility cannot be controlled except by miracles. 8 The miracle turns the defense of Atonement to your real protection, and as you become more and more secure **in your real protection**, you assume your natural talent of protecting others, knowing yourself as both a brother and a Son.

Note # 12: ACIM's use of the term "Atonement" differs than how it is understood by most religious circles. Western fundamental religions define the atonement as a process in which someone or something must be sacrificed to make amends (atone) for someone's errors, which are called sins against God. ACIM utilizes the word 'Atonement" as the acceptance of the truth that God's Son could never be guilty of any sin since God created him to be changeless perfection. Without the belief in separation, there is no one to sin against. Our denial of the fact that we are an indivisible Oneness is not viewed as a sin but merely as an error in thinking that needs to be corrected. No punishment is warranted since an illusion has no impact on truth. A make-believe illusion that calls for the shattering of a Oneness can have no affect on the Oneness that is the Mind of God. No sin has occurred since an illusion has no power to change reality.

III. The Altar of God

T-2.III.1. The Atonement can only be accepted within you by releasing the inner light. 2 Since the separation, defenses have been used almost entirely to defend <*against*> the Atonement, and thus maintain the separation. 3 **The defenses of the separation are** generally seen as a need to protect the body. 4 The many body fantasies in which minds engage arise from the distorted belief that the body can be used as a means for attaining "atonement." 5 Perceiving the body as a temple is only the first step in correcting this distortion, **because perceiving the body as a temple** alters only part of **this distortion**. 6 **Perceiving the body as a temple** <*does*> recognize that Atonement in physical terms is impossible. 7 The next step, however, is to realize that a temple is not a structure at all. 8 **A temple's** true holiness lies at the inner altar around which the structure is built. 9 The emphasis on beautiful structures is a sign of the fear of Atonement, and an unwillingness to reach the altar itself. 10 The real beauty of the temple cannot be seen with the physical eye. 11 Spiritual sight, on the other hand, cannot see the structure at all because **spiritual sight** is perfect vision. 12 **Spiritual sight** can, however, see the altar with perfect clarity.

Note # 13: Atonement for ACIM purpose takes place at the level of Mind. It was at the level of the Mind that the problem of the belief in separation, sin, guilt and fear arose. It is at the level of Mind that healing must takes place. ACIM's Atonement has nothing to do with the physical level of the body.
Note: The term light is often used interchangeably with truth and symbolizes truth.

T-2.III.2. For perfect effectiveness the Atonement belongs at the center of the inner altar, where **the Atonement** undoes the separation and restores the wholeness of the mind. 2 Before the separation the mind was invulnerable to fear, because fear did not exist. 3 Both the separation and the fear are miscreations that must be undone for the restoration of the temple, and for the opening of the altar to receive the Atonement. 4 **The undoing of the miscreation of both the separation and fear is the restoration of the temple that** heals the separation by placing within you the one effective defense **(the Atonement)** against all separation thoughts and making you perfectly invulnerable.

<u>Note # 14:</u> The Atonement process is the acceptance of the truth that God's creations remain as God created them. We remain sinless and guiltless.

T-2.III.3. The acceptance of the Atonement by everyone is only a matter of time. 2 This **acceptance of the Atonement by everyone** may appear to contradict free will because of the inevitability of the final decision, but this is not so. 3 You can temporize and you are capable of enormous procrastination, but you cannot depart entirely from your Creator, Who set the limits on your ability to miscreate. 4 An imprisoned will engenders a situation, which, in the extreme, becomes altogether intolerable. 5 Tolerance for pain may be high, but **tolerance for pain** is not without limit. 6 Eventually everyone begins to recognize, however dimly, that there <*must*> be a better way. 7 As this recognition becomes more firmly established, **this recognition that there <*must*> be a better way** becomes a turning point. 8 This **recognition that there <*must*> be a better way** ultimately reawakens spiritual vision, simultaneously weakening the investment in physical sight. 9 The alternating investment in the two levels of perception is usually experienced as conflict, which can become very acute. 10 But the outcome is as certain as God.

<u>Note # 15:</u> Eventually, we suffer so much pain that we voluntarily decide to reevaluate who we are. We reexamine our egoic belief system. We decide there must be another way. The egoic thought system only results in dissatisfaction and pain. There must be something better than the ego's plan and thought system. We ask our Inner Guide to show us another way. Eventually, by listening to the Voice Within, we realize that we are not an ego-body but rather a spiritual being, a Son of God. We start to view ourselves more and more as spiritual beings, perfect, whole and complete as God created us. We drop our misguided belief that we are the physical body. We change our level of thinking from the physical level to the spirit level.

T-2.III.4. Spiritual vision literally cannot see error, and merely looks for Atonement. 2 All solutions the physical eye seeks dissolve. 3 Spiritual vision looks within **ourselves to our temple** and recognizes immediately that the altar has been defiled **by our erroneous belief we are a separate body** and **that the altar** needs to be repaired and protected. 4 Perfectly aware of the right defense which is the Atonement, spiritual vision passes over all others defense, looking past error to truth. 5 Because of the strength of **spiritual** vision, it brings the mind into the **spirit's** service. 6 This re-establishes the power of the mind and makes **the mind** increasingly unable to tolerate delay, realizing that **delay** only adds unnecessary pain. 7 As a result **of the spirit's re-establishing its power over the mind,** the mind becomes increasingly sensitive to what **the mind** would once have regarded as very minor intrusions of discomfort.

<u>Note # 16:</u> As we turn our mind over to the influence of the thought system of the Holy Spirit, we realize that the egoic thought system does not work. The favorable results that are achieved by utilizing the guidance of the Holy Spirit only increase our continued use of our Inner Voice for truth. We have flashes of inner peace that only lead us to wanting more such experiences. The false egoic belief that we are limited ego-bodies becomes distasteful.

T-2.III.5. The children of God are entitled to the perfect comfort that comes from perfect trust. 2 Until **the children of God** achieve **this perfect comfort that comes from prefect trust,** they waste themselves and their true creative powers on useless attempts to make themselves more comfortable by inappropriate means. 3 But the real means **(the Atonement)** are already provided, and do not involve any effort at all on their part. 4 The Atonement is the only gift that is worthy of being offered at the altar of God, because of the value of the altar itself. 5 **The altar** was created perfect and is entirely worthy of receiving perfection. **This altar, which is God's Son as God created His Son was defiled by both the son's belief in the separation and of fear.** 6 God and His creations are completely dependent on Each Other. 7 **God** depends on **His creations** *<because>* **God** created **His creations** perfect. 8 **God** gave **His creations** His peace so **His creations** could not be shaken and could not be deceived. 9 Whenever you are afraid you *<are>* deceived, and your mind cannot serve the Holy Spirit. 10 This starves you by denying you your daily bread. 11 God is lonely without His Sons, and **His Sons** are lonely without **God**. 12 **His Sons** must learn to look upon the world as a means of healing the separation. 13 The Atonement is the guarantee that **His Sons** will ultimately succeed.

Note # 17: Our safety lies in the truth of what we are. Because we are an extension of the Mind of God, we must be like our Creator. God is the Cause and the Son is the Effect. They are inseparable. The egoic belief that an effect can somehow change its original source or cause is impossible. Without its cause, which is the Mind of God, the effect would cease to exist. Both cause and effect are interrelated and thus are "joined at the hip." Cause without its effect is no longer cause. Each completes the other and is inseparable. Since there is only the Mind of God, which is Truth, the effect must also rest in the truth. Being of one Will, the effect must mirror its cause. In this case, the Mind of God is the first Cause. The Atonement merely acknowledges the truth that we, the Effect, remain as we were created, perfect, whole and complete. We are an inseparable part of the entire Oneness that is the Mind of God. We are that One. This is the "At-Onement" of the Atonement. There is no separation.

IV. Healing as Release from Fear

T-2.IV.1. Our emphasis is now on healing. 2 The miracle is the means **to heal**, the Atonement is the principle **to heal**, and healing is the result. 3 To speak of "a miracle of healing" is to combine two orders of reality inappropriately. 4 Healing is not a miracle. 5 The Atonement, or the final miracle, is a remedy and any type of healing is a result. 6 The kind of error to which Atonement is applied is irrelevant. 7 All healing is essentially the release from fear. 8 To undertake this **healing from fear**, you cannot be fearful yourself. 9 You do not understand healing because of your own fear.

Note # 18: Fear is birthed out of our belief that separation from our Source, the Mind of God, is possible. It is the thinking of the fearful person that must be corrected. By our mind's acceptance of the Atonement principle, which is the truth about our sinless and guiltless nature, all fear is dissolved. The Atonement is the acceptance of the truth about our divine birthright and that separation from our Source is an impossibility.

T-2.IV.2.A major step in the Atonement plan is to undo error at all levels. 2 Sickness or "not-right-mindedness" is the result of level confusion, because **sickness** always entails the belief that what is amiss on one level can adversely affect another. 3 We have referred to miracles as the means of correcting level confusion, for all mistakes must be corrected at the level on which they occur. 4 Only the mind is capable of error. 5 The body can act wrongly only when **the body** is responding to misthought **of the mind**. 6 The body cannot create, and the belief that **the body** can **create is** a fundamental error. **The fundamental error that the body can create** produces all physical symptoms. 7 Physical illness represents a belief in magic. 8 The whole distortion that made magic rests on the belief that there is a creative ability in matter which the mind cannot control. 9 This error can take two forms; **one form of this error** can be **the belief** that the mind can miscreate in the body, or **the second form of this error is** that the body can miscreate in the mind. 10 When it is understood that the mind, **not the body, is** the only level of creation and **that the mind** cannot create beyond itself, neither type of confusion need occur.

Note # 19: Mind is the level of creation. The body is the projection of the mind. As such, the body is an effect of the mind. Just as the Son cannot change the Father, the body cannot change its cause, which is mind. Magic denies our own creative powers of the mind. Magic claims that there is something outside our mind that we lack and that this "something outside" has creative powers that can change our reality. Magic is based on the belief that due to the separation, we are not perfect and that something outside of mind can make us whole again. Magic claims that creative power exists at some level other than mind. It claims that an illusion at the level of bodily form can change or affect the level of mind.

T-2.IV.3. Only the mind can create because spirit has already been created, and the body is a learning device for the mind. 2 Learning devices are not lessons in themselves. 3 All learning devices, like the body, purpose is merely to facilitate learning. 4 The worst a faulty use of a learning device can do is to fail to facilitate learning. 5 **The learning device** has no power in itself to introduce actual learning errors. 6 The body, if properly understood, shares the invulnerability of the Atonement to two-edged application. 7 This is not because the body is a miracle, but because **the body** is not inherently open to misinterpretation. 8 The body is merely part of your experience in the physical world. 9 **The body's** abilities can be and frequently are overevaluated. 10 However, it is almost impossible to deny **the body's** existence in this world. 11 **Those who do deny the body's existence in this world** are engaging in a particularly unworthy form of denial. 12 The term "unworthy" here implies only that **this denial** is not necessary to protect the mind by denying the unmindful. 13 If one denies this unfortunate aspect of the mind's power **(the mind's ability to make or miscreate on behalf of the ego),** one is also denying the power itself **(the mind's power to create like God).**

Note # 20: The body, along with this physical world, is evidence of our ability to create or make, which is miscreation. Only when we come from our true spiritual essence as Sons of God's Love do we have the ability to create like our Father. If we come from the split mind of the ego, we have the ability to make or miscreate. Our split mind can only project illusionary forms that are based on fear and limitation. When we believe that we are limited to the body, we cannot create like the Father because we come from lack. When we attempt to use the learning device of the body as the source of our creative power, we simply fail to create. This failure is not a sin but merely an unsuccessful attempt at creation. As such, it is a mistake that has no affect on the Mind of God.

T-2.IV.4. All material means that you accept as remedies for bodily ills are restatements of magic principles. 2 This **acceptance of physical remedies for bodily ills** is the first step in believing that the body makes its own illness. 3 It is a second misstep to attempt to heal **the body** through non-creative agents. 4 It does not follow, however, that the use of such agents for corrective purposes is evil. 5 Sometimes the illness has a sufficiently strong hold over the mind to render a person temporarily inaccessible to the Atonement. 6 In this case **when a person is temporarily inaccessible to the Atonement,** it may be wise to utilize a compromise approach to mind and body, in which something from the outside is temporarily given healing belief. 7 This is because the last thing that can help the non-right-minded, or the sick, is an increase in fear. 8 **The non-right-minded** are already in a fear-weakened state **of mind**. 9 If **the non-right-minded** are prematurely exposed to a miracle, **the sick-minded** may be precipitated into panic. 10 This is likely to occur when upside-down perception has induced the belief that miracles are frightening.

Note # 21: The body is a neutral learning device. Although the spirit cannot be sick, you can erroneously believe that you are a body. Due to this error in thinking, the mind takes the learning device of the body and makes it "sick." If you believe you are a body, your mind may become too frightened to accept the reality that you are spirit and not a body. The "sick" person's mind may not be able to handle the fact that its own erroneous thinking has caused its body to be "sick." Rather than frighten the sick person more, it may be advisable to utilize "conventional medical treatments" since the mind is temporarily incapable of overriding its egoic mind's belief that it is a "sick physical body." This sick person's belief in the power of an outside agent to affect change within its body will allow the sick person's own creative powers of mind to correct and heal its own body. It is the patient's mind, not the outside agent, which causes the healing.

General Note about doctors and medicine: Although all healing is at the level of mind, ACIM states that you should never do anything that would increase the fear of a patient or your own. Instead, ACIM suggests that we utilize a "magic pill." This "pill" will help reduce the patient's fear and thus, allow the patient's mind to recover its creative ability and if desired to go about doing the actual healing which may include the physical body. ACIM thus does not suggest that you refuse medical treatment to prove that the learning device of the body is not real. Rather, we should maintain and honor the body as a learning device that aids us in our rediscovering of what we are. Aided by the body, we learn about our true spiritual essence and that our real purpose is to be and teach only love. Ignoring or abusing our body may not be the best way to teach and be only love.

T-2.IV.5. The value of the Atonement does not lie in the manner in which **the Atonement** is expressed. 2 In fact, if **the Atonement** is used truly, **the Atonement** will inevitably be expressed in whatever way is most helpful to the receiver. 3 This means that a miracle, to attain its full efficacy **(power to produce),** must be expressed in a language that the recipient can understand without fear. 4 This does not necessarily mean that this **language that the recipient can understand without fear** is the highest level of communication of which he is capable. 5 It does mean, however, that **this language** is the highest level of communication of which he is capable of <*now.* > 6 The whole aim of the miracle is to raise the level of communication, not to lower **the level of communication** by increasing fear.

Note # 22: The underlying principle that rules the thought system of the Holy Spirit is to never do anything that would increase someone's fear. In healing, like all other experience in time and space, our goal should never be to do anything that would increase the level of fear in our brother or ourselves. Fear is counterproductive and makes the illusion of separation from our Source appear real. We must meet our brother at the highest level of understanding that he is currently capable of achieving in the <now> of this present moment. We, like the Holy Spirit, may have to help him "baby-step his way back to the truth. Yet due to the Atonement principle, we know that the return to truth is the inevitable result of God's Plan for His Son's reawakening to his divine birthright.

V. The Function of the Miracle Worker

T-2.V.1.Before miracle workers are ready to undertake their function in this world, it is essential that **the miracle worker** fully understand the fear of release. 2 **Unless they fully understand the fear of release, the miracle worker** may unwittingly foster the belief that release is imprisonment, a belief that is already very prevalent. 3 This misperception **that release is imprisonment** arises in turn from the belief that harm can be limited to the body. 4 That is because of the underlying fear that the mind can hurt itself. 5 None of these errors is meaningful, because the miscreations of the mind do not really exist. 6 This recognition **that the miscreations of the mind do not really exist** is a far better protective device than any form of level confusion, because **the recognition that the miscreations of the mind do not exist**, introduces correction at the level of the error. 7 It is essential to remember that only the mind can create, and that correction belongs at the thought level. 8 To amplify an earlier statement, spirit is already perfect and therefore does not require correction. 9 The body does not exist except as a learning device for the mind. 10 This learning device **of the body** is not subject to errors of its own, because **the body as a learning device** cannot create. 11 It is obvious, then, that inducing the mind to give up **the mind's** miscreations is the only application of creative ability that is truly meaningful.

Note # 23: For a correction to be meaningful, we must deal with the actual error, not with some effect that is the result of the error. Since the body is not the source of the error, the error cannot be corrected at the level of the body. The error is at the level of mind. It is the thought of separation that must be healed. Separation from the Oneness is the cause of fear. By correcting this erroneous thought, all the effects of fear also disappear. To attempt to resolve the problem at the body level is only a futile attempt at masking the problem. Until the root cause is corrected, the problem will not go away. We need only realize that our past thoughts that sought to deny the truth cannot change the truth. We still remain unlimited spirit as God created us. We remain perfect, whole and complete; a Oneness of "All That Is".

T-2.V.2.Magic is the mindless or the miscreative use of mind. 2 Physical medications are forms of "spells," but if you are afraid to use the mind to heal, you should not attempt to-do so. 3 The very fact that you are afraid makes your mind vulnerable to miscreation. 4 You are therefore likely to misunderstand any healing that might occur, and because egocentricity and fear usually occur together, you may be unable to accept the real Source of the healing. 5 Under these conditions **where you are afraid to use the mind to heal,** it is safer for you to rely temporarily on physical healing devices, because you cannot misperceive **the physical healing devices** as your own creations. 6 As long as your sense of vulnerability persists, you should not attempt to perform miracles.

Note # 24: Magic is the use of outside devises to heal or modify a perceived problem. Magic's only power comes from the person's own belief that they are not perfect, not whole, nor complete. Magic has no power unless you choose to abdicate your own power as the creator of your own experience. Magic is the belief that you lack something and that something outside yourself can give you what you are missing. As Child of God, you have been given everything. You cannot lack anything. You can choose to deny your divine birthright. When you do this, you believe and make your illusion of separation from the Oneness appear real.

T-2.V.3.I have already said that miracles are expressions of miracle-mindedness, and miracle-mindedness means right-mindedness. 2 The right-minded neither exalt nor depreciate the mind of the miracle worker or the miracle receiver. 3 However, as a correction, the miracle need not await the right-mindedness of the receiver. 4 In fact, **the miracles** purpose is to restore **the receiver** <to> his right mind. 5 It is essential, however, that the miracle worker be in his right mind, however briefly, or **the miracle worker** will be unable to re-establish right-mindedness in someone else.

Note # 25: The miracle restores the receiver's mind to correct thinking. In order for a miracle to occur, someone must be willing to follow the guidance of the Holy Spirit. If both parties are under the guidance of their egoic thought system, the Holy Spirit will be unable to correct the mind's misperception. Someone must be willing, at least momentarily, to ask and follow his or her Inner Guide, which is the Holy Spirit or Christ consciousness. If the Holy Spirit were to act alone without some party's invitation, this would only increase that party's fear. The Holy Spirit will do nothing that would increase fear and, therefore, He waits patiently on the "sidelines" until someone invites Him to take charge.

T-2.V.4. The healer who relies on his own readiness is endangering his understanding. 2 You are perfectly safe as long as you are completely unconcerned about your readiness, but maintain a consistent trust in **my (Jesus or the Holy Spirit's) readiness**. 3 If your miracle working inclinations are not functioning properly, **the malfunction** is always because fear has intruded on your right-mindedness and has turned **your right-mindedness** upside down. 4 All forms of not-right-mindedness are the result of refusal to accept the Atonement for yourself. 5 If you do accept **the Atonement for yourself**, you are in a position to recognize that those who need healing are simply those who have not realized that right-mindedness <is> healing.

Note # 26: We are responsible for controlling our fear. By accepting the Atonement for ourselves, all fear dissipates. This is due to the fact that you understand that you are the perfect, sinless and guiltless extension of the Mind of God. There is no separation so there can be nothing to fear.

T-2.V.5. *<The sole responsibility of the miracle worker is to accept the Atonement for himself.>* 2 This means you recognize that mind is the only creative level, and that **the mind's** errors are healed by the Atonement. 3 Once you accept this, your mind can only heal. 4 By denying your mind any destructive potential and reinstating **the mind's** purely constructive powers, you place yourself in a position to undo the level confusion of others. 5 The message you then give to **the confused** is the truth that their minds are similarly constructive, and their miscreations cannot hurt them. 6 By affirming this **truth that their minds are similarly constructive, and their miscreations cannot hurt them** you release the mind from over evaluating its own learning device **(the body),** and restore the mind to **the mind's** true position as the learner.

Note # 27: By accepting the Atonement for yourself, you reclaim the truth about yourself. Once you know the truth of what you are, you are in a position to help others rediscover that same truth about themselves. Prior to this, it was only one deluded mind trying to help another, similarly deluded mind. It is foolish to seek advice from the insane.

T-2.V.6. It should be emphasized again that the body does not learn any more than **the body** creates. 2 As a learning device **the body** merely follows the learner, but if **the learning device, the body,** is falsely endowed with self-initiative, **the body** becomes a serious obstruction to the very learning **the body** should facilitate. 3 Only the mind is capable of illumination. 4 Spirit is already illuminated and the body in itself is too dense. 5 The mind, however, can bring **the mind's** illumination to the body by recognizing that **the body** is not the learner, and **therefore, the body is** unamenable to learning. 6 The body is, however, easily brought into alignment with a mind that has learned to look beyond **the body** toward the light.

Note # 28: The body follows the mind's direction. It is only when the mind abdicates its creative responsibility to the body that the body appears to be in charge. The actual cause of this role reversal is the "victim's" own desire to pretend that the body controls the mind. Ultimately, even in the deepest state of victim consciousness, it is the victim's own mind that is in control.

T-2.V.7. Corrective learning always begins with the awakening of spirit, and the turning away from the belief in physical sight. 2 This **turning away from the belief in physical sight** often entails fear, because you are afraid of what your spiritual sight will show you. 3 I said before that the Holy Spirit cannot see error, and **the Holy Spirit** is capable only of looking beyond **error** to the defense of Atonement. 4 There is no doubt that **looking beyond error** may produce discomfort, yet the discomfort is not the final outcome of the perception. 5 When the Holy Spirit is permitted to look upon the defilement of the altar, **the Holy Spirit** also looks immediately toward the Atonement. 6 Nothing **the Holy Spirit** perceives can induce fear. 7 Everything that results from spiritual awareness is merely channelized toward correction. 8 Discomfort is aroused only to bring the need for correction into awareness.

Note # 29: The Holy Spirit is aware that what you perceive to be our reality is merely the illusion of separation. It is not part of the Mind of God. The Oneness remains unbroken and unharmed. Yet until the dreamer awakens to the truth that he or she was merely dreaming, the dream will appear to be real within his or her egoic split-mind. In the awakening process, we disregard or look past the physical senses. We understand that we are not the body. Until we began to realize that we are a spiritual being having a temporary physical experience in time and space, we will remain trapped in the egoic thinking that the separation is real and that we have something to fear.

T-2.V.8. The fear of healing arises in the end from an unwillingness to accept unequivocally that healing is necessary. 2 What the physical eye sees is not corrective, nor can error be corrected by any device that can be seen physically. 3 As long as you believe in what your physical sight tells you, your attempts at correction will be misdirected. 4 The real vision **(spiritual sight)** is obscured, because you cannot endure to see your own defiled altar. 5 But since the altar has been defiled, your state becomes doubly dangerous unless **the defiled altar** <*is*> perceived.

Note # 30: The defiled altar is your true self as God created you. In truth, you remain a sinless and perfect oneness. Yet, you perceive yourself to be something other than God's Child. Your true Big "S" Self is defiled due to your belief in the separation and your view of yourself as a physical body. This error cannot be corrected at the physical (body) level since the error is at the level of creation. The level of creation is the mind and the healing/correction must occur at this level.

T-2.V.9. Healing is an ability that developed after the separation, before **the separation** healing was unnecessary. 2 Like all aspects of the belief in space and time, **healing** is temporary. 3 However, as long as time persists, healing is needed as a means of protection. 4 This is because healing rests on charity, and charity is a way of perceiving the perfection of another even if you cannot perceive **the perfection** in yourself. 5 Most of the loftier concepts of which you are capable now are time-dependent. 6 Charity is really a weaker reflection of a much more powerful love-encompassment that is far beyond any form of charity you can conceive of as yet. 7 Charity is essential to right-mindedness in the limited sense in which **right-mindedness** can now be attained.

Note # 31: Charity allows us to look past our physical senses to the spiritual truth that our brother is much more than a body. We perceive our brother to be spirit or mind. We accord him the truth of his perfect "higher" nature. His spiritual reality is something that our physical sense would deny to him and ourselves.

T-2.V.10. Charity is a way of looking at another as if **the other person** had already gone far beyond his actual accomplishments in time. 2 Since **the other person's** own thinking is faulty he cannot see the Atonement for himself, or he would have no need of charity. 3 The charity that is accorded **the other person** is both an acknowledgment that he needs help, and a recognition that he will accept **help**. 4 Both of these perceptions **that he needs and will accept help** clearly imply their dependence on time, making it apparent that charity still lies within the limitations of this world. 5 I said before that only revelation transcends time. 6 The miracle, as an expression of charity, can only shorten **time**. 7 It must be understood, however, that whenever you offer a miracle to another, you are shortening the suffering of both of you. 8 This **miracle** corrects retroactively as well as progressively.

<u>Note # 32:</u> The miracle grants to another person's split-mind the truth of what they truly are as opposed to how they may currently, incorrectly perceive themselves to be. Their incorrect perception is based on their erroneous belief that they are a limited ego-body. By looking past the physical toward their true spiritual nature, the other person moves both the giver and receiver of the miracle down the time line towards their full acceptance of the Atonement for themselves. The miracle is a change in the mind's misperception. As such, it implies change that requires time for change is what time measures.

A. Special Principles of Miracle Workers

T-2.V.A.11.(1) The miracle abolishes the need for lower-order concerns. 2 Since **the miracle** is an out-of-pattern time interval, the ordinary considerations of time and space do not apply. 3 When you perform a miracle, I will arrange both time and space to adjust to **the miracle**.

<u>Note # 33:</u> The miracle is not bound by time and space. The miracle occurs at the level of mind, which is "higher up the ladder" and thus, closer to the truth than the level of physical time and space. The miracle utilizes the laws of God instead of the laws of egoic misperception.

T-2.V.A.12.(2) A clear distinction between what is created and what is made is essential. 2 All forms of healing rest on this fundamental correction in level perception.

<u>Note # 34:</u> When the mind believes it is an ego-body, the mind cannot create because it believes in lack and fear. Under this condition, the split mind can only "make" since the mind is under the control of the ego and wrong-mindedness. "Made things" are not perfect, whole and complete. "Made things" are subject to change and thus, only exist in our temporary dream state of provisional reality. Only creation, which is the shared extension of love, is eternal and changeless. When we "make", we miscreate because we fail to create in our true spiritual image as God's Child, who is always perfect, whole and complete. It is our erroneous belief of what we are that prevents us from creating. Creation is an extension of what we truly are. We are part of the holographic Mind of God, which is the Oneness of "All That Is." We are love and love can be extended without any loss to the giver. When a mind is under the influence of the ego (wrong-mindedness), the mind is in a state of fear and, therefore, cannot create because the mind falsely believes it lacks something. Under this perceived condition of fear and lack, love does not appear to exist and the split mind cannot create. Only Love can create or extend since only Love gives all without any expectation of return. God is the embodiment of Love. Being His Son

made in His image, we must also be Love. Due to our free will we have the ability to forget who we are but we do not have the ability to loose what we are. What God has given us can never be lost since this is not God's will for His creations. We are not a body since God did not create this "physical thing" we call our body. In our dream of separation, we perceive that we are physical form and have made a body. It is this erroneous egoic thinking, not God's thinking, that made the body. In eternity, we are always as God created us, a perfect, whole and complete Oneness within the Mind of God.

T-2.V.A.13.(3) Never confuse right- and wrong-mindedness. 2 Responding to any form of error with anything except a desire to heal is an expression of this confusion.

Note # 35: Right-mindedness is associated with the thought system of the Holy Spirit; wrong-mindedness with the thought system of the ego.

T-2.V.A.14.(4) The miracle is always a denial of this error **of wrong-mindedness** and an affirmation of the truth **of right-mindedness**. 2 Only right-mindedness can correct in a way that has any real effect. 3 Pragmatically, what has no real effect has no real existence. 4 **What has no real** effect, then, is emptiness. 5 Being without substantial content, **wrong-mindedness** lends itself to projection.

Note # 36: This error in perception is ultimately the erroneous belief that we are separate. Our belief in separateness leads to the wrong-mindedness of the split mind. If we attempt to correct one misperception with another misperception, we still remain in confusion. Both misperceptions are equally false and thus have no impact on the reality of truth.

T-2.V.A.15.(5) The level-adjustment power of the miracle induces the right perception for healing. 2 Until this **right perception** has occurred healing cannot be understood. 3 Forgiveness is an empty gesture unless **forgiveness** entails correction. 4 Without this **correction, forgiveness** is essentially judgmental, rather than healing.

Note # 37: The miracle changes misperception into correct perception. It replaces the belief in separation with the belief in unity and Oneness.

T-2.V.A.16.(6) Miracle-minded forgiveness is <*only*> correction. 2 **Miracle-minded forgiveness** has no element of judgment at all. 3 The statement "Father forgive them for they know not what they do" in no way evaluates <*what*> they do. 4 **This statement** is an appeal to God to heal their minds. 5 **In this statement** there is no reference to the outcome of the error. 6 **The outcome of the error** does not matter.

Note # 38: Error is treated simply as a mistake from which we are asked to choose again. There is no judgment of wrongdoing or repentance extracted from the error-maker. The deluded mind is not punished. Instead the wrong-minded are told to choose again. The miracle-maker understands that illusions can have no affect on the Mind of God or the Sonship's divine inheritance.

T-2.V.A.17.(7) The injunction "Be of one mind" is the statement for revelation-readiness. 2 My request "Do this in remembrance of me" is the appeal for cooperation from miracle workers. 3 The two statements are not in the same order of reality. 4 Only the latter **statement "do this in remembrance of me",** involves an awareness of time, since to remember is to recall the past in the present. 5 Time is under my direction, but timelessness belongs to God. 6 In time we exist for and with each other. 7 In timelessness we coexist with God.

Note # 39: While under the illusion that the separation is real, we perceive ourselves to be in the realm of time. Time measures change in perception. Knowledge or truth does not change and, therefore, is timeless. Time exists as long as the united Sonship believes Itself to be incomplete, different and separate. With the end of time, the once apparently fragmented Sonship is returned to the wholeness of correct-mindedness.

T-2.V.A.18. (8) You can do much on behalf of your own healing and that of others if, in a situation calling for help, you think of **the situation calling for help** this way:
2 I am here only to be truly helpful.
3 I am here to represent Him Who sent me.
4 I do not have to worry about what to say or what to do, because He Who sent me will direct me.
5 I am content to be wherever He wishes, knowing He goes there with me.
6 I will be healed as I let Him teach me to heal.

Note # 40: Being an extension of our Creator, we are a conduit for God's love. The Holy Spirit is the Voice for God. By following the thought system of the Holy Spirit, we will heal the mind of the Sonship and return the once split mind to right-mindedness. God's plan for His Child's return to knowledge will be accomplished for it is God's Will.

VI. Fear and Conflict

T-2.VI.1. Being afraid seems to be involuntary; something beyond your own control. 2 Yet I have said already that only constructive acts should be involuntary. 3 My control can take over everything that does not matter, while my guidance can direct everything that does **matter**, if you so choose. 4 Fear cannot be controlled by me, but **fear** can be self-controlled. 5 **Your** fear prevents me from giving you my control. 6 The presence of fear shows that you have raised body thoughts to the level of the mind. 7 **When you raise body thoughts to the level of the mind,** this removes these **body thoughts** from my control, and makes you feel personally responsible for **these body thoughts**. 8 This is an obvious confusion of levels.

Note # 41: Since fear is self-induced, we must learn to control our fear. Jesus, a symbol for the Holy Spirit, can guide our mind in all areas that matter. Only love is real and our return to knowledge requires placing our mind under the guidance of the Holy Spirit. Thoughts of love and forgiveness become the only thoughts that matter since they are real. Illusionary thought projections based on the belief of separation and lack are not real and of no consequence. These egoic thought projections can and are being reinterpreted by the Holy Spirit to bring about the return of the split-minded back to the truth of what they are. These same egoic thought projections when reinterpreted by the Holy Spirit now become part of God's Plan to return the Sonship to knowledge. When we are in fear-based thought patterns, we can control our fear by stopping what we are thinking and asking for the Holy Spirit's guidance. We must claim responsibility for our thoughts. Fear is the result of mistakenly identifying your spiritual essence as a limited ego-body. When we do this, we have made the body the apparent controller of our mind. This is an attempt by our ego to make the false appear real. This results in level confusion, which is the egoic attempt to mix or replace the true with the false. Fear arises when we value an illusion over the truth. We fear that we might lose this imagined projection that we value. We have attempted to raise a bodily illusion to the creative level of mind and thus, denied that we bear responsibility for the illusion in the first place.

Constructive acts, which within the dream of separation are acts of love and forgiveness, should flow involuntary since they are our natural state. Miracle-mindedness is the mindset of our Christ consciousness.

T-2.VI.2.I do not foster level confusion, but you must choose to correct **level confusion**. 2 You would not excuse insane behavior on your part by saying you could not help it. 3 Why should you condone insane thinking? 4 There is a confusion here that you would do well to look at clearly. 5 You may believe that you are responsible for what you do, but not for what you think. 6 The truth is that you are responsible for what you think, because it is only at this level **of thought** that you can exercise choice. 7 What you do comes from what you think. 8 You cannot separate yourself from the truth by "giving" autonomy to behavior. 9 **Behavior** is controlled by me automatically as soon as you place what you think under my guidance. 10 Whenever you are afraid, it is a sure sign that you have allowed your mind to miscreate and have not allowed me to guide **your mind**.

<u>Note # 42:</u> Thoughts are things. Everything we do originates from thought. We control our thoughts. It is the denial of the belief that we control our thoughts that leads us down the self-imposed road of victim consciousness. It has been said. "Sow a thought; you reap an action. Sow an action; you reap a habit. Sow a habit: you reap a character. Sow a character; you reap a destiny." We need to take responsibility for what we think because thinking is the creative aspect of the mind. Once the thought has been released, the mind will "make or create" the desired outcome. The behavior is the effect of the thought. The thought is the cause of the behavior. Thoughts are things. But be careful what you think since you will get what you really thought about; not what you said or what you meant to say. Fear based thoughts result in miscreations that are made out of the belief in lack. These fear-based thoughts result in behavior or activity on the body level that support the belief that we exist as separate, limited ego-bodies in competition with other ego-bodies. As such, they engender fear, conflict and struggle. These egoic miscreations make the illusion appear real within the mind of the dreamer. Thoughts always precede the behavior. Thoughts are causative, not the other way around. The ego claims that your thoughts are the reactions to behaviors that are outside your control. This misperceiving of cause for effect and effect for cause is level confusion.

T-2.VI.3. It is pointless to believe that controlling the outcome of misthought can result in healing. 2 When you are fearful, you have chosen wrongly. 3 **Your fearful misthinking** is why you feel responsible for **choosing wrongly**. 4 You must change your mind, not your behavior, and this < *changing of your mind is* > a matter of willingness. 5 You do not need guidance except at the mind level. 6 Correction belongs only at the **mind** level where change is possible. 7 Change does not mean anything at the symptom level, where **change** cannot work.

<u>Note # 43:</u> Since the error is at the level of creative mind, we need guidance and correction at that same level of mind since this is where the problem occurred. To attempt correction on the level of the behavior is attempting to heal the effect rather than deal with the cause. The cause is always at the higher level of the mind, which is where the power of creation or making resides. Correct the mistaken thought and healing will result. Level confusion takes place when we attempt to correct something on one level with something from another level. In this case, we attempt to treat the effect rather than the cause. We need to go to the source of the original error, which is always our belief in the separation from our Source. We have temporarily forgotten that we are spirit, not a body. We need the Holy Spirit's guidance to remember that we are God's Creation; always sinless and guiltless as God created

His Child.

T-2.VI.4. The correction of fear <*is*> your responsibility. 2 When you ask for release from fear, you are implying that **fear is not your responsibility**. 3 You should ask, instead, for help in the conditions that have brought the fear about. 4 These conditions always entail a willingness to be separate. 5 At that level **(level of the mind)** you <*can*> help **correct the fear.** 6 You are much too tolerant of mind wandering, and are passively condoning your mind's miscreations. 7 The particular result does not matter, but the fundamental error does **matter.** 8 The correction is always the same. 9 Before you choose to do anything, ask me if your choice is in accord with mine. 10 If you are sure that **your choice is in accord with mine** there will be no fear.

Note # 44: Whatever form the result takes does not matter because the result is not the cause. To correct the error we need to be on the level of the error. The error occurs at the level of the mind. We need to correct the mistaken thought. The fundamental error is the erroneous belief in the separation. It is our split-minded egoic attempts at separation that need correction. The ego has once again raised body thoughts to the level of mind. This identification of yourself as the body is the cause of your fear.

T-2.VI.5. Fear is always a sign of strain. **Fear and strain** arising whenever what you want conflicts with what you do. 2 This **conflicting** situation **of what you want, conflicting with what you do** arises in two ways: First, you can choose to do conflicting things, either simultaneously or successively. 3 This produces conflicted behavior, which is intolerable to you because the part of the mind that wants to do something else is outraged. 4 Second, you can behave as you think you should, but without entirely wanting to do so. 5 This produces consistent behavior, but entails great strain. 6 In both cases, the mind and the behavior are out of accord **and this conflicting mind / behavior pattern**, resulting in a situation in which you are doing what you do not wholly want to do. 7 **Out of** this **conflicting thought / behavior pattern of doing what you do not wholly want to do**, arouses a sense of coercion that usually produces rage, and projection is likely to follow. 8 Whenever there is fear, it is because you have not made up your mind. 9 Your mind is therefore split, and your behavior inevitably becomes erratic. 10 Correcting at the behavioral level can shift the error from the first type of conflicting situations, to the second type, but will not obliterate the fear.

Note # 45: When our thoughts align with the thought system of the ego, we are in conflict with our true nature, which is our Christ conscious Self or Big "S" Self's goals and desire. This internal conflict births fear. Our Big "S" Self knows that we are unlimited, invulnerable spirit or mind. As such, we are only extension of God's Love. When we have fearful thoughts, these are by definition unloving thoughts. This results in a conflict within our mind that now appears to be split into two separate parts. One part represents our egoic thinking; the other, the thought system of the Holy Spirit. Fear and conflict dissipate when we align with the Holy Spirit. Our feelings are the indicator of our alignment to our true Big "S" Self's nature. Bad feelings indicate that we are out of alignment and moving into fear. Good feelings indicate that we are moving into proper alignment with love.

T-2.VI.6. It is possible to reach a state in which you bring your mind under my guidance without conscious effort, but this implies a willingness that you have not developed as yet. 2 The Holy Spirit cannot ask more than you are willing to do. 3 The strength to do comes from your undivided decision. 4 There is no strain in doing God's Will as soon as you recognize that **God's Will** is also your own. 5 The lesson here is quite simple, but particularly apt to be overlooked. 6 I will therefore repeat **this lesson,** urging you to listen. 7 Only your mind can produce fear. 8 **The mind produces fear** whenever **the mind** is conflicted in what the mind wants. **This conflict between what the mind wants produces** inevitable strain because wanting and doing are discordant. 9 This **conflict between wanting and doing**

can be corrected only by accepting a unified goal.

Note # 46: Being an extension of God, our true will must equate with God's Will. God's Will is that we be happy. Being love, we cannot be happy by thinking fearful or unloving thoughts. We can only be happy when we align our current experience with forgiving and loving thoughts. Our feelings are our inner guidance system's gage that allows our mind to know in current time how well our current thoughts and actions are aligning with our Big "S" Self's will, which is also God's Will. Bad feelings indicate that we are out of alignment and moving into fear. Good feelings indicate that we are moving into proper alignment with love.

T-2.VI.7. The first corrective step in undoing the error **of conflict between wanting and doing** is to know first that the conflict is an expression of fear. 2 Say to yourself that you must somehow have chosen not to love, or the fear could not have arisen. 3 Then the whole process of correction becomes nothing more than a series of pragmatic steps in the larger process of accepting the Atonement as the remedy. 4 These steps may be summarized in this way:
5 Know first that **conflict** is fear.
6 Fear arises from lack of love.
7 The only remedy for lack of love is perfect love.
8 Perfect love is the Atonement.

Note # 47: The choice is always between love and fear. If we have lost our inner peace, we are coming from fear. We have raised body thoughts to the level of mind. We have made the illusionary dream of the fragmentation of our Oneness appear real. It is our belief in separation that leads to the making of conflict and fear.

T-2.VI.8.I have emphasized that the miracle, or the expression of Atonement, is always a sign of respect <from> the worthy <to> the worthy. 2 The recognition of this worth is re-established by the Atonement. 3 It is obvious, then, that when you are afraid, you have placed yourself in a position where you need Atonement. 4 You have done something loveless, having chosen without love. 5 This **having chosen without love** is precisely the situation for which the Atonement was offered. 6 The need for the remedy **to having chosen without love** inspired **the remedy's** establishment, **which is the Atonement.** 7 As long as you recognize only the need for the remedy, you will remain fearful. p30 8 However, as soon as you accept the remedy, you have abolished the fear **of having chosen without love with the remedy, which is the Atonement.** 9 **Accepting the Atonement for one's self** is how true healing occurs.

Note # 48: By accepting the Atonement for ourselves, we accept the truth that we, as God's Creations, must remain guiltless and sinless like our Source. We realize that an illusion, which is an unloving thought, is a mistaken belief that can have no impact on the Mind of God. We remain as God created us, perfect, whole and complete. We recognize both our brother and our own worthiness to be love and loved.

T-2.VI.9. Everyone experiences fear. 2 Yet it would take very little right thinking to realize why fear occurs. 3 Few appreciate the real power of the mind, and no one remains fully aware **of the real power of the mind** all the time. 4 However, if you hope to spare yourself from fear there are some things you must realize, and realize fully. 5 The mind is very powerful, and **the mind** never loses **the mind's** creative force. 6 **The mind** never sleeps. 7 Every instant **the mind** is creating. 8 It is hard to recognize that thought and belief combine into a power surge that can literally move mountains. 9 It appears at first glance that to believe such power about yourself **as your minds ability to move mountains** is arrogant, but that is not the real reason you do not believe **your mind can do this.** 10 You prefer to believe that your thoughts cannot exert real influence because you are actually afraid of your **thoughts.** 11 This belief **that your thoughts cannot exert real influence and are thus, not causative** may allay awareness of the guilt, but this **allaying the awareness of guilt comes** at the cost of perceiving the mind as impotent. 12 If you believe that what you think is ineffectual you may cease to be afraid of **what you think**, but you are hardly likely to respect **what you think**. 13 There <*are*> no idle thoughts. 14 All thinking produces form at some level.

Note # 49: Thoughts become things. We are constantly creating our own experiences by what we are thinking. The only question is, "Are you creating deliberately or by default." When we claim that we are powerless to affect our experience, we are creating by default. This denial of our own creative powers results in a state of victim consciousness. We believe that we are the innocent victims of some known or unknown force, but we are sure we are not the cause of our plight. Since our thoughts determine our experiences, it becomes a question of what we will choose to create. Loving thoughts create. They are inclusive and unite. They are real. Fear-based thoughts make or miscreate and they exclude, separate and limit. Fear-based thoughts are at the level of bodily illusion and are not real. Miscreation is not part of the Mind of God. We either create or make depending on the thought system we choose to follow. But in either case, we are the decision-makers. There are no accidents. Our thoughts cause our "provisional reality" that we perceive as real.

VII. Cause and Effect

T-2.VII.1. You may still complain about fear, but you nevertheless persist in making yourself fearful. 2 I have already indicated that you cannot ask me to release you from fear. 3 I know **fear** does not exist, but you do not **know fear does not exist**. 4 If I intervened between your thoughts and their results, I would be tampering with a basic law of cause and effect; **which is** the most fundamental law there is. 5 I would hardly help you if I depreciated the power of your own thinking. 6 This would be in direct opposition to the purpose of this course **which is for you to reclaim and remember who you really are, which is God's Son.** 7 It is much more helpful to remind you that you do not guard your thoughts carefully enough. 8 You may feel that at this point it would take a miracle to enable you **to guard your thoughts carefully enough,** which is perfectly true. 9 You are not used to miracle-minded thinking, but you can be trained to think that way. 10 All miracle workers need that kind of training **in miracle minded thinking**.

Note # 50: Fear is not part of the Mind of God and, therefore, is not real. Fear does appear very real within the deluded mind of the dreamer who claims to not know what his divine birthright is. We were created to be a creator just like our Source. The basic law of the universe is that cause must have its effect and that like begets like. When we choose to pretend we are something we are not, we miscreate a similar thought projection of this same deluded mental state. Thus, believing we are in a state of lack, we place limitations on what we make. Since we are the source of our own fear, we must look within ourselves if we are to correct the source of this fear, which is our own split mind belief in separation.

T-2.VII.2.I cannot let you leave your mind unguarded, or you will not be able to help me. 2 Miracle working entails a full realization of the power of thought in order to avoid miscreation. 3 **You must realize the full power of thought in order to avoid miscreation or else** a miracle will be necessary to set the mind itself straight, a circular process that would not foster the time collapse for which the miracle was intended. 4 The miracle worker must have genuine respect for true cause and effect as a necessary condition for the miracle to occur.

Note # 51: The miracle worker must respect the creative power of the mind and realize that his thinking determined his perception. By changing your thinking from the thought system of the ego to the Holy Spirit, you change your perceived results. You go from misperception to correct perception.

T-2.VII.3. Both miracles and fear come from thoughts. 2 If you are not free to choose **either miracles or fear**, you would also not be free to choose the other. 3 By choosing the miracle you <*have*> rejected fear, if only temporarily. 4 You have been fearful of everyone and everything. 5 You are afraid of God, of me and of yourself. 6 You have misperceived or miscreated Us **(God, me and yourself),** and believe in what you have made **through your misperception**. 7 You would not have done this **miscreating of God, me and yourself** if you were not afraid of your own thoughts. 8 The fearful <*must*> miscreate, because **the fearful** misperceive creation. 9 When you miscreate you are in pain. 10 The cause and effect principle now becomes a real expediter, though only temporarily. 11 Actually, "Cause" is a term properly belonging to God, and His "Effect" is His Son. 12 This entails a set of Cause and Effect relationships totally different from those you introduce into miscreation. 13 The fundamental conflict in this world, then, is between creation and miscreation. 14 All fear is implicit in the second, **miscreation**, and all love in the first, creation. 15 The conflict is therefore one between love and fear.

Note # 52: Free will allows us to act as our own decision-maker. In the world of perception, we have only two choices, love or fear. Each is represented by a different thought system and each choice is also a choice for the true or the false. In our deluded state of claiming we are other than what God created, we have lost knowledge. Perception was born out of the insane belief that there is something other than God's Will; that the Oneness had been shattered into separate parts that are now different than the whole. This is the Sonship's misperception of what creation is. Within the split-minded Sonship, the separation appeared to be real and now there is an observer and something to observe. Rather than the truth that there is just a Oneness of everything, there now appears something to fear. When we think fearful thoughts, we miscreate. Miscreation results in conflict and more fear.

God is the Cause and we are the Effect. The Sonship is all that God created as He created it and is the Effect of God. An effect cannot change its cause. For the child to be able to change its cause would be to change its parentage. This is impossible. Source always comes first and is changeless. The Sonship cannot change God, the Father.

T-2.VII.4. It has already been said that you believe you cannot control fear because you yourself made **fear,** and your belief in **fear** seems to render **fear** out of your control. 2 Yet any attempt to resolve the error **of your belief in fear,** through attempting the mastery of fear is useless. 3 In fact, it asserts the power of fear by the very assumption that **fear** need be mastered. 4 The true resolution **of fear** rests entirely on mastery **of fear** through love. 5 In the interim, however, the sense of conflict is inevitable, since you have placed yourself in a position where you believe in the power of what does not exist **which is fear.**

Note # 53: Fear is not real in the Mind of God. It is something that we have made up within our egoic thought system. Only love is real since love is all that exists. In our illusionary state of separation, we believe that both love and fear exist. When fear is brought in front of love's light, fear disappears. When we oppose fear and attempt to resist it, we make it real. If something exists only in the mind of the dreamer, we need only to awaken the dreamer and the dream dissipates. To do battle against an imaginary enemy is to make the enemy appear real. Fear's only power is the power we choose to give it.

T-2.VII.5. Nothing and everything cannot coexist. 2 To believe in one is to deny the other. 3 Fear is really nothing and love is everything. 4 Whenever light enters darkness, the darkness is abolished. 5 What you believe is true for you. 6 In this sense, **because you believe in the separation**, the separation <has> occurred, and to deny **that the separation has occurred to you** is merely to use denial inappropriately. 7 However, to concentrate on error is only a further error. 8 The initial corrective procedure is to recognize temporarily that there is a problem, but only as an indication that immediate correction is needed. 9 This establishes a state of mind in which the Atonement can be accepted without delay. 10 It should be emphasized, however, that ultimately no compromise is possible between everything and nothing. 11 Time is essentially a device by which all compromise **between everything and nothing** can be given up 12 **Compromise between everything and nothing** only seems to be abolished by degrees, because time itself involves intervals that do not exist. 13 Miscreation made this **compromise** necessary as a corrective device. 14 The statement "For God so loved the world that he gave his only begotten Son, that whosoever believeth in him should not perish but have everlasting life" needs only one slight correction to be meaningful in this context; "He gave it, **everlasting life,** <to> His only begotten Son."

Note # 54: God is everything. Therefore, when God extended Himself, He created or gave His creations everything. He created His Son in His image, which is perfect Love. God's Son is everything God created. What God created can have no opposite for extension is merely the expansion of the Oneness of "All That Is". God is everything and there is nothing outside or apart from this Oneness. Within the illusion of separation, we believe that there can be opposites. We believe that our decision-maker has a choice between separation and oneness, fear and love. Time is the device that allows us to change our belief from the false to the true. As long as we perceive that the choice for the false is possible, time will be needed. Time is only truth oriented in its direction. Whatever moment you find yourself to be in, it is exactly where you need to be. The Holy Spirit uses time and the miracle to bring us back to right-mindedness as quickly as possible.

T-2.VII.6. It should especially be noted that God has only <one> Son. 2 If all His creations are His Sons, every one must be an integral part of the whole Sonship. 3 The Sonship in its Oneness transcends the sum of **the Sonship's** parts. 4 However, this **Oneness** is obscured as long as any of its parts is missing. 5 That is why the conflict, **our belief in the separation,** cannot ultimately be resolved until all the parts of the Sonship have returned **to Oneness.** 6 Only then can the meaning of wholeness in the true sense be understood. 7 Any part of the Sonship can believe in error or incompleteness if he so chooses. 8 However, if he does **choose to believe in incompleteness,** he is believing in the existence of nothingness. 9 The correction of this error **of the belief in incompleteness or nothingness** is the Atonement.

Note # 55: The Sonship is everything God created as God created it. The Sonship cannot be separated into indivisible parts, as it is holographic in nature. Even in its vain attempt to shatter the wholeness, the Sonship remains a Oneness of The Mind of God.

T-2.VII.7. I have already briefly spoken about readiness, but some additional points might be helpful here. 2 Readiness is only the prerequisite for accomplishment. 3 The two, **readiness and accomplishment,** should not be confused. 4 As soon as a state of readiness occurs, there is usually some degree of desire to accomplish, but **the desire to accomplish** is by no means necessarily undivided. 5 The state **of readiness** does not imply more than a potential for a change of mind. 6 Confidence cannot develop fully until mastery has been accomplished. 7 We have already attempted to correct the fundamental error that fear can be mastered, and have emphasized that the only real mastery is through love. 8 Readiness is only the beginning of confidence. 9 You may think this implies that an enormous amount of time is necessary between readiness and mastery, but let me remind you that time and space are under my control.

Note # 56: **As** we turn more of our thinking over to the thought system of the Holy Spirit, our confidence will grow in its ability to produce our desired goal of forgiveness and love, which leads to our inner-peace. Eventually we will decide to totally abandon the thought system of the ego and side only with the Holy Spirit's. Love will replace fear and mastery will be accomplished.

VIII. The Meaning of the Last Judgment

T-2.VIII.1. One of the ways in which you can correct the magic-miracle confusion is to remember that you did not create yourself, **God did**. 2 You are apt to forget this when you become egocentric, and **your belief that you created yourself** puts you in a position where a belief in magic is virtually inevitable. 3 Your will to create was given you by your Creator, Who was expressing the same Will in His creation. 4 Since creative ability rests in the mind, everything you create is necessarily a matter of will. 5 It also follows that whatever you alone make is real in your own sight, though not in the Mind of God. 6 This basic distinction **that whatever you alone make is real in your own sight, though not in the Mind of God**, leads directly into the real meaning of the Last Judgment.

Note # 57: When you believe in separation, whatever you make is "real" only to you in your own limited egoic mind or sight but it is not real in the Mind of God. What you miscreate is only an erroneous thought projection based on your mind's belief in fear and lack. This is what is referred to as provisional reality. Provisional reality is momentarily "true" for you because you believe it is. Provisional reality is what your mind has projected into your own "dream world". Provisional reality exists only in the mind of the one projecting it. Because provisional reality is subject to change, it is not permanent and, therefore, not eternal or real. Creation is an extension, which is based on inclusion and true love. True love gives everything because it is everything. This is how God and His right-minded Son create. These creations are real in the mind of God because they are extensions of what is perfect, eternal and thus, changeless. God is love and thus, to co-create with God requires that we also must come from loving thoughts.

T-2.VIII.2. The Last Judgment is one of the most threatening ideas in your thinking. 2 This is because you do not understand **the meaning of the Last Judgment**. 3 Judgment is not an attribute of God. 4 **Judgment** was brought into being only after the separation, when **judgment** became one of the many learning devices to be built into the overall plan. 5 Just as the separation occurred over millions of years, the Last Judgment will extend over a similarly long period, and perhaps an even longer one. 6 **The Last Judgment's** length can, however, be greatly shortened by miracles, which is the device for shortening **time** but not abolishing time. 7 If a sufficient number become truly miracle-minded, this shortening process can be virtually immeasurable. 8 It is essential, however, that you free yourself from fear quickly, because you must emerge from the conflict **of fear**, if you are to bring peace to other minds.

Note # 58: God does not judge since a Oneness of Everything has nothing outside itself to judge. It is only the egoic mind that perceives separation that judges. As long as one remnant of egoic thinking remains, time will be needed. We, not God, are the ones who have chosen to judge. When the Sonship stops judging and accepts the Atonement for itself, its last judgment will be at hand.

T-2.VIII.3. The Last Judgment is generally thought of as a procedure undertaken by God. 2 Actually, **the Last Judgment** will be undertaken by my brothers with my help. 3 **The Last Judgment** is a final healing rather than a meting out of punishment, however much you may think that punishment is deserved. 4 Punishment is a concept totally opposed to right-mindedness, and the aim of the Last Judgment is to restore right-mindedness to you. 5 The Last Judgment might be called a process of right evaluation. 6 **This process of right evaluation, which is the Last Judgment**, simply means that everyone will finally come to understand what is worthy and what is not **worthy**. 7 **After right evaluation is achieved,** the ability to choose can be directed rationally. 8 Until this distinction is made **between what is worthy and what is not worthy**, however, the vacillations between free and imprisoned will cannot but continue.

Note # 59: Currently we value our belief in separation. We have judged the dream to be more desirable than the truth. Right evaluation will determine that only truth or love is worthy. The false will be cast aside as unworthy.

T-2.VIII.4. The first step toward freedom involves a sorting out of the false from the true. 2 This is a process of separation in the constructive sense, and reflects the true meaning of the Apocalypse. 3 Everyone will ultimately look upon his own creations and choose to preserve only what is good, just as God Himself looked upon what He had created and knew that **what He created** was good. 4 At this point, the mind can begin to look with love on its own creations because of their worthiness. 5 At the same time the mind will inevitably disown its miscreations which, without belief, **which originally came from in the mind's creative power to be causes, its miscreation** will no longer exist.

Note # 60: It is our continuing belief that we are separate and have miscreated that results in our provisional reality remaining constantly warped. Without the creative power of our mind to continually project and make its own "dream world," our own provisional reality would disappear. When we realize our true nature, our mind will continue to support only the creations that extend and reflect the truth that God's Son is only unlimited love.

T-2.VIII.5. The term "Last Judgment" is frightening not only because **the ego's trait of judgment** has been projected onto God, but also because of the association of "last" with death. 2 This is an outstanding example of upside-down perception. 3 If the meaning of the Last Judgment is objectively examined, it is quite apparent that **the Last Judgment** is really the doorway to life. 4 No one who lives in fear is really alive. 5 Your own last judgment cannot be directed toward yourself, because you are not your own creation. 6 You can, however, apply **judgment** meaningfully and at any time to everything you have made, and retain in your memory only what is creative and good. 7 **Retaining in your memory only what is creative and good** is what your right-mindedness cannot but dictate. 8 The purpose of time is solely to "give you time" to achieve this judgment. 9 **The Last Judgment** is your own perfect judgment of your own perfect creations. 10 When everything you retain is lovable, there is no reason for fear to remain with you. 11 This **removal of all your fears** is your part in the Atonement.

Note # 61: When fear, which is all the obstacles that we have placed before love is removed, only love remains. The last judgment is the acceptance of the truth that only love is real and we are that love. Love is life and only love remains. Before this judgment, we believed that we could will ourselves to be something other than the extension of the Mind of God. The Sonship is now ready to exchange his misperception for correct perception or right-mindedness. God, the Father, will then return His Child to knowledge. We will know that we were, are and always will be the Oneness of Everything, perfect, whole and complete.

Chapter 3. THE INNOCENT PERCEPTION

I. Atonement without Sacrifice

T-3.I.1.A further point must be perfectly clear before any residual fear still associated with miracles can disappear. 2 The crucifixion did not establish the Atonement; the resurrection did. 3 Many sincere Christians have misunderstood this **and believe the crucifixion, not the resurrection, established the Atonement**. 4 No one who is free of the belief in scarcity could possibly make this mistake. 5 If the crucifixion is seen from an upside-down point of view, **the crucifixion** does appear as if God permitted and even encouraged one of His Sons to suffer because he was good. 6 This particularly unfortunate interpretation **that God would let one of His Sons suffer because he was good,** which arose out of projection, has led many people to be bitterly afraid of God. 7 Such anti-religious concepts enter into many religions. 8 Yet the real Christian should pause and ask, "How could this be?" 9 Is it likely that God Himself would be capable of the kind of thinking which His Own words have clearly stated is unworthy of His Son?

<u>Note # 1:</u> Jesus dismisses the Christian fundamentalist's concept of the crucifixion as totally illogical. Jesus said that the resurrection established the Atonement. It is the resurrection that proved that we are not a body; instead we are eternal unlimited spirit.

T-3.I.2. The best defense, as always, is not to attack another's position, but rather to protect the truth. 2 It is unwise to accept any concept if you have to invert a whole frame of reference in order to justify the concept. 3 This procedure **having to invert a whole frame of reference** is painful in its minor applications and genuinely tragic on a wider scale. 4 Persecution frequently results in an attempt to "justify" the terrible misperception that God Himself persecuted His Own Son on behalf of salvation. 5 The very words are meaningless. 6 It has been particularly difficult to overcome this misperception **that God would persecute His Own Son on behalf of salvation,** because, although the error itself is no harder to correct than any other **error**, many have been unwilling to give this error up in view of **this error's** prominent value as a defense. 7 In milder forms **this type of error allows** a parent says, "This hurts me more than it hurts you," and feels exonerated in beating a child. 8 Can you believe our Father really thinks this way **that our Father would persecute His Own Son on behalf of salvation?** 9 It is so essential that all such thinking be dispelled that we must be sure that nothing of this kind **of upside down thinking** remains in your mind. 10 I was not "punished" because <*you*> were bad. 11 The wholly benign lesson the Atonement teaches is lost if **the Atonement** is tainted with this kind of **distorted thinking that God could persecute His Own Son** in any form.

<u>Note # 2:</u> Love allows. It is unconditional. It does not make demands that are punishable if we fail to

obey. The idea that God would punish an innocent victim, His only Son, in place of the wrongdoer is even more insane. Insanity disguised as love is truly tragic. Our western, traditional religious view of a judgmental, vindicate and petty god does not make any sense. This is even more illogical, when Christian fundamentalists proclaim this type of god as a god of love.

T-3.I.3. The statement "Vengeance is mine, saith the Lord" is a misperception by which one assigns his own "evil" past to God. 2 The "evil" past has nothing to do with God. 3 **God** did not create **your own "evil" thinking**, and **God** does not maintain **your "evil" thinking**. 4 God does not believe in retribution. 5 **God's** Mind does not create that way. 6 **God** does not hold your "evil" deeds against you. 7 Is it likely that **God** would hold **your "evil" deeds** against me? 8 Be very sure that you recognize how utterly impossible this assumption is, and how entirely this assumption **that God would punish me, Jesus, for your "evil" deeds,** arises from projection. 9 This kind of error is responsible for a host of related errors, including the belief that God rejected Adam and forced him out of the Garden of Eden. 10 **This kind of error, that God rejected His Child and forced him out of Heaven,** is also why you may believe from time to time that I am misdirecting you. 11 I have made every effort to use words that are almost impossible to distort, but it is always possible to twist symbols around if you wish.

<u>Note # 3:</u> Projection is the action or thought of blaming or punishing someone else for your deeds. In the egoic error of projection, we attempt to transfer and attribute our actions to something or someone outside ourselves. Rather than recognize that the "error" comes from our own thinking and thus, needs to be corrected within our mind, we seek to ignore our own sourceness for the error and focus our attention somewhere else. We fail to take ownership and responsibility for our own creations. We claim to be powerless to correct our erroneous thoughts since by our own projection and denial, the error that we created now appears to come from somewhere outside our own mind. We then claim that if the error is from an outside cause or source, we are powerless to correct the error. God knows His creations are extensions of Himself. Being a Oneness how could there be anyone to judge or punish?

T-3.I.4. Sacrifice is a notion totally unknown to God. 2 **Sacrifice** arises solely from fear, and frightened people can be vicious. 3 Sacrificing in any way is a violation of my injunction that you should be merciful even as your Father in Heaven is merciful. 4 It has been hard for many Christians to realize that this **prohibition on sacrifice** applies to themselves **as Christians**. 5 Good teachers never terrorize their students. 6 To terrorize is to attack, and this **attacking by teachers of their students,** results in rejection of what the teacher offers. 7 The result is learning failure.

<u>Note # 4:</u> What can be sacrificed if there is no lack? Sin and hell are a foreign concept to a Oneness of Everything. Who could the Oneness sin against? The belief in guilt, sin and hell are needed and very useful only if you wish to control another. These concepts of sin, guilt and hell form the bedrock for the fear based egoic thought system.

T-3.I.5.I have been correctly referred to as "the lamb of God who taketh away the sins of the world," but those who represent the lamb as blood-stained do not understand the meaning of the symbol. 2 Correctly understood **this symbol of the "lamb of God"** is a very simple symbol that speaks of my innocence. 3 The lion and the lamb lying down together symbolize that strength and innocence are not in conflict, but naturally live in peace. 4 "Blessed are the pure in heart for they shall see God" is another way of saying the same thing. 5 A pure mind knows the truth and this is **a pure mind's** strength. 6 **A pure mind** does not confuse destruction with innocence because **a pure mind** associates innocence with strength, not **innocence** with weakness.

<u>Note # 5:</u> When you know your strength comes from God, Herself, you know that you are invulnerable.

True strength requires neither defenses nor weapons for attack. When you believe that you are a limited ego-body, attack and defense are synonymous.

T-3.I.6. Innocence is incapable of sacrificing anything, because the innocent mind has everything and strives only to protect **the innocent mind's** wholeness. 2 **The innocent mind** cannot project. 3 **The innocent mind** can only honor other minds, because honor is the natural greeting of the truly loved to others who are like them. 4 The lamb "taketh away the sins of the world" in the sense that the state of innocence, or grace, is one in which the meaning of the Atonement is perfectly apparent. 5 The Atonement is entirely unambiguous. 6 The Atonement is perfectly clear because **the Atonement** exists in light **of truth**. 7 Only the attempts to shroud **the Atonement** in darkness have made **the Atonement** inaccessible to those who do not choose to see.

Note # 6: The Atonement is the acceptance of the truth about God's Son. Truth abolishes all illusions and errors in thinking. You and your brothers and sisters are innocent, sinless and guiltless. The Sonship remains God's perfect extension of only Herself, which is only Love.

T-3.I.7. The Atonement itself radiates nothing but truth. 2 **The Atonement** therefore epitomizes harmlessness and sheds only blessing. 3 **The Atonement** could not do this if **the Atonement** arose from anything but perfect innocence. 4 Innocence is wisdom because **innocence** is unaware of evil, and evil does not exist. 5 **Innocence** is, however, perfectly aware of everything that is true. 6 The resurrection demonstrated that nothing can destroy truth. 7 Good can withstand any form of evil, as light abolishes forms of darkness. 8 The Atonement is therefore the perfect lesson. 9 **The Atonement** is the final demonstration that all the other lessons I taught are true. 10 If you can accept this one generalization now **that the Atonement is the final demonstration that all the other lessons I taught are true**, there will be no need to learn from many smaller lessons. 11 You are released from all errors if you believe this **lesson of accepting the Atonement for yourself.**

Note # 7: Salvation is just one decision away. All will freely choose for the Atonement. It is just a matter of time. Do you wish to baby-step your way to recovery of your divine birthright or achieve it in one giant leap? Our free will determines the timing of when we decide to accept the Atonement for ourselves.

T-3.I.8. The innocence of God is the true state of the mind of His Son. 2 In this **innocence** state your mind knows God, for God is not symbolic; He is Fact. 3 **By you** knowing His Son as he is, you realize that the Atonement, not sacrifice, is the only appropriate gift for God's altar, where nothing except perfection belongs. 4 The understanding of the innocent is truth. 5 That is why **the** altars **of the innocent** are truly radiant.

Note # 8: God's Mind is changeless. God's Plan is that His Creations be happy. As such, God created you eternally perfect, whole and complete. What part of God's Plan is so difficult to accept? Why would you wish to follow your ego's plan, which claims you are a guilty sinner in need of punishment? Would a sane mind freely choose to be limited and fearful when God's Plan offers that same mind everything without any pain or sacrifice? God's Plan offers total freedom and love. The ego's plan offers limitation, fear, enslavement and then finally death.
"Hum… Let me think about that for a while. Is it such a hard choice?"

II. Miracles as True Perception

T-3.II.1.I have stated that the basic concepts referred to in this course are not matters of degree. 2 Certain fundamental concepts cannot be understood in terms of opposites. 3 It is impossible to conceive of light and darkness or everything and nothing as joint possibilities. 4 They are all true or all false. 5 It is essential that you realize your thinking will be erratic until a firm commitment to one (**light versus darkness or spirit versus ego-body**) or the other is made. 6 A firm commitment to darkness or nothingness, however, is impossible. 7 No one has ever lived who has not experienced <*some*> light and <*some*> thing. 8 No one, therefore, is able to deny truth totally, even if he thinks he can **deny truth totally**.

Note # 9: ACIM is black and white. What is not changeless is not real. Something is either true or false. The false has no reality and thus, is the belief in nothing. For ACIM's purpose, something is not sometimes true and sometimes false. There is no gray. The choice for love is real and fear cannot exist except as an illusion in a deluded mind. Truth and love are our Source or Cause. Effect cannot be separate from its cause. It is impossible to totally restrict or deny our connectiveness to Source Energy or First Cause, which is the Mind of God. Even if on the egoic level you believed and claimed that you were totally disconnected to God, your Christ consciousness or Holy Spirit would maintain the connection. It is against God's Will that you be separate from His Oneness.

T-3.II.2. Innocence is not a partial attribute. 2 **Innocence** is not real <*until*> innocence is total. 3 The partly innocent are apt to be quite foolish at times. 4 It is not until their innocence becomes a viewpoint with universal application that **innocence** becomes wisdom. 5 Innocent or true perception means that you never misperceive and always see truly. 6 More simply, **innocence or true perception** means that you never see what does not exist, and always see what does.

Note # 10: Innocence means that you always follow the thought system of the Holy Spirit. In the egoic dream state of separation, only the Holy Spirit knows the truth about your oneness and is also aware of your dream experience that you call limitation and separation. By understanding both, the Holy Spirit is in the unique position to be able to translate our misperception into correct perception.

T-3.II.3. When you lack confidence in what someone will do, you are attesting to your belief that he is not in his right mind. 2 This **lack of confidence in what someone will do** is hardly a miracle-based frame of reference. 3 **Attesting to your belief that an individual is not in his right mind**, also has the disastrous effect of denying the power of the miracle. 4 The miracle perceives everything as it **truly** is. 5 If nothing but the truth exists, right-minded seeing cannot see anything but perfection. 6 I have said that only what God creates or what you create with the same Will has any real existence. 7 This, then (**only what is created in God's image**) is all the innocent can see. 8 **The innocent** do not suffer from distorted perception.

Note # 11: The innocent only perceive the truth. They look past the body to the spiritual essence of all they perceive. They "look" only through the eyes of love. Even when a brother appears to be acting out his desire to experience fear or lack, the innocent realize that each one's own thoughts make their experience. They understand the sourceness of each brother's perception and the freedom this entails.

T-3.II.4. You are afraid of God's Will because you have used your own mind, which **God** created in the likeness of His Own **Will**, to miscreate. 2 The mind can miscreate only when **the mind** believes **the**

mind is not free. 3 An "imprisoned" mind is not free because **the "imprisoned mind"** is possessed, or held back, by itself. 4 **The "imprisoned mind"** is therefore limited, and the will **of the "imprisoned mind"** is not free to assert itself. 5 To be one is to be of one mind or will. 6 When the Will of the Sonship and the Father are One, their perfect accord is Heaven.

Note # 12: A mind that believes it is something other than perfect, whole and complete limits itself. Believing it is limited, the egoic mind passes on this same false concept whenever it attempts to create. This results in projection, which is miscreation. Creation only extends its true Big "S" Self. An attempt to beget something other than your Big "S" Self is impossible. The belief in "littleness" is the denial of the truth and can only appear real in an illusionary state of make-believe. Only the fearful would choose limitation over freedom.

T-3.II.5. Nothing can prevail against a Son of God who commends his spirit into the Hands of his Father. 2 **By a Son of God commending his spirit into the Hands of His Father**, the mind awakens from its sleep and **the mind of the Son** remembers its Creator. 3 All sense of separation disappears. 4 The Son of God is part of the Holy Trinity, but the Trinity Itself is One. 5 There is no confusion within Its Levels, because They are of one Mind and one Will. 6 This single purpose creates perfect integration and establishes the peace of God. 7 Yet this vision **of perfect integration that establishes the peace of God** can be perceived only by the truly innocent. 8 Because **the truly innocent's** hearts are pure, the **truly** innocent defend true perception instead of defending themselves against **true perception**. 9 Understanding the lesson of the Atonement, **the truly innocent,** are without the wish to attack, and therefore the **innocent** see truly. 10 This is what the Bible means when it says, "When he shall appear (or be perceived) we shall be like him, for we shall see him as he is."

Note # 13: Due to our belief that duality exists, ACIM must use language to describe what we perceive. ACIM speaks as if there is a separation within the Trinity because that is how our dualistic mind perceives it. In truth, there is just the One Self. There is no difference between God the Father, God the Son and God the Holy Spirit. They are the one indivisible "All That Is". The Mind of God is holographic. Each inseparable part contains the whole and the whole contains each part. There is no difference.

T-3.II.6. The way to correct distortions is to withdraw your faith in **distortions** and invest **your faith** only in what is true. 2 You cannot make untruth true. 3 If you are willing to accept what is true in everything you perceive, you let **what is true** be true for you. 4 Truth overcomes all error, and those who live in error and emptiness can never find lasting solace. 5 If you perceive truly you are cancelling out misperceptions in yourself and **misperceptions** in others simultaneously. 6 Because you see **others** as they **truly** are, **a spiritual being that is part of the Sonship,** you offer them your acceptance of their truth so they can accept **the truth** for themselves. 7 This **acceptance of the truth for themselves** is the healing that the miracle induces.

Note # 14: The truth is not someone's misperceptions about himself or herself as a limited ego-body. It is not the "truth" of the egoic misperception, but rather the truth of the Holy Spirit's correct perception that "sees" the eternal spiritual nature in all that is. When you follow the thought system of the Holy Spirit, you offer your brother the truth about what he truly is. You let him see his Big "S" Self. You allow him to "see" himself as a Son of God, perfect, whole and complete. He sees himself as sinless and guiltless like His Source. This is the healing the miracle induces.

III. Perception versus Knowledge

T-3.III.1. We have been emphasizing perception, and have said very little about knowledge as yet. 2 This is because perception must be straightened out before you can know anything. 3 To know is to be certain. 4 Uncertainty means that you do not know. 5 Knowledge is power because **knowledge** is certain, and certainty is strength. 6 Perception is temporary. 7 As an attribute of the belief in space and time, **perception** is subject to either fear or love. 8 Misperceptions produce fear and true perceptions foster love, but neither brings certainty because all perception varies. 9 That is why **perception** is not knowledge. 10 True perception is the basis for knowledge, but knowing is the affirmation of truth and beyond all perceptions.

Note # 15: Knowledge like truth never changes. For ACIM's purposes, knowledge is the truth and not a generally accepted belief. For example, although past human "so called knowledge" would include the "fact" that the earth was the center of the universe, this could not be knowledge since it was not true. Certainty without truth is not knowledge. Perception changes as your viewpoint shifts. It differs from person to person based on their unique past beliefs and experiences. Perception is based on what you choose to put your awareness upon. The two thought systems produce radically different perceptions although the "external happening" or experience is theoretically the same. The ego's perception is fearful while the Holy Spirit's is loving.

T-3.III.2. All your difficulties stem from the fact that you do not recognize yourself, your brother or God. 2 To recognize means to "know again," implying that you knew before. 3 You can see in many ways because perception involves interpretation, and this means that **perception** is not whole or consistent. 4 The miracle, being a way of perceiving, is not knowledge. 5 **The miracle** is the right answer to a question, but you do not question when you know. 6 Questioning illusions is the first step in undoing **illusions**. 7 The miracle, or the right answer, corrects **illusions**. 8 Since perceptions change, **perceptions'** dependence on time is obvious. 9 How you perceive at any given time determines what you do, and actions must occur in time. 10 Knowledge is timeless, because certainty is not questionable. 11 You know when you have ceased to ask questions.

Note # 16: We must first question the logic of the egoic thought system before we will decide that there must be another way to interpret the experience. Our difficulty arose when we chose to believe that we did not know what we are. The egoic thought system's goal is to keep us from remembering that we are a Oneness of "All That Is." The Holy Spirit's goal is to return us to the remembrance that we are "That One".

T-3.III.3. The questioning mind perceives itself in time, and therefore, **the questioning** mind looks for future answers **in time**. 2 The closed mind believes the future and the present will be the same. **3 The closed mind's belief that the future and the present will be the same** establishes a seemingly stable state that is usually an attempt to counteract an underlying fear that the future will be worse than the present. 4 This fear **that the future will be worse than the present** inhibits the tendency to question at all.

Note # 17: Since perceptions change and time is the measure of change, the world of perception is also the world of time. Change is often frightening and, therefore, they who are closed minded attempt to control their fear by limiting the amount of change they are willing to experience. Coming from fear, the universe is viewed as an unsupportive place that is ruled by lack and competition. To the ego, life is a "zero sum game". If I am to win, someone must lose. Conflict and competition is the norm and thus, the ego's belief system projects, makes and then perceives a fearful world.

T-3.III.4. True vision is the natural perception of spiritual sight, but **true vision** is still a correction rather than a fact. 2 Spiritual sight is symbolic, and therefore not a device for knowing. 3 **Spiritual sight** is, however, a means of right perception, which brings **spiritual sight** into the proper domain of the miracle. 4 A "vision of God" would be a miracle rather than a revelation. 5 The fact that perception is involved at all removes the experience from the realm of knowledge **since perception always involves interpretation, which means that perception is not consistent.** 6 That is why visions, however holy, do not last.

Note # 18: Perception involves questioning, thinking and judgment, which are all subject to change and interpretation. With knowledge, you just know. Knowing does not question. It does not think; it just knows.

T-3.III.5. The Bible tells you to know yourself, or to be certain. 2 Certainty is always of God. 3 When you love someone you have perceived him as he is, and this makes it possible for you to know him. 4 Until you first perceive him as he is you cannot know him. 5 While you ask questions about him you are clearly implying that you do not know God. 6 Certainty does not require action. 7 When you say you are acting on the basis of knowledge, you are really confusing knowledge with perception **since knowledge is certainty and does not require action**. 8 Knowledge provides the strength for creative thinking, but not for right doing. 9 Perception, miracles and doing are closely related. 10 Knowledge is the result of revelation and induces only thought. 11 Even in **perception's** most spiritualized form perception involves the body. 12 Knowledge comes from the altar within and is timeless because **knowledge** is certain. 13 To perceive the truth is not the same as to know **the truth**.

Note # 19: Perception always implies the belief in separation. It requires both an observer and something to observe. Even when you perceive correctly and conclude that there is only the Oneness and that you are that one, you have arrived at the correct conclusion based on the original belief that there could be something outside of the Oneness that you observed. Knowing requires no action since knowledge just is. Being truth, there is nothing to change and nothing that could be changed. Action is only relevant to the mind that believes change is possible. At the level of the illusionary non-real world of time and perception, change is believed possible and action induces change. Physical action is not required, but changing your thinking is necessary. Thoughts become things. Mind, not the body, is the seat of all creation or miscreation.

T-3.III.6. Right perception is necessary before God can communicate directly to His altars, which **God** established in His Sons. 2 There **God** can communicate His certainty, and His knowledge will bring peace without question. 3 God is not a stranger to His Sons, and His Sons are not strangers to each other. 4 Knowledge preceded both perception and time, and will ultimately replace **perception and time**. 5 That is the real meaning of "Alpha and Omega, the beginning and the end," and "Before Abraham was I am." 6 Perception can and must be stabilized, but knowledge <is> stable. 7 "Fear God and keep His commandments" becomes "Know God and accept His certainty."

Note # 20: To know God, we must drop all egoic thinking and follow the guidance to the Holy Spirit. Only the Holy Spirit knows the path that will reawaken our sleeping minds to the truth.

T-3.III.7. If you attack error in another, you will hurt yourself. 2 You cannot know your brother when you attack him. 3 Attack is always made upon a stranger. 4 You are making **your brother** a stranger by misperceiving **your brother**, and so you cannot know **your brother**. 5 It is because you have made **your brother** a stranger that you are afraid of **your brother**. 6 Perceive **your brother** correctly so that you can know **your brother**. 7 There are no strangers in God's creation. 8 To create as **God** created you can create only what you know, and therefore accept as yours. 9 God knows His children with perfect certainty. 10 **God** created **His children** by knowing **His children**. 11 **God** recognizes **His children** perfectly. 12 When **His children** do not recognize each other, **His children** do not recognize **God**.

Note # 21: As long as we view our brother as a limited ego-body, we will fail to perceive the truth about him. With the guidance of the Holy Spirit, we can look past the physical body and correctly perceive his Christ consciousness, his Big "S" Self. When we do this, we see our own true self and we recognize God. We realize that we are all joined and are the One Self of the shared holographic Mind of God.

IV. Error and the Ego

T-3.IV.1. The abilities you now possess are only shadows of your real strength. 2 All of your present functions are divided and open to question and doubt. 3 This **questioning and doubt of your present functions** is because you are not certain how you will use **your abilities because their functions are divided**, and therefore **you are** incapable of knowledge. 4 You are also incapable of knowledge because you can still perceive lovelessly. 5 Perception did not exist until the separation introduced degrees, aspects and intervals. 6 Spirit has no levels, and all conflict arises from the concept of levels. 7 Only the Levels of the Trinity are capable of unity. 8 The levels created by the separation cannot but conflict. 9 This is because **the levels created by the separation** are meaningless to each other.

Note # 22: Since we do not recognize what we are, we do not understand our own creative power. Because we come from fear and lack, we limit our own power to create. We attempt to serve two masters. One is love and the other fear or lovelessness. Believing ourselves to be limited ego-bodies, we cannot help but perceive a world of conflict and competition. Our belief in separation has not only introduced the concept of the false, we also have the concept of "sometimes". Truth now can vacillate back and forth and both the true and the false become conditional at best. In the world of perception, there are no absolutes. Everything is questionable and changeable. On the non-real level of time, space and perception, stability does not exist.

T-3.IV.2. Consciousness, the level of perception, was the first split introduced into the mind after the separation, making the mind a perceiver rather than a creator. 2 Consciousness is correctly identified as the domain of the ego. 3 The ego is a wrong-minded attempt to perceive yourself as you wish to be, rather than as you are. 4 Yet you can know yourself only as you are, because that is all you can be sure of. 5 Everything else **except knowing yourself only as you are** <*is*> open to question.

Note # 23: This is an important paragraph **(T-3.IV.2).** This is referencing the splitting of the mind into the "higher mind" which is under the jurisdiction of spirit and the "lower mind" which is in the domain of the ego. Part of the indivisible Sonship of God has "fallen" from a creator to a perceiver and has lost their ability to know. This supposed separation, however, is only in the mind of the perceiver, not in the Mind of God. This idea correlates with the definition of the ego, which is defined as a wrong-minded attempt to perceive yourself as you wish to be, rather than as you are. You cannot change what you truly are since God has created you perfect and changeless. You can, however, forget (misperceive) who you are. This misperception leads to levels created by the separation, which are irreconcilable to each other. Level confusion is the result and is a device, which is used by the ego to verify that you are indeed a limited ego-body, not a "Oneness of Everything". As an ego-body you believe you are separate, fearful, and come from lack. Prior to the separation there were no levels since there was only the knowing of the One Self. Consciousness is the level of perception. Since the ego is the result of a misperception, the ego is a miscreation. The result of a miscreation is not real in God's mind and is only perceived as real in the mind of the perceiver. This initial miscreation of the split mind is the start of individual, provisional reality. Provisional reality is a world that appears true only to the mind of the one perceiving (dreaming) it. Based on the fact that God did not create the ego, (you did within your dream world of provisional reality), the ego does not exist. The ego was made (miscreated) by the split mind that perceived itself to be separate and was an attempt to make the false appear real. The ego was not created by God and is not a part of the Mind of God.

The belief in separation is necessary for perception to exist. Without the belief of separation, there could be nothing outside the perceiver to perceive. There would just be a Oneness of the One Self. With the concept of separation, we now have two. We have an observer and something outside itself to observe. We have something to compete with and conflict with. The world of changeable perception has been born. Time, which is the measure of change, now becomes relevant. The separation birthed the concepts of perception, change, time and fear. The ego, which is our split mind's claim that it does not know what it is, now takes up its residency in the illusionary non-real world of perception.

T-3.IV.3. The ego is the questioning aspect of the post-separation self, which was made rather than created. 2 **The ego** is capable of asking questions but not of perceiving meaningful answers, because **meaningful answers** would involve knowledge and cannot be perceived. 3 The mind is therefore confused, because only One-mindedness can be without confusion. 4 A separated or divided mind <*must*> be confused. 5 **A separated or divided mind** is necessarily uncertain about what it is. 6 **A separated mind** has to be in conflict because **a divided mind** is out of accord with itself. 7 This makes **a divided mind's** aspects strangers to each other, and this **lack of accord among the separated mind's various aspects** is the essence of the fear-prone condition, in which attack is always possible. 8 You have every reason to feel afraid as you perceive yourself. 9 This is why you cannot escape from fear **of how you perceive yourself**, until you realize that you did not and could not create yourself. 10 You can never make your misperceptions true, and your creation is beyond your own error. 11 That is why you must eventually choose to heal the separation.

Note # 24: To correct something, you must go to the source of the error. The source is the mad idea that you can usurp God's Will and somehow are separate from God. Since God created all that is, God is the Cause and you are God's Effect. The effect cannot birth itself. Creation is an extension of itself and thus, cause can only extend what it is. The effect must be just as changeless as its cause. Misperceptions, no matter how hard you choose to believe them, will always be false. Just because you believe the world is flat, does not make it true. You can choose to live your life under the misperception that your world is flat but "reality" will be that the "real" world is round. We can deny our divine birthright but we can never lose it. Our divine inheritance always remains waiting patiently within us for the moment when we will cease playing the game of separation. This game will stop when we cease valuing our self-made ego that claims we could not know that we are Sons of God.

T-3.IV.4. Right-mindedness is not to be confused with the knowing mind, because **right-mindedness** is applicable only to right perception. 2 You can be right-minded or wrong-minded, and even this is subject to degrees. **The possibility of various degrees, or outcomes, demonstrates that this clearly requires perception** and that knowledge is not involved. 3 The term "right-mindedness" is properly used as the correction for "wrong-mindedness," and applies to the state of mind that induces accurate perception. 4 **Right-mindedness** is miracle-minded because **right-mindedness induces accurate perception, which** heals misperception, and this **change in perception** is indeed a miracle in view of how you perceive yourself.

Note # 25: The miracle is a change in the viewer's perception. Knowledge is beyond the realm of perception since it is certain. Knowledge is not found at the non-real, illusionary level of separation, time and space.

T-3.IV.5. Perception always involves some misuse of mind, because **perception** brings the mind into areas of uncertainty. 2 The mind is very active 3 When **the mind** chooses to be separated, **the mind** chooses to perceive. 4 Until the **mind chooses to perceive, the mind** wills only to know. 5 Afterwards **the mind chooses to perceive, the mind** can only choose ambiguously, and the only way out of ambiguity is clear perception. 6 The mind returns to **the mind's** proper function only when **the mind** wills to know. 7 **When the mind's will to know**, this places **the mind** in the service of spirit, where perception is changed. 8 The mind chooses to divide itself when **the mind** chooses to make its own levels. **(Perception is a separate level from Oneness of God, which would be the state of mind called Heaven)** 9 But it **(the perceiving mind)** could not entirely separate itself from spirit, because **the mind** is from spirit that **the mind** derives **the mind's** whole power to make or create **from spirit**. 10 Even in miscreation the mind is affirming its Source **(Spirit)** or **the mind** would merely cease to be. 11 This **ceasing of the mind to be** is impossible, because the mind belongs to spirit which God created and which is therefore eternal.

Note # 26: Even in our mind's most delusional state, we still remain connected to our Source Energy or God. Our Christ-consciousness remembers who we are. The Holy Spirit maintains its eternal vigilance within our split mind patiently awaiting our call for Its guidance that cannot fail. Our mind or spirit always remains connected to its Cause. Cause and effect are inseparable. You cannot have one without the other.

T-3.IV.6. The ability to perceive made the body possible, because you must perceive <*something*> and <*with*> something. 2 That is why perception involves an exchange or translation, which knowledge does not need. 3 The interpretative function of perception, a distorted form of creation, then permits you to interpret the body as yourself in an attempt to escape from the conflict you have induced **(the separation)**. 4 Spirit, which knows, could not be reconciled with this loss of power, because **spirit** is incapable of darkness. 5 This makes spirit almost inaccessible to the **split-minded** and entirely inaccessible to the body. 6 Thereafter, spirit is perceived as a threat, because light abolishes darkness merely by showing you **darkness** is not there. 7 Truth will always overcome error in this way. 8 This **overcoming of error by truth** cannot be an active process of correction because, as I have already emphasized, knowledge does not do anything. 9 **Knowledge** can be perceived as an attacker, but **knowledge** cannot attack. 10 What you perceive as **knowledge's** attack is your own vague recognition that knowledge can always be remembered, **since knowledge has** never been destroyed.

Note # 27: Within our split mind our Christ consciousness or Big "S" Self holds the remembrance of our true beingness. By seeking the guidance of the Holy Spirit, we reawaken the Christ within.

T-3.IV.7. God and His creations remain in surety, and therefore know that no miscreation exists. 2 Truth cannot deal with errors that you want. 3 I was a man who remembered spirit and **spirit's** knowledge. 4 As a man I did not attempt to counteract error with knowledge, but to correct error from the bottom up. 5 I demonstrated both the powerlessness of the body and the power of the mind. 6 By uniting my will with that of my Creator, I naturally remembered spirit and **spirit's** real purpose. 7 I cannot unite your will with God's **Will** for you, but I can erase all misperceptions from your mind if you will bring **your mind** under my guidance. 8 Only your misperceptions stand in your way **of my guidance**. 9 Without **your misperceptions** your choice is certain. 10 Sane perception induces sane choosing. 11 I cannot choose for you, but I can help you make your own right choice. 12 "Many are called but few are chosen" should be, 'All are called but few choose to listen." 13 Therefore, they do not choose right. 14 The "chosen ones" are merely those who choose right sooner. 15 Right minds can do this now, and **right minds** will find rest unto their souls. 16 God knows you only in peace, and this <*is*> your reality.

Note # 28: Your true reality was, is, and always will be, as God created you – a Oneness, perfect, whole and complete. You remain sinless and guiltless as your Father created you. You can choose to misperceive who you are, but you cannot change what God created. In the misperception that we call the dream of separation, we create our personal dream world of provisional reality. We ultimately will choose to freely dissolve this world of provisional reality since "God's Will is not mocked." God wills you to be an extension of God, Himself. Thus, you must remain an eternal Oneness of Everything. Ultimately there is only one choice and only one true option available to your decision-making mind. The only option that rests in truth is that you must assume your rightful place within the One Mind of God. The choice of separation is not a choice since it is a choice for an illusional fantasy, which is a choice for nothingness.

V. Beyond Perception

T-3.V.1.I have said that the abilities you possess are only shadows of your real strength, and that perception, which is inherently judgmental, was introduced only after the separation. 2 No one has been sure of anything since **perception was exchanged for knowledge due to the separation.** 3 I have also made it clear that the resurrection was the means for the return to knowledge, which was accomplished by the union of my will with the Father's **Will**. 4 We can now establish a distinction that will clarify some of our subsequent statements.

Note # 29: The resurrection, which is the proof that the body is not you, is the foundation for the return to truth. Jesus demonstrated through the resurrection that mind or spirit is unlimited and the egoic body has nothing of value.

T-3.V.2.Since the separation, the words "create" and "make" have become confused. 2 When you make something, you do so out of a specific sense of lack or need. 3 Anything made for a specific purpose has no true generalizability. 4 When you make something to fill a perceived lack, you are tacitly implying that you believe in separation. 5 The ego has invented many ingenious thought systems for this purpose **of reinforcing your belief in lack or need.** 6 None **of the ego's thought systems are** creative. 7 Inventiveness is wasted effort even in **inventiveness's** most ingenious form. 8 The highly specific nature of invention is not worthy of the abstract creativity of God's creations.

Note # 30: The specific nature of invention or "making" assisted the ego in the ego's desire to convince your split mind that you are separate and not a Oneness with your brother and the Mind of God. If you believe that you are whole (a Oneness), what could you lack? Anything that is for a specific purpose rather than applicable to everything implies that there is something "out there" that you are missing and, therefore, you are not perfect, whole and complete. You believe that you are separate. To the ego, this confirms that you are something other than God's Son. Creation comes from the mindset that you have everything, and, therefore, you can and do give everything. When someone creates, there is no sacrifice or diminishment. By sharing, both giver and receiver are strengthened. The creator shares its wholeness and perfection rather than makes something that it perceives it lacks. Creation is inclusion. Making is exclusion.

T-3.V.3. Knowing, as we have already observed, does not lead to doing. 2 The confusion between your real creation and what you have made of yourself is so profound that **due to the confusion of what your real creation is (a spirit, the Son of God) versus what you have made or believe yourself to be (an ego body)**, it has become literally impossible for you to know anything. 3 Knowledge is always stable, and it is quite evident that you are not **stable**. 4 Nevertheless, you are perfectly stable as God created you. 5 In this sense, when your behavior is unstable, you are disagreeing with God's idea of your creation. 6 You can **disagree with God's idea of your creation** if you choose, but you would hardly want to **disagree with God's idea of your creation** if you were in your right mind.

<u>Note # 31:</u> God sees us as perfect, whole and complete. What part in your own perfection do you wish to reject? Only an insane mind would choose limitation and lack over everything.

T-3.V.4. The fundamental question you continually ask yourself cannot properly be directed to yourself at all. 2 You keep asking what it is you are. 3 **The question "What it is you are?"** implies that the answer is not only one you know, but **the answer** is also one that is up to you to supply. 4 Yet you cannot perceive yourself correctly. 5 You have no image to be perceived. 6 The word "image" is always perception-related, and not a part of knowledge. 7 Images are symbolic and stand for something else. 8 The idea of "changing your image" recognizes the power of perception, but **the idea of "changing your image" also implies** that there is nothing stable to know **since perception is open to interpretation**.

<u>Note # 32:</u> The insane mind does not know the truth. Yet your egoic mind would claim not only that you know the truth but the ego, also, claims that you are the arbitrator of truth. The insane believe that by their own choice, they create what will be the truth and when it will be truth. To the insane, truth is unstable and constantly changing. In our egoic dream of separation, individual perception is the arbitrator of truth. Knowledge knows that truth is eternal and changeless.

T-3.V.5. Knowing is not open to interpretation. 2 You may try to "interpret" meaning, but **to "interpret" meaning** is always open to error because **to "interpret" meaning** refers to the <perception> of meaning. 3 Such incongruities **between knowledge and perception of meanings** are the result of attempts to regard yourself as separated and unseparated at the same time. 4 It is impossible to make so fundamental a confusion **(regard yourself as separated and not separated at the same time)** without increasing your overall confusion still further. 5 Your mind may have become very ingenious, but as always happens when method and content are separated, **the ingenious mind** is utilized in a futile attempt to escape from an inescapable impasse. 6 Ingenuity is totally divorced from knowledge, because knowledge does not require ingenuity. 7 Ingenious thinking is <not> the truth that shall set you free, but you are free of the need to engage in **ingenious thinking** when you are willing to let **ingenious thinking** go.

<u>Note # 33:</u> In this world of perception and time, we need to understand that due to our loss of knowledge, we cannot perceive anything correctly. The way around this impasse is to seek the guidance of someone who knows the truth. Only the Holy Spirit knows the truth about what you are and is also

aware of our current state of illusion or insanity. We need only ask the help of our Inner Guide, the Holy Spirit, for His correct perception. The utilization of the Holy Spirit's thought system is the pathway to the eventual return of the Sonship to knowledge.

T-3.V.6.Prayer is a way of asking for something. 2 **Prayer** is the medium of miracles. 3 But the only meaningful prayer is for forgiveness, because those who have been forgiven have everything. 4 Once forgiveness has been accepted, prayer in the usual sense becomes utterly meaningless **since you realize you already have everything**. 5 The prayer for forgiveness is nothing more than a request that you may be able to recognize what you already have. 6 In electing perception instead of knowledge, you placed yourself in a position where you could resemble your Father only by perceiving miraculously. 7 You have lost the knowledge that you yourself are a miracle of God. 8 Creation is your Source and your only real function.

Note # 34: A "correct" prayer would be asking to remember who you really are. You are spirit, not the ego-body that you incorrectly perceive yourself to be. As God's Son, you are creation and your function is to extend creation. In the prayer of forgiveness, we are giving ourselves permission to remember who we are. We, not God, need to forgive ourselves for our own stupidity. The ego would have you cling to your illusion of separateness so that you can claim to be right. The Holy Spirit would merely tell you to choose again. The Holy Spirit knows that an illusion is not real and where there is no harm, there can be no foul. The Holy Spirit asks you to not judge yourself. Instead It asks that you choose again. This time choose to be happy instead of the egoic decision to sacrifice your happiness so that you can pretend to be "right".

T-3.V.7.The statement "God created man in his own image and likeness" needs reinterpretation. 2 "Image" can be understood as "thought," and "likeness" as "of a like quality." 3 God did create spirit in His Own Thought and of a quality like to His Own. 4 There <is> nothing else. 5 Perception, on the other hand, is impossible without a belief in "more" and "less." 6 At every level **perception** involves selectivity. 7 Perception is a continual process of accepting and rejecting, organizing and reorganizing, shifting and changing. 8 Evaluation is an essential part of perception, because judgments are necessary in order to select.

Note # 35: Spirit is everything. There is no lack in spirit. Perception requires that there is something outside "the everything." which contradicts the definition of "everything." Lack is impossible in a Oneness of "All That Is." Perception attempts to divide the inseparable and then judge what it claims has been removed from the whole. Spirit is holographic. Each inseparable part contains the whole because it is the whole. The whole is in each part and each part is in the whole. Spirit is not form but the Thought of God.

T-3.V.8.What happens to perceptions if there are no judgments and nothing but perfect equality? 2 Perception becomes impossible. 3 Truth can only be known. 4 All of **truth** is equally true, and knowing any part of **truth** is to know all of **truth** 5 Only perception involves partial awareness. 6 Knowledge transcends the laws governing perception, because partial knowledge is impossible. 7 **Knowledge** is all one and has no separate parts. 8 You who are really one with **knowledge** need but know yourself and your knowledge is complete. 9 To know God's miracle is to know **God**

Note # 36: Judgment is required for perception. If you judge not, you look past form to content. Content is the truth that only love is real. The ego is a big judging machine. When you quiet the voice of the judgmental ego, you will finally be able to hear the Voice for the remembrance of God and the truth of what you are. When you set aside all judgment, you will accept the Atonement for yourself. The Father will return the Sonship to knowledge and perception will be no more. We will know that we all are unlimited spirit, part of the One Self that is the Mind of God. The Mind of God extends. It does not separate.

In this paragraph, it clearly states the knowledge is holographic in nature. Partial knowledge is impossible since knowledge is all one and has no separate parts.

T-3.V.9. Forgiveness is the healing of the perception of separation. 2 Correct perception of your brother is necessary, because **without correct perception of your brother,** minds have chosen to see themselves as separate. 3 Spirit knows God completely. 4 **Spirit's complete knowledge of God** is **spirit's** miraculous power. 5 The fact that each one has this power **to know God** completely is a condition entirely alien to the world's thinking. 6 The world believes that if anyone has everything, there is nothing left. 7 But God's miracles are as total as His Thoughts because **God's miracles** <are> **God's** Thoughts.

<u>Note # 37:</u> We need to abandon the current paradigm of dualistic thinking. We currently operate under the belief that a whole can be divided into smaller parts and the each part is less than the whole. This leads us into egoic thinking that claims each part is a separate, limited ego-body in competition with other separate, limited ego-bodies. Struggle and conflict result with each party trying to get what they need from a world of fear and lack. Yet, if we shift to a new holographic paradigm, we will have a better conceptual understanding of how ACIM views the universe of the Mind of God. In a true hologram, you can cut the whole into smaller and smaller parts. Yet, whenever you shine a laser beam through any separate piece of the hologram, no matter how small, the entire holographic projection will reappear. Any and all parts have all the information needed to recreate the whole. In the Holographic Model of the Mind of God, each part contains the whole and the whole contains each part. When we realize that we are all created from the same stuff called spirit, we understand that although form may appear to vary, the content, which is spirit is all the same. There is equality in the parts and connectiveness in all parts. There is no separation since all are interconnected on the holographic web of life, that we call the Mind of God. When any part of the hologram shares or extends itself, all parts share and extend. Because of the inter-connectiveness within a hologram, to give is to receive. In the holographic Oneness of Spirit, the Father, the Sonship, the Holy Spirit, your brother and sister and you are all One Self.

T-3.V.10. As long as perception lasts prayer has a place. 2 Since perception rests on lack, those who perceive have not totally accepted the Atonement and given themselves over to truth **since they still believe in lack.** 3 Perception is based on a separated state, so that anyone who perceives at all needs healing. 4 Communion, not prayer, is the natural state of those who know. 5 God and **God's** miracle are inseparable. 6 How beautiful indeed are the Thoughts of God who live in **God's** light! 7 Your worth is beyond perception because **your worth** is beyond doubt. 8 Do not perceive yourself in different lights. 9 Know yourself in the One Light **of God** where the miracle that is you is perfectly clear.

<u>Note # 38:</u> You are the Thoughts of God. You need but to know who you really are. Realize your oneness. Your worthiness is undeniable for you are the One Light of God's Thoughts. Do not perceive yourself in the "light" of littleness and limitation. This egoic "light" is not light but rather a cloak for darkness. Any perception of yourself as different from the Light that is God's Thoughts, is symbolic of your belief in the separation. Do not perceive yourself to be different, separate and not whole.

VI. Judgment and the Authority Problem

T-3.VI.1.We have already discussed the Last Judgment, but in insufficient detail. 2 After the Last Judgment there will be no more **judgment**. 3 Judgment is symbolic because beyond perception there is no judgment. 4 When the Bible says "Judge not that ye be not judged," **the Bible** means that if you judge the reality of others you will be unable to avoid judging your own **reality**.

Note # 39: The ego judges. Knowledge is truth, which is beyond perception. In a Oneness of everything to judge or condemn another is to judge and condemn yourself.

T-3.VI.2.The choice to judge rather than to know is the cause of the loss of peace. 2 Judgment is the process on which perception but not knowledge rests. 3 I have discussed this before in terms of the selectivity of perception, pointing out that evaluation is **perception's** obvious prerequisite. 4 Judgment always involves rejection. 5 **Judgment** never emphasizes only the positive aspects of what is judged, whether in you or in others. 6 What has been perceived and rejected, or judged and found wanting, remains in your mind because **what has been perceived and rejected, or judged and found wanting,** has been perceived. 7 One of the illusions from which you suffer is the belief that what you judged against has no effect. 8 **What you judged against has no effect** cannot be true unless you also believe that what you judged against does not exist. 9 You evidently do not believe **what you judged against does not exist,** or you would not have judged against it. 10 In the end it does not matter whether your judgment is right or wrong. 11 Either way, **whether your judgment is right or wrong,** you are placing your belief in the unreal. 12 This **placing of your belief in the unreal** cannot be avoided in any type of judgment, **because placing your belief in the unreal** implies the belief that reality is yours to select <from.>

Note # 40: Truth is truth. Reality is reality. Our belief in what we choose to perceive as our own personal "provisional reality" has no impact on truth. The ego claims you are the arbitrator of truth. The ego is wrong. God, not you, determined what is the changelessness Truth. Reality and Truth are permanently fixed in the Mind of God. When you perceive something to be apart from you, you confirm your belief that the separation is real. By seeing another as something other than unlimited spirit, you deny both parties their divine inheritance.

T-3.VI.3.You have no idea of the tremendous release and deep peace that comes from meeting yourself and your brothers totally without judgment. 2 When you recognize what you are and what your brothers are, you will realize that judging **your brothers** in any way is without meaning. 3 In fact, **your brothers'** meaning is lost to you precisely <because> you are judging **your brothers**. 4 All uncertainty comes from the belief that you are under the coercion of judgment. 5 You do not need judgment to organize your life, and you certainly do not need **judgment** to organize yourself. 6 In the presence of knowledge all judgment is automatically suspended, and this **automatic suspension of judgment** is the process that enables recognition to replace perception.

Note # 41: When you suspend all judgments, you can be in the <now> of the moment. Judgment robs you of your peace and happiness. Drop egoic judgment and all that remains is love. What was perceived as fearful and separate is now seen as a cry for joining and love. When we drop the judgments of the egoic split mind, all that we hear is the Voice of the Holy Spirit and right-mindedness.

T-3.VI.4.You are very fearful of everything you have perceived but have refused to accept **everything**

you have perceived. 2 You believe that, because you have refused to accept **everything you have perceived**, you have lost control over **everything you have perceived**. 3 This is why you see **everything you have perceived** in nightmares, or in pleasant disguises in what seem to be your happier dreams. 4 Nothing that you have refused to accept can be brought into awareness. 5 **The perception that you have refused to accept** is not dangerous in itself, but you have made **the perceptions that you have refused to accept** seem dangerous to you.

Note # 42: Until we are willing to accept ownership for our own perception, we will never be in a position to dissolve them. As long as we claim that we are causeless over our own perception, we will remain in victim consciousness. If we do not realize that we are the dreamer, we will never realize that by awakening our mind to the truth, the dream will disappear. The dream of separation is not the problem. The problem is that we have forgotten that we are the dreamer. We have allowed love to be replaced by fear. As the Bible states, "That a deep sleep fell upon Adam." yet it never states that Adam awoke. We are that "Adam." We have forgotten that we chose to experience what it would be like to pretend that we had a body and now believe that we are that body. We, the dreamer, have identified ourselves as a character in the dream rather than realizing that we are the dreamer. In our personal world of provisional reality, we are the writer, director, and star in our own movie of make believe that we call our private, bodily, life experience. Only when you claim ownership of the script, do you have the power to change it. Your thoughts make your perception and your perception is your world.

T-3.VI.5. When you feel tired, **your tiredness** is because you have judged yourself as capable of being tired. 2 When you laugh at someone, **you laugh at someone** because you have judged him as unworthy. 3 When you laugh at yourself you must laugh at others, if only because you cannot tolerate the idea of being more unworthy than they are. 4 All this makes you feel tired because it is essentially disheartening. 5 You are not really capable of being tired, but you are very capable of wearying yourself. 6 The strain of constant judgment is virtually intolerable. 7 It is curious that **the ability of judgment, which is** so debilitating would be so deeply cherished. 8 Yet if you wish to be the author of reality, you will insist on holding on to judgment. 9 You will also regard judgment with fear, believing that **judgment** will someday be used against you. 10 This belief **that judgment will someday be used against you** can exist only to the extent that you believe in the efficacy of judgment as a weapon of defense for your own authority.

Note # 43: Judgment blocks and restricts the flow of source energy or connectiveness to our mind. This sense of disconnectedness with our Big "S" Self is perceived as tiring because you have chosen to be out of alignment with your Source, which is what you truly are. Your egoic thinking is denying your true nature as unlimited spirit.

T-3.VI.6. God offers only mercy. 2 Your words should reflect only mercy, because that is what you have received **from God**, and **only mercy** is what you should give. 3 Justice is a temporary expedient, or an attempt to teach you the meaning of mercy. 4 **Justice** is judgmental only because you are capable of injustice.

Note # 44: Because we perceive ourselves as unworthy, fearful sinners, we seek and demand retribution. God's mercy or judgment is only that His Child is sinless and guiltless because that is how God created you. You are an extension of God, Herself. God knows the truth that you can only be perfect, whole and complete.

T-3.VI.7. I have spoken of different symptoms, and at that level **where judgment exists,** there is almost endless variation **of different symptoms.** 2 There is, however, only one cause for all of **the different**

symptoms, the authority problem. 3 **The authority problem** <is> "the root of all evil." 4 Every symptom the ego makes involves a contradiction in terms, because the mind is split between the ego and the Holy Spirit, so that whatever the ego makes is incomplete and contradictory. 5 This untenable position **that whatever the ego makes is incomplete and contradictory** is the result of the authority problem which, because **the mind** accepts the one inconceivable thought as its premise, can produce only ideas that are inconceivable.

<u>Note # 45:</u> The "authority problem" is a question of who is the author of reality. Is God the creator or are you? If God is the creator, reality is stable and changeless and you will always be as God created you, perfect, whole and complete. If you are the creator of yourself, you have somehow usurped the authority of God and are separate and have something to fear. The authority problem now centers on what you are. Are you an ego-body? Or, are you Spirit? You cannot be both. If one is true, the other must be an illusion or dream. Due to your false belief that you are separate, your split-mind must decide which view point it should follow. Your higher mind and the Holy Spirit represent right-mindedness. This is your Big "S" Self. Wrong-mindedness is represented by the ego and its ally, the body. This is your little "s" self. The core belief of wrong-mindedness is that you are separate and come from lack and limitation. As such, you are no longer perceived as God created you. The ego tells you that you are not the Son of God but rather are something other than as God created you. The core belief of right-mindedness is that you are created by God in His Image. As such, you will always be a Oneness with God for you are an extension of God. You can deny, or forget, your birthright, but your inheritance will always be there for you to reclaim whenever you choose to remember. God made you, perfect, whole and complete, and this and only this is what you are.

T-3.VI.8.The issue of authority is really a question of authorship. 2 When you have an authority problem, it is always because you believe you are the author of yourself and project your delusion onto others. 3 You then perceive the situation as one in which others are literally fighting you for your authorship. 4 This is the fundamental error of all those who believe they have usurped the power of God. 5 This belief **that they have usurped the power of God** is very frightening to them, but hardly troubles God. 6 **God** is, however, eager to undo **this belief that you have usurped the power of God**, not to punish His children. but only because **God** knows that **this belief that you have usurped the power of God** makes **His children** unhappy. 7 God's creations are given their true Authorship, but you prefer to be anonymous when you choose to separate yourself from your Author, which **is God**. 8 Being uncertain of your true Authorship, you believe that your creation was anonymous. 9 This leaves you in a position where it sounds meaningful to believe that you created yourself. 10 The dispute over authorship has left such uncertainty in your mind that **your mind** may even doubt whether you really exist at all.

<u>Note # 46:</u> There is only one will and that is the shared Will of God. God wills that His Child be happy and know Itself. When we deny our Source, we also claim that we are unlike our Source. Yet, because we have been given God's power of creation, we are a co-creator with God. Even in the deluded state of split-mindedness, our creative power is never lost. Coming from lack, we make or miscreate through the use of projection. Although it is our thoughts that make, we disown our own authorship over our thoughts. We claim something outside ourselves created them. We also claim that what we perceive to be outside ourselves was self-created and that we are powerless to alter our circumstances. When we believe we lack, we send these thoughts of lack outward into the world of perception. When these same thought patterns return to the sender, the sender's sense then confirms that something that we claim we have no control over exists outside and separate from the mind of the sender, who is also the perceiver. Projection allows the ego to claim that perhaps we, like our outside world, was self-created.

     God's Thought is the Cause and we are God's Effect. Only in the insane logic of the egoic thought system can an effect be its own cause.

T-3.VI.9. Only those who give over all desire to reject can know that their own rejection is impossible. 2 You have not usurped the power of God, but you *<have>* lost **the power of God**. 3 Fortunately, to lose something does not mean that it has gone. 4 **To lose something** merely means that you do not remember where **what you lost** is. 5 **The** existence **of what you have lost** does not depend on your ability to identify **what you have lost**, or even to place **where what you have lost is**. 6 It is possible to look on reality without judgment and merely know that **what you have lost** is there.

Note # 47: It is impossible to lose our divine inheritance for this is not God's Will. We can deny or forget that we have, but we cannot change what God has given us. Denial does not change the truth. We merely have to believe that we have it and it will be made available to us. The mind's beliefs and thoughts are that powerful. Our divine inheritance is that God's creations remain as God created them. God's creations are eternally pure, perfect and innocent. Being spirit, these thoughts of God are invulnerable to change.

T-3.VI.10. Peace is a natural heritage of spirit. 2 Everyone is free to refuse to accept his inheritance, but he is not free to establish what his inheritance is. 3 The problem everyone must decide is the fundamental question of authorship. 4 All fear comes ultimately, and sometimes by way of very devious routes, from the denial of Authorship. 5 The offense **of the denial of Authorship** is never to God, but only to those who deny **God's Authorship**. 6 To deny **God's** Authorship is to deny yourself the reason for your peace. **Your peace is the natural heritage of spirit, which is your birthright as God's Son. When you deny God's Authorship** you see yourself only in segments. 7 This strange perception **that you, not God, created yourself** *<is>* the authority problem.

Note # 48: The denial of your birthright as a child of God, results in your belief that you are separate. This belief in separation leaves the mind split and gives rise to the illusionary world of the ego. In this dream world of the ego, you are a victim of limitation and fear. You are no longer perfect, whole and complete in this dream world of egoic making. By your denial of your divine birthright, you deny your inherited ability to co-create with your Father. Belief in lack results in miscreation because you believe yourself to be separate from the Oneness that is the Source of your creative power.

T-3.VI.11. There is no one who does not feel that he is imprisoned in some way. 2 If this **imprisonment** is the result of his own free will he must regard his will as not free, or the circular reasoning in this position would be quite apparent. 3 Free will must lead to freedom. 4 Judgment always imprisons because **judgment** separates segments of reality by the unstable scales of desire. 5 Wishes are not facts. 6 To wish is to imply that willing is not sufficient. 7 Yet no one in his right mind believes that what is wished is as real as what is willed. 8 Instead of "Seek ye first the Kingdom of Heaven" say, "*<Will>* ye first the Kingdom of Heaven," and you have said, "I know what I am and I accept my own inheritance."

Note # 49: Claim the truth of your divine birthright and it is yours. Claim that you are limited and you will imprison yourself. Only you, not God, judge yourself guilty and unworthy. Only you hold the keys to your own prison cell. When will you choose for only truth and unlock the door?

VII. Creating versus the Self-Image

T-3.VII.1.Every system of thought must have a starting point. 2 A starting point begins with a making or a creating, a difference we have already discussed. 3 Their resemblance lies **between a making or a creating**, in their power as foundations. 4 Their difference **in the power of the foundation of a making (egoic thought system) or a creating (Holy Spirit's) thought system** lies in what rests upon them. 5 Both **the power of a making or a creating** are cornerstones for systems of belief by which one lives. 6 It is a mistake to believe that a thought system based on lies is weak. 7 Nothing made by a child of God is without power. 8 It is essential to realize **that nothing made by a child of God is without power**, because otherwise you will be unable to escape from the prison you have made.

Note # 50: Due to free will, your mind has the creative power to manifest whatever you will. This is true even if you falsely believe you are a powerless victim trapped in an ego-body. Making is based on limitation and, therefore, lacks permanency and only exists in the dream state of your mind. This projected dream world is neither real nor part of the Mind of God. Yet if one believes the dream to be real, the dream has the power to entrap the dreamer within the dream itself. Creation comes from oneness and is unalterable. Coming from truth and love, creation frees, includes and joins. The two thought systems are both powerful in their creative abilities. The ego's thought system rests on the false belief in fear, separation, lack and limitation. Due to its false beliefs, the egoic split mind lacks the creative power of love, yet, it still has the power to miscreate. Although the egoic thought system is based on the false, it can make a personal, provisional reality that evolves into an entire planet that appears to be ruled by fear. The creative power of the mind is a powerful force even when it rests on lies and false beliefs. This creative power is even more powerful when its foundation rests upon the truth. The thought system of the Holy Spirit creates, rather than makes since it is based on love. Creation, being real and part of the Mind of God, is more powerful than making. When the false is brought into the light of truth, the false fades away and only love remains.

T-3.VII.2.You cannot resolve the authority problem by depreciating the power of your mind. 2 To do so **(depreciating the power of your mind),** is to deceive yourself, and this will hurt you because you really understand the strength of the mind. 3 You also realize that you cannot weaken **the power of your mind**, any more than you can weaken God. 4 The "devil" is a frightening concept because **the "devil"** seems to be extremely powerful and extremely active. 5 **The "devil"** is perceived as a force in combat with God, battling **God** for possession of **God's** creations. 6 The devil deceives by lies, and builds kingdoms in which everything is in direct opposition to God. 7 Yet **the "devil"** attracts men rather than repels **men**, and **men** are willing to "sell" **the "devil"** their souls in return for gifts of no real worth. 8 This makes absolutely no sense.

Note # 51: The mind's belief in separation is the "Devil." To the split minded, separation is very real and fearful. Our egoic thought system represents the "devil." It is based on the belief in the false, which opposes the Will of God. The false is not real and has no real intrinsic value, yet, the illusions of the false is what we seem to prize.

T-3.VII.3.We have discussed the fall or separation before, but **the fall or separation's meaning** must be clearly understood. 2 The separation is a system of thought real enough in time, though not in eternity. 3 All beliefs are real to the believer. 4 The fruit of only one tree was "forbidden" in the symbolic garden. 5 But God could not have forbidden **the fruit**, or **the fruit** could not have <been> eaten. 6 If God knows His children, and I assure you that **God** does, would **God** have put them in a position where their own destruction was possible? 7 The "forbidden tree" was named the "tree of knowledge." 8 Yet God created knowledge and gave knowledge freely to His creations. 9 The symbolism here has been given many interpretations, but you may be sure that any interpretation that sees either God or His creations as capable of destroying Their Own purpose is in error.

Note # 52: On the level of the world of perception, time and space, there are two thought systems available from which to choose. The egoic thought system made this false dream of separation appear real. The thought system of the Holy Spirit will remove the false and leave only what is created from love. The false cannot destroy the truth. The Atonement principle insures that "Adam" will wake up. It is only our denial of our divine birthright that keeps us from our remembrance of the truth that we are part of the One Self.

T-3.VII.4. Eating of the fruit of the tree of knowledge is a symbolic expression for usurping the ability for self-creating. 2 **The ability for self-creating** is the only sense in which God and His creations are not co-creators. 3 The belief that **God's creation**s are **self-created** is implicit in the "self-concept," or the tendency of the self to make an image of itself. 4 Images are perceived, not known. 5 Knowledge cannot deceive, but perception can. 6 You can perceive yourself as self-creating, but you cannot do more than believe it. 7 You cannot make **self-creating** true. 8 And, as I said before, when you finally perceive correctly you can only be glad that you cannot **self-create**. 9 Until then, however, the belief that you can **self-create** is the foundation stone in your thought system, and all your defenses are used to attack ideas that might bring **the fallacy that you can self-create** to light. 10 You still believe you are an image of your own making. 11 Your mind is split with the Holy Spirit on this point, and there is no resolution while you believe **in the fallacy that you can self-create which** is the one thing **which is** literally inconceivable. 12 **Because your mind is split with the Holy Spirit on this point,** that is why you cannot create and are filled with fear about what you make.

Note # 53: God or Source Energy is the First Cause. This "Force" always was and always will be. This "Force" is everywhere and in everything. This "Force" cannot be lost or destroyed. This "Force" is constantly moving in, out and through form. Theologians call this "Force" God. Scientists currently choose to call this "Force" energy. Both define it the same way. Call it whatever makes you feel most comfortable. ACIM calls this universal force, God. The only difference from God and everything else is that this "God Force" has no cause. This is why we describe It as always was and always will be. As such, this God Force is "self-created." Everything else that follows arose from this Causeless Force, that ACIM calls God. This God Force is the Primary Source or First Cause for all that follows after It. The Law of Creation states that like begets like. This is extension and thus, we possess all the attributes of our Original Source or Creator except that we are not causeless. God is Cause and we are God's Effect. Other than that there is no difference between this God Force and us.

The ego claims that you are self-created. This egoic claim for self–creation means you can be something other than God. If God is everything, if you believe that you are different from God, then you must be less than God. Thus, while God is perfect, whole and complete, the ego would tell you that you are not perfect, not whole and very incomplete. The ego's belief that you are self-created is the root cause of the belief in the separation and lack. From this belief that we could be separate from our Source, the entire egoic thought system arose. Separation, sin, guilt and fear are the logical outcomes of this impossible egoic belief that you gave birth to yourself. We are not self-created and we are not causeless. Being God's thoughts, we trace our origin or Source back to the Mind of our Father.

T-3.VII.5. The mind can make the belief in separation very real and very fearful, and this belief **in separation** <*is*> the "devil." 2 **The belief in separation, the "devil,"** is powerful, active, destructive and clearly in opposition to God, because **the belief in separation** literally denies **God's** Fatherhood. 3

Look at your life and see what the devil has made. 4 But realize that this making will surely dissolve in the light of truth, because its foundation, **the belief in separation**, is a lie. 5 Your creation by God is the only Foundation that cannot be shaken, because the light is in it **(the truth of your creation by God)**. 6 Your starting point is truth, and you must return to your Beginning **(Truth)**. 7 Much has been seen since then, but nothing has really happened. 8 Your Self is still in peace, even though your mind is in conflict. 9 You have not yet gone back far enough, and that is why you become so fearful. 10 As you approach the Beginning, you feel the fear of the destruction of your **egoic** thought system upon you as if **the destruction of your thought system** were the fear of death. 11 There is no death, but there <*is*> a belief in death.

Note # 54: Since our foundation rests in truth, which is real, we must return to truth. In this regard, our journey is different than what we would call the normal evolutionary cycle. Rather than evolve beyond our parent's state of being, we need to return to our "primitive" origins. We need to go back to our Source and return to the truth that we are a Child of God.

T-3.VII.6. The branch that bears no fruit will be cut off and will wither away. 2 Be glad! 3 The light will shine from the true Foundation of life, and your own thought system will stand corrected. 4 **Your own egoic thought system** cannot stand otherwise. 5 You who fear salvation are choosing death. 6 Life and death, light and darkness, knowledge and perception, are irreconcilable. 7 **To believe that Life and death, light and darkness, knowledge and perception** can be reconciled is to believe that God and His Son can <*not*> **be reconciled.** 8 Only the oneness of knowledge is free of conflict. 9 Your Kingdom is not of this world because **the Kingdom** was given you from beyond this world. 10 Only in this world **(your ego world of misperception)** is the idea of an authority problem meaningful. 11 The world is not left by death but by truth, and truth can be known by all those for whom the Kingdom was created, and for whom **the Kingdom** waits.

Note # 55: Reject the thought system of the ego. It is based on the false beliefs of self-creation, separation, limitation, lack and fear. Instead, embrace the thought system of the Holy Spirit that represents truth and love. Love is life. Nothing truly living can survive on the thought system of the ego. The false cannot support life for the false is an illusion of nothing. The loving flow of Source Energy is what gives life. This is your divine birthright and inheritance. Follow the thought system of the Holy Spirit and reawaken to the truth. By accepting the Atonement for yourself, your path to the return to the knowledge that resides in the Kingdom of Heaven is assured.

Chapter 4. THE ILLUSIONS OF THE EGO

Introduction

T-4.in.1.The Bible says that you should go with a brother twice as far as **a brother** asks. 2 It certainly does not suggest that you set him back on his journey. 3 Devotion to a brother cannot set you back either. 4 **Devotion to a brother** can lead only to mutual progress. 5 The result of genuine devotion is inspiration, a word which properly understood is the opposite of fatigue. 6 To be fatigued is to be dis-spirited, but to be inspired is to be in the spirit. 7 To be egocentric is to be dis-spirited, but to be Self-centered in the right sense is to be inspired or in spirit. 8 The truly inspired are enlightened and cannot abide in darkness.

Note # 1: To be Self-centered is to be in alignment with your Big "S" Self's nature. It acknowledges your spiritual roots and encourages joining, not separation. Being a Oneness, when you assist another on their journey back to the light this also aids yourself. We assist a brother when we see his spiritual nature rather than view him as a limited ego-body. By realizing that his action can only be an expression of love or a cry for love, we allow him to be his true Self.

T-4.in.2.You can speak from the spirit or from the ego, as you choose. 2 If you speak from spirit you have chosen to "Be still and know that I am God." 3 These words are inspired because they reflect knowledge. 4 If you speak from the ego you are disclaiming knowledge instead of affirming **knowledge**, and are thus dis-spiriting yourself. 5 Do not embark on useless journeys, because **useless journeys** are indeed in vain. 6 The ego may desire **useless journeys**, but spirit cannot embark on useless journeys because **spirit** is forever unwilling to depart from **spirit's** Foundation.

Note # 2: Only seek and witness for the truth of our Big "S" Self. Follow the voice of the Holy Spirit. If you utilize egoic thinking, you will judge wrongly and will misperceive.

T-4.in.3.The journey to the cross should be the last "useless journey." 2 Do not dwell upon **the journey to the cross**, but dismiss **the journey to the cross** as accomplished. 3 If you can accept **the journey to the cross** as your own last useless journey, you are also free to join my resurrection. 4 Until you do so your life is indeed wasted. 5 **Your life** merely re-enacts the separation, the loss of power, the futile attempts of the ego at reparation, and finally the crucifixion of the body, or death. 6 Such repetitions are endless until they are voluntarily given up. 7 Do not make the pathetic error of "clinging to the old rugged cross." 8 The only message of the crucifixion is that you can overcome the cross. 9 Until then you are free to crucify yourself as often as you choose. 10 This **pathetic error of "clinging to the old rugged cross"** is not the gospel I intended to offer you. 11 We have another journey to undertake, and if you will read these lessons carefully **these lessons** will help prepare you to undertake **this other**

journey.

Note # 3: By our abandoning the egoic thought system and accepting the Atonement for ourselves, we accomplish the journey back to the truth that we are the "Christ." Following the guidance of the Holy Spirit does this.

I. Right Teaching and Right Learning

T-4.I.1.A good teacher clarifies his own ideas and strengthens **his own ideas** by teaching **his own ideas.** 2 Teacher and pupil are alike in the learning process. 3 **Teacher and pupil** are in the same order of learning, and unless **teacher and pupil** share their lessons conviction will be lacking. 4 A good teacher must believe in the ideas he teaches, but **a good teacher** must meet another condition; **a good teacher** must believe in the students to whom he offers the ideas.

Note # 4: Both teacher and pupil aid each other when they both share the belief that the learning goal will be accomplished. We are all teachers and we are all students. We are on the journey together.

T-4.I.2.Many stand guard over their ideas because they want to protect their thought systems as they are, and learning means change. 2 Change is always fearful to the separated, because **the separated** cannot conceive of **change** as a move towards healing the separation. 3 **The separated** always perceive **change** as a move toward further separation, because the separation was their first experience of change. 4 You believe that if you allow no change to enter into your ego you will find peace. 5 This profound confusion **of the separated to not conceive of change as a move towards healing the separation**. is possible only if you maintain that the same thought system can stand on two foundations. 6 Nothing can reach spirit from the ego, and nothing can reach the ego from spirit. 7 Spirit can neither strengthen the ego nor reduce the conflict within **the ego.** 8 The ego <is> a contradiction. 9 Your self **(ego-self)** and God's Self <are> in opposition. 10 **Your self (ego-self) and God's Self** are opposed in source, in direction and in outcome. 11 **Your self (ego-self) and God's Self** are fundamentally irreconcilable, because spirit cannot perceive and the ego cannot know. 12 **Your self (ego-self) and God's Self** are therefore not in communication and can never be in communication. 13 Nevertheless, the ego can learn, even though its maker **(your split-minded self)** can be misguided. 14 **The ego's maker** cannot, however, make the totally lifeless out of the life-given.

Note # 5: The thought systems of the ego and the Holy Spirit are mutually exclusive. They are like two parallel lines; they never cross. They always contradict each other. The true and the false do not mix to become "sometimes." When we realize that each system represents a different level of thinking, we can understand why both cannot take us to the truth. The only way to the truth is by total abandonment of the egoic ladder of separation. The ego's ladder only takes us to different degrees of fear. We can never reach the truth by following the false. If we follow the thought system of the Holy Spirit, the split-minded can relearn the truth about themselves.

T-4.I.3.Spirit need not be taught, but the ego must be **taught**. 2 Learning is ultimately perceived as frightening because **learning** leads to the relinquishment, not the destruction, of the ego to the light of spirit. 3 This **relinquishment, not the destruction, of the ego to the light of spirit** is the change the ego must fear, because **the ego** does not share my charity. 4 My lesson was like yours, and because I learned **my lesson** I can teach **my lesson**. 5 I will never attack your ego, but I am trying to teach you how **your ego's** thought system arose. 6 When I remind you of your true creation, your ego cannot but respond with fear.

Note # 6: Jesus wants us to recover our decision-making ability. We each have our own decision-maker in our mind. It is your decision-maker that determines which thought system you will choose to follow at any given moment in time. Jesus asks us to reclaim our mind's decision-making ability and realize that we have the power to choose again. When we choose a different thought system, we get different results. Thus, we get change. The ego does not want change for change means you have decided to remove some of your allegiance from the ego to the Holy Spirit. ACIM and Jesus know that by teaching us the truth about the egoic thought system, we will come to our senses and freely decide to seek the guidance of the Holy Spirit.

T-4.I.4. Teaching and learning are your greatest strengths now, because **teaching and learning** enable you to change your mind and help others to change their **minds**. 2 Refusing to change your mind will not prove that the separation has not occurred. 3 The dreamer who doubts the reality of his dream while he is still dreaming is not really healing his split mind. 4 You dream of a separated ego and believe in a world that rests upon **a separated ego**. 5 This **dream world that rests upon a separated ego** is very real to you. 6 You cannot undo **this dream world that rests upon a separated ego** by not changing your mind about **this dream world that rests upon a separated ego**. 7 If you are willing to renounce the role of guardian of your thought system and open **the role of guardian of your thought system** to me, I will correct **your thought system** very gently and lead you back to God.

Note # 7: The insane cannot expect to be healed by continuing to follow an insane thought system. Only someone who is sane and is aware of your current delusional state of mind can offer correction and return you to right-mindedness. Jesus is the representative for the Holy Spirit's guidance system. This guide and teacher stands ready to help us retrain our mind. We need only ask for His advice and it will be given.

T-4.I.5. Every good teacher hopes to give his students so much of his own learning that **his students** will one day no longer need **the teacher**. 2 This is the one true goal of the teacher. 3 It is impossible to convince the ego **that the one true goal of the good teacher is to no longer be needed by your students**, because **this** goes against all of **the ego's** own laws. 4 But remember that laws are set up to protect the continuity of the system in which the lawmaker believes. 5 It is natural for the ego to try to protect itself once you have made **the ego your teacher**, but it is not natural for you to want to obey **the ego's** laws unless <you> believe **the ego's laws**. 6 The ego cannot make this choice because of the nature of **the ego's** origin. 7 You can, because of the nature of your **origin**.

Note # 8: The ego wants you to always follow it for the ego's very existence depends upon you. The ego was not self-created. It was your mind that birthed your ego. You are the cause and the ego is the effect of your thinking. The ego is the result of your belief that the separation is real. It is your thinking that birthed your ego and the ego's existence is contingent on your decision to allow it to continue to be your adviser for your experiences of separation. Because of your divine birthright, you have the power of creation and also the power of the decision-maker.

The decision-maker is your free will. You have free will to imagine and experience whatever you want. If you wish to pretend or imagine that you are something you are not, free will gives you this power. Free will does not give you the power to change the truth, but it does allow you to pretend that you are anything you want to be, even self-created if you dare to will that type of experience for yourself. When we believe we are self-created, we birth our ego and the egoic thought system. Self-creation allows us to experience what it would be like to be limited and separate from our Source. There was nothing wrong with us desiring the experience of separation, but somehow during the process, we forgot that we were pretending and we took the dream seriously. We identified ourselves as real participant, rather than merely an actor in a stage play. We, the dreamer, forgot that it was our own dream. We took the dream of separation seriously and in our minds it became real to us, the actors. When we choose to reclaim our right to control our own decision-maker, we will be able to decide that we no longer want to play the game of separation. The ego never wants us to rediscover that we, not the ego, have always been in control of the decision-maker.

T-4.I.6. Egos can clash in any situation, but spirit cannot clash at all. 2 If you perceive a teacher as merely "a larger ego" you will be afraid, because to enlarge an ego would be to increase anxiety about separation. 3 I will teach with you and live with you if you will think with me, but my goal will always be to absolve you finally from the need for a teacher. 4 This is the opposite of the ego-oriented teacher's goal. 5 **The ego-oriented teacher** is concerned with the effect of his ego on other egos, and therefore interprets their interaction as a means of ego preservation. 6 I would not be able to devote myself to teaching if I believed this, and you will not be a devoted teacher as long as you believe **that the role of a teacher's interaction with the student is a means of ego preservation.** 7 I am constantly being perceived as a teacher either to be exalted or rejected, but I do not accept either perception for myself.

Note # 9: An ego-oriented teacher wants his student to always be dependent on him and never outgrow his need for a teacher. This is similar to the psychologist or doctor who wants his patients to get better but not so well that their patients no longer need their services.

T-4.I.7. Your worth is not established by teaching or learning. 2 Your worth is established by God. 3 As long as you dispute that **your worth is established by God** everything you do will be fearful, particularly any situation that lends itself to the belief in superiority and inferiority. 4 Teachers must be patient and repeat their lessons until **their lessons** are learned. 5 I am willing to do this, because I have no right to set your learning limits for you. 6 Again,–nothing you do or think or wish or make is necessary to establish your worth. 7 This point **that your worth is established by God** is not debatable except in delusions. 8 Your ego is never at stake because God did not create **your ego.** 9 Your spirit is never at stake because He did **create your spirit.** 10 Any confusion on this point is delusional, and no form of devotion is possible as long as **the** delusion lasts **regarding the fact that your worth is established by God and not by anything you do.**

Note # 10: This egoic world teaches that our worth is determined by what we do. The ego teaches that love must be earned. The thought system of the Holy Spirit knows that God established your worth and that there is nothing you can do to increase or decrease your worth in God's eyes. God so loved His Creation that He gave everything that He is to them. God has established that our birthright is our worth. He created you perfect, whole and complete. The egoic thought system wants to limit you, don't let it. Reclaim your truth as unlimited spirit. We are a Oneness of Everything. Our will and God's Will are One.

T-4.I.8. The ego tries to exploit all situations into forms of praise for itself in order to overcome **the ego's** doubts. 2 **The ego** will remain doubtful as long as you believe in **the ego's** existence. 3 You who made **the ego** cannot trust **the ego,** because in your right mind you realize **the ego** is not real. 4 The only sane solution is not to try to change reality, which is indeed a fearful attempt, but to accept **reality** as **reality** is. 5 You are part of reality, which stands unchanged beyond the reach of your ego but within easy reach of spirit. 6 When you are afraid, be still and know that God is real, and you are His beloved

Son in whom He is well pleased. 7 Do not let your ego dispute **that you are His beloved Son in whom He is well pleased,** because the ego cannot know what is as far beyond **the ego's** reach as you are.

Note # 11: Our Christ consciousness and our ego belief system are opposite. One is truth and the other represents illusion. When we choose the thought system of the Holy Spirit, we align with the truth. God is well pleased because He knows the truth that we are His changeless extension. We eternally are as God created us, His Children, perfect, whole and complete.

T-4.I.9. God is not the author of fear. 2 You are **the author of fear.** 3 You have chosen to create unlike Him, and have therefore made fear for yourself. 4 You are not at peace because you are not fulfilling your function **to create like God.** 5 God gave you a very lofty function that you are not meeting. 6 Your ego has chosen to be afraid instead of meeting **your function to create like God.** 7 When you awaken you will not be able to understand **that you chose to be afraid instead of meeting your function,** because it is literally incredible. 8 <Do not believe the incredible now.> 9 Any attempt to increase its believableness, **that you chose to be afraid instead of meeting your function to create like God,** is merely to postpone the inevitable. 10 The word "inevitable" is fearful to the ego, but joyous to the spirit. 11 God is inevitable, and you cannot avoid Him any more than He can avoid you.

Note # 12: Our function is to create like God. We are designed to extend the love of God. We do this by being love. Due to identification with the egoic thought system, we have attempted to create out of fear. Fear is our miscreation and, thus, it is not real. Miscreation is not our destiny and can never give us lasting joy. Being love, we must extend the truth of our "Beingness." which is only love. When we learn to control our fear, we will once again reclaim our rightful place as co-creator with Our Father. This result is certain. Time patiently waits upon our inevitable decision to accept the Atonement for ourselves and be the truth of what we are.

T-4.I.10. The ego is afraid of the spirit's joy, because once you have experienced **the spirit's joy** you will withdraw all protection from the ego, and become totally without investment in fear. 2 Your investment **in fear** is great now because fear is a witness to the separation, and your ego rejoices when you witness to **the separation.** 3 Leave **the ego and the separation** behind! 4 Do not listen to **the ego** and do not preserve **the separation and the ego.** 5 Listen only to God, Who is as incapable of deception as is the spirit He created. 6 Release yourself and release others. 7 Do not present a false and unworthy picture of yourself to others, and do not accept such **a false and unworthy** picture of them yourself.

Note # 13: Our ego's self-image of littleness is totally false and unworthy of a Son of God. When we realize that we control our own decision-maker, we will allow ourselves to choose again. We will recover right-mindedness. Who but the insane would choose the fantasy of littleness over the reality of their Big "S" Self?

T-4.I.11. The ego has built a shabby and unsheltering home for you, because **the ego** cannot build otherwise. 2 Do not try to make this impoverished house stand. 3 **The ego's impoverished house's** weakness is your strength. 4 Only God could make a home that is worthy of His creations. **His creations have chosen to leave the home that God made for His creations** empty by **His creations'** own dispossession **of God's home.** 5 Yet His home will stand forever, and is ready for you when you choose to enter **His home.** 6 Of this you can be wholly certain. 7 God is as incapable of creating the perishable as the ego is of making the eternal.

Note # 14: Our birthright cannot be lost or stolen. Our true Home awaits our decision to bear witness only for the truth. God never took away our Home. We freely chose to move out. The Holy Spirit has kept God's Home for us and we will return to God's Home whenever we decide to accept the Atonement for ourselves. Our return is only one decision away. The Holy Spirit asks our decision-maker to choose again.

T-4.I.12. Of your ego you can do nothing to save yourself or others, but of your spirit you can do everything for the salvation of both **yourself or others**. 2 Humility is a lesson for the ego, not for the spirit. 3 Spirit is beyond humility, because **spirit** recognizes its radiance and gladly sheds its light everywhere. 4 The meek shall inherit the earth because their egos are humble, and this gives **the meek** truer perception. 5 The Kingdom of Heaven is the spirit's right, whose beauty and dignity are far beyond doubt, beyond perception, and stand forever as the mark of the Love of God for His creations, who are wholly worthy of Him and only of Him. 6 Nothing else **but the Kingdom of Heaven** is sufficiently worthy to be a gift for a creation of God Himself.

Note # 15: The ego's thought system has a plan for everything that you choose to experience. This egoic plan is based on its erroneous beliefs in separation and limitation. From this error laden thought system, the ego judges incorrectly and then determines what must be done to fix what it misperceived and then also misjudged in the first place. This egoic thought system is bankrupt. The false can do nothing to change to truth. The false can only replace one illusion with another equally false illusion. Only the Holy Spirit, Who knows both the truth and your illusion, can return you to right-mindedness. Once in your right-mind, Spirit can do everything through you to return you and your brother to knowledge.

T-4.I.13.I will substitute for your ego if you wish, but **I will** never **substitute** for your spirit. 2 A father can safely leave a child with an elder brother who has shown himself responsible, but this involves no confusion about the child's origin. 3 The brother can protect the child's body and **child's** ego, but the **brother** does not confuse himself with the father because he does this. 4 I can be entrusted with your body and your ego only because this enables you not to be concerned with **your body and your ego**, and lets me teach you **your body and your ego's** unimportance. 5 I could not understand their importance to you if I had not once been tempted to believe in **my body and my ego** myself. 6 Let us undertake to learn this lesson together so we can be free of **the body and the ego** together. 7 I need devoted teachers who share my aim of healing the mind. 8 Spirit is far beyond the need of your protection or mine. 9 Remember this:

10 In this world you need not have tribulation because I have overcome the world. 11 **Because I have overcome this world (world of the ego body),** this is why you should be of good cheer.

Note # 16: Jesus has "been there and done that." As such, he is the perfect teacher, who can act as our mentor and guide. Jesus is the "way shower" because he has completed the journey back Home. Jesus is an experienced, older brother who was just like us. Jesus, like us, is a Child of God. Jesus, unlike us, has learned that he was not self-created and that all power resided in our Source. Jesus knows that the Sonship could never usurp God's power and thus he will teach us that we remain the sinless and guiltless Child of God. God is Cause and we are His Effect. Jesus brings news that our inheritance has not been lost and we should rejoice. This egoic world of body and form is not real. It is an illusion.

II. The Ego and False Autonomy

T-4.II.1. It is reasonable to ask how the mind could ever have made the ego. 2 In fact, **how the mind could ever have made the ego** is the best question you could ask. 3 There is, however, no point in giving an answer **to the question of how the mind could ever have made the ego** in terms of the past because the past does not matter, and history would not exist if the same errors were not being repeated in the present. 4 Abstract thought applies to knowledge because knowledge is completely impersonal, and examples are irrelevant to **knowledge's** understanding. 5 Perception, however, is always specific, and therefore quite concrete.

<u>Note # 17:</u> It does not matter how the mind made the ego, but ACIM states that we are still making the same choice in this moment. Our experience is based on what we choose to believe. Our beliefs or thoughts generate our experiences. Thoughts become things. "As a Man thinks, so he becomes." We are constantly creating our world of provisional reality.

T-4.II.2. Everyone makes an ego or a self for himself, which is subject to enormous variation because of **the ego's** instability. 2 He also makes an ego for everyone else he perceives, which is equally variable **or unstable.** 3 Their interaction **(your own ego and the ego you made for someone else)** is a process that alters both, because they **(your own ego and the ego you made for someone else)** were not made by or with the Unalterable, **it is not shared with the Mind of God.** 4 It is important to realize that this alteration **between your own ego and the ego you made for someone else** can and does occur as readily when the interaction takes place in the mind as when **the interaction** involves physical proximity. 5 Thinking about another ego is as effective in changing **your** relative perception **about that other ego that you created** as is physical interaction. 6 There could be no better example that the ego is only an idea and not a fact.

<u>Note # 18:</u> We create our ego, which determines how we perceive ourselves to be. We also create an ego for everything else. Perception, since it is not knowledge, is subject to change based on the mind of the perceiver   Since these egos are our own perception which is subject to change, the egos that we make and project upon ourselves and others are unstable and subject to change. Being only thought projections, egos represent the idea that we hold in our mind about any subject. It is our story, not the "facts." As we change our thinking, we change our perception of what we believe. This change in our thinking also changes our egoic projections about ourselves and others. Our perception forms the basis for our own "provisional reality," "dream state" or "illusionary world." By changing our thinking, we can change our "provisional reality."

<u>**IMPORTANT NOTE:**</u> Paragraph **T-4.II.2** contains a critically concept if someone is to escape from a fear-based thought system. It states that we are constantly creating an ego, not just for ourselves, but also for everyone and everything that we perceive. Our ability to create these egos for all that we perceive requires a split mind that believes the separation to be real. We live in a world of private individuated perception. This private world is being evaluated and judged through our own mind's egoic filters and belief system. Our belief system determines what experiences we are willing to allow within our state of consciousness. This helps insures that the outer world that we perceive confirms and conforms to the inner world that we have created within our own mind. We claim to see an outside world that is separate and autonomous from us. This is not so. We are only seeing through our own personal egoic sunglasses that color everything that we perceive. Thus, the interactions that we claim to be having with other ego-bodies are actually occurring within our own mind. This interplay is not

between two separate autonomous entities but rather it is an internal mind game that is played out between our own ego and the ego we made for someone else. Everything is an inside job that is originating within each party's own mind. Yet we behave as if we are interacting with another separate autonomous being. In reality, each party is reacting to their own mind's projections about what they believe that other person's role is supposed to be. This role, of course, is our egoic image that we have created for them. By the same token, the other party is not reacting to you, but rather to the egoic role that they created for you. Thus, through the process of individuated egoic creation, each party's mind is controlling how they personally will perceive the situation. Neither party is in the <now> since each is reacting and cultivating their own egoic story. Each is living in their own private fantasy world of egoic projection.

T-4.II.3. Your own state of mind is a good example of how the ego was made. 2 When you threw knowledge away it is as if you never had **knowledge.** 3 This is so apparent that one need only recognize **that, when you throw knowledge away it is as if you never had knowledge,** to see that it does happen. 4 If this occurs **(throwing knowledge away and then forgetting that you once had it)** in the present, why is it surprising that it occurred in the past? 5 Surprise is a reasonable response to the unfamiliar, though hardly to something that occurs with such persistence. 6 But do not forget that the mind need not work that way, even though **the mind** does work that way now.

<u>Note # 19:</u> When our mind chooses to believe something different, all past knowledge that would be contradictory to the new belief is temporarily forgotten. Knowledge requires certainty. When we choose to perceive, we lose certainty and with it knowledge.

T-4.II.4. Think of the love of animals for their offspring, and the need the **animals** feel to protect **their offspring** 2 That is because they regard **their offspring** as part of themselves. 3 No one dismisses something he considers part of himself. 4 You react to your ego much as God does to His creations,– with love, protection and charity. 5 Your reactions to the self you made are not surprising. 6 In fact, **your reactions to the self you made (your ego)** resemble in many ways how you will one day react to your real creations, which are as timeless as you are. 7 The question is not how you respond to the ego, but what you believe you are. 8 Belief is an ego function, and as long as your origin is open to belief you are regarding, **or questioning, what you believe you are,** from an ego viewpoint. 9 When teaching is no longer necessary you will merely know God. 10 Belief that there is another way of perceiving is the loftiest idea of which ego thinking is capable. 11 That is because **belief that there is another way of perceiving,** contains a hint of recognition that the ego is not the Self.

<u>Note # 20:</u> The "problem" of the ego comes from our faulty belief in what we are. Are we spirit (Son of God), perfect, whole and complete? Or, are we ego-bodies subject to lack and limitation? We cannot create like God when we are under the false belief that we are something other than as God created us. The ego claims that we are self-created. Yet, when the ego changes its beliefs and thinking, it admits that perception can change and that our ego is not always right. It confirms that the ego is not sure what it is. Our Big "S" Self is in the "I AM" state. The ego is in the "WHAT AM I?" state. The ego's instability in thinking hints that anything the ego claims to be truth is subject to change. If this is the case, can we trust and believe the ego's definition of what we are?

T-4.II.5. Undermining the ego's thought system must be perceived as painful, even though this is anything but true. 2 Babies scream in rage if you take away a knife or scissors, although **the babies** may well harm themselves if you do not **take away the knife** 3 In this sense you are still a baby. 4 You have no sense of real self-preservation, and are likely to decide that you need precisely what would hurt you most. 5 Yet whether or not you recognize it now, you have agreed to cooperate in the effort to become both harmless and helpful, attributes that must go together. 6 Your attitudes even toward **both harmless and helpful** are necessarily conflicted, because all attitudes are ego-based. 7 This **conflict** will not last. 8 Be patient a while and remember that the outcome is as certain as God.

Note # 21: We have been brought up to believe that we are a separate, limited ego-body. Although the belief that we are a body is detrimental to the happiness of our true Self, we have adopted the belief that the egoic thought system protects and defends our reality. In truth, the egoic thought system defends only the dream of separation while attacking the truth of your reality as Spirit, your Big "S" Self.

T-4.II.6. Only those who have a real and lasting sense of abundance can be truly charitable. 2 This is obvious when you consider what is involved **to be truly charitable**. 3 To the ego, to give anything implies that you will have to do without it. 4 When you associate giving with sacrifice, you give only because you believe that you are somehow getting something better, and can therefore do without the thing you give. 5 "Giving to get" is an inescapable law of the ego, **since the ego** always evaluates itself in relation to other egos. 6 **The ego** is therefore continually preoccupied with the belief in scarcity that gave rise to **the ego**. 7 **The ego's** whole perception of other egos as real is only an attempt to convince itself that <the ego> is real. 8 "Self-esteem" in ego terms means nothing more than that the ego has deluded itself into accepting **the ego's** reality, and is therefore temporarily less predatory. 9 This "self-esteem" is always vulnerable to stress, a term which refers to any perceived threat to the ego's existence.

Note # 22: ACIM also points out that egoic "charity" is not true, unconditional giving but rather we give to get. Egoic charity is an exchange in which we believe we will get something better than what we gave up. We will get our reward in heaven or we will be blessed tenfold. This is why ACIM states most charitable giving is an exchange to get.
ACIM gives its definition of **"STRESS"** as any perceived threat to the ego. Stress is in the domain of the ego and its insistence on lack. It is not a function of the body but a misperception based on what you are.

T-4.II.7. The ego literally lives by comparisons. 2 Equality is beyond grasp, and charity becomes impossible. 3 The ego never gives out of abundance, because **the ego** was made as a substitute for **abundance**. 4 That is why the concept of "getting" arose in the ego's thought system. 5 Appetites are "getting" mechanisms, representing the ego's need to confirm itself. 6 **The ego's need to confirm itself** is as true of body appetites as **the ego's need to confirm itself** is **true** of the so-called appetites of the "higher ego needs." 7 Body appetites are not physical in origin. 8 The ego regards the body as **the ego's** home, and tries to satisfy itself through the body. 9 But the idea **that through the body the ego can satisfy itself** is possible, is a decision of the mind **yet the mind has** become completely confused about what is really possible.

Note # 23: Although the mind is the true seat of power, your uncertainty as to what you are has allowed you to abdicate that power to the ego's belief system. The ego's thought system is design to bear false witness against the truth and claim that you are either self-created or that you have a will that opposes God's Will. Since you arose from lack, you must get what you need from outside yourself. This is further proof that you are separate and apart from the Mind of God and cannot be a Oneness of Everything.

T-4.II.8. The ego believes it is completely on its own, which is merely another way of describing how **the ego** thinks it originated. 2 This **belief that the ego is completely on its own** is such a fearful state that **the ego** can only turn to other egos and try to unite with **the other egos** in a feeble attempt at identification, or attack **the other egos** in an equally feeble show of strength. 3 **The ego** is not free, however, to open the premise to question, because the premise **(the belief that the ego is completely on its own)** is **the ego's** foundation. 4 The ego is the mind's belief that **the mind** is completely on its own. 5 The ego's ceaseless attempts to gain the spirit's acknowledgment and thus establish **the ego's** own existence are useless. 6 Spirit in its knowledge is unaware of the ego. 7 **Spirit** does not attack **the ego**; **Spirit** merely cannot conceive of **the ego** at all. 8 While the ego is equally unaware of spirit, **the ego** does perceive itself as being rejected by something greater than itself **(Spirit).** 9 This is why self-esteem in ego terms must be delusional. 10 The creations of God do not create myths, although creative effort can be turned to mythology. 11 **Creative efforts can be turned to mythology**, however, only under one condition; what **creative effort egoically** makes is then no longer creative. 12 Myths are entirely perceptual, and so ambiguous in form and characteristically good-and-evil in nature that the most benevolent of **the myths are** not without fearful connotations.

Note # 24: The self-creation myth of the ego is the seat of all fear. It is the bedrock for the belief that God's creation could usurp God's authority and oppose God's Will. This idea that we could be something other than our God, our Source, has led to the ego's unholy alliance with sin, guilt and fear. These three "kissing cousins" always show up together as a threesome upon our acceptance of the belief in separation.

T-4.II.9. Myths and magic are closely associated, since myths are usually related to ego origins, and magic to the powers the ego ascribes to itself. 2 Mythological systems generally include some account of "the creation," and associate **its' account of "the creation,"** with its particular form of magic. 3 The so-called "battle for survival" is only the ego's struggle to preserve itself, and **the ego's** interpretation of its own beginning. 4 This beginning is usually associated with physical birth, because it is hard to maintain that the ego existed before that point in time **(physical birth).** 5 The more "religiously" ego-oriented may believe that the soul existed before, and will continue to exist after a temporary lapse into ego life. 6 Some even believe that the soul will be punished for this lapse **into ego life.** 7 However, salvation does not apply to spirit, **since spirit** is not in danger and does not need to be salvaged.

Note # 25: Spirit, being one with God, has no need for salvation for it eternally rests in the Mind of God. Only a belief system that claims that separation from God happened, would require and develop a mythology of salvation for its return to God.

T-4.II.10. Salvation is nothing more than "right-mindedness," which is not the One-mindedness of the Holy Spirit, but **"right-mindedness"** must be achieved before One-mindedness is restored. 2 Right-mindedness leads to the next step automatically, because right perception is uniformly without attack, and therefore wrong-mindedness is obliterated. 3 The ego cannot survive without judgment, and **the ego** is laid aside accordingly **when right-mindedness is achieved.** 4 **Since wrong-mindedness has been obliterated because of right perception**, the mind then has only one direction in which **the mind** can move. 5 **The mind's** direction is always automatic, because **the direction** cannot but be dictated by the thought system to which **the mind** adheres.

Note # 26: The ego must judge in order to survive. Judgment is used by the ego to confirm that the ego is separate from something "out there." If there is only a Oneness, who could the ego judge against?
Once we start to request the guidance of the Holy Spirit, we will automatically gravitate more and more toward the help of the Holy Spirit. We feel positive emotions when we drop our egoic judgments and respond to a brother with love and forgiveness. These positive emotions testify to the effectiveness of love's ability to remove fear. This pull toward the inner peace found in the thought system of the Holy Spirit is magnetic and goes in one direction. Once begun, there is no turning back. It is merely a question of time before the thought system of the ego is abandoned entirely.

T-4.II.11. It cannot be emphasized too often that correcting perception is merely a temporary expedient. 2 **Correct perception** is necessary only because misperception is a block to knowledge, while accurate perception is a steppingstone towards **knowledge**. 3 The whole value of right perception lies in the inevitable realization that <*all*> perception is unnecessary. 4 This **realization that <*all*> perception is unnecessary** removes the block entirely. 5 You may ask how **this removal of the block** is possible as long as you appear to be living in this world. 6 That is a reasonable question. 7 You must be careful, however, that you really understand **the question**. 8 Who is the "you" who are living in this world? 9 Spirit is immortal, and immortality is a constant state. 10 **Spirit is immortal, and immortality is a constant state** is as true now as it ever was or ever will be, because **immortality, like spirit,** implies no change at all. 11 **Immortality** is not a continuum, nor is i**mmortality** understood by being compared to an opposite. 12 Knowledge never involves comparisons. 13 That **knowledge never involves comparisons** is **knowledge's** main difference from everything else the mind can grasp.

Note # 27: We seek oneness, which is the result of knowledge. When the separation occurred in our minds, we "lost" knowledge and replaced knowledge with perception. Perception can vary from person to person. Perception is not stable since it arises out of a split-mind. The mind is under the influence of right-mindedness when it is following the guidance of the Holy Spirit. Right perception arises from the decision to ask for the Holy Spirit's guidance. The mind is under the influence of wrong-mindedness when it is under the belief system of the ego. When we misperceive, knowledge is blocked. To correct this block, it is necessary to recover right-mindedness.

This block, like all other fear based thoughts are the product of illusion. They appear to exist only in the mind of the perceiver of the dream of separation. Awaken the power of the decision-maker to his ability to choose again and he will freely choose to awaken to truth. Our tolerance for pain is high but it is not infinite. Eventually we will ask to be shown another way to look at our experiences. When we do this, the Holy Spirit will be there.

III. Love without Conflict

T-4.III.1. It is hard to understand what "The Kingdom of Heaven is within you" really means. 2 This is because **what "The Kingdom of Heaven is within you" really means** is not understandable to the ego, which interprets **this statement** as if something outside is inside, and this does not mean anything. 3 The word "within" is unnecessary. 4 The Kingdom of Heaven <*is*> you. 5 What else <*but*> you did the Creator create, and what else <*but*> you is His Kingdom? 6 This is the whole message of the Atonement; a message which in its totality transcends the sum of its parts. 7 You, too, have a Kingdom that your spirit created. 8 **Your spirit** has not ceased to create because of the ego's illusions. 9 Your creations are no more fatherless than you are. 10 Your ego and your spirit will never be co-creators, but your spirit and your Creator will always be. 11 Be confident that your creations are as safe as you are.

12 The Kingdom is perfectly united and perfectly protected, and the ego will not prevail against **the Kingdom**. 13 Amen.

Note # 28: Heaven is not a place. It is a state of mind or Spirit. As long as we believe ourselves to be a body, we cannot understand how this could be. ACIM is mind training. It asks us to question everything the ego has taught us so that we can choose differently. To abandon everything you have been taught to be true requires either great courage or great desperation. You need to ask yourself, has the egoic thought system brought you lasting peace, joy and happiness? If not, why not try something else? If that something else does not give you improved results, you can always go back to your old ways of thinking.

ACIM has an accompanying workbook consisting of 365 daily lessons. These lessons are to retrain your mind to a new paradigm of thinking. The workbook lessons will move the teachings of ACIM from your head to your heart. If you are serious about changing your life's direction, you need to do these lessons. To claim you know and not to live it is not to know.

T-4.III.2. This **(T-4 III.1.12. The Kingdom is perfectly united and perfectly protected, and the ego will not prevail against the Kingdom. 13 Amen.)**
is written in the form of a prayer because it is useful in moments of temptation. 2 **This prayer, (T-4 III.12.)** is a declaration of independence. 3 You will find it **(T-4 III.12.)** very helpful if you understand it fully. 4 The reason you need my help is because you have denied your own Guide and therefore need guidance. 5 My role is to separate the true from the false, so truth can break through the barriers the ego has set up and **truth** can shine into your mind. 6 Against our united strength the ego cannot prevail.

Note # 29: Egoic thinking has brainwashed us so effectively that we cannot see the forest through the trees. Only someone above the level of the trees can direct us home .It is impossible to change error thinking when you are being constantly told that this is just the way it is and you have no power to affect change over your experience. You need to be told that you have the ability to choose again.

T-4.III.3. It is surely apparent by now why the ego regards spirit as **the ego's** "enemy." 2 The ego arose from the separation, and **the ego's** continued existence depends on your continuing belief in the separation. 3 The ego must offer you some sort of reward for maintaining this belief **in the separation.** 4 All **the ego** can offer is a sense of temporary existence, which begins with **the ego's** own beginning and ends with **the ego's** own ending. 5 **The ego** tells you this life is your existence because **this life** is **the ego's** own existence. 6 Against this sense of temporary existence spirit offers you the knowledge of permanence and unshakable being. 7 No one who has experienced the revelation of **the spirit's knowledge of permanence and unshakable being** can ever fully believe in the ego again. 8 How can **the ego's** meager offering to you **of temporary existence** prevail against the glorious gift of God **which is permanence and unshakable being**?

Note # 30: When we compare what each thought system promise their followers, only an insane mind would choose the egoic thought system. Because of this fact, the ego never wants you to rediscover that you have the ability to choose again. ACIM goal is to reawaken the decision-maker within you to the fact that you still have free will and, therefore, can choose differently. You can choose to follow the Holy Spirit's thought system and accept the Atonement, which is the Truth about yourself.

T-4.III.4. You who identify with your ego cannot believe God loves you. 2 You do not love what you made **(the ego)**, and what you made **(the ego)** does not love you. 3 Being made out of the denial of the Father, the ego has no allegiance to **you**, its maker. 4 You cannot conceive of the real relationship that exists between God and His creations because of your hatred for the self you made. 5 You project onto the ego the decision to separate, and this conflicts with the love you feel for the ego because you made **the ego**. 6 No love in this world is without this ambivalence, and since no ego has experienced love without ambivalence the concept **of love without this ambivalence** is beyond **the ego's** understanding. 7 Love will enter immediately into any mind that truly wants **love**, but **the mind** must want **love** truly. 8 This means that **the mind** wants **love** without ambivalence, and this kind of wanting is wholly without the ego's "drive to get."

Note # 31: The ego is incapable of love or of understanding the meaning of love. Because the ego was miscreated by our belief in lack, the ego believes that the only purpose of giving is to get. Unconditional love, which is the only love that exists, gives without expectation of some return or payoff. The ego is incapable of understanding that to give is to receive since its beliefs are rooted in separation, limitation and struggle. To the ego, its home is the body form. The ego demands that everything must be a "good trade" if the body is to continue to exist. Unconditional love gives all because it is all. By giving love, you prove that you are love for it is impossible to give what you do not have.

T-4.III.5. There is a kind of experience so different from anything the ego can offer that you will never want to cover or hide **this experience** again. 2 It is necessary to repeat that your belief in darkness and hiding is why the light cannot enter. 3 The Bible gives many references to the immeasurable gifts which are for you, but for which you must ask. 4 This **asking** is not a condition as the ego sets conditions. 5 It is the glorious condition of what you are.

Note # 32: Because you are God's Son, created in God's image, all is given you. Because you have free will, you are allowed to claim your birthright at any time. Your birthright is always yours for the asking. It cannot be denied you, since this is how God created you. It is God's Will that you be perfect, whole, and complete. What God created is changeless. You can choose not to remember your birthright and in the realm of time, even reject your inheritance. Yet, it is never lost, just forgotten. When you choose to temporarily reject your inheritance, you make your belief in the separation appear real. Yet, even while you use time to experience the dream of separation, you still remain God's child. You only need to wake up and reclaim (ask for) your inheritance. Upon reawakening, you will remember that you are unlimited Spirit, not an ego-body, and you will remember your Father, Who created you. The prodigal son has return to His Home.

T-4.III.6. No force except your own will is strong enough or worthy enough to guide you. 2 In this, **your will**, you are as free as God, and must remain so forever. 3 Let us ask the Father in my name to keep you mindful of His Love for you and **your love** for Him. 4 **God** has never failed to answer this request **to keep you mindful of His Love for you and your love for Him**, because it asks only for what He has already willed. 5 Those who call truly are always answered. 6 Thou shalt have no other gods before Him because there <are> **no other gods.**

Note # 33: We have been given free will, which is the power of choice. Yet, free will does not give us the power to change our Source. We are the Effect of God's Thought and thus, God must always be our Cause. We are not self-created. Being an extension of the Mind or Thought of God, we remain a Oneness within that Mind. Since there is only one Mind and one will, our will and God's Will must be the same. Free will allows us to deny this truth, but our denial cannot change this truth.

T-4.III.7. It has never really entered your mind to give up every idea you ever had that opposes knowledge. 2 You retain thousands of little scraps of fear that prevent the Holy One from entering. 3 Light cannot penetrate through the walls you make to block **the light**, and **light** is forever unwilling to destroy what you have made. 4 No one can see through a wall, but I can step around **a wall**. 5 Watch your mind for the scraps of fear, or you will be unable to ask me to **step around your wall.** 6 I can help you only as our Father created us. 7 I will love you and honor you and maintain complete respect for what you have made, but I will not uphold **what you have made** unless **what you have made** is true. 8 I will never forsake you any more than God will, but I must wait as long as you choose to forsake yourself. 9 Because I wait in love and not in impatience, you will surely ask me truly. 10 I will come in response to a single unequivocal call.

Note # 34: Because you have free will, neither Jesus, nor the Holy Spirit, would attempt to impose the Truth upon you. Their will merely speaks for the Truth but Truth never attacks. Truth just is. Only by your asking for their guidance will their assistance be made available to you. But when you ask for their help, it will be provided. This is what was meant by the statement that you must ask for the gifts God has given you. When you ask, you acknowledge your willingness to question the validity of your egoic belief system. If asked, the Holy Spirit will gently remind you Who created you and what you really are.

T-4.III.8. Watch carefully and see what it is you are really asking for. 2 Be very honest with yourself in **what it is you are really asking for,** for we must hide nothing from each other. 3 If you will really try to do this **(be honest with yourself)**, you have taken the first step toward preparing your mind for the Holy One to enter **your mind.** 4 We will prepare for this together, for once **the Holy One** has come, you will be ready to help me make other minds ready for **the Holy One.** 5 How long will you deny **the Holy One** His Kingdom?

Note # 35: When we accept the truth about our Big "S" Self, we become a teacher of this truth. To teach the truth, we must be the truth. By our giving the truth to others, we prove we have it. For in a Oneness, to give is to receive.

T-4.III.9. In your own mind, though denied by the ego, is the declaration of your release. 2 <*God has given you everything.*> 3 This one fact **that God has given you everything** means the ego does not exist, and this makes **the ego** profoundly afraid. 4 In the ego's language, "to have" and "to be" are different, but they are identical to the Holy Spirit. 5 The Holy Spirit knows that you both <*have*> everything and <*are*> everything. 6 Any distinction in this respect is meaningful only when the idea of "getting," which implies a lack, has already been accepted. 7 That is why we make no distinction between <*having*> the Kingdom of God and <*being*> the Kingdom of God.

Note # 36: Because the ego comes from lack, the ego believes in a "zero-sum game." If someone wins the other side must lose. There is no possibility of a win-win situation. Because of this sense of lack to the ego, to have is to get. You cannot just BE when you need to protect what you have gotten. Having is a constant battle for the ego since the ego "lives" in constant fear of losing what it has. The ego believes that you are form and form cannot be shared. If I give you my pencil, I now lack one pencil. Sharing of form always requires sacrifice on the givers part. Due to the ego's belief that to give is to get, the ego always demands a 'good trade."
  To Spirit, having and being are the same since Spirit comes from abundance and oneness. Spirit knows it is not a body and there is nothing to fear. There is only the Oneness, which is Spirit, Mind or the Thought of God. Thoughts can be shared with no loss to the giver. Shared thoughts are extended and strengthened, not diminished. Spirit is everything and Spirit has everything. Spirit knows there is no lack. Spirit knows that having and being are the same. Being is the creative process of extending what It is.

T-4.III.10. The calm being of God's Kingdom, which in your sane mind is perfectly conscious, is ruthlessly banished from the part of the mind the ego rules. 2 The ego is desperate because **the ego** opposes literally invincible odds, whether you are asleep or awake. 3 Consider how much vigilance you have been willing to exert to protect your ego, and how little to protect your right mind. 4 Who but the insane would undertake to believe what is not true, and then protect this belief at the cost of truth?

Note # 37: The calm being is he who knows that he is the Son of God. It is the Christ consciousness part of our mind. When the separation occurred, the mind was split into right-mindedness, which is under the guidance of the Holy Spirit and wrong-mindedness, which is under the guidance of the ego and the ego's belief in lack. The Son of God has fallen asleep and does not remember His birthright. The mind has fallen under to the guidance of the ego, and the mind believes that it is an ego-body rather than a spiritual being. Because you believe that you are an ego-body, this becomes your "provisional reality." Ultimately this egoic dream world ("your provisional reality") that you miscreated will surrender to right-mindedness. You cannot change the truth of what God created. You must accept the truth that you were and always will be perfect, whole and complete. The ego can oppose God's Will, but it cannot triumph over God's Will.

IV. This Need Not Be

T-4.IV.1. If you cannot hear the Voice for God, it is because you do not choose to listen **to the Voice for God.** 2 That you <do> listen to the voice of your ego is demonstrated by your attitudes, your feelings and your behavior. 3 Yet **to** listen to the voice of your ego is what you want. 4 **The voice of your ego** is what you are fighting to keep, and **the voice of your ego is** what you are vigilant to save. 5 Your mind is filled with schemes to save the face of your ego, and you do not seek the face of Christ. 6 The glass in which the ego seeks to see its face is dark indeed. 7 How can **the ego** maintain the trick of **the ego's** existence except with mirrors? 8 But where you look to find yourself is up to you.

<u>Note # 38:</u> You can choose to see yourself as a Son of God (the face of Christ), or you can choose to see yourself as an ego-body. When the voice of the ego controls attitudes, feelings and behavior, you cannot change your mind as to who you are. You need to choose for the Voice of God, the Holy Spirit.

T-4.IV.2.I have said that you cannot change your mind by changing your behavior, but I have also said, and many times, that you <can> change your mind. 2 When your mood tells you that you have chosen wrongly, and **chosen wrongly** is whenever you are not joyous, then <know this *lack of joy* need not be>. 3 In every case you have thought wrongly about some brother God created, and are perceiving images your ego makes in a darkened glass. 4 Think honestly what you have thought that God would not have thought, and what you have not thought that God would have you think. 5 Search sincerely for what you have done and left undone accordingly, and then change your mind to think with God's. 6 This **changing your mind to think with God's mind** may seem hard to do, but it is much easier than trying to think against **God**. 7 Your mind is one with God's **mind**. 8 Denying **that your mind is one with God's mind**, and thinking **that you were separate** has held your ego together, but has literally split your mind. 9 As a loving brother I am deeply concerned with your mind, and urge you to follow my example as you look at yourself and at your brother, and see in both **yourself and your brother** the glorious creations of a glorious Father.

<u>Note # 39:</u> Jesus wants us to follow our bliss, which is thoughts that align with God's Will that we be happy. When we are not joyous and have lost our peace of mind, our Big "S" Self is telling us that we are not in alignment with right-mindedness.

T-4.IV.3. When you are sad, <know this *need not be*>. 2 Depression comes from a sense of being deprived of something you want and do not have. 3 Remember that you are deprived of nothing except by your own decisions, and then decide otherwise.

<u>Note # 40:</u> Free will makes you the master to choose whatever you wish to experience. There are neither

victims nor accidents.

T-4.IV.4. When you are anxious, realize that anxiety comes from the capriciousness of the ego, and <*know this need not be*>. 2 You can be as vigilant against the ego's dictates as for **the ego's dictates**.

<u>Note # 41:</u> Whatever thought system you value, you will be vigilant for that one.

T-4.IV.5. When you feel guilty, remember that the ego has indeed violated the laws of God, but <*you*> have not **violated the laws of God**. 2 Leave the "sins" of the ego to me. 3 **Leaving the "sins" of the ego** is what Atonement is for. 4 But until you change your mind about those whom your ego has hurt, the Atonement cannot release you. 5 While you feel guilty **about those whom your ego has hurt**, your ego is in command, because only the ego can experience guilt. 6 <*This **guilt** need not be*>.

<u>Note # 42:</u> You are a Child of God. The Atonement is the acceptance of our guiltlessness and sinlessness. Yet, until you are willing to extend this same guiltlessness and sinlessness to your brother, it cannot be yours. To give is to receive and you cannot give what you do not have. When you accept the Atonement for yourself, you accept and extend it to all.

T-4.IV.6. Watch your mind for the temptations of the ego, and do not be deceived by **the temptations of the ego**. 2 **The ego's temptations** offer you nothing. 3 When you have given up **this** voluntary dis-spiriting **by the ego**, you will see how your mind can focus and rise above fatigue and heal. 4 Yet you are not sufficiently vigilant against the demands of the ego to disengage yourself. 5 <*This need not be*>.

<u>Note # 43:</u> We cannot accept the Atonement for ourselves partially. Unless we give our allegiance totally to the Holy Spirit, we will remain trapped in fear. Partial denial of our birthright is total denial. In the illusion of time and space, we can pretend that there are exceptions to truth but this lie will keep as trapped in the insanity of wrong-mindedness.

T-4.IV.7. The habit of engaging with God and His creations is easily made if you actively refuse to let your mind slip away. 2 The problem is not one of concentration; **the problem** is the belief that no one, including yourself, is worth consistent effort. 3 Side with me consistently against this deception **that no one, including yourself, is worth consistent effort,** and do not permit this shabby belief to pull you back. 4 The disheartened are useless to themselves and to me, but only the ego can <*be*> disheartened.

<u>Note # 44:</u> Unless you see the value and worth of something, you will not put forth consistent effort or maintain your relationship with it. Currently, we do not believe anything is worth the effort required to maintain right-mindedness.

T-4.IV.8. Have you really considered how many opportunities you have had to gladden yourself, and how many **opportunities to gladden yourself,** you have refused? 2 There is no limit to the power of a Son of God, but **a Son of God** can limit the expression of his power as much as **a Son of God** chooses. 3 Your mind and mine can unite in shining your ego away, **thus** releasing the strength of God into everything you think and do. 4 Do not settle for anything less than this, **releasing the strength of God into everything you think and do,** and refuse to accept anything but this **(releasing the strength of God into everything you think and do)** as your goal. 5 Watch your mind carefully for any beliefs that hinder **your mind's** accomplishment, and step away from **any beliefs that hinder your mind's accomplishment.** 6 Judge how well you have done this **(uniting with God's Will)** by your own feelings, for this is the one right use of judgment. 7 Judgment, like any other defense, can be used to attack or protect; to hurt or to heal. 8 The ego <*should*> be brought to judgment and found wanting there. 9 Without your own allegiance, protection and love, the ego cannot exist. 10 Let **the ego** be judged truly and you must withdraw allegiance, protection and love from **the ego**.

Note # 45: The ego demands that we be right. The Holy Spirit knows that God wills that you be happy. By following your feelings, you can tell how your current thinking aligns with your Big "S" Self. Good feelings like joy and peace indicate alignment with your Source. Bad or fearful feelings warn you of your alignment with the egoic belief system of lack. Would you rather be right or happy? By following your feeling toward your bliss, you will return to the peace of God.

T-4.IV.9. You are a mirror of truth, in which God Himself shines in perfect light. 2 To the ego's dark glass you need but say, "I will not look there **(in ego's dark glass or viewpoint)** because I know these images **in the ego's dark glass** are not true." 3 Then let the Holy One shine on you in peace, knowing that **peace** and only **peace** must be. 4 **The Holy One's** Mind shone on you in your creation and brought your mind into being. 5 **The Holy One's** Mind still shines on you and must shine through you. 6 Your ego cannot prevent **the Holy One** from shining on you, but **your ego** can prevent you from letting **the Holy One** shine through you.

Note # 46: What you perceive is based on what you choose to value. Your decision-maker is constantly choosing between the two thought systems. If given a chance, the Holy Spirit can reinterpret any egoic experience into a holy one. Perception follows your purpose. Is your purpose inclusion or separation? If separation, we merely need to choose again.

T-4.IV.10. The First Coming of Christ is merely another name for the creation, for Christ is the Son of God. 2 The Second Coming of Christ means nothing more than the end of the ego's rule and the healing of the mind. 3 I was created like you in the First **(the creation),** and I have called you to join with me in the Second **(the end of the ego's rule and the healing of the mind).** 4 I am in charge of the Second Coming, and my judgment, which is used only for protection, cannot be wrong because **my judgment** never attacks. 5 Your **judgment** may be so distorted that you believe I was mistaken in choosing you. 6 I assure you this is a mistake of your ego. 7 Do not mistake **your belief that I was mistaken in choosing you** for humility. 8 Your ego is trying to convince you that **the ego** is real and I am not, because if I am real, I am no more real than you are **since I was created like you in the Creation.** 9 That knowledge **that I was created like you in the Creation**, and I assure you that it <*is*> knowledge, means that Christ has come into your mind and healed **your mind**.

Note # 47: Jesus states that we are ready to join him in ending the ego's rule over our split mind. Our ego will tell us that this is not so. The ego will claim that Jesus was different from us and, therefore, we are incapable of following in his footsteps. Jesus states that this is not so. We are the same Child of God and are ready to join with Jesus to remove egoic rule and heal our split minds.

T-4.IV.11. I do not attack your ego. 2 I do work with your higher mind, the home of the Holy Spirit, whether you are asleep or awake, just as your ego does with your lower mind, which is **the ego's** home. 3 I am your vigilance in this **(working with your higher mind),** because you are too confused to recognize your own hope **(that you to were created like me, a Son of God).** 4 I am not mistaken. 5 Your mind will elect to join with mine, and together we are invincible. 6 You and your brother will yet come together in my name, and your sanity will be restored. 7 I raised the dead by knowing that life is an eternal attribute of everything that the living God created. 8 Why do you believe it is harder for me to inspire the dis-spirited or to stabilize the unstable? 9 I do not believe that there is an order of difficulty in miracles; you do. 10 I have called and you will answer. 11 I understand that miracles are natural, because they are expressions of love. 12 My calling you is as natural as your answer, and as inevitable.

Note # 48: The Higher mind is the home of the Holy Spirit and is based on the idea that you are God's Son, perfect, whole and complete. The lower mind is the home of the ego. This lower mind is fear based. Our egoic belief in self-creation and separation resulted in the apparent splitting of the Sonship's mind into two. This lower egoic mind is the part that claims it does not know who and what you are. Most people currently view their world from the perception of the egoic mind. Jesus has called us to join him in the restoration of the Sonship to right-mindedness.

V. The Ego-Body Illusion

T-4.V.1. All things work together for good. 2 There are no exceptions **that all things work together for good**, except in the ego's judgment. 3 The ego exerts maximal vigilance about what the ego permits into awareness, and this **limitation on what the ego permits into awareness** is not the way a balanced mind holds together. 4 The ego is thrown further off balance because the ego keeps its primary motivation from your awareness, and **the ego** raises control rather than sanity to predominance. 5 The ego has every reason to do this according to the thought system which gave rise to **the ego** and which **the ego** serves. 6 Sane judgment would inevitably judge against the ego and **therefore, sane judgment** must be obliterated by the ego in the interest of the ego's self-preservation.

Note #49: By placing limitations on what the ego permits into the mind's awareness, the ego corrupts the thought system of the whole mind (right-mindedness), thereby producing the insane thought system of the lower mind (wrong-mindedness). Selectivity of focus fragmentizes and corrupts the appearance of Oneness from the mind's awareness. What you are allowed to perceive is based on the ego's purpose. The egoic mind's belief in the separation, not the "power" of the ego, is the catalyst for this insane thought system. The ego itself is powerless to control the mind unless the mind believes that you are not God's Son but rather are a limited ego-body created out of lack. The "authority problem" becomes the foundation to the insane thought system of the split mind. The ego is the servant of this insane thought system since this insane thought system gives rise to the ego. This insane thought system of the split-minded must limit awareness since the awareness of what you truly are (Son of God) would result in the return to sanity and right-mindedness. Control and the seeking of truth is the goal of the ego.

T-4.V.2.A major source of the ego's off-balanced state is its **insane thought system's** lack of discrimination between the body and the Thoughts of God. 2 Thoughts of God are unacceptable to the ego, because **thoughts of God** clearly point to the nonexistence of the ego itself. 3 The ego therefore either distorts **the thoughts of God** or refuses to accept **the thoughts of God**. 4 **The ego** cannot, however, make **the thoughts of God** cease to be. 5 **The ego** therefore tries to conceal not only "unacceptable" body impulses, but also the Thoughts of God, because both are threatening to **the ego**. 6 Being concerned primarily with the ego's own preservation in the face of threat, the ego perceives **both "unacceptable" body impulses and the Thoughts of God**, as the same. 7 By perceiving **both "unacceptable" body impulses and the Thoughts of God** as the same, the ego attempts to save itself from being swept away, as **the ego** would surely be in the presence of knowledge.

Note # 50: The ego is a champion for thoughts that engender fear and the belief that you are incomplete and, thus, need to get something outside yourself. It opposes loving and forgiving thoughts that would promote joining and wholeness. The ego protects your belief in littleness and victimization.

T-4.V.3. Any thought system that confuses God and the body must be insane. 2 Yet this confusion **between God and the body** is essential to the ego, which judges only in terms of threat or non-threat to itself. 3 In one sense the ego's fear of God is at least logical, since the idea of **God** does dispel the ego. 4 But fear of the body, with which the ego identifies so closely, makes no sense at all.

Note # 51: The ego is a judging machine. Its judgment is based on the criteria of maintaining control over your mind so that your decision-maker will never realize that it has a choice other than the egoic thought system. Fear paralyzes our decision-maker's ability to choose again. This is why ACIM states that we must learn to control our fear.

T-4.V.4. The body is the ego's home by **the ego's** own election. 2 It **(the body)** is the only identification with which the ego feels safe, since the body's vulnerability is **the ego's** own best argument that you cannot be of God. 3 This **belief that you are a body and cannot be of God** is the belief that the ego sponsors eagerly. 4 Yet the ego hates the body, because **the ego** cannot accept **the body** as good enough to be **the ego's** home. 5 Here is where the mind becomes actually dazed. 6 Being told by the ego that **the mind** is really part of the body and that the body is **the mind's** protector, the mind is also told that the body cannot protect **the mind**. 7 Therefore, the mind asks, "Where can I go for protection?" to which the ego replies, "Turn to me." 8 The mind, and not without cause, reminds the ego that **the ego** has itself insisted that **the ego** is identified with the body, so there is no point in turning to <*the ego* > for **the mind's** protection. 9 The ego has no real answer to this because there is none, but **the ego** does have a typical solution. 10 **The ego** obliterates the question from the mind's awareness. 11 Once out of awareness the question can and does produce uneasiness, but **the question** cannot be answered because **the question** cannot be asked.

Note # 52: The ego's goal is to have the mind, which is actually unlimited spirit, identify itself as the body. The ego tells us that the mind is the body-part we call the brain. Since the body is separate, weak and vulnerable the mind must also be the same. Fearful thoughts of death and destruction imprison the mind within the illusion of the body and make the body unquestionably appear real. The egoic thought system claims to be the protector of both the mind and the body.

T-4.V.5. This is the question that <*must*> be asked: "Where can I go for protection?" 2 "Seek and ye shall find" does not mean that you should seek blindly and desperately for something you would not recognize. 3 Meaningful seeking is consciously undertaken, consciously organized and consciously directed. 4 The goal **of meaningful seeking** must be formulated clearly and kept in mind. 5 Learning and wanting to learn are inseparable. 6 You learn best when you believe what you are trying to learn is of value to you. 7 However, not everything you may want to learn has lasting value. 8 Indeed, many of the things you want to learn may be chosen <*because*> their value will not last.

Note # 53: The ego tells us that being a body, we need physical substance or we will die. Life is believed to be a struggle. We believe that we exist in a universe of lack, competition and struggle and ultimately death. Our happiness is secondary to our body's survival. Getting is the goal of relationships. We are told that we need to get love instead of being love. Form, not content, is what the ego values. We are told by the ego that due to our limited nature, we must seek outside ourselves for our sustenance and happiness. The ego tells us that our happiness rests outside of us and is not under our control. Outside things are the source of our happiness. The ego never advises us to seek within our split-mind to rediscover our divine birthright. The ego never wants us to find the truth that we are not of this world, but rather unlimited Spirit.

T-4.V.6. The ego thinks it is an advantage not to commit itself to anything that is eternal, because the eternal must come from God. 2 Eternalness is the one function the ego has tried to develop, but has systematically failed to achieve. 3 The ego compromises with the issue of the eternal, just as **the ego compromises** with all issues touching on the real question (**"Where can I go for protection?"),** in any way. 4 By becoming involved with tangential issues, **the ego** hopes to hide the real question, **"Where can I go for protection?"** and keep **this question** out of mind. 5 The ego's characteristic busyness with nonessentials is for precisely **the** purpose **of keeping this question out of mind.** 6 Preoccupations with problems set up to be incapable of solution are favorite ego devices for impeding learning progress. 7 In all these diversionary tactics, however, the one question that is never asked by those who pursue them is, "What for?" 8 This is the question that <*you*> must learn to ask in connection with everything. 9 What is the purpose? 10 Whatever **the purpose** is, it will direct your efforts automatically. 11 When you make a decision of purpose, then, you have made a decision about your future effort; a decision that will remain in effect unless you change your mind.

<u>Note # 54:</u> Is your purpose to confirm or justify your belief that you are an ego-body or the Son of God? Is your purpose to be happy or right? The ego wants to be right. God wants you to be happy.

VI. The Rewards of God

T-4.VI.1. The ego does not recognize the real source of "threat," and if you associate yourself with the ego, you do not understand the situation as it is. 2 Only your allegiance to **the ego** gives the ego any power over you. 3 I have spoken of the ego as if **the ego** were a separate thing, acting on its own. 4 This idea that the ego is a separate thing, acting on its own was necessary to persuade you, that you cannot dismiss **the ego** lightly, and must realize how much of your thinking is ego-directed. 5 We cannot safely let it go at that, however, or you will regard yourself as necessarily conflicted as long as you are here, or as long as you believe that you are here. 6 The ego is nothing more than a part of your belief about yourself. 7 Your other life **as a spiritual Son of God** has continued without interruption, and has been and always will be totally unaffected by your attempts to dissociate **yourself by claiming you are an ego-body rather than what you truly are, a spiritual Son of God.**

<u>Note # 55:</u> The ego is defined as nothing more than a part of your belief about yourself. It is not your totality but rather only a small part of your overall beliefs about yourself. It is that part of you that allowed doubt to enter your mind and ask the question "What Am I?" It claims to have lost knowledge of what it was, is and will eternally be. Your Big "S" Self knows very well what you are and continues to be the thought of God or a conduit for love.

T-4.VI.2. In learning to escape from illusions, your debt to your brother is something you must never forget. 2 **Your debt to your brother** is the same debt that you owe to me. 3 Whenever you act egotistically towards another, you are throwing away the graciousness of your indebtedness and the holy perception **your indebtedness** would produce. 4 The term "holy" can be used here because, as you learn how much you are indebted to the whole Sonship, which includes me, you come as close to knowledge as perception can. 5 The gap **between knowledge and perception** is then so small that knowledge can easily flow across **the gap** and obliterate **perception** forever.

<u>Note # 56:</u> Being connected, our salvation rests on all the parts of the Sonship. By giving, we receive

and by giving, we know that we have it. Holiness means wholeness.

T-4.VI.3. You have very little trust in me as yet, but **your trust in me** will increase as you turn more and more often to me instead of to your ego for guidance. 2 The results **in turning to me for guidance** will convince you increasingly that this choice **in turning to me** is the only sane **choice** you can make. 3 No one who learns from experience that one choice **(the choice to side with high-self, right-mindedness or the spiritual self)** brings peace and joy while another **(the choice to side with low-self, wrong–mindedness or the ego)** brings chaos and disaster needs additional convincing. 4 Learning through rewards is more effective than learning through pain, because pain is an ego illusion, and **an ego illusion** can never induce more than a temporary effect. 5 The rewards of God, however, are immediately recognized as eternal. 6 Since **the recognition of the rewards of God** is made by you and not the ego, the recognition itself establishes that you and your ego cannot be identical. 7 You may believe that you have already accepted this difference **that you and your ego cannot be identical**, but you are by no means convinced as yet **that you and your ego cannot be identical**. 8 The fact that you believe you must escape from the ego shows **that you have not accepted that you and your ego cannot be identical,** but you cannot escape from the ego by humbling **the ego** or controlling **the ego** or punishing **the ego**.

Note # 57: By the results of their advice, you will know which thought system you should follow. When you follow your bliss, you will know you are moving in the right direction. Aligning with your Big "S" Self will bring you joy and peace
The ego is a part of your belief system about you. The ego is not a separate thing acting on its own. The ego is the part of the mind that believes your existence rests on or is defined by separateness from your Source. All and any power that the ego seems to have has been given to the ego by the mind's belief that you are not who you are. The ego claims self-creation and that you are not God's Son, perfect, whole, complete, eternal, and changeless. Change your belief in what you are from a body to unlimited spirit and the ego dissolves into the nothingness from which the ego arose, which is your split mind's insane belief in the fantasy that it could be something it is not.

T-4.VI.4. The ego and the spirit do not know each other. 2 The separated mind cannot maintain the separation except by dissociating. 3 Having done this **dissociating, the separated mind** denies all truly natural impulses, not because the ego is a separate thing, but because you want to believe that <you> are **a separate thing**. 4 The ego is a device for maintaining this belief **that you are a separate thing,** but it is still only your decision **of your mind** to use the device **of the ego** that enables **the ego to be used for maintaining your belief that you are a separate thing** to endure **against God's Will**.

Note # 58: Due to the belief in the separation, the mind made the ego as part of an elaborate plan to confirm its separation from God. This "plan" involves the idea of lack and fear, which are unknown to the Mind of God since God is Love. The mind made the ego to confirm that the mind was something other than God. It is only from the wrong-mindedness of your mind that the ego exists. Since it was your choice to believe in the separation, the ego becomes part of your own provisional reality. The ego, like all parts of your deluded world of provisional reality is perceived as very real to your split-mind, but it is nonexistent in the Mind of God. Your illusion of provisional reality is miscreated and opposite to God's Will. It cannot be real. In your upside down, insane thought system, your mind made the ego exist only to confirm your belief that you are something that you are not.

T-4.VI.5. How can you teach someone the value of something he has deliberately thrown away? 2 He must have thrown it away because he did not value it. 3 You can only show him how miserable he is without **what he has deliberately thrown away**, and slowly bring **what he has deliberately thrown**

away nearer so he can learn how his misery lessens as he approaches **what he has deliberately thrown away**. 4 This teaches him to associate his misery with the absence **of what he has deliberately thrown away**, and the opposite of misery with its presence. 5 **What he has deliberately thrown away** gradually becomes desirable as he changes his mind about **the** worth **of what he had deliberately thrown away**. 6 I am teaching you to associate misery with the ego and joy with the spirit. 7 You have taught yourself the opposite, **which is to associate misery with the spirit and joy with the ego**. 8 You are still free to choose, but can you really want the rewards of the ego in the presence of the rewards of God?

Note # 59: When we remember the joy and peace associated with being God's Son, we will once again value and want to reclaim our divine inheritance.

T-4.VI.6. My trust in you is greater than your **trust** in me at the moment, but it will not always be that way. 2 Your mission is very simple. 3 You are asked to live so as to demonstrate that you are not an ego, and I do not choose God's channels wrongly. 4 The Holy One shares my trust, and accepts my Atonement decisions because my will is never out of accord with His **Will**. 5 I have said before that I am in charge of the Atonement. 6 **I am in charge of the Atonement** only because I completed my part in **the Atonement** as a man, and can now complete **the Atonement** through others. 7 My chosen channels cannot fail, because I will lend **my chosen channels** my strength as long as theirs is wanting.

Note # 60: Jesus states that we have been selected to demonstrate to our brothers that we are not ego-bodies. By our doing this, others will also learn to accept the truth.

T-4.VI.7.I will go with you to the Holy One, and through my perception He can bridge the little gap. 2 Your gratitude to your brother is the only gift I want. 3 I will bring **your gratitude of your brother** to God for you, knowing that to know your brother *is* to know God. 4 If you are grateful to your brother, you are grateful to God for what **God** created. 5 Through your gratitude you come to know your brother, and one moment of real recognition makes everyone your brother because each of them is of your Father. 6 Love does not conquer all things, but **love** does set all things right. 7 Because you are the Kingdom of God I can lead you back to your own creations. 8 You do not recognize **your own cre**ations now, but what has been dissociated is still there.

Note # 61: Our creations are any loving or forgiving thoughts. These are the things that are real and they are kept safe awaiting the Sonship's return to knowledge. We and our brothers are one and the Father is us. God is Cause and We are His Effect. Cause and Effect cannot be separate. The combined They are the indivisible Oneness of Everything. We are that One Self.

T-4.VI.8. As you come closer to a brother you approach me, and as you withdraw from **a brother** I become distant to you. 2 Salvation is a collaborative venture. 3 **Salvation** cannot be undertaken successfully by those who disengage themselves from the Sonship, because they **who disengage themselves from the Sonship** are disengaging themselves from me. 4 God will come to you only as you will give Him to your brothers. 5 Learn first of **your brother** and you will be ready to hear God. 6 That is because the function of love is one.

Note # 62: Oneness is a state in which you are perfect, whole, and complete. Your wholeness and completeness make you part of your brother, who like you, is part of God. God's creations are an extension of the Father and are one with the Father. Because to give is to receive, you cannot withhold the Oneness of Everything and exclude anyone. To exclude someone is to deny wholeness to all. Love is unconditional.

VII. Creation and Communication

T-4.VII.1.It is clear that while the content of any particular ego illusion does not matter, **the correction of any particular ego illusion** is more helpful in a specific context. 2 Ego illusions are quite specific, although the mind is naturally abstract. 3 Part of the mind becomes concrete, however, when the mind splits. 4 The concrete part believes in the ego, because the ego depends on the concrete. 5 The ego is the part of the mind that believes your existence is defined by separation.

<u>Note # 63:</u> To the split mind, there appears to be degrees of difficulty. Although one illusion is no more difficult to correct than any other illusion since all are equally false, it may assist the learning process by correcting each illusion independently. This allows for gradual learning and does not increase fear in the learner. If all illusions were brought before truth at one time, this shattering of the entire belief system of deluded mind could induce panic. The Holy Spirit will not do anything that would increase fear in the student. The Holy Spirit is patient and allows each person to baby-step their way back to truth.

The concrete mind learns by going from specific example to the general concept. The abstract mind just needs the general concept and knows it applies to all related forms.

Ego is defined as the part of the mind that believes your existence is defined by separation. Prior to the separation, it did not exist. Before the separation, there were no specific items since everything was all and nothingness was unknown. Thus, the natural state of mind was abstract since it was not differentiated. During the separation, the mind split from an abstract Oneness into the High Self, which maintained its oneness (Son of God) and the lower self (egoic part of mind) that defined itself as separate from its Cause. The lower mind (wrong-mindedness) made up its own dream world based on the egoic thought system in an attempt to make the separation appear real. The ego's thought system defines everything as specific (concrete) individual things. Form helps define the part as separate and different from the whole. Oneness does not exist in egoic thinking because everything must lack something. The ego defines itself by what it is not. The ego needs darkness to know the light. The Mind of God is abstract and only knows Light. Unlike the ego, It does not require contrast or comparison. In the Mind of God, Light is everything and darkness is nothing and, therefore, does not exist.
(Also, see note 18 above about the ego.)

T-4.VII.2.Everything the ego perceives is a separate whole, without the relationships that imply being. 2 The ego is thus against communication, except insofar as **communication** is utilized to establish separateness rather than to abolish **separateness**. 3 The communication system of the ego is based on **the ego's** own thought system, as is everything else **the ego** dictates **is based on the ego's own thought system of separation**. 4 **The ego's** communication is controlled by **the ego's** need to protect itself, and **the ego** will disrupt communication when **the ego** experiences threat. 5 This disruption **in communication** is a reaction to a specific person or persons. 6 The specificity of the ego's thinking, then, results in spurious generalization which is really not abstract at all. 7 **The ego** merely responds in certain specific ways to everything **the ego** perceives as related.

<u>Note # 64:</u> The ego is interested in maintaining control by keeping the decision-maker unaware of its power to choose again. If the egoic communication does not appear to increase control over the mind, the ego will break off communication. The ego is not interested in happiness or truth; instead it demands that it be right.

The ego's thought system utilizes inductive reasoning. Inductive reasoning takes specific examples and draws general conclusions. Inductive reasoning requires specific (separate) items in order to be able to work. Prior to the separation, inductive reasoning did not exist since there was just oneness and, therefore, nothing to compare or judge against. There was just BEING. With the concept of separation, we have separate items so now the ego perceives a difference between HAVING and BEING. When there was just a Oneness, there was nothing to get since oneness was everything. With separate items, if you have something, I do not have it. Now I lack something. Form cannot be shared, so the previous owner must be asked to sacrifice. Because form cannot be shared, the ego is determined to imprison the mind in a body. Thoughts can be share and each party is strengthened.

T-4.VII.3. In contrast, spirit reacts in the same way to everything **spirit** knows is true, and does not respond at all to anything else. 2 Nor does **spirit** make any attempt to establish what is true. 3 **Spirit** knows that what is true is everything that God created. 4 **Spirit** is in complete and direct communication with every aspect of creation, because **Spirit** is in complete and direct communication with its Creator. 5 **Spirit's** communication **with its Creator** is the Will of God. 6 Creation and communication are synonymous. 7 God created every mind by communicating His Mind to it, thus establishing **every mind** forever as a channel for the reception of His Mind and **His** Will. 8 Since only beings of a like order can truly communicate, **God's** creations naturally communicate with Him and like Him. 9 This communication is perfectly abstract, since **this communication's** quality is universal in application and not subject to any judgment, any exception or any alteration. 10 God created you by **this communication** and for **this communication**. 11 The mind can distort **this communication's** function, but **the mind** cannot endow itself with functions **the mind** was not given. 12 That is why the mind cannot totally lose the ability to communicate, even though **the mind** may refuse to utilize **this ability to communicate** on behalf of being.

Note # 65: The Mind of God does not utilize inductive reasoning for everything has universal application. This is how God created since our mind is an extension of Our Father's Mind. This Oneness allows complete and direct communication since all are one in Being. There is no separation or distinction since there is nothing to judge against. Creation and communication are synonymous and we are invested by God's Mind to co-create like our Father.

T-4.VII.4. Existence as well as being rest on communication. 2 Existence, however, is specific in how, what and with whom communication is judged to be worth undertaking. 3 Being is completely without these distinctions. **(The distinctions are in how, what and with whom communication is judged to be worth undertaking.)** 4 **Being** is a state in which the mind is in communication with everything that is real. 5 To whatever extent you permit this state **of Being** to be curtailed you are limiting your sense of your own reality, which becomes total only by recognizing all reality in the glorious context of its real relationship to you. 6 This is your reality. 7 Do not desecrate it, **(your true state of reality which is a state of Being),** or recoil from it. **(Your true state of reality which is a state of Being)** 8 It, **(your true state of reality which is a state of Being)** is your real home, your real temple and your real Self.

Note # 66: Love allows all. Love does not judge or exclude. This is "Being." "Existence" is more synonymous to egoic miscreation. "Existence" limits, judges and excludes. Thus, "Existence" is fear based. "Being" is our true reality. "Existence" is our "provisional reality." Our provisional reality is based on lack and exclusion. We judge (perceive) that we are missing something since we believe we come from lack. "Having" is no longer "Being" in our illusionary world of provisional reality. We "EXIST" rather than just allowing ourselves to "BE" since we judge what is worthy to communicate with. Due to our judgment that we are not whole, we have limited our ability to just "BE."

T-4.VII.5. God, Who encompasses all being, created beings who have everything individually, but who want to share it **(everything)** to increase their joy. 2 Nothing real can be increased except by sharing. 3 That is why God created you. 4 Divine Abstraction takes joy in sharing. 5 That **(sharing)** is what creation means. 6 "How," "what" and "to whom" are irrelevant, because real creation gives everything, since **creation** can create only like itself. 7 Remember that in the Kingdom there is no difference between <having> and <being,> as there is in existence. 8 In the state of being the mind gives everything always.

Note # 67: What is real are thoughts, not form. Content, not the temporary form it may appear as, is what is shared. Loving thoughts can be shared and extended. Love allows and does not judge or attack.

Perhaps the closest model for how the Mind of God appears to function would be to consider its holographic nature. All parts contain the whole and the whole is contained in each part. A part cannot be separated from the whole, but if it were, that part would remain in constant and instant communication with all other parts. To affect any part affects all parts simultaneously.

T-4.VII.6. The Bible repeatedly states that you should praise God. 2 This hardly means that you should tell **God** how wonderful He is. 3 **God has** no ego with which to accept such praise, and **God has** no perception with which to judge **such praise.** 4 But unless you take your part in the creation, **God's** joy is not complete because your **joy** is incomplete. 5 And this **(your part in the creation)** God does know. 6 **God** knows it **(your part in the creation)** in His Own Being and **God knows the** experience of His Son's experience. 7 The constant going out of **God's** Love is blocked when **God's** channels are closed, and **God** is lonely when the minds **God** created do not communicate fully with Him.

Note # 68: Being holographic in nature, God is aware when the hologram is extended by any of its "parts" own creative thoughts. When we miscreate, we fail to extend the message throughout the hologram. The creative process shares and communicates its extension with all. The Oneness extends Itself yet remains whole, perfect and complete.

T-4.VII.7. God has kept your Kingdom for you, but **God** cannot share His joy with you until you know **your Kingdom** with your whole mind. 2 Revelation is not enough, because **revelation** is only communication <from> God. 3 God does not need revelation returned to Him, which would clearly be impossible, but He does want **revelation** brought to others. 4 **Bringing revelations to others** cannot be done with the actual revelation; **since revelation's** content cannot be expressed, because **revelation's content** is intensely personal to the mind that receives **the revelation.** 5 **Revelation** can, however, be returned by that mind to other minds, through the attitudes the knowledge from the revelation brings.

Note # 69: To know and not to act according to that knowing is to not know. If we are love, we will have that attitude of love extended to all. There can be no exceptions. To teach love, you must be love. To teach peace, you must be peace. You demonstrate what you value by what you are. You must walk your talk. By their actions you will know them and you will know yourself.

T-4.VII.8. God is praised whenever any mind learns to be wholly helpful. 2 **Being wholly helpful** is impossible without being wholly harmless, because the two beliefs must coexist. 3 The truly helpful are invulnerable, because **the truly helpful** are not protecting their egos and so nothing can hurt **the truly helpful.** 4 Their helpfulness is their praise of God, and **God** will return their praise of Him because **the truly helpful** are like Him, and they can rejoice together. 5 God goes out to **the truly helpful** and through **the truly helpful**, and there is great joy throughout the Kingdom. 6 Every mind that is changed adds to this joy with its individual willingness to share in **this joy of the Kingdom.** 7 The truly helpful are God's miracle workers, whom I direct until we are all united in the joy of the Kingdom. 8 I will direct you to wherever you can be truly helpful, and to whoever can follow my guidance through you.

Note # 70: Jesus will direct those who accept his call to where they can be most helpful in the Sonship's return to knowledge. To be wholly helpful, you must be wholly harmless. In your invulnerability lies your strength to aid your brother.

Definition: BEING is the state in which mind is in communication with everything that is real.
Definition: EXISTENCE is the state in which mind communicates with only those who it, the ego controlled mind, judges to be worthy of communication.
 BEING does not equal EXISTENCE. BEING only knows reality. EXISTENCE judges based on separation. EXISTENCE only "lives" in your own mind's "provisional reality."

Chapter 5. HEALING AND WHOLENESS

Introduction

T-5.in.1. To heal is to make happy. 2 I have told you to think how many opportunities you have had to gladden yourself, and how many you have refused. 3 This **refusal to gladden yourself** is the same as telling you that you have refused to heal yourself. 4 The light that belongs to you is the light of joy. 5 Radiance is not associated with sorrow. 6 Joy calls forth an integrated willingness to share **joy**, and **joy** promotes the mind's natural impulse to respond as one **mind**. 7 Those who attempt to heal without being wholly joyous themselves call forth different kinds of responses at the same time, and thus deprive others of the joy of responding wholeheartedly.

Note # 1: Healing is at the level of mind. If you are not joyous or happy, which is God's Will for His Children, you are sick. Sickness starts first at the spiritual level, moves to the emotional level, and lastly manifests upon the physical level of the body. If the healer wishes to teach another to heal themselves, the healer needs to be healed. You need to be healed in spirit, which means that you need to be happy and joyous yourself. To teach joy, be joy.

T-5.in.2. To be wholehearted you must be happy. 2 If fear and love cannot coexist, and if it is impossible to be wholly fearful and remain alive, the only possible whole state is that of love. 3 There is no difference between love and joy. 4 Therefore, the only possible whole state is the wholly joyous. 5 To heal or to make joyous is therefore the same as to integrate and to make one. 6 That is why it makes no difference to what part or by what part of the Sonship the healing is offered. 7 Every **part of the Sonship** benefits, and benefits equally.

Note # 2: By healing yourself everyone benefits. All minds are interconnected. Healing takes place in the mind. Only the mind is sick. Any bodily sickness is only the effect of mind "DIS- EASE." You need to heal your "stinking thinking."

T-5.in.3. You are being blessed by every beneficent thought of any of your brothers anywhere. 2 You should want to bless **your brothers** in return, out of gratitude **to your brothers.** 3 You need not know **your brothers** individually, or they **need not know** you **individually.** 4 The light is so strong that **the light** radiates throughout the Sonship and **the Sonship** returns thanks to the Father for radiating His joy upon **the Sonship.** 5 Only God's holy children are worthy channels of His beautiful joy, because only **God's holy children** are beautiful enough to hold **God's beautiful joy** by sharing **His beautiful joy**. 6 It is impossible for a child of God to love his neighbor except as himself. 7 That is why the healer's prayer is:

8 *Let me know this brother as I know myself.*

Note # 3: The Sonship, being part of the holographic Mind of God, must also be part of that same hologram. Each brother is part of this holographic Mind. Since in a hologram each part is the whole and the whole is in each part, to know yourself is to know the whole. Know your true Big "S" Self and you know all parts of the hologram. Your Big "S" Self is the One Self of "All That Is."

I. The Invitation to the Holy Spirit

T-5.I.1.Healing is a thought by which two minds perceive their oneness and become glad. 2 This gladness calls to every part of the Sonship to rejoice with **the two minds that perceive their oneness and become glad,** and lets God go out into **these same two minds** and through **these same two minds.** 3 Only the healed mind can experience revelation with lasting effect, because revelation is an experience of pure joy. 4 If you do not choose to be wholly joyous, your mind cannot have what it does not choose to be. **It cannot be wholly joyous.** 5 Remember that spirit knows no difference between *<having>* and *<being.>* 6 The higher mind thinks according to the laws spirit obeys, and therefore **the higher mind** honors only the laws of God. 7 To spirit getting is meaningless and **to spirit** giving is all. 8 Having everything, spirit holds everything by giving **everything,** and thus creates as the Father created. 9 While this kind of thinking is totally alien to having things, even to the lower mind **this kind of thinking** is quite comprehensible in connection with ideas. 10 If you share a physical possession, you do divide its ownership. 11 If you share an idea, however, you do not lessen **the idea.** 12 All of **the idea** is still yours although all of **the idea** has been given away. 13 Further, if the one to whom you give **the idea** accepts **the idea** as his **own,** he reinforces **the idea** in your mind and thus increases **the idea.** 14 If you can accept the concept that the world is one of ideas, the whole belief in the false association the ego makes between giving and losing is gone.

Note # 4: Form cannot be shared without "sacrifice" on the part of the giver. Yet, ideas can be shared and the sharing can strengthen both parties. Thoughts become things. Share the idea that your brother is perfect, whole and complete and you give him everything. Yet, at the same time, this sharing strengthens and extends your own perfection. Content is shared, which is at the level of mind or ideas, not form. The content's form is not the focus of the sharing. Sharing loving thoughts allows joy, happiness and healing to be made available to both parties.

T-5.I.2.Let us start our process of reawakening with just a few simple concepts:

2 *Thoughts increase by being given away.*
3 *The more who believe in **the thought**, the stronger **the thought** becomes.*
4 *Everything is an idea.*
5 *How, then, **with an idea** can giving and losing be associated?*

Note # 5: When we realize everything is thought, the idea that giving requires no sacrifice makes sense. Being interconnected, to give is to receive. By sharing an idea you prove you have it and the idea grows stronger in your mind. There is no loss or diminishment.

T-5.I.3. This **simple concept** is the invitation to the Holy Spirit. 2 I have said already that I can reach up and bring the Holy Spirit down to you, but I can bring Him to you only at your own invitation. 3 The Holy Spirit is in your right mind, **just** as **the Holy Spirit** was in **my right mind**. 4 The Bible says, "May the mind be in you that was also in Christ Jesus," and uses this as a blessing. 5 **This Bible saying** is the blessing of miracle-mindedness. 6 **This Bible saying** asks that you may think as I thought, joining with me in Christ thinking.

<u>Note # 6:</u> You are your own mind's decision-maker. You have free will and can make the choice to accept the ideas that Jesus shares with us and join him in right-mindedness. By your acceptance of these shared ideas, miracle-mindedness is extended and strengthened.

T-5.I.4. The Holy Spirit is the only part of the Holy Trinity that has a symbolic function. 2 **The Holy Spirit** is referred to as the Healer, the Comforter and the Guide. 3 **The Holy Spirit** is also described as something "separate," apart from the Father and from the Son. 4 I myself said, "If I go I will send you another Comforter **(the Holy Spirit)** and he will abide with you." 5 **The Holy Spirit's** symbolic function makes the Holy Spirit difficult to understand, because symbolism is open to different interpretations. 6 As a man and also one of God's creations, my right thinking, which came from the Holy Spirit or the Universal Inspiration, taught me first and foremost that this Inspiration, **which came from the Holy Spirit,** is for all. 7 I could not have **this Inspiration which came from the Holy Spirit** myself without knowing **this Inspiration is for all**. 8 The word "know" is proper in this context, because the Holy Spirit is so close to knowledge that **the Holy Spirit** calls **this Inspiration** forth; or better, allows **this Inspiration** to come. 9 I have spoken before of the higher or "true" perception, which is so near to truth that God Himself can flow across the little gap. 10 Knowledge is always ready to flow everywhere, but **knowledge** cannot oppose. 11 Therefore you can obstruct **knowledge**, although you can never lose **knowledge**.

<u>Note # 7:</u> Jesus states that although we have talked of the Sonship's loss of knowledge, knowledge was not lost. We merely chose to temporarily block our access to it. We resisted, rather than accepted, the natural flow of ideas, which comprise the basis for knowledge. This blocked knowledge is available to us through the Holy Spirit or what we might call "inspiration." During moments of true "inspiration," we reconnect to this previously blocked pool of knowledge. Another way to understand "inspiration" is "In - Spirit." We have reconnected to our Source Energy.

<u>General Note:</u> All words are symbolic attempts to translate ideas. Jesus must meet the student at the student's level of understanding. Jesus' words attempt to offer the student a better understanding of these concepts that are often impossible or difficult to translate into words.

T-5.I.5. The Holy Spirit is the Christ Mind which is aware of the knowledge that lies beyond perception. 2 **The Holy Spirit, which is the Christ Mind,** came into being with the separation as a protection, inspiring the Atonement principle at the same time. 3 Before **the separation** there was no need for healing, for no one was comfortless. 4 The Voice of the Holy Spirit is the Call to Atonement, or the restoration of the integrity of the mind. 5 When the Atonement is complete and the whole Sonship is healed there will be no Call to return. 6 But what God creates is eternal. 7 The Holy Spirit will remain with the Sons of God, to bless their creations and keep **the Sons' of God creations** in the light of joy.

<u>Note # 8:</u> The Holy Spirit is defined as the Christ Mind, which is aware of the knowledge that lies beyond perception. The Holy Spirit is described in many ways and in many terms. The term used is not as important as the concept that it is designed to represent. These terms may be used interchangeably and with some poetic license. Do not let yourself be "turned off" by the term. If the term does not resonate with you, substitute the terminology that does. If you don't like the Holy Spirit, try Universal

Inspiration or just Inspiration. Use whatever will help with your understanding.

T-5.I.6. God honored even the miscreations of His children because **God's children** had made even **these miscreations**. 2 But **God** also blessed His children with a way of thinking that could raise **His children's** perceptions so high **His children** could reach almost back to **God**. 3 The Holy Spirit is the Mind of the Atonement. 4 **The Holy Spirit** represents a state of mind close enough to One-mindedness that transfer to **One-mindedness** is at last possible. 5 Perception is not knowledge, but **perception** can be transferred to knowledge or cross over into **knowledge**. 6 It might even be more helpful here to use the literal meaning of transferred or "carried over," since the last step is taken by God.

Note # 9: Miscreations arise out of our false belief in lack due to our failure to remember who we are. Because we have free will, God does not prevent us from creating, which is technically called "making" our own "dream world." God does not prevent whatever we choose to "dream up" in our provisional reality's world of illusion since God honors all of our dreams. This allows the creative power of our mind to function. Thoughts are things. Our mind's creative power constantly functions since we are created in God's Image. As long as we fail to remember what we are, we only "make" in our own dream world. Making comes from our belief in lack and is fear based. This making is not real to God or to the Kingdom, since what is made comes from lack and is not perfect, whole and complete as God created us. Thus, what we "make" is not real, existing only in our dream world of provisional reality. God does not prevent His Children from dreaming, but God has a plan to reawaken His Children as gently as possible. This is the Atonement process. The Holy Spirit is the Mind of the Atonement and will gently awaken us from our dream.

T-5.I.7. The Holy Spirit, the shared Inspiration of all the Sonship, induces a kind of perception in which many elements **of this shared Inspiration of all the Sonship** are like those in the Kingdom of Heaven itself:
2 First, **this kind of inspired perception's** universality is perfectly clear, and no one who attains **this shared Inspiration of all the Sonship** could believe for one instant that sharing **the Holy Spirit's inspired perception** involves anything but gain.
3 Second, **the Holy Spirit** is incapable of attack and is therefore truly open. 4 This means that although **this shared Inspiration of all the Sonship** does not engender knowledge, **this kind of inspired perception** does not obstruct **knowledge** in any way.
5 Finally, **the Holy Spirit** points the way beyond the healing that **this shared Inspiration of all the Sonship** brings, and leads the mind beyond **the mind's** own integration toward the paths of creation. 6 It is at this point that sufficient quantitative change occurs to produce a real qualitative shift.

Note # 10: The shared Inspiration of all the Sonship or Holy Spirit brings about a change in viewpoint in the mind of the perceiver. When we ask for the Holy Spirit's guidance, our perception is reinterpreted based on the concepts of universal love and Oneness. We are able to shift out of fear and into love and forgiveness. This change of perception is the miracle.

II. The Voice for God

T-5.II.1. Healing is not creating; **healing** is reparation. 2 The Holy Spirit promotes healing by looking beyond **healing** to what the children of God were before healing was needed, and **to what the children of God** will be when they have been healed. 3 This alteration of the time sequence should be quite familiar, because **this alteration of the time sequence** is very similar to the shift in the perception of time that the miracle introduces. 4 The Holy Spirit is the motivation for miracle-mindedness, **which is** the decision to heal the separation by letting **the belief in separation** go. 5 Your will **which you share with God's Will** is still in you because God placed **this shared will** in your mind, and although you can keep **this shared will** asleep you cannot obliterate **this shared will**. 6 God Himself keeps your **shared** will alive by transmitting **this shared will** from His Mind to **your mind** as long as there is time. 7 The miracle itself is a reflection of this union of Will between Father and Son.

<u>Note # 11:</u> Healing is repairing our connection to our Source which we perceive to be broken and lost. This perceived separation is healed by the realization that nothing can change our true will that is joined with the Father's Will. We denied this connection but this denial cannot change the truth. Our true will resides in our Big "S" Self and is the home of the Holy Spirit, which keeps us in contact with our Source. Our true will and the Will of God are the same shared Will of the One Self.

T-5.II.2. The Holy Spirit is the spirit of joy. 2 **The Holy Spirit** is the Call to return with which God blessed the minds of His separated Sons. 3 This **Call to return** is the vocation of the mind. 4 The mind had no calling until the separation, because before **the separation the mind** had only being, and would not have understood the Call to right thinking. 5 The Holy Spirit is God's Answer to the separation. **The Holy Spirit** is the means by which the Atonement heals until the whole mind returns to creating.

<u>Note # 12:</u> During the separation, the split-mind is "making" not creating since the lower-mind is under the influence of the egoic belief in lack. Creation is an extension of our true self, not the limited ego-body you have dreamed you are. The Holy Spirit calls for those who are split-minded to return to true creation and extension. As God's Child, our purpose is to co-create with God and extend the Oneness that is the Mind of God. The Holy Spirit's purpose is to guide us back to this truth of what we are. Before the separation began God placed the Holy Spirit within our mind to insure our mind's safe return to sanity.

T-5.II.3. The principle of Atonement and the separation began at the same time. 2 When the ego was made, God placed in the mind the Call to joy. 3 This Call **to joy** is so strong that the ego always dissolves at **the Call to joy's** sound. 4 That is why you must choose to hear one of two voices within you. 5 One, **the call of the ego**, you made yourself, and **the call of the ego** is not of God. 6 But the other, **the Call to joy,** is given you by God, Who asks you only to listen to **the Call to joy**. 7 The Holy Spirit is in you in a very literal sense. 8 **The Holy Spirit** is the Voice that calls you back to where you were before **the separation** and **where you** will be again **after the separation**. 9 It is possible even in this world **of perception** to hear only that Voice **(the Holy Spirit's)**, and no other **voice**. 10 **To hear only the Holy Spirit's Voice** takes effort and great willingness to learn. 11 **To hear only the Holy Spirit's Voice** is the final lesson that I learned, and God's Sons are as equal as learners as they are as Sons.

<u>Note # 13:</u> Jesus states that we are all capable of learning to listen and follow the Holy Spirit's guidance. We must, however, quiet the voice of the ego if we are to hear the Voice for God. In this world of perception, the ego will always judge and talk first. Before we can hear the Voice for God, we must silence the ego and ask for the guidance from the Holy Spirit. The Holy Spirit will not fail to answer our call.

T-5.II.4. You <are> the Kingdom of Heaven, but you have let the belief in darkness enter your mind and so you need a new light. 2 The Holy Spirit is the radiance that you must let banish the idea of darkness. 3 **The Holy Spirit** is the glory before which dissociation falls away, and the Kingdom of Heaven breaks through into its own. 4 Before the separation you did not need guidance. 5 **Before the separation** you knew as you will know again, but as you do not know now.

Note # 14: The Holy Spirit knows the truth that you are the Kingdom of Heaven. If asked, the Holy Spirit's knowledge of truth will dissolve all egoic judgments and misperceptions and transform them into correct perception.

T-5.II.5. God does not guide, because **God** can share only perfect knowledge. 2 Guidance is evaluative, because **guidance** implies there is a right way and also a wrong way, one to be chosen and the other to be avoided. 3 By choosing one **way** you give up the other **way.** 4 The choice for the Holy Spirit is the choice for God. 5 God is not in you in a literal sense; you are part of **God.** 6 When you chose to leave Him, **God** gave you a Voice to speak for Him, **which is the Holy Spirit,** because **God** could no longer share His knowledge with you without hindrance. 7 Direct communication was broken because you had made another voice, **which was the voice of the ego and wrong mindedness.**

Note # 15: The Holy Spirit can properly evaluate since it knows both the truth and our perceived state of illusion. God, the Father, does not evaluate because God just "knows" the changeless truth of what is the eternal Will and Mind of God. To the Father there is no choice and, therefore, there is nothing that requires evaluation. Only in the illusions of the world of perception is choice and thus, evaluation possible and needed. In the world of time, we can misperceive or correctly perceive.

T-5.II.6. The Holy Spirit calls you both to remember and to forget. 2 You have chosen to be in a state of opposition in which opposites are possible. 3 As a result, there are choices you must make. 4 In the holy state the will is free, so that **the will's** creative power is unlimited and choice is meaningless. 5 Freedom to choose is the same power as freedom to create, but **freedom of choices** application is different. 6 Choosing depends on a split mind. 7 The Holy Spirit is one way of choosing. 8 God did not leave His children comfortless, even though **His children** chose to leave **God.** 9 The voice **His children** put in their minds was **the voice of the ego and wrong mindedness,** not the Voice for **God's** Will, for which the Holy Spirit speaks.

Note # 16: Only in the split-minded world of egoic perception does choice appear possible. This is because we appear to have the choice between the true and the false. There is nothing that can oppose God's Will. Illusions are nothing and thus, cannot have an impact on reality. The Holy Spirit calls us to remember God's Oneness and forget the illusion of egoic separation.

T-5.II.7. The Voice of the Holy Spirit does not command, because **the Holy Spirit** is incapable of arrogance. 2 **The Voice of the Holy Spirit** does not demand, because **the Holy Spirit** does not seek control. 3 **The Voice of the Holy Spirit** does not overcome, because **the Holy Spirit** does not attack. 4 **The Holy Spirit** merely reminds. 5 **The Voice of the Holy Spirit** is compelling only because of what It reminds you <of.> 6 **The Voice of the Holy Spirit** brings to your mind the other way, remaining quiet even in the midst of the turmoil you may make. 7 The Voice for God is always quiet, because **the Voice of the Holy Spirit** speaks of peace. 8 Peace is stronger than war because **peace** heals. 9 War is division, not increase. 10 No one gains from strife. 11 What profiteth it a man if he gain the whole world and lose his own soul? 12 If you listen to the wrong voice **(voice of the ego)** you <have> lost sight of your soul. 13 You cannot lose **your soul,** but you can not know **your soul.** 14 **Your soul** is therefore "lost" to you until you choose right. **(Choose to follow the guidance of the Holy Spirit)**

Note # 17: The Holy Spirit respects your free will and does nothing without your permission. The Holy Spirit is infinitely patient since It knows that your return to Its thought system is inevitable as this is God's Will.

T-5.II.8. The Holy Spirit is your Guide in choosing. 2 **The Holy Spirit** is in the part of your mind that always speaks for the right choice, because **the Holy Spirit** speaks for God. 3 **The Holy Spirit** is your remaining communication with God, which you can interrupt but cannot destroy. 4 The Holy Spirit is the way in which God's Will is done on earth as **God's Will** is **done** in Heaven. 5 Both Heaven and earth are in you, because the call of both **voices** is in your mind. 6 The Voice for God comes from your own altars to Him. 7 These altars are not things; **these altars** are devotions. 8 Yet you have other devotions now. 9 Your divided devotion has given you the two voices, and you must choose at which altar you want to serve. 10 The call you answer now is an evaluation because **the call you answer** is a decision. 11 The decision is very simple. 12 **The decision** is made on the basis of which call **(call of the ego verses Call of the Holy Spirit,)** is worth more to you.

Note # 18: Heaven is in the High or Christ conscious part of your split mind (right mindedness). The earth is under your lower or egoic influence and is part of your split mind (wrong-mindedness). Heaven and earth are not places but rather, states of mind. Our decision-maker must decide which thought system he will choose to follow. This choice will be based on what the decision-maker values most. It is a choice between Oneness and separation. The value that separation offers to the split-minded is that it fulfills the desire of the ego to be special. In a Oneness nothing can be special since all are equally the same. The One Self is indivisible.

T-5.II.9. My mind will always be like your **mind**, because we were created as equals. 2 It was only my decision that gave me all power in Heaven and earth. 3 My only gift to you is to help you make the same decision. 4 This decision is the choice to share it, because the decision itself <*is*> the decision to share. 5 **The decision to share** is made by giving, and is therefore the one choice that resembles true creation. 6 I am your model for decision. 7 By deciding for God I showed you that this decision **to share** can be made, and that you can make the decision to share.

Note # 19: Jesus' decision was to follow the guidance of the Holy Spirit. The Holy Spirit's thought system is based on love, which is inclusive and sharing in nature. Jesus' wish is to share that same decision with us. Ideas, not form, can be shared. When we accept someone's idea, the idea is strengthened.

T-5.II.10.I have assured you that the Mind that decided for me is also in you, and that you can let **your High-mind under the guidance of the Holy Spirit** change you just as **my High-mind under the guidance of the Holy Spirit** changed me. 2 This Mind, **which is under the guidance of the Holy Spirit,** is unequivocal, because **this Mind** hears only one Voice and answers in only one way. **The High-Mind or Christ consciousness chooses to do God's Will.** 3 You are the light of the world with me. 4 Rest does not come from sleeping but from waking. 5 The Holy Spirit is the Call to awaken and be glad. 6 The world **of perception, time and space** is very tired, because **the world** is the idea of weariness. 7 Our task is the joyous one of waking **the mind** to the Call for God. 8 Everyone will answer the Call of the Holy Spirit, or the Sonship cannot be as One. 9 What better vocation could there be for any part of the Kingdom than to restore **the Kingdom** to the perfect integration that can make **the Kingdom** whole? 10 Hear only **the Call for God** through the Holy Spirit within you, and teach your brothers to listen **for the Call of the Holy Spirit**, as I am teaching you.

Note # 20: Jesus implores us to make the same decision to follow the guidance of the Holy Spirit as he did. All brothers must do their part in the reuniting and returning of the Sonship to the Truth of the Kingdom.

T-5.II.11.When you are tempted by the wrong voice **(voice for the ego),** call on me to remind you how to heal by sharing my decision and making **my decision** stronger. 2 As we share this goal **(to hear only the Voice of the Holy Spirit),** we increase **this goal's** power to attract the whole Sonship, and to bring **the whole Sonship** back into the oneness in which **the Sonship** was created. 3 Remember that "yoke" means "join together," and "burden" means "message." 4 Let us restate "My yoke is easy and my burden light" in this way; "Let us join together, for my message is light."

<u>Note # 21:</u> By our joining and accepting Jesus' message, it is strengthened.

T-5.II.12.I have enjoined you to behave as I behaved, but we must respond to the same Mind to do this. 2 This Mind is the Holy Spirit, Whose Will is for God always. 3 **The Holy Spirit** teaches you how to keep me as the model for your thought, and to behave like me as a result. 4 The power of our joint motivation is beyond belief, but not beyond accomplishment. 5 What we can accomplish together has no limits, because the Call for God is the Call to the unlimited. 6 Child of God, my message is for you, to hear **my message** and give away **my message** as you answer the Holy Spirit within you. **Child of God, you are not separate, you are unlimited.**

<u>Note # 22:</u> Jesus asks us to make the same decision as he did. You are asked to return to right-mindedness and follow the Voice for God, which is the Holy Spirit. This Mind is called by various names, the High Self, Christ consciousness, right-mindedness, the Higher Mind to name a few. This is the home of the Holy Spirit. At the time of the Separation the Holy Spirit was placed in your now split mind to gently reawaken you to the truth of who and what you really are. The Holy Spirit guides you back to the understanding that your will is the same as God's Will. This heals the split-mind and leads to the return to Oneness. The Sonship and the Mind are made whole.

III. The Guide to Salvation

T-5.III.1.The way to recognize your brother is by recognizing the Holy Spirit in **your brother**. 2 I have already said that the Holy Spirit is the Bridge for the transfer of perception to knowledge, so we can use the terms, **perception and knowledge,** as if **perception and knowledge** were related, because in **the Holy Spirit's** Mind **perception and knowledge are related.** 3 This relationship **between perception and knowledge** must be in **the Holy Spirit's** Mind because, unless it were, the separation between the two ways of thinking would not be open to healing. 4 **The Holy Spirit** is part of the Holy Trinity, because **the Holy Spirit's** Mind is partly your **mind** and also partly God's **Mind.** 5 This concept that the Holy Spirit's Mind is partly your mind and also partly God's **Mind** needs clarification, not in statement but in experience.

<u>Note # 23:</u> The Holy Spirit is like the bridge between your Higher Mind and the Mind of God. The Holy Spirit is said to "reside" in the Christ consciousness, which is also the seat of awareness to the remembrance of God. Again, due to the holographic nature of the Mind of God, the Holy Trinity is but One Mind. The Trinity is presented as three separate parts for ease of discussion purposes only. They are

One.

T-5.III.2. The Holy Spirit is the idea of healing. 2 Being thought, the idea **of healing** gains as **the idea of healing** is shared. 3 **The Holy Spirit is** the Call <*for*> God. **The Holy Spirit and the idea of healing** is also the idea <*of*> God. 4 Since you are part of God it **(the Holy Spirit and the idea of healing)** is also the idea of yourself, as well as of all His creations. 5 The idea of the Holy Spirit shares the property of other ideas because **the idea of the Holy Spirit** follows the laws of the universe of which **the idea of the Holy Spirit** is a part. 6 **The idea of healing, the idea of the Holy Spirit and the idea of God are** strengthened by being given away. 7 **The three ideas of God, the Holy Spirit and healing** increases in you as you give **these three ideas** to your brother. 8 Your brother does not have to be aware of the Holy Spirit in himself or in you for this miracle to occur. 9 **Your brother** may have dissociated the Call for God, just as you have. 10 This dissociation is healed in both of you as you become aware of the Call for God in **your brother**, and thus acknowledge **the Holy Spirit's** being **in both your brother and yourself**.

Note #24: The idea of the Holy Spirit is the Call for God. Ideas can be shared with others and thus, they can be strengthened when the idea has been accepted by another. Ideas are not necessarily true. Yet, if enough people believe that an idea is true, that idea becomes the basis for that group's collective consciousness or that group's "provisional reality." Thoughts are things. If we believe or think that we are an ego-body, this becomes our provisional reality. The Holy Spirit's Call for God is the call for a return to truth. It is a call to remember what and who we really are. We are God's Beloved Child. We are called to heal our split-mind and once again remember that we are an extension of God and, therefore, must be perfect, whole and complete. Our dissociation with God was the result of the separation; the mad idea that we could be something we were not. With the guidance of the Holy Spirit, our dissociation with God and our brother will be healed.

T-5.III.3. There are two diametrically opposed ways of seeing your brother. 2 **These two ways of seeing your brother** must both be in your mind, because you are the perceiver. 3 **These two ways of seeing your brother** must also be in **your brother's mind** because you are perceiving **your brother**. 4 See **your brother** through the Holy Spirit in **your brother's** mind, and you will recognize **your brother and the Holy Spirit** in your **mind**. 5 What you acknowledge in your brother you are acknowledging in yourself, and what you share you strengthen.

Note #25: Perception is your viewpoint. As such, your perception may or may not be true in reality but it is always perceived to be true for you in your provisional reality because you believe it to be so. What you choose to perceive, you project out towards others. Your brother or the world you perceive to be outside yourself, acts as a mirror and reflects back what you originally projected out. Since thoughts are things, if you see your brother as handicapped, he will be handicapped. If you see him as hateful, he will be hateful. The course's two ways of seeing your brother reflect how you see yourself. Am I an ego-body, in competition with other ego bodies in a world of lack and limitation? OR Am I a Son of God Who has reclaimed His birthright and is perfect, whole and complete? The thoughts that you project out towards another are strengthened when your brother reflects your thoughts or perceptions, back to you. The Holy Spirit asks you to choose to see your brother's true Big "S" Self, perfect whole and complete, not his ego-body. In this way, what will be reflected back to you will be your true Big "S" Self, as God created you.

Also, an important note about projection is the fact that for your projected ideas to be reflected back to you, some element of what you project out must also be held in the "mirror's mind." This common element in both minds is needed in order to provide the resistance to reflect the idea back from the receiver to the sender. If the object or mirror does not have that element within it, the projection will pass through looking for something else that it can reflect against and thus, return to the sender. Because of this, in an example of a projected hateful thought towards you, if there is no hate in you, no hateful thought is able to reflect back from you. It simply passes through you looking for a "willing victim." Like seeks like. This is a very empowering concept since it means that you are never a victim of someone else's thinking. If there is something "wrong" in my provisional reality, I need to look within and correct my own mistaken beliefs about myself.

T-5.III.4. The Voice of the Holy Spirit is weak in you. 2 That is why you must share **the Voice of the Holy Spirit**. 3 **The Voice of the Holy Spirit** must be increased in strength before you can hear It. 4 It is impossible to hear **the Voice of the Holy Spirit** in yourself while **the Voice of the Holy Spirit** is so weak in your mind. 5 **The Voice of the Holy Spirit** is not weak in Itself, but **the Voice of the Holy Spirit** is limited by your unwillingness to hear **the Voice of the Holy Spirit**. 6 If you make the mistake of looking for the Holy Spirit in yourself alone your thoughts will frighten you because, by adopting the ego's viewpoint, you are undertaking an ego-alien journey with the ego as guide. 7 This is bound to produce fear.

Note # 26: The ego's viewpoint is that you are separate from everything else and that in order for you to gain, someone must lose. Having is associated with getting, not Being. If you make the mistake of looking for the Holy Spirit in you alone, you are confirming your belief that you are not a Oneness. You are proclaiming that you are a limited ego-body in competition with other limited ego-bodies. This puts your mind under the control of the ego's thought system, which in turn strengths the belief in the ego's thought system. By sharing the Voice of the Holy Spirit with your brother, It is strengthened.

T-5.III.5. Delay is of the ego, because time is **the ego's** concept. 2 Both time and delay are meaningless in eternity. 3 I have said before that the Holy Spirit is God's Answer to the ego. 4 Everything of which the Holy Spirit reminds you is in direct opposition to the ego's notions, because true and false perceptions are themselves opposed. 5 The Holy Spirit has the task of undoing what the ego has made. 6 **The Holy Spirit** undoes **what the ego has made** at the same level on which the ego operates, or the mind would be unable to understand the change.

Note # 27: The ego operates on the level of perception in a physical world according to time and space that is subject to limitations. The ego does not operate on the spiritual world of true reality. Instead, the ego is part of the dream world of your provisional reality. Your split-mind gave "life" to your ego only in your "dream world." The Holy Spirit will work to undo the error of the separation at the same level the ego operates on, which is the level of our own "provisional reality" of time and space. This is where you imagine and perceive yourself to be. Ultimately, all healing takes place at the level of mind for this is where the source of the error in thinking occurred.

T-5.III.6.I have repeatedly emphasized that one level of the mind is not understandable to another. 2 So it is with the ego and the Holy Spirit; with time and eternity. 3 Eternity is an idea of God, so the Holy Spirit understands **the idea of eternity** perfectly. 4 Time is a belief of the ego, so the lower mind, which is the ego's domain, accepts **time** without question. 5 The only aspect of time that is eternal is <now.>

Note # 28: Everything happens in the<now>. We only experience in the <now>. Every thought, even if it is of the past, can only be remembered in the <now>.

T-5.III.7. The Holy Spirit is the Mediator between the interpretations of the ego and the knowledge of the spirit. 2 **The Holy Spirit's** ability to deal with symbols enables **the Holy Spirit** to work with the ego's beliefs in **the ego's** own language. 3 **The Holy Spirit's** ability to look beyond symbols into eternity enables **the Holy Spirit** to understand the laws of God, for which **the Holy Spirit** speaks. 4 **The Holy Spirit** can therefore perform the function of reinterpreting what the ego makes, not by destruction but by understanding **what the ego makes**. 5 Understanding is light, and light leads to knowledge. 6 The Holy Spirit is in light because **the Holy Spirit** is in you who are light, but you yourself do not know **you are in light**. 7 It is therefore the task of the Holy Spirit to reinterpret you on behalf of God.

Note # 29: The task of the Holy Spirit is to reinterpret what you falsely perceive yourself to be (an ego body) and reawaken you to the true reality of your spiritual magnificence which is your divine birthright. The Holy Spirit, when asked, takes your egoic misperception and reinterprets them into correct perception. Correct perception is in alignment with the truth that joins and connects what was originally perceived as separate.

T-5.III.8. You cannot understand yourself alone. 2 This is because you have no meaning apart from your rightful place in the Sonship, and the rightful place of the Sonship is God. 3 **Your rightful place in the Sonship, which is in God,** is your life, your eternity and your Self. 4 **Your rightful place in the Sonship** is of this that the Holy Spirit reminds you, **which is God.** 5 **Your rightful place in the Sonship** is this that the Holy Spirit sees, **which is God.** 6 This vision, **your rightful place in the Sonship,** frightens the ego because **your rightful place in the Sonship, which is God,** is so calm. 7 Peace is the ego's greatest enemy because, according to **the egoic** interpretation of reality, war is the guarantee of **the ego's** survival. 8 The ego becomes strong in strife. 9 If you believe there is strife you will react viciously, because the idea of danger has entered your mind. 10 The idea itself **(belief there is strife)** is an appeal to the ego. 11 The Holy Spirit is as vigilant as the ego to the call of danger, opposing **the call of danger and strife** with **the Holy Spirit's** strength just as the ego welcomes **the same call of danger with war**. 12 The Holy Spirit counters this welcome **by the ego to war with the Holy Spirit's** welcoming peace. 13 Eternity and peace are as closely related as are time and war.

Note # 30: The Big "S" Self is part of the Mind of God. The task of the Holy Spirit is to return us to the remembrance of God. With this remembrance of God comes the Peace of God. The Holy Spirit does not oppose. It merely allows the strength of truth to dissolve all that is false. To oppose or make war against the ego would be to make the false appear real. There is only God. The Father is First Cause. The Son is the Father's Effect. The Holy Spirit is the commune of the Two as One. Together, They are intertwined as the inseparable One holographic Mind of God. This is "All That Is." This Trinity is the One Self that we all share.

T-5.III.9. Perception derives meaning from relationships. 2 Those **relationships** you accept are the foundations of your beliefs. 3 The separation is merely another term for a split mind. 4 The ego is the symbol of separation, just as the Holy Spirit is the symbol of peace. 5 What you perceive in others you are strengthening in yourself. 6 You may let your mind misperceive, but the Holy Spirit lets your mind reinterpret its own misperceptions.

Note # 31: When we misperceive, we base our relationship on the beliefs of fear and separation. The Holy Spirit allows the same relationship to be viewed based on love, forgiveness and joining for a common purpose.

T-5.III.10. The Holy Spirit is the perfect Teacher. 2 **The Holy Spirit** uses only what your mind already understands to teach you that you do not understand **what your mind thought it understood.** 3 The Holy Spirit can deal with a reluctant learner without going counter to his mind, because part of **a reluctant learner's mind** is still for God. 4 Despite the ego's attempts to conceal this part **of the reluctant learner's mind that is still for God, which is the High-Self, this Big "S" Self** is still much stronger than the ego, although the ego does not recognize this **fact that the High-Self's mind is stronger than the ego.** 5 The Holy Spirit recognizes **the fact that the High-Self's mind is stronger than the ego** perfectly because **the High-Self's mind** is **the Holy Spirit's** Own dwelling place; the place in the mind where **the Holy Spirit** is at home. 6 You are at home there, too, because **the High-Self's mind** is a place of peace, and peace is of God. 7 You who are part of God are not at home except in God's peace. 8 If peace is eternal, you are at home only in eternity.

Note # 32: The reluctant learner's mind that is still for God is the High-Self, Christ consciousness, higher mind or Big "S" Self, which is the part of the mind from which right-mindedness arises. It is the Home of the Holy Spirit. The Holy Spirit utilizes the Big "S" Self's mind to reinterpret egoic misperception into correct perception.

T-5.III.11. The ego made the world **of perception, time and space** as **the ego** perceives **the world**, but the Holy Spirit, the reinterpreter of what the ego made, sees the world as a teaching device for bringing you home. 2 The Holy Spirit must perceive time, and reinterpret **time** into the timeless. 3 **The Holy Spirit** must work through opposites, because **the Holy Spirit** must work with and for a mind that is in opposition **with itself.** 4 Correct and learn, and be open to learning. 5 You have not made truth, but truth can still set you free. 6 Look as the Holy Spirit looks, and understand as **the Holy Spirit** understands. 7 **The Holy Spirit's** understanding looks back to God in remembrance of me. 8 **The Holy Spirit** is in communion with God always, and **the Holy Spirit** is part of you. 9 **The Holy Spirit** is your Guide to salvation, because **the Holy Spirit** holds the remembrance of things past and to come, and brings **the remembrance of your true birthright** to the present. 10 **The Holy Spirit** holds this gladness **(your true birthright as the Son of God)** gently in your mind, asking only that you increase it **(your true birthright)** in His Name by sharing it **(your true birthright)** to increase His joy in you.

Note # 33: The Holy Spirit utilizes all that the ego miscreated out of the ego's belief in lack and transforms them into teaching devices to return the Sonship to the truth of His divine inheritance. The experiences from the egoic world of perception, time and space are reinterpreted by the Holy Spirit to become examples to teach love and forgiveness through sharing and joining. When transformed by love, these same experiences are realigned with truth.

IV. Teaching and Healing

T-5.IV.1. What fear has hidden still is part of you. 2 Joining the Atonement is the way out of fear. 3 The Holy Spirit will help you reinterpret everything that you perceive as fearful, and teach you that only what is loving is true. 4 Truth is beyond your ability to destroy, but **truth is** entirely within your ability to accept. 5 **Truth** belongs to you because, as an extension of God, you created **truth** with **God.** 6 **Truth** is yours because **truth** is part of you, just as you are part of God because **God** created you. 7 Nothing that is good can be lost because **what is good** comes from the Holy Spirit, the Voice for creation. 8 Nothing that is not good was ever created, and therefore **what is not good** cannot be protected. 9 The Atonement is the guarantee of the safety of the Kingdom, and the union of the Sonship is **the Atonement's** protection. 10 The ego cannot prevail against the Kingdom because the Sonship is united. 11 In the presence of those who hear the Holy Spirit's Call to be as one, the ego fades away and is undone.

Note # 34: The Sonship rests safely protected in the truth that there is only union within the Sonship and Its Cause. God and all He created are of One Mind and One Will. The Sonship can deny truth but cannot change it. The ego will dissolve before the reality of the eternal truth and the Sonship will once again become aware of Its wholeness.

T-5.IV.2. What the ego makes **the ego** keeps to itself, and so **what the ego makes** is without strength. 2 **Whatever the ego makes,** its existence is unshared. 3 **What the ego makes** does not die; **what the ego makes** was merely never born. 4 Physical birth is not a beginning; **physical birth** is a continuing. 5 Everything that continues has already been born. 6 **What has already been born** will increase, as you are willing to return the unhealed part of your mind to the higher part, returning **your mind** undivided to creation. 7 I have come to give you the foundation, so your own thoughts can make you really free. 8 You have carried the burden of unshared ideas that are too weak to increase, but having made **the unshared ideas that are too weak to increase,** you did not realize how to undo **these unshared ideas.** 9 You cannot cancel out your past errors alone. 10 **Your past errors, (the unshared ideas that are too weak to increase)** will not disappear from your mind without the Atonement, a remedy not of your making. 11 The Atonement must be understood as a pure act of sharing. 12 That is what I meant when I said it is possible even in this world to listen to one Voice. 13 If you are part of God and the Sonship is One, you cannot be limited to the self the ego sees.

Note # 35: Unloving, judgmental and unforgiving thoughts cannot be shared. These "private thoughts" remain part of our personal provisional reality of illusion-based thinking. If they are given to the Holy Spirit's thought system, these private thoughts can be reinterpreted and made holy. These "misperceptions" can be transformed with love and forgiveness into correct perception. The Atonement Principle is the basis for this transformation.

T-5.IV.3. Every loving thought held in any part of the Sonship belongs to every part **of the Sonship.** 2 **Every loving thought** is shared <*because*> **every loving thought** is loving. 3 Sharing is God's way of creating, and also your **way of creating.** 4 The ego can keep you in exile from the Kingdom, but in the Kingdom itself **the ego** has no power. 5 Ideas of the spirit do not leave the mind that thinks them, nor can **ideas of the spirit** conflict with each other. 6 However, ideas of the ego can conflict because **ideas of the ego** occur at different levels and also include opposite thoughts at the same level. 7 <*It is impossible to share opposing thoughts.*> 8 You can share only the thoughts that are of God and that **God** keeps for you. 9 And of such is the Kingdom of Heaven. 10 The rest **(the conflicting ideas of the ego),** remains with you until the Holy Spirit has reinterpreted them **(the conflicting ideas of the ego),** in the light of the Kingdom, making them **(the conflicting ideas of the ego)** too, worthy of being shared. 11 When they **(the conflicting ideas of the ego),** have been sufficiently purified **by the Holy Spirit, the Holy Spirit** lets you give them **(the conflicting ideas of the ego that have been purified)** away. 12 The decision to share them, **(the conflicting ideas of the ego),** <*is*> their purification.

Note # 36: God is Truth and only ideas that align with the truth can be shared, strengthened and extended. Egoic ideas based on fear, limitation and separation support the false and thus, cannot be real. Illusions, being nothing, cannot be shared. When the false is brought before the Holy Spirit's light of truth, only the truth remains. Now where there was the false, only correct perception remains. By sharing this with another, it is made real.

T-5.IV.4. I heard one Voice because I understood that I could not atone for myself alone. 2 Listening to one Voice implies the decision to share **the one Voice** in order to hear **the one Voice for** yourself. 3 The Mind that was in me is still irresistibly drawn to every mind created by God, because God's Wholeness is the Wholeness of His Son. 4 You cannot be hurt, and do not want to show your brother anything except your wholeness. 5 Show **your brother** that **your brother** cannot hurt you and hold nothing against **your brother**, or you hold **that same thing** against yourself. 6 This is the meaning of "turning the other cheek."

Note # 37: Jesus saw the Oneness of the Father in everything that he experienced. Realizing the Oneness of the Sonship, giving and receiving became the same. Jesus understood the holographic nature of the Mind of God.

T-5.IV.5. Teaching is done in many ways, above all by example. 2 Teaching should be healing, because **teaching** is the sharing of ideas and the recognition that to share ideas is to strengthen **the shared ideas**. 3 I cannot forget my need to teach what I have learned, which arose in me *<because>* I learned it. 4 I call upon you to teach what you have learned, because by so doing you can depend on **what you have learned**. 5 Make **what you have learned** dependable in my name because my name is the Name of God's Son. 6 What I learned I give you freely, and the Mind that was in me rejoices as you choose to hear **what I learned**.

Note # 38: The best teaching is by example. To teach love, you must be love. By being, you demonstrate that you have incorporated the idea into your being and now can give it away. By being, we move a thought form, a word lesson, to a world lesson. A world lesson is the experience of being it. It demonstrates that you know it and now are teaching it. By sharing, the idea grows stronger in both teacher and pupil.

T-5.IV.6. The Holy Spirit atones in all of us by undoing, and thus **the Holy Spirit** lifts the burden you have placed in your mind. 2 By following **the Holy Spirit,** you are led back to God where you belong, and how can you find the way except by taking your brother with you? 3 My part in the Atonement is not complete until you join **the Atonement** and give **the Atonement** away. 4 As you teach so shall you learn. 5 I will never leave you or forsake you, because to forsake you would be to forsake myself and God Who created me. 6 You forsake yourself and God if you forsake any of your brothers. 7 You must learn to see **your brothers** as **your brothers truly** are, and understand **your brothers** belong to God as you do. 8 How could you treat your brother better than by rendering unto God the things that are God's?

Note # 39: The Atonement is the forgiveness that comes from accepting the truth that God's Son was, is and always will be sinless and guiltless. As such, there is nothing to forgive but our own misperception that we could be something other than as God created us. Since "All That Is" is a Oneness, to withhold the Atonement from any of God's creations is to withhold it from all.

T-5.IV.7. The Atonement gives you the power of a healed mind, but the power to create is of God. 2 Therefore, those who have been forgiven must devote themselves first to healing because, having received the idea of healing, they must give, **(share) the idea of healing with all,** to hold **the idea of healing**. 3 The full power of creation cannot be expressed as long as any of God's ideas is withheld from the Kingdom. 4 The joint will of the Sonship is the only creator that can create like the Father, because only the **joint will of the** complete **Sonship** can think completely, and the thinking of God lacks nothing. 5 Everything you think that is not through the Holy Spirit *<is>* lacking.

Note # 40: All egoic thinking must give way to the thought system of the Holy Spirit in order for the Sonship to return to wholeness and One-Mindedness.

T-5.IV.8. How can you who are so holy suffer? 2 All your past except its beauty is gone, and nothing is left but a blessing. 3 I have saved all your kindnesses and every loving thought you ever had. 4 I have purified them, **all your kindnesses and every loving thought you ever had,** of the errors that hid their light, and kept them, **all your kindnesses and every loving thought you ever had,** for you in their own perfect radiance. 5 They, **your loving thoughts that I have purified,** are beyond destruction and beyond guilt. 6 They, **your loving thoughts that I have purified,** came from the Holy Spirit within you, and we know what God creates is eternal. 7 You can indeed depart in peace because I have loved you as I loved myself. 8 You go with my blessing and for my blessing. 9 Hold **my blessing** and share **my blessing** that **my blessing** may always be our **blessing.** 10 I place the peace of God in your heart and in your hands, to hold and share. 11 The heart is pure to hold **the peace of God**, and the hands are strong to give **the peace of God**. 12 We cannot lose **the peace of God**. 13 My judgment is as strong as the wisdom of God, in Whose Heart and Hands we have our being. 14 His quiet children are His blessed Sons. 15 The Thoughts of God are with you.

Note # 41: While in time, our function is forgiveness, our purpose is love and our destiny is the Peace of God. Jesus and the Holy Spirit will guide us there. No loving thought can ever be lost. They are preserved in eternity by the Holy Spirit and await the Sonship's return to knowledge.

V. The Ego's Use of Guilt

T-5.V.1.Perhaps some of our concepts will become clearer and more personally meaningful if the ego's use of guilt is clarified. 2 The ego has a purpose, just as the Holy Spirit has. 3 The ego's purpose is fear, because only the fearful can be egotistic. 4 The ego's logic is as impeccable as that of the Holy Spirit, because your mind has the means at **the mind's** disposal to side with Heaven or earth, as **the mind** elects. 5 But again, remember that both **the higher mind and the lower mind** are in you **since you believe in the separation.**

Note # 42: Due to our belief in the separation, we appear to have split our mind into two opposing and competing parts. The ego, which claims that we have a different will than God's Will, is one component. The other is the Big "S" Self, which is represented by the thought system of the Holy Spirit. Our decision-maker is being constantly asked who it will follow. It will follow the one that it values the most.

T-5.V.2.In Heaven there is no guilt, because the Kingdom is attained through the Atonement, which releases you to create. 2 The word "create" is appropriate here because, once what you have made is undone by the Holy Spirit, the blessed residue is restored and therefore continues in creation. 3 What is truly blessed is incapable of giving rise to guilt, and must give rise to joy. 4 This makes **what is truly blessed** invulnerable to the ego because **the peace of what is truly blessed** is unassailable. 5 **What is truly blessed** is invulnerable to disruption because **what is truly blessed** is whole. 6 Guilt is <*always*> disruptive. 7 Anything that engenders fear is divisive because **anything that engenders fear** obeys the law of division. 8 If the ego is the symbol of the separation, **the ego** is also the symbol of guilt. 9 Guilt is more than merely not of God. 10 **Guilt** is the symbol of attack on God. 11 **Guilt's attack on God** is a totally meaningless concept except to the ego, but do not underestimate the power of the ego's belief in **guilt.** 12 **The ego's belief that it has attacked God and therefore is guilty** is the belief from which all guilt really stems.

Note # 43: Guilt is the egoic symbol of attack on God. Guilt is the feeling you have when you deny yourself the total freedom God gave you. When you claim that you are not perfect, whole and complete, you deny your invulnerability. The ego believes that it has attacked God by rejecting your own perfection and, therefore, you feel guilty. It is the belief in this perceived attack on God from which all guilt really stems.

T-5.V.3. The ego is the part of the mind that believes in division. 2 How could part of God detach itself without believing **the ego's mind** is attacking **God**? 3 We spoke before of the authority problem as based on the concept of usurping God's power. 4 The ego believes that **usurping God's power** is what you did because **the ego** believes that **the ego** <*is*> you. 5 If you identify with the ego, you must perceive yourself as guilty **as the ego**. 6 Whenever you respond to your ego you will experience guilt, and you will fear punishment. 7 The ego is quite literally a fearful thought. 8 However ridiculous the idea of attacking God may be to the sane mind, never forget that the ego is not sane. 9 **The ego** represents a delusional system, and speaks for **this delusional system**. 10 Listening to the ego's voice means that you believe it is possible to attack God, and that a part of **God** has been torn away by you. 11 Fear of retaliation from without follows, because the severity of the guilt is so acute that **the guilt** must be projected.

Note # 44: Believing that it has separated from the Oneness that was the Mind of God, the ego believes that it has attacked God. Fear arises from the belief that due to separation, there is now something outside itself. The ego believes that having been attacked, God will seek retribution and retaliate against His attacker, the ego. The egoic thought system is designed as a means to hide from God's retribution and minimize this guilt. The ego tries to control this guilt by the use of projection. In projection, the ego attempts to transfer its own guilt upon another by blaming another for its own thoughts and experiences. Projection claims, "I'm not guilty, you are!"

T-5.V.4. Whatever you accept into your mind has reality for you. 2 It is your acceptance of **whatever you accept into your mind** that makes it real. 3 If you enthrone the ego in your mind, your allowing **the ego** to enter makes **the ego** your reality. 4 This is because the mind is capable of creating reality or making illusions. 5 I said before that you must learn to think with God. 6 To think with **God** is to think like **God**. 7 This engenders joy, not guilt, because **to think with God** is natural. 8 Guilt is a sure sign that your thinking is unnatural. 9 Unnatural thinking will always be attended with guilt, because **unnatural thinking (not thinking with God)** is the belief in sin. 10 The ego does not perceive sin as a lack of love, but **the ego perceives** sin as a positive act of assault. 11 This is necessary to the ego's survival because, as soon as you regard sin as a lack, you will automatically attempt to remedy the situation. 12 And you will succeed. 13 The ego regards this **(the removal of the ego's belief in lack)**, as doom, but you must learn to regard it **(the removal of the ego's belief in lack)**, as freedom.

Note # 45: If we define sin as attack, it makes sense to prepare ourselves for God's inevitable counterattack. This solution protects the belief that the separation was real. If we define sin as lack of love, the response is to want to remove all blocks to love. One definition for sin engenders fear, the other love. Whichever definition we accept will determine which thought system we will follow.

T-5.V.5. The guiltless mind cannot suffer. 2 Being sane, the **guiltless** mind heals the body because <*the mind*> has been healed. 3 The sane mind cannot conceive of illness because **the sane mind** cannot conceive of attacking anyone or anything. 4 I said before that illness is a form of magic. 5 It might be better to say that **illness** is a form of magical solution. 6 The ego believes that by punishing itself **the ego** will mitigate the punishment of God. 7 Yet even in this **belief that by punishing itself, the ego**

will mitigate the punishment of God, the ego is arrogant. 8 **The ego** attributes to God a punishing intent, and then takes this **punishing** intent **it has attributed to God** as **the ego's** own prerogative **to mitigate and minimize**. 9 **The ego** tries to usurp all the functions of God as **the ego** perceives **the functions of God to be**, because **the ego** recognizes that only total allegiance can be trusted.

<u>Note # 46:</u> Sickness is the ego's attempt to punish itself. Sickness is not from God. The egoic thought system dictates that due to sin, which it defined as our attack against God, God must demand retribution. The ego than further usurped God's authority by defining what sin is and then determined what God's proper response to the ego's imagined sin should be. Since the ego believed that God must require someone be punished, the ego attempts to extract God's "pound of flesh" from the body. The ego makes the body sick. The ego believes that it is better to suffer a little now then wait for God's judgment. Thus, the ego seeks to mitigate the punishment. The ego tells us that we can further mitigate the damages by transferring our punishment to another innocent victim. This is done by our mind's use of projection. Even illness itself is the ego's projection of the mind's punishment of the body for the mind's sins against God. The ego "knows" that it was the mind that actually did the crime; yet, the ego is willing to extract "God's retribution" from anyone, even the innocent.

T-5.V.6. The ego cannot oppose the laws of God any more than you **can oppose the laws of God**, but **the ego** can interpret **the laws of God** according to what **the ego** wants, just as you can. 2 That is why the question, "What do you want?" must be answered. 3 You are answering **the question, "What do you want?"** every minute and every second, and each moment of decision is a judgment that is anything but ineffectual. 4 **The effects of your answer of the question, "What do you want?"** will follow automatically until the decision is changed. 5 Remember, though, that the alternatives themselves are unalterable. 6 The Holy Spirit, like the ego, is a decision. 7 Together they **(the Holy Spirit and the ego)** constitute all the alternatives the mind can accept and obey. 8 The Holy Spirit and the ego are the only choices open to you. 9 God created one **(the choice for the Holy Spirit),** and so you cannot eradicate it **(the choice for the Holy Spirit).** 10 You made the other **(the ego),** and so you can **eradicate the choice for the ego**. 11 Only what God creates is irreversible and unchangeable. 12 What you made can always be changed because, when you do not think like God, you are not really thinking at all. 13 Delusional ideas are not real thoughts, although you can believe in **your delusional ideas**. 14 But you are wrong **to believe in your delusional ideas**. 15 The function of thought comes from God and is in God. 16 **Since you are a part of God's Thought**, you <*cannot*> think apart from **God**.

<u>Note # 47:</u> The thoughts of the egoic mind make up our own "provisional reality." Since these thought are not shared with God, they are not God's Will nor are they the thoughts of your whole mind. These thoughts only exist in your ego's world of delusions. They do not exist in God's reality. Reality is the eternal and thus, changeless. The world of delusion is the world of time, choice and change. Ultimately, the choice is between the two thought systems, one representing the true and the other the false. Since the false is not real, a choice for the egoic thought system only binds the deluded mind. The choice for the ego is a mistake, not a sin. A mistake only requires correction. The Holy Spirit merely asks that we choose again. Eventually, our decision-maker will pick the choice for the Holy Spirit and truth. It is only in the world of time and perception that the false appears to be a viable choice.

T-5.V.7. Irrational thought is disordered thought. 2 God Himself orders your thought because your thought was created by **God**. 3 Guilt feelings are always a sign that you do not know **that your thought was created by God**. 4 **Guilt feelings** also show that you believe you can think apart from God, and want to **think apart from God**. 5 Every disordered thought is attended by guilt at **the disordered thought's** inception, and maintained by guilt in **the disordered thought's** continuance. 6 Guilt is inescapable by those who believe they, **rather than God,** order their own thoughts, and must therefore obey their dictates. 7 This makes **those who believe they order their own thoughts** feel responsible for their errors without recognizing that, by accepting this responsibility, they are reacting irresponsibly. 8 If the sole responsibility of the miracle worker is to accept the Atonement for himself, and I assure you that it is **to accept the Atonement for himself**, then the responsibility for <*what*> is atoned for cannot be yours. 9 The dilemma cannot be resolved except by accepting the solution of undoing. 10 You <*would*> be responsible for the effects of all your wrong thinking if **your wrong thinking** could not be undone. 11 The purpose of the Atonement is to save the past in purified form only. 12 If you accept the remedy for disordered thought, a remedy whose efficacy is beyond doubt, how can **disordered thought's** symptoms remain?

<u>Note # 48:</u> **Efficacy** is the power to produce results.
You are not responsible for what you believe that you made since it never happened. The egoic mind is incapable of creating because it believes in separation and lack. When the split mind is following the egoic thought system, it only makes in the delusional and imagined world that is misperceived by the insane mind of the ego. This egoic world of misperception is not real and only exists in the dream world of your egoic provisional reality. When you realize that unloving thoughts do not come from the Mind of God, you will give them no reality. God did not create the dream world of the ego and by accepting the Atonement for oneself, this egoic world of delusion disappears. By accepting the Atonement for yourself, you accept that your ego's dream world never happened in reality. The ego's dreams are undone (fade away). You cannot feel guilty for something that never happened.

God does not judge. God allows. When God creates, He extends the One Self of "All that Is." We are an extension of the Mind of God. A thought is an idea in the Mind of God. Thoughts are just thoughts. They are neutral. It is our judgment that gives them their "good" or 'bad' characteristic. When we judge a thought, we move it outside the realm of an aspect of the indivisible "All That Is." We claim that the judged thought is now separate and apart. Now, instead of the thought being a part of the Oneness, we believe that we have a thought that is private and excluded from the Mind of God. We have judged and rejected part of our wholeness. Guilt feelings are always associated with these thoughts since we believe these thoughts are self-created. We do not know and so deny that God created our thoughts. Instead of allowing all thoughts, we choose to separate, reject and judge these thoughts. Guilt feelings show that you believe you can think apart from God and that you want to think apart from God. Guilt feelings show that you believe you can oppose God's Will and have a will other than God's Will. It is this belief that we have self-created or judged something to be outside of the Mind of God that is the source in our belief in sin, guilt and fear. This belief that we have private thoughts is part of the illusion of separation. Private thoughts are not real. They only "exist" in the imagination of the deluded mind of the dreamer.

T-5.V.8. The continuing decision to remain separated is the only possible reason for continuing guilt feelings. 2 We have said this before, but did not emphasize the destructive results of the decision **to remain separated**. 3 Any decision of the mind will affect both behavior and experience. 4 What you want you expect. 5 This is not delusional. 6 Your mind <*does*> make your future, and **your mind** will turn **your future** back to full creation at any minute if **your mind** accepts the Atonement first. 7 **Your mind** will also return to full creation the instant **your mind** has done so, **(accept the Atonement for yourself)**. 8 Having given up **your mind's** disordered thought, the proper ordering of thought becomes quite apparent.

<u>Note # 49:</u> The proper ordering of thought comes from God. God's thought created us perfect, whole and complete. We cannot go against this and create something of limitation. The egoic world of misperception is nothing since it is not real. Anything that the ego mind dreams up that is fear-based is, therefore, also unreal. From nothing comes nothing. Proper order of thought is restored when we

remember what we are, the Son of God. We accept the fact that our reality and the reality that is the truth of the Mind of God are one and the same.

VI. Time and Eternity

T-5.VI.1. God in His knowledge is not waiting, but His Kingdom is bereft while <**you**> wait **for His knowledge**. 2 All the Sons of God are waiting for your return, just as you are waiting for their **return**. 3 Delay does not matter in eternity, but **delay** is tragic in time. 4 You have elected to be in time rather than eternity, and therefore believe you <*are*> in time. 5 Yet your election is both free and alterable. 6 You do not belong in time. 7 Your place is only in eternity, where God Himself placed you forever.

Note # 50: Time arose out of the belief in separation. Prior to the separation there was just Oneness and Being. In order for time to "exist," you need to have different points of reference. Time could be viewed as the time or distance that it takes to get from one point to another. Time is a measure of change. It can measure the time it takes to change not only physical positions, which are associated with distance, but also mental positions, which are associated with perception and beliefs. Time can measure how long it takes to move from misperception to the return to knowledge. If there is only oneness, there is no distance to go because being One you are already there. Both time and space are related and are needed to make each other relevant Both time and space are learning devices that exist in our dream world of provisional reality since they both require belief in separation. Time and space are relevenant in a world of perception and form. As long as we find value in the belief in separation from God's Will, time is needed. When we freely decide our will and our Father's Will are one, the need for time will disappear. Time allows us to experience what it would be like to be something other than God, which is All-Knowing. To have forgotten knowledge is to imagine you are separate from God. Time allows us to pretend we do not know what we are. If we wish to not be aware of some idea and to have no access to that idea, we place it in the future. If there is an idea that we would like to have out of our mind's present awareness yet, still have access to that idea, we place it in the past. This "past" idea is then accessible in our memory. What we choose to be aware of at this moment, we call our present.

T-5.VI.2. Guilt feelings are the preservers of time. 2 **Guilt feelings** induce fears of retaliation or abandonment, and thus **guilt feelings** ensure that the future will be like the past. 3 **By insuring that the future will be like the past** is the ego's continuity **maintained**. 4 **Insuring that the future will be like the past** gives the ego a false sense of security by believing that you cannot escape **from time and the ego's belief in separation**. 5 But you can and must escape **from this belief in separation from which time arose**. 6 God offers you the continuity of eternity in exchange. 7 When you choose to make this exchange, **(time for eternity),** you will simultaneously exchange guilt for joy, viciousness for love, and pain for peace. 8 My role is only to unchain your will and set **your will** free. 9 Your ego cannot accept this freedom **of your will**, and will oppose **the freeing of your will** at every possible moment and in every possible way. 10 And as **the ego's** maker, **which is your mind's will,** you recognize what **the ego** can do because you gave **the ego** the power to do it.

Note # 51: Due to our belief in separation, the mind made the ego. The ego derives its power and existence from our mind. The ego cannot create anything but the mind can follow or obtain its guidance from the belief system of the ego. The ego's belief system is rooted in its belief in the separation. Our belief in sin, guilt and fear are interrelated concepts that help keep our ego "alive and well" within our mind.

T-5.VI.3. Remember the Kingdom always, and remember that you who are part of the Kingdom cannot be lost. 2 The Mind that was in me <*is*> in you, for God creates with perfect fairness. 3 Let the Holy Spirit remind you always of **God's** fairness, and let me teach you how to share **this reminder of God's fairness, which comes from the Holy Spirit** with your brothers. 4 How else can the chance to claim **God's fairness** for yourself be given you? 5 The two voices (**voices of the ego and the Holy Spirit**) speak for different interpretations of the same thing simultaneously; or almost simultaneously, for the ego always speaks first, 6 Alternate interpretations were unnecessary until the first one (**the ego interpretation based on separation**) was made.

<u>Note # 52:</u> The ego always speaks first. This speaking takes many forms but is based on the belief in separation, sin, guilt and fear. The ego's voice is judgmental and comparing. The Holy Spirit will respond to egoic misperception with correct perception whenever asked.

T-5.VI.4. The ego speaks in judgment, and the Holy Spirit reverses **the ego's** decision, much as a higher court has the power to reverse a lower court's decisions in this world. 2 The ego's decisions are always wrong, because **the ego's decisions** are based on the error **the ego's decisions** were made to uphold. 3 Nothing the ego perceives is interpreted correctly. 4 Not only does the ego cite Scripture for its purpose, but **the ego** even interprets Scripture as a witness for itself. 5 The Bible is a fearful thing in the ego's judgment. 6 Perceiving the **Bible** as frightening, **the ego** interprets **the Bible** fearfully. 7 Being afraid, you do not appeal to the Higher Court because you believe its judgment (**the Holy Spirit's judgment**), would also be against you.

<u>Note # 53:</u> Because the egoic thought system is based on the false belief that God's Will can be opposed and changed, all conclusions that the ego reaches are incorrect. The ego judges everything based on wrong assumptions and thus, reaches wrong conclusions. Because its thought system is based in fear, the ego interprets everything fearfully. The ego does not comprehend love and thus, interprets the Bible based on its egoic version of an unloving god. This egoic version of god is not a God of love, but rather a god who is arbitrary, petty, vengeful and full of insecurity. ACIM states that such an unloving god could only exist in the insane mind of the ego. The Holy Spirit knows that God is love and thus, interprets the Bible in accordance with a loving God. ACIM suggests that we appeal all egoic judgments to the Holy Spirit for correction.

T-5.VI.5. There are many examples of how the ego's interpretations are misleading, but a few will suffice to show how the Holy Spirit can reinterpret **the ego's misinterpretations** in **the Holy Spirit's** Own light.

<u>Note # 54:</u> Jesus will now demonstrate interpretations of biblical verse under both thought systems.

T-5.VI.6."As ye sow, so shall ye reap" **the Holy Spirit** interprets to mean what you consider worth cultivating you will cultivate in yourself. 2 Your judgment of what is worthy makes it worthy for you.

<u>Note # 55:</u> What you hold in your consciousness, you will sow and reap. Thoughts become things. You experience what you place your attention upon.

T-5.VI.7."Vengeance is mine, saith the Lord" is easily reinterpreted if you remember that ideas increase only by being shared. 2 The statement emphasizes that vengeance cannot be shared. 3 Give **vengeance**

therefore to the Holy Spirit, Who will undo **vengeance** in you because **vengeance** does not belong in your mind, which is part of God.

Note # 54: Give all your fear-based thoughts to the Holy Spirit for reinterpretation and undoing. God judges not, for the ego's concept of sin is erroneous. There can be no victims.

T-5.VI.8."I will visit the sins of the fathers unto the third and fourth generation," as interpreted by the ego, is particularly vicious. 2 It becomes merely an attempt to guarantee the ego's own survival. 3 To the Holy Spirit, the statement **"I will visit the sins of the fathers unto the third and fourth generation,"** means that in later generations **the Holy Spirit** can still reinterpret what former generations had misunderstood, and thus release the thoughts **that the former generations had misunderstood** from **their** ability to produce fear **in you**.

Note # 56: Egoic beliefs are based on the past. Unless we choose to follow a different thought system, we will continue to recreate our past errors in our present and future. Give these egoic misperceptions over to the Holy Spirit for correction and these past misperceptions will have no power over you.

T-5.VI.9."The wicked shall perish" becomes a statement of Atonement, if the word "perish" is understood as "be undone." 2 Every loveless thought must be undone, a word the ego cannot even understand. 3 To the ego, to be undone means to be destroyed. 4 The ego will not be destroyed because **the ego** is part of your thought, but because **the ego** is uncreative and therefore unsharing, **the ego** will be reinterpreted to release you from fear. 5 The part of your mind that you have given to the ego will merely return to the Kingdom, where your whole mind belongs. 6 You can delay the completion of the Kingdom, but you cannot introduce the concept of fear into **the Kingdom**.

Note # 57: The wicked, or fearful, will be undone. The Holy Spirit will reinterpret and remove all fear-based thoughts into loving and forgiving thoughts. Fear will be undone.

T-5.VI.10.   You need not fear **that** the Higher Court **of the Holy Spirit** will condemn you. 2 **The Higher Court of the Holy Spirit** will merely dismiss the case against you. 3 There can be no case against a child of God, and every witness to guilt in God's creations is bearing false witness to God Himself. 4 Appeal everything you believe gladly to God's Own Higher Court, because **God's Own Higher Court (the Holy Spirit)** speaks for **God** and therefore speaks truly. 5 **God's Own Higher Court (the Holy Spirit),** will dismiss the case against you, however carefully you have built **the case against you** up. 6 The case may be fool-proof, but **the case against you** is not God-proof. 7 The Holy Spirit will not hear **the case against you**, because **the Holy Spirit** can only witness truly. 8 **The Holy Spirit's** verdict will always be "thine is the Kingdom," because **the Holy Spirit** was given to you to remind you of what you are.

Note # 58: Both the ego's and the Holy Spirit's thought systems follow the rules of logic perfectly. Yet due to their differing initial premises, they arrive at totally opposite conclusions. ACIM states that the egoic thought system is flawed because it is based on the false belief that we were self-created and separate from God. If this major premise is wrong, everything that follows will not be correct. The logic can be impeccable but the conclusions will be wrong. ACIM states that only the thought system of the Holy Spirit can produce correct conclusions since not only is its logic perfect, its major premise is also correct. The decision-maker must decide what he chooses to value. Ultimately, truth will stand the test of time and we will freely choose the thought system of the Holy Spirit.

T-5.VI.11. When I said "I am come as a light into the world," I meant that I came to share the light with you. 2 Remember my reference to the ego's dark glass, and remember also that I said, "Do not look there." 3 It is still true that where you look to find yourself is up to you. 4 Your patience with your brother is your patience with yourself. 5 Is not a child of God worth patience? 6 I have shown you infinite patience because my will is that of our Father, from Whom I learned of infinite patience. 7 His Voice was in me as **the Holy Spirit's Voice** is in you, speaking for patience towards the Sonship in the Name of its Creator **(God, the Father).**

Note # 59: The light Jesus speaks of is the light of truth. See your brother not as a body, but as Spirit, the extension of his Creator.

T-5.VI.12. Now you must learn that only infinite patience produces immediate effects. 2 **Infinite patience** is the way in which time is exchanged for eternity. 3 Infinite patience calls upon infinite love, and by producing results <*now*> **infinite patience and love** renders time unnecessary. 4 We have repeatedly said that time is a learning device to be abolished when **time** is no longer useful. 5 The Holy Spirit, Who speaks for God in time, also knows that time is meaningless. 6 **The Holy Spirit** reminds you **that time is meaningless** in every passing moment of time, because it is **the Holy Spirit's** special function to return you to eternity and remain to bless your creations there **in eternity.** 7 **The Holy Spirit** is the only blessing you can truly give, because **the Holy Spirit** is truly blessed. 8 Because **the Holy Spirit** has been given you freely by God, you must give **the Holy Spirit freely** as you received **the Holy Spirit freely from God.**

Note # 60: To give is to receive. We demonstrate that we have something by giving it away. When only love remains, time no longer has a purpose to serve.

VII. The Decision for God

T-5.VII.1. Do you really believe you **(your egoic self)** can make a voice, **the call for egoic separation that** can drown out God's? 2 Do you really believe **that your egoic self** can devise a thought system)** that can separate you from **God?** 3 Do you really believe **your egoic self** can plan for your safety and joy**, better than **God** can **plan for your safety and joy? The ego's plan is that you are a unique, limited ego body in competition with other ego bodies.** 4 You need be neither careful nor careless; you need merely cast your cares upon **God** because **God** careth for you. 5 You are **God's** care because **God** loves you. 6 **God's** Voice reminds you always that all hope is yours because of **God's** care. 7 You cannot choose to escape **God's** care because that is not **God's** Will, but you can choose to accept **God's** care and use the infinite power of **God's** care for all those **God** created by **God's care and Love**

Note # 61: Although we can choose not to believe that we are in God's care, this belief only appears true in our insane world of provisional reality. We can never escape the eternal care of God since God created us by extension of Himself in an act of God's Love. It is God's Will that we be perfect, whole, and complete. The Will of God is also His Son's Will since we are created in God's image. We share completely in God's Oneness.

T-5.VII.2. There have been many healers who did not heal themselves. 2 **The healers who did not heal themselves** have not moved mountains by their faith because **these unhealed healers'** faith was not whole. 3 Some of **these unhealed healers** have healed the sick at times, but **these unhealed healers** have not raised the dead. 4 Unless the healer heals himself, **the healer** cannot believe that there is no order of difficulty in miracles. 5 **The unhealed healer** has not learned that every mind God created is equally worthy of being healed <*because*> God created **every mind** whole. 6 You are merely asked to return to God the mind as **God** created **the mind**. 7 **God** asks you only for what **God** gave, knowing that this giving will heal you. 8 Sanity is wholeness, and the sanity of your brothers is your **sanity**.

Note # 62: Unhealed healers would still perceive some separation within the Sonship and the Oneness. Not seeing all as God created them to be, they still believe there is some form of magic outside the power of truth that will bring about the healing of the patient's mind or body. When we speak of healing, we are speaking at the level of mind, not the body. The "unhealed healer" believes in the basic inequality between the "healer" and the patient. The healer believes that he or she has some magic power to heal the patient. Healing only occurs within the mind of the patient. It is the patient, not the healer that cures the perceived illness. The healer merely aids the patient in the patient's rediscovery of the power of truth over an illusion. The healer reminds the patient of the truth that we are spirit and not a body.

T-5.VII.3. Why should you listen to the endless insane calls you think are made upon you, **(the calls or voice for the ego and separation),** when you can know the Voice for God is in you? 2 God commended His Spirit to you, and asks that you commend your **spirit** to Him. 3 **God** wills to keep **your spirit** in perfect peace, because you are of one mind and spirit with **God**. 4 Excluding yourself from the Atonement is the ego's last-ditch defense of **the ego's** own existence. 5 **Excluding yourself from the Atonement** reflects both the ego's need to separate, and your willingness to side with **the ego's** separateness. 6 This willingness **to excluding yourself from the Atonement** means that you do not want to be healed.

Note # 63: Our purpose is to accept the Atonement for ourselves. We cannot feel "At-One-ment" when we refuse anyone this same gift. To give, we must have and to give is to receive.

T-5.VII.4. But the time is now **for you to be healed**. 2 You have not been asked to work out the plan of salvation yourself because, as I told you before, the remedy could not be of your making. 3 God Himself gave you the perfect Correction for everything you made that is not in accord with His holy Will. 4 I am making His plan perfectly explicit to you, and **I** will also tell you of your part in **God's Plan**, and how urgent **your part** is to fulfill **God's Plan**. 5 God weeps at the "sacrifice" of His children who believe they are lost to **God**.

Note # 64: The remedy for our salvation cannot be our own ego's plan. Any egoic plan is on the level of "making" since what we have made is not real and only exist in our provisional reality. Provisional reality is not on the same level as our true nature. Our true nature is God's nature. God's plan corrects the problem, the belief in the separation, at its source and restores or corrects our mistaken belief of whom and what we are. God's plan undoes our dream world of provisional reality. We cannot correct this alone because of our deep-seated guilt, which we believe would require someone's (God's) forgiveness. As long as you believe your dream world is real, you believe your guilt is justified.
God's plan reawakens you out of the nightmare of your dream world, back to the reality of your true Big "S" Self, perfect whole and complete. Only the Holy Spirit, God's Voice for the truth, can assure you that you have done nothing wrong and, therefore, are sinless and guiltless as God created you. For this is God's Will which He shares with you. Your true will and God's Will are one and the same. You only need to accept the Atonement for yourself.

T-5.VII.5. Whenever you are not wholly joyous, **your lack of joy** is because you have reacted with a lack of love to one of God's creations. 2 Perceiving **your lack of love to one of God's creations** as "sin" you become defensive because you expect attack. 3 The decision to react in this way is **your decision** and can therefore be undone. **This reaction is based on your perceived unloving act toward another that you perceive as a sin. You then expect that your brother will retaliate with his own attack against you.** 4 This reaction, **your lack of love toward another and your expectation for attack,** cannot be undone by repentance in the usual sense, because **repentance** implies guilt. 5 If you allow yourself to feel guilty, you will reinforce the error rather than allow **the error** to be undone for you.

Note # 65: Anytime you are in fear, you will not react to a brother's cry for love with love. If you are not in love, you are in fear. The error is always your lack of love toward another and your expectation for attack in return. Your sense of guilt reinforces the error because by feeling guilty, you are claiming you must have done something to feel guilty about. By your own judgment, you have made your "sin" real. You cannot be a oneness since you perceive something outside yourself to feel guilty about. This sense of guilt confirms and reinforces your ego's belief in separation. It proves that there must be something outside you that needs to forgive you. The ego then warns you that if that something outside yourself fails to forgive you, it will decide to attack you. Whether it forgives or attacks, in either case, the egoic thought system has reaffirmed that you are separate and lack wholeness. Both results imply and confirm that you are not perfect, whole and complete. Thus, under the ego's thought system, you cannot be God's Son. You must be an ego-body, subject to lack and limitation.

T-5.VII.6. Decision cannot be difficult. 2 This is obvious, if you realize that you must already have decided not to be wholly joyous if that is how you feel. 3 Therefore, the first step in the undoing **this lack of joy** is to recognize that you actively decided wrongly, but can as actively decide otherwise. 4 Be very firm with yourself in this, **(that you can choose again)** and keep yourself fully aware that the undoing process, which does not come from you, is nevertheless within you because God placed **the undoing process to choose again within you.** 5 Your part is merely to return your thinking to the point at which the error was made, and give **your thinking which made the error** over to the Atonement in peace. 6 Say this to yourself as sincerely as you can, remembering that the Holy Spirit will respond fully to your slightest invitation:

7 *I must have decided wrongly, because I am not at peace.*
8 *I made the decision* **for the ego** *myself, but I can also decide otherwise.*
9 *I want to decide otherwise, because I want to be at peace.*
10 *I do not feel guilty, because the Holy Spirit will undo all the consequences of my wrong decision if I will let* **the Holy Spirit.**
11 *I choose to let* **the Holy Spirit**, *by allowing* **the Holy Spirit** *to decide for God for me.*

Note # 66: The Atonement prayer process basically says that by taking responsibility for your decision, you have given yourself the right to reclaim your power to decide to undo that same decision. You can choose again. The Holy Spirit will undo the consequences of your wrong decision. This is easy for the Holy Spirit since It knows that your actions were just in the dream world of your provisional reality. The Holy Spirit knows that your dream world is not reality. The Holy Spirit utilizes your provisional reality, which is the level of ego misperception, as a schoolroom. The purpose of the schoolroom is to act as a learning device and playfield for you to relearn and remember what and who you really are. Under the guidance of the Holy Spirit, you are told that your answer was wrong and that you can choose again. The purpose of a schoolroom is to allow the student to learn, or in our case, to remember what is truth without placing the pupil in harm's way. Thus, the Holy Spirit has reinterpreted the ego's fearful and guilt ridden world of provisional reality into a learning device to bring us back home.

To determine which thought system we are following at any given moment, we merely need to check with how we feel. Our feelings indicate the degree that our current thinking aligns with our Big "S" Self. If we are not in a state of joy and peace, we are not following the thought system of the Holy Spirit. Loss of inner peace indicates that we have slipped into fear-based, egoic thought patterns.

Chapter 6. THE LESSONS OF LOVE

Introduction

T-6.in.1. The relationship of anger to attack is obvious, but the relationship of anger to fear is not always so apparent. 2 Anger always involves projection of separation. **Projection of separation** must ultimately be accepted as one's own responsibility, rather than **blaming projection of separation** on others. 3 Anger cannot occur unless you believe that you have been attacked, that your attack is justified in return, and that you are in no way responsible for **the attack**. 4 Given these three wholly irrational premises, the equally irrational conclusion that a brother is worthy of attack rather than of love must follow. 5 What can be expected from insane **egoic** premises except an insane conclusion? 6 The way to undo an insane **egoic** conclusion is to consider the sanity of the premises on which **the insane egoic conclusion** rests. 7 You cannot <*be*> attacked, attack <*has*> no justification, and you <*are*> responsible for what you believe.

NOTE # 1: The thought system of the Holy Spirit, your Higher-Self, or right-mindedness is as follows: You cannot <*be*> attacked. Attack <*has*> no justification, and you <*are*> responsible for what you believe.

The thought system of the ego, your lower mind or wrong-mindedness is as follows: You <*can be*> attacked. Attack <*is*> justified and you <*are not*> responsible for what you believe. Both thought systems follow the rules of logic but they have opposite originating beliefs and, therefore, yield opposite conclusions. If the major or first premise is found to be incorrect, any conclusion that follows cannot be relied upon to be true.

T-6.in.2. You have been asked to take me as your model for learning, since an extreme example is a particularly helpful learning device. 2 Everyone teaches, and teaches all the time. 3 This **idea that everyone teaches, and teaches all the time**, is a responsibility you inevitably assume the moment you accept any premise at all, and no one can organize his life without some thought system. 4 Once you have developed a thought system of any kind, you live by **your thought system** and teach **your thought system**. 5 Your capacity for allegiance to a thought system may be misplaced, but **your allegiance to a thought system** is still a form of faith and can be redirected.

NOTE # 2: Your thought system originates from you and, therefore, you can change it. Your thought system is based on your beliefs about yourself and your world's experiences. Change your beliefs and the world that you perceive will automatically change to align with your new thinking. Thoughts become your perceived experiences.

I. The Message of the Crucifixion

T-6.I.1.For learning purposes, let us consider the crucifixion again. 2 I did not dwell on **the crucifixion** before because of the fearful connotations you may associate with **the crucifixion**. 3 The only emphasis laid upon **the crucifixion** so far has been that **the crucifixion** was not a form of punishment. 4 Nothing, however, can be explained in negative terms only. 5 There is a positive interpretation of the crucifixion that is wholly devoid of fear, and therefore wholly benign in **what this positive interpretation of the crucifixion** teaches, if **the crucifixion** is properly understood.

NOTE # 3: Jesus states that the crucifixion has been falsely interpreted based on fear. His crucifixion was not God punishing His one Son because others were bad. To do this would mean that the so-called "God of Love" must be equally insane. Jesus is about to explain the correct meaning of the crucifixion.

T-6.I.2.The crucifixion is nothing more than an extreme example. 2 **The crucifixion's** value, like the value of any teaching device, lies solely in the kind of learning **the crucifixion** facilitates. 3 **The crucifixion** can be, and has been, misunderstood. 4 This is only because the fearful are apt to perceive fearfully. 5 I have already told you that you can always call on me to share my decision, and thus make my decision stronger. 6 I have also told you that the crucifixion was the last useless journey the Sonship need take, and that **the crucifixion** represents release from fear to anyone who understands **the crucifixion**. 7 While I emphasized only the resurrection before, the purpose of the crucifixion and how **the crucifixion** actually led to the resurrection was not clarified then. 8 Nevertheless, **the crucifixion** has a definite contribution to make to your own life, and if you will consider **the crucifixion** without fear, **the crucifixion** will help you understand your own role as a teacher.

NOTE # 4: Jesus asks us to understand the crucifixion without fear. Then, we need not believe that we must repeat it and will understand its correct symbolic meaning.

T-6.I.3.You have probably reacted for years as if you were being crucified. 2 This is a marked tendency of the separated, who always refuse to consider what they, **who believe they are separate,** have done to themselves. 3 Projection means anger, anger fosters assault, and assault promotes fear. 4 The real meaning of the crucifixion lies in the <apparent> intensity of the assault of some of the Sons of God upon another. 5 This <apparent> assault, of course, is impossible, and must be fully understood <as> impossible. 6 Otherwise, I cannot serve as a model for learning.

NOTE # 5: We act out our lives as if some outside force were crucifying us. Since we are the masters of our thoughts, this is impossible. Our thoughts become our experience.

T-6.I.4.Assault can ultimately be made only on the body. 2 There is little doubt that one body can assault another, and can even destroy **another body**. 3 Yet if destruction itself is impossible, anything that is destructible cannot be real **and, therefore, the body cannot be real**. 4 **The body's** destruction, therefore, does not justify anger **because the body cannot be real**. 5 To the extent to which you believe that **the body's destruction does justify anger**, you are accepting false premises and teaching to others **these false premises that the body is real**. 6 The message the crucifixion was intended to teach was that it is not necessary to perceive any form of assault in persecution, because you cannot <be> persecuted. 7 If you respond with anger, you must be equating yourself with the destructible, and are therefore regarding yourself insanely.

NOTE # 6: You are invulnerable, unlimited spirit. We are not a body. Attack can only exist in your mind's imaginary dream world of provisional reality, which is part of the ego's insane belief system. Attack does not exist in the thought system of the Holy Spirit. When you believe that you have been attacked, you equate yourself with the body. The Holy Spirit reinterprets this erroneous belief and asks you to choose again and follow the thought system of the Holy Spirit. **See Chapter Six NOTE # 1 for the description of the two thought systems.**

T-6.I.5.I have made it perfectly clear that I am like you and you are like me, but our fundamental equality can be demonstrated only through joint decision. 2 You are free to perceive yourself as persecuted if you choose. 3 When you do choose to react that way, however, you might remember that I was persecuted as the world judges, and did not share this evaluation for myself. 4 And because I did not share **that I was persecuted**, I did not strengthen **the belief that I, a Child of God, could be persecuted**. 5 I therefore offered a different interpretation of attack, and one which I want to share with you. 6 If you will believe **this different interpretation of attack**, you will help me teach **this different interpretation of attack.**

NOTE # 7: By accepting Jesus' interpretation of the crucifixion, we will help Jesus teach the truth about our spiritual nature and that attack is never justified.

T-6.I.6. As I have said before, "As you teach so shall you learn." 2 If you react as if you are persecuted, you are teaching persecution. 3 This **teaching of persecution** is not a lesson a Son of God should want to teach if he is to realize his own salvation. 4 Rather, teach your own perfect immunity, which is the truth in you, and realize that **your own perfect immunity** cannot <be> assailed. 5 Do not try to protect **your own perfect immunity** yourself, or you are believing that **your own perfect immunity** is assailable. 6 You are not asked to be crucified, which was part of my own teaching contribution. 7 You are merely asked to follow my example in the face of much less extreme temptations to misperceive, and not to accept them as false justifications for anger. 8 There can be no justification for the unjustifiable. 9 Do not believe there is **a justification for anger**, and do not teach that there is **a justification for anger**. 10 Remember always that what you believe you will teach. 11 Believe with me, and we will become equal as teachers.

NOTE # 8: Jesus states that since you are Spirit, you cannot be persecuted nor attacked. Thus, anger is never justified. Being Spirit, you remain invulnerable since that is how God created you.

T-6.I.7. Your resurrection is your reawakening. 2 I am the model for rebirth, but rebirth itself is merely the dawning on your mind of what is already in **your mind**. 3 God placed **your rebirth and reawakening** there Himself, and so your reawakening is true forever. 4 I believed in **your reawakening**, and therefore accepted **your reawakening** as true for me. 5 Help me to teach **your reawakening** to our brothers in the name of the Kingdom of God, but first believe that **your reawakening** is true for you, or you will teach amiss. 6 My brothers slept during the so-called "agony in the garden," but I could not be angry with **my brothers** because I knew I could not <be> abandoned.

NOTE # 9: We must believe the truth that as God's Creation, we are invulnerable Spirit. Without a belief in our reawakening to our true nature, we will respond with fear and perceive our brother's cry for love as an attempt to persecute us. If we perceive ourselves as a body, we will respond with fear instead of love.

T-6.I.8.I am sorry when my brothers do not share my decision to hear only one Voice, because **when my brothers do not share my decision to hear only one Voice**, it weakens them as teachers and as learners. 2 Yet I know **my brothers** cannot really betray themselves or me, and that it is still on **my brothers** that I must build my church. 3 There is no choice in this, because only you can be the foundation of God's church. 4 A church is where an altar is, and the presence of the altar is what makes the church holy. 5 A church that does not inspire love has a hidden altar that is not serving the purpose for which God intended **the church and its altar to serve which is to inspire love.** 6 I must found His church on you, because those who accept me as a model are literally my disciples. 7 Disciples are followers, and if the model **the disciples** follow has chosen to save them pain in all respects, **the disciples who accept me as their model,** are unwise not to follow **me.**

NOTE # 10: Jesus states that he understands that only love is real. We, being the extension of God, can only be love. Jesus will build his church, which is the belief system that inspires only love, upon us. Jesus has faith and sees the truth that as Spirit, we are God's altars to and for love.

T-6.I.9.I elected, for your sake and mine, to demonstrate that the most outrageous assault, as judged by the ego, does not matter. 2 As the world judges these things, but not as God knows them, I was betrayed, abandoned, beaten, torn, and finally killed. 3 It was clear that this **assault upon the body** was only because of the projection of others onto me, since I had not harmed anyone and had healed many.

NOTE #11: Jesus states that he was sinless and had harmed no one. In the eyes of this egoic world, Jesus was betrayed and wrongly persecuted. Yet, Jesus did not respond with anger since he knew he was not the body, but invulnerable Spirit.

T-6.I.10. We are still equal as learners, although we do not need to have equal experiences. 2 The Holy Spirit is glad when you can learn from **my experiences**, and be reawakened by **my experiences**. 3 That **you can be reawakened by my experiences** is their only purpose, and that is the only way in which I can be perceived as the way, the truth and the life. 4 When you hear only one Voice, **which is the Holy Spirit's,** you are never called on to sacrifice. 5 On the contrary, by being able to hear the Holy Spirit in others you can learn from their experiences, and can gain from **their experiences** without experiencing them directly yourself. 6 That is because the Holy Spirit is One, and anyone who listens is inevitably led to demonstrate **the Holy Spirit's** way for all.

NOTE # 12: The Sonship, being part of the Mind of God, is holographic in nature. We are all interconnected. By one member experiencing something, all parties of the Sonship can benefit from that same experience. We do not have to individually experience that same event to receive the benefits of that experience. If the event has been experienced with love by any part of the Sonship, it has been shared with all. By accepting that shared idea for ourselves, we reap the same benefits without having to experience the event directly. The Holy Spirit communicates these loving and real thoughts throughout the Sonship for the benefit of all.

T-6.I.11. You are not persecuted, nor was I **persecuted**. 2 You are not asked to repeat my experiences because the Holy Spirit, Whom we share, makes this unnecessary. 3 To use my experiences constructively, however, you must still follow my example in how to perceive **my experiences**. 4 My brothers and your **brothers** are constantly engaged in justifying the unjustifiable. 5 My one lesson, which I must teach as I learned **my one lesson,** is that no perception that is out of accord with the judgment of the Holy Spirit can be justified. 6 I undertook to show **that no perception that is out of accord with the judgment of the Holy Spirit can be justified** was true in an extreme case **of the crucifixion,** merely because **my experience of the crucifixion** would serve as a good teaching aid to those whose temptation to give in to anger and assault would not be so extreme. 7 I will with God that none of His Sons should suffer.

NOTE # 13: Jesus' crucifixion was an extreme example that demonstrates that Spirit is invulnerable to any form of attack. Thus, anger, attack or the belief that you have been persecuted can never be justified. By following the thought system of the Holy Spirit, we also will realize this truth for ourselves. By accepting this shared truth from the personal experience of Jesus, we do not have to relive or repeat them ourselves.

T-6.I.12. The crucifixion cannot be shared because **the crucifixion** is the symbol of projection, but the resurrection is the symbol of sharing because the reawakening of every Son of God is necessary to enable the Sonship to know **the Sonship's** Wholeness. 2 Only this, **the reawakening of every Son of God,** is knowledge.

NOTE # 14: Projection results from anger. The source of anger is fear. Being a miscreation, fear cannot be real and shared.

T-6.I.13. The message of the crucifixion is perfectly clear:
2 *Teach only love, for **love** is what you are.*

NOTE # 15: The crucifixion represents the release of fear. Fear is the opposite of love. With the release of fear as symbolized by the crucifixion, you are reawakened or resurrected, to what you are. Being love, you teach only love. The crucifixion taught that anger can never be justified.

T-6.I.14. If you interpret the crucifixion in any other way **other than to "teach only love, for love is what you are,"** you are using **the crucifixion** as a weapon for assault rather than as the call for peace for which **the crucifixion** was intended. 2 The Apostles often misunderstood **that the crucifixion was a call for peace, not a weapon for assault.** And for the same reason that anyone misunderstands **the crucifixion, the apostle and others have turned the crucifixion into a weapon for assault.** 3 **The Apostles'** own imperfect love made **the Apostles** vulnerable to projection, and out of **the Apostles'** own fear they spoke of the "wrath of God" as **God's** retaliatory weapon. 4 Nor could **the Apostles** speak of the crucifixion entirely without anger, because **the Apostles'** sense of guilt had made **the Apostles** angry.

NOTE # 16: The apostles had not accepted the thought system of the Holy Spirit totally. They wished to withhold some egoic experiences from the guidance of the Holy Spirit. This demonstrates that they still perceived some illusions to be more real than others. They had not truly accepted the fact that we are not the body. To the Apostles, love still had conditions and, therefore, they judged themselves and others as unworthy of unconditional love. Unworthiness results in guilt and guilt results in projection as we attempt to give our guilt to another.

T-6.I.15. These are some of the examples of upside-down thinking in the New Testament, although **the New Testament's** gospel is really only the message of love. 2 If the Apostles had not felt guilty, **the Apostles** never could have quoted me as saying, "I come not to bring peace but a sword." 3 This **quotation** is clearly the opposite of everything I taught. 4 Nor could they have described my reactions to Judas as **the Apostles** did, if **the Apostles** had really understood me. 5 I could not have said, "Betrayest thou the Son of man with a kiss?" unless I believed in betrayal. 6 The whole message of the crucifixion was simply that I did not **believe in betrayal.** 7 The "punishment" I was said to have called forth upon Judas was a similar mistake. 8 Judas was my brother and a Son of God, as much a part of the Sonship as myself. 9 Was it likely that I would condemn **Judas** when I was ready to demonstrate that condemnation is impossible?

NOTE # 17: Jesus states that he was misquoted and sometimes misrepresented in the Bible. He, like the Holy Spirit, teaches only the message of love.

T-6.I.16. As you read the teachings of the Apostles, remember that I told **the Apostles** myself that there was much **the Apostles** would understand later, because **the Apostles** were not wholly ready to follow me at the time. 2 I do not want you to allow any fear to enter into the thought system toward which I am guiding you. 3 I do not call for martyrs but for teachers. 4 No one is punished for sins, and the Sons of God are not sinners. 5 Any concept of punishment involves the projection of blame, and reinforces the idea that blame is justified. 6 The result is a lesson in blame, for all behavior teaches the beliefs that motivate **the behavior**. 7 The crucifixion was the result of clearly opposed thought systems. **The crucifixion was** the perfect symbol of the "conflict" between the ego and the Son of God. 8 This conflict **between the ego and the Son of God** seems just as real now, and **this conflict's** lessons must be learned now as well as then.

NOTE # 18: After the ego judges, it than looks for someone to blame and punish. When we follow the Holy Spirit's guidance, we realize that we are unable to judge correctly and thus, we must not judge. Instead, we should ask and follow the Holy Spirit's lead. The Holy Spirit sees all God's creations as sinless and guiltless since that is God's Will. Without sin, there is no need for punishment.

Conflict is the loss of peace and joy due to our split mind's struggle between the two thought systems. The ego is the symbol of conflict. Whenever we feel conflicted in any way, this is a sign that we have chosen to follow the egoic thought system. This places our thought out of alignment with our Christ consciousness and we feel conflicted. To correct this, we need to silence our ego and ask for the guidance of the Holy Spirit. We will than hear this Inner Voice for the remembrance of God and our inner peace will be restored.

T-6.I.17. I do not need gratitude, but you need to develop your weakened ability to be grateful, or you cannot appreciate God. 2 **God** does not need your appreciation, but <*you*> do **need your appreciation**. 3 You cannot love what you do not appreciate, for fear makes appreciation impossible. 4 When you are afraid of what you are, you do not appreciate **what you are**, and will therefore reject **what you are**. 5 As a result, you will teach rejection.

NOTE # 19: Gratitude and appreciation go hand in hand with love. If you cannot love yourself, you cannot love another. You must "be" love in order to give love away.

T-6.I.18. The power of the Sons of God is present all the time, because **the Sons of God** were created as creators. 2 **The Sons of God's** influence on each other is without limit, and must be used for **the Sons of God's** joint salvation. 3 Each **Son of God** must learn to teach that all forms of rejection are meaningless. 4 The separation is the notion of rejection. 5 As long as you teach this **rejection due to separation**, you will believe **in the separation due to your rejection of your oneness**. 6 This **belief in the separation due to your rejection of your oneness** is not as God thinks, and you must think as **God** thinks if you are to know **God** again.

NOTE # 20: Rejection is exclusion. The egoic thought system of fear is based on exclusion and results in miscreation. Love is inclusive and is creation. Love is "thinking" as God "thinks." In our Oneness, we are connected to "All That is." The Father, the Son and the Holy Spirit are that One Self.

T-6.I.19. Remember that the Holy Spirit is the Communication Link between God the Father and His separated Sons. 2 If you will listen to **the Holy Spirit's** Voice you will know that you cannot either hurt or be hurt, and that many need your blessing to help them hear this **Voice for this same lesson, that they cannot either hurt or be hurt**, for themselves. 3 When you perceive only this need in them **to hear this same lesson of spirit's invulnerability**, and do not respond to any other **need in them**, you will have learned of me and will be as eager to share your learning **that you cannot either hurt or be hurt** as I am.

NOTE #21: The Holy Spirit is the bridge back to the Father and knowledge. As long as we perceive ourselves as separate from our Source, we will need to seek and follow the guidance of the Holy Spirit. The Holy Spirit is the Voice for God and our Big "S" Self. This Voice teaches that as unlimited Spirit, we cannot be the body nor can we hurt or be hurt. We are only Love.

II. The Alternative to Projection

T-6.II.1.Any split in mind must involve a rejection of part of **the mind**, and this **rejection of part of the mind** <*is*> the belief in separation. 2 The Wholeness of God, which is **God's** peace, cannot be appreciated except by a whole mind that recognizes the Wholeness of God's creation. 3 By this recognition **in the Wholeness of God's creation, a whole mind** knows its Creator. 4 Exclusion and separation are synonymous, as are separation and dissociation. 5 We have said before that the separation was and is dissociation, and that once it, **separation and dissociation** occurs projection becomes **separation's** main defense, or the device that keeps **the separation** going. 6 The reason **projection keeps the separation going**, however, may not be so obvious as you think.

NOTE # 22: The peace of God is associated with whole-mindedness.

T-6.II.2.What you project you disown, and therefore **what you project you** do not believe is yours. 2 You are excluding yourself by the very judgment that you are different from the one on whom you project. 3 Since you have also judged against what you project, you continue to attack **what you project** because you continue to keep **what you project** separated. 4 By doing this unconsciously, **(your belief that you are different from the one on whom you project),** you try to keep the fact that you attacked yourself out of awareness, and thus imagine that you have made yourself safe.

Note # 23: Projection is the ego's attempt to get rid of something by seeing or projecting that something outside itself. We first judge and then we disown our own thought. The hope of projection is that by perceiving that your own projected idea is something that is not a part of you, you can freely attack or destroy the projection thus, keeping yourself safe. Projection requires judgment and to judge means that there is something separate to judge. This judgment reinforces your belief in separation. It confirms the ego's belief that you are not a Oneness. The attack on your true nature must be unconscious because if you knew there was no one to attack but yourself, who would attack themselves when they are prefect, whole and complete? Only the insane would attack themselves. When you already are everything, self-attack is self-destruction.

T-6.II.3.Yet projection will always hurt you. 2 **Projection** reinforces your belief in your own split mind, and **projection's** only purpose is to keep the separation going. 3 **Projection** is solely a device of the ego to make you feel different from your brothers and separated from **your brothers**. 4 The ego justifies

your belief that you are different from the one upon whom you project, on the grounds that it makes you seem "better" than they are, thus obscuring your equality with **the one upon whom you project,** still further. 5 Projection and attack are inevitably related, because projection is always a means of justifying attack. 6 Anger without projection is impossible. 7 The ego uses projection only to destroy your perception of both yourself and your brothers. 8 The process **of projection** begins by excluding something that exists in you but which you do not want, and leads directly to excluding you from your brothers. **Thus, projection destroys your true perception of both yourself and your brothers.**

<u>NOTE # 24:</u> Projection and attack are related because projection is always a means of justifying attack upon another. Anger results in projection and keeps your separation from the Oneness real within your split mind. When we project, we select a thought of an aspect of the whole of creation that we are. We separate and judge that aspect and we reject it as incomplete and not being a part of ourselves. This disowned thought is then projected out of our mind so that we perceive the thought to be outside and a threat to our existence. Perceiving ourselves to be separate, we now are free to attack this "outside force" to protect our safety and well-being. Judgment is based on preferring, choosing and rejecting some aspect of creation that you no longer wish to claim responsibility for. You will not allow your mind to claim ownership of this thought. Projection limits your ability to experience the whole thus, confirming your belief that you are not whole, are separate and lack something that is outside yourself.

T-6.II.4. We have learned, however, that there <*is*> an alternative to projection. 2 Every ability of the ego has a better use, because **the ego's** abilities are directed by the mind, which has a better Voice, **the Voice of Holy Spirit.** 3 The Holy Spirit extends and the ego projects. 4 As **the** goals **of the Holy Spirit and the ego** are opposed, so is the result **of the Holy Spirit and the ego opposite.**

<u>Note # 25:</u> The goal of the Holy Spirit is to reawaken you to who you really are, a Oneness. The tool of the Holy Spirit is extension through the use of miracles. Miracles transform egoic misperception into correct perception or right-mindedness. The goal of the ego is to confirm that you are something you are not, an ego-body, separate and limited. The tool of the ego is projection, which arises out of judgment and anger. All three, projection, judgment and anger, are used in conjunction by the ego to confirm that you must be something other than as God created you. The ego concludes that you must have created yourself. The separation is "confirmed" and wrong-mindedness continues in your split-mind as long as you continue to value your dream of egoic specialness over the Oneness that the Holy Spirit offers.

T-6.II.5. The Holy Spirit begins by perceiving you as perfect. 2 Knowing this perfection is shared **and the Holy Spirit** recognizes **this perfection** in others, thus strengthening this perfection in both **you and your brother**. 3 Instead of anger this **shared perfection** arouses love for both, because **this shared perfection** establishes inclusion. 4 Perceiving equality, the Holy Spirit perceives equal needs. 5 **Perceived equal needs** invite Atonement automatically, because Atonement is the one need in this world that is universal. 6 To perceive yourself this way, **as shared perfection,** is the only way in which you can find happiness in the world. 7 That is because **shared perfection, which is happiness,** is the acknowledgment that you are not in this world, for the world <*is*> unhappy.

<u>NOTE # 26:</u> The Holy Sprit's thought system rests on the knowledge that God's creation must be a perfect Oneness. The ego argues for your littleness and separation. Being created as a Oneness of everything, we cannot be happy by becoming a limited ego-body. The lure of specialness, leads to the unhappiness of separation.

T-6.II.6. How else can you find joy in a joyless place except by realizing that you are not there? 2 You cannot be anywhere God did not put you, and God created you as part of **God**. 3 That **part of God that is you** is both where you are and what you are. 4 **How God created you** is completely unalterable. 5 **How God created you** is total inclusion. 6 You cannot change **how God created you** now or ever. 7 **How God created you** is forever true. 8 **How God created you** is not a belief, but a Fact. 9 Anything that God created is as true as **God** is. 10 Its truth lies only in its perfect inclusion in **God** Who alone is perfect. 11 To deny this, **that you are part of God**, is to deny yourself and **God,** since it is impossible to accept one without the other.

NOTE # 27: God did not create a world of limitation and unhappiness. We made this world of limitation in our own imagined dream world of provisional reality. Our world of unhappiness cannot exist in the Mind of God because God Wills that His Children be happy. Our dream world cannot change the truth about reality. We can choose to dream that we are something that we are not, but we cannot change what we truly are. We are God's Effect. We need to reawaken to our divine birthright. We are a Oneness, perfect, whole and complete. We are part of God and cannot change this eternal truth since that is not Our Creator's Will.

T-6.II.7.The perfect equality of the Holy Spirit's perception is the reflection of the perfect equality of God's knowing. 2 The ego's perception has no counterpart in God, but the Holy Spirit remains the Bridge between perception and knowledge. 3 By enabling you to use perception in a way that reflects knowledge, **the Holy Spirit guides you and** you will ultimately remember **the perfect equality of the Sonship and that you are part of God**. 4 The ego would prefer to believe that this memory is impossible, yet **to this memory, (the perfect equality of the Sonship and that you are part of God),** is <*your*> perception **guided by** the Holy Spirit. 5 Your perception will end where it began. 6 Everything meets in God, because everything was created by **God** and in **God.**

NOTE # 28: The Holy Spirit's purpose is to return the split-minded to whole-mindedness. This must eventually happen since this is God's Will.

T-6.II.8.God created His Sons by extending His Thought, and retaining the extensions of **God's** Thought in **God's** Mind. 2 All **God's** Thoughts are thus perfectly united within themselves and with each other. 3 The Holy Spirit enables you to perceive this wholeness <*now.*> 4 God created you to create. 5 You cannot extend **God's** Kingdom until you know of **the** wholeness **of God's Kingdom**.

NOTE # 29: As extensions of the Mind of God, our minds possess the creative power of God. Thus, our purpose is to co-create with and like our Father. We can only create when we accept the truth that we are only love. Your free will allows you the absolute freedom to either create or to imagine whatever you would like to experience. You can even imagine that you are separate and self-created if you would like to experience fear. Imagination is fear based and thus, making. It excludes rather than joins. Creation is love-based sharing and extension of the everything that you are. We can only create like God, when we believe we share and are part of the Oneness that is the Mind of God.

T-6.II.9.Thoughts begin in the mind of the thinker, from which **the thinker's thoughts** reach outward. 2 This is as true of God's Thinking as it is of your **thinking.** 3 Because your mind is split, you can perceive as well as think. 4 Yet perception cannot escape the basic laws of mind. 5 You perceive from your mind and project your perceptions outward. 6 Although perception of any kind is unreal, you made **perception** and the Holy Spirit can therefore use **perception as** well. 7 **The Holy Spirit** can inspire perception and lead **perception** toward God. 8 This convergence seems to be far in the future only because your mind is not in perfect alignment with the idea, and therefore does not want **this convergence that leads perception toward God** now.

Note # 30: The Mind of God does not perceive since the Mind of God only knows. To perceive requires judgment that there is something that you are not. God is a Oneness.

The Holy Spirit is aware of both sides of the split-mind. The Holy Spirit can take egoic perception and reinterpret the ego's misperception into correct perception. It is only the egoic mind that is out of alignment with God's Will. Our Big "S" Self, which is the home of the Holy Spirit, continues to align with the truth. Until our split-mind is made whole, time will remain necessary. Time allows for learning. Learning is our changing perception of what we believe ourselves to be. We move from our false beliefs to the truth of what we truly were created to be. In time, we learn that we are not a body but rather, unlimited spirit. When our learning is complete and we remember God, the need for time will be over and we will reawaken in eternity to the knowledge of our divine birthright.

T-6.II.10. The Holy Spirit uses time, but does not believe in **time**. 2 Coming from God, **the Holy Spirit** uses everything for good, but **the Holy Spirit** does not believe in what is not true. 3 Since the Holy Spirit is in your mind, your mind can also believe only what is true. 4 The Holy Spirit can speak only for **what is true**, because **the Holy Spirit** speaks for God. 5 **The Holy Spirit** tells you to return your whole mind to God, because **your whole mind** has never left Him. 6 If **your whole mind** has never left Him, you need only perceive **your whole mind** as **your whole mind** is to be returned **to God**. 7 The full awareness of the Atonement, then, is the recognition that <*the separation never occurred.*> 8 The ego cannot prevail against **this recognition that** <*the separation never occurred.*> because **the Atonement** is an explicit statement that the ego never occurred.

NOTE # 31: The Atonement does not change the truth. It only states that what is true is always the changeless truth. God's Creation must remain as His Father created him. Thus the idea of separation is a mistake that has no power to change reality. Being a fantasy, the dreamer needs merely to awaken from the dream to have the illusion of separation disappear. The Holy Spirit's job is to reawaken sleeping minds to their own spiritual magnificence.

T-6.II.11. The ego can accept the idea that return is necessary because **the ego** can so easily make the idea seem difficult. 2 Yet the Holy Spirit tells you that even return is unnecessary, because what never happened cannot be difficult. 3 However, you can <*make*> the idea of return both necessary and difficult. 4 Yet it is surely clear that the perfect need nothing, and you cannot experience perfection as a difficult accomplishment, because that is what you are. 5 This is the way in which you must perceive God's creations, bringing all of your perceptions into the one line the Holy Spirit sees. 6 This line is the direct line of communication with God, and lets your mind converge with **God's Mind**. 7 There is no conflict anywhere in this perception **brought to the Holy Spirit**, because it means that all perception is guided by the Holy Spirit, Whose Mind is fixed on God. 8 Only the Holy Spirit can resolve conflict, because only the Holy Spirit is conflict-free. 9 **The Holy Spirit** perceives only what is true in your mind, and extends outward only to what is true in other minds.

Note # 32: The Holy Spirit is the bridge that knows the truth of your Spirit, yet, is also aware of the ego's imagined world of provisional reality and the ego's misperceptions. The Holy Spirit is able to reinterpret the misperceptions of the ego into right-mindedness. This leads the split-mind back to correct perception. Since all perception is ultimately based on the belief in separation, the Holy Spirit gently reminds the split-mind that the separation never happened and that we have never left, and always will remain, part of God. The Holy Spirit only perceives what is true and, therefore, knows our mind must be whole because that is how we were created. The correction is easy since it requires no new abilities or skills. It merely requires the removal of all of imagined block that we placed against love. We merely need to be what we are, which is only love. Rather than become something new, we merely allow ourselves to "BE" what we already are.

T-6.II.12. The difference between the ego's projection and the Holy Spirit's extension is very simple. 2 The ego projects to exclude, and therefore to deceive. 3 The Holy Spirit extends by recognizing Himself in every mind, and thus perceives **every mind** as one. 4 Nothing conflicts in this perception **that every mind is one**, because what the Holy Spirit perceives is all the same. 5 Wherever **the Holy Spirit** looks **the Holy Spirit** sees Himself, and because **the Holy Spirit** is united **the Holy Spirit** offers the whole Kingdom always. 6 This is the one message God gave to **the Holy Spirit** and for which **the Holy Spirit** must speak, because that is what **the Holy Spirit** is. **The Holy Spirit is the message or Voice for God.** 7 The peace of God lies in that message, and so the peace of God lies in you. 8 The great peace of the Kingdom shines in your mind forever, but **that message** must shine outward to make you aware **that the peace of God lies in you.**

NOTE # 33: Since the ego sees itself as separate, its purpose for projection is to exclude and deceive your mind into believing that your mind is something that it is not, a limited ego-body. Projection differs from creation because it excludes and limits. The Holy Spirit knows itself to be the whole of the Oneness. As such, the Holy Spirit extends Itself to all, as One. The Holy Spirit is all and It offers the entire Kingdom to all. Extension is inclusion into the totality of Oneness. The Holy Spirit's message is that as God's Creation, you are guiltless, sinless and reside in complete safety and freedom that is the Oneness of the Mind of God. There is but One and You are that One. There is no separation. Cause and Effect are indivisible.

T-6.II.13. The Holy Spirit was given you with perfect impartiality, and only by recognizing **the Holy Spirit** impartially can you recognize **the Holy Spirit** at all. 2 The ego is legion, but the Holy Spirit is One. 3 No darkness abides anywhere in the Kingdom, but your part is only to allow no darkness to abide in your own mind. 4 This alignment, **which allows no darkness to abide in your own mind,** with light is unlimited, because it is in alignment with the light of the world. 5 Each of us is the light of the world, and by joining our minds in this light we proclaim the Kingdom of God together and as one

NOTE # 34: There is only One Holy Spirit just as there is only one Truth and only One Mind of God. The Holy Spirit sees only sameness because that is all there can be in a Oneness of Everything. With a reality of a Oneness, only in an illusion can there appear to be many. There appears to be many egos. The ego sees specialness in its illusions of separation. The belief in separation demands that there must be differentiation or specialness. Only when we value the exclusive truth of the Oneness over our desire to be special can the split minded be made whole again.

III. The Relinquishment of Attack

T-6.III.1. As we have already emphasized, every idea begins in the mind of the thinker. 2 Therefore, what extends from the mind is still in **the mind**, and from <*what*> the mind extends **the mind** knows itself. 3 The word "knows" is correct here, because the Holy Spirit still holds knowledge safe in your mind through **the Holy Spirit's** impartial perception. 4 By attacking nothing, **the Holy Spirit** presents no barrier to the communication of God. 5 Therefore **since the Holy Spirit attacks nothing**, being is never threatened. 6 Your Godlike mind can never be defiled. 7 The ego never was and never will be part of **your Godlike mind**, but through the ego you can hear and teach and learn what is not true. 8 You have taught yourself **through the ego**, to believe that you are not what you are. 9 You cannot teach what you have not learned, and what you teach you strengthen in yourself because you are sharing what you teach. 10 Every lesson you teach you are learning.

NOTE # 35: In this dualistic world of perception, we learn by contrast and comparison. From thoughts, come your experiences. By utilizing what the ego would teach, you learn what you are not, which in turn teaches you to "BE" what you are.

T-6.III.2.Because every lesson you teach you are learning. this is why you must teach only one lesson. 2 If you are to be conflict-free yourself, you must learn only from the Holy Spirit and teach only by Him. 3 You are only love, but when you deny **that you are only love**, you make what you are something you must learn to remember. 4 I said before that the message of the crucifixion was, "Teach only love, for that is what you are." 5 This is the one lesson, **"Teach only love, for that is what you are,"** that is perfectly unified, because it **("Teach only love, for that is what you are.")**, is the only lesson that is one. 6 Only by teaching **love** can you learn **love**. 7 "As you teach **only love**, so will you learn **that you are only love**." 8 If that is true **that you are only love**, and it is true indeed, do not forget that what you teach is teaching you. 9 And what you project or extend you believe.

Note # 36: The one lesson that we must learn is to follow the thought system of the Holy Spirit instead of the thought system of the ego. The thought system of the Holy Spirit is based on the knowledge that you are everything. The thought system of the ego is based on nothingness. Nothingness is the opposite of everything and nothing is what the ego is. The ego has no existence other than the belief and power you choose to give it within your own split-mind. The ego does not exist in the Mind of God. The ego only exists in your mind's dream world of your self-created provisional reality. What you value, you will call into your experience and this will be what you teach and learn. The only lesson the Holy Spirit would have you learn is the truth that you are only love. This is the only knowledge that we need seek.

T-6.III.3.The only safety lies in extending the Holy Spirit, because as you see **the Holy Spirit's** gentleness in others your own mind perceives itself as totally harmless. 2 Once **your own mind** can accept this fully, **(your own mind perceives itself as totally harmless)**, **your own mind** sees no need to protect itself. 3 The protection of God then dawns upon **your own mind**, assuring **your own mind** that **your own mind** is perfectly safe forever. 4 The perfectly safe are wholly benign. 5 **The perfectly safe** bless because **the perfectly safe** know that **the perfectly safe** are blessed. 6 Without anxiety the mind is wholly kind, and because **the mind** extends beneficence **the mind** is beneficent. 7 Safety is the complete relinquishment of attack. 8 No compromise is possible in this. 9 Teach attack in any form and you have learned **attack,** and attack will hurt you. 10 Yet this learning, **to teach attack,** is not immortal, and you can unlearn **to teach attack,** by not teaching **attack**.

NOTE 37: Learning arises out of perception. Learning implies that you don't know. Due to our belief in the separation, we lost or forgot, knowledge. By unlearning the belief in the separation, knowledge will be recovered and our split-mind will be healed. See only the Christ in your brother and only understand that no harm can befall a Oneness of everything. Spirit cannot be harmed.
NOTE: You unlearn attack rather than learn not to attack. To learn not to attack implies that there is something outside yourself, which reinforces your belief in the separation. If you are a Oneness, what is there for you to attack?

T-6.III.4.Since you cannot <*not*> teach, your salvation lies in teaching the exact opposite of everything the ego believes. 2 This is how you will learn the truth that will set you free, and will keep you free as others learn it of you. 3 The only way to have peace is to teach peace. 4 By teaching peace you must learn **peace** yourself, because you cannot teach what you still dissociate. 5 Only thus can you win back the knowledge that you threw away. 6 An idea that you share you must have. 7 **An idea** awakens in your mind through the conviction of teaching **the idea**. 8 Everything you teach you are learning. 9 Teach only love, and learn that love is yours and you are love.

NOTE # 38: We are always teaching what we value. The choice is between oneness and separation. Based on this one choice, we will have automatically decided to teach either love or fear.

IV. The Only Answer

T-6.IV.1.Remember that the Holy Spirit is the Answer, **the Holy Spirit is** not the question. 2 The ego always speaks first. 3 **The ego** is capricious and does not mean its maker well. **(Your mind is the ego's maker.)** 4 **The ego** believes, and correctly, that its maker, **your mind**, may withdraw **your mind's** support from **the ego** at any moment. 5 If **the ego** meant you well **the ego** would be glad, as the Holy Spirit will be glad when **the Holy Spirit** has brought you home and you no longer need **the Holy Spirit's** guidance. 6 The ego does not regard itself as part of you. 7 Herein lies **the ego's** primary error **of separation, which is** the foundation of **the ego's** whole thought system.

NOTE # 39: The ego sees everything as separate and does not view itself as part of the Oneness of Everything, perfect, whole and complete. The ego does not regard itself as part of you. You are spirit, which is mind, not a body. Because the ego does not consider itself to be you, the ego does not have your well-being or your best interest as its purpose and goal. Instead, the ego has its own continued existence as its goal. Since your mind created the ego, it is the goal of the ego to obliterate all remembrance of this truth from your mind. If the mind remembered that it created the ego, the mind would also know it could discreate the ego. The ego is always questioning what you are. It is the ego's thought system, which is based on its belief that you are not your Big "S" Self. This questioning of what you are forms the basis for the ego's attack upon your spiritual essence. The ego does not wish to attack itself and, therefore, believes that it is separate from your mind. The ego constantly attacks your mind thus, hoping to keep your mind in a state of powerless victim consciousness. Unfortunately for the ego, since you created (made) it, your mind is the source of any powers the ego appears to have. If you reclaim your true nature as a Child of God, the ego's control or voice will disappear. The ego's goal is to falsely convince you that you are separate and thus, powerless to change your provisional reality.

T-6.IV.2.When God created you God made you part of Him. 2 **Since God made you part of Him,** this is why attack within the Kingdom is impossible. 3 You made the ego without love, and so **the ego** does not love you. 4 You could not remain within the Kingdom without love, and since the Kingdom <is> love, you believe that you are without **the Kingdom**. 5 **This belief that you are outside the Kingdom** enables the ego to regard itself as separate and outside its maker, which is **your mind.** Thus **the ego** speaks for the part of your mind that believes <you> are separate and outside the Mind of God, which is **the Kingdom.** 6 The ego, then, raised the first question that was ever asked, but one **the ego** can never answer. 7 That question, "What are you?" was the beginning of doubt. 8 The ego has never answered any questions since, although **the ego** has raised a great many. 9 The most inventive activities of the ego have never done more than obscure the question **of "What are you?"** because you have the answer and

*<the ego is afraid of you, **your True Self.** >*

NOTE # 40: Ego cannot answer the question," What are you?" truthfully since the answer if comprehended would terminate the ego's control over your split-mind. The answer is that you are a Child of God. As God's thought, you are perfect, whole, and complete. You are as God created you, part of a Oneness of everything. The ego asks the question, "What are you?" But the ego does not want you to rediscover the answer. By asking the question "What Am I?" our whole mind seems to split in two. Certainty is lost as your mind moves from the "I AM" State of Consciousness, which is the domain of the Big "S" Self into the "What Am I?" State of Consciousness, which is the domain of the ego. If you found the true answer to the question of "What Am I?" the ego's rule would end.

T6.IV.3. You cannot understand the conflict until you fully understand the basic fact that the ego cannot know anything. 2 The Holy Spirit does not speak first, *<but **the Holy Spirit** always answers.>* 3 Everyone has called upon **the Holy Spirit** for help at one time or another and in one way or another, and has been answered. 4 Since the Holy Spirit answers truly **the Holy Spirit** answers for all time, which means that everyone has the answer *<now.>*

NOTE # 41: Since we are part of the One Mind of God, the answer has always been inside us. We have just refused to ask. Ask, then be still and listen to the Holy Spirit's reply.

T-6.IV.4. The ego cannot hear the Holy Spirit, but **the ego** does believe that part of the mind that made **the ego** is against **the ego**. 2 **The ego** interprets this as a justification for attacking its maker, **your mind.** 3 **The ego** believes that the best defense is attack, and wants *<you>* to believe **that the best defense is attack.** 4 Unless you do believe **that the best defense is attack,** you will not side with **the ego**, and the ego feels badly in need of allies, though not of brothers. 5 Perceiving something alien to itself in your mind, the ego turns to the body as **the ego's** ally, because the body is *<not>* part of you, **whose true essence is spirit or mind.** 6 This makes the body the ego's friend. 7 **The ego and its friend, the body** is an alliance frankly based on separation. 8 If you side with this alliance **of the ego and the body,** you will be afraid, because you are siding with an alliance of fear.

NOTE # 42: If we perceive ourselves as the body, we will believe that the vulnerable body must be defended at all costs. We cannot perceive ourselves as unlimited sprit if our home is the body. The body is the ego's proof that we are not part of the Mind of God and that we must be separate.

T-6.IV.5. The ego uses the body to conspire against your mind, and because the ego realizes that its "enemy," **the mind,** can end them both, **(the ego and the body)** merely by recognizing they **(ego and body)** are not part of you, **therefore both the ego and body** join in the attack on **your mind** together. 2 This is perhaps the strangest perception of all, if you consider what it really involves. 3 The ego, which is not real, attempts to persuade the mind, which *<is>* real, that the mind is the ego's learning device; and further, that the body is more real than the mind is. 4 No one in his right mind could possibly believe this, and no one in his right mind does believe **that the mind is the ego's learning device and that the body is more real than the mind.**

NOTE 43: Since all creative power resides in the mind, the ego's entire thought system relies on your mind not recalling that the mind is the decision-maker. The thought system of the Holy Spirit, corrects this misperception, and reinterprets the body correctly as a learning device to rediscover who we really are. The mind is the cause. The ego and the body are the mind's effect. To believe that an effect controls its cause is insane.

T-6.IV.6.Hear, then, the one answer of the Holy Spirit to all the questions the ego raises: You are a child of God, a priceless part of His Kingdom, which **God** created as part of **God**. 2 Nothing else exists and only this is real. 3 You have chosen a sleep in which you have had bad dreams, but the sleep is not real and God calls you to awake. 4 There will be nothing left of your dream when you hear **God**, because you will awaken. 5 Your dreams contain many of the ego's symbols and **your dreams** have confused you. 6 Yet that was only because you were asleep and did not know. 7 When you wake you will see the truth around you and in you, and you will no longer believe in dreams because **your dreams** will have no reality for you. 8 Yet the Kingdom and all that you have created there will have great reality for you, because **the Kingdom and all that you have created** are beautiful and true.

NOTE 44: This is the thought system of the Holy Spirit. You are and always will be as God created you because you are part of God. This is truth and this is reality. Nothing can change the Mind or Will of God. The world of the ego never existed since it was an imagined dream. You are sinless and guiltless. The Holy Spirit's task is to gently awaken God's sleeping Son to the fact that his mind was merely having a bad dream. Dreams can have no affect on the reality of the Kingdom.

T-6.IV.7.In the Kingdom, where you are and what you are is perfectly certain. 2 There is no doubt, because the first question, which is "**What are you?**" was never asked. 3 Having finally been wholly answered, <it has never been.> 4 <Being> alone lives in the Kingdom, where everything lives in God without question. 5 The time spent on questioning in the dream has given way to creation and to its eternity. 6 You are as certain as God because you are as true as **God** is, but what was once certain in your mind has become only the ability for certainty.

NOTE 45: The answer to the question removes the question. If you are as God created you, a Oneness, there was never someone to ask the question to. Only if there is doubt, can the question be asked. Since you are part of God, God does not doubt. God just <IS>. God is just <BEING>. Because you doubt your true nature, certainty is forgotten. Knowledge is certain. It does not waiver or doubt. With loss of certainty, knowing gives way to perception. Because of doubt, you place limits on your own power as God's Son. The limits that you place on yourself now change your unlimitedness into the ability to relearn and remember your unlimitedness. Abilities leave doubt as to if and when they will be realized because abilities are just potentials. With the introduction of doubt you have lost <Beingness> and introduced <Doingness> <Doing> implies the belief in limitation and separation. If you are everything what is there to do? You just are <Being>.

T-6.IV.8.The introduction of abilities into being was the beginning of uncertainty, because abilities are potentials, not accomplishments. 2 Your abilities are useless in the presence of God's accomplishments, and also of **your accomplishments.** 3 Accomplishments are results that have been achieved. 4 When **accomplishments** are perfect, abilities are meaningless. 5 It is curious that the perfect must now be perfected. 6 In fact it is impossible **for the perfect be perfected since this implies they were not perfect to being with.** 7 Remember, however, that when you put yourself in an impossible situation you believe that the impossible <is> possible.

NOTE # 46: We always remain as God created us, perfect, whole and complete. Because we have free will, we have the power to pretend something that is not true. This denial of reality does not change the truth, but it does change what we choose to experience as our current awareness. Time allows us to play with uncertainty and to relearn what we have temporarily chosen to forget. We claim to not know what we are. When we remember that we are a conduit for God's love, our learning will be over. We will have transformed our abilities into our accomplishments. Time and the game of separation will end.

T-6.IV.9. Abilities must be developed before you can use **those abilities**. 2 This is not true of anything that God created, but **the idea that abilities must be developed before you can use your abilities** is the kindest solution possible for what you made. 3 In an impossible situation, you can develop your abilities to the point where they can get you out of **the impossible situation**. 4 You have a Guide **in the Holy Spirit to help you in** how to develop **your abilities**, but you have no commander except yourself. 5 This leaves you in charge of the Kingdom, with both a Guide to find **the Kingdom** and a means, **your abilities,** to keep **the Kingdom**. 6 You have a model to follow who will strengthen your command, and never detract from **your command** in any way. 7 You therefore retain the central place in your imagined enslavement, which in itself demonstrates that you are not enslaved.

NOTE 47: You are always the ultimate controller of your mind. You are the decision-maker and you have been given free will to determine for yourself what you choose to value. Jesus can serve as your model and as a way shower. The Holy Spirit can act as a guide but you must decide what belief system you will follow. You only have two choices. Your decision-maker must choose between either the belief system of the Holy Spirit or the belief system of the ego. There is no other choice and the choice is totally one or the other. It cannot be both.

T-6.IV.10. You are in an impossible situation only because you think it is possible to be in **an impossible situation**. 2 You <*would*> be in an impossible situation if God showed you your perfection, and proved to you that you were wrong. 3 This would demonstrate that the perfect are inadequate to bring themselves to the awareness of their perfection, and thus side with the belief that those who have everything need help and are therefore helpless. 4 This is the kind of "reasoning" in which the ego engages. 5 God, Who knows that His creations are perfect, does not affront **His perfect creation by telling the perfect that they are helpless and in need of fixing**. 6 This would be as impossible as the ego's notion that **the ego** has affronted **God**.

NOTE 48: If God acknowledged that you needed help, God would be acknowledging the idea that you were not perfect. If this were the case, God would not be perfect since you are part of God. This idea would reinforce your belief in your limitation. The solution is to gently allow you to reawaken yourself to what you are. Once awake, the question "What are you?" disappears since the question itself is impossible. With the return to knowledge, certainty of what you are has also been returned. The question is never asked.

T-6.IV.11. That is why the Holy Spirit never commands. 2 To command is to assume inequality, which the Holy Spirit demonstrates **that inequality** does not exist. 3 Fidelity to premises is a law of mind, and everything God created is faithful to **God's** laws. 4 Fidelity to other laws is also possible, however, not because the laws are true, but because you made **the decision to make the laws "true" only in your limited split mind**. 5 What would be gained if God proved to you that you have thought insanely? 6 Can God lose His Own certainty? 7 I have frequently said that what you teach you are. 8 Would you have God teach you that you have sinned? 9 If **God** confronted the self you made with the truth **God** created for you, what could you be but afraid? 10 You would doubt your right mind, which is the only place where you can find the sanity **God** gave you.

NOTE 49: The Holy Spirit, which is the Voice for God in you, like God the Father, knows truth. The Holy Spirit's job is to reawaken your mind to the truth about yourself. The Holy Spirit will not do anything that would increase your fear. To command would imply that you are not capable of self-correction. This would reinforce your belief in separation. The Holy Spirit, therefore, never commands but rather offers guidance by reinterpreting the thought system of the ego back to the reality of your perfect Oneness. The Holy Spirit knows what you really are and your reawakening is inevitable, since your whole mind and God's Mind are one.

T-6.IV.12. God does not teach. 2 To teach is to imply a lack, which God knows is not there. 3 God is not conflicted. 4 Teaching aims at change, but God created only the changeless. 5 The separation was not a loss of perfection, but a failure in communication. 6 A harsh and strident form of communication arose as the ego's voice. 7 **The ego's voice** could not shatter the peace of God, but **the ego's voice** could shatter <*your*> peace. 8 God did not blot **the ego's voice** out, because to eradicate **the ego's voice** would be to attack **the ego's voice**. 9 Being questioned **by the ego's voice**, **God** did not question **the ego**. 10 **God** merely gave the Answer. 11 His Answer is your Teacher, **the Holy Spirit.**

<u>NOTE 50:</u> God's Answer is the Voice of the Holy Spirit. God placed that Voice within your mind the moment the question of "What am I?" was asked. Your teacher is the Holy Spirit. By accepting the Atonement for ourselves, we demonstrate that relearning is complete.

V. The Lessons of the Holy Spirit

T-6.V.1. Like any good teacher, the Holy Spirit knows more than you do now, but **the Holy Spirit** teaches only to make you equal with **the Holy Spirit**. 2 You had already taught yourself wrongly, having believed what was not true. 3 You did not believe in your own perfection. 4 Would God teach you that you had made a split mind, when **God** knows your mind only as whole? 5 What God does know is that **God's** communication channels are not open to **God**, so that **God** cannot impart **God's** joy and know that His children are wholly joyous. 6 Giving **God's** joy is an ongoing process, not in time but in eternity. 7 God's extending outward, though not **God's** completeness, is blocked when the Sonship does not communicate with **God** as one. 8 So **God** thought, "My children sleep and must be awakened."

<u>NOTE # 51:</u> When we do not co-create with our Source, we fail to extend the Mind of God. God and His Creation remain a perfect and complete Oneness but the continued expansion and sharing of the Mind of God is not maximal.

T-6.V.2. How can you wake children in a more kindly way than by a gentle Voice that will not frighten **the sleeping children**, but will merely remind **the sleeping children** that the night is over and the light has come? 2 You do not inform **the sleeping children** that the nightmares that frightened **the sleeping children** so badly are not real, because children believe in magic. 3 You merely reassure **the sleeping children** that **the children** are safe <*now.*> 4 Then you train **the children** to recognize the difference between sleeping and waking, so **the children** will understand they need not be afraid of dreams. 5 And so when bad dreams come, **the children** will themselves call on the light to dispel **the bad dreams**.

<u>NOTE # 52:</u> The plan of awakening teaches God's Children the difference between miscreating out of fear and creating out of love. By learning this lesson, we experience what it is like to choose only love.

T-6.V.3. A wise teacher teaches through approach, not avoidance. 2 **A wise teacher** does not emphasize what you must avoid to escape from harm, but what you need to learn to have joy. 3 Consider the fear and confusion a child would experience if **a child** were told, "Do not do this because it will hurt you and make you unsafe; but if you do that instead, you will escape from harm and be safe, and then you will not be afraid." 4 It is surely better to use only three words: "Do only that!" 5 This simple statement is perfectly clear, easily understood and very easily remembered.

NOTE # 53: It is best to teach someone what to do rather than all the possible things not to do. Teaching what not to do only increases the pupil's apprehension and fear.

T-6.V.4.The Holy Spirit never itemizes errors because **the Holy Spirit** does not frighten children, and those who lack wisdom <*are*> children. 2 Yet **the Holy Spirit** always answers the **child's** call, and **the Holy Spirit's** dependability makes **the child** more certain. 3 Children <*do*> confuse fantasy and reality, and **children** are frightened because **children** do not recognize the difference **between fantasy and reality**. 4 The Holy Spirit makes no distinction among dreams. 5 **The Holy Spirit** merely shines **the dreams** away. 6 **The Holy Spirit's** light is always the Call to awaken, whatever you have been dreaming. 7 Nothing lasting lies in dreams, and the Holy Spirit, shining with the light from God Himself, speaks only for what lasts forever.

NOTE # 54: Anything not of love is not real. Truth awakens the dreamer from all illusions. Whether it is a "bad" dream or a "good" dream, it is still an illusion. The goal of the Holy Spirit is to dissolve all illusions away by gently awakening the sleeping child to the truth of the Kingdom.

A. To Have, Give All to All

T-6.V.A.1.When your body and your ego and your dreams are gone, you will know that you will last forever. 2 Perhaps you think this is accomplished through death, but nothing is accomplished through death, because death is nothing. 3 Everything is accomplished through life, and life is of the mind and in the mind. 4 The body neither lives nor dies, because **the body** cannot contain you who are life. 5 If we share the same mind, you can overcome death because I did **overcome death**. 6 Death is an attempt to resolve conflict by not deciding at all. 7 Like any other impossible solution the ego attempts, <*it (death) will not work*>.

NOTE # 55: The "death" of the body does not grant us eternal life in either heaven or hell. It merely means that we failed to decide to be vigilant for God. We have not learned who we are and have continued to find value in the illusion of separation and specialness. Eventually, we must resolve the conflict between fear and love and decide that love is only real. Death merely postpones the moment that we will freely choose to unite our will with our Father's Will.

T-6.V.A.2.God did not make the body, because **the body** is destructible, and therefore **the body is** not of the Kingdom. 2 The body is the symbol of what you think you are. 3 **The body** is clearly a separation device, and therefore **the body** does not exist. 4 The Holy Spirit, as always, takes what you have made and translates **the body** into a learning device. 5 Again as always, **the Holy Spirit** reinterprets what the ego uses as an argument for separation into a demonstration against separation. 6 If the mind can heal the body, but the body cannot heal the mind, then the mind must be stronger than the body. 7 Every miracle demonstrates **that the mind must be stronger than the body**.

NOTE # 56: God did not make the body. The body is the ego's symbol of what we believe we are. The body was made to prove that the separation is real. The Holy Spirit utilizes the body to teach that we are not the body but instead mind or spirit.

T-6.V.A.3.I have said that the Holy Spirit is the motivation for miracles. 2 **The Holy Spirit** always tells you that only the mind is real, because only the mind can be shared. 3 The body is separate, and therefore cannot be part of you. 4 To be of one mind is meaningful, but to be one body is meaningless. 5 By the laws of mind, then, the body is meaningless.

NOTE # 57: The body is the ego's proof that separation occurred and that the mind is under the control of the body. The ego utilizes the body as a separation device. The Holy Spirit utilizes the body as a learning devise to demonstrate that the mind is the controlling force since only the mind can heal the body. The course also points out that the mind, not the body, is real since only the mind can be shared. What is real is shared because extension, which is creation, is sharing. Thoughts can expand (be shared) without decreasing the thought itself. Sharing strengthens the idea. The body, which is physical form, cannot be shared without diminishment and, thus, the body cannot be real. The body is a symbol of what you believe you are when your mind accepts the ego as its guide.

T-6.V.A.4. To the Holy Spirit, there is no order of difficulty in miracles. 2 **That there is no order of difficulty in miracles** is familiar enough to you by now, but **the concept that there is no order of difficulty in miracles,** has not yet become believable. 3 Therefore, you do not understand **the concept that there is no order of difficulty in miracles** and **therefore you** cannot use **this concept that there is no order of difficulty in miracles**. 4 We have too much to accomplish on behalf of the Kingdom to let this crucial concept **(that there is no order of difficulty in miracles)**, slip away. 5 **This crucial concept, (that there is no order of difficulty in miracles),** is a real foundation stone of the thought system I teach and want you to teach. 6 You cannot perform miracles without believing **that there is no order of difficulty in miracles**, because **this crucial concept** is a belief in perfect equality. 7 Only one equal gift can be offered to the equal Sons of God, and that is full appreciation. 8 Nothing more and nothing less **than full appreciation**. 9 Without a range, order of difficulty is meaningless, and there must be no range in what you offer to your brother **which is full appreciation**.

NOTE # 58: Since the basis of all creation is that it is an extension of God, creation, which is God's Son, must be everything. All creation is part of the whole, therefore, in reality, there is only the One. There is only equality in the One and the only gift is that of full appreciation since the One is everything. Having everything what can be given it? Only appreciation for Its <BEINGNESS> is in order. Appreciation is a response of being loving. Being everything, there must be no limits on what you will share with your brother. The only range being offered and shared is the everything that you are. Creation, like miracles, is maximal. Nothing is held back.

T-6.V.A.5. The Holy Spirit, Who leads to God, translates communication into being, just as **the Holy Spirit** ultimately translates perception into knowledge. 2 You do not lose what you communicate. 3 The ego uses the body for attack, for pleasure and for pride. 4 The insanity of this perception **that the body is for attack, for pleasure and for pride** makes **the ego's perception of the body** a fearful one indeed. 5 The Holy Spirit sees the body only as a means of communication, and because communicating is sharing **the body** becomes communion. 6 Perhaps you think that fear as well as love can be communicated; and therefore **you think fear** can be shared. 7 Yet this **idea that fear can be shared** is not so real as it may appear. 8 Those who communicate fear are promoting attack, and attack always breaks communication, making **communication** impossible. 9 Egos do join together in temporary allegiance, but always for what each one can get <separately.> 10 The Holy Spirit communicates only what each one can give to all. 11 **The Holy Spirit** never takes anything back, because **the Holy Spirit wants you to keep everything the Holy Spirit gives you.** 12 Therefore, **the Holy Spirit's** teaching begins with the lesson:

13 *To have, give all to all.*

Note # 59: The Holy Spirit reinterprets the ego's body into a device for communication. Communication can be shared. The Holy Spirit sees you as God created you and communicates to you what you truly are. Full appreciation of what you are can be shared with your brother because you are equal. God did not create specialness. God, being All, extended Himself to All. The Holy Spirit teaches this lesson of equality and inclusion which is "To have, give all to all." By giving, we prove that we have.

Communication is "Being," which is different than egoic thinking with its emphasis on "having." When you are "Being", you are experiencing or feeling. Our feelings indicate or communicate our connectiveness with our Source Energy. If we are feeling fearful and lack inner peace, we are out of alignment with our Big "S" Self. When we feel good and are at peace, we are following the guidance of the Holy Spirit.

T-6.V.A.6. This **lesson**, "**To have, give all to all,**" is a very preliminary step, and the only one you must take for yourself. 2 It is not even necessary that you complete the step **of this lesson of "To have, give all to all,"** yourself, but it is necessary that you turn in that direction **of the belief that "to have, give all to all."** 3 Having chosen to go that way, **this belief that "to have, give all to all,"** allows you to place yourself in charge of the journey, where you and only you must remain. 4 This step **of placing yourself in charge of the journey and following the belief that "to have, give all to all,"** may appear to exacerbate conflict rather than resolve **conflict,** because **this new role of placing yourself in charge of the journey and following the belief that "to have, give all to all,"** is the beginning step in reversing your perception and turning **your perception** right-side up. 5 This conflicts with the upside-down perception you have not yet abandoned, or the change in direction would not have been necessary. 6 Some **with the upside-down perception** remain at this step for a long time, experiencing very acute conflict. 7 At this point **they with the upside-down perception** may try to accept the conflict, rather than take the next step towards **the conflict's** resolution. 8 Having taken the first step **of following the belief that "to have, give all to all,"** however, they **with the upside-down perception** will be helped. 9 Once **a brother** has chosen **the belief that "to have, give all to all," which is a belief that** they cannot complete alone **without another,** they are no longer alone.

NOTE # 60: This first lesson, "To have, give all to all," is the first step to retraining the mind. Under the egoic belief system, to give means we lose. This is due to the egoic belief in lack and that you are a body. Form cannot be shared without sacrifice. Yet, ideas can be shared and result in strengthening the original idea. No sacrifice is required when loving ideas are shared. This lesson, which is "To have, give all to all." is a lesson in oneness and sharing. It requires joining and thus, begins the healing of the fragmented Sonship.

B. To Have Peace, Teach Peace to Learn It

T-6.V.B.1. All who believe in separation have a basic fear of retaliation and abandonment. 2 **All who believe in separation** believe in attack and rejection, so that is what **all who believe in separation** perceive and teach and learn. 3 These insane ideas are clearly the result of dissociation and projection. 4 What you teach you are, but it is quite apparent that you can teach wrongly, and can therefore teach yourself wrong. 5 Many thought I was attacking them, even though it was apparent I was not **attacking them.** 6 An insane learner learns strange lessons. 7 What you must recognize is that when you do not share a thought system, you are weakening **that thought system.** 8 Those who believe in **that thought system** therefore perceive **that when you do not share their thought system, it is** an attack on **those who believe in that same thought system.** 9 This is because everyone identifies himself with his thought system, and every thought system centers on what you believe you are. 10 If the center of the thought system is true, only truth extends from **the thought system.** 11 But if **the thought system has** a lie at its center, only deception proceeds from **the thought system, which has a lie at its center.**

NOTE # 61: If someone believes that they are a body, they will follow the egoic thought system of fear, lack and separation. When they come in contact with someone like Jesus who follows the thought system of the Holy Spirit, Jesus' love would be perceived by the fearful as an attack on their person and their egoic belief system. At the center of each thought system is your belief in what you are. Are you unlimited Spirit or a body? If they get the first answer wrong, everything else that follows will be based on incorrect data.

T-6.V.B.2. All good teachers realize that only fundamental change will last, but **all good teachers** do not begin at that **fundamental** level. 2 Strengthening motivation for change is **all good teachers'** first and foremost goal. 3 **Strengthening motivation for change** is also their last and final one **goal.** 4 Increasing motivation for change in the learner is all that a teacher need do to guarantee change. 5 Change in motivation is a change of mind, and this **change of mind** will inevitably produce fundamental change because the mind <*is*> fundamental.

NOTE # 62: When you are motivated, the task at hand automatically becomes easier to achieve. Learning only can occur within the mind of the learner. The Holy Spirit wants you to be happy. The ego wants to claim that it is right even when it is wrong. When you change your motivation from the need to be right to the need to be happy, change is guaranteed. Ask yourself this simple question. **"Would I rather be right or happy?"** Choose happiness and follow your bliss and you will follow the pathway to the Kingdom.

T-6.V.B.3. The first step in the reversal or undoing process is the undoing of the getting concept. 2 Accordingly, the Holy Spirit's first lesson was "To have, give all to all." 3 I said that this **concept, "To have, give all to all,"** is apt to increase conflict temporarily, and we can clarify this still further now. 4 At this point, the equality of <**having**> and <**being**> is not yet perceived. 5 Until **the equality of** <*having*> **and** <*being*> **is perceived,** <*having*> appears to be the opposite of <*giving.*> 6 Therefore, the first lesson,(**"To have, give all to all"),** seems to contain a contradiction, since **the first lesson, ("To have, give all to all"),** is being learned by a conflicted mind. 7 **A conflicted mind** means conflicting motivation, and so the lesson cannot be learned consistently as yet. 8 Further, the mind of the learner projects **the learner's own conflict,** and thus does not perceive consistency in the minds of others, making him suspicious of **the other's** motivation. 9 This is the real reason why, in many respects, the first lesson, (**"To have, give all to all"),** is the hardest **lesson** to learn. 10 Still strongly aware of the ego in yourself, and responding primarily to the ego in others, you are being taught to react to both **yours and the others' egos,** as if what you **egoically** do believe, **which is that giving and having are opposites,** is not true.

NOTE # 63: The Holy Spirit understands that having and being are the same. The Holy Spirit's thought system is actually your own true thought system. The egoic thought system's belief is "To have, take all from all." This is the opposite of what the Holy Spirit teaches, which is "To have, give all to all." Because we have been under the guidance of the ego, we now find ourselves in conflict with our true thought system of the Big "S" Self. The ego's thought system is "insane" because its major premise is incorrect. The ego's system is based on separation and the belief that you are an ego body rather than Mind or Spirit. These lessons of the Holy Spirit are a call to motivate you to change your belief in what you are. Until you abandon your belief that you are a body, you will remain conflicted as you seek to follow the guidance of the Holy Spirit. Conflict always follows when you seek to serve two masters. You must choose to follow only the Voice for Truth.

T-6.V.B.4. Upside down as always, the ego perceives the first lesson **of the Holy Spirit which was, "To have, give all to all,"** as insane. 2 In fact, **the belief by the ego that the lesson of the Holy Spirit is insane** is **the ego's** only alternative since the other possibility, which would be much less acceptable to **the ego**, would obviously be that <*the ego* > is insane. 3 The ego's judgment, here as always, is predetermined by what **the ego** is. 4 The fundamental change will still occur with the change of mind in the thinker. 5 Meanwhile, the increasing clarity of the Holy Spirit's Voice makes it impossible for the learner not to listen. 6 For a time, then, **the learner** is receiving conflicting messages and accepting both **messages**.

NOTE # 64: The two conflicting messages that we hear at this stage of our journey are:
   1) The ego's message is "To have. Take all from all." It is based on the belief that you are a separate body in competition with other ego-bodies.
   2) The Holy Spirit's message is, "To have, give all to all." It is based on the belief that you are unlimited mind or spirit, which is part of the Oneness that is the holographic Mind of God.

T-6.V.B.5. The way out of conflict between two opposing thought systems is clearly to choose one **thought system** and relinquish the other **thought system**. 2 If you identify with your thought system and you cannot escape this **identification with your thought system**, and if you accept two thought systems which are in complete disagreement, peace of mind is impossible. 3 If you teach both **thought systems**, which you will surely do as long as you accept both **thought systems**, you are teaching conflict and learning **conflict**. 4 Yet you do want peace, or you would not have called upon the Voice for peace to help you, **which is the Voice of the Holy Spirit**. 5 **The Holy Spirit's** lesson is not insane; the conflict is **insane.**

NOTE # 65: Until we value only the truth that we are unlimited Spirit, a part of the Oneness of everything, our split-mind will be in conflict. When we value specialness and oneness, we also guarantee a conflicted mind.

T-6.V.B.6. There can be no conflict between sanity and insanity. 2 Only one is true, and therefore only one is real. 3 The ego tries to persuade you that it is up to you to decide which voice is true, but the Holy Spirit teaches you that truth was created by God, and your decision cannot change **truth**. 4 As you begin to realize the quiet power of the Holy Spirit's Voice, and **the Holy Spirit's** perfect consistency, it must dawn on your mind that you are trying to undo a decision that was irrevocably made for you. 5 That is why I suggested before that you remind yourself to allow the Holy Spirit to decide for God for you.

NOTE # 66: The ego claims that we, not God, are the arbitrators for truth. Truth is not arbitrary. Truth just is. We cannot change what God created. Truth and reality are changeless. Because we have free will, we can dream that the truth is something it is not. This is what we do when we make our private world of provisional reality. We actively choose to follow the ego's belief system of separation and lack for its promise of specialness. Our miscreation does not change reality. The Holy Spirit consistently and lovingly calls us to reawaken from our dream and reaffirm what we truly are, God's Beloved Child.

T-6.V.B.7. You are not asked to make insane decisions, although you can think you are **asked to make insane decisions.** 2 It must, however, be insane to believe that it is up to you to decide what God's creations are. 3 The Holy Spirit perceives the conflict exactly as **the conflict** is. 4 Therefore, **the Holy Spirit's** second lesson is:

5 *To have peace, teach peace to learn* **peace**.

NOTE # 67: What you are, you automatically teach. To teach peace, you must be peace. Since perception follows our purpose, we most first decide what our purpose is. In this lesson, our decision-maker has decided that its learning objective is peace. Our future perceptions will now begin to align with our new purpose of achieving peace.

T-6.V.B.8. "To have peace, teach peace to learn peace," is still a preliminary step, since *<having>* and *<being>* are still not equated. 2 This **second step of "To have peace, teach peace to learn peace,"** is, however, more advanced than the first step, **which was "To have, give all to all,"** which is really only the beginning of the thought reversal. 3 The second step **of "To have peace, teach peace to learn peace,"** is a positive affirmation of what you want. 4 This **positive affirmation of what you want**, then, is a step in the direction out of conflict, since **this affirmation, "To have peace, teach peace to learn peace,"** means that alternatives have been considered, and one **alternative** has been chosen as more desirable **than the other alternative.** 5 Nevertheless, the term "more desirable" still implies that the desirable has degrees. 6 Therefore, although this step **is a positive affirmation of what you want and** is essential for the ultimate decision, **this second step** is clearly not the final **step.** 7 Lack of order of difficulty in miracles has not yet been accepted, because nothing is difficult that is *<wholly>* desired. 8 To desire wholly is to create, and creating cannot be difficult if God Himself created you as a creator.

NOTE # 68: In this lesson our decision-maker has reclaimed some of his power. He has considered some option and made a decision. Until we make a clear decision as to what we desire, it is difficult to create or make. Unless we choose that we want, our mind's creative power lies dormant. When we realize that we have lost our peace and we fail to choose again, we "waste" time.

T-6.V.B.9. The second step, **the positive affirmation "To have peace, teach peace to learn peace,"** then, is still perceptual, although **the second step** is a giant step toward the unified perception that reflects God's knowing. 2 As you take this step, **"To have peace, teach peace to learn peace,"** and hold this **second step's** direction, you will be pushing toward the center of your **egoic** thought system, where the fundamental change will occur. 3 At the second step progress is intermittent, but the second step is easier than the first **step** because **the second step** follows **the first step.** 4 Realizing that **the second step, which is "To have peace, teach peace to learn peace,"** *<must>* follow **the first step which was "To have, give all to all.,"** is a demonstration of a growing awareness that the Holy Spirit will lead you on **toward your mind's return to sanity and remembering who you really are, a Oneness as God created you.**

NOTE # 69: To achieve the Holy Spirit's goal of reawakening the sleeping mind, It must first release the mind's decision-making ability from egoic victim consciousness. Until we realize that our mind and not the outside world is the cause of our experience, we will not realize that we can choose again. When you believe you are powerless, there is no reason to choose differently. Only when we start to believe that our mind's decisions have consequence that cause and attract future experiences, does it matter what we think. Step number two continues us down the path to the idea that thoughts are things. It teaches that your ideas have creative power and determine your experience. We are beginning to realize that we make or create our own provisional reality. There are no innocent victims.

C. Be Vigilant Only for God and His Kingdom

T-6.V.C.1. We said before that the Holy Spirit is evaluative, and must be **evaluative**. 2 **The Holy Spirit** sorts out the true from the false in your mind, and **the Holy Spirit** teaches you to judge every thought you allow to enter **your mind** in the light of what God put there **in your mind**. 3 Whatever is in accord with this light **that God put in your mind, the Holy Spirit** retains, to strengthen the Kingdom in you. 4 What is partly in accord with **the Kingdom in you, the Holy Spirit** accepts and purifies. 5 But what is out of accord entirely **with the Kingdom in you, the Holy Spirit** rejects by judging against **what is out of accord entirely with the Kingdom in you**. 6 This is how **the Holy Spirit** keeps the Kingdom perfectly consistent and perfectly unified. 7 Remember, however, that what the Holy Spirit rejects the ego accepts. 8 This is because **the Holy Spirit and the ego** are in fundamental disagreement about everything, **since the Holy Spirit and the ego are** in fundamental disagreement about what you are. 9 The ego's beliefs on this crucial issue **about what you are** vary, and that is why **the ego** promotes different moods. 10 The Holy Spirit never varies on this point **about what you are**, and so the one mood **the Holy Spirit** engenders is joy. 11 **The Holy Spirit** protects **joy** by rejecting everything that does not foster joy, and so **the Holy Spirit** alone can keep you wholly joyous.

<u>**NOTE # 70:**</u> The Holy Spirit's role as the Voice for God requires that the Holy Spirit evaluate the correctness of what is perceived by your mind. The Holy Spirit's evaluation is always based on the knowledge that as Spirit you are as God created you. The Holy Spirit has both the ability to know because the Holy Spirit is part of God. He perceives and evaluates correctly because the Holy Spirit was sent by the Father to reawaken His sleeping Son to the truth. The Holy Spirit is the link between God and God's split-minded Son. The Holy Spirit reinterprets the ego's misperception in view of the fact that you are always God's Son as God created you. This reinterpretation judges what is out of accord with what you really are and guides you to chose again based on the thought system of the Holy Spirit.

T-6.V.C.2. The Holy Spirit does not teach you to judge others, because **the Holy Spirit** does not want you to teach error and learn **to judge others** yourself. 2 **The Holy Spirit** would hardly be consistent if **the Holy Spirit** allowed you to strengthen what you must learn to avoid **which is egoic judgment**. 3 In the mind of the thinker, then, **the Holy Spirit** <is> judgmental, but only in order to unify the mind so **the mind of the thinker** can perceive without judgment. 4 **By unifying the mind so the mind of the thinker can perceive without judgment, the Holy Spirit** enables the **student's** mind to teach without judgment, and therefore to learn to <be> without judgment. 5 The undoing **of the student's mind to teach without judgment, and therefore to learn to <be> without judgment,** is necessary only in your **split** mind, so that you will not project, instead of extend. 6 God Himself has established what you can extend with perfect safety. 7 Therefore, the Holy Spirit's third lesson is:

8 Be vigilant only for God and His Kingdom.

NOTE # 71: The ego is a judging machine, which is constantly judging in error. Since the ego's basic premise is faulty, its reasoning is equally flawed. The ego judges based on past misperceptions and thus, continues to perpetuate the errors of the past. The only correct judgment that we can make is that we are unable to judge correctly. We must not judge. We need to turn our perceptions over to the Holy Spirit for His evaluation and guidance.

T-6.V.C.3. This **Being vigilant only for God and His Kingdom** is a major step toward fundamental change. 2 Yet, **this third lesson of the Holy Spirit, "Be vigilant only for God and His Kingdom,"** still has an aspect of thought reversal, since b**eing vigilant only for God and His Kingdom** implies that there is something you must be vigilant <*against.*> 3 **This third lesson of the Holy Spirit, "Be vigilant only for God and His Kingdom,"** has advanced far from the first lesson, **"To have, give all to all,"** which is merely the beginning of the thought reversal, and also from the second **lesson of "To have peace, teach peace to learn peace,"** which is essentially the identification of what is more desirable. 4 **This third lesson or step of the Holy Spirit, which is "Be vigilant only for God and His Kingdom,** follows from the second **lesson.** The second **lesson of "To have peace, teach peace to learn peace,"** follows from the first **lesson, which was "To have, give all to all." The second lesson of "To have peace, teach peace to learn peace,"** emphasizes the dichotomy between the desirable and the undesirable. 5 **This third lesson or step of the Holy Spirit of being vigilant only for God and His Kingdom** therefore makes the ultimate choice inevitable.

NOTE # 72: The inevitable choice is that we will reject the thought system of the ego in favor of the Holy Spirit's thought system. Ultimately, there is only one viable choice since the choice for fantasy is the choice for nothingness. We must eventually choose for truth. The choice for God is inevitable since we share God's Will. Ultimately, God's Will and our will are the same since we are an extension of God, a part of God. Being only vigilant for God and His Kingdom is the decision for reality over illusion.

T-6.V.C.4. While the first step, **"To have, give all to all."** seems to increase conflict and the second **step, "To have peace, teach peace to learn peace."** may still entail conflict to some extent, this **third** step **of being vigilant only for God and His Kingdom,** calls for consistent vigilance against **conflict which arises from the ego's thought system.** 2 I have already told you that you can be as vigilant against the ego as for the ego. 3 This **third** lesson **of being vigilant only for God and His Kingdom** teaches not only that you can be **vigilant against the ego** but that you <*must*> be **vigilant against the ego. 4 This third lesson of being vigilant only for God and His Kingdom** does not concern itself with order of difficulty, but with clear-cut priority for vigilance **for only God, not the ego.** 5 **This third lesson of being vigilant only for God and His Kingdom,** is unequivocal in that **this third lesson** teaches there must be no exceptions, although **this third lesson of being vigilant only for God and His Kingdom** does not deny that the temptation to make exceptions will occur. 6 Here, then, your consistency is called on despite chaos. 7 Yet chaos and consistency cannot coexist for long, since **chaos and consistency** are mutually exclusive. 8 As long as you must be vigilant against anything, however, you are not recognizing this mutual exclusiveness, and still believe that you can choose either one **of the thought systems.** 9 By teaching <*what*> to choose, the Holy Spirit will ultimately teach you that you need not choose at all. 10 This will finally liberate your mind from choice, and direct **your mind** towards creation within the Kingdom.

NOTE # 73: Chaos represents the thought system of the ego. Because the egoic thought system is based on the false, this allows for many versions to exist. Thus, the ego's advice is constantly changing as its objectives shift. It is an unstable platform to base our universe upon. The Holy Spirit's thought system is always consistent because it is based on truth, which never changes. Knowledge, unlike perception, is not a matter of choice. Knowledge, like truth, just is. Choice resides in our mind's imagined world of perception.

T-6.V.C.5. Choosing through the Holy Spirit will lead you to the Kingdom. 2 You create by your true being, but what you are, (**your true being as a Son of God),** you must learn to remember. 3 The way to remember **your true being as a Son of God** is inherent in the third step **of being vigilant only for God and His Kingdom. This third step** brings together the lessons implied in the others, and goes beyond **the first two steps** towards real integration. **The first two step were "To have, give all to all" and "To have peace, teach peace to learn peace."** 4 If you allow yourself to have in your mind only what God put there, you are acknowledging your mind as God created **your mind.** 5 Therefore, you are accepting **your mind** as **your mind** is. 6 Since **your mind** is whole, you are teaching peace <*because*> you believe in **peace.** 7 The final step will still be taken for you by God, but by the third step **of being vigilant only for God and His Kingdom,** the Holy Spirit has prepared you for God. 8 **The Holy Spirit** is getting you ready for the translation of <*having*> into <*being*> by the very nature of the steps you must take with **the Holy Spirit.**

<u>NOTE # 74:</u> The Holy Spirit is slowly teaching us to move from egoic judgmental thinking to just being. Being is associated with experience or feeling. Being does not judge or figure things out, it just experiences. Egoic "having" is associated with the belief in lack, limitation and fear. When we choose the thought system of the Holy Spirit, we are starting to "live or be" the truth of what we are. We are being vigilant only for love.

T-6.V.C.6. You learn first that <*having*> rests on giving, and not on getting. 2 Next you learn that you learn what you teach, and that you want to learn peace. 3 This **wanting to learn peace** is the condition for identifying with the Kingdom, since **peace** is the condition <*of*> the Kingdom. 4 You have believed that you are without the Kingdom, and have therefore excluded yourself from **the peace of the Kingdom by** your belief **that you are without the Kingdom** 5 It is therefore essential to teach you that you must be included **with the Kingdom,** and that the belief that you are not **with the Kingdom** is the only thing that you must exclude.

<u>NOTE # 75:</u> Being part of the Oneness of Everything, our divine birthright is the Kingdom. It is only by our own denial of our heritage that we have decided to exclude ourselves from the Kingdom. This denial of our Source is self-imposed. Only when we accept the Atonement for ourselves, will we give ourselves permission to reawaken within the Kingdom. The Kingdom was never lost, we chose to forget the truth.

T-6.V.C.7. The third step **of being vigilant only for God and His Kingdom** is thus one of protection for your mind, allowing you to identify only with the center **for truth,** where God placed the altar to Himself. 2 Altars are beliefs, but God and His creations are beyond belief because **God and His creations** are beyond question. 3 The Voice for God speaks only for belief beyond question, which is the preparation for <*being*> without question. 4 As long as belief in God and His Kingdom is assailed by any doubts in your mind, **God's** perfect accomplishment, **which is you,** is not apparent to you. 5 This **belief in God and His Kingdom without any doubts in your mind** is why you must be vigilant on God's behalf. 6 The ego speaks against **God's** creation, and therefore **the ego** engenders doubt **in your mind.** 7 You cannot go beyond belief until you believe fully **that you are part of God's Kingdom.**

<u>NOTE # 76:</u> Our center is our One Self, which is our Big "S" Self. Altars are beliefs. What is your core belief? Are you an ego-body or Son of God? What thought or belief system is your altar built on? God's

altar is built on only truth. You are part of the Shared Oneness that is the Mind of God.

T-6.V.C.8. To teach the whole Sonship without exception demonstrates that you perceive **the whole Sonship's** wholeness, and have learned that **the Sonship** is one. 2 Now you must be vigilant to hold **the Sonship's** oneness in your mind because, if you let doubt enter **your mind**, you will lose awareness of **the Sonship's** wholeness and will be unable to teach **the Sonship's wholeness**. 3 The wholeness of the Kingdom does not depend on your perception **of the wholeness of the Kingdom**, but your awareness of **the Kingdom's** wholeness does **depend on your perception**. 4 It is only your awareness that needs protection, since being cannot be assailed. 5 Yet a real sense of being cannot be yours while you are doubtful of what you are. **6 Since a real sense of being cannot be yours while you are doubtful of what you are,** this is why vigilance **for God and His Kingdom** is essential. 7 Doubts about being must not enter your mind, or you cannot know what you are with certainty. 8 Certainty is of God for you. 9 Vigilance is not necessary for truth, but **vigilance** is necessary against illusions.

<u>NOTE # 77:</u> Our perception depends on our purpose. Will you be vigilant for the truth of wholeness or the illusion of separation?

T-6.V.C.9. Truth is without illusions and therefore **truth is** within the Kingdom. 2 Everything outside the Kingdom is illusion. 3 When you threw truth away **due to your belief in the separation,** you saw yourself as if you were without **the Kingdom**. 4 By making another kingdom that you valued, **which is the ego's kingdom of separation, specialness and individuality,** you did not keep <*only*> the Kingdom of God in your mind, and thus placed part of your mind outside **the Kingdom of God in your mind**. 5 What you made has imprisoned your will, and given you a sick mind that must be healed. 6 Your vigilance against this sickness **of the now split mind's allegiance to conflicting thought systems** is the way to heal sick mind. 7 Once your mind is healed **your mind** radiates health, and thereby teaches healing. 8 This **healed mind** establishes you as a teacher who teaches like me. 9 Vigilance was required of me as much as of you, and those who choose to teach the same thing must be in agreement about what they believe.

<u>NOTE # 78:</u> This placing of part of your mind outside the Kingdom of God is referred to as the splitting of your mind. This "splitting" only occurred in your provisional reality. It never occurred in the Mind of God, nor in your High Self, which is the Home of the Holy Spirit. It is only your belief that it occurred that makes it "real" to you. The "split mind" is a "sick mind." The ego's thought system, which is based on the belief in separation and lack, acts as a prison for your split mind. This prison can only be maintained by your ego convincing your mind that the mind is something that it is not. The ego tells the mind that it is a limited ego-body, not unlimited spirit. It is this mistaken identification of our mind as the body that forms the prison walls. The ego imprisons the mind by disempowering your decision-making ability to choose again. The split mind slips into victim consciousness. Your split mind is in conflict over the two opposing thought systems of the ego and the Holy Spirit. With step three, the decision-maker has decided to attempt to exclusively follow the thought system of the Holy Spirit.

T-6.V.C.10.The third step **of being vigilant only for God and His Kingdom** then, is a statement of what you want to believe, and entails a willingness to relinquish everything else. 2 The Holy Spirit will enable you to take this step **of being vigilant only for God and His Kingdom**, if you follow **the Holy Spirit's guidance**. 3 Your vigilance is the sign that you <*want*> **the Holy Spirit** to guide you. 4 Vigilance does require effort, but only until you learn that effort itself is unnecessary. 5 You have exerted great effort to preserve what you made because **what you made** was not true. 6 Therefore, you must now turn your effort against **what you made that was not true**. 7 Only this **effort and vigilance against what you made that was not true** can cancel out the need for effort, and call upon the being which you both *<have>* and *<are.>* 8 This recognition **of the being which you both *<have>* and *<are>*,** is wholly without effort since **the being which you both *<have>* and *<are>*** is already true and needs no protection. 9 **The being which you both *<have>* and *<are>*** is in the perfect safety of God. 10 Therefore, inclusion is total and creation is without limit.

NOTE # 79: The being which you both <have> and <are> requires no effort since this is what you truly are, which is God's Son. What does require effort and vigilance is the reawakening from the illusion in which you envision yourself to be a special and separate ego-body. This requires vigilance against the thought system of the ego. The "split or sick" mind must be healed and made whole. By the Atonement process, the Holy Spirit aids us in the healing of our split mind. Being what you are requires no effort since in the Mind of God you can only be as God created you, perfect whole and complete - an extension of God the Father. Effort is only required when you attempt to be something that you are not.

Chapter 7. THE GIFTS OF THE KINGDOM

I. The Last Step

T-7.I.1.The creative power of God and His creations is limitless, but **the creative power of God and His creations** are not in reciprocal relationship. 2 You communicate fully with God, as He does with you. 3 This **communication** is an ongoing process in which you share **with God**, and because you share **this communication**, you are inspired to create like God. 4 Yet in creation you are not in a reciprocal relation to God, since **God** created you but you did not create **God**. 5 I have already told you that only in this respect, **which is that God created you but you did not create God, is** your creative power **different** from **God's creative powers**. 6 Even in this world there is a parallel. 7 Parents give birth to children, but children do not give birth to parents. 8 **Children** do, however, give birth to their children, and thus give birth as their parents do.

Note # 1: We replicate God in every way except that God as First Cause created us. We are an Effect of God. Being an Effect of God, we do not have any ability to change our parent. We cannot be self-created as the ego claims that we are.

T-7.I.2.If you created God and **God** created you, the Kingdom could not increase through **the Kingdom's** own creative thought. 2 **If the Kingdom could not increase through the Kingdom's own creative thought**, creation would therefore be limited, and you would not be co-creator with God. 3 As God's creative Thought proceeds from **God** to you, so must your creative thought proceed from you to your creations. 4 Only in this way, **if your creative thought proceed from you to your creations,** can all creative power extend outward. 5 God's accomplishments are not your **accomplishments, but your accomplishments** are like **God's accomplishments**. 6 **God** created the Sonship and you increase **the Sonship**. 7 You have the power to add to the Kingdom, though not to add to the Creator of the Kingdom. 8 You claim this power **to add to the Kingdom** when you become vigilant only for God and **God's** Kingdom. 9 By accepting this power **to add to the Kingdom** as yours, you have learned to remember what you are.

Note # 2: When you are vigilant only for God and His kingdom, which is the third lesson of the Holy Spirit, you are able to create like God. At that moment you are under the guidance of the thought system of the Holy Spirit and are no longer coming from the ego's thought system of lack. You can only create like God when you know that you are God's Son, which is a co-creator with your Father.

T-7.I.3.Your creations belong in you, as you belong in God. 2 You are part of God, as your sons are part of His Sons. 3 To create is to love. 4 Love extends outward simply because **love** cannot be contained. 5

Being limitless **love** does not stop. 6 **Love** creates forever, but **love does** not **create** in time. 7 God's creations have always been, because **God** has always been. 8 Your creations have always been, because you can create only as God creates. 9 Eternity is yours, because **God** created you eternal.

Note # 3: Love does not create in time because time itself is only a learning device that arose from the separation. Due to this fact, time will dissolve or disappear when the Atonement process is completed. If love created in time, love's creations would not be eternal and, therefore, would be limited.

T-7.I.4. The ego, on the other hand, always demands reciprocal rights, because **the ego** is competitive rather than loving. 2 **The ego** is always willing to strike a bargain, but **the ego** cannot understand that to be like another means that no bargains are possible. 3 To gain you must give, not bargain. 4 To bargain is to limit giving, and **thus to bargain** is not God's Will. 5 To will with God is to create like **God**. 6 God does not limit **God's** gifts in any way. 7 You <are> **God's** gifts, and so your gifts must be like **God's gifts**. 8 Your gifts to the Kingdom must be like **God's** gifts to you.

Note # 4: To gain, you must give, not bargain. This statement is a natural result of the first lesson of the Holy Spirit, which is "To Have, Give All to All." When we bargain, we are looking for a "good trade" that will make us feel more complete than before. Yet, since bargaining means giving up something in return, the ego insures that we remain not whole and complete. We now lack what we give up in exchange.

T-7.I.5. I gave only love to the Kingdom because I believed that **love** was what I was. 2 What you believe you are determines your gifts, and if God created you by extending Himself as you, you can only extend yourself as **God** did. 3 Only joy increases forever, since joy and eternity are inseparable. 4 God extends outward beyond limits and beyond time and you who are co-creator with **God** extend **God's** Kingdom forever and beyond limit. 5 Eternity is the indelible stamp of creation. 6 The eternal are in peace and joy forever.

Note # 5: We were created to create like our Source. We cannot be happy unless we fulfill this function of extending the Oneness of everything.

T-7.I.6. To think like God is to share **God's** certainty of what you are, and to create like **God** is to share the perfect Love **God** shares with you. 2 To **share the perfect Love God shares with you,** the Holy Spirit leads you, that your joy may be complete because the Kingdom of God is whole. 3 I have said that the last step in the reawakening of knowledge is taken by God. **4 It is true that the last step in the reawakening of knowledge is taken by God,** but **this last step** is hard to explain in words because words are symbols, and nothing that is true need be explained. 5 However, the Holy Spirit has the task of translating the useless into the useful, the meaningless into the meaningful, and the temporary into the timeless. 6 **The Holy Spirit** can therefore tell you something about this last step **in the reawakening process, which is taken by God**.

Note # 6: The Holy Spirit takes our misperceptions and reinterprets them through the eyes of love. The Holy Spirit saves what can be transformed by forgiveness and love into something that can be shared throughout the Sonship. He disregards any illusions that are not transformable into love as unworthy of the Son of God.

T-7.I.7. God does not take steps, because **God's** accomplishments are not gradual. 2 **God** does not teach, because **God's** creations are changeless. 3 **God** does nothing last, because **God** created first and for always. 4 It must be understood that the word "first" as applied to **God** is not a time concept. 5 **God** is first in the sense that **God** is the First in the Holy Trinity Itself. 6 **God** is the Prime Creator, because **God** created **God's** co-creators. 7 Because **God** did, time applies neither to **God** nor to what **God** created. 8 The "last step" that God will take was therefore true in the beginning, is true now, and will be true forever. 9 What is timeless is always there, because its being is eternally changeless. 10 **What God created** does not change by increase, because **what God created** was forever created to increase. 11 If you perceive **what God created** as not increasing you do not know what **God's creation** is. 12 You also do not know Who created **what God created**. 13 God does not reveal this to you because **what God created** was never hidden. 14 His light was never obscured, because **His light** is His Will to share **His light.** 15 How can what is fully shared be withheld and then revealed?

Note # 7: God's creative powers follow that lesson of the Holy Spirit, "To Have All, Give All to All." In the creative process God gives all and, therefore, withholds nothing. Since when God creates nothing is withheld, there is nothing that was ever left out that could be revealed at some later time. God is First Cause. As First Cause, what God sourced into being was the ever-expanding changeless Love of God. Being Love, this is all God could extend because you can only give away what you are, have and be. Unconditional Love can only expand and extend outwardly remaining constantly perfect, whole and complete. Time measures change. Unconditional Love is changeless and, therefore, is timeless.

II. The Law of the Kingdom

T-7.II.1. To heal is the only kind of thinking in this world that resembles the Thought of God, and because of the elements **to healing and the Thought of God** share, **to heal** can transfer easily to **the Thought of God.** 2 When a brother perceives himself as sick, **a brother** is perceiving himself as not whole, and therefore in need. 3 If you, too, see him **sick and, therefore, in need**, you are seeing **your brother** as if **your brother** were absent from the Kingdom or separated from **the Kingdom**, thus making the Kingdom itself obscure to both you **and your brother.** 4 Sickness and separation are not of God, but the Kingdom is **of God.** 5 If you obscure the Kingdom, you are perceiving what is not of God.

Note # 8: When we perceive based on fear, we feel that we must protect and guard others or ourselves from the fear and danger. When fear enters into the picture, we are denying that we are invulnerable spirit and accepting the belief that we are a limited ego-body. This gives the illusion a false power and makes it appear real within our own mind. If you agree that a brother needs to be "fixed," you are confirming his belief that he is not perfect, whole and complete. You are allowing his illusion to become yours. By his sharing and you accepting his idea of sickness, you have strengthened this false idea. When you heal, you deny the false and allow only the truth to shine forth.

T-7.II.2. To heal, then, is to correct **the wrong** perception in your brother and yourself by sharing the Holy Spirit with **your brother.** 2 This places you both within the Kingdom, and restores **the Kingdom's** wholeness in your mind. 3 This reflects creation, because **to heal places you both within the Kingdom and, therefore, this** unifies by increasing and integrates by extending. 4 What you project or extend is real for you. 5 **What you project or extend is real for you** is an immutable law of the mind in this world as well as in the Kingdom. 6 However, the content is different in this world, because the thoughts **in this world that the law of mind** governs are very different from the Thoughts in the Kingdom. **The law of mind is that what you project or extend is real for you.** 7 Laws must be adapted to circumstances if they are to maintain order. 8 The outstanding characteristic of the laws of mind as operate in this world is that by obeying **the laws of mind**, and I assure you that you must obey **the laws of mind,** you can arrive at diametrically opposed results. 9 This **diametrically opposed result** is because the laws have been adapted to the circumstances of this world, in which diametrically opposed outcomes seem possible because you can respond to two conflicting voices.

<u>Note # 9:</u> Our provisional reality is a world in which we believe that we are the arbitrator of truth. We believe that we can decide between the true and the false and by choosing the false, make the false real and the true unreal. Only in illusions does this appear possible since the law of mind is that what you project or extend is real for you. Outside the deluded mind of the dreamer, the illusion, which is thought projection, has no power to change the real world, which ACIM calls the Kingdom.

Because you believe that you are separate in your world of provisional reality, there are two voices that you can follow. Each voice supports opposite conclusions. By following the voice for egoic fear, your dream world becomes a very scary and real place to you. By following the Holy Spirit's voice, you are called to remember that you are Spirit, a Oneness of God. The ego leads you to a world of limitation, pain, guilt, and fear. The Holy Spirit leads you back to the truth of the Kingdom.

T-7.II.3. Outside the Kingdom, the law that prevails inside **the Kingdom** is adapted to "What you project you believe." 2 **"What you project you believe" is the law of mind that prevails outside the Kingdom's."** What you project you believe" is **this law's adapted** teaching form **outside the Kingdom**, because outside the Kingdom learning is essential. 3 This **adapted** form **of the law of mind, which is "What you project you believe,"** implies that you will learn what you are from what you have projected onto others, and therefore believe **the others** are **what you have projected onto them.** 4 In the Kingdom there is no teaching or learning, because there is no belief. 5 There is only certainty **in the Kingdom.** 6 God and His Sons, in the surety of being, know that what you extend you are. 7 That form of the law is not adapted at all, being the law of creation. 8 God Himself created the law by creating <by> **the law of creation, which is "when you create, you extend the totality of what you are and thus, what you extend you are."** 9 And His Sons, who create like Him, follow **the law of creation** gladly, knowing that the increase of the Kingdom depends on **the law of creation,** just as their own creation did **depend on the law of creation**.

<u>Note # 10:</u> In the Kingdom, there is no teaching or learning, because there is knowledge. Knowledge is truth and therefore just is. In the world of time and perception, knowledge has been lost and has been replaced by perception.
The Law of creation is the total extension of everything that you are. It states that what you extend you are. When God created, nothing was held back. Being All, God gave All. In the world of our provisional reality this law has been modified to fit your viewpoint that you are a limited ego-body. The law is modified to read' "What you project you believe." This modification is necessary because you cannot create if you believe that you are a limited ego-body. Creation is extension of what you really are, which is an unlimited Son of God. When we are under the guidance of the ego, we believe that we are something we are not. We believe that we are a limited ego-body. Because we project outside ourselves something that we are not, what we perceive back is what we projected out. This reflection, confirms our belief in how we perceive ourselves to be and thus, we conclude that we are a limited ego-body. If the law of creation, "What you extend you are," was not modified when applied outside the Kingdom, our belief in separation would force us to become something God did not create, an ego-body. If this were the case, God's Will would not be honored and we would be changing God, which is the First Cause. It is impossible for an effect to change its cause. Because an effect cannot change its cause, extension belongs in the Kingdom (the Mind of God), and projection is held outside the Kingdom and

confined to our imagined dream world of provisional reality, perception, time and space.

T-7.II.4. Laws must be communicated if they are to be helpful. 2 In effect, Laws must be translated for those who speak different languages. 3 Nevertheless, a good translator, although he must alter the form of what he translates, **a good translator** never changes the meaning. 4 In fact, **a good translator's** whole purpose is to change the form so that the original meaning is retained. 5 The Holy Spirit is the Translator of the laws of God to those who do not understand **the laws of God**. 6 You could not **translate the laws of God** yourself because a conflicted mind cannot be faithful to one meaning, and will therefore change the meaning to preserve the form.

<u>Note # 11:</u> Only the Holy Spirit knows the big picture and can properly interpret our experiences to align with the truth. The ego, not knowing the truth, cannot uphold to truth. To the ego, the illusion of form is more important than the content, which is the true message.

T-7.II.5. The Holy Spirit's purpose in translating is exactly the opposite **of changing the meaning to preserve the form.** 2 **The Holy Spirit** translates only to preserve the original meaning in all respects and in all languages. 3 Therefore, the Holy Spirit opposes the idea that differences in form are meaningful, emphasizing always that <these differences **in form** do not matter.> 4 The meaning of **the Holy Spirit's** message is always the same; only the meaning matters. 5 God's law of creation does not involve the use of truth to convince **God's** Sons of truth. 6 The extension of truth, which <is> the law of the Kingdom, rests only on the knowledge of what truth is. 7 This **knowledge of what truth is** is your inheritance and requires no learning at all, but when you disinherited yourself you became a learner of necessity.

<u>Note # 12:</u> The Holy Spirit resides in and as our Big "S" Self and retains knowledge. We never truly lose our connection to our Source. The Holy Spirit protects and preserves our divine inheritance until our split mind is healed through relearning and acceptance of the truth.

T-7.II.6. No one questions the connection of learning and memory. 2 Learning is impossible without memory since **learning** must be consistent to be remembered. 3 That is why the Holy Spirit's teaching is a lesson in remembering. 4 I said before that **the Holy Spirit** teaches remembering and forgetting, but the forgetting is only to make the remembering consistent. 5 You forget in order to remember better. 6 You will not understand **the Holy Spirit's** translations while you listen to two ways of interpreting **these translations.** 7 Therefore you must forget or relinquish one to understand the other. 8 This **forgetting and relinquishing one thought system's interpretation to understand the other thought system's interpretation,** is the only way you can learn consistency, so that you can finally <be> consistent.

<u>Note # 13:</u> You listen to both the ego's and Holy Spirit's interpretation of what you perceive. Therefore, the Holy Spirit's goal is to help you remember what He teaches and to forget what the ego teaches. Until you follow only the Holy Spirit's teachings, you will be inconsistent.

T-7.II.7. What can the perfect consistency of the Kingdom mean to those who are confused? 2 It is apparent that confusion interferes with meaning, and therefore prevents the learner from appreciating **the meaning.** 3 There is no confusion in the Kingdom, because there is only one meaning. 4 This **one** meaning comes from God and <is> God. **God is Love.** 5 Because **this one meaning** is also you, you share **this one meaning** and extend **this one meaning** as your Creator did. 6 This **one meaning** needs no translation because **this one meaning** is perfectly understood, but **this one meaning** does need extension because **this one meaning** <means> extension. 7 Communication is perfectly direct and perfectly united. 8 Communication is totally free, because nothing discordant ever enters. 9 That is why communication is the Kingdom of God. 10 **Communication** belongs to **God** and is therefore like **God**. 11 That is **the Kingdom's** reality and nothing can assail **the Kingdom's reality.**

<u>Note # 14:</u> In the kingdom, which is the Mind of God, there is only being. Knowledge has not been lost and what is true just is. There is only one meaning since there is only undifferentiated Oneness. The Mind is whole and one. God being Love, the one meaning is love. You, being an extension of God, can only be love. Love is extension. Love is universal and needs no translation. Love needs to be shared or extended and this is how we communicate love. Love is life. Love is the reality of the Kingdom. Only love is real since only unconditional love is changeless. Love is all that is; one meaning, one message, one reality.

III. The Reality of the Kingdom

T-7.III.1. The Holy Spirit teaches one lesson, and applies **one lesson** to all individuals in all situations. 2 Being conflict-free, **the Holy Spirit** maximizes all efforts and all results. 3 By teaching the power of the Kingdom of God Himself, **the Holy Spirit** teaches you that all power is yours. 4 **The power of the Kingdom of God's** application does not matter. 5 **The power of the Kingdom of God** is always maximal. 6 Your vigilance does not establish **the power of the Kingdom of God** as your **power**, but **your vigilance** does enable you to use **the power of the Kingdom of God** always and in all ways. 7 When I said "I am with you always," I meant it literally. 8 I am not absent to anyone in any situation. 9 Because I am always with you, <*you*> are the way, the truth and the life. 10 You did not make this power **of the power of the Kingdom of God**, any more than I **made this power of the Kingdom of God**. 11 **The power of the Kingdom of God** was created to be shared, and, therefore, **the power of the Kingdom of God** cannot be meaningfully perceived as belonging to anyone at the expense of another. 12 Such a perception makes **the power of the Kingdom of God** meaningless by eliminating or overlooking **the power of the Kingdom of God's** real and only meaning **which is sharing.**

<u>Note # 15:</u> Truth is the power of the Kingdom of God. God is love and being love He extended Himself totally to all of Creation. There is no separation; just the extension of the Oneness that is the Mind of God. God shares completely "All That He Is."

T-7.III.2. God's meaning waits in the Kingdom, because that is where **God** placed **His meaning**. 2 **God's meaning** does not wait in time. 3 **God's meaning** merely rests in the Kingdom because **God's meaning** belongs **in the Kingdom** there, as you **belong in the Kingdom**. 4 How can you who are God's meaning perceive yourself as absent from **God's meaning and the Kingdom**? 5 You can see yourself as separated from your meaning only by experiencing yourself as unreal. 6 This is why the ego is insane; **the ego** teaches that you are not what you are. 7 **The ego's teaching that you are not what you are,** is so contradictory **the ego's teaching** is clearly impossible. 8 **The ego's teaching that you are not what you are,** is therefore a lesson you cannot really learn, and therefore **you** cannot really teach **the ego's teaching that you are not what you are**. 9 Yet you are always teaching. 10 You must, therefore, be teaching something else, even though the ego does not know what **your teaching** is. 11 **Because you are always teaching even though the ego does not know what your teaching is,** the ego, then, is always being undone, and does suspect your motives **since the ego does not know what you are really teaching.** 12 Your mind cannot be unified in allegiance to the ego, because the mind does not belong to

the ego. 13 Yet what is "treacherous" to the ego, **(your mind's Big "S" Self),** is faithful to peace. 14 The ego's "enemy", **(your mind's Big "S" Self),** is therefore your friend.

<u>Note # 16</u>: God's meaning is you, which is only an extension of God's Love. God is Cause and we are God's Effect. We, or Creation, are the extension of God's Love. God's meaning is not found in your dream world of provisional reality because your dream does not exist in the Mind of God. It is not found in time since both time and space are temporary teaching devices only found in your transitory world of provisional reality. Provisional reality, time and space all are outside the Kingdom and thus, are not part of the Mind of God. They appear to reside only within the imagination of the mind of the dreamer.
You are God's meaning and anytime that you believe yourself to be something that you are not, this something can only exist in your own provisional reality. It cannot exist in the Mind of God, which is changeless and real. Your Real Self never left the Mind of God. Only due to your split-mind's belief in the dream world can you imagine what you are not. Our imagination is the tool that allows us to perceive ourselves as something we are not and yet remain totally safe in the truth of what we are. Our imagination has no ability to change the truth. You are God's Kingdom and God's Kingdom is what you are. There is just a wholeness and oneness in love.

T-7.III.3.I said before that the ego's friend, **the body,** is not part of you, because the ego perceives itself at war and therefore in need of allies. 2 You who are not at war must look for brothers and recognize all whom you see as brothers, because only equals are at peace. 3 Because God's equal Sons have everything, **God's equal Sons** cannot compete. 4 Yet if **God's equal Sons** perceive any of their brothers as anything other than their perfect equals, the idea of competition has entered **into the minds of God's equal Sons.** 5 Do not underestimate your need to be vigilant <*against*> this idea **that God's equal sons are somehow not equal,** because all your conflicts come from **this idea that God's equal sons are somehow not equal.** 6 **That God's equal sons are somehow not equal** <*is*> the belief that conflicting interests are possible, and therefore you have accepted the impossible **belief that conflicting interests are possible,** as true. 7 Is that different from saying you perceive yourself as unreal?

<u>Note # 18:</u> Equality of Sons of God allows for Oneness. Without equality, you would lack something. There would be something outside yourself that you are not. Competition is the natural result of inequality since now there are limited things and, therefore, to get I must take. Due to our belief in lack of equality, we have specialness and differentiation that allow for the concept of winners and loser. Because they are equal, God's Children have everything and they are everything. If we view the split-minded Sonship as a true hologram, we can understand how each part would contain the whole and the whole would be in each part. With the acceptance of the holographic nature of the Mind of God, competition and conflict disappear. Everyone already has "All That Is."

T-7.III.4. To be in the Kingdom is merely to focus your full attention on **the Kingdom.** 2 As long as you believe you can attend to what is not true, you are accepting conflict as your choice. 3 Is **your belief that you can attend to what is not true** really a choice? 4 **Your belief that you can attend to what is not true** seems to be **a choice,** but seeming and reality are hardly the same. 5 You who <*are*> the Kingdom are not concerned with seeming. 6 Reality is yours because you are reality. 7 This is how <*having*> and <*being*> are ultimately reconciled, not in the Kingdom, but in your mind. 8 The altar there is the only reality. 9 The altar is perfectly clear in thought, because **the altar** is a reflection of perfect Thought. 10 Your right mind sees only brothers, because **your right mind** sees only in its own light, **which is truth.**

<u>Note # 19:</u> The altar is your truth. The altar is your core truth of what you really are. You can temporarily choose to worship or believe that you are something you are not, but you cannot change

what God created since you abide in the Mind of God. You can build a temporary altar to egoic idols that represent your belief in the false but you can never destroy God's altar, which is your One Self. Your real altar is your "right mind." Your right mind sees equality in all it perceives. Your right mind's full attention is on the truth of what you really are as Spirit and a Son of God. The Son of God is God's Kingdom. The altar is the reflection of this perfect thought.

T-7.III.5. God has lit your mind Himself, and **God** keeps your mind lit by **God's** light because **God's** light is what your mind is. 2 **God keeps your mind lit** is totally beyond question, and when you question **if God keeps your mind lit,** you are answered. 3 The Answer merely undoes the question by establishing the fact that to question reality is to question meaninglessly. 4 **The fact that to question reality is to question meaninglessly** is why the Holy Spirit never questions. 5 **The Holy Spirit's** sole function is to undo the questionable and thus lead to certainty. 6 The certain are perfectly calm, because **the certain** are not in doubt. 7 **The certain** do not raise questions, because nothing questionable enters **the** minds **of the certain**. 8 This **having no questions** holds **the certain** in perfect serenity **with the truth**, because this is what **the certain** share, knowing what they are.

<u>Note # 20:</u> Reality is reality. The truth is reality. To question the truth is useless since questioning the truth cannot change the truth. It can only open the door to your own doubt. The Holy Spirit's purpose is to remove all doubt, which will ultimately lead to certainty. We need to be certain of the truth of what we are. By accepting the Atonement for ourselves, we become certain. What can be more certain than not to have any questions, or doubts, about the truth? Perception leads to doubt since perception is always subject to interpretation. Knowledge is not perception since knowledge simply knows the true. Knowledge is certain. The Holy Spirit's role is to reawaken your mind to the truth of what you are. You are God's Kingdom for that is what you are. This is God's Will. Only love is real and you are only love.

IV. Healing as the Recognition of Truth

T-7.IV.1.Truth can only <be> recognized and **truth** <need> only be recognized. 2 Inspiration is of the Holy Spirit, and certainty is of God according to **God's** laws. 3 Both, **inspiration and certainty**, therefore, come from the same Source, since inspiration comes from the Voice for God and certainty comes from the laws of God. 4 Healing does not come directly from God, **since God the Father,** knows His creations as perfectly whole. 5 Yet healing is still of God, because **healing** proceeds from **God's** Voice and from **God's** laws. 6 **Healing proceeds as the** result **of God's Voice and God's laws** in a state of mind that does not know **God**. 7 The state **of the split-mind that does not know God and therefore requires healing** is unknown to **God, the Father,** and therefore does not exist, but those who sleep are unaware **that a state of mind that does not know God cannot exist.** 8 Because **those who sleep** are unaware, **these split-minds** do not know **themselves as prefect creations of God, the Father., and therefore believe they can be something other than whole and perfect.**

<u>Note # 21:</u> When it says that healing does not come from God since God knows his creations as perfect, we are speaking of God the Father. God the Father is the source of all. He is the original, first and primary source of everything. God the Father extended Himself, Who is only Love and only knows His

Creations as this truth because that is what God, is. Our misperceptions are not part of the truth and, therefore, are not known by God the Father.

God's Voice is the Holy Spirit's. The Holy Spirit knows the truth like God the Father, but also has the ability to be aware that God's Son has forgotten, or lost, his true nature and has fallen into a "deep sleep." This allows the Holy Spirit to reinterpret the misperception of our ego-based dreams and thus, reawaken or heal our dreaming split-mind.

The state of mind that is asleep is under the guidance of the ego's thought system, which believes in separation and individuality. Because they believe in the separation, truth's certainty has given away to perception. The split–minded fails to remember what it is. In contrast, the Father always and only knows His creations as He created them. His creations have never left His Mind. Because the split-minded do not know themselves as prefect creations of God, the Father, they believe they can be something other than love. The Holy Spirit utilizes the truth and God's Laws to teach the sleeping mind to heal its belief system and thus, return itself to whole-mindedness.

T-7.IV.2. The Holy Spirit must work <*through*> you to teach you **the Holy Spirit** is <*in*> you. 2 **Teaching you that the Holy Spirit is <*in*> you,** is an intermediary step toward the knowledge that you are in God because you are part of **God** 3 The miracles the Holy Spirit inspires can have no order of difficulty, because every part of creation is of one order. **This one order is the Oneness of Everything that is God.** 4 **That every part of creation is of one order** is God's Will and your **will.** 5 The laws of God establish **that every part of creation is of one order**, and the Holy Spirit reminds you **that every part of creation is of one order.** 6 When you heal, you are remembering the laws of God and forgetting the laws of the ego. 7 I said before that forgetting is merely a way of remembering better. 8 **Forgetting** is therefore not the opposite of remembering when **forgetting** is properly perceived. 9 Perceived improperly **forgetting** induces a perception of conflict with something else, as all incorrect perception does **induce a perception of conflict with something else.** 10 Properly perceived **forgetting** can be used as a way out of conflict, as all proper perception can **be used as a way out of conflict.**

<u>Note # 22:</u> The Holy Spirit guides you to forget the thought system of the ego. Once forgotten, the Voice for God, the Holy Spirit, remains unchallenged. There are no longer two thought systems to conflict with each other. When we forget our egoic misperception, we are only left with correct perception.

T-7.IV.3. The ego does not want to teach everyone all **the ego** has learned, because **to teach everyone all the ego has learned** would defeat **the ego's** purpose. 2 Therefore **the ego** does not really learn at all. 3 The Holy Spirit teaches you to use what the ego has made, **and** to teach the opposite of what the ego has "learned." 4 The kind of learning is as irrelevant as is the particular ability that was applied to the learning. 5 All you need do is make the effort to learn, for the Holy Spirit has a unified goal for the effort. 6 If different abilities are applied long enough to one goal, the abilities themselves become unified. 7 **The abilities themselves become unified** because **the different abilities** are channelized in one direction, or in one way. 8 Ultimately, then, **the different abilities that are channelized in one direction,** all contribute to one result, and by so doing, **the different abilities'** similarity rather than **the different abilities'** differences **are** emphasized.

<u>Note # 23:</u> The Holy Spirit reinterprets based of the truth and the Laws of God what the ego's thought system has misperceived. The Holy Spirit knows that you and your brother are One Self, which is the Big "S" Self, but the Holy Spirit is also aware of your dream world in which you believe you have lost your birthright as a Child of God. The one goal of the Holy Spirit is to reawaken you to your spiritual magnificence. If allowed, the Holy Spirit will take all egoic misperceptions and convert them into

witnesses for the reuniting and healing of the Sonship.

T-7.IV.4. All abilities should therefore be given over to the Holy Spirit, Who understands how to use them properly. 2 **The Holy Spirit** uses **all abilities** only for healing, because **the Holy Spirit** knows you only as whole. 3 By healing you learn of wholeness, and by learning of wholeness you learn to remember God. 4 You have forgotten **God**, but the Holy Spirit understands that your forgetting must be translated into a way of remembering.

<u>Note # 24:</u> The Holy Spirit takes everything that the ego claims will prove that the separation was real and translates them into correct perception that then witnesses only for the truth that only love is real. This is the call for the remembrance of God.

T-7.IV.5. The ego's goal is as unified as the Holy Spirit's, and it is because of this that **the ego's and Holy Spirit's** goals can never be reconciled in any way or to any extent. 2 The ego always seeks to divide and separate. 3 The Holy Spirit always seeks to unify and heal. 4 As you heal you are healed, because the Holy Spirit sees no order of difficulty in healing. 5 Healing is the way to undo the belief in differences, being the only way of perceiving the Sonship as one. 6 This perception **that there is no differences in the Sonship** is therefore in accord with the laws of God, even in a state of mind that is out of accord with **God's Mind**. 7 The strength of right perception is so great that **right perception** brings the mind into accord with **God's Mind**, because **right perception** serves **God's** Voice, **which is the Holy Spirit**, which is in all of you.

<u>Note # 25:</u> The only way to perceive the Sonship as one is to remove all misperceptions in your mind that God's Sons are not equal. Equality results on Oneness. Right perception brings the split-mind into proper alignment with your Big "S" Self's state of awareness. Your Big "S" Self is the home of the Holy Spirit and right perception.

T-7.IV.6. To think you can oppose the Will of God is a real delusion. 2 The ego believes that **the ego can oppose the Will of God**, and that **the ego** can offer you **the ego's** own "will" as a gift. 3 <*You do not want the ego's own "will" as a gift.*> 4 **The ego's own "will"** is not a gift. 5 **The ego's own "will"** is nothing at all. 6 God has given you a gift, **which is the shared Will of God,** that you both <*have*> and <*are.*> 7 When you do not use **the gift of God's Will**, you forget that you have **the gift of God's Will**. 8 By not remembering **the gift of God's Will**, you do not know what you are. 9 Healing, then, is a way of approaching knowledge by thinking in accordance with the laws of God, and recognizing **the laws of God's** universality. 10 Without this recognition **of the universality of God's laws**, you have made the laws **of God** meaningless to you. 11 Yet the laws **of God** are not meaningless, since all meaning is contained by **the laws of God** and in **the laws of God**.

<u>Note # 26:</u> God's laws apply in all situations. Even in the dream world of perception and separation, God's Laws apply. The dreamer is not aware that they apply and thus, is under the delusion that his dream has actually changed God's Will. Yet once reawakened, the dreamer discovers that the illusion had no effect on the reality that is the Mind of God. God's laws have maintained the Oneness of the Truth that only love is real.

T-7.IV.7. Seek ye first the Kingdom of Heaven, because that is where the laws of God operate truly, and **the laws of God** can operate only truly because **the laws of God** are the laws of truth. 2 But seek only **the laws of God**, because you can find nothing else. 3 There <*is*> nothing else. 4 God is All in all in a very literal sense. 5 All being is in **God** Who is all Being. 6 You are therefore in **God** since your being is **God's Being**. 7 Healing is a way of forgetting the sense of danger the ego has induced in you, by not recognizing **the ego's** existence in your brother. 8 This strengthens the Holy Spirit in both **you and your brother,** because **by not recognizing the ego's existence in your brother, this** is a refusal to acknowledge fear. 9 Love needs only this invitation**, which is your refusal to acknowledge fear.** 10 **Love** comes freely to all the Sonship, **love** being what the Sonship is. 11 By your awakening to **love,** you are merely forgetting what you are not. 12 This **forgetting what you are not** enables you to remember what you are.

Note # 27: The ego's goal is to divide and separate. The Holy Spirit's goal is to unify and heal. As you heal, you are healed. Healing is the undoing of the belief in differences that arose as a result of your belief in the separation. Difference is the lure of the egoic thought system since differences allow us to claim that we are special. It is this desire to be special that keeps us under the influence of the egoic thought system. Undoing the belief of specialness and differences within the Sonship allows you to perceive yourself and your brother as one with a common goal. Right perception has the power to heal the "sick or split-minded" and bring them back into accord with their Big "S" Self and the Will of God. When we heal, we align with God and our Big "S" Self. We realize the truth that love is all there is and we are that One.

V. Healing and the Changelessness of Mind

T-7.V.1. The body is nothing more than a framework for developing abilities, which is quite apart from what **developing abilities** are used for. 2 <*What developing abilities are used for,*> is a decision. 3 The effects of the ego's decision in this matter **of what developing abilities are used for** are so apparent that **what developing abilities are used for** need no elaboration, but the Holy Spirit's decision to use the body only for communication has such a direct connection with healing that **the Holy Spirit's decision to use the body only for communication** does need clarification. 4 The unhealed healer obviously does not understand his own vocation.

Note #28: The ego uses our developed abilities for the purpose of demonstrating that you are indeed special and different from your brother. This specialness verifies your individuality and, therefore, your belief in the separation is increased. The ego's purpose is always to try to confirm the impossible. The ego claims that you have the option and ability to decide not to do God's Will. It attempts to show that you somehow self-created yourself. To the ego, the body and our abilities are used for attacking other parts of the unified Sonship, which is an attack upon your Big "S" Self's reality.

T-7.V.2. Only minds communicate. 2 Since the ego cannot obliterate the impulse to communicate because **to communicate** is also the impulse to create, **the ego** can only teach you that the body can both communicate and create, and therefore **the body** does not need the mind. 3 The ego thus tries to teach you that the body can act like the mind, and **that the body** is therefore self-sufficient. 4 Yet we have learned that behavior is not the level for either teaching or learning, since you can act in accordance with what **your Big "S" Self does** not believe. 5 To **act in accordance with what your Big "S" Self does not believe,** however, will weaken you as a teacher and a learner because, as has been repeatedly emphasized, you teach what you <do> believe. 6 An inconsistent lesson will be poorly taught and poorly learned. 7 If you teach both sickness <and> healing, you are both a poor teacher and a poor learner.

Note # 29: Since only mind can communicate and to communicate is to create, the ego attempts to confuse the mind into thinking that the mind is really part of the body. When the mind comes under the guidance of the ego's thought system, the mind confuses itself with the body. The "split mind" sees itself as limited and separated just like the body. In this state of limitation and fear, the mind can only make (miscreate) and misperceive. In order to correct this state, we need to control our fear and ask for the guidance of the Holy Spirit.

Note # 30: The split mind teaches both sickness and healing due to its confusion about what you are. The ego tells you that you are a body. Yet your Big "S" Self and Holy Spirit know the truth that you are spirit. If you perceive yourself as a body, you will act accordingly. You will use the body for attack and thus, your behavior will support the idea of separation. Are you God's Son, under the guidance of the Holy Spirit's thought system? Or, are you an ego-body, under the guidance of the ego's thought system?

T-7.V.3. Healing is the one ability everyone can develop and **one's ability to heal** must develop if he, **the healer**, is to be healed. 2 Healing is the Holy Spirit's form of communication in this world, and the only **form of communication that the Holy Spirit** accepts. 3 **The Holy Spirit** recognizes no other **form of communication**, because **the Holy Spirit** does not accept the ego's confusion of mind and body. 4 Minds can communicate, but **minds** cannot hurt. 5 The body in the service of the ego can hurt other bodies, but this **ability of the body to hurt other bodies** cannot occur unless the body has already been confused with the mind. 6 This situation, too, **confusing the body with the mind,** can be used either for healing or for magic, but you must remember that magic always involves the belief that healing is harmful. 7 This belief **of confusing the body with the mind and therefore believing that the body has the some powers and abilities of the minds'** is **the ego's** totally insane premise, and so **the ego** proceeds accordingly.

Note # 31: The goal of the ego's thought system is to make the mind believe that it is something that it is not. When you identify your mind as the body, your mind has forgotten what you are. You have forgotten that all seeming separate parts are all one and equal. Spirit cannot be divided or made limited.

T-7.V.4. Healing only strengthens. 2 Magic always tries to weaken. 3 Healing perceives nothing in the healer that everyone else does not share with **the healer**. 4 Magic always sees something "special" in the healer, which **the healer** believes **the healer** can offer as a gift to someone who does not have **the gift of something "special" that the healer possesses.** 5 **The healer** may believe that the gift **of the something "special" that the healer possesses** comes from God to **the healer**, but it is quite evident that **the healer** does not understand God if **the healer** thinks **the healer** has something that others lack.

Note # 32: In order to heal, the healer must see the equality and truth in all. The healer must see his brother's High Self and teach his brother this truth that all brothers are equal Children of God. If the healer believes that he has special gifts to give, he does not come from equality but rather from belief in lack and specialness. Magic always involves the belief in specialness and means someone must lack what the "healer" has.

T-7.V.5. The Holy Spirit does not work by chance, and healing that is of **the Holy Spirit** <always> works. 2 Unless the healer always heals by **the Holy Spirit,** the results will vary. 3 Yet healing itself is consistent, since only consistency is conflict-free, and only the conflict-free are whole. 4 By accepting exceptions and acknowledging that **the healer** can sometimes heal and sometimes not, the healer is obviously accepting inconsistency. 5 **The healer** is therefore in conflict, and **the healer** is teaching conflict. 6 Can anything of God not be for all and for always? 7 Love is incapable of any exceptions. 8

Only if there is fear does the idea of exceptions seem to be meaningful. 9 Exceptions are fearful because **any exceptions** are made by fear. 10 The "fearful healer" is a contradiction in terms, and **the "fearful healer"** is therefore a concept that only a conflicted mind could possibly perceive as meaningful.

Note # 33: The "fearful healer" does not see the Oneness of everything, in everything.
He still perceives the separation to be real and thus, correction of sickness or belief in split-mindedness requires a force outside the mind of the sick person. Healing always takes place within the mind of the "sick" person. It is the "sick" person's correction of their own error in thinking that takes place. The healer merely helps them see the light of truth within themselves.

T-7.V.6. Fear does not gladden. 2 Healing does **gladden.** 3 Fear always makes exceptions. 4 Healing never **makes exceptions**. 5 Fear produces dissociation, because **fear** induces separation. 6 Healing always produces harmony, because **healing** proceeds from integration. 7 **Healing** is predictable because **healing** can be counted on. 8 Everything that is of God can be counted on, because everything of God is wholly real. 9 Healing can be counted on because **healing** is inspired by God's Voice, **which is the Voice of the Holy Spirit**, and is in accord with **God's** laws. 10 Yet if healing is consistent, **healing** cannot be inconsistently understood. 11 Understanding means consistency because God means consistency. 12 Since **consistency** is **God's** meaning, **consistency** is also **your meaning**. 13 Your meaning cannot be out of accord with **God's meaning,** because your whole meaning and your only meaning comes from **God's meaning** and is like **God's meaning**. 14 God cannot be out of accord with Himself, and you cannot be out of accord with **God**. 15 You cannot separate your Self from your Creator, Who created you by sharing His Being with you.

Note # 34: Your true reality is that you are part of the indivisible Oneness with God, your Creator. There is no other option but wholeness in the Mind of God, which is changeless and eternal. Only in your dreams can you be something you are not. Sickness is the illusion that you be something you are not. There is no order of difficulty in miracles. All illusions simply fade away before the healing light of truth.

T-7.V.7. The unhealed healer wants gratitude from his brothers, but **the unhealed healer** is not grateful to **his brothers**. 2 **The unhealed healer is not grateful to his brothers** because **the unhealed healer** thinks **the unhealed healer** is giving something to **his brothers,** and **that the unhealed healer** is not receiving something equally desirable in return **from his brothers**. 3 **The unhealed healer's** teaching is limited because **the unhealed healer** is learning so little. 4 **The unhealed healer's** healing lesson is limited by **the unhealed healer's** own ingratitude, which is a lesson in sickness. 5 True learning is constant, and so vital in **true learning's** power for change that a Son of God can recognize his power **as a Son of God** in one instant and change the world in the next **instant**. 6 **This recognizing his power as a Son of God in one instant and change the world in the next instant is possible** because, by changing his mind, **a Son of God** has changed the most powerful device, **which is his mind**, that was ever given **a Son of God** for change. 7 This **changing of a Son of God's mind,** in no way contradicts the changelessness of mind as God created **the Son's mind**, but you think that you have changed **the Son's mind** as long as you learn through the ego. 8 This **learning through the ego** places you in a position of needing to learn a lesson that seems contradictory;–you must learn to change your mind about your mind. 9 Only by this can you learn that **the Son's mind** <*is*> changeless.

Note # 35: The lesson that seems contradictory is that by "changing" your egoic mind, you can prove that your Big "S" Self's mind cannot change. What you are to change is your mistaken belief that you can actually change your mind because you believe that you are separate from the Mind of God. It is this belief in your separateness that you are asked to change. Your true state of mind, your Big "S" Self's mind, is one with the Mind of God. Your Big "S" Self remains changeless as God created it.

T-7.V.8. When you heal, that is exactly what you <are> learning. 2 You are recognizing the changeless mind in your brother by realizing that **your brother** could not have changed his mind. 3 **By recognizing the changeless mind in your brother,** that is how you perceive the Holy Spirit in **your brother.** 4 It, **the changeless mind in your brother,** is only the Holy Spirit in **your brother** that never changes His Mind. **(Your brother's High-Self or High-Mind)** 5 **Your brother** himself may think he can **change his mind,** or **your brother** would not perceive himself as sick. 6 **Your brother** therefore does not know what his **Big "S"** Self is. 7 If you see only the changeless in **your brother** you have not really changed **your brother.** 8 By changing your mind about **your belief about your brother's changeless mind** <for> your brother, you help **your brother** undo the change his ego thinks **his ego** has made in him.

Note # 36: Healing restores your mind to its state of oneness, which is the Mind of God. You remember what you really are and what your brother really is. You realize that your mind and your brother's mind are changeless. You see Mind as the One Self as God created it.

In healing, you, the healer, are not concerned with changing your brother, for your brother's Big "S" Self is as changeless as your mind since both are from the Mind of God. You are changing your belief that your brother's mind could be something that it is not and thus, truly be split-minded. You are recognizing that your brother's mind cannot change. The ego cannot change your brother's Big "S" Self because the ego has no power over the mind. The only power that the ego appears to possess comes only from the deluded mind's choice to follow the thought system of the ego. This is a decision in your brother's mind, not by his ego. He has erred as to which thought system his mind has temporarily chosen to listen to. Healing is your brother's choice to follow the thought system of the Holy Spirit and correct this illusion of split-mindedness.

T-7.V.9. As you can hear two voices, so you can see in two ways. 2 One way, **the way of the ego's thought system,** shows you an image, or an idol that you may worship out of fear, but will never love. 3 The other, **the way of the Holy Spirit's thought system,** shows you only truth, which you will love because you will understand **truth.** 4 Understanding is appreciation, because what you understand you can identify with, and by making **what you understand** part of you, you have accepted **what you understand** with love. 5 That, **truth, understanding, appreciation, and love,** is how God Himself created you; in understanding, in appreciation and in love. 6 The ego is totally unable to understand this **creative process of extension,** because **the ego** does not understand what **the ego** makes, **the ego** does not appreciate **what the ego makes** and **the ego** does not love **what the ego makes.** 7 **The ego** incorporates to take away. 8 **The ego** literally believes that every time **the ego** deprives someone of something, **the ego** has increased. 9 I have spoken often of the increase of the Kingdom by your creations, which can only be created as you were. 10 The whole glory and perfect joy that <is> the Kingdom lies in you to give. 11 Do you not want to give **the whole glory and perfect joy that <is> the Kingdom?**

Note # 37: The ego's thought system is based on getting by taking away. The ego believes that life is a "zero-sum" game. If I'm to win, someone must lose. This is not creation, but rather making through projection. It is based on the egoic belief of exclusion and that "to have" is "to get." This is not how God created His Son. Therefore, God's Son can only create like his Father, which is by extending unconditional Love. To have all, give all to all, which is the first lesson of the Holy Spirit. This is the basis for creation.

T-7.V.10. You cannot forget the Father because I am with you, and I cannot forget **the Father.** 2 To forget me is to forget yourself and **the Father,** Who created you. 3 Our brothers are forgetful. 4 **Because**

our brothers are forgetful, that is why **our brothers** need your remembrance of me and of **the Father, Who created me.** 5 Through **your remembrance of me and of the Father, Who created me**, you can change **our brothers'** minds about themselves, as I can change your **mind about yourselves.** 6 Your mind is so powerful a light that you can look into their **mind** and enlighten **their mind**, as I can enlighten **your mind.** 7 I do not want to share my body in communion because **to share my body** is to share nothing. 8 Would I try to share an illusion, **which would be that I am an ego-body**, with the most holy children of a most holy Father? 9 Yet I do want to share my mind with you because we are of one Mind, and that Mind is ours. 10 See only this **one** Mind everywhere, because only this is everywhere and in everything. 11 **Mind** is everything because **Mind** encompasses all things within itself. 12 Blessed are you who perceive only **the Mind, which encompasses all things within itself**, because you perceive only what is true.

Note # 38: You are Mind or Spirit. You are not an ego-body. This is truth. You are not an individual; you are the Oneness of Mind. Jesus tells us that he will always share this remembrance of God with us so that we can share it with another. Due to the holographic nature of Mind, all must have access to the truth of this Oneness. By sharing and holding this truth with and for another, a brother can end their own denial of this truth. They can accept the Atonement for themselves and be healed.

T-7.V.11.Come therefore unto me, and learn of the truth in you. 2 The mind we share is shared by all our brothers, and as we see **all our brothers** truly **as the One Self, all our brothers** will be healed. 3 Let your mind shine with **my mind** upon **all our brothers'** minds, and by our gratitude to **all our brothers** make **all our brothers** aware of the light in **all our brothers**. 4 This light will shine back upon you and on the whole Sonship, because this **light** is your proper gift to God. 5 **God** will accept **this light** and give **this light** to the Sonship, because **the sharing of this light** is acceptable to **God** and therefore to **God's Sons.** 6 **The sharing of this light** is true communion with the Holy Spirit, Who sees the altar of God in everyone, and by **the Holy Spirit** bringing **the sharing of this light** to your appreciation, **the Holy Spirit** calls upon you to love God and **God's** creation. 7 You can appreciate the Sonship only as one. 8 **The appreciation of the Sonship only as one** is part of the law of creation, and therefore governs all thought.

Note # 39: The law of creation is the law of Oneness as demonstrated in the first lesson of the Holy Spirit, which is, "To have all, give all to all." It is the extension of the Oneness. Nothing is held back and nothing is excluded. Unconditional love is just continually expanded and extended out to all.

VI. From Vigilance to Peace

T-7.VI.1.Although you can love the Sonship only as one, you can perceive **the Sonship** as fragmented. 2 It is impossible, however, to see something in part of **the Sonship** that you will not attribute to all of **the Sonship.** 3 That is why attack is never discrete, and why **attack** must be relinquished entirely. 4 If **attack** is not relinquished entirely **attack** is not relinquished at all. 5 Fear and love make or create, depending on whether the ego or the Holy Spirit begets or inspires **the creation**, but **fear or love** <*will*> return to the mind of the thinker and **fear or love** will affect **the mind of the thinker's** total perception. 6 That fear or love will affect the mind of the thinker's total perception includes his concept of God, of **God's** creations and of his own **creations.** 7 **The thinker** will not appreciate any of **his concepts of**

God, of God's creations and of his own creations if he regards Them, **God, God's creations and the thinker's own creations,** fearfully **through the eyes of the ego.** 8 He will appreciate all of Them, **which is the thinker's concept of God, of God's creations and of his own creations,** if he regards **God, God's creations and the thinker's own creations** with **the** love **of the Holy Spirit.**

Note # 40: The ego's thought system is based on fear and, therefore, can only make since the ego comes from the fear-based belief in lack. The Holy Spirit's thought system is based on love and, therefore, creates since it comes from love and extends what it truly is which is love. Due to the Oneness, to attack any part of the Sonship is an attack on the whole. Thoughts never leave the mind of the thinker. They may be shared or projected outside oneself but they always maintain their roots in the soil of the mind that birthed the thought.

T-7.VI.2. The mind that accepts attack cannot love. 2 That is because **the mind that accepts attack** believes **attack** can destroy love, and therefore does not understand what love is. 3 If **the mind that accepts attack** does not understand what love is, **the mind that accepts attack** cannot perceive itself as loving. 4 **The mind that cannot perceive itself as loving,** loses the awareness of being, induces feelings of unreality and results in utter confusion. 5 Your thinking has done this **loss of the awareness of being, which induces feelings of unreality that results in utter confusion,** because of **the mind's** power, but your thinking can also save you from this **loss of the awareness of being, which induces feelings of unreality that results in utter confusion,** because **the mind's** power is not of your making. 6 Your ability to direct your thinking as you choose is part of **the mind's** power. 7 If you do not believe you can **direct your thinking** you have denied the power of your thought, and thus rendered **the power of your thought** powerless in your belief.

Note # 41: The power of the mind lays in your belief in your ability or inability to direct your thinking. It is a question of first reclaiming your mind's decision-making ability and then next determining which thought system your decision-maker is going to value. If you deny that you can direct your thinking, you deny that you are the decision-maker and, therefore, render the mind powerless. The mind is never powerless since God has given you free will to choose. Yet, you can choose to believe that you are the powerless victim of outside forces and thus, deny and rob your decision-maker of its power. It is your thought that the mind is powerless that makes your decision-maker appear impotent. Thus, thoughts are things. It is your decision to be powerless that has become your provisional reality.

T-7.VI.3. The ingeniousness of the ego to preserve itself is enormous, but **the preservation of the ego** stems from the very power of the mind **that** the ego denies, **which is your mind's ability to direct your thinking.** 2 This means that the ego attacks what is serving it, **which is your mind's ability to direct your thinking. This attack by the ego** must result in extreme anxiety. 3 **Due to the extreme anxiety that results from the ego's attack on your mind's ability to direct your thinking,** the ego never recognizes what **the ego** is doing. 4 **The ego** is perfectly logical but clearly insane. 5 The ego draws upon the one source, **which is your mind's ability to direct your thinking,** that is totally inimical, **(hostile or unfriendly)** to the ego's existence <*for*> the ego's existence. 6 Fearful of perceiving the power of this source, **which is your mind's ability to be the decision-maker, the ego** is forced to depreciate **your mind's ability to be the decision-maker.** 7 **Your mind's ability to be the decision-maker** threatens **the ego's** own existence. **This threat is** a state which **the ego** finds intolerable. 8 Remaining logical but still insane, the ego resolves this completely insane dilemma in a completely insane way. 9 **The ego** does not perceive <*the ego's*> existence as threatened by projecting the threat onto <*you, your decision-maker*> and perceiving your being as nonexistent. 10 This **projecting the threat onto <you> and perceiving your being as nonexistent** ensures **the ego's** continuance if you side with **the ego,** by guaranteeing that you, *your decision-maker,* will not know your own safety.

Note # 42: The ego's goal is to attack your mind's ability to be the decision-maker. If the ego can aid the mind in forgetting that the mind's decision-maker controls the power to either make or create, the ego will insure its existence. If you forget that you are the decision-maker, you have lost your ability to reject the thought system of the ego since you no longer remember that you are spirit. You have abdicated your free will and your right to choose again. You believe yourself to be a victim of outside forces that are beyond your control. You disavow your divine birthright to be the cause of all you choose to call into your awareness. Believing you are powerless to choose again, you remain stuck under the control of the tyrannical thought system of the ego.

T-7.VI.4. The ego cannot afford to know anything. 2 Knowledge is total, and the ego does not believe in totality. 3 This unbelief, **and the rejection of knowledge which leads to birth of perception,** is **the ego's** origin, and while the ego does not love you **the ego** *<is>* faithful to **the ego's** own antecedents, **which are anything logically preceding from the ego's thought system,** begetting **out of fear** as **the ego** was begotten. 4 Mind always produces as it was produced. 5 Produced by fear, the ego reproduces fear. 6 This **fact that the ego was produced out of fear and the ego reproduces out of fear,** is **the ego's** allegiance, and this allegiance **to fear** makes **the ego** treacherous to love because you *<are>* love. 7 Love is your power, which the ego must deny. 8 **The ego** must also deny everything this power **of love** gives you *<because>* **this power of love** gives you everything. 9 No one who has everything wants the ego. 10 Its own maker, **your mind,** then, does not want **the ego.** 11 Rejection is therefore the only decision the ego could possibly encounter, if the mind that made **the ego** knew itself. 12 And if **the mind that made the ego** recognized any part of the Sonship, **the mind that made the ego** *<would>* know itself.

Note # 43: The ego was born when knowledge was lost and perception replaced it. Perception requires separation and individuality, since it needs something "out there" to observe. The ego's thought system is based on perception and projection. Under the fear based guidance of the ego, the mind "makes" through perception rather than extending with love and knowledge. What the ego perceives is what will be produced and experienced. Perception proceeds from our thoughts and our thoughts are what we choose to value.

T-7.VI.5. The ego therefore opposes all appreciation, all recognition, all sane perception and all knowledge. 2 **The ego** perceives **all appreciation, all recognition, all sane perception and all knowledge as a total** threat because **the ego** senses that all commitments the mind makes are total. 3 **The ego** forced, therefore, to detach itself from you, is willing to attach itself to anything else. 4 But there *<is>* nothing else **for the ego to attach itself to.** 5 The mind can, however, make up illusions, and if **the mind** does **make up illusions, the mind** will believe in **the illusions,** because that is how **the mind** made **the illusions.**

Note # 44: What you project you believe. The creative power of the mind allows us to "make" out of fear and exclusion. Making is not real except within the imagination of the deluded mind of the dreamer. If we want to believe that we are separate, we can make a body to "prove" this illusion to be "true." Our projections become our provisional reality, which can imprison our mind in self-imposed temporary insanity.

T-7.VI.6. The Holy Spirit undoes illusions without attacking **the illusions,** because **the Holy Spirit** cannot perceive **the illusions** at all. 2 **The illusions** therefore do not exist for **the Holy Spirit.** 3 **The Holy Spirit** resolves the apparent conflict **the illusions** engender by perceiving conflict as meaningless.

4 I have said before that the Holy Spirit perceives the conflict exactly as **the conflict** is, and **the conflict** <*is*> meaningless. 5 The Holy Spirit does not want you to understand conflict; **the Holy Spirit** wants you to realize that, because conflict is meaningless, **conflict** is not understandable. 6 As I have already said, understanding brings appreciation and appreciation brings love. 7 Nothing else can be understood, because nothing else is real and therefore nothing else has meaning.

Note # 45: The Holy Spirit does not attack the illusion since such an attack would appear to make the fantasy real and thus, fearful to the dreamer. Rather than increase fear, the Holy Spirit merely recognizes that only truth is real and with that, the memory of the dream seemingly fades from the dreamer's mind. Being not real, the dream of making slips back into the nothingness from which it arose.

T-7.VI.7. If you will keep in mind what the Holy Spirit offers you, you cannot be vigilant for anything <*but*> God and His Kingdom. 2 The only reason you may find this **fact that the apparent conflict that illusions engender is meaningless because the illusion is not real,** hard to accept is because you may still think there is something else. 3 Belief does not require vigilance unless **belief** is conflicted. 4 If **belief** is **conflicted**, there are conflicting components within **the belief** that have led to a state of war, and vigilance has therefore become essential. 5 Vigilance has no place in peace. 6 **Vigilance** is necessary against beliefs that are not true, and **vigilance** would never have been called upon by the Holy Spirit if you had not believed the untrue. 7 When you believe something, you have made **what you believe** true for you. 8 When you believe what God does not know, your thought seems to contradict **God's thought system**, and this makes it appear as if you are attacking **God**.

Note # 46: Because we value our egoic specialness, we find it hard to relinquish all the values of the egoic thought system. If we knew the truth that we already have everything because we are unlimited spirit, we would not be conflicted. It is our conflicted belief as to whom we are that we must guard against. The split-minded, appear to have two allegiances. The ego values separation and specialness. The Big "S" Self knows that we are the shared Oneness of Everything. The Holy Spirit calls for the remembrance of God and the return to whole-mindedness. The Holy Spirit asks us to be vigilant only for God.

T-7.VI.8.I have repeatedly emphasized that the ego does believe **that the ego** can attack God, and tries to persuade you that you have done this **attack on God**. 2 If the mind cannot attack, the ego proceeds perfectly logically to the belief that you must be a body **rather than mind which, as spirit is incapable of attack**. 3 By not seeing you as you are, **which is mind or spirit, the ego** can see itself as **the ego** wants to be. 4 Aware of **the ego's** weakness the ego wants your allegiance, but not as you really are. 5 The ego therefore wants to engage your mind in **the ego's** own delusional **thought** system, because otherwise the light of your understanding would dispel **the ego**. 6 **The ego** wants no part of truth, because the ego itself is not true. 7 If truth is total, the untrue cannot exist. 8 Commitment to either **truth or untruth** must be total. **Truth or untruth** cannot coexist in your mind without splitting **your mind**. 9 If **truth or untruth** cannot coexist in peace, and if you want peace, you must give up the idea of conflict entirely and for all time. 10 This requires vigilance only as long as you do not recognize what is true. 11 While you believe that **the** two totally contradictory thought systems **of the ego and the Holy Spirit** share truth, your need for vigilance is apparent.

Note # 47: The ego wants your allegiance to the idea that you are a body, not unlimited spirit or mind. As long as we believe that an illusion of the false is a viable choice, we need to be vigilant only for the truth. All fear-based thoughts must be abandoned. With the abandonment of the egoic thought system, all blocks to love are removed.

T-7.VI.9. Your mind is dividing **your mind's** allegiance between two kingdoms, and you are totally committed to neither **kingdom**. 2 Your identification with the Kingdom is totally beyond question except by you, when you are thinking insanely. 3 What you are is not established by your perception, and **what you are** is not influenced by **your perception** at all. 4 Perceived problems in identification at any level are not problems of fact. 5 **Perceived problems in identification** are problems of understanding, since **the** presence **of perceived problems in identification** implies a belief that what you are is up to you to decide. 6 The ego believes **that what you are is up to you to decide** totally, **and the ego is** fully committed to **the belief that what you are is up to you to decide.** 7 **The belief that what you are is up to you to decide** is not true. 8 The ego therefore is totally committed to untruth, perceiving in total contradiction to the Holy Spirit and to the knowledge of God.

Note # 48: This belief that it is up to you to decide what you are is the foundation of the ego's thought system. This erroneous belief insures your claim to the "reality" of the separation and your individuality. The ego tells us that we are the arbitrators of truth and that truth is conditional and changeable. Truth just is. Our denial of the truth cannot change the truth. Only the insane would believe that they control what is the truth.

T-7.VI.10. You can be perceived with meaning only by the Holy Spirit because your being <*is*> the knowledge of God. 2 Any belief you accept apart from this will obscure God's Voice in you, and will therefore obscure God to you. 3 Unless you perceive **God's** creation truly you cannot know the Creator, since God and **God's** creation are not separate. 4 The Oneness of the Creator and the creation is your wholeness, your sanity and your limitless power. 5 This limitless power is God's gift to you, because **this limitless power** is what you are. 6 If you dissociate your mind from **this limitless power which is what you are** you are perceiving the most powerful force in the universe as if **this limitless power** were weak, because you do not believe you are part of **this limitless power which is your Oneness with the Creator**.

Note # 49: Your power to create is the same as God, Your Father's. It is the same power due to your shared Oneness. When God creates, He extends everything that God is to His creations. Only your belief that you can be something other than as God created you, limits your ability to create like the Father. "To have all, give all to all." The ego does not believe this first lesson of the Holy Spirit. Instead, the ego prefers to claim that what you choose to believe will change the truth. The ego claims that you have a will that can oppose and overrule God's Will.

T-7.VI.11. Perceived without your part in **the Oneness**, God's creation is seen as weak, and those who see themselves as weakened do attack. 2 The attack must be blind, however, because there is nothing to attack. 3 Therefore they, **who see themselves as outside the Oneness**, make up images, perceive **these made up images** as unworthy and attack **these made up images** for their unworthiness. 4 That is all the world of the ego is. It is a projection of made up images. 5 The world of the ego is nothing. 6 **The world of the ego** has no meaning. 7 **The world of the ego** does not exist. 8 Do not try to understand **the world of the ego** because, if you do **try to understand the world of the ego,** you are believing that **the world of the ego** can be understood and **the world of the ego** is therefore capable of being appreciated and loved. 9 That **if the world of the ego is capable of being appreciated and loved, then this** would justify **the world of the ego's** existence, which cannot be justified. 10 You cannot make the **world of the ego, which is** meaningless, meaningful. 11 This **attempt to make the world of the ego meaningful** can only be an insane attempt.

Note # 50: Do not value the world of the ego. It is an illusion based on fantasy and is not real. There can be no value in possessing what does not exist. What does not exist is nothing. When we attempt to give the egoic illusion of specialness and separation any value, we are empowering the illusion and making it appear real.

T-7.VI.12. Allowing insanity to enter your mind means that you have not judged sanity as wholly desirable. 2 If you want something else you will make something else, but because it is something else, it will attack your thought system and divide your allegiance. 3 You cannot create in this divided state **of the split-mind**, and you must be vigilant against this divided state because only peace can be extended. 4 Your divided mind is blocking the extension of the Kingdom, and **the Kingdom's** extension is your joy. 5 If you do not extend the Kingdom, you are not thinking with your Creator and creating as **your Creator** created.

<u>Note # 51:</u> Since you are the Oneness of "All That Is,' there is nothing more to want. This truth is your reality. To want something other than the truth that you are the Oneness of "All That Is" only leaves the option of pretending that you are an illusion of limitation. This leads us into an egoic, made-up world of illusion that becomes our own "provisional reality" in which we claim to be the arbitrator for truth. This dream world is the ego's battleground for its perceived attack against God and Truth. The ego attacks our Big "S" Self's certainty on what it is. The ego attempts to usurp your Big "S" Self's control over your mind's decision- making ability. This leaves your mind in a powerless state of self-delusion.

T-7.VI.13. In this depressing state the Holy Spirit reminds you gently that you are sad because you are not fulfilling your function as co-creator with God, and **because you are not fulfilling your function as co-creator with God, you** are therefore depriving yourself of joy. 2 **To deprive yourself of joy** is not God's choice but your **choice**. 3 If your mind could be out of accord with God's, you would be willing without meaning. 4 Yet because God's Will is unchangeable, no conflict of will is possible. 5 That **God's Will is unchangeable and that no conflict of will is possible** is the Holy Spirit's perfectly consistent teaching. 6 Creation, not separation, is your will <*because*> **creation, not separation** is God's **Will**, and nothing that opposes **God's Will** means anything at all. 7 Being a perfect accomplishment, the Sonship can only accomplish perfectly, extending the joy in which **the Sonship** was created, and identifying itself**, the Sonship,** with both **the Sonship's** Creator and **the Sonship's** creations, knowing They are One.

<u>Note # 52:</u> If you are sad, you are not fulfilling your function as co-creator with God, your Father. God wills that His Child be happy. Being a Oneness of Everything, we cannot be happy pretending we are limited and frightened. We can only be happy when we are extending love for this is our co-creative nature and purpose. To be love, we must teach only love.

VII. The Totality of the Kingdom

T-7.VII.1. Whenever you deny a blessing to a brother <*you*> **in the world of the ego** will feel deprived, because denial is as total as love. 2 It is as impossible to deny part of the Sonship as it is to love part **of the Sonship**. 3 Nor is it possible to love **the Sonship** totally at times. 4 You cannot be totally committed sometimes. 5 Denial has no power in itself, but you can give **denial** the power of your mind, whose power, **(your mind's power),** is without limit. 6 If you use **the power of your mind** to deny reality, reality is gone for you. 7 <*Reality*> cannot be partly appreciated. 8 Because <*Reality*> cannot be partly appreciated, that is why denying any part of <Reality> means you have lost the awareness of all of <Reality>. 9 Yet denial is a defense, and so **denial** is as capable of being used positively as well as negatively. 10 **Denial** used negatively will be destructive, because **denial** will be used for attack. 11 But in the service of the Holy Spirit, **denial** can help you recognize part of reality, and thus appreciate all of **reality**. 12 Mind is too powerful to be subject to exclusion. 13 You will never be able to exclude yourself from your thoughts.

Note #53: You are the product of your thoughts. You are mind and the world you perceive is produced by your thoughts. Thoughts never leave the mind of the thinker.
Denial of the false is a proper use of denial, but to use it to reject the truth is an improper use of denial. You cannot be partially committed to the truth sometimes. It is an all or nothing decision. To value the false sometimes is not to be committed to the obtainment of the truth. Whatever you value you will attract into your awareness and experience.

T-7.VII.2. When a brother acts insanely, **a brother** is offering you an opportunity to bless **your brother**. 2 **Your brother's** need is your **need**. 3 You need the blessing you can offer **your brother**. 4 There is no way for you to have **the blessing you can offer your brother** except by giving **the blessing to your brother**. 5 **What you give is what you receive.** This is the law of God, and the Law of God has no exceptions. **Thus, to receive a blessing, you must give a blessing,** 6 What you deny you lack, not because **what you deny** is lacking, but because you have denied it in another and are therefore not aware of **what you deny to another** in yourself. 7 Every response you make is determined by what you think you are, and what you want to be <is> what you think you are. 8 What you want to be, then, must determine every response you make.

Note # 54: Thoughts are things. This, coupled with the law of God that states what you give, you receive, results in what you perceive yourself to be. Thus, if you are confused as to what you truly are and believe that you are a product of lack; you project this same lack out from our own mind into your world. What you want to be is thus, what you think you are. The goal of this course is not that you change the world, but rather change your thinking about the world. Your response to anything is predicated on what you think you are. What you think you are, you become due to the power of your mind and this Law of God. "What you give, you receive.

T-7.VII.3. You do not need God's blessing because **God's blessing** you have forever, but you do need your **blessing**. 2 The ego's picture of you is deprived, unloving and vulnerable. 3 You cannot love **the ego's picture of you**. 4 Yet you can very easily escape from this image **that you are deprived, unloving and vulnerable** by leaving **the ego's picture of you** behind. 5 You are not there **in the ego's image of you,** and **the ego's image of you,** is not you. 6 Do not see this picture, **the ego's image of you,** in anyone, or you have accepted **the ego's picture of you,** <as> you. 7 All illusions about the Sonship are dispelled together **as all illusions about the Sonship** were made together. 8 Teach no one that he is what you would not want to be. 9 Your brother is the mirror in which you see the image of yourself as long as perception lasts. 10 And perception will last until the Sonship knows itself as whole. 11 You made perception and **perception** must last as long as you want **perception to last**.

Note # 55: Your brother is the mirror of how you see yourself. See your brother as limited in any way, and you place that same limitation on yourself. The Sonship is not complete until all that has been created, including you, are seen by you as whole, perfect and complete.
To deny the ego's false image of you is an example of the proper use of denial. In this case, you are simply denying the false which leaves you only with the truth.

T-7.VII.4. Illusions are investments. 2 **Illusions** will last as long as you value **illusions**. 3 Values are relative, but **values** are powerful because **values** are mental judgments. 4 The only way to dispel illusions is to withdraw all investment from **illusions**, and **illusions** will have no life for you because you will have put **illusions** out of your mind. 5 While you include **illusions** in **your mind**, you are giving life to **illusions**. 6 Except **since an illusion is nothing,** there is nothing there **in an illusion** to receive your gift **of life and thus, make it real**.

Note # 56: There is nothing to receive the illusion since illusions have no reality in truth. Illusions only exist in your dream world of provisional reality. You cannot give life to an illusion since an illusion by definition does not exist. What you value, you include in your thoughts. The powers of our thoughts make the illusion appear real within your dreamer's mind. When the dreamer ceases to value the unreal, the illusion will disappear from his mind.

T-7.VII.5. The gift of life is yours to give, because **the gift of life** was given you. 2 You are unaware of your gift **of life** because you do not give **the gift of life**. 3 You cannot make nothing live. (**Nothing is your illusions that you have created from your belief in limitation and fear.**) 3 You cannot make nothing live since nothing, **your illusions,** cannot be enlivened. 4 Therefore, you are not extending the gift **of life,** you both <*have*> and <*are,*> and so you do not know your being. 5 All confusion comes from not extending life, because **not extending life** is not the Will of your Creator. 6 You can do nothing apart from **your Creator**, and you <*do*> do nothing apart from **your Creator**. 7 Keep **your Creator's** way, **which is extending the gift of life,** to remember yourself, and teach **your Creator's** way, **which is extending the gift of life,** lest you forget yourself. 8 Give only honor to the Sons of the living God, and count yourself among **the Sons of the living God** gladly.

Note # 57: Love is life. Being created by love, you are love and must extend love. This extension is in compliance with God's Law that to give is to receive. You cannot give life to an illusion. An illusion is basically everything that is not a Oneness of love because that is how the Father created you. To create is to extend. Since you are wholly love, you must extent love's wholeness to create. Since you see yourself as incomplete and as a separate individual, you can only project the false. Coming from fear and lack, these projected illusions have no reality in Truth and lack love and thus, life.

T-7.VII.6. Only honor is a fitting gift for those whom God Himself created worthy of honor, and whom **God** honors. 2 Give **those whom God Himself created** the appreciation God accords **those whom God Himself created** always, because they, are **God's** beloved Sons in whom **God** is well pleased. 3 You cannot be apart from **those whom God Himself created and honor**, because you are not apart from **God**. 4 **You** rest in **God's** Love and protect your rest by loving. 5 But love everything **God** created, of which you are a part, or you cannot learn of **God's** peace and accept **God's** gift for yourself and as yourself. 6 You cannot know your own perfection until you have honored all those who were created **perfect** like you.

Note # 58: To reawaken to what you are, you must once again remember what you are. Since what you give, you receive; you must see the Oneness in all that God created in order to rediscover your own Oneness. If you cannot love yourself, you cannot love your brother.

T-7.VII.7. One child of God is the only teacher sufficiently worthy to teach another **child of God**. 2 One Teacher, **the Holy Spirit,** is in all minds and **the Holy Spirit** teaches the same lesson to all. 3 **The Holy Spirit** always teaches you the inestimable worth of every Son of God, teaching **you the inestimable worth of every Son of God,** with infinite patience born of the infinite Love for which **the Holy Spirit** speaks. 4 Every attack is a call for **the Holy Spirit's** patience, since **the Holy Spirit's** patience can translate attack into blessing. 5 Those who attack do not know they, **who choose to attack** are blessed. 6 **Those who choose to attack,** attack because they believe they are deprived. 7 Give, therefore, of your abundance, and teach your brothers, **who choose to attack** their **abundance**. 8 Do not share **your brothers'** illusions of scarcity, or you will perceive yourself as lacking.

Note # 59: We are all teachers. We teach what we value. We can choose to teach what our Big "S" Self values or, what our little "s" self values. Our Big "S" Self values the truth of the Holy Spirit's thought system. If this is what you value, you will deny your brother's false image of himself as a body and see him only as unlimited spirit. The vision you give your brother will be the same vision you receive and hold for yourselves.

T-7.VII.8. Attack could never promote attack unless you perceived **attack** as a means of depriving you of something you want. 2 Yet you cannot lose anything unless you do not value it, **the thing you cannot lose,** and therefore do not want it. 3 This **not valuing it** makes you feel deprived of it, **the thing you cannot lose,** and by projecting your own rejection you then believe that others are taking it, **the thing you cannot lose,** from you. 4 You must be fearful if you believe that your brother is attacking you to tear the Kingdom of Heaven from you. 5 This **fear that your brother is attacking you to tear the Kingdom of Heaven from you** is the ultimate basis for all the ego's projection.

Note # 60: Fear destroys your sense of Oneness. To be fearful you must believe that there is something outside of you of which to be afraid. Since your egoic self claims you are not everything, you must lack what it perceives as outside of you. And what you perceive as separate from you can attempt to take what you have and also resist giving you what they possess. Thus, attack becomes the natural result of the ego's thought system. Yet, because you are unlimited spirit, you cannot truly lack for anything. Our Big "S" Self values the truth and thus, we can never lose our divine birthright. When we value egoic littleness, we deny our spiritual being. Not valuing our spirit, we believe our divine birthright has been lost. It has not been lost. Rather, by our denial, we have chosen not to access it.

T-7.VII.9. Being the part of your mind that does not believe it is responsible for itself, **(the part of mind under the guidance of the ego),** and being without allegiance to God, the ego is incapable of trust. 2 **By the ego p**rojecting its insane belief that you have been treacherous to your Creator, **the ego** believes that your brothers, who are as incapable of **being treacherous to your Creator** as you are, **are treacherous. Your ego believes that your brothers** are out to take God from you. 3 Whenever a brother attacks another, that <is> what he believes. **(That you are out to take God from him, your brother.)** 4 Projection always sees your wishes **as another brother's wishes.** 5 If you choose to separate yourself from God that is what you will think others are doing to you. **(Separating you from God)**

Note # 61: The egoic mind claims that you are not responsible for what you experience. It claims that you are an innocent victim of outside forces that are beyond your control. The ego utilizes projection as the tool to convince you that this is so. Projection takes your own thoughts and transfers or projects these same thought upon another. We then claim that the originator of our thought was the other person. This allows us to shift the blame and guilt from our own mind to another. Thus, when we attack another, the ego claims that we are merely defending ourselves from our brother's original attack.

T-7.VII.10. You <are> the Will of God. 2 Do not accept anything else as your will, or you are denying what you are, **which is the Will of God.** 3 Deny this, **that you <are> the Will of God,** and you will attack, believing you have been attacked. 4 But see the Love of God in you, and you will see **the Love of God** everywhere because **the Love of God** <is> everywhere. 5 See **God's** abundance in everyone and you will know that you are in **God** with everyone. 6 **Everyone is** a part of you, as you are part of

God. 7 You are as lonely without understanding this, **that everyone is a part of you, as you are part of God**, as God Himself is lonely when **God's** Sons do not know **God**. 8 The peace of God is understanding this, **that everyone is a part of you, as you are part of God**. 9 There is only one way out of the world's thinking, just as there was only one way into **the world's thinking**. 10 Understand totally by understanding totality.

Note # 62: Understand totality rests on the understanding that you are not an individual but a Oneness. Each indivisible part is a hologram of the totality. A true hologram contains the whole. If you cut a true hologram apart, as soon as you shine a laser beam through any part, you see the entire whole. We are a hologram of God; just as our brother is a hologram of God and us. There can be no separation but only equality within that One Self. We are all the Oneness of that One Self. Cause and Its Effect are inseparable.

T-7.VII.11. Perceive any part of the ego's thought system as wholly insane, wholly delusional and wholly undesirable, and you have correctly evaluated all of **the ego's thought system**. 2 This correction **to perceive any part of the ego's thought system as wholly insane** enables you to perceive any part of creation as wholly real, wholly perfect and wholly desirable. 3 **By** wanting only **to perceive any part of creation as wholly real, wholly perfect and wholly desirable**, you will <*have*> this only and giving this only, **(the perception of creation as wholly real, perfect and desirable)**, you will <*be*> only this, **which is the wholly real, perfect and desirable**. 4 The gifts you offer to the ego are always experienced as sacrifices, but the gifts you offer to the Kingdom are gifts to you. 5 **The gifts you offer to the Kingdom** will always be treasured by God because **the gifts you offer to the Kingdom** belong to **God's** beloved Sons, who belong to **God**. 6 All power and glory are yours because the Kingdom is **God's**.

Note # 63: By perceiving the ego's thought system as insane, you have made the choice to follow the thought system of the Holy Spirit. This change in your thought system's allegiance opens the door to reawakening the memory of what you really are. What you value, you call into your awareness and this becomes your experience.
Egoic giving is always perceived to be a sacrifice because the ego believes that "having" and "being" are not the same. To the ego, to have you must possess and to give you must lose what you originally possessed. Form cannot be shared since someone must be made to sacrifice what he or she had. To the ego, all are separate from each other and thus, to give and to receive are mutually exclusive.

VIII. The Unbelievable Belief

T-7.VIII.1. We have said that without projection there can be no anger, but it is also true that without extension there can be no love. 2 These, **(without projection there can be no anger, and without extension there can be no love)**, reflect a fundamental law of the mind, and therefore one that always operates. 3 **This fundamental law of the mind** is the law by which you create and were created. 4 **This fundamental law of the mind** is the law that unifies the Kingdom, and keeps **the Kingdom** in the Mind of God. 5 To the ego, **this fundamental law of the mind** is perceived as a means of getting rid of something **the ego** does not want. 6 To the Holy Spirit, **this fundamental law of the mind** is the fundamental law of sharing, by which you give what you value in order to keep **what you value** in your mind. 7 To the Holy Spirit **this fundamental law of the mind, which is the law of sharing,** is **also** the law of extension. 8 To the ego **this fundamental law of the mind has been modified to become the law of projection, which** is the law of deprivation. 9 **This fundamental law of the mind** therefore produces abundance or scarcity, depending on how you choose to apply **this fundamental law of the mind.** 10 This choice **of how you choose to apply this law** is up to you, but it is not up to you to decide whether or not you will utilize **this fundamental law of the mind.** 11 Every mind must project or extend, because that is how **every mind** lives, and every mind is life.

Note # 64: This fundamental law of the mind is the law of sharing, which is also called the law of extension. This fundamental law of the mind states that mind must project or extend, because that is how mind lives, and every mind is life. The name that the law of sharing goes by may vary depending on what thought system your mind is following at any moment. Whether the mind is following the fearful ego or the loving Holy Spirit the results are the same, "what you share is returned onto you." This is why it is called the law of sharing. This law of the mind works automatically. It is not something one can elect not to participate in. It is a mandatory requirement of life, which is what mind is. Mind expands, extends and creates.

When the mind believes in lack, the law of sharing becomes the law of deprivation since the split-mind is driven by fear and anger. The egoic mind uses projection as a means to attack. Projection is a tool to exclude some aspect of Creation from wholeness. Projection, which is based on lack, will result in anger and fear since that is what you are attempting to share. You are sharing your belief in lack which is the opposite of how God creates. When the ego "shares" and projects its own lack, fear, anger, sin, and guilt, the power of the mind has been utilized to "make" rather than "create." "Making" is not real since it is not love-based and thus not shared with the Mind of God. Since the split mind is creating unlike God, the law of sharing has been egoically modified to make and imagine the false and could be more accurately called the law of deprivation.

The Holy Spirit's Law of Sharing is the law of extension or creation since the Holy Spirit operates under the principle "that to be all, give all to all." Thus, the law of creation comes from love. In the sharing of love, cause and effect become so intertwined that they become the inseparably joined. You cannot have one without the other and thus, they become one. We share what we give to others and this is what we become.

T-7.VIII.2. The ego's use of projection must be fully understood before the inevitable association between projection and anger can be finally undone. 2 The ego always tries to preserve conflict. 3 **The ego** is very ingenious in devising ways that seem to diminish conflict, because **the ego** does not want you to find conflict so intolerable that you will insist on giving **conflict** up. 4 The ego therefore tries to persuade you that <*the ego* > can free you of conflict, lest you give the ego up and free yourself **of conflict.** 5 Using **the ego's** own warped version of the laws of God, **(the law of deprivation),** the ego utilizes the power of the mind only to defeat the mind's real purpose, **which is to create like the Father, which is the law of extension.** 6 **The ego** projects conflict from your mind to other minds, in an attempt to persuade you that you have gotten rid of the problem **of conflict.**

Note # 65: The ego attempts to get rid of what it does not want by projecting that item onto someone else. The "Law of Deprivation," which is the fundamental law of the egoic mind, returns the thoughts that you projected out to another back upon yourself. It appears that you have gotten rid of the problem, but the problem will return to you, its source, since the Law of Sharing/ Extension/ Deprivation must work. Therefore, what you give, which is conflict, is what you get. The law of sharing states that thoughts never leave the mind of the thinker. What you project, you get to keep.

T-7.VIII.3. There are two major errors involved in this, **the ego's** attempt **to get rid of conflict by**

projecting the problem of the conflict onto others. 2 First, strictly speaking, conflict cannot be projected because **conflict** cannot be shared. 3 Any attempt to keep part of **conflict** and get rid of another part **of conflict** does not really mean anything. 4 Remember that a conflicted teacher is a poor teacher and a poor learner. 5 **A conflicted teacher's** lessons are confused, and **the lessons** transfer value is limited by **the conflicted teacher's** confusion. 6 The second error is the idea that you can get rid of something you do not want by giving **what you do not want** away. 7 Giving **what you do not want away** is how you <keep> **what you do not want.** 8 The belief that by seeing **what you do not want** outside you, **you** have excluded **what you do not want away** from within **you** is a complete distortion of the power of extension. 9 **This complete distortion of the power of extension** is why those who project are vigilant for their own safety. 10 **Those that project** are afraid that their projections will return and hurt **them who were the original source of the projection.** 11 Believing they, **(those who project),** have blotted their projections from their own minds, **those who project** also believe their projections are trying to creep back **into their mind.** 12 Since the projections have not left their minds, **those who project** are forced to engage in constant activity in order not to recognize this **projection has returned into their own mind, which was the source of the initial projection.**

<u>Note # 66:</u> Since to give is to receive, a thought can never leave its source. Thoughts that are shared or projected always remain with the thinker.

T-7.VIII.4. You cannot perpetuate an illusion about another without perpetuating **an illusion** about yourself. 2 There is no way out of this **perpetuating cycle of the illusion about yourself** because it is impossible to fragment the mind. 3 To fragment is to break into pieces, and mind cannot attack or be attacked. 4 The belief that **the mind can attack or be attacked is** an error the ego always makes. **The belief that the mind can attack or be attacked** underlies **the ego's** whole use of projection. 5 **The ego** does not understand what mind is, and therefore **the ego** does not understand what <you> are. 6 Yet **the ego's** existence is dependent on your mind, because the ego is your **mind's** belief. 7 The ego is a confusion in identification. 8 **Since the ego** never had a consistent model, **the ego** never developed consistently. 9 **The ego** is the product of the misapplication of the laws of God by distorted minds that are misusing their **mind's** power.

<u>Note # 67:</u> The illusion about your self-identity arose due to the distorted, or split-mind's belief in the separation. The belief in separation, or individuality, resulted from your belief in lack. Perception leads to projection and judgment, which perpetuates the belief in separation. The Law of Sharing or Extension is misapplied since you do not remember what you are. Rather than extending the everything that you are, you have chosen to project a fear-based image of lack. The ego arose out of the error that what you are could be something other than the Will of God. Projection perpetuates this error.

T-7.VIII.5. <Do not be afraid of the ego.> 2 **The ego** depends on your mind, and as you made **the ego** by believing in **the ego**, so you can dispel **the ego** by withdrawing **your mind's** belief from **the ego.** 3 Do not project the responsibility for your belief in **the ego** onto anyone else, or you will preserve the belief **in the ego existence.** 4 When you are willing to accept sole responsibility for the ego's existence you will have laid aside all anger and all attack, because **all anger and all attack** come from an attempt to project responsibility **onto others**, for your own errors. 5 But having accepted the errors as yours, do not keep **the errors.** 6 Give **the errors** over quickly to the Holy Spirit to be undone completely, so that all **these errors'** effects will vanish from your mind and from the Sonship as a whole.

<u>Note # 68:</u> You must be willing to accept responsibility for your own sourceness before you can correct your own mind's error. If you claim that the source of the error is outside you, you lack the power to change your creation. Only cause can stop its own effect. Once you realize you are responsible for an

error, give the error over to the Holy Spirit's thought system so that the Holy Spirit can remove or reinterpret the error correctly. When you are under the influence of the thought system of the ego, your mind is split. Being split-minded, it is impossible to correct the error without help. The Holy Spirit, Who knows who you really are, will have no problem correcting the error since the Holy Spirit has knowledge of the truth that you are spirit. As God's Beloved Son you remain perfect, whole and complete.

In this world of perception, we often claim that how we define ourselves is based on other people's opinions of what we are. We claim that outside forces make us what we are. We must understand that we are the masters of our mind and take personal responsibility for how we define ourselves. Just because the "outside" world tells us that we are limited-ego-bodies does not make it true. We need to understand that our beliefs and thoughts determine our private provisional reality. Each can freely choose what thought system they will follow. You are the decision-maker of your own consciousness. We can pretend to project this responsibility upon another yet, this denial cannot change the fact that it is our own mind's free will that decides what we choose to value.

T-7.VIII.6. The Holy Spirit will teach you to perceive beyond your belief, because truth is beyond belief and **the Holy Spirit's** perception is true. 2 The ego can be completely forgotten at any time, because **the ego** is a totally incredible belief, and no one can keep a belief he has judged to be unbelievable. 3 The more you learn about the ego, the more you realize that **the ego** cannot be believed. 4 The incredible cannot be understood because **the incredible** is unbelievable. 5 The meaninglessness of perception based on the unbelievable is apparent, but **the meaninglessness of perception based on the unbelievable** may not be recognized as being beyond belief, because it, **the meaninglessness of perception based on the unbelievable,** is made <by> belief.

Note # 69: Because you have free will, you have the option to dream up any illusion that you want to believe to be true in your provisional reality. This, your dream, of course, does nothing to change reality, which is the Will of God, but it does become "real" for you, the perceiver. Free will does not mean that you can establish the curriculum. God's curriculum that was established at the moment of the separation is the path to your remembering who you are. God's curriculum will reestablish your knowledge that you are a Oneness with God. Free will means only that you can elect what you want to take of God's curriculum at any given time. The Holy Spirit is your true teacher in this classroom of your dream world of provisional reality. The ego that knows nothing can teach nothing.

T-7.VIII.7. The whole purpose of this course is to teach you that the ego is unbelievable and will forever be unbelievable. 2 You who made the ego by believing the unbelievable cannot make this judgment **that the ego is unbelievable** alone. 3 By accepting the Atonement for yourself, you are deciding against the belief that you can be alone, thus dispelling the idea of separation and affirming your true identification with the whole Kingdom as literally part of you. 4 This identification **that the whole Kingdom as literally part of you** is as beyond doubt as it is beyond belief. 5 Your wholeness has no limits because being is infinity.

Note # 70: God's curriculum is the Atonement process. The Atonement states that everything the egoic thought system claims to be true is actually false. Only through the acceptance of the Atonement for yourself is your return to Oneness guaranteed. By the Atonement, the "split-mind" is healed and you reclaim your birthright in the shared Mind of God. The fact that the whole Kingdom is literally part of you is as beyond doubt as it is beyond belief because it is true. Truth is certain and is not contingent upon your belief. We can deny this truth but our denial cannot affect or change this truth. The truth of the Oneness just is.

IX. The Extension of the Kingdom

T-7.IX.1. Only you can limit your creative power, but God wills to release **your creative power**. 2 **God** no more wills you to deprive yourself of your creations than **God** wills to deprive Himself of **His creations**. 3 Do not withhold your gifts to the Sonship, or you withhold yourself from God! 4 Selfishness is of the ego, but Self-fullness is of spirit because that is how God created **spirit**. 5 The Holy Spirit is in the part of the mind that lies between the ego and the spirit. **The Holy Spirit** mediating between **the ego and the spirit** always in favor of the spirit. 6 To the ego this is partiality, and **the ego** responds as if **the ego** were being sided against **by the Holy Spirit**. 7 To spirit this is truth, because **spirit** knows **spirit's** fullness and cannot conceive of any part from which **spirit** is excluded

Note # 71: Selfishness is ego based. Selfishness is the egoic attempt to be excluded from the Oneness. The selfish ones claim that they are not whole and have needs. The selfish believe they must get and keep something from outside themselves that they perceive they lack. Self-fullness is based in spirit. Since it is complete and whole, Self-fullness includes, extends and shares. Self-fullness is part of the natural expansion of the Sonship. Your reality is that you are spirit and not an ego-body. The Holy Spirit has the ability to know both the truth that you are spirit and also to understand the activities of the part of your mind that is under the guidance of the ego. Since the Holy Spirit knows who you are, It always reinterprets the activities of the lower self, which follows the ego's thought system, in favor of the thought system of the Holy Spirit which speaks for truth.

NOTE: When the course uses the term, spirit it also means your High Self or the Christ conscious part of your mind. Before the separation, there was only the wholeness of Spirit.

T-7.IX.2. Spirit knows that the awareness of all its brothers is included in **spirit's** own **awareness**, as **awareness** is included in God. 2 The power of the whole Sonship and of **the Sonship's** Creator is therefore spirit's own fullness, rendering s**pirit's** creations equally whole and equal in perfection. 3 The ego cannot prevail against a totality that includes God, and any totality <*must*> include God. 4 Everything **God** created is given all **God's** power, because **everything God created** is part of **God** and shares **God's** Being with God. 5 Creating is the opposite of loss, as blessing is the opposite of sacrifice. 6 Being <*must*> be extended. 7 **Extension** is how **being** retains the knowledge of itself. 8 Spirit yearns to share its being as spirit's Creator, **God the Father**, did. 9 Created by sharing, **spirit's** will is to create. 10 **Spirit** does not wish to contain God, but **Spirit** wills to extend **God's** Being.

Note # 72: To contain would be to limit. God cannot be limited and, therefore, spirit, which is the Son of God, wills to extend God's Being by extending itself like the Father.
Extension or creation is how being retains the knowledge of itself. When the Sonship refused to co-create with God, it lost the knowledge of itself. Losing knowledge of what it was, the Sonship moved into the illusionary world of perception, projection and making. The egoic little "s" self was born.

T-7.IX.3. The extension of God's Being is spirit's only function. 2 **Spirit's** fullness cannot be contained, any more than can the fullness of **spirit's** Creator. 3 Fullness is extension. 4 The ego's whole thought system blocks extension, and thus **the ego's whole thought system** blocks your only function, which **is extension or creation**. 5 **The ego's whole thought system** therefore blocks your joy, so that you perceive yourself as unfulfilled. 6 Unless you create you <*are*> unfulfilled, but God does not know unfulfillment and therefore you must create. 7 You may not know your own creations, but this can no more interfere with **your own creations'** reality than your unawareness of your spirit can interfere with **spirit's** being.

Note # 73: You must create like the Father since that is how you were created. This is God's Will. While under the influence of the ego's thought system, our mind is "asleep" and, therefore, is not aware of truth and reality. When our awareness is placed in the world of perception, time and space, our true mind is safe and asleep in heaven. In our imagination, our split-mind plays the game of "What am I?" known as the separation. This dream state however, cannot change the Will of God. God continues to know His Son as a creator or extender of God's Own Being.

T-7.IX.4. The Kingdom is forever extending because **the Kingdom** is in the Mind of God. 2 You do not know your joy because you do not know your own Self-fullness. 3 Exclude any part of the Kingdom from yourself and you are not whole. 4 A split mind cannot perceive its **split mind's** fullness, and needs the miracle of the mind's wholeness to dawn upon **the split mind** and heal **the split mind**. 5 This reawakens the wholeness in **the split mind**, and restores **the split mind** to the Kingdom because of **the split mind's** acceptance of wholeness. 6 The full appreciation of the mind's Self-fullness makes selfishness impossible and extension inevitable. 7 **Since Self-fullness makes selfishness impossible and extension inevitable, this** is why there is perfect peace in the Kingdom. 8 Spirit is fulfilling **spirit's** function, and only complete fulfillment is peace.

Note # 74: The extension of the Kingdom, which is the Mind of God, is inevitable since this is God's Will. Nothing can stop this as we cannot oppose God's Will that we share. Only in the illusions of the ego's insane thought system can God's Will be opposed. Our true Big "S" Self has never left the peace of God because it is impossible for us not to do God's Will. Pretending has no impact on Heaven.

T-7.IX.5. Your creations are protected for you because the Holy Spirit, Who is in your mind, knows of **your creations** and can bring **your creations** into your awareness whenever you will let **the Holy Spirit**. 2 **Your creations** are there **in your mind** as part of your own being, because your fulfillment includes **your creations**. 3 The creations of every Son of God are your **creations**, since every creation belongs to everyone, being created for the Sonship as a whole.

Note # 75: The reality of the Sonship, which is all that God created, is that the Sonship remains a oneness or wholeness as God created it. As such, the Sonship never experienced the separation and is still whole. However, the split-minded are currently failing to recognize this fact. As part of the whole, everything in the Sonship belongs to everyone. There is only equality in the Sonship as each indivisible part is a hologram of the whole. The Sonship, like God, its Creator, is a Oneness of "All That Is."

T-7.IX.6. You have not failed to increase the inheritance of the Sons of God, and thus have not failed to secure **the inheritance of the Sons of God** for yourself. 2 Since it was the Will of God to give you **this inheritance**, God gave **this inheritance** forever. 3 Since **the inheritance of the Sons of God** was **God's** Will that you have **this inheritance** forever, **God** gave you the means for keeping **the inheritance**. 4 <*And you have done so and have this inheritance forever.* > 5 Disobeying God's Will is meaningful only to the insane. 6 In truth **disobeying God's Will** is impossible. 7 Your Self-fullness is as boundless as God's 8 Like **God's, Your Inheritance** extends forever and in perfect peace. 9 **Like God's, Your Inheritance's** radiance is so intense that **Your Inheritance** creates in perfect joy, and only the whole can be born of **Your Inheritance's** Wholeness.

Note # 76: It is God's Will that His Son's create like Him. This is our divine birthright that cannot be lost. Our function, as God's Son, is to create or extend our "Beingness" to our creations. Thus, we extend God's Kingdom. Our inheritance, being of God and from God, cannot be lost. In our insanity, we can temporarily forget where we put our inheritance, but paradise cannot be lost.

T-7.IX.7. Be confident that you have never lost your Identity and the extensions which maintain **your Identity** in wholeness and peace. 2 Miracles are an expression of this confidence **that you have never lost your Identity**. 3 **Miracles** are reflections of both your proper identification with your brothers, and of your awareness that your identification is maintained by extension. 4 The miracle is a lesson in total perception. 5 By including any part of totality in the lesson, you have included the whole **of totality in the lesson**.

Note # 77: Our true reality is that we are a Oneness. Whenever we share or extend, we experience or know our One Self as this Oneness. The lesson of the Holy Spirit is, "To have, give all to all." Having and being are the same in the "eyes" of the Holy Spirit, Who keeps us in communication within the Mind of God.

X. The Confusion of Pain and Joy

T-7.X.1. The Kingdom is the result of premises, just as this world is **the result of premises**. 2 You may have carried the ego's reasoning to **the ego's** logical conclusion, which is total confusion about everything. 3 If you really **saw that the ego's logical conclusion of its' reasoning is total confusion about everything,** you could not want **this result**. 4 The only reason you could possibly want any part of **the ego's thought system, which results in total confusion about everything,** is because you do not see the whole of **the ego's thought system**. 5 You are willing to look at the ego's premises, but not at **the ego's premises'** logical outcome. 6 Is it not possible that you have done the same thing with the premises of God? **(Not looked at their logical outcome)** 7 Your creations are the logical outcome of **God's** premises. 8 **God's** thinking has established **your creations as the logical outcome of God's premises** for you. 9 **Your creations** are exactly where **your creations** belong. 10 **Your creations** belong in your mind as part of your identification with **God's Mind**, but your state of mind and your recognition of what is in **your mind** depend on what you believe about your mind. 11 Whatever these beliefs may be, **these beliefs** are the premises that will determine what you accept into your mind.

Note # 78: As decision-maker, your mind must decide what thought system it will follow. It must choose between either the ego's or the Holy Spirit's thought system. Based on this decision, the results will be the logical outcome as determined by the basic premise of either lack or abundance, fear or love, separation or oneness.

T-7.X.2. It is surely clear that you can both accept into your mind what is not there, and deny what is **there in your mind**. 2 Yet the function God Himself gave your mind through His **Mind** you may deny, but you cannot prevent **the function God Himself gave your mind**. 3 **The function God Himself gave your mind** is the logical outcome of what you are, **which is a Son of God**. 4 The ability to see a logical outcome depends on the willingness to see **the logical outcome**, but **the logical outcome's** truth has nothing to do with your willingness **to see the logical outcome**. 5 Truth is God's Will. 6 Share **God's**

Will and you share what **God** knows. 7 Deny **God's** Will as your **will**, and you are denying **God's** Kingdom <*and*> **denying** your **own kingdom, which is the same as God's Kingdom.**

Note # 79: God's Will is truth and thus, changeless. You can deny or not accept God's Will only in your dream world of provisional reality. Ultimately, we all must reawaken to what we are and follow God's Will. This Will is the same and only will we have since we live in the Mind of God. Our dream world must give way to God's Kingdom, which is Truth. Truth is not based on your perception but on the Knowledge of God. Although we can deny the truth, our denial does not change the truth.

T-7.X.3. The Holy Spirit will direct you only so as to avoid pain. 2 Surely no one would object to this goal if he recognized **that the Holy Spirit's goal is to avoid pain**. 3 The problem is not whether what the Holy Spirit says is true, but whether you want to listen to what **the Holy Spirit** says. 4 You no more recognize what is painful than you know what is joyful, and are, in fact, very apt to confuse **pain with joy**. 5 The Holy Spirit's main function is to teach you to tell **pain and joy** apart. 6 What is joyful to you is painful to the ego, and as long as you are in doubt about what you are, you will be confused about joy and pain. 7 This confusion **about joy and pain** is the cause of the whole idea of sacrifice. 8 Obey the Holy Spirit, and you will be giving up the ego. 9 But if **you obey the Holy Spirit,** you will be sacrificing nothing. 10 On the contrary, **if you obey the Holy Spirit**, you will be gaining everything. 11 If you believed **that by obeying the Holy Spirit, you would be gaining everything,** there would be no conflict.

Note # 80: Conflict is the result of not following your purpose. You cannot know your purpose if you do not know that you are spirit. The Holy Spirit's thought system reminds you of what you are. You remember that you are spirit and, therefore, a Oneness. The outcome is the logical result of what thought system you choose to belief in. Spirit is everything and illusions are nothing. To give up nothing for everything cannot be a sacrifice.

T-7.X.4. That is why you need to demonstrate the obvious to yourself. 2 **The obvious, which is doing God's Will,** is not obvious to you. 3 You believe that doing the opposite of God's Will can be better for you. 4 You also believe that it is possible to <*do*> the opposite of God's Will. 5 Therefore, you believe that an impossible choice **of doing the opposite of God's Will** is open to you, and **this choice is** one which is both fearful and desirable. 6 Yet God wills. 7 **God** does not wish. 8 Your will is as powerful as **God's Will** because **your will** <*is*> God's Will. 9 The ego's wishes do not mean anything, because the ego wishes for the impossible, **which is not doing God's Will.** 10 You can wish for the impossible, but you can will only with God. 11 This is the ego's weakness and your strength.

Note # 81: Since ego is not mind, ego has no will of its own. The ego can only wish and the split-minded can only imagine that the false is possible. The ego must rely on your mind to utilize your mind's will on behalf of the ego's goals. The ego can only wish for your mind's decision to choose to make rather than create. Your strength is that you are mind and, therefore, you are the decision-maker. Your mind has the power to will. Will, not wishes, become reality. Wishes, like the false, belong to the realm of fantasy.

T-7.X.5. The Holy Spirit always sides with you and with your strength, **which is the will you share with God's Will.** 2 As long as you avoid **the Holy Spirit's** guidance in any way, you want to be weak. 3 Yet weakness is frightening. 4 What else, then, can this decision **to avoid the Holy Spirit's guidance in any way,** mean except that you want to be fearful? 5 The Holy Spirit never asks for sacrifice, but the ego always does **asks for sacrifice.** 6 When you are confused about this distinction in motivation, **this confusion** can only be due to projection. 7 Projection is a confusion in motivation, and given this confusion **in motivation**, trust becomes impossible. 8 No one gladly obeys a guide he does not trust, but this does not mean that the guide is untrustworthy. 9 In this case, it always means that the follower is **untrustworthy**. 10 However, this **untrustworthiness of the follower**, too, is merely a matter of **the follower's** own belief. 11 Believing that **the follower** can betray, **the follower** believes that everything can betray him. 12 Yet this is only because **the follower** has elected to follow **the** false guidance **of the ego**. 13 Unable to follow **the ego's** guidance without fear, **the follower** associates fear with guidance, and refuses to follow any guidance at all. 14 If the result of this decision is confusion, this is hardly surprising.

Note # 82: Confusion and conflict results from the belief in two opposing thought systems. Projection is the result of the ego's thought system, which always arises as some form of attack. Attack demonstrates your fear that confirms your separateness. Trust is impossible when you come from fear. Lacking trust, one is fearful of placing their trust in the guidance of the Holy Spirit. Your Big "S" Self always trusts the Holy Spirit, but your little "s" self believes it has two possible choices to choose from. This egoic belief that you can pick the false leads to confusion, conflict and fear.

T-7.X.6. The Holy Spirit is perfectly trustworthy, as you are **perfectly trustworthy**. 2 God Himself trusts you, and therefore your trustworthiness is beyond question. 3 **Your trustworthiness** will always remain beyond question, however much you may question **your trustworthiness**. 4 I said before that you are the Will of God. 5 **God's** Will is not an idle wish, and your identification with **God's** Will is not optional, since **God's Will** is what you are. 6 Sharing **God's** Will with me is not really open to choice, though **sharing God's Will with me** may seem to be **open to choice**. 7 The whole separation lies in this error **that we have a choice to share or follow God's Will**. 8 The only way out of the error **that we have a choice to share or follow God's Will** is to decide that you do not have to decide anything. 9 Everything has been given you by God's decision. 10 That **everything has been given you by God's decision** is **God's** Will, and you cannot undo **God's Will which gave you everything.**

Note # 83: The "authority problem" is based on the erroneous belief that we have a choice to do or not do God's Will. This "mad idea" is the cause of the separation and the belief in individuality rather than Oneness. It claims that we are self-created and are the arbitrators of truth. We have no choice to make these decisions since truth has already been established for us in the Mind of God, and God's Will is changeless.

T-7.X.7. Even the relinquishment of your false decision-making prerogative, which the ego guards so jealously, is not accomplished by your wish. 2 **The relinquishment of your false decision-making prerogative** was accomplished for you by the Will of God, Who has not left you comfortless. 3 **God's** Voice, **which is the Holy Spirit,** will teach you how to distinguish between pain and joy, and **the Holy Spirit** will lead you out of the confusion you have made. 4 There is no confusion in the mind of a Son of God, whose will must be the Will of the Father, because the Father's Will <is> His Son's **will**.

Note # 84: When this "mad idea" that we had decision-making prerogative in regards to the choice to follow God's Will, God placed within our split mind the Voice for God, which is the Holy Spirit. Since creation is extension, our true will and God's will must be One. This idea that we could oppose God's Will is at the heart of the "Authority Problem" which forms the basis for the ego's thought system. By placing our mind under the guidance of the Holy Spirit, we remember the truth and are gently reawakened into God's Kingdom, which is our home and divine inheritance.

T-7.X.8. Miracles are in accord with the Will of God. **God's** Will you do not know because you are confused about what <you> will. 2 This means that you are confused about what you are. 3 If you are

God's Will and do not accept **God's** Will, you are denying joy. 4 The miracle is therefore a lesson in what joy is. 5 Being a lesson in sharing, **the miracle** is a lesson in love, which <*is*> joy. 6 Every miracle is thus a lesson in truth, and by offering truth you are learning the difference between pain and joy.

Note # 85: God's will is that we be happy. A miracle is a change in perception or thinking from the ego's thought system to the Holy Spirit's thought system. The ego's thought system is based on individual competition and brings pain. The miracle shifts misperception to correct perception. It recalls your oneness with another and your common purpose. This sharing and joining in mind results in joy.

XI. The State of Grace

T-7.XI.1.The Holy Spirit will always guide you truly, because your joy is **the Holy Spirit's joy**. 2 This **joy** is **the Holy Spirit's** Will for everyone because **the Holy Spirit** speaks for the Kingdom of God, which <*is*> joy. 3 Following **the Holy Spirit** is therefore the easiest thing in the world, and the only thing that is easy, because **following the Holy Spirit** is not of the world. 4 **Following the Holy Spirit** is therefore natural. 5 The world goes against your nature, being out of accord with God's laws. 6 The world perceives orders of difficulty in everything. 7 **This perception of orders of difficulty in everything in this world** is because the ego perceives nothing as wholly desirable. 8 By demonstrating to yourself there is no order of difficulty in miracles, you will convince yourself that, in your natural state, there is no difficulty at all <*because*> **your natural state** is a state of grace.

Note # 86: We are a spiritual essence dreaming that we are having an earthly experience. Our natural state is unlimited spirit. To pretend that we are a limited ego-body is unnatural since it is foreign to our "beingness." It is easy to be yourself. It is difficult to be something you are not. Conflict is the result of lack of certainty. When we deny our spiritual essences, we become conflicted and slip into fear. Any time we are not in a joyous and peaceful state, we have slipped into egoic fear-based thinking.

T-7.XI.2.Grace is the natural state of every Son of God. 2 When **a Son of God** is not in a state of grace, **a Son of God** is out of his natural environment and does not function well. 3 Everything **a Son of God** does becomes a strain, because **a Son of God** was not created for the environment that **a Son of God** has made, **which is the illusionary world of egoic perception, time and space**. 4 **A Son of God** therefore cannot adapt to **the illusionary world of the ego**, nor can **a Son of God** adapt **the illusionary world of the ego** to **his natural state as a Son of God**. 5 There is no point in trying. 6 A Son of God is happy only when **a Son of God,** knows he, **as a Son of God,** is with God. 7 **Being with God** is the only environment in which **a Son of God** will not experience strain, because **being with God** is where **a Son of God** belongs. 8 **Being with God** is also the only environment that is worthy of **a Son of God,** because **a Son of God's** own worth is beyond anything **a Son of God** can make.

Note # 87: Grace is the natural state of the Son of God. Grace maintains the realization that our being rests with God. As Sons of God, we are one with our Father. God's Son can only be happy when he is joined with His Father. In the egoic world made from our fears and limitations, we are out of our natural element. Our Big "S" Self is spirit and part of the holographic Mind of God. Being in extension of God, we can only be love. Love, not fear, is the only reality worthy of a Son of God.

T-7.XI.3. Consider the kingdom you have made and judge **the** worth **of this illusionary world of the ego** fairly. 2 Is **this illusionary world of the ego** worthy to be a home for a child of God? 3 Does **this illusionary world of the ego** protect **a child of God's** peace and shine love upon **a child of God**? 4 Does **this illusionary world of the ego** keep **a child of God's** heart untouched by fear, and allow **a child of God** to give always, without any sense of loss? 5 Does **this illusionary world of the ego** teach **a child of God** that this giving is his joy, and that God Himself thanks **a child of God** for **the child of God's** giving? 6 That is the only environment in which you can be happy. 7 You cannot make **an environment in which you can be happy**, any more than you can make yourself. 8 **An environment in which you can be happy** has been created for you, as you were created for **God's environment in which you can be happy**. 9 God watches over His children and denies them nothing. 10 Yet when **children of God** deny **God, they** do not know **that God watches over His children and denies His children nothing. Yet because of their denial of God, they** deny themselves everything. 11 You who could give the Love of God to everything you see and touch and remember are literally denying Heaven to yourself.

Note # 88: God gives everything to His creations. God denies them nothing. God's children can refuse to accept this knowledge of what they really are and thus, perceive they have "fallen from grace." This false perception needs to be corrected within the deluded mind. Yet, the true nature of how and what God created remains unchanged. Only in your ego's dream world of provisional reality can you deny yourself heaven, which is the Kingdom.

T-7.XI.4.I call upon you to remember that I have chosen you to teach the Kingdom <to> the Kingdom. 2 There are no exceptions to this lesson **for you to teach the Kingdom <to> the Kingdom,** because the lack of exceptions <is> the lesson. 3 Every Son who returns to the Kingdom with this lesson **that you must teach the Kingdom <to> the Kingdom with no exceptions,** in his heart has healed the Sonship and given thanks to God. 4 Everyone who learns this lesson **that you must teach the Kingdom <to> the Kingdom with no exceptions** has become the perfect teacher, because he has learned it of the Holy Spirit. p136

Note # 89: We cannot exclude any of God's creations from the truth of the Kingdom. There can be no exception since all God's creations are equally blessed with the same divine birthright and inheritance. God gives only equally since God gives everything to everything. Extension of the hologram is the creative process of the Mind of God.

T-7.XI.5. When a mind has only light, **a mind** knows only light. 2 **A mind's** own radiance shines all around **itself,** and extends out into the darkness of other minds, transforming **other minds** into majesty. 3 The Majesty of God is there **in other minds**, for you to recognize and appreciate and know. 4 Recognizing the Majesty of God as your brother is to accept your own inheritance. 5 God gives only equally. 6 If you recognize **God's** gift **and know the Majesty of God is** in anyone, you have acknowledged what **God** has given you. 7 Nothing is so easy to recognize as truth. 8 This **truth of what God has given you, your inheritance**, is the recognition that is immediate, clear and natural. 9 You have trained yourself not to recognize **your inheritance that God's Majesty is you** and this has been very difficult for you.

Note # 90: Because we have free will, we can dream or forget that we are Sons of God. As such, we can deny our inheritance, but we cannot lose it. It cannot be lost because God has given us this inheritance and God's Will is changeless. Since giving is receiving, when we choose to see only the Big "S" Self in our brother, we realize that same Big "S" Self in ourselves.

T-7.XI.6. Out of your natural environment, **which is the illusionary world of the ego,** you may well ask, "What is truth?" since truth is the environment by which and for which you were created. 2 You do not know yourself, because you do not know your Creator. 3 You do not know your creations because you do not know your brothers, who created **your creations** with you. 4 I have already said that only the whole Sonship is worthy to be co-creator with God, because only the whole Sonship can create like **the Father.** 5 Whenever you heal a brother by recognizing his worth, you are acknowledging **a brother's** power to create and **your power to create.** 6 **A brother** cannot have lost what you recognize, and you must have the glory you see in **your brother.** 7 **A brother** is a co-creator with God with you. 8 Deny **a brother's** creative power and you are denying your **creative power** and **the creative power** of God Who created you.

Note # 91: To create like the Father, the Sonship must see itself as whole to be whole. Only the Oneness of the Sonship can create like the Father. If we attempt to exclude any part of the Sonship from sharing in our creation, we are engaged in making, not creating. Only a Oneness can extend the One Self that is the holographic Mind of God.

T-7.XI.7. You cannot deny part of truth. 2 You do not know your creations because you do not know their creator, **which is the whole Sonship.** 3 You do not know yourself because you do not know **your creations.** 4 Your creations cannot establish your reality, any more than you can establish God's **reality.** 5 But you can <know> both **your creations and your true reality.** 6 Being is known by sharing. 7 Because God shared His Being with you, you can know **God.** 8 But you must also know all **God** created, to know what **all God created** have shared. 9 Without your Father you will not know your fatherhood. 10 The Kingdom of God includes all His Sons and **all His Sons'** children, who are as like the Sons as **all His Sons' children** are like the Father. 11 Know, then, the Sons of God, and you will know all creation.

Note # 92: All God's creation is a Oneness. This is why there is equality in the Kingdom. All creations, being an extension of everything that created them, are an indivisible part of the wholeness of everything. Each part is a holographic oneness of the whole, for each part is one with the Mind of God. Only the whole Sonship is worthy to be co-creator with God, because only the whole Sonship can create like God. Deny your brother's creative power and you have denied your own creative power. Being is known by sharing. Since we are spirit, the only way to know our true Self is to <be>. True creation, or extension, is <Being>. Spirit feels, experiences and just is. The egoic mind thinks, compares, divides and then judges. Creation and making involve two different mindsets.

Chapter 8. THE JOURNEY BACK

I. The Direction of the Curriculum

T-8.I.1. Knowledge is not the motivation for learning this course. 2 Peace is **the motivation for learning this course.** 3 **Peace** is the prerequisite for knowledge only because those who are in conflict are not peaceful, and peace is the condition of knowledge because **peace** is the condition of the Kingdom. 4 Knowledge can be restored only when you meet **knowledge's** conditions. 5 **The requirement that peace is the prerequisite for knowledge** is not a bargain made by God, Who makes no bargains. 6 **The requirement that peace is the prerequisite for knowledge** is merely the result of your misuse of **God's** laws on behalf of an imaginary will that is not **God's Will.** 7 Knowledge <is> **God's** Will. 8 If you are opposing **God's** Will, how can you have knowledge? 9 I have told you what knowledge offers you, but perhaps you do not yet regard **what knowledge offers you** as wholly desirable. 10 If you did **regard what knowledge offers you as wholly desirable,** you would not be so ready to throw **knowledge** away when the ego asks for your allegiance.

<u>Note #1:</u> Knowledge is truth. Knowledge is lost as long as your mind is split due to the ego's belief in separation. Egoic beliefs lead us into conflict and the loss of inner peace.

T-8.I.2. The distractions of the ego may seem to interfere with your learning, but the ego has no power to distract you unless you give **the ego** the power to **distract you.** 2 The ego's voice is an hallucination. 3 You cannot expect **the ego** to say "I, **the ego,** am not real." 4 Yet you are not asked to dispel your hallucinations alone. 5 You are merely asked to evaluate **your hallucinations of the ego,** in terms of **your hallucinations'** results to you. 6 If you do not want **your hallucinations' results** on the basis of loss of peace, **your hallucinations' results** will be removed from your mind for you.

<u>Note # 2:</u> Since the ego is a creation of your mind, the only power that the ego has is what your mind gives it. Your mind remains the decision-maker. You will only want to keep the ego if you value the results given to you by following its belief system. The egoic belief system says that you are a separate autonomous individual. It claims that you are special.

T-8.I.3. Every response to the ego is a call to war, and war does deprive you of peace. 2 Yet in this war **of the ego** there is no opponent. 3 **The realization that there is no opponent for the ego to war against** is the reinterpretation of reality that you must make to secure peace, and the only **response to the ego** you need ever make. 4 Those whom you perceive as opponents are part of your peace, which you are giving up by attacking **those whom you perceive as opponents.** 5 How can you have what you give up? 6 You share to have **peace,** but you do not give **peace** up yourself. 7 When you give up peace, you are excluding yourself from **peace.** 8 **Excluding yourself from peace** is a condition so alien to the Kingdom that you cannot understand the state that prevails within **the Kingdom.**

Note # 3: You, as decision-maker, always have a choice as to which thought system the mind will follow. The ego's thought system offers war while the Holy Spirit's thought system offers peace. If we claim we are separate and special, we will have to protect our "assets" against outside attack. By claiming specialness, we deny the reality of our spirit. We deny the reality of our oneness with everything. We now have opponents and attack becomes possible.

T-8.I.4. Your past **egoic** learning must have taught you the wrong things, simply because **your past learning** has not made you happy. 2 On this basis alone **(The fact that your past egoic learning has not made you happy.) your egoic learning** value should be questioned. 3 If learning aims at change, and that is always **learning's** purpose, are you satisfied with the changes your **egoic** learning has brought you? 4 Dissatisfaction with learning outcomes is a sign of learning failure, since **dissatisfaction with learning outcomes** means that you did not get what you wanted.

Note # 4: If you are not happy, the Holy Spirit asks you to choose again and follow the guidance of the Holy Spirit. The egoic thought system is designed to value your claim to be right over your happiness.

T-8.I.5. The curriculum of the Atonement is the opposite of the curriculum you have established for yourself, but so is **the curriculum of the Atonement's** outcome. 2 If the outcome of **your ego's curriculum** has made you unhappy, and if you want a different **outcome**, a change in the curriculum is obviously necessary. 3 The first change to be introduced is a change in direction. 4 A meaningful curriculum cannot be inconsistent. 5 If it is planned by two teachers, each believing in diametrically opposed ideas, **each teacher's curriculum** cannot be integrated. 6 If **the curriculum** is carried out by these two teachers simultaneously, each **teacher's curriculum** merely interferes with the other **teacher's curriculum**. 7 **These conflicting teacher's curriculums** leads to fluctuation, but not to change. 8 The volatile have no direction. 9 **The students** cannot choose one **teacher's curriculum** because **the students,** cannot relinquish the other **teacher's curriculum**, even if **the other teacher's curriculum** does not exist. 10 Their conflicted curriculum teaches **the student** that <all> directions exist, and gives **the student** no rationale for choice.

Note # 5: Your mind cannot serve two opposing teachers. You must choose only one teacher's voice to follow.

T-8.I.6. The total senselessness of such a **conflicted** curriculum must be fully recognized before a real change in direction becomes possible. 2 You cannot learn simultaneously from two teachers who are in total disagreement about everything. 3 Their joint curriculum presents an impossible learning task. 4 **The two teachers who are in total disagreement about everything** are teaching you entirely different things in entirely different ways, which might be possible except that both are teaching you about yourself. 5 Your reality is unaffected by both **teachers**, but if you listen to both **teachers**, your mind will be split about what your reality is.

Note # 6: To reunify your split mind, you must choose only to follow the guidance of the Holy Spirit. The ego teaches us that we are special and separate. The price for specialness is limitation and the acceptance of the body as our reality. The ego's teachings result in the loss of our peace and happiness. It gives us conflict, fear, competition and lack. The Holy Spirit teaches us that we are unlimited spirit and part of the Oneness that is the holographic Mind of God. Knowing we are everything, It teaches equality and extension. The Holy Spirit's teachings result in our obtainment of love, peace and happiness.

II. The Difference between Imprisonment and Freedom

T-8.II.1. There <*is*> a rationale for choice. 2 Only one Teacher knows what your reality is. 3 If learning to remove the obstacles to that knowledge is the purpose of the curriculum, you must learn **to remove the obstacles to that knowledge** of Him, **the Holy Spirit, the one Teacher that knows what your reality is.** 4 The ego does not know what **the ego** is trying to teach. 5 **The ego** is trying to teach you what you are without knowing what you are. 6 **The ego** is expert only in confusion. 7 **The ego** does not understand anything else **but confusion.** 8 As a teacher, then, the ego is totally confused and totally confusing. 9 Even if you could disregard the Holy Spirit entirely, which is impossible, you could still learn nothing from the ego, because the ego knows nothing.

Note # 7: The ego knows nothing because its entire thought system is based on not knowing what you are. It is based on the belief in separation and that you can do something other than God's Will. The ego claims you are an individual ego-body, not an unlimited spiritual essence The Holy Spirit's thought system is based on knowledge and its goal is your return to knowledge. Knowledge is God's Will.

T-8.II.2. Is there any possible reason for choosing a teacher such as **the ego who knows nothing**? 2 Does the total disregard of anything **the ego** teaches make anything but sense? 3 Is **the ego that knows nothing** the teacher to whom a Son of God should turn to find himself? 4 The ego has never given you a sensible answer to anything. 5 Simply on the grounds of your own experience with **the ego's** teaching, should not this alone disqualify **the ego** as your future teacher? 6 Yet the ego has done more harm to your learning than this alone. 7 Learning is joyful if **learning** leads you along your natural path, and facilitates the development of what you have. 8 When you are taught against your nature, however, you will lose by your learning because your learning will imprison you. 9 Your will is <*in*> your nature, and therefore cannot go against **your nature**.

Note # 8: The ego teaches that you are not your mind, but rather a body. This goes against your nature as unlimited spirit. If you are a body, you become a victim to outside forces. You lose your ability to be the decision-maker in charge of choosing your own experiences and awareness.

T-8.II.3. The ego cannot teach you anything as long as your will is free, because you will not listen to **the ego if your will is free**. 2 It is not your will to be imprisoned because your will is free. 3 **Because the ego would imprison your will, this** is why the ego is the denial of free will. 4 It is never God Who coerces you, because **God** shares **God's** Will with you. 5 **God's** Voice teaches only in accordance with **God's** Will, but that is not the Holy Spirit's lesson because that is what you <*are.*> 6 The lesson **of the Holy Spirit** is that your will and God's Will cannot be out of accord because **your will and God's Will** are one. 7 **That your will and God's Will are one** is the undoing of everything the ego tries to teach. 8 It is not, then, only the direction of the curriculum that must be unconflicted, but also the content **of the curriculum that must be unconflicted**.

Note # 9: The entire egoic thought system is predicated on the belief that you have a will that is different from God's and that your will can and does oppose God's Will. The ego's "will" claims that it is more important to claim that you are right even when you are wrong than it is to be happy. God and the Holy Spirit and your Big "S" Self all agree that Their one joint Will is that you be happy.

T-8.II.4. The ego tries to teach that you want to oppose God's Will. 2 **That you want to oppose God's Will is an** unnatural lesson **that** cannot be learned, and the attempt to learn **the unnatural lesson that you want to oppose God's Will** is a violation of your own freedom, making you afraid of your will <because> **your will** is free. 3 The Holy Spirit opposes any imprisoning of the will of a Son of God, knowing that the Will of the Son is the Father's **Will**. 4 The Holy Spirit leads you steadily along the path of freedom, teaching you how to disregard or look beyond everything that would hold you back.

Note # 10: Since you are an extension of the Mind of God, you have been created in God's image. As such, your will and God's Will are the same. The ego attempts to teach you that what is the same, your joint Will, is actually different. This is unnatural since it is contradictory to what you are and, therefore, false. Your Big "S" Self knows the truth and looks upon the ego's thought system as unnatural and imprisoning since it opposes your divine birthright.

T-8.II.5. We have said that the Holy Spirit teaches you the difference between pain and joy. 2 **The difference between pain and joy** is the same as saying **the Holy Spirit** teaches you the difference between imprisonment and freedom. 3 You cannot make this distinction **between imprisonment and freedom** without **the Holy Spirit** because you have taught yourself that imprisonment is freedom. 4 Believing **imprisonment and freedom** to be the same how can you tell **imprisonment and freedom** apart? 5 Can you ask the part of your mind, **your ego that** taught you to believe **imprisonment and freedom** are the same, to teach you how **imprisonment and freedom** are different?

Note # 11: A teacher who knows nothing and only teaches the false cannot be expected to miraculously start teaching the truth. To teach truth, the teacher must have knowledge of the truth. The ego's thought system imprisons your free will by removing the mind as the decision-maker, and then claims that you are free to oppose God's Will. It is only in your decision to be one with the Mind of God that you can be free since that is what you are. The goal of the Holy Spirit is to "Know Thyself." The ego's goal is that you "Never Know Thyself." As long as you view yourself as a separate individual, you cannot know yourself as the whole. You need unity with your brother, who is a part of you, to realize that you are part of God, Who is everything.

T-8.II.6. The Holy Spirit's teaching takes only <one> direction and has only <one> goal. 2 **The Holy Spirit's** direction is freedom and **the Holy Spirit's** goal is God. 3 Yet **the Holy Spirit** cannot conceive of God without you, because it is not God's Will to <be> without you. 4 When you have learned that your will is God's Will, you could no more will to be without **God** than **God** could will to be without you. 5 This **learning that your will is God's Will,** is freedom and this **learning that your will is God's Will** is joy. 6 Deny yourself this **learning that your will is God's Will** and you are denying God His Kingdom, because **God** created you for this **learning that your will is God's Will**.

Note # 12: God created you as an extension of Himself. God is the cause and we are the Effect. Cause and effect are inseparable. We are God's completion. Our purpose is to extend the Kingdom by becoming co-creators with our Father.

T-8.II.7. When I said, "All power and glory are yours because the Kingdom is **God's**," this is what I meant: The Will of God is without limit, and all power and glory lie within **the Will of God**. 2 **The Will of God** is boundless in strength and in love and in peace. 3 **The Will of God** has no boundaries because **the Will of God's** extension is unlimited, and **the Will of God** encompasses all things because **the Will of God** created all things. 4 By creating all things, **the Will of God** made **all things** part of itself. 5 You are the Will of God because that is how you were created. 6 Because your Creator creates only like

Himself, you are like **your Creator**. 7 You are part of **your Creator** Who is all power and glory, and **you** are therefore, as unlimited as **God, your Creator** is.

Note # 13: Because creation is an extension, we share all the powers of our source. Our powers only difference is that the Father is the First Cause. We did not self-create ourselves. We are the extension of the universal hologram that is the Mind of God.

T-8.II.8. To what else except all power and glory can the Holy Spirit appeal to restore God's Kingdom? 2 **The Holy Spirit's** appeal, then, is merely to what the Kingdom is, and for **the Kingdom's** own acknowledgment of what **the Kingdom** is. 3 When you acknowledge **what the Kingdom is** you bring the acknowledgment automatically to everyone, because you <*have*> acknowledged everyone. 4 By your recognition you awaken their **recognition**, and through their **recognition** your **recognition** is extended. 5 Awakening runs easily and gladly through the Kingdom, in answer to the Call for God. 6 This **recognition and acknowledgement of what the Kingdom is**, is the natural response of every Son of God to the Voice for his Creator, because **this recognition and acknowledgement of what the Kingdom is,** is the Voice for his son's creations and for his son's own extension. **This recognition is the acknowledgment that all power and glory has been given to God's creations since God's creations are the extensions of the Will of God**

Note # 14: The Kingdom is the Truth. When we realize that our divine birthright is the truth that we are the Oneness of Everything, we will freely embrace this truth and share it with our brother. Being One with the God of "All That Is," we cannot be content with egoic littleness.

III. The Holy Encounter

T-8.III.1. Glory to God in the highest, and to you because **God** has so willed **glory to you**. 2 Ask and **glory to you** shall be given you, because **glory to you** has already <*been*> given **to you**. 3 Ask for light and learn that you <*are*> light. 4 If you want understanding and enlightenment you will learn **understanding and enlightenment**, because your decision to learn **understanding and enlightenment** is the decision to listen to the Teacher Who knows of light, **which is the Holy Spirit,** and can therefore teach **understanding and enlightenment** to you. 5 There is no limit on your learning because there is no limit on your mind. 6 There is no limit on **the Holy Spirit's** teaching because **the Holy Spirit** was created to teach. 7 Understanding **the Holy Spirit's** function perfectly **the Holy Spirit** fulfills **the Holy Spirit's function** perfectly, because that is **the Holy Spirit's** joy and **your joy**.

Note # 15: God gave the Holy Spirit the purpose of returning the Sonship to the Kingdom. The Holy Spirit cannot fail in this mission since Its purpose is backed by the Will of God. It will teach us the truth because It knows the truth.

T-8.III.2. To fulfill the Will of God perfectly is the only joy and peace that can be fully known, because **to fulfill the Will of God perfectly** is the only function that can be fully experienced. 2 When **fulfilling the Will of God perfectly** is accomplished, then, there is no other experience **than to fulfill the Will of God perfectly**. 3 Yet the wish for other experience will block **the** accomplishment **of the fulfillment of the Will of God perfectly**, because God's Will cannot be forced upon you, **because God's Will is** being an experience of total willingness. 4 The Holy Spirit understands how to teach **the fulfillment of the Will of God perfectly** but you do not **understand how to teach the fulfillment of the Will of God perfectly**. 5 **Because you do not understand how to teach the fulfillment of the Will of God perfectly this** is why you need **the Holy Spirit**, and why God gave **the Holy Spirit** to you. 6 Only **the Holy Spirit's** teaching will release your will to God's **Will**, uniting **your will** with **God's** power and glory and establishing **God's power and glory** as **your power and glory**. 7 You share **God's power and glory** as God shares **God's power and glory**, because **God's power and glory** is the natural outcome of **God's power and glory's** being.

Note # 16: Our function is to perfectly fulfill and experience the Will of God. We do this by extending ourselves to our own creations as the Father extended Himself to His Son. We cannot create like our Father if we do not know and accept our divine inheritance as unlimited spirit. Since to give is to receive, by sharing or extending our inheritance to others, we accept and receive our inheritance. Creation is "being" It is a participatory process. We cannot participate in co-creation when we attempt to exclude anything from the Oneness that is the holographic Mind of God.

T-8.III.3. The Will of the Father and of the Son are One, by Their extension. 2 **The** extension **of the One Will of the Father and Son** is the result of **the Father and Son's** Oneness holding Their unity together by extending **the Father and Son's** joint Will. 3 This **extension** is perfect creation by the perfectly created **Son** of God in union with the perfect Creator, **God, the Father**. 4 The Father must give fatherhood to His Son, because **God's** Own Fatherhood must be extended outward. 5 You who belong in God have the holy function of extending **God's** Fatherhood by placing no limits upon **God's Fatherhood**. 6 Let the Holy Spirit teach you how to do this **holy function of extending God's Fatherhood by placing no limits upon God's Fatherhood**, for you can know what **this function of extending God's Fatherhood** means only of God Himself.

Note # 17: We must not place any limits on the extension of God, the Father. To limit is to not extend. To have all, give all, to all. This is the first lesson of the Holy Spirit. If God did not give us all His powers, including the power of creation, we would not have been created in His image. By our failure to utilize this power, we are attempting to limit the extension of God. This cannot be done. Our function is to be co-creator with God. This is how we share God's Will.

T-8.III.4. When you meet anyone, remember **any meeting** is a holy encounter. 2 As you see him you will see yourself. 3 As you treat him you will treat yourself. 4 As you think of him you will think of yourself. 5 Never forget this, for in **your brother** you will find yourself or lose yourself. 6 Whenever two Sons of God meet, they are given another chance at salvation. 7 Do not leave anyone without giving salvation to him and receiving **salvation** yourself. 8 For I am always there with you, in remembrance of <you.>

Note # 18: We receive what we give. What we perceive, we project out to others and this same projection is reflected back on us. What we think, we become. We can only perceive in another what we believe that we hold inside ourselves. Our purpose will determine what we allow ourselves to perceive. We cannot love another if we do not love ourselves.

T-8.III.5. The goal of the curriculum, regardless of the teacher you choose, is "Know thyself." 2 There is nothing else to seek **but to "Know thyself."** 3 Everyone is looking for himself and for the power and glory he thinks he has lost. 4 Whenever you are with anyone, you have another opportunity to find them. 5 Your power and glory are in him because **his power and glory** are yours. 6 The ego tries to find **power and glory** in yourself alone, because **the ego** does not know where to look **for your power and**

glory. 7 The Holy Spirit teaches you that if you look only at yourself you cannot find yourself, because that is not what you are. 8 Whenever you are with a brother, you are learning what you are because you are teaching what you are **to your brother**. 9 **Your brother** will respond either with pain or with joy, depending on which teacher, **the ego or the Holy Spirit,** you are following. 10 **Your brother** will be imprisoned or released according to your decision **on which teacher, the ego or the Holy Spirit, you are choosing to follow**, and so will you **be imprisoned or released by your decision**. 11 Never forget your responsibility to **your brother**, because **your responsibility for your choice of teacher** is your responsibility to yourself. 12 Give **your brother** his place in the Kingdom and you will have **given yourself your place in the Kingdom**.

Note # 19: When we follow the thought system of the Holy Spirit, we look past bodily form, and see the Christ in our brother. If not, we see limitation and imperfection. Since to give is to receive, we will be placing that same self-image upon ourselves. By seeing our brother as limited, we imprison ourselves as his jail warden.

T-8.III.6. The Kingdom cannot be found alone, and you who are the Kingdom cannot find yourself alone. 2 To achieve the goal of the curriculum, **which is to know thyself and thus, extend God's Kingdom,** then, you cannot listen to the ego, whose purpose is to defeat its own goal **of knowing thyself**. 3 The ego does not know this, because **the ego** does not know anything. 4 But you can know **not to listen to the ego**, and you will know **not to listen to the ego** if you are willing to look at what the ego would make of you. 5 **To look at what the ego would make of you** is your responsibility, because once you have really looked at **what the ego would make of you,** you <*will*> accept the Atonement for yourself. 6 What other choice could you make? 7 Having made this choice **of accepting the Atonement for yourself,** you will understand why you once believed that, when you met someone else, you thought he <*was*> someone else. 8 And every holy encounter in which you enter fully will teach you **the idea of your separateness** is not so.

Note # 20: Since the Sonship is also a Oneness, all God's creations are part of the whole. In seeing the oneness of you and your entire brotherhood, the Sonship becomes reunited in perfect equality. Every holy encounter is utilized to teach and experience union with each other. These once egoic relationships have been transformed into a means of sharing and joining. The Holy Spirit has taken the teaching devices of egoic learning and turned them into learning lessons for the truth of the Oneness.

T-8.III.7. You can encounter only part of yourself because you are part of God, Who is everything. 2 **God's** power and glory are everywhere, and you cannot be excluded from **God's power and glory**. 3 The ego teaches that your strength is in you alone. 4 The Holy Spirit teaches that all strength is in God and <*therefore*> **all strength is** in you **since you are part of God**. 5 God wills no one suffer. 6 **God** does not will anyone to suffer for a wrong decision, including you. 7 That is why **God** has given you the means for undoing **a wrong decision**. 8 Through **God's** power and glory all your wrong decisions are undone completely, releasing you and your brother from every imprisoning thought any part of the Sonship holds. 9 Wrong decisions have no power, because **wrong decisions** are not true. 10 The imprisonment **that wrong decisions** seem to produce is no more true than **the wrong decision is true**.

Note # 21: God only wills that His Child be happy. God does not condemn a child, when a child errs. Mistakes are not sin. They merely require correction. God asks through the Holy Spirit that His Child choose again. Punishment is not part of the Mind of God since God knows His Child only as He was created, perfect, whole and complete.

T-8.III.8. Power and glory belong to God alone. 2 So do you **belong to God alone** 3 God gives whatever belongs to **God** because **God** gives of Himself, and everything belongs to **God**. 4 Giving of yourself is the function **God** gave you. 5 Fulfilling **the function of giving of yourself** perfectly will let you remember what you <have> of **God**, and by this **giving of yourself perfectly** you will remember also what you <are> in **God**. 6 You cannot be powerless to do this **giving of yourself perfectly**, because this **giving of yourself perfectly** is your power. 7 Glory is God's gift to you, because **glory** is what **God** is. 8 See this glory **of God** everywhere to remember what you are, **for you are the glory of God**.

Note # 22: Giving of yourself is the function God gave you. By giving, you receive and remember that you are unlimited spirit. You are "being" what God created you to be. Creation is the giving of yourself, which is everything, to everything. By giving, you know you have. Being and having are the same under the thought system of the Holy Spirit, Who represents God's Laws. By your being a co-creator with God, you extend the holographic Mind of God. This is God's glory.

IV. The Gift of Freedom

T-8.IV.1.If God's Will for you is complete peace and joy, unless you experience only **complete peace and joy** you must be refusing to acknowledge **God's** Will. 2 **God's** Will does not vacillate, being changeless forever. 3 When you are not at peace it can only be because you do not believe you are in **God**. 4 Yet **God** is All in all. 5 **God's** peace is complete, and you must be included in **God's peace**. 6 **God's** laws govern you because **God's laws** govern everything. 7 You cannot exempt yourself from **God's** laws, although you can disobey **God's laws**. 8 Yet if you do **disobey God's laws**, and only if you do **disobey God's laws**, you will feel lonely and helpless, because you are denying yourself everything.

Note # 23: Because we have free will, our ego can temporarily choose to deny that the Laws of God apply to us. Yet, this denial can only result in our unhappiness since our Big "S" Self feels our lack of alignment with our true Source. Our split mind is in conflict and needs to be brought back into wholeness with God's Will. God's Will is that we be happy and know ourselves to be the completion of God, Herself.

T-8.IV.2.I am come as a light into a world that does deny itself everything. 2 **This world that denies itself everything** does this simply by dissociating itself, **(our dream world of provisional reality)**, from everything **that is real**. 3 **Our dream world of provisional reality** is therefore an illusion of isolation, maintained by fear of the same loneliness that <is> our dream world's illusion, **which is the belief in the separation**. 4 I said that I am with you always, even unto the end of the world. 5 **Because I am with you always**, that is why I am the light of the world. 6 If I am with you in the loneliness of the world, the loneliness is gone. 7 You cannot maintain the illusion of loneliness if you are not alone. 8 My purpose, then, is still to overcome the world **of illusion**. 9 I do not attack **the world of illusion**, but my light must dispel **the world of illusion** because of what **the world** is. 10 Light does not attack darkness, but **light** does shine **darkness** away. 11 If my light goes with you everywhere, you shine **darkness** away with me. 12 The light becomes **our light**, and you cannot abide in darkness any more than darkness can abide wherever you go. 13 The remembrance of me is the remembrance of yourself, and of **God,** Who sent me to you.

Note # 24: By denying our spiritual essence, we deny the fact that we are a Oneness of "All That Is." Instead, we make an illusionary world in which we hide in fear. Jesus, as the way-shower, dispels our illusions with his light of truth. As we share his light with our brother, his light becomes our light. We discover we were never alone, only sleeping.

T-8.IV.3. You were in darkness until God's Will was done completely by any part of the Sonship. 2 When **God's Will was done completely by any part of the Sonship,** it was perfectly accomplished by all **of the Sonship**. 3 How else could **God's Will** be perfectly accomplished? 4 My mission was simply to unite the will of the Sonship with the Will of the Father by being aware of the Father's Will myself. 5 This is the awareness I came to give you, and your problem in accepting **the unity of the will of the Sonship with the Will of the Father** is the problem of this world. 6 Dispelling **the world's problem of not accepting the unity of the will of the Sonship with the Will of the Father** is salvation, and in this sense I <am> the salvation of the world. 7 The world must therefore despise and reject me, because the world <is> the belief that love is impossible. 8 If you will accept the fact that I am with you, you are denying the world and accepting God. 9 My will is **God's Will**, and your decision to hear me is the decision to hear **God's** Voice and abide in **God's** Will. 10 As God sent me to you so will I send you to others. 11 And I will go to **the others** with you, so we can teach **the others** peace and union.

Note # 25: Jesus' mission was to unite the will of the Sonship with the Will of the Father. Jesus accomplished this by being aware of God's Will within himself. Our part in the salvation process is to accept God's Will within ourselves as Jesus did and thus, unite the will of the Sonship with God's Will. The Sonship is one and is also holographic. When Jesus completed his remembrance of God, the entire Sonship benefited from this unification.

T-8.IV.4. Do you not think the world needs peace as much as you do? 2 Do you not want to give **peace** to the world as much as you want to receive **peace**? 3 For unless you do **want to give peace**, you will not receive **peace**. 4 If you want to have **the peace** of me, you must give **peace**. 5 Healing does not come from anyone else. 6 You must accept guidance from within. 7 The guidance must be what you want, or **the guidance** will be meaningless to you. 8 That **you must want guidance, or the guidance will be meaningless to you,** is why healing is a collaborative venture. 9 I can tell you what to do, but you must collaborate by believing that I know what you should do. 10 Only then **by believing that I know what you should do**, will your mind choose to follow me. 11 Without this choice **to follow me** you could not be healed because you would have decided against healing, and this rejection of my decision for you makes healing impossible.

Note # 26: Because we have free will, we must be willing to accept Jesus' or the Holy Spirit's guidance. Without our collaboration, the guidance of the High –Self will not be followed. Healing must come from within you. Only you can choose to be healed. Healing cannot be imposed upon someone by an outside force. If this were the case, it would prove that we are indeed separate and not created equally. Since our mind is split, you must accept guidance from the Holy Spirit and collaborate with this guide by believing the Holy Spirit knows what you should do. Healing reflects the joining of our Big "S" Self with another High-Self's will by which the "mad idea" of the separation is overcome by union. By sharing, truth overcomes the fear of the false.

T-8.IV.5. Healing reflects our joint will. 2 This is obvious when you consider what healing is for. 3 Healing is the way in which the separation is overcome. 4 Separation is overcome by union. 5 **Separation** cannot be overcome by separating. 6 The decision to unite must be unequivocal, or the mind itself is divided and not whole. 7 Your mind is the means by which you determine your own condition, because mind is the mechanism of decision. 8 **Mind's mechanism of decision** is the power by which you separate or join, and experience pain or joy accordingly. 9 My decision cannot overcome **your decision**, because **your decision** is as powerful as **my decision**. 10 If **your decision was not as powerful as my decision,** the Sons of God would be unequal. 11 All things are possible through our joint decision, but **my decision** alone cannot help you. 12 Your will is as free as mine, and God Himself would not go against **your free will**. 13 I cannot will what God does not will **and God Wills your will be free**. 14 I can offer my strength **of my will** to make **your will** invincible, but I cannot oppose your decision without competing with **your decision** and thereby violating God's Will for you.

Note # 27: Due to our free will, we must willingly join in any decision making process. Our mind is the decision-maker and our free will insures equality among the Sonship. Only by collaboration with the thought system of the Holy Spirit can we heal our split mind. We control every experience we call into our awareness. There are no victims and no outside force controls our destiny. God's love allows us perfect freedom to co-create or to imagine anything that we want.

This also means that there are no "innocent victims." Any experience that involves others is a collaborative effort. Someone must choose to be the "victim" and the other must choose to be the "victimizer." No one, not even Jesus, can force us to do something against our free will. God wills that His Children be free to experience anything that we want. We can co-create like and with God or we can imagine the false in the non-real world of individual perception, time and space with the fragmented Sonship.

T-8.IV.6. Nothing God created can oppose your decision, as nothing God created can oppose **God's Will**. 2 God gave your will its power, which I can only acknowledge in honor of **God's Will**. 3 If you want to be like me I will help you, knowing that we are alike. 4 If you want to be different, I will wait until you change your mind. 5 I can teach you, but only you can choose to listen to my teaching. 6 How else can it be, if God's Kingdom is freedom? 7 Freedom cannot be learned by tyranny of any kind, and the perfect equality of all God's Sons cannot be recognized through the dominion of one mind over another **mind**. 8 God's Sons are equal in will, all being the Will of their Father. 9 **That God's Sons are equal in will, all being the Will of their Father,** is the only lesson I came to teach.

Note # 28: Due to equality within the Sonship, our free will prevents Jesus or the Holy Spirit from forcing their Will upon another. Both are willing to wait patiently until we freely ask for their guidance. This asking is inevitable because God's Will is that we be whole. The joining or union of our split mind is the goal of healing. This reestablishes the Will of God in our minds, which always remain part of the One Mind of God.

T-8.IV.7. If your will were not **my will, your will** would not be our Father's **Will**. 2 This would mean you have imprisoned **your will**, and have not let **your will** be free. 3 Of yourself you can do nothing, because of yourself you <are> nothing. 4 I am nothing without the Father and you are nothing without me, because by denying the Father you deny yourself. 5 I will always remember you, and in my remembrance of you lies your remembrance of yourself. 6 In our remembrance of each other lies our remembrance of God. 7 And in this remembrance lies your freedom because your freedom is in **God**. 8 Join, then, with me in praise of **God** and you whom **God** created. 9 This **joining in praise of God and His creations** is our gift of gratitude to **God**, which **God** will share with all **God's** creations, to whom **God** gives equally whatever is acceptable to **God**. 10 Because **our joint praise of God and His creations** is acceptable to **God, our joint praise of God and His creations** is the gift of freedom, which is **God's** Will for all **God's** Sons. 11 By offering freedom you will be free.

Note # 29: It is our joining freely as one will and extending our true Self, (creation), that our praise of the Father is demonstrated. Since there is only One Will, to deny God's Will to any part of the indivisible Oneness is to deny it to all. We can deny God's Will but we cannot change God's Will. Our denial has no affect upon the Kingdom.

God's Will is that you be free. When we accept the Atonement for ourselves, we are accepting our total freedom. The Atonement states that we are sinless and guiltless. It states that our fear-based thoughts have no consequences and, therefore, cannot affect the reality of what we are. God allows all and does not judge. God's love provides us this absolute freedom and safety.

T-8.IV.8. Freedom is the only gift you can offer to God's Sons, being an acknowledgment of what **God's Sons** are and what **God** is. 2 Freedom is creation, because **freedom** is love. 3 Whom you seek to imprison you do not love. 4 Therefore, when you seek to imprison anyone, including yourself, you do not love him and you cannot identify with him. 5 When you imprison yourself you are losing sight of your true identification with me and with the Father. 6 Your identification is with the Father <*and*> with the Son. 7 **Your identification** cannot be with **only** One, **either Father or Son,** and not the Other. 8 If you are part of One, **either Father or Son,** you must be part of the Other because **the Father and Son** are One. 9 The Holy Trinity is holy <*because*> the **Holy Trinity** is One. 10 If you exclude yourself from this union **of the Holy Trinity,** you are perceiving the Holy Trinity as separated. 11 You must be included in **the Holy Trinity**, because **the Holy Trinity** is everything. 12 Unless you take your place in **the Holy Trinity** and fulfill your function as part of **the Holy Trinity**, the Holy Trinity is as bereft as you are. 13 No part of **the Holy Trinity** can be imprisoned if **the Holy Trinity's** truth is to be known.

<u>Note #30:</u> The Holy Trinity is the Oneness of everything. It encompasses everything and, therefore, we are part of it. This Holy Trinity is comprised of the Father, the Sonship, and the Holy Spirit. The function of the Sonship is to continue the extension of the Mind of God by creating like the Father. The function of the Holy Spirit is to be the bridge that connects the Father with His Son. We are part of this hologram of Oneness. Our reuniting of the Sonship through the Atonement process is the renunciations of the ego and the mad idea of the separation.

V. The Undivided Will of the Sonship

T-8.V.1. Can you be separated from your identification and be at peace? 2 Dissociation is not a solution; **dissociation or, separation from your identification**, is a delusion. 3 The delusional believe that truth will assail them, and they, **who did not remember that they are unified spirit,** do not recognize **this delusional belief** because they prefer the delusion **of separation from their own identity.** 4 Judging truth as something they, **who did not remember what they are,** do not want, **these deluded minds** perceive their illusions which block knowledge. 5 Help them, **who did not remember their own identity,** by offering them **who are deluded,** your unified mind on their behalf, as I am offering you **my unified mind** on behalf of your **mind**. 6 Alone we can do nothing, but together our minds fuse into something whose power is far beyond the power of **our minds'** separate parts. 7 By not being separate, the Mind of God is established in our mind and as our **mind**. 8 **The Mind of God** is invincible because **the Mind of God** is undivided.

<u>Note # 31:</u> Alone we can do nothing because only by sharing are ideas strengthened. Unshared ideas foster the belief in separation. Sharing thought is joining, union and creation.

T-8.V.2. The undivided will of the Sonship is the perfect creator, being wholly in the likeness of God, Whose Will is **also the undivided will of the Sonship**. 2 You cannot be exempt from **the undivided will of the Sonship** if you are to understand what **the undivided will of the Sonship** is and what you are. 3 By the belief that your will is separate from mine, you are exempting yourself from the Will of God which <*is*> yourself. 4 Yet to heal is still to make whole. 5 Therefore, to heal is to unite with those who are like you, because perceiving this likeness is to recognize the Father. 6 If your perfection is in **the Father** and only in **the Father**, how can you know **the undivided will of the Sonship** without recognizing **the Father**? 7 The recognition of God is the recognition of yourself. 8 There is no separation of God and **God's** creation. 9 You will realize this when you understand that there is no separation between your will and **my will**. 10 Let the Love of God shine upon you by your acceptance of me. 11 My reality is **your reality** and **God's reality**. 12 By joining your mind with mine you are signifying your awareness that the Will of God is One.

Note # 32: By the belief that your will is separate from Jesus and God's, you are claiming that you do not know what you are. This denial of our joint one Will is the underlying belief that birthed the idea of the separation and specialness.

T-8.V.3. God's Oneness and **our oneness** are not separate, because His Oneness encompasses **our oneness**. 2 To join with me is to restore **God's** power to you because we are sharing **our oneness**. 3 I offer you only the recognition of **God's** power in you, **but in that recognition that God's power is in you**, lays all truth. 4 As we unite, we unite with **God**. 5 Glory be to the union of God and **God's** holy Sons! 6 All glory lies in **the union of God and God's holy Sons** <*because*> God and God's holy Sons are united. 7 The miracles we do bear witness to the Will of the Father for His Son, and to our joy in uniting with **God's Will** for us, **God's Sons**.

Note # 33: There is just the Oneness of "All That Is." Miracles, which are a change from misperception to correct perception, are natural because truth is the only reality of the One Self. Miracles merely allow deluded minds to reawaken to the truth that there is just One and we are that One. The Mind of God is perfect, whole and complete and nothing is outside of It.

T-8.V.4. When you unite with me you are uniting without the ego, because I have renounced the ego in myself and therefore **I** cannot unite with **your ego**. 2 Our union is therefore the way to renounce the ego in you. 3 The truth in both of us is beyond the ego. 4 Our success in transcending the ego is guaranteed by God, and I share this confidence for both of us and all of us **that we can transcend the ego because it is God's Will.** 5 I bring God's peace back to all **God's** children because I received **the peace** of **God** for us all. 6 Nothing can prevail against our united wills because nothing can prevail against God's **Will.**

Note # 34: God's oneness encompasses our oneness and our union of the Sonship with Jesus in the way that our Oneness renounces the ego and the belief in the separation. By joining with our brother, we reject the thought system of the ego, for the ego cannot join. With this rejection of the belief in separation, our ego fades into the nothingness from which it arose.

T-8.V.5. Would you know the Will of God for you? 2 Ask it of me who know **the Will of God** for you and you will find **the Will of God** 3 I will deny you nothing, as God denies me nothing. 4 **Our journey** is simply the journey back to God Who is our home. 5 Whenever fear intrudes anywhere along the road to peace, **this fear** is because the ego has attempted to join the journey with us and **the ego** cannot do so. 6 **The ego** sensing defeat and angered by **potential defeat,** the ego regards itself as rejected and becomes retaliative. 7 You are invulnerable to **the ego's** retaliation because I am with you. 8 On this journey you have chosen me as your companion <*instead*> of the ego. 9 Do not attempt to hold on to both the ego and me, or you will try to go in different directions and will lose the way.

Note # 35: We cannot follow two opposing thought systems. By accepting Jesus or the Holy Spirit's guidance, we are rejecting the thought system of the ego. The ego must be left behind. The ego, the representative of the false and darkness, cannot stand the light of truth.

T-8.V.6. The ego's way is not **my way**, but **the ego's way** is also not **your way**. 2 The Holy Spirit has one direction for all minds, and the one **way the Holy Spirit** taught me is **your way, which is your Big "S" Self**. 3 Let us not lose sight of **the Holy Spirit's** direction through illusions, for only illusions of another direction can obscure the one for which God's Voice, **the Holy Spirit's voice**, speaks in all of us. 4 Never accord the ego the power to interfere with the journey. 5 **The ego** has **no power**, because the journey is the way to what is true. 6 Leave all illusions behind, and reach beyond all attempts of the ego to hold you back. 7 I go before you because I am beyond the ego. 8 Reach, therefore, for my hand because you want to transcend the ego. 9 My strength will never be wanting, and if you choose to share **my strength** you will do so. 10 I give **my strength** willingly and gladly, because I need you as much as you need me.

Note # 36: We, as decision makers, have to decide which of the two thought system's we will follow. The ego's thought system teaches that your strength lies in you alone. Therefore, your egoic belief in separation, individuality and specialness is stressed. The ego reinforces these beliefs with false witness that we misperceive. We see ourselves as limited ego-bodies in our dream world of provisional reality. We live in fear, lack and vulnerability.

The Holy Spirit's thought system teaches that your strength lies in God. Its goal is to reawaken you to what you really are. Its message is that you are a Oneness and not an individual. It seeks to awaken you to your divine birthright as the Son of God. As God's extension, you have been given everything because you are One with the Mind of God.

VI. The Treasure of God

T-8.VI.1. We are the joint will of the Sonship, whose Wholeness is for all. 2 We begin the journey back **to the Oneness of what we really are** by setting out together, and gather in our brothers as we continue together. 3 Every gain in our strength is offered for all, so **our brothers** too can lay aside their weakness and add their strength to us. 4 God's welcome waits for us all, and **God** will welcome us as I am welcoming you. 5 Forget not the Kingdom of God for anything the world has to offer.

Note # 37: You cannot desire and value your provisional dream world of specialness and also know God. What you value, you will choose to perceive. If you value separation, individuality and specialness, you will choose to remain deluded. God cannot be found in your fantasy world for God is real and the Sonship has never left his home, which is the Mind of God. In the world of perception, what you choose to believe becomes your provisional reality. It seems real only in the deluded mind of the dreamer.

T-8.VI.2. The world **of perception** can add nothing to the power and the glory of God and **God's** holy Sons, but **the world of perception** can blind the Sons to the Father if **God's holy Sons** behold **the

world of perception. 2 You cannot behold the world **of perception** and know God. 3 Only one, **either the world of perception or God,** is true. 4 I am come to tell you that the choice of which is true **that you believe to be your choice of between either the world of perception or God's reality,** is not yours to make. 5 If **the choice of which is true** were **yours to make** you would have destroyed yourself. 6 Yet God did not will the destruction of **God's** creations, having created **God's creations** for eternity. 7 **God's** Will has saved you, not from yourself but from your illusion of yourself. 8 **God** has saved you <*for*> yourself.

Note # 38: When ACIM states that if we "behold" the world of perception, it "can blind the Sons to the Father," the word "behold" should be understood to mean that you have upgraded the dream of separation from a fantasy and given it a reality of its own. If you give all your perceptions over to the Holy Spirit, this world of perception will become the tool for your return to the truth. By following the egoic misperceptions of this world, your mind makes the fantasy of separation appear real. The acceptance of the dream of separation becomes your provisional reality that blinds you from the vision of God's Oneness.

T-8.VI.3. Let us glorify **God** Whom the world denies, for over **God's** Kingdom the world has no power. 2 No one created by God can find joy in anything except the eternal; not because he is deprived of anything else, but because nothing else is worthy of him **who was created by God.** 3 What God and His Sons create is eternal, and in this, **the eternal,** and this only is their joy.

Note # 39: God's Will has saved us from our own illusions that we made into our dream world of separation. Our world of illusion adds nothing to the power of God or the Kingdom since it is nothing. Reality is changeless. It is eternal. Nothing in our world of provisional reality has permanence. Our world is based on our perceptions, beliefs and judgments, which change daily. Only in God's Kingdom can we find peace and joy. The Will of God insures that the eternal joy of the Kingdom will always be our reality. We can deny reality but our denial will not change the eternal reality of God's creations. Our illusions cannot change our divine spiritual nature that has been given to us by Our Creator.

T-8.VI.4. Listen to the story of the prodigal son, and learn what God's treasure is and **what your treasure is**: This son of a loving father left his home and thought he, **the son,** had squandered everything for nothing of any value, although **the son** had not understood its worthlessness at the time. 2 **The son** was ashamed to return to his father, because **the son** thought he, **the son,** had hurt **his father.** 3 Yet when **the son** came home the father welcomed **the son** with joy, because the son himself <*was*> his father's treasure. 4 **His father** wanted nothing else.

Note # 40: God does not judge. He only wills that His Son be happy. We are happy when we co-create with our Father. By this co-creative process, we complete God. We join our will with His Will as One. This is the extension of the Mind of God.

T-8.VI.5. God wants only His Son because **God's** Son is **God's** only treasure. 2 You want your creations as **God** wants His **creations**. 3 Your creations are your gift to the Holy Trinity. **Your creations are** created in gratitude for your creation. 4 **Your creations** do not leave you any more than you left your Creator, but **your creations** extend your creation as God extended Himself to you. 5 Can the creations of God Himself take joy in what is not real, **which is the egoic world of perception**? 6 And what is real except the creations of God and those that are created like **God's creations**? 7 Your creations love you as you love your Father for the gift of creation. 8 There is no other gift that is eternal, and therefore there is no other gift that is true. 9 How, then, can you accept anything else **than eternal creations** or give anything else **than eternal creations**, and expect joy in return? 10 And what else but joy would you want? 11 You made neither yourself nor your function. 12 You made only the **egoic** decision to be unworthy of both **yourself and your function**. 13 Yet you cannot make yourself unworthy because you are the treasure of God, and what **God** values, is valuable. 14 There can be no question **of the** worth **of what God values** because its value lies in God's sharing Himself with **whatever God values** and **thus** establishing **the** value **of whatever God values** forever.

Note # 41: We are God's treasure because the Sonship is God's creation. The function of the Sonship is to continue to extend or create as their Father created them. This extension of the Son of God is the Son's gift to His Father and to the Kingdom. It is God, not our ego, which establishes our worth. God knows His creations to be only perfect, whole and complete.

T-8.VI.6. Your function is to add to God's treasure by creating **your treasure**. 2 **God's** Will <*to*> you is **God's** Will <*for*> you. 3 **God** would not withhold creation from you because **God's** joy is in **creation**. 4 You cannot find joy except as God does **by creating like your Father.** 5 **God's** joy lay in creating you, and **God** extends **God's** Fatherhood to you so that you can extend yourself as **God** did. 6 You do not understand **that you can extend yourself as God did** because you do not understand **God**. 7 No one who does not accept his function can understand what **his function** is, and no one can accept his function unless he knows what <*he*> is. 8 Creation is the Will of God. 9 **God's** Will created you to create. 10 Your will was not created separate from **God's Will**, and so you must will as **God** wills.

Note # 42: Your function is to create as God created you, perfect whole and complete. Since you have free will, you can make the decision to believe that you are unworthy of your divine birthright, but you cannot change yourself or your function. Both were given by God to you and thus are eternal and changeless. This is God's Will.
Joy is to be found in creation, which is the sharing and extending of oneself. It is by this extension of your Big "S" Self that one knows and realizes their own spiritual magnificence.

T-8.VI.7. An "unwilling will" does not mean anything, being a contradiction in terms that actually means nothing. 2 When you think you are unwilling to will with God, you are not thinking. 3 God's Will <*is*> Thought. 4 **God's Will being Thought** cannot be contradicted <*by*> thought. 5 God does not contradict Himself, and **God's** Sons, who are like **God**, cannot contradict themselves or **God**. 6 Yet **God's Sons'** thought is so powerful that **God's Sons' thought** can even imprison the mind of God's Son, if **God's Sons** so choose **to imagine the imprisonment of his own mind**. 7 This choice **for the imagined self-imprisonment of the mind of God's own Son** does make the Son's function unknown to **the Son**, but never to his Creator. 8 And because **this choice by the Son to imagine the imprisonment of his own mind** is not unknown to **God,** the Creator, **the Son's ability to will with God's Will** is forever knowable to **God's Son.**

Note # 43: In reality there is only God's Will, which is Thought. Before the mad idea of the separation, only the thoughts harmonious with love, which are the Thoughts of God, existed. This was and is the thought system of the Holy Spirit, which knows that we are part of the Oneness. With the rise of the ego's thought system, we believed that we could think without God. These "private thoughts" that exist only in our imagination are projected into your delusional world of provisional reality. Your private thoughts have the ability to imprison your mind since your split mind projects these ideas out into its own dream world thus, "confirming" the error that the ego is real and that we exist separate from God. In the changeless Mind of God, your true power to create like God waits your reawakening from the erroneous belief that you could be a limited ego-body. True creation only occurs when you think with God. When we think like God, we give all, to all. This is the co-creative function of creation.
Although the Son can imagine he is separate from his Source, God knows that His Son is, and always

will be, perfect, whole and complete. The Father sees His Son merely asleep, dreaming or pretending to be something that the child is not. The Father does not accept the Son's illusionary game as having any impact on the truth since to do so would be to attempt to make the false real. This is impossible. In a sleeping mind, the false can be mistaken for the truth but this error does not change the truth. God grants His Child the perfect freedom to be or imagine anything the child wants knowing that the Child remains perfectly safe within the Mind of God. This is because God knows that a game of make believe cannot change the reality of what the Child truly is. God knows that a sleeping Child will and must reawaken and reclaim His divine inheritance. This inheritance can be temporarily forgotten or denied by the child, but it can never be lost.

T-8.VI.8. There is no question but one **question** you should ever ask of yourself;–"Do I want to know my Father's Will for me?" 2 **God** will not hide **His Will for you**. 3 **God** has revealed **His Will for you** to me because I asked **the question** of God, and learned of what **God** had already given. 4 Our function, **which is to create like Our Father,** is to work together, because apart from each other we cannot function at all. 5 The whole power of God's Son lies in all of us, but not in any of us alone. 6 God would not have us be alone because <*God*> does not will to be alone. 7 That is why **God** created His Son, and gave **His Son** the power to create with **God, their Father**. 8 Our creations are as holy as we are, and we are the Sons of God Himself, as holy as **God** is. 9 Through our creations we extend our love, and thus increase the joy of the Holy Trinity. 10 You do not understand **that we are as holy as God is and that we must extend our love like our Father. This is** because you who are God's Own treasure do not regard yourself as valuable. 11 Given this belief **that you are not valuable**, you cannot understand anything.

<u>Note # 44:</u> We are God's prodigal sons. God holds and guards our birthright and awaits our return to the Kingdom. We, the Thoughts of God, are God's treasure. Because we do not know what we are, we do not understand our value to Our Father. We fail to realize that we are the completion of Our Father. He is Cause and we His Effect. As such we are inseparable and priceless.

T-8.VI.9.I share with God the knowledge of the value **God** puts upon you. 2 My devotion to you is of **God**, being born of my knowledge of myself and **God**. 3 We, **the Sonship and God,** cannot be separated. 4 Whom God has joined cannot be separated, and God has joined all His Sons with Himself. 5 Can you be separated from your life and your being? 6 The journey to God is merely the reawakening of the knowledge of where you are always, and what you are forever. 7 **The journey to God** is a journey without distance to a goal that has never changed. 8 Truth can only be experienced. 9 **Truth** cannot be described and **truth** cannot be explained. 10 I can make you aware of the conditions of truth, but the experience **of truth** is of God. 11 Together we can meet **truth's** conditions, but truth will dawn upon you of itself.

<u>Note # 45:</u> Truth will dawn upon you only when you choose to follow the thought system of the Holy Spirit. This is your reawakening to the truth of what and where you are. The truth is that you have never left the holographic Mind of God since what God Wills is eternal and thus, changeless. We cannot change our Cause. We must remain Its eternal Effect.

T-8.VI.10. What God has willed for you <*is*> yours. 2 **God** has given **God's** Will to His treasure, whose treasure **God's Will** is. 3 Your heart lies where your treasure is, **which is in your creations just** as does **God's heart lies with His treasure, which is God's Son**.4 You who are beloved of God are wholly blessed. 5 Learn **that you who are beloved of God are wholly blessed** of me, and free the holy will of all those who are as blessed as you are.

Note # 46: By accepting the truth of the Atonement for yourself, you accept the Atonement for all your brothers. All parts of the Sonship are equal. The Sonship, being indivisible is joined as one.

VII. The Body as a Means of Communication

T-8.VII.1. Attack is always physical. 2 When attack in any form enters your mind you are equating yourself with a body, since this **belief that you are a body** is the ego's interpretation of the body. 3 You do not have to attack physically to accept this interpretation **that you are a body**. 4 You are accepting **this interpretation that you are a body** simply by the belief that attack can get you something you want. 5 If you did not believe **that you are a body**, the idea of attack would have no appeal for you. 6 When you equate yourself with a body you will always experience depression. 7 When a child of God thinks of himself in this way he is belittling himself, and seeing his brothers as similarly belittled. 8 Since he can find himself only in **his brother**, he has cut himself off from salvation.

Note #47: You are mind or spirit, and not the body. The idea that you are a body, confirms the ego's claim that you are a separate, special and unique individual. Separation and specialness are the natural outcome of the egoic thought system. Spirit or mind is a shared Oneness of Everything. When you already are "Everything," to argue for your "littleness" is a depressing thought. Anytime we block the natural flow of God's love to and through our mind, we will feel depressed, sad and lonely. Blocking this flow prevents us from fulfilling our function of co-creation. Being God's Child, we are joyous only when we create and extend like Our Father.

T-8.VII.2. Remember that the Holy Spirit interprets the body only as a means of communication. 2 Being the Communication Link between God and **God's** separated Sons, the Holy Spirit interprets everything you have made in the light of what **God** is. 3 The ego separates through the body. 4 The Holy Spirit reaches through **the body** to others. 5 You do not perceive your brothers as the Holy Spirit does, because you do not regard bodies solely as a means of joining minds and uniting **your brothers' mind** with yours and mine. 6 This interpretation of the body **as a means of communication and for the joining of minds** will change your mind entirely about **the body's** value. 7 Of itself **the body** has **no value**.

Note # 48: The Holy Spirit utilizes the ego created body as a learning device to communicate with the various parts of the split Sonship to reawaken them to the truth of who they really are. A learning device has no value by itself. Its value comes from the usage of the learning device.

T-8.VII.3. If you use the body for attack, the body is harmful to you. 2 If you use **the body** only to reach the minds of those who believe they are bodies, and teach **the minds of those who believe they are bodies** <*through*> the body that this is not so, you will understand the power of the mind that is in you. 3 If you use the body for this and only for this, **which is the teaching that your brothers are not a body,** you cannot use **the body** for attack. 4 In the service of uniting **the body** becomes a beautiful lesson in communion, which has value until communion <*is.*> 5 This **lesson in communion** is God's way of making unlimited what you have limited. 6 The Holy Spirit does not see the body as you do, because the Holy Spirit knows the only reality of anything is the service **anything** renders God on behalf of the function **God** gives it.

Note #49: In the world of egoic perception, the body was made to symbolize and prove that we are a limited ego-body in competition with other ego-bodies. The Holy Spirit has reinterpreted the function of the body and utilizes it as a learning device to teach that the Sonship is not the body, but rather a Oneness united with God. This is the truth that is taught through the Atonement process.

T-8.VII.4. Communication ends separation. 2 Attack promotes **separation**. 3 The body is beautiful or ugly, peaceful or savage, helpful or harmful, according to the use to which **the body** is put. 4 And in the body of another you will see the use to which you have put **your body**. 5 If the body becomes a means you give to the Holy Spirit to use on behalf of union of the Sonship, you will not see anything physical except as what **the body** is. 6 Use **the body** for truth and you will see **the body** truly. 7 Misuse **the body** and you will misunderstand **the body**, because you have already **misunderstand the body** <*by*> misusing **the body**. 8 Interpret anything apart from the Holy Spirit and you will mistrust **whatever you have interpreted apart from the Holy Spirit**. 9 This **mistrust caused by misinterpretation** will lead you to hatred and attack and loss of peace.

Note # 50: The body should be used only as a communication device to communicate only forgiveness and love. If we identify ourselves as the body, we will become fearful and use the body for attack.

T-8.VII.5. Yet all loss comes only from your own misunderstanding. 2 Loss of any kind is impossible. 3 But when you look upon a brother as a physical entity, his power and glory are "lost" to you and so are **your own power and glory "lost" to yourself.** 4 You have attacked **a brother**, but you must have attacked yourself first. 5 Do not see **a brother** this way for your own salvation, which must bring **a brother** his **salvation**. 6 Do not allow **a brother** to belittle himself in your mind, but give **a brother** freedom from his belief in littleness, and thus escape from **your belief in littleness**. 7 As part of you, **a brother** is holy. 8 As part of me, you are **holy**. 9 To communicate with part of God Himself is to reach beyond the Kingdom to its Creator, through **God's** Voice, **which is the Holy Spirit,** which **God** has established as part of you.

Note # 51: We only can see in another what we believe is also in our mind. Thoughts never leave the mind of the thinker. Minds are joined and by discovering the Big "S" Self in another, we receive and give that same understanding to ourselves.

T-8.VII.6. Rejoice, then, that of yourself you can do nothing. 2 You are not <*of*> yourself. 3 **God** of Whom you are has willed your power and glory for you, with which you can perfectly accomplish **God's** holy Will for you when you accept God's holy Will for yourself. 4 **God** has not withdrawn **God's** gifts **of His holy Will** from you, but you believe you have withdrawn **God's gifts of His holy Will** from God. 5 Let no Son of God remain hidden for **God's** Name's sake, because **God's** Name is yours.

Note # 52: Without our Cause, we would cease to be. This is impossible since that would change God by making Him incomplete without His Effect. Our denial of our birthright did not impact our inheritance or our Source. Cause and Effect remain eternally linked as One. Our power flows from our Source, through us and extends beyond. We cannot hide from our Source. Only the egoic self attempts to deny its birthright by claiming that it does not know what it is.

T-8.VII.7. The Bible says, "The Word (or thought) was made flesh." 2 Strictly speaking this **idea that "The Word (or thought) was made flesh."** is impossible, since **this idea that "The Word or thought was made flesh."** seems to involve the translation of one order of reality into another **order of reality.**

3 Different orders of reality merely appear to exist, just as different orders of miracles **appear to exist**. 4 Thought cannot be made into flesh except by belief, since thought is not physical. 5 Yet thought is communication, for which the body can be used. 6 **Communication** is the only natural use to which **the body** can be put **to use**. 7 To use the body unnaturally is to lose sight of the Holy Spirit's purpose **which is to reawaken, or communicate, to you what you really are**, and thus to confuse the goal of **the Holy Spirit's** curriculum, **which is to reawaken God's Son to his divine birthright and thus reclaim joy, peace, and knowledge.**

Note # 53: The Holy Spirit can use the body for communication so that the split-minded can once again know themselves. The body, being form, cannot be shared and is not real. God did not make the body; our deluded mind did. God does not create other than like Himself.

T-8.VII.8. There is nothing so frustrating to a learner as a curriculum he cannot learn. 2 **A learner's** sense of adequacy suffers, and **the learner** must become depressed. 3 Being faced with an impossible learning situation is the most depressing thing in the world. 4 In fact, **being faced with an impossible learning situation** is ultimately why the world itself is depressing. 5 The Holy Spirit's curriculum is never depressing, because **the Holy Spirit's curriculum** is a curriculum of joy. 6 Whenever the reaction to learning is depression, **the reaction** is because the true goal of the curriculum has been lost sight of.

Note # 54: The Holy Spirit utilizes the body to communicate that you are not the body; you are mind. The Holy Spirit's goal is the end of your belief in separation. The goal of the Holy Spirit's curriculum is that you know yourself. The ego utilizes the body for attack, which promotes the belief in separation. The ego's goal is that you never know yourself. Our true goal is to be happy. The ego's goal is to deny the truth that you are only love and God's joy. We cannot be happy trying to find love and joy in an illusion designed to embody fear, loneliness and separation.

T-8.VII.9. In this world, not even the body is perceived as whole. 2 **The body's** purpose is seen as fragmented into many functions with little or no relationship to each other, so that **the body** appears to be ruled by chaos. 3 **The body's purpose as** guided by the ego <is.> chaos. 4 **The body's purpose as** guided by the Holy Spirit is not **chaos**. 5 Under **the guidance of the Holy Spirit the body** becomes a means by which the part of the mind you tried to separate <from> spirit can reach beyond **the split mind's** distortions and return <to> spirit. 6 The ego's temple, **which is the body,** thus becomes the temple of the Holy Spirit, where devotion to **the Holy Spirit** replaces devotion to the ego. 7 In this sense the body does become a temple to God; His Voice, **the Holy Spirit,** abides in **the body** by directing the use to which **the body** is put **to use**.

Note # 55: The Holy Spirit abides in the High-Self or Christ conscious part of mind. The Holy Spirit's home cannot be the physical body since the body is part of the illusion of separateness. The Holy Spirit reinterprets the ego's temple for separation, which is the body, and transforms it into a communication device to teach only union and truth.

T-8.VII.10. Healing is the result of using the body solely for communication. 2 Since **using the body solely for communication** is natural **using the body solely for communication** heals by making whole, which is also natural. 3 All mind is whole, and the belief that part of **the mind** is physical, or not mind, is a fragmented or sick interpretation. 4 Mind cannot be made physical, but **the mind** can be made manifest <through> the physical if **the mind** uses the body to go beyond itself. 5 By reaching out, the mind extends itself. 6 **The mind** does not stop at the body, for if **the mind** does **stop at the body, the mind** is blocked in **the mind's** purpose, **which is extension or creation**. 7 A mind that has been blocked has allowed itself to be vulnerable to attack, because **a blocked mind** has turned against itself.

Note # 56: The mind is spirit. The mind is not the physical brain. A split mind is not whole and, therefore, is unable or blocked in its ability to create or extend itself like the Father creates. The body is used by the Holy Spirit to teach forgiveness and to reestablish the unity of the Sonship. Teaching forgiveness is the function of the Holy Spirit and leads to our acceptance of the Atonement for ourselves. The block that needs to be removed is the thought system of the ego. This removal returns the mind to its natural state of wholeness.

T-8.VII.11. The removal of blocks, then, is the only way to guarantee help and healing. 2 Help and healing are the normal expressions of a mind that is working through the body, but not <in> **the body**. 3 If the mind believes the body is **the mind's** goal **the mind** will distort **the mind's** perception of the body, and by blocking **the mind's** own extension beyond **the body, the mind** will induce illness by fostering separation 4 Perceiving the body as a separate entity cannot but foster illness, because **perceiving the body, as a separate entity** is not true. 5 A medium of communication loses its usefulness if **the medium of communication** is used for anything else. 6 To use a medium of communication as a medium of attack is an obvious confusion in purpose.

Note # 57: Our purpose forms the basis for our perception. If we have differing purposes such as communication versus attack, we will have differing perceptions of the same experience. Purpose determines our perception. Split proposes result in conflict and confusion.

T-8.VII.12. To communicate is to join and to attack is to separate. 2 How can you do both simultaneously with the same thing and not suffer? 3 Perception of the body can be unified only by one purpose, **which is the purpose of healing, or joining**. 4 This **unified purpose of healing, or joining** releases the mind from the temptation to see the body in many lights, and gives **the body** over entirely to the One Light in which **the body** can be really understood. 5 To confuse a learning device, **the body,** with a curriculum goal, **which is to know thyself through extension,** is a fundamental confusion that blocks the understanding of both **the learning device and the curriculum.** 6 Learning must lead beyond the body to the re-establishment of the power of the mind in **the mind.** 7 **This re-establishment of the power of the mind can** be accomplished only if the mind extends to other minds, and does not arrest itself in **the mind's** extension. 8 This arrest **of the mind's extension to other minds** is the cause of all illness, because only extension is the mind's function.

Note # 58: The Holy Spirit utilizes the body as a learning device for joining one brother's mind to another. The ego utilizes the body to prove separation and, therefore, the body becomes an instrument for attacking a brother. The Holy Spirit's learning curriculum is a process to lead the mind beyond the limiting belief that the mind is a body, thus re-establishing the power of the mind. The power of the mind is re-established by the reuniting of the mind of one brother with another. By healing, the Sonship to the reality of its wholeness, the power of extension, or creation, is returned to the Sonship.

T-8.VII.13. The opposite of joy is depression. 2 When your learning promotes depression instead of joy, you cannot be listening to God's joyous Teacher, **the Holy Spirit,** and learning **the Holy Spirit's** lessons. 3 To see a body as anything except a means of communication is to limit your mind and to hurt yourself. 4 Health is therefore nothing more than united purpose. 5 If the body is brought under the purpose of the mind, **the mind** becomes whole because the mind's purpose is one. 6 Attack can only be an assumed purpose of the body, because apart from the mind the body has no purpose at all.

Note # 59: Health is the united purpose of the mind. When we speak of healing, we are not speaking of physical healing, since the body is not "real." Rather, it is the healing of the split-mind and thus, the healing of the Sonship from the insane idea that it could be separate from the Mind of God. By healing, we realize that our will and God's Will are One. We understand that cause and effect are forever intertwined as one.

T-8.VII.14. You are not limited by the body, and thought cannot be made flesh. 2 Yet mind can be manifested through the body if **the mind** goes beyond **the body** and does not interpret **the body** as **a limitation of the mind**. 3 Whenever you see another as limited to or by the body, you are imposing this **same limitation to or by the body upon** yourself. 4 Are you willing to accept this **limitation of the body**, when your whole purpose for learning should be to escape from limitations? 5 To conceive of the body as a means of attack and to believe that joy could possibly result **from attack** is a clear-cut indication of a poor learner. 6 **The poor learner** has accepted **an egoic** learning goal **of attack and is thus promoting separation. This inappropriate learning goal is** in obvious contradiction to the unified purpose of the **Holy Spirit's** curriculum, **which is health and joining**, and **the contradictory egoic goal of attack** is interfering with **the poor learner's** ability to accept **the curriculum's** purpose **of healing** as his own **purpose**.

<u>Note # 60:</u> Being created as a Oneness of Everything, we can never be happy with being less. To misperceive any part of the Oneness as limited is to place that same limitation on oneself. Separation and Oneness are like parallel lines; they never meet. We cannot have a purpose different than the purpose God established for His Son. Our unified purpose must be the co-creative extension of the Mind of God. Creation is the joy of God.

T-8.VII.15. Joy is unified purpose, and unified purpose is only God's **purpose.** 2 When **your purpose** is unified **your purpose** is **God's purpose.** 3 Believe you can interfere with **God's** purpose, and you need salvation. 4 You have condemned yourself, but condemnation is not of God. 5 Therefore**, since condemnation is not of God, condemnation** is not true. 6 No more are any of **condemnation's** seeming results **true.** 7 When you see a brother as a body, you are condemning **a brother** because you have condemned yourself **as a body.** 8 Yet if all condemnation is unreal, and **condemnation** must be unreal since **condemnation** is a form of attack, then **condemnation** can <*have*> no results.

<u>Note # 61:</u> God does not judge. If God's child chooses to pretend that he is something that he is not, God allows the child to play his childish games. The only thing God insures is that when the child grows tired of his war games, the child will always find his way back to his Father's house. God placed the Holy Spirit within our playful mind to insure our safe return.

<u>**T-8.VII.16.**</u>Do not allow yourself to suffer from imagined results of **condemnation which are** not true. 2 Free your mind from the belief that **condemnation** is possible. 3 In **condemnation's** complete impossibility lies your only hope for release **from condemnation.** 4 But what other hope would you want? 5 Freedom from illusions lies only in not believing **the illusions.** 6 There is no attack, but there <*is*> unlimited communication and therefore unlimited power and wholeness. 7 The power of wholeness is extension. 8 Do not arrest your thought in this world **of illusion**, and you will open your mind to creation in God.

<u>Note # 62:</u> Freedom from illusion lies in you not believing, actually, never even perceiving the illusion as a threat to your true reality. Freedom lies in truth. Illusion is false and, therefore, has no basis in reality, which is the Kingdom. What is false is false and what is true has never changed. The Holy Spirit's task is to gently awaken a sleeping child's mind to the fact that it was only dreaming. Once the child realizes that he is the dreamer, he can choose to release himself from all of his childish fears. He can leave the game of separation behind and rejoin the Kingdom and co-create with His Father.

VIII. The Body as Means or End

T-8.VIII.1. Attitudes toward the body are attitudes toward attack. 2 The ego's definitions of anything are childish, and **the ego's definitions** are always based on what **the ego** believes the thing is <*for.*> 3 **The ego's definitions are always based on what the ego believes the thing is <*for.*>** because **the ego** is incapable of true generalizations, and equates what **the ego** sees with the function **the ego** ascribes to **the thing.** 4 **The ego** does not equate **the thing** with what **the thing** <*is.*> 5 To the ego the body is to attack <*with.*> 6 Equating you with the body, **the ego** teaches that <*you*> are to attack with. 7 The body, then, is not the source of **the body's** own health. 8 The body's condition lies solely in your interpretation of **the body's** function. 9 Functions are part of being since **functions** arise from **being,** but the relationship is not reciprocal **and therefore being does not arise from functions.** 10 The whole does define the part, but the part does not define the whole. 11 Yet to know in part is to know entirely because of the fundamental difference between knowledge and perception. 12 In perception the whole is built up of parts that can separate and reassemble in different constellations. 13 But knowledge never changes, so **knowledge's** constellation is permanent. 14 The idea of part-whole relationships has meaning only at the level of perception, where change is possible. 15 Otherwise, there is no difference between the part and whole.

Note # 63: Knowledge is unchanging and like a hologram since each part contains the whole. If truth were changeable, it would not be truth. Perception is based on interpretation and, therefore, changes as judgments shift. The perceptions of the mind under the thought system of the ego change from time to time because the ego knows nothing and is always uncertain. Time is the measure of change. Time exists and has a function in the ego's thought system since there is something that changes and, therefore, is available to measure. The ego's thought system is based on individuality and inequality of the parts, so different combinations result in different answers. The Holy Spirit's thought system is based on equality. In the thought system of the Holy Spirit, all parts are the same since all parts contain everything. These indivisible parts are eternal. They do not change and thus, time in the Kingdom does not exist since there is no change to measure. Time is only necessary in the unreal world of perception. In the world of perception, time allows the split-minded to relearn what they are by healing and rejoining as one whole mind.

T-8.VIII.2. The body exists in a world that seems to contain two voices, **the ego's and the Holy Spirit's. Both voices appear to be** fighting for **the** possession **of the body.** 2 In this perceived constellation the body is seen as capable of shifting **the body's** allegiance from one **voice** to the other **voice,** making the concepts of both health and sickness meaningful. 3 The ego makes a fundamental confusion between means and end as **the ego** always does. 4 Regarding the body as an end, the ego has no real use for **the body** because **the body** is <*not*> an end. 5 You must have noticed an outstanding characteristic of every end that the ego has accepted as **the ego's** own. 6 When you have achieved **the end,** <*the end has not satisfied you.*> 7 This is why the ego is forced to shift ceaselessly from one goal to another, so that you will continue to hope **the ego** can yet offer you something.

Note # 64: The body, to the Holy Spirit, is a learning device, a means, which can be utilized for communication and joining. The thought system of the ego promises you happiness when you obtain something outside yourself. Yet, once the goal is achieved, you realize that it did not bring about the promised result. Due to this failure in obtaining happiness and peace, the ego then must substitute a new goal with the same promised results of happiness and completeness. The ego's motto is, "Seek and never find."

T-8.VIII.3. It has been particularly difficult to overcome the ego's belief in the body as an end, because **the ego's belief in the body as an end** is synonymous with the belief in attack as an end. 2 The ego has a profound investment in sickness. 3 If you are sick, how can you object to the ego's firm belief that you are not invulnerable? 4 This **idea that since the body is sick, you are not invulnerable** is an appealing argument from the ego's point of view, because **the argument** obscures the obvious attack that underlies the sickness. 5 If you recognized **the obvious attack that underlies the sickness** and also decided against attack, you could not give **or allow** this false witness **of sickness** to the ego's **belief in the body as an end** stand.

Note # 65: You must decide whether you are a separate ego-body in competition with other ego-bodies, or if you are a Child of God, a Oneness, prefect, whole and complete. Is the body what you are (an end), or is the body a learning device (a means)? Are you limitless spirit, or are you a limited body?

T-8.VIII.4. It is hard to perceive sickness as a false witness, because you do not realize that **sickness** is entirely out of keeping with what you want. 2 This witness, **called sickness**, then, appears to be innocent and trustworthy because you have not seriously cross-examined **this witness, called sickness**. 3 If you had **seriously cross-examined this witness, called sickness**, you would not consider sickness such a strong witness on behalf of the ego's views. 4 A more honest statement would be that those who want the ego are predisposed to defend **the ego**. 5 Therefore, **those who are predisposed to defend the ego's** choice of witnesses should be suspect from the beginning. 6 The ego does not call upon witnesses who would disagree with **the ego's** case, nor does the Holy Spirit **call upon witnesses who would disagree with the ego's case**. 7 I have said that judgment is the function of the Holy Spirit, and **the function of judgment is** one **the Holy Spirit** is perfectly equipped to fulfill. 8 The ego as a judge gives anything but an impartial judgment. 9 When the ego calls on a witness, **the ego** has already made the witness an ally.

Note # 66: The Holy Spirit does not call witness to testify against the ego since that would be an attack that would confirm the existence of the ego. The ego is not real as it is only a product of false thinking. The Holy Spirit takes the witnesses that the ego has called into your experience and converts them into witnesses for the truth. When we ask for guidance, we choose again and transform egoic misperception into correct perception. When the thinking is corrected, the ego disappears.

T-8.VIII.5. It is still true that the body has no function of itself, because **the body** is not an end. 2 The ego, however, establishes **the body** as an end because, as such, **the body's** true function **as a learning device to facilitate communication and joining** is obscured. 3 **To obscure something's true function** is the purpose of everything the ego does. 4 **The ego's** sole aim is to lose sight of the function of everything. 5 A sick body does not make any sense. 6 **A sick body** could not make sense because sickness is not what the body is for. 7 Sickness is meaningful only if the two basic premises on which the ego's interpretation of the body rests are true; **the first basic premises is** that the body is for attack, and **the second basic premises is** that you are a body. 8 Without these **two** premises **that the body is for attack and you are a body,** sickness is inconceivable.

Note # 67: Perception follows purpose. For the ego, the body's purpose is to prove that you are not unlimited, invulnerable spirit. A sick body is the ego's proof in the reality of the separation.

T-8.VIII.6. Sickness is a way of demonstrating that you can be hurt. 2 **Sickness** is a witness to your frailty, your vulnerability, and your extreme need to depend on external guidance. 3 The ego uses **sickness** as **the ego's** best argument for your need for < *the ego's*> guidance. 4 **The ego** dictates endless prescriptions for avoiding catastrophic outcomes. 5 The Holy Spirit, perfectly aware of the same situation, does not bother to analyze **the same situation** at all. 6 If data are meaningless there is no point in analyzing **the meaningless data**. 7 The function of truth is to collect information that is true. 8 <*Any*> way you handle error results in nothing. 9 The more complicated the results become the harder it may be to recognize **the** nothingness **of the error,** but it is not necessary to examine all possible outcomes to which premises give rise in order to judge **the error** truly.

Note # 68: It is not necessary to review all possible outcomes that may follow from insane thinking. Once the original idea is determined to be insane, we need not follow it down to all its logical conclusions. The Holy Spirit knows what you really are and, therefore, understands that the entire thought system of the ego rests on the ego's false idea that the separation occurred and that you are a body. Once you accept the falseness of the ego's first premise, anything that follows logically from the ego's thought system cannot be trusted.
 Example: Only humans have feathers. Birds have feathers. Therefore, birds are human. This is a logical conclusion but it is false since the major premise, "Only humans have feathers" is wrong.

T-8.VIII.7. A learning device is not a teacher. 2 **A learning device** cannot tell you how you feel. 3 You do not know how you feel because you have accepted the ego's confusion, and you therefore believe that a learning device, **the body,** <*can*> tell you how you feel. 4 Sickness is merely another example of your insistence on asking guidance of a teacher, **the ego,** who does not know the answer. 5 The ego is incapable of knowing how you feel. 6 When I said that the ego does not know anything, I said the one thing about the ego that is wholly true. 7 But there is a corollary **to fact that the ego does not know anything. This corollary is** if only knowledge has being and the ego has no knowledge, then the ego has no being.

Note # 69: The ego's only existence comes from the power your mind chooses to give the ego. The ego was "made" by a split mind. Heal the split mind and the ego disappears. The ego has no power of being for it is not real and, therefore, the ego has no reality in the Mind of God.

T-8.VIII.8. You might well ask how the voice of something that does not exist, **the ego,** can be so insistent. 2 Have you thought about the distorting power of something you want, even if **that something** is not real? 3 There are many instances of how what you want distorts perception. 4 No one can doubt the ego's skill in building up false cases. 5 Nor can anyone doubt your willingness to listen **to the ego's false cases** until you choose not to accept anything except truth. 6 When you lay the ego aside, **the ego** will be gone. 7 The Holy Spirit's Voice is as loud as your willingness to listen. 8 **The Holy Spirit's Voice** cannot be louder without violating your freedom of choice, which the Holy Spirit seeks to restore, never to undermine.

Note # 70: What we value, we call into our experience. Because we value the egoic promise of specialness and individuality that comes along with the belief in separation from the Oneness, we want and falsely choose the separation to be our "truth." Because of free will, we have been given the power to either create the real or make the false appear real. When we choose to "create" differently from God (technically make) we choose to exclude and thus, refuse to extend perfection. It is our desire for specialness that makes the voice for the ego so insistent. Unfortunately, for the decision-maker, with the choice for specialness comes the unwanted baggage of limitation, sin, guilt and fear. We want specialness and individuality, but we get littleness and vulnerability instead.

T-8.VIII.9. The Holy Spirit teaches you to use your body only to reach your brothers, so **the Holy Spirit** can teach **the Holy Spirit's** message through you. 2 **Teaching the Holy Spirit's message through you** will heal **your brothers** and therefore heal you. 3 Everything used in accordance with its function as the Holy Spirit sees it cannot be sick. 4 Everything used **not in accordance with its function as the Holy Spirit sees it, is sick.** 5 Do not allow the body to be a mirror of a split mind. 6 Do not let **the body** be an image of your own perception of littleness. 7 Do not let **the body** reflect your decision to attack. 8 Health is seen as the natural state of everything when interpretation is left to the Holy Spirit, Who perceives no attack on anything. 9 Health is the result of relinquishing all attempts to use the body lovelessly. 10 Health is the beginning of the proper perspective on life under the guidance of the one Teacher, **the Holy Spirit,** Who knows what life is, **the Holy Spirit** being the Voice for Life Itself.

<u>Note # 71:</u> The Holt Spirit utilizes the body as a teaching device. As such, the body is a means to communicate the Holy Spirit's message to you and your brothers that you are unlimited spirit and part of the unified Sonship. This is done by forgiveness and the eventual acceptance of the Atonement for yourself. The Holy Spirit is the Voice for Life, which is the Spirit of God. God is Love and Love is Life. We are the Children of the Living God.

IX. Healing as Corrected Perception

T-8.IX.1.I said before that the Holy Spirit is the Answer. 2 **The Holy Spirit** is the Answer to everything, because **the Holy Spirit** knows what the answer to everything is. 3 The ego does not know what a real question is, although **the ego** asks an endless number **of questions.** 4 Yet you can learn **that the ego does not know what a real question is**, as you learn to question the value of the ego, and thus establish your ability to evaluate **the ego's** questions. 5 When the ego tempts you to sickness do not ask the Holy Spirit to heal the body, for **to heal the body** would merely be to accept the ego's belief that the body is the proper aim of healing. 6 Ask, rather, that the Holy Spirit teach you the right <*perception*> of the body, for perception alone can be distorted. 7 Only perception can be sick, because only perception can be wrong.

<u>Note # 72:</u> Ask that the Holy Spirit correct your misperception of the purpose of the body. The body's purpose is that of a learning device for communication. It is a means not an end. It is your mind's misperception not that of the body's that leads to the sickness of the body.

T-8.IX.2. Wrong perception is the wish that things be as **the things** are not. 2 The reality of everything is totally harmless, because total harmlessness is the condition of **everything's real** reality. 3 **Total harmlessness** is also the condition of your awareness of **everything's real** reality. 4 You do not have to seek reality. 5 **Reality** will seek you and find you when you meet **reality's** conditions. 6 **Reality's harmless** conditions are part of what **reality** is. 7 And this part only, **that you be totally harmless,** is up to you. 8 The rest is of **reality,** itself. 9 You need do so little because your little part **of being totally harmless** is so powerful that **being totally harmless** will bring the whole to you. 10 Accept, then, your little part, and let the whole be yours.

Note # 73: Your part is to correct your wrong perception that you are a body that can attack and be attacked. Wrong perception only requires the acceptance of reality as it is. Truth can be obscured by the false but truth still remains hidden behind the cloak of darkness. Reality is found in the Mind of God, which we share. Reality is rediscovering what you really are. The ego's thought system utilizes the world of your provisional reality to attempt to "prove" that you are not the Son of God, created perfect, whole and complete. Fantasy is not your true reality.

Being totally harmless means that we are powerless to change the Will of God. Our misperceptions have no ability to impact or change the truth about God's perfect Creation. Our egoic thoughts cannot change the Oneness that is the Mind of God.

T-8.IX.3. Wholeness heals because **wholeness** is of the mind. 2 All forms of sickness, even unto death, are physical expressions of the fear of awakening **to the wholeness of the mind**. 3 **All forms of sickness** are attempts to reinforce sleeping out of fear of waking. 4 This **"sleeping" out of fear of waking,** is a pathetic way of trying not to see by rendering the faculties for seeing, **which is the mind, not the physical eyes,** ineffectual. 5 "Rest in peace" is a blessing for the living, not the dead, because rest comes from waking, not from sleeping. 6 Sleep is withdrawing; waking is joining. 7 Dreams are illusions of joining, because **dreams** reflect the ego's distorted notions about what joining is. 8 Yet the Holy Spirit, too, has use for sleep, and can use dreams on behalf of waking if you will let Him.

Note # 74: Sickness is the result of the splitting of our mind that arose from our belief in the separation. The split mind holds within it two conflicting thought systems. The ego's thought system believes in separation, individual "littleness" and limitation. Your world of provisional reality is the ego's witness that you are a limited ego-body. The Holy Spirit's thought system knows the truth about what you really are, and always "sees" you as an unlimited spirit, part of the Mind of God. The Holy Spirit utilizes your world of provisional reality and reinterprets this "dream world" based on truth. He asks you to choose again. By choosing for the guidance of the Holy Spirit, we are called to reawaken from the deep sleep that we have fallen into. The Holy Spirit can transform our egoic misperception by removing the false aspects of fear and allowing only loving and forgiving aspects to remain. Thus, egoic misperceptions are realigned with the truth and become correct perception that witnesses for only joining and union as one.

T-8.IX.4. How you wake is the sign of how you have used sleep. 2 To whom did you give **your sleep and dreams**? 3 Under which teacher did you place **your sleep**? 4 Whenever you wake dispiritedly, **your sleep** was not given to the Holy Spirit. 5 Only when you awaken joyously have you utilized sleep according to **the Holy Spirit's** purpose. 6 You can indeed be "drugged" by sleep, if you have misused **sleep** on behalf of sickness. 7 Sleep is no more a form of death than death is a form of unconsciousness. 8 Complete unconsciousness is impossible. 9 You can rest in peace only because you are awake.

Note # 75: The mind is always awake even when we appear to be physically sleeping. Sleeping is the withdrawal or resting of our conscious mind. Yet, our subconscious mind is active and continues to function. If we have given our subconscious mind over to the though system of the ego, our subconscious mind will continue to manifest and call into our experiences proof that we are a vulnerable and limited ego-body. If the subconscious mind is given over to the Holy Spirit's thought system, it will attempt to remember what we really are. Sleep, therefore, can be utilized to "withdraw" or awaken from our dream world of provisional reality into the truth that we are unlimited Spirit.

T-8.IX.5. Healing is release from the fear of waking and the substitution of the decision to wake. 2 The decision to wake is the reflection of the will to love, since all healing involves replacing fear with love. 3 The Holy Spirit cannot distinguish among degrees of error, for if **the Holy Spirit** taught that one form of sickness is more serious than another, **the Holy Spirit** would be teaching that one error can be more real than another **error**. 4 **The Holy Spirit's** function is to distinguish only between the false and the true, replacing the false with the true.

Note # 76: There is no degree of difficulty because there is nothing more false than the false. To the Holy Spirit, everything is either black or white. There is just the choice between the true and the false. Yet, if choice does not result in a change in outcome, can it be a viable choice? The Holy Spirit recognizes that black, the false, is really no choice since it has no lasting and real effect. The Holy Spirit, therefore, merely advises that you simply choose again. When the choice for truth is finally made, the false always fades away into the nothingness from which it came.

T-8.IX.6. The ego, which always wants to weaken the mind, tries to separate **the mind** from the body in an attempt to destroy **the mind**. 2 Yet the ego actually believes that **the ego** is protecting **the body**. 3 **This belief that the ego is protecting the body** is because the ego believes that mind is dangerous, and that to make **the body** mindless is to heal. 4 But to make **mind** mindless is impossible, since **to make mind mindless** would mean to make nothing out of what God created, **which is only mind or spirit**. 5 The ego despises weakness, even though **the ego** makes every effort to induce **weakness**. 6 The ego wants only what **the ego** hates. 7 To the ego **wanting only what the ego hates** is perfectly sensible. 8 Believing in the power of attack, the ego wants attack.

Note # 77: The ego wants the mind to forget that the mind is the decision-maker. If the ego can successfully convince the mind that the mind is only a body instead of spirit, the mind will "forget" that it alone is the ultimate decision-maker. If the mind abdicates its decision-making abilities, the egoic thought system can fill this void. As such, the ego's "existence" depends upon keeping the mind in this deluded state of consciousness. The ego's goal is to keep you mindless and for you to identify yourself only as the body. Attack is the way to reinforce this belief that you are a limited ego-body in competition with other ego-bodies.

T-8.IX.7. The Bible enjoins you to be perfect, to heal all errors, to take no thought of the body as separate and to accomplish all things in my name. 2 This is not my name alone, for our **being** is a shared identification. 3 The Name of God's Son is One, and you are enjoined to do the works of love because we share this Oneness. 4 Our minds are whole because **our minds** are one. 5 If you are sick you are withdrawing from me. 6 Yet you cannot withdraw from me alone. 7 You can only withdraw from yourself <*and*> me.

Note # 78: You withdraw from the Oneness when you make yourself sick and claim that you are little. Sickness arises from your belief in split-mindedness. When we are sick, we have chosen to withdraw from the truth of our Big "S" Self and all others. We deny our Oneness with the Mind of God.

T-8.IX.8. You have surely begun to realize that <u>**A Course In Miracles**</u> is a very practical course, and one that means exactly what it says. 2 I would not ask you to do things you cannot do, and it is impossible that I could do things you cannot do. 3 Given **that it is impossible that I could do things you cannot do**, and given this quite literally, nothing can prevent you from doing exactly what I ask, and everything argues <*for*> your doing **exactly what I ask**. 4 I give you no limits because God lays **no limits** upon you. 5 When you limit yourself we are not of one mind, and that is sickness. 6 Yet sickness is not of the body, but **sickness is** of the mind. 7 All forms of sickness are signs that the mind is split, and **that the mind** does not accept a unified purpose.

Note # 79: All parts of the Sonship, including Jesus, are equal. When we see differences and limitations, it is due to our valuing specialness, individuality and separation. Our mind is split trying to serve two masters. Healing requires one unified purpose to return wholeness to the split-minded. Our Big "S" Self can never accept the ego's thought system. Jesus has demonstrated that only the Holy Spirit's thought system can unify the split-mind and thus, conquer the illusion of the body and its associated death.

T-8.IX.9. The unification of purpose, then, is the Holy Spirit's only way of healing **your mind's belief that it is separate and therefore split.** 2 This is because **the mind** is the only level at which healing means anything. 3 The re-establishing of meaning in a chaotic thought system <*is*> the way to heal a chaotic thought system. 4 Your task is only to meet the conditions for meaning, since meaning itself is of God. 5 Yet your return to meaning is essential to **God**, because your meaning is part of **God**. 6 Your healing, then, is part of **God's** health, since **your health** is part of His Wholeness. 7 **God** cannot lose **His Wholeness**, but you <*can*> not know **God's Wholeness**. 8 Yet **God's Wholeness** is still **God's** Will for you, and **God's** Will must stand forever and in all things

Note # 80: Sickness is of the mind and, therefore, the mind must be healed because it is at that level that the problem occurred. To attempt to heal the body would be addressing the symptom rather than the cause. The cause of sickness is the belief in separation, which resulted in the appearance of false choices for our purpose. These different choices in purpose results in conflict and competition within a now "split mind" that claims that it did not know what it was. The split mind gave rise to the ego and the egoic thought system. By healing, the Holy Spirit re-establishes the wholeness of the mind by once again unifying the purpose of the mind. This unified purpose is the reestablishment of the Sonship to the truth of the Oneness, the Sonship return to knowledge and the fulfilling of the Son's function as a co-creator with His Father. The ego's chaotic thought system is discarded for the thought system of truth, which is the Holy Spirit's thought system. Our will and God's Will are recognized as the same Will. Thus, healing re-established the wholeness of our minds with the Mind of God.

Chapter 9. THE ACCEPTANCE OF THE ATONEMENT

I. The Acceptance of Reality

T-9.I.1. Fear of the Will of God is one of the strangest beliefs the human mind has ever made. 2 **Fear of the Will of God** could not possibly have occurred unless the mind were already profoundly split, making it possible for **the split minded** to be afraid of what **the Will of God and the mind** really is. 3 Reality cannot "threaten" anything except illusions, since reality can only uphold truth. 4 The very fact that the Will of God, which is what you are, is perceived as fearful, demonstrates that you <are> afraid of what you are. 5 It is not, then, the Will of God of which you are afraid, but **your will.**

<u>Note # 1:</u> Because we perceive ourselves to be separate from God, we believe that we can oppose God's Will. If we understood that we are God's Will, there would be nothing to oppose. The truth of love just is. Love is not fearful. It is our denial of the fact that we are only the expression of God's Love that is the source of our fear. We then project our misperception of what we are upon God. Our misperception of ourselves as a fearful being leads to our mind's egoic projection that God is something to fear. Instead of God being only Love, the split-minded make up an egoic god of fear. Being split-minded, we are afraid of what we perceive our own "egoic" will to represent. We believe that we are something other than love. Our perceived provisional reality now becomes a frightening place.

T-9.I.2. Your will is not the ego's **will**, and that is why the ego is against you. 2 What seems to be the fear of God is really the fear of your own **egoic provisional** reality. 3 It is impossible to learn anything consistently in a state of panic. 4 If the purpose of this course is to help you remember what you are, and if you believe that what you are is fearful, then it must follow that you will not learn this course **because you believe that what you are is fearful**. 5 Yet the reason for the course is that you do not know what you are.

<u>Note # 2:</u> The ego's thought system is based on fear. If we adopt the viewpoint of our egoic mind, we can only learn what is false. The opposite of love is fear and this is only what the ego would teach us. Only by seeking a different teacher will we find a spokesman for love and truth.

T-9.I.3. If you do not know what your reality is, why would you be so sure that **your reality** is fearful? 2 The association of truth and fear, which would be highly artificial at most, is particularly inappropriate in the minds of those who do not know what truth is. 3 All this **association of truth with egoic fear**

could mean is that you are arbitrarily associating something beyond your awareness, **which is truth,** with something you do not want, **which is fear**. 4 **Because you are arbitrarily associating truth with egoic fear, which is something you do not want**, it is evident, then, that you are judging something of which you are totally unaware **of which is truth**. 5 You have set up this strange situation **of judging something of which you are totally unaware of, which is the truth,** so that it is impossible to escape from **this strange situation** without a Guide, **the Holy Spirit**, Who <*does*> know what your reality is. 6 The purpose of this Guide, **the Holy Spirit,** is merely to remind you of what you want. 7 **The Holy Spirit** is not attempting to force an alien will upon you. 8 **The Holy Spirit** is merely making every possible effort within the limits you impose on **the Holy Spirit** to re-establish your own will in your awareness.

Note # 3: You believe that you are something you are not and are fearful. Therefore, it is impossible for you to self-correct because you are coming from a false belief that you are a limited ego body. Since you believe that you are a limited ego body, you can never "find" yourself. Claiming that you are the frail body, you will never look past the bodily shroud to rediscover your inner Big "S" Self, which is the unlimited spirit that you are. You will search every other place within your dream world of provisional reality for something that can bring you happiness and wholeness. Since you have forgotten what you really are, you have forgotten that you already are what you seek. Only the Holy Spirit, Who knows your true reality and also is aware of your dream state, can guide you back home and awaken you to the remembrance that you are the Shared Mind of God.

T-9.I.4. You have imprisoned your will beyond your own awareness, where **your will** remains, but **where your true will** cannot help you. 2 When I said that the Holy Spirit's function is to sort out the true from the false in your mind, I meant that **the Holy Spirit** has the power to look into what you have hidden and recognize the Will of God there **in what you have hidden.** 3 **The Holy Spirit's** recognition of this **true** Will can make **this true Will** real to you because **the Holy Spirit** is in your mind, and therefore **the Holy Spirit** is your reality. 4 If, then, **the Holy Spirit's** perception of your mind brings **your mind's** reality to you, **the Holy Spirit** <*is*> helping you to remember what you are. 5 The only source of fear in this process **of helping you to remember what you are** is what you think you will lose. 6 Yet it is only what the Holy Spirit sees, **which is your true Big "S" Self** that you can possibly have because **this true Will** is **what you are**

Note # 4: The Holy Spirit knows the truth and, therefore, guides you back to the truth that you are God's Son and as such, you cannot be a limited ego body. Outside your mind's delusional dream world, you can only be as God created you.

T-9.I.5. I have emphasized many times that the Holy Spirit will never call upon you to sacrifice anything. 2 But if you ask the sacrifice of reality of yourself, the Holy Spirit must remind you that **this self-imposed sacrifice of the reality about yourself** is not God's Will because **this self-imposed sacrifice of the reality about yourself** is not **your true Will**. 3 There is no difference between your will and God's **Will**. 4 If you did not have a split mind, you would recognize that willing is salvation because **willing** is communication.

Note # 5: Perceiving ourselves to be split-minded, we believe that we have a will that could be different from our Source. This error is based on your ego's misinterpretation of what creation is. God's Creation is the extension of God, Herself. To have a will other than God's would be to claim that we are self-created, which has already been defined as the "authority problem." God is Cause and we are Her Effect. We cannot be self-created.

T-9.I.6. It is impossible to communicate in alien tongues. 2 You and your Creator can communicate through creation, because **creation** and only **creation** is Your joint Will **and thus, your true reality**. 3 A divided mind cannot communicate, because **a divided mind** speaks for different things to the same mind. 4 **Since a divided mind speaks for different things to the same mind, the divided mind** loses the ability to communicate simply because confused communication does not mean anything. 5 A message cannot be communicated unless **a message** makes sense. 6 How sensible can your messages be, when you ask for what you do not want? 7 Yet as long as you are afraid of your will, **asking for what you do not want** is precisely what you are asking for.

Note # 6: The Holy Spirit follows your true Will, which is the Will of God. The Holy Spirit does not follow or attack the false egoic will that you have dreamed up in your illusionary world of provisional reality. To do so would only increase your fear by making the false appear real. The Holy Spirit's goal is to release you from your self-imposed fear about your true will. You fear the false and illusionary will of your ego. Only by awakening to the truth can you rediscover your true will is one with the Will of God. God wills only that you be happy. You cannot be happy when you fail to co-create with God. Creation is communication.

T-9.I.7. You may insist that the Holy Spirit does not answer you, but it might be wiser to consider the kind of questioner you are. 2 You do not ask only for what you want. 3 **You do not ask only for what you want** because you are afraid you might receive **only what you want**, and you would **receive only what you want from the Holy Spirit who knows your true Will**. 4 That is why you persist in asking the teacher**, the ego,** who could not possibly give you what you want **since the ego does not know your true Will**. 5 Of **the ego** you can never learn what it is **that you really want**, and **not to be able to get what you really want from the ego** gives you the illusion of safety. 6 Yet you cannot be safe <*from*> truth, but **you can** only **be safe** <*in*> truth. 7 Reality is the only safety. 8 Your will is your salvation because **your true Will** is the same as God's **Will**. 9 The separation is nothing more than the belief that **your will** is different **from God's Will**.

Note # 7: Because you believe you are an ego-body, you desire to believe that you are separate. We want to be special and different from how God created us. By refusing to choose the Holy Spirit as your guide, you never are reminded of what you really are, which is a Oneness of "All That Is." Instead, you take the ego as your guide. The ego cannot tell you what you are because the ego does not know. The ego can only teach the false and claim that you have a special, separate and autonomous will that is different from God's Will.

T-9.I.8. No right mind can believe that its will is stronger than God's **Will**. 2 If, then, a mind believes that its will is different from **God's Will, the "non right-minded"** can only decide either that there is no God or that God's Will is fearful. 3 The former, **that there is no God,** accounts for the atheist and the latter, **that God's Will is fearful, accounts** for the martyr, who believes that God demands sacrifices. 4 Either of these insane decisions, **that there is no God or that God's Will is fearful,** will induce panic, because the atheist believes he is alone, and the martyr believes that God is crucifying him. 5 Yet no one really wants either abandonment or retaliation, even though many may seek both **abandonment and retaliation**. 6 Can you ask the Holy Spirit for "gifts" such as **abandonment or retaliation** and actually expect to receive them? **(Abandonment or retaliation)** 7 **The Holy Spirit** cannot give you something you do not want **with your true Will**. 8 When you ask the Universal Giver, **the Holy Spirit,** for what you do not want, you are asking for what cannot be given because **what you do not want** was never created. 9 **What you do not want** was never created, because **what you do not want** was never your will for <*you.*>

Note # 8: God's Will, of which you are an extension, only created joy and love, because that is what God willed for His Son. God never created anything that was harmful. To do so in a Oneness of Everything would mean God would have to will that He harm Himself. This would be insanity. Therefore, there can be nothing harmful within the Will of God.

T-9.I.9. Ultimately everyone must remember the Will of God, because ultimately everyone must recognize himself, **which is the Will of God.** . 2 This recognition **of yourself** is the recognition that **your** will and God's Will are one. 3 In the presence of truth, there are no unbelievers and no sacrifices. 4 In the security of reality, fear is totally meaningless. 5 To deny what is can only <*seem*> to be fearful. 6 Fear cannot be real without a cause, and God is the only Cause. 7 God is Love and you do want **God.** 8 This, **Love** <*is*> your will. 9 Ask for this, **God's Love,** and you will be answered, because you will be asking only for what belongs to you, **which is God's Love, your inheritance.**

Note # 9: Like the prodigal son, God insures that you will never lose your inheritance. You can forget what you are, but you can never lose what you are. Our reawakening is assured because it is God's Will that His Son be joyous and loved.

T-9.I.10. When you ask the Holy Spirit for what would hurt you **the Holy Spirit** cannot answer because nothing can hurt you, and so you are asking for nothing. 2 Any wish that stems from the ego is a wish for nothing, and to ask for **a wish that stems from the ego** is not a request. 3 A **wish that stems from the ego** is merely a denial in the form of a request. 4 The Holy Spirit is not concerned with form, being aware only of meaning. 5 The ego cannot ask the Holy Spirit for anything, because there is complete communication failure between **the ego and the Holy Spirit.** 6 Yet <*you*> can ask for everything of **the Holy Spirit,** because your requests to **be everything** are real, being of your right mind. 7 Would the Holy Spirit deny the Will of God? 8 And could **the Holy Spirit** fail to recognize **the Will of God** in **God's** Son?

Note # 10: The Holy Spirit hears only requests from the true "High-Self." To respond to the request from the insane egoic thought system would only increase fear and thus, "confirm" the split-mind's belief in the separation. This cannot be the Will of God and thus, it cannot be your true will. Requests for littleness and limitation are only the insane requests of the ego. Egoic requests are asking for the denial of the truth. The ego always requests that the false be made true. This is impossible.

T-9.I.11. You do not recognize the enormous waste of energy you expend in denying truth. 2 What would you say of someone who persists in attempting the impossible, believing that to achieve **the impossible** is to succeed? 3 The belief that you must have the impossible in order to be happy is totally at variance with the principle of creation. 4 God could not will that happiness depended on what you could never have. 5 The fact that God is Love does not require belief, but **the fact that God is Love** does require acceptance. 6 It is indeed possible for you to deny facts, although it is impossible for you to change **facts.** 7 If you hold your hands over your eyes, you will not see because you are interfering with the laws of seeing. 8 If you deny love, you will not know **love** because your cooperation is the law of **love's** being. 9 You cannot change laws you did not make, and the laws of happiness were created for you, not by you.

Note # 11: God's love allows you total freedom. It flows constantly to and through you. Due to free will, we can pretend that we are not the recipients of God's love. Yet, our denial of the truth cannot change the truth.

T-9.I.12. Any attempt to deny what <*is*> must be fearful, and if the attempt is strong **this denial of what**

<is> will induce panic. 2 Willing against reality, though impossible, can be made into a very persistent goal even though you, **your Big "S" Self,** do not want **to will against reality.** 3 But consider the result of this strange decision **of willing against what you really want.** 4 You are devoting your mind to what you do not want. 5 How real can this devotion be? 6 If you do not want it, it was never created. 7 If it were never created, it is nothing. 8 Can you really devote yourself to nothing?

Note # 12: Willing against what you really want is an insane wish of a split-mind under the influence of the ego's guidance. Since the mind is split, the mind does not know what it really is. Not knowing what it really is, the split-minded cannot know what it really wants. The split-minded refuse to listen to the request of their Big "S" Self. The Holy Spirit does not respond to the ego, since both are not on the same level of communication. One only hears the voice for truth. The ego only asks for the false.

T-9.I.13. God in **God's** devotion to you created you devoted to everything, and gave you what you are devoted *<to>*, **which is everything.** 2 Otherwise **without being given everything,** you would not have been created perfect. 3 Reality is everything, and you have everything because you are real. 4 You cannot make the unreal because the absence of reality is fearful, and fear cannot be created. 5 As long as you believe that fear is possible, you will not create. 6 Opposing orders of reality, **which are fear and love,** make reality meaningless, and reality *<is>* meaning.

Note # 13: Being everything, what is there to fear? Love is the only reality and Love is everything. As long as you believe that you are not everything, you cannot create because your beliefs are artificially limiting your creative ability. You cannot limit the Power of God, which is your inheritance, but you can fail to acknowledge that this power exists in you. Argue for your limitations and they will be yours. This limitation, however, only exist in your world of provisional reality. Your creative power can be denied, but it cannot be lost.

T-9.I.14. Remember, then, that God's Will is already possible, and nothing else will ever be. 2 **That God's Will is already possible and nothing else will ever be,** is the simple acceptance of reality, because only **this fact** that **God's Will is already possible, and nothing else will ever be,** is real. 3 You cannot distort reality and know what **reality** is. 4 And if you do distort reality you will experience anxiety, depression and ultimately panic, because you are trying to make yourself unreal. 5 When you feel these things, **anxiety, depression and ultimately panic,** do not try to look beyond yourself for truth, for truth can only be within you. 6 Say, therefore:

7 *Christ is in me, and where **Christ** is God must be, for Christ is part of **God**.*

Note # 14: Do not go beyond yourself for truth because there is nothing that could be beyond you. Beyond yourself can only "exist" in an egoic dream world of your own provisional reality. Truth can only be found to the thought system of the Holy Spirit. Since the ego's thought system is based on the insane and false belief that you can oppose the Will of God, you should not seek answers from the ego for it does not know who you are.

II. The Answer to Prayer

T-9.II.1.Everyone who ever tried to use prayer to ask for something has experienced what appears to be failure. 2 This **experience of what appears to be failure in prayer** is not only true in connection with specific things that might be harmful, but also in connection with requests that are strictly in line with this course. 3 The latter **requests that are strictly in line with this course**, in particular might be incorrectly interpreted as "proof" that the course does not mean what **the course** says. 4 You must remember, however, that the course states, and repeatedly, that **the course's** purpose is the escape from fear.

Note # 15: The Holy Spirit cannot answer your legitimate request affirmatively, if the answer would result in an increase in your fear. To do so, would only make your belief in the separation appear more real to your already deluded mind. This would be counterproductive and against the Holy Spirit's function and purpose.

T-9.II.2.Let us suppose, then, that what you ask of the Holy Spirit is what you really want, but you are still afraid of **what you ask of the Holy Spirit**. 2 Should this be the case **that you are still afraid of what you ask of the Holy Spirit**, your attainment of **what you ask of the Holy Spirit which if received would still frighten you,** would no longer <be> what you want. 3 Because **this would no longer <be> what you want, this** is why certain specific forms of healing are not achieved, even when the state of healing is **achieved**. 4 An individual may ask for physical healing because **the individual** is fearful of bodily harm. 5 At the same time, if **the individual** were healed physically, the threat to **the individual's** thought system might be considerably more fearful to **the individual** than **the sickness'** physical expression. 6 In this case **the individual** is not really asking for release from fear, but for the removal of a symptom that **the individual** himself selected. 7 This request **for the removal of a symptom that the individual himself selected** is, therefore, not **a request** for healing at all.

Note # 16: All prayer is answered. Yet, because the Holy Spirit will not do anything that might increase your fear, the answer may not be recognized. Any increase in your level of fear would reinforce the belief in separation. Prayer is a request for healing which is a request for a release of fear. This is in alignment with the goal of the Holy Spirit. Since sickness' source is the mind's misperception of what you are, the Holy Spirit must heal at the problem's source, which is at the level of the mind. The symptom may appear at the physical level of the body, yet, it is the mind, not the body where the healing must take place. The body is part of your dream world of provisional reality. The Holy Spirit will answer all requests but you may choose not to listen or recognize the answer. If the mind is healed, the imagined symptom in the body may or may not appear to change. Yet, when healed, the whole mind will recognize that you are not the body.

T-9.II.3.The Bible emphasizes that all prayer is answered, and this is indeed true **that all prayer is answered**. 2 The very fact that the Holy Spirit has been asked for anything will ensure a response. 3 Yet it is equally certain that no response given by **the Holy Spirit** will ever be one that would increase fear. 4 It is possible that **the Holy Spirit's** answer will not be heard. 5 It is impossible, however, that **the answer of the Holy Spirit** will be lost. 6 There are many answers you have already received but have not yet heard. 7 I assure you that **the answers of the Holy Spirit** are waiting for you.

Note # 17: The Holy Spirit answers all requests, but you may choose not to listen or recognize the answer. If this is the case, the answer will not be wasted. It will be preserved for you until your free will chooses to listen and accept the answer.

T-9.II.4.If you would know your prayers are answered, never doubt a Son of God. 2 Do not question **a Son of God** and do not confound **a Son of God**, for your faith in **a Son of God** is your faith in yourself.

3 If you would know God and **God's** Answer, believe in me whose faith in you cannot be shaken. 4 Can you ask of the Holy Spirit truly, and doubt your brother? 5 Believe **your brother's** words are true because of the truth that is in **your brother**. 6 You will unite with the truth in **your brother**, and **your brother's** words will <*be*> true. 7 As you hear **your brother** you will hear me. 8 Listening to truth is the only way you can hear **truth** now, and finally know **truth**.

Note # 18: We must look beyond our brother's body to the truth of his Big "S" Self. We must perceive our brother's actions as only communicating love or a cry for love. This is how we listen only for truth. The proper response to a brother's cry for love is to respond with love, not attack.

T-9.II.5. The message your brother gives you is up to you. 2 What does **your brother** say to you? 3 What would you have **your brother** say? 4 Your decision about **your brother** determines the message you receive. 5 Remember that the Holy Spirit is in **your brother**, and **the Holy Spirit's** Voice speaks to you through **your brother**. 6 What can so holy a brother tell you except truth? 7 But are you listening to **the truth that your holy brother tells you**? 8 Your brother may not know who he is, but there is a light in **your brother's** mind that does know **the truth**. 9 This light can shine into **your mind,** giving truth to **your brother's** words and making you able to hear **your brother's words** 10 **Your brother's** words are the Holy Spirit's answer to you. 11 Is your faith in **your brother** strong enough to let you hear **the Holy Spirit's answer to you**?

Note # 19: Your brother's Big 'S" Self lies hidden by his bodily form. If you quiet your egoic mind and stop and listen, the Holy Spirit will speak the truth about your brother's Big 'S" Self and your Big "S" Self will respond with love and forgiveness. You will join together for your common holiness is one.

T-9.II.6. You can no more pray for yourself alone than you can find joy for yourself alone. 2 Prayer is the restatement of inclusion, directed by the Holy Spirit under the laws of God. 3 Salvation is of your brother. 4 The Holy Spirit extends from your mind to **your brother's mind**, and answers <*you.*> 5 You cannot hear the Voice for God, **the Holy Spirit,** in yourself alone, because you are not alone. 6 And **the Holy Spirit's** answer is only for what you are. 7 You will not know the trust I have in you unless you extend **the trust I have in you**. 8 You will not trust the guidance of the Holy Spirit, or believe that **the guidance of the Holy Spirit** is for you unless you hear **the guidance of the Holy Spirit** in others. 9 **The guidance of the Holy Spirit** must be for your brother <*because*> **the guidance of the Holy Spirit** is for you. 10 Would God have created a Voice **of the Holy Spirit** for you alone? 11 Could you hear **the Holy Spirit's** answer except as **the Holy Spirit** answers all of God's Sons? 12 Hear of your brother what you would have me hear of you, for you would not want me to be deceived.

Note # 20: Since prayer is inclusive, you cannot pray alone. Prayer is answered through your brothers for the removal of fear is shared by all. The guidance of the Holy Spirit has universal application since we are all Sons of God. Although denied by the egoic mind, we remain connected with our brother in the holographic web of God's Mind. Healing is the coming together of those who once perceived themselves as separate. The Laws of God state that "To give is to receive." for we are all joined as One.

T-9.II.7. I love you for the truth in you, as God does. 2 Your deceptions may deceive you, but **your deceptions** cannot deceive me. 3 I knowing what you are, I cannot doubt you. 4 I hear only the Holy Spirit in you **and the Holy Spirit** speaks to me through you. 5 If you would hear me, hear my brothers in whom God's Voice speaks. 6 The answer to all prayers lies in **our brothers**. 7 You will be answered **by God's Voice** as you hear the answer in everyone. 8 Do not listen to anything else or you will not hear truly.

Note # 21: The answer comes from the thought system of the Holy Spirit's eyes of love. Do not listen to the thought system of the ego. The ego's goal is to deceive and keep you from reclaiming your power to choose again.

T-9.II.8. Believe in your brothers because I believe in you, and you will learn that my belief in you is justified. 2 Believe in me <*by*> believing in **your brothers**, for the sake of what God gave **your brothers**. 3 **Your brothers** will answer you if you learn to ask only truth of **your brothers**. 4 Do not ask for blessings without blessing **your brothers**, for only in this way **of blessing your brothers first,** can you learn how blessed you are. 5 By following this way **of blessing your brothers first,** you are seeking the truth in you. 6 **Blessing your brothers first** is not going beyond yourself but toward yourself. 7 Hear only God's Answer in His Sons, and you are answered.

Note # 22: What we perceive ourselves to be, we extend or project upon another. Loving thoughts are extended, shared and strengthened. Fear-based thoughts make by excluding and separating. They are not shared. How we perceive another is how we view ourselves. We only give what we believe we have and by giving we prove we have it. We can either teach love or fear but not both.

T-9.II.9. To disbelieve is to side against, or to attack. 2 To believe is to accept, and to side with. 3 To believe is not to be credulous, but to accept and appreciate. 4 What you do not believe you do not appreciate and you cannot be grateful for what you do not value. 5 There is a price you will pay for judgment, because judgment is the setting of a price. 6 And as you set **the price** you will pay **the price**.

Note # 23: Since giving is receiving, any judgments you rendered will return upon yourself. Condemn your brother and you condemn yourself. Thoughts never leave their source. What we value, we will perceive to be our experience.

T-9.II.10. If paying is equated with getting, you will set the price low but demand a high return. 2 You will have forgotten, however, that to price is to value, so that your return is in proportion to your judgment of worth. 3 If paying is associated with giving **paying** cannot be perceived as loss, and the reciprocal relationship of giving and receiving will be recognized. 4 **If paying is associated with giving**, the price will then be set high, because of the value of the return. 5 The price for getting is to lose sight of value, making it inevitable that you will not value what you receive. 6 Valuing **the item a** little, you will not appreciate **the item** and you will not want **the item**.

Note # 24: The judgment that you place on the item will set the price for the item. If you believe paying is getting, you are following the belief system of the ego, which believes in limitation and, therefore, always seeks a "bargain." To the ego, having is getting. You only give to get more of something you perceive you lack and need. You will want to pay little but want to receive a lot. The ego always wants a "good trade." If you believe paying is sharing or giving, you are under the thought system of the Holy Spirit which knows "to have all, give all to all." You will be willing to pay a high price because it will be shared or returned to you. This is why creation is the giving of all you are to everything. By giving all, you demonstrate that you really are all. Having and being are the same under the thought system of the Holy Spirit.

T-9.II.11. Never forget, then, that you set the value on what you receive, and price **the value on what you receive** by what you give **for the item**. 2 To believe that it is possible to get much for little is to believe that you can bargain with God. 3 God's laws are always fair and perfectly consistent. 4 By giving you receive. 5 But to receive is to accept, not to get. 6 It is impossible not to have, but it is possible not to know you have. 7 The recognition of having is the willingness for giving, and only by this willingness **for giving** can you recognize what you have. 8 What you give is therefore the value you put on what you have, being the exact measure of the value you put upon **what you have**. 9 And **the value you put on what you have**, in turn, is the measure of how much you want **what you have**.

Note # 25: You can only give what you have. Being only one, we can never lose what we have by giving it to the Oneness that is ourselves. By sharing thoughts, ideas are extended and strengthened. It is thought's experience that is shared. The body form cannot be shared; only the holographic Mind of God can be shared.

T-9.II.12. You can ask of the Holy Spirit, then, only by giving to **the Holy Spirit**, and you can give to **the Holy Spirit** only where you recognize **the Holy Spirit**. 2 If you recognize **the Holy Spirit** in everyone, consider how much you will be asking of **the Holy Spirit**, and how much you will receive **from the Holy Spirit**. 3 **The Holy Spirit** will deny you nothing because you have denied **the Holy Spirit** nothing, and so you can share everything **with the Holy Spirit**. 4 **By denying nothing to the Holy Spirit,** this is the way, and the only way to have **the Holy Spirit's** answer, because **the Holy Spirit's** answer is all you can ask for and **all you can** want. 5 Say, then, to everyone:

6 *Because I will to know myself, I see you as God's Son and my brother.*

Note # 26: The price is set by what we give. The Law of Love states that by giving, you receive. Receiving is accepting, not getting. The recognition of having is based on our willingness to give. The first lesson of the Holy Spirit is to have all, give all to all. We cannot love God if we do not love our brothers and ourselves. All three are One. If we refuse to give all our misperceptions over to the Holy Spirit's thought system, we are attempting to exclude some part from the Oneness. This cannot be love. To withhold love from any part is to withhold love from God, every brother and ourselves. All share equally because all are connected as One. Our denial cannot change the reality of our One Self, but denial does prevent us from remembering and recognizing our spiritual magnificence as "That One."

III. The Correction of Error

T-9.III.1. The alertness of the ego to the errors of other egos is not the kind of vigilance the Holy Spirit would have you maintain. 2 Egos are critical in terms of the kind of "sense" **the ego's** stand for. 3 Egos understand this kind of sense **that alerts the ego to the errors of other egos,** because **finding errors in others** is sensible to **the ego**. 4 To the Holy Spirit **finding errors in others** makes no sense at all.

Note # 27: To the Holy Spirit, any judgment is self-judgment. Why would a Oneness want to condemn itself? To the ego, judging another proves that you are separate and special. Thus, the ego perceives itself to be one big judging machine. The ego places its need to be right above your need to be happy.

T-9.III.2. To the ego, **finding errors in others** is kind and right and good to point out errors and "correct" **these errors in others**. 2 **Finding errors in others** makes perfect sense to the ego, which is unaware of what errors are and what correction is. 3 Errors are of the ego, and correction of errors lies in the relinquishment of the ego. 4 When you correct a brother, you are telling **a brother** that **the brother** is wrong. 5 **A brother** may be making no sense at the time, and it is certain that, if **a brother** is speaking from the ego, **the brother** will not be making sense. 6 But your task is still to tell **a brother** he is right. 7 You do not tell **a brother** this verbally, if **a brother** is speaking foolishly. 8 **A brother** needs correction at another level, because **the brother's** error is at another level. 9 **The brother** is still right, because **the brother** is a Son of God. 10 **A brother's** ego is always wrong, no matter what **a brother's ego** says or what **a brother's ego does**.

Note # 28: Our ego always wants to be right and goes to great lengths to maintain that it judged correctly even when it is wrong. The ego wants to fix others since this confirms its correctness and specialness. The Holy Spirit knows that the ego knows nothing and, therefore, cannot judge correctly. This is why the Holy Spirit looks past the form and focuses on content. The Holy Spirit sees the Big "S" Self in all because the Love of Christ is all that we are. Everything is judged by this simple test, "What would love have me do?" This is the only criterion that the Holy Spirit used to respond to a brother's cry for love. This is the only criterion that our Big "S" Self knows is not insane.

T-9.III.3. If you point out the errors of your brother's ego you must be seeing through **your ego**, because the Holy Spirit does not perceive **your brother's** errors. 2 This **seeing of the errors of your brother's ego through your egoic mind** <*must*> be true, since there is no communication between the ego and the Holy Spirit. 3 The ego makes no sense, and the Holy Spirit does not attempt to understand anything that arises from **the ego since the ego makes no sense**. 4 Since **the Holy Spirit** does not understand **the ego, the Holy Spirit** does not judge **the ego,** knowing that nothing the ego makes means anything.

Note # 29: The ego is on the level of illusion. Egoic illusions have no impact on the Mind of God. Because of this, any perceived error that the ego observes are ignored and dismissed as meaningless. The Holy Spirit does not attack them since to do so would be giving the dream a false sense of reality. Instead of judging the illusion, the Holy Spirit dismisses the non-reality of the dream itself. This dismissal paves the way for the light of truth to resurface.

T-9.III.4. When you react at all to errors, you are not listening to the Holy Spirit. 2 **The Holy Spirit** has merely disregarded **all errors**, and if you attend to **errors** you are not hearing **the Holy Spirit**. 3 If you do not hear **the Holy Spirit,** you are listening to your ego and making as little sense as the brother whose errors you perceive. 4 This **listening to your ego and making your brother wrong for errors you perceive in your brother** cannot be correction. 5 Yet **listening to your ego and making your brother wrong for errors you perceive in your brother** is more than merely a lack of correction for **your brother**. 6 **This listening to your ego and making your brother wrong for errors you perceive in your brother** is the giving up of correction in yourself.

Note # 30: The ego relies on what it wants to perceive and makes judgments based on its false past perception and beliefs. Since the ego does not know what you are, all it "sees" are misperceptions. The split-minded, under the guidance of the ego, projects upon others, its own fear-based thoughts that it believes about itself but wishes to deny. It than judges the object of its projection based on what the ego has rejected in itself. The ego, not knowing what you are, always judges incorrectly. Since ideas cannot leave their source, this projection of limitation toward others, always returns to the mind of the sender. Thus, when you see your brother as less than a Son of God, you also deny the divinity of your Big "S" Self.

T-9.III.5. When a brother behaves insanely, you can heal **a brother** only by perceiving the sanity in **this brother**. 2 If you perceive **a brother's** errors and accept **a brother's errors,** you are accepting **your errors**. 3 If you want to give **your errors** over to the Holy Spirit, you must do this **by giving your brother's errors over to the Holy Spirit**. 4 Unless this **giving your brother's errors over to the Holy**

Spirit to free yourself of your errors becomes the one way in which you handle all errors, you cannot understand how all errors are undone. 5 How is this **giving your brother's errors over to the Holy Spirit to free yourself of your errors** different from telling you that what you teach you learn? 6 Your brother is as right as you are, and if you think **your brother** is wrong you are condemning yourself.

Note # 31: Since to give is to receive, whenever we see a brother as something other than perfect, whole and complete, we lay that same judgment upon ourselves. Because you are a Oneness, you must turn all misperception and egoic judgments over to the Holy Spirit. You cannot hate a little and be only Love. Any remnant of fear resists and blocks the flow of love.

T-9.III.6. *<You>* cannot correct yourself. 2 Is it possible, then, for you to correct another? 3 Yet you can see **your brother** truly, because it is possible for you to see yourself truly. 4 It is not up to you to change your brother, but merely to accept **your brother** as **your brother** is. 5 **Your brother's** errors do not come from the truth that is in **your brother's Big "S" Self,"** and only this truth, is your **truth**. 6 **Your brother's egoic** errors cannot change this **truth of your brother's Big "S" Self** and **these errors** can have no effect at all on the truth in you **that you also are unlimited spirit**. 7 To perceive errors in anyone, and to react to **the perceived errors in anyone** as if **perceived errors in anyone** were real, is to make **perceived errors in anyone** real to you. 8 You will not escape paying the price for **making the perceived errors in anyone real to you,** not because you are being punished for **making the perceived errors real to you,** but because you are following the wrong guide, **the ego,** and will therefore lose your way.

Note # 32: When you believe yourself to be a limited ego-body, you are under the guidance of the ego and, therefore, are unable to self-correct. The insane cannot correct themselves since they do not realize that both they and their egoic guide are equally insane. Only by choosing a new guide, the Holy Spirit, will you be able to once again remember what you and your brother really are. The Holy Spirit reinterprets your misperceptions of yourself and your brother by acknowledging the fact that nothing from the ego belief system has any impact on the reality of God's Kingdom. The only "reality" of egoic errors lies in the dreamer's false world of provisional reality. Since you are the dreamer, you have the power to reawaken from your dream whenever you choose to follow the guidance of the Holy Spirit.

T-9.III.7. Your brother's errors are not of him, any more than yours are of you. 2 Accept **your brother's** errors as real, and you have attacked yourself. 3 If you would find your way and keep **your way**, see only truth beside you for you walk together **with your brother**. 4 The Holy Spirit in you forgives all things in you and in your brother. 5 **Your brother's** errors are forgiven with your **errors**. 6 Atonement is no more separate than love. 7 Atonement cannot be separate because **Atonement** comes from love. 8 Any attempt you make to correct a brother means that you believe correction by you is possible, and this can only be the arrogance of the ego. 9 Correction is of God, Who does not know of arrogance.

Note # 33: The ego will attempt to tell you that you can fix or save another person with your own egoic plan for salvation. Anytime you need to fix another, you are confirming our ego's belief that you are a separate ego-body. You are claiming that your brother is not as God created him. You have judged your brother to be a child of a "lesser god." This is making your brother's error in thinking real and making his error your own. The Atonement is the acceptance of the fact that God's Creations can only be perfect as God created them. Thus, your brother, like yourself remains sinless and guiltless. God's correction is the Atonement. It says that what is true is true and can never be threatened or changed.

T-9.III.8. The Holy Spirit forgives everything because God created everything. 2 Do not undertake **the Holy Spirit's** function **to forgive,** or you will forget your **function, which is to create like God, the**

Father. 3 Accept only the function of healing in time, because **the function of healing** is what time is for. 4 God gave you the function to create in eternity. 5 You do not need to learn **to forgive**, but you do need to learn to want **to forgive**. 6 For that **you should forgive is what** all learning was made **for**. 7 **The function of healing in time** is the Holy Spirit's use of an ability that you do not need, but that you made. 8 Give **the function of healing** to **the Holy Spirit**! 9 You do not understand how to use **the function of healing**. 10 **The Holy Spirit** will teach you how to see yourself without condemnation, by learning how to look on everything without **condemnation**. 11 Condemnation will then not be real to you, and all your errors will be forgiven.

Note # 34: Because of your belief in the separation, you perceive yourself and others as sick and in need of healing. This "sickness" is found only in your split-mind's provisional reality, which is the unreal world of perception, time and space. Since the separation never really occurred in the Mind of God, time was "created" so that the Holy Spirit could heal your belief in split-mindedness. Time and space is where the dream world of your provisional reality occurs. Time is relevant here since change is possible in dreams. The Holy Spirit will teach the split-minded to stop denying their true One Self. The Holy Spirit uses time to teach you that the world of perception is only a dream and, therefore, nothing that is perceived in this dream can affect the changeless Mind of God. Thus, there is nothing in this fantasy that could require forgiveness. Illusions can have no affect on the real world, which is the Kingdom or Heaven. Self-condemnation is unnecessary since this world of perception was made in error. God did not create this world. Instead we **made** this world in error. Error needs correction, not judgment and condemnation.

Give all your perception to the Holy Spirit so that He can correct them. Once healed, you can freely choose to reclaim your oneness with God's Will and you can fulfill your function to co-create in eternity as God's Child.

IV. The Holy Spirit's Plan of Forgiveness

T-9.IV.1. Atonement is for all, because **Atonement** is the way to undo the belief that anything is for you alone. 2 To forgive is to overlook. 3 Look, then, beyond error and do not let your perception rest upon **perceived error**, for you will believe what your perception holds. 4 Accept as true only what your brother is, **(his Big "S" Self)** if you would know yourself. 5 Perceive what **your brother** is not **(his little "s" self)** and you cannot know what you are, because you see **your brother** falsely. 6 Remember always that your Identity **as the Son of God** is shared, and that Its sharing is **the Son of God's** reality.

Note # 35: You will identify with what you value. What you perceive follows your purpose. Value oneness and you will perceive the Christ in all. Value the specialness of littleness and you will perceive everything limited, different and separate. The Atonement asks you to look beyond all past egoic misperception and accept the truth of your divine birthright.

T-9.IV.2. You have a part to play in the Atonement, but the plan of the Atonement is beyond you. 2 You do not understand how to overlook errors, or you would not make **errors**. 3 It would merely be further error to believe either that you do not make **perceived errors**, or that you can correct **perceived errors** without **the Holy Spirit's** Guide to correction. 4 And if you do not follow **the Holy Spirit's** Guide your errors will not be corrected. 5 The plan **of the Atonement** is not yours because of your limited ideas about what you are. 6 This sense of limitation is where all errors arise. 7 The way to undo **all errors**, therefore, is not <*of*> you but <*for*> you.

Note # 36: The plan for the Sonship's return to knowledge comes from God, the Father. The Holy Spirit is given to be our Guide to follow in the implementation of God's Plan of the Atonement. Being unaware of what we are and falsely believing that we are a limited body, how can we expect our little "s" self to lead us back safely to knowledge. Our ego is the part of our mind that claims it does not know what we are. Only the foolish would expect the ignorant or insane to develop a plan for would return the split-minded to the sanity of whole mindedness.

T-9.IV.3. The Atonement is a lesson in sharing, which is given you because <*you have forgotten how to share.*> 2 The Holy Spirit merely reminds you of the natural use of your abilities. 3 **The Holy Spirit merely reminds you** by reinterpreting the ability to attack into the ability to share. **The Holy Spirit** translates what you have made into what God created. 4 If you would accomplish this **reinterpreting of what you have made into what God created** through **the Holy Spirit,** you cannot look on your abilities through the eyes of the ego, or you will judge **your abilities** as <*the ego*> does. 5 All **your abilities'** harmfulness lies in the ego's judgment. 6 All **your abilities** helpfulness lies in the judgment of the Holy Spirit.

Note # 37: The Holy Spirit reinterprets your attack thoughts and converts them into lessons of sharing and forgiveness. This reinterpretation results in a new vision that is based on sharing. Since sharing is creating or extending, this new vision aligns more closely to the reality of Heaven. You learn this new vision by sharing forgiveness with your brother. This new vision is the correct perception that comes from forgiveness and love. Forgiveness is overlooking that we originally perceived as an error and remembering the true nature of everything. Content, not form, represents the true nature or essence of something.

T-9.IV.4. The ego, too, has a plan of forgiveness because you are asking for **a plan of forgiveness,** though not of the right teacher, **which is the Holy Spirit.** 2 The ego's plan **of forgiveness,** of course, makes no sense and will not work. 3 By following **the ego's** plan you will merely place yourself in an impossible situation, to which the ego always leads you. 4 The ego's plan is to have you see error clearly first, and then overlook **the error.** 5 Yet how can you overlook what you have made real, **which was the perceived error**? 6 By seeing **the error** clearly, you have made **the error** real and <*cannot*> overlook **the error.** 7 This **inability of your mind to overlook an error you have made real** is where the ego is forced to appeal to "mysteries," insisting that you must accept the meaningless, **which is your perceived or imagined error,** to save yourself. 8 Many have tried to do this, **accept the meaningless error as real and then overlook the error** in my name, forgetting that my words make perfect sense because **my words** come from God. 9 **My words** are as sensible now as **my words** ever were, because **my words** speak of ideas that are eternal.

Note # 38: The ego's plan of forgiveness is to first make an error in our perception real and then to ask you to overlook the error. This is something that our mind finds impossible to do.
Example: You perceive that your brother has wronged or harmed you. Since you are unlimited spirit and not a body, you cannot be harmed. Yet, your ego has already convinced you that you are a body and, therefore, vulnerable to harm. Because of this untrue belief that you are body, your mind makes the body sick and it suffers pain. Sickness and hurt now become your provisional reality. The ego then asks you to forgive the wrongdoer, who you perceive to be your brother. Your mind is unable to "forgive and forget" since the mind has already made the sickness and pain the mind's imagined reality. It has made the illusion of the body real. Your ego next tells the mind that your brother had unjustly wronged you

and then asks that you to give up your rights of retribution. Giving up this right to revenge requires sacrifice. This sacrifice means that you must admit to inequality between your brother and yourself. This inequality proves you are separate, limited and very vulnerable. Egoic forgiveness thus, teaches the lesson that the separation is real. Egoic forgiveness teaches that you and your brother are not equal or do not share one mind.

The Holy Spirit takes this same misperception and takes you back to the original point that the error in perception occurred. This is your belief that you are a body. The Holy Spirit then tells you that since you are not a body, you could not be hurt. Since it could never have happened, this perceived hurt is easy to overlook, forget and forgive since it was not real. No sacrifice is required since the Holy Spirit is merely asking you to accept the truth that you are spirit and a part of the shared Sonship.

T-9.IV.5.Forgiveness that is learned of me, **who represents the Holy Spirit,** does not use fear to undo fear. 2 Nor does **forgiveness that is learned of me** make real the unreal and then destroy **the unreal**. 3 Forgiveness through the Holy Spirit lies simply in looking beyond error from the beginning, and thus keeping **the error** unreal for you. 4 Do not let any belief in **the error's** realness enter your mind, or you will also believe that you must undo what you have made in order to be forgiven. 5 What has no effect does not exist, and to the Holy Spirit the effects of error are nonexistent. 6 By steadily and consistently cancelling out all **the error's** effects, everywhere and in all respects, **the Holy Spirit** teaches that the ego does not exist and proves **that the ego does not exist**.

Note # 39: The Holy Spirit does not lift an illusion up to the status of reality. The Holy Spirit does not raise the misperception that you are the body to the level of the truth. By maintaining that the perceived error has no effect on the truth and thus, is not real, the Holy Spirit merely allows the error to dissipate. Now there is no error to forgive. To "forgive and forget" the nothingness of the once perceived error is now easily accomplished.

T-9.IV.6.Follow the Holy Spirit's teaching in forgiveness, then, because forgiveness is **the Holy Spirit's** function and **the Holy Spirit** knows how to fulfill **the Holy Spirit's function** perfectly. 2 That is what I meant when I said that miracles are natural, and when **miracles** do not occur something has gone wrong. 3 Miracles are merely the sign of your willingness to follow the Holy Spirit's plan of salvation, recognizing that you do not understand what **the Holy Spirit's plan of salvation** is. 4 **The Holy Spirit's** work is not your function, and unless you accept **that the Holy Spirit's work is not your function,** you cannot learn what your function is, **which is to co-create in eternity**.

Note # 40: Miracles are natural because they are the return to right-mindedness. This is the natural thought process of your Big "S" Self. This is how the One Self of the Mind of God operates. Your Big "S" Self knows the truth that only love is real and that love is sharing and the extension of the Oneness.

T-9.IV.7.The confusion of functions is so typical of the ego that you should be quite familiar with **the confusion of functions by the ego** by now. 2 The ego believes that all functions belong to **the ego,** even though **the ego** has no idea what **your function truly is.** 3 This **belief that all functions belong to the ego, even though the ego has no idea what your function truly is,** is more than mere confusion. 4 **This belief that all functions belong to the ego, even though the ego has no idea what your function truly is,** is a particularly dangerous combination of grandiosity and confusion that makes the ego likely to attack anyone and anything for no reason at all. 5 **Being confused, the ego is likely to attack anyone and anything for no reason and** this is exactly what the ego does. 6 **The ego** is unpredictable in **the ego's** responses, because **the ego** has no idea of what **the ego** perceives.

Note # 41: The ego believes that one of its functions is to save you and your brother from what the ego perceives as your combined errors, sins and mistakes. The ego claims that it has a plan to make you happy. The ego equates happiness with being right even if it is wrong. The ego believes its plan is always right and sets about the task of correcting, changing, fixing and if necessary, killing anyone or anything that would get in its way. Since the ego claims to be right, attacking anything that opposes its "rightness" is justified. The need to be right and attack are inseparable. Since the ego has no real plan that can make you happy; the ego is unpredictable as its plan shifts with each new failed attempt at happiness. Attack becomes the ego's best defense of its "rightness."

T-9.IV.8. If you have no idea what is happening, how appropriately can you expect to react? 2 You might ask yourself, regardless of how you may account for the reaction, whether **the ego's** unpredictability places the ego in a sound position as your guide. 3 Let me repeat that the ego's qualifications as a guide are singularly unfortunate, and that **the ego** is a remarkably poor choice as a teacher of salvation. 4 Anyone who elects a totally insane guide **like the ego** must be totally insane himself. 5 Nor is it true that you do not realize the guide is insane. 6 You realize **the ego is an insane guide,** because I realize **the ego is an insane guide**, and you have judged **the ego** by the same standard I have **judged the ego**.

Note # 42: Only the insane would trust their return to sanity by following the advice of the equally insane ego. Jesus recognized this fact that the egoic thought system is insane. We too have that same decision-maker inside our mind and thus, can also decide with Jesus to choose again.

T-9.IV.9. The ego literally lives on borrowed time, and **the ego's** days are numbered. 2 Do not fear the Last Judgment, but welcome **the Last Judgment** and do not wait, for the ego's time is "borrowed" from your eternity. 3 **The Last Judgment** is the Second Coming that was made for you as the First was created. 4 The Second Coming is merely the return of sense. 5 Can this, **the return of sense**, possibly be fearful?

Note # 43: The First Coming was the creation of the Sonship by God. The Second Coming is the return to Oneness of the Sonship with the Father. It is the remembrance of what you are and thus, the return to knowledge. Whole-mindedness is your reality. This return to the One Self is the truth that is, always was, and always will be, for it is eternal.

T-9.IV.10. What can be fearful but fantasy and who turns to fantasy unless he despairs of finding satisfaction in reality? 2 Yet it is certain that you will never find satisfaction in fantasy, so that your only hope is to change your mind about reality. 3 Only if the decision that reality is fearful is wrong can God be right. 4 And I assure you that God <is> right. 5 Be glad, then, that you have been wrong **to believe that reality was fearful,** but this was only because you did not know who you were. 6 Had you known **who you were**, you could no more have been wrong than God can **be wrong**.

Note # 44: God preserves the Truth for all of His Creations. We have been given free will and thus, we can deny the truth but our denial cannot change the Truth. Eventually, we will freely realize that there is just the One Self, and we are that One.

T-9.IV.11. The impossible can happen only in fantasy. 2 When you search for reality in fantasies you will not find **reality in fantasy**. 3 The symbols of fantasy are of the ego, and of these **symbols of egoic fantasy,** you will find many. 4 But do not look for meaning in **the ego's symbols of fantasy**. 5 **The symbols of egoic fantasy** have no more meaning than the fantasies into which **the symbols** are woven. 6 Fairy tales can be pleasant or fearful, but no one calls **the fairy tales** true. 7 Children may believe **the fairy tales**, and so, for a while, the tales are true for **the children who believe in the fairy tale**. 8 Yet when reality dawns, the fantasies are gone. 9 Reality has not gone in the meanwhile. 10 The Second Coming is the awareness of reality. **The Second Coming is** not **the** return **of reality**.

Note # 45: Fantasies do not change reality; they merely hide reality for a brief moment before the fantasy disappears and reality reappears from behind fantasy's veil. The Bible states that a deep sleep fell upon Adam, but it never states that Adam awoke. The second coming is when "Adam," the Son of God, awakens from this deep sleep. This is the Sonship's awakening from the world of perception into the reality of the Kingdom, which is Heaven.

T-9.IV.12. Behold, my child, reality is here. 2 **Reality** belongs to you and me and God, and **reality** is perfectly satisfying to all of Us. 3 Only this awareness **that reality is perfectly satisfying to all of Us** heals, because this awareness **that reality is perfectly satisfying to all of Us** is the awareness of truth.

Note # 46: Our reality is that everything is a Oneness with God, and that nothing else is needed or wanted. Since we are everything, what is there to want? We are the One Self that is the holographic Mind of God.

V. The Unhealed Healer

T-9.V.1. The ego's plan for forgiveness is far more widely used than God's **plan for forgiveness**. 2 **The ego's plan for forgiveness is far more widely used** because it is undertaken by unhealed healers, and is therefore of the ego. 3 Let us consider the unhealed healer more carefully now. 4 By definition, **the unhealed healer** is trying to give what **the unhealed healer** has not received. 5 If an unhealed healer is a theologian, for example, **unhealed theologian healer** may begin with the premise, "I am a miserable sinner, and so are you." 6 If **unhealed healer** is a psychotherapist, he is more likely to start with the equally incredible belief that attack is real for both himself and the patient, but that **attack** does not matter for either **himself or the patient**.

Note # 47: The unhealed healer does not know the truth that he, like you are unlimited Spirit. Coming from the false egoic belief that we are something that we are not, the unhealed healers mistakenly believe that the patient is a body or a sinner. They come from the egoic belief in lack, fear and limitation. Coming from a false premise, their healing technique should be questioned and challenged.

T-9.V.2.I have repeatedly said that beliefs of the ego cannot be shared, and **because beliefs of the ego cannot be shared this** is why **beliefs of the ego** are unreal. 2 How, then, can "uncovering" **the unreal beliefs of the ego** make them real? 3 Every healer who searches fantasies for truth must be unhealed, because **every healer who searches fantasies for truth** does not know where to look for truth, and therefore does not have the answer to the problem of healing.

Note # 48: You cannot come to a correct solution by following an illogical or insane belief system. Truth cannot be found in the false. It is useless to look for your keys in a different country when you lost them in your own home.

T-9.V.3. There is an advantage to bringing nightmares into awareness, but only to teach that **nightmares**

are not real, and that anything **nightmares** contain is meaningless. 2 The unhealed healer cannot **teach that nightmares are not real** because **the unhealed healer** does not believe **that the nightmares are meaningless**. 3 All unhealed healers follow the ego's plan for forgiveness in one form or another. 4 If **the unhealed healers** are theologians, **the unhealed theologians** are likely to condemn themselves, teach condemnation and advocate a fearful solution. 5 Projecting condemnation onto God, **the unhealed theologians** make **God** appear retaliative, and fear **God's** retribution. 6 What **the unhealed theologians** have done is merely to identify with the ego, and by perceiving what <*the ego*> does, condemn themselves because of **the ego's** confusion. 7 It is understandable that there have been revolts against this concept **of projecting condemnation onto God and thus making God appear retaliative and, therefore, fearing God's retribution**, but to revolt against **this concept** is still to believe in **this concept of projecting condemnation onto God and thus making God appear retaliative, and, therefore, fearing God's retribution**.

<u>Note # 49:</u> The unhealed theologian sees himself and all his brother's as sinners and subject to limitations. Therefore, he cannot heal since he does not know what he is. The unhealed theologian would judge and condemn his brother for any "wrongs" done against him because sinners should be condemned for their sins against God. Because the unhealed theologian believes in retribution, he projects this same trait onto God. Fear must follow. Fear reinforces separation, not joining. Healing becomes impossible and the ego's thought system is reinforced. We remain sinners rather than Sons of God, perfect, whole and complete. You cannot heal if you see yourself as a limited sinner.

T-9.V.4. Some newer forms of the ego's plan are as unhelpful as the older ones, because form does not matter and the content has not changed. 2 In one of the newer forms, for example, a psychotherapist may interpret the ego's symbols in a nightmare, and then use **the ego's symbols in the nightmare** to prove that the nightmare is real. 3 Having made **the nightmare** real, **the unhealed psychotherapist** then attempts to dispel **the nightmare's** effects by depreciating the importance of the dreamer. 4 This **dispelling of the nightmare's effects by depreciating the importance of the dreamer** would be a healing approach if the dreamer were also identified as unreal. 5 Yet if the dreamer is equated with the mind, the mind's corrective power through the Holy Spirit is denied. 6 This **depreciating the importance of the dreamer and the denial of the mind's corrective power** is a contradiction even in the ego's terms, and one which **the dreamer** usually notes even in **the dreamer's state of** confusion.

<u>Note # 50:</u> The unhealed psychotherapist first makes real the nightmare of the misperception that you are the body. He starts with the belief that you are a limited ego-body and fails to question the validity of this erroneous assumption. He then tells you not to worry about the nightmare since the dream, like you are insignificant and limited. The unhealed psychotherapist copes with the problem but does not correct the cause, which is your failure to remember who you are. The empowering value of your mind that lies with the decision maker is reduced by this limiting belief. The unhealed psychotherapist's focus is on the effect and the behavior rather than the cause. By the failure of the unhealed psychotherapist to address and correct the true cause, the problem is never resolved. The patient's ability to cope with the problem may improve but the source of the problem remains lurking in the background to reappear whenever an opportunity presents itself.

T-9.V.5. If the way to counteract fear is to reduce the importance of the mind, how can this build ego strength? 2 Such evident inconsistencies account for why no one has really explained what happens in psychotherapy. 3 Nothing really does **happen in psychotherapy**. 4 Nothing real has happened to the unhealed healer, and **the unhealed healer** must learn from his own teaching. 5 **The unhealed psychotherapist's** ego will always seek to get something from the situation. 6 The unhealed **psychotherapist** healer therefore does not know how to give, and consequently cannot share. 7 **The**

unhealed psychotherapist cannot correct because **the unhealed healer** is not working correctively. 8 **The unhealed psychotherapist** believes that it is up to him to teach the patient what is real, although **the unhealed healer** does not know **what is real** himself.

<u>Note # 51:</u> If you do not know what you are, how can you teach someone what they are? You do not even know the truth about yourself and, therefore, do not know reality. Because the unhealed healer is coming from the thought system of the ego, fear and limitation are the primary motivating factors. "Sharing" your lack of wholeness cannot make the "sick person" well. It only reconfirms that everybody is sick and that "healing" is learning how to manage your sickness. The unhealed healer believes in specialness rather than oneness. The unhealed healer believes that he has some power or magic that the patient needs in order to be healed. He views himself as the healer and the other person as someone incapable of healing themselves. He does not believe that giving and receiving are the same. Nor does he understand that it is only the patient's own mind that can heal the patient. A healer who himself is healed, knows that all healing takes place in the patient's mind through the recovery of the patient's own sense of Oneness. We need to correct the cause of the problem, not cover up the effect. The cause is at the level of mind. Any attempt to heal the body is only an attempt at covering up the symptoms.

T-9.V.6. What, then, should happen? 2 When God said, "Let there be light," there <*was*> light. 3 Can you find light by analyzing darkness, as the psychotherapist does, or like the theologian, by acknowledging darkness in yourself and looking for a distant light to remove the darkness in yourself, while emphasizing the distance **you are from the light**? 4 Healing is not mysterious. 5 Nothing will change unless **the nothingness of darkness** is understood, since light <*is*> understanding. 6 A "miserable sinner" cannot be healed without magic, nor can an "unimportant mind" esteem itself without magic.

<u>Note # 52:</u> Magic is the belief that something outside you is needed to make or fix the perceived problem. Sickness arises anytime that you believe that you are not perfect, whole and complete. It is based on the belief in lack and separation. Seeing the "sick" person as incomplete, the unhealed healer claims that only something outside the "sick" person can return the sick person to wholeness again. This confirms that you are incomplete and incapable of finding wholeness within yourself.

T-9.V.7. Both forms of the ego's approach **to healing**, then, must arrive at an impasse; the characteristic "impossible situation" to which the ego always leads. 2 **The ego's approach to healing** may help someone to point out where **"that someone"** is heading, but the point is lost unless **"that someone"** is also helped to change his direction. 3 The unhealed healer cannot **help "his patient" to change "the patient's direction,** since **the unhealed healer** cannot change **the unhealed healer's own direction** for himself. 4 The only meaningful contribution the healer can make is to present an example of one whose direction has been changed <*for*> **the healer, himself,** and **that the healer** no longer believes in nightmares of any kind. 5 The light in **the healer's** mind will therefore answer the questioner. **The questioner** must decide with God that there is light <*because*> **the questioner** sees **light**. 6 And by **the healer's** acknowledgment **of the light,** the healer knows **the light** is there. 7 **By this acknowledgment of the light by the healer, the healer knows the light, and this** is how perception ultimately is translated into knowledge. 8 The miracle worker begins by perceiving light, and translates **the miracle worker's** perception into sureness by continually extending **the light** and accepting **the light's** acknowledgment. 9 **The light's** effects assure **the miracle worker that the light** is there.

<u>Note # 53:</u> Unlike the ego's method of healing, the Holy Spirit's method is to demonstrate and give witness to the truth about what you and the other person really are. The Holy Spirit does this by having the healer "be" the role model for the truth that we are only our Big "S" Self. The other person must

ultimately "see" the truth that they are spirit and a part of the One Self. Since everyone has "free will," you cannot heal someone else. Forcing someone to be "healed" is confirming the belief that the "sick person's mind does not have the creative power to correct its own misperceptions. Rather than heal, this confirms to both the unhealed healer and the "sick person" that both are separate and not whole.
Light is understanding the truth and thus, knowing the truth.

T-9.V.8.A therapist does not heal; < *a therapist lets healing be.*> 2 **A therapist** can point to darkness but **a therapist** cannot bring light of himself, for light is not of **the therapist**. 3 Yet, **light** being <*for*> **a therapist**, **this same light** must also be for **a therapist's** patient. 4 The Holy Spirit is the only Therapist. 5 **The Holy Spirit** makes healing clear in any situation in which **the Holy Spirit** is the Guide. 6 You can only let **the Holy Spirit** fulfill **the Holy Spirit's** function **of healing**. 7 **The Holy Spirit** needs no help **to fulfill the Holy Spirit's, function, which is healing the split-minded of all misperception**. 8 **The Holy Spirit** will tell you exactly what to do to help anyone **the Holy Spirit** sends to you for help, and will speak to **that same anyone that the Holy Spirit sent to you for help** through you if you do not interfere. 9 Remember that you choose the guide for helping, and the wrong choice, **the ego's method for healing,** will not help. 10 But remember also that the right **choice for the Holy Spirit's method for healing** will **help**. 11 Trust **the Holy Spirit**, for help is **the Holy Spirit's** function, and **the Holy Spirit** is of God. 12 As you awaken other minds to the Holy Spirit through **the Holy Spirit**, and not **through your egoic self**, you will understand that you are not obeying the laws of this world **of perception, time and space**. 13 But the laws **of God** you are obeying work. 14 "The good is what works" is a sound though insufficient statement. 15 Only the good <*can*> work. 16 Nothing else works at all.

Note # 54: Since you can only be "sick" in your dream world of provisional reality, the healer acknowledges the truth about himself and his brother and thus, allows the healing to <be>. Remove the belief in the illusion and healing becomes the only reality. The healer simple acknowledges that the "sick person" could not be sick in the Mind of God, which is where reality and truth reside. The healer is only a witness to the truth about what both he and his brother must be since there is only One Mind.
Healing is accepting the Laws of God and rejecting to false laws that seem to govern the egoic world of our own misperception. Healing does not come from you. Healing comes from reawakening to the truth of what you really are. This truth has never been lost but it has been misplaced. In the Mind of God, you can only be perfect, whole and complete. Peace and joy are our birthright. We can dream that we have lost our birthright, but the Holy Spirit will guard and protect our inheritance for us. The function of the Holy Spirit is to gently reawaken us from our dream of not remembering what we are.
Only the good can work since the Laws of God are the Laws that govern the Kingdom, which is eternal reality. The good is what is real and true always. This is the Will of God, which has been extended to become our will since we share and are the Oneness of God.

T-9.V.9.This course offers a very direct and a very simple learning situation, and provides the Guide, **the Holy Spirit,** Who tells you what to do. 2 If you do **what the Holy Spirit guides you to do**, you will see that **what the Holy Spirit guides you to do** works. 3 **The** results **of what the Holy Spirit guides you to do** are more convincing than **the Holy Spirit's** words. 4 **The results of what the Holy Spirit guides you to do** will convince you that the words **of the Holy Spirit** are true. 5 By following the right Guide, **which is the Holy Spirit,** you will learn the simplest of all lessons:

6 By their fruits ye shall know them, and they shall know themselves.

Note # 55: We are asked by the Holy Spirit to accept the Laws of God and reject the false laws that the ego has made up. Healing does not come from you but from the Holy Spirit. Healing comes from reawakening to the truth that you are unlimited Spirit. Your spiritual nature can never be lost. In the Mind of God, you can only be perfect, whole and complete. Peace and joy are your birthright. You can dream that you have lost your birthright, but the Holy Spirit will guard and protect your birthright for you. The function of the Holy Spirit is to gently reawaken you from your dream that you are separate from your Creator and have lost knowledge.

We are asked by the Holy Spirit to look at the results of the two thought systems and then make the choice. If we are not satisfied with the results of the guide that we are following, we are asked to choose again. If we want joy and peace, we need to choose the Holy Spirit for our guide. The Holy Spirit will help us relearn what we are.

Light is understanding. Once we understand that our dream world of provisional reality is nothing but an illusion, the Holy Spirit will "heal" us by changing, or reinterpreting, our false perceptions into correct perceptions. When we understanding that our dream is a veil hiding the truth, we can choose to remove this veil and reclaim the truth about us. This reclamation of our spiritual truth as the Big "S" Self can be easily done because an illusion is "nothing." Since the Holy Spirit knows that "nothing" really is "nothing", this illusion of nothingness cannot change the truth of the Kingdom. We remain our Big "S" Self that is part of the holographic Oneness of the Mind of God. This One Self is our reality.

VI. The Acceptance of Your Brother

T-9.VI.1.How can you become increasingly aware of the Holy Spirit in you except by **the Holy Spirit's** effects? 2 You cannot see **the Holy Spirit** with your eyes nor hear **the Holy Spirit** with your ears. 3 How, then, can you perceive **the Holy Spirit** at all? 4 If you inspire joy and others react to you with joy, even though you are not experiencing joy yourself there must be something in you that is capable of producing **joy**. 5 If **what is capable of producing joy** is in you and can produce joy, and if you see that **what is capable of producing joy** does produce joy in others, you must be dissociating **from what is capable of producing joy** in yourself.

Note # 56: We deny the recognition of the Holy Spirit within us when we are not in a joyous state. Since God's Will is that His Son be happy, our natural state must be peace, joy and happiness. If we are not at peace, we have failed to align our thinking with our Big "S" Self and the Holy Spirit's thought system.

T-9.VI.2.It seems to you that the Holy Spirit does not produce joy consistently in you only because you do not consistently arouse joy in others. 2 **These other people's** reactions to you are your evaluations of **the Holy Spirit** consistency. 3 When you are inconsistent you will not always give rise to joy, and so you will not always recognize **the Holy Spirit's** consistency. 4 What you offer to your brother you offer to **the Holy Spirit**, because **the Holy Spirit** cannot go beyond your offering in **the Holy Spirit's** giving. 5 This is not because **the Holy Spirit** limits **the Holy Spirit's** giving, but simply because you have limited your receiving. 6 The decision to receive is the decision to accept.

Note # 57: Unless you accept the gifts of the Holy Spirit, you cannot receive them. Since you have "free will," the Holy Spirit will not force you to take something you are not willing to accept. To do so would only serve to increase your fear. You must be willing to freely choose to accept the Joy of the Holy Spirit. If we choose to selectively give some of our egoic misperception over to the Holy Spirit, while retaining some for our ego's misperceptions, we are inconsistent in our purpose. Differing purposes will result in our brother receiving mixed signals. We will be alternating between forgiveness and attack. What we give, we will receive. If we give all our perception over to the Holy Spirit, we will receive the consistent Joy of the Holy Spirit.

T-9.VI.3. If your brothers are part of you, will you accept **your brothers**? 2 Only **your brothers** can teach you what you are, for your learning is the result of what you taught **your brothers**. 3 What you call upon in **your brothers** you call upon in yourself. 4 And as you call upon **something** in **your brothers that something** becomes real to you. 5 God has but one Son, knowing **God's Son** all as One. 6 Only God Himself is more than **God's one Son** but **God's one Son is** not less than **God** is. 7 Would you know what this means? 8 If what you do to my brother you do to me, and if you do everything for yourself because we are part of you, everything we do belongs to you as well. 9 Everyone God created is part of you and shares **God's** glory with you. 10 **God's** glory belongs to **God**, but **God's glory** is equally **to your glory**. 11 You cannot, then, be less glorious than **God** is.

<u>Note # 58:</u> God is more than you only because God is the First Cause. God created you. Since creation is the sharing and extension of the Mind of God, God created a "carbon copy" of Himself when He extended Himself to His Son. God is Cause and we are His Effect. As such, we complete each other and are inseparable. God gave everything to His Son since God is everything. Creation is the extension of the Oneness. Since we are of one mind, we are joined in the holographic Mind of God. Each indivisible part contains the whole and the whole contains each part. What we perceive in our brother, we perceive in ourselves through this holographic web of consciousness.

T-9.VI.4. God is more than you only because He created you, but not even this would **God** keep from you. 2 Therefore you can create as **God** did, and your dissociation will not alter **your ability to create as God did**. 3 Neither God's light nor **your light** is dimmed because you do not see **your light**. 4 Because the Sonship must create as one, you remember creation whenever you recognize part of creation. 5 Each part **of your creation** you remember adds to your wholeness because each part **of your creation** <*is*> whole. 6 Wholeness is indivisible, but you cannot learn of your wholeness until you see **your wholeness** everywhere. 7 You can know yourself only as God knows His Son, for knowledge is shared with God. 8 When you awake in **God** you will know your magnitude by accepting **God's** limitlessness as **your limitlessness**. 9 But meanwhile you will judge **your limitlessness** as you judge your brother's **limitlessness**, and will accept **your limitlessness** as you accept his **limitlessness**.

<u>Note # 59:</u> In the Laws of God, receiving and giving are tied together. You cannot receive unless you give. You cannot receive or give if you are unwilling to accept. Judge your brother as less than whole and you condemn yourself to that same littleness.

God is creation and when God creates He Gives His Son the same power to create. Our creations, however, must be "carbon copies" of ourselves as God created us since creation by God's Law is extension and complete sharing. God's creation is the Sonship. The Sonship is perfect, whole and complete and, therefore, our creations must be perfect. Our true creations are different than the things we "make" in our dream world of limitation. Making comes when we attempt to use our creative powers out of fear and littleness. When we make, we attempt to exclude, rather than include. Making is not sharing our Big "S" Self but rather trying to protect and project from our egoic little "s" self.

T-9.VI.5. You are not yet awake, but you can learn how to awaken. 2 Very simply, the Holy Spirit teaches you to awaken others. 3 As you see **others** waken you will learn what waking means, and because you have chosen to wake **others their** gratitude and their appreciation of what you have given them will teach you the value **of being awake**. 4 **These awakened others** will become the witnesses to your reality, as you were created witness to God's **reality**. 5 Yet when the Sonship comes together and accepts **the Sonship's** Oneness **the Sonship** will be known by **the Sonship's** creations, who witness to **the Sonship's** reality as the Son **witnesses to the reality of** the Father.

Note # 60: Our true reality is unlimited Spirit. Unless we create by giving all to our creations, we have not created under the Laws of God. The Sonship's Reality, as God created it, is perfect, whole and complete. God knows Himself through the Sonship. We are God's Effect. Similarly, we know ourselves through our creations. Our creations are our Effects. Our creations are our reality. When we "make" rather than create, we are coming from fear due to our belief in separateness and limitation. As a result, we make a false image in our dream world of provisional reality. This image is based on fear and is not part of the Mind of God. This illusionary world seems real to us. However, it has no reality in the Mind of God and cannot be shared since it is not a carbon copy of God's Mind. Our false image of ourselves lacks the holographic nature of true creation. It claims to be less than "the everything" that we are.

T-9.VI.6. Miracles have no place in eternity, because **miracles** are reparative. 2 Yet while you still need healing, your miracles are the only witnesses to your reality that you can recognize. 3 You cannot perform a miracle for yourself, because miracles are a way of giving acceptance and receiving **acceptance.** 4 In time the giving comes first, though **giving and receiving** are simultaneous in eternity, where **giving and receiving** cannot be separated. 5 When you have learned **giving and receiving** are the same, the need for time is over.

Note # 61: Miracles take place in the world of perception. This world of time and space is what the split-mind made to imagine that it could hide from God. It is the place where we play at not being our true Big "S" Selves. It is the playfield for the game of "What Am I?" It is also the "place" that the Holy Spirit uses to teach us how to correct our misperception so that we can rediscover what we are. After this reawakening, we will discover that we had never left the Oneness. Being a Oneness of Everything, where could we have gone? Only in time can we learn what it would be like to pretend that we can change from being unlike God and becoming One with God. This is how we relearn about God and remember Our own Spiritual Magnificence.

T-9.VI.7. Eternity is one time, **eternity's** only dimension being "always." 2 That **eternity's only dimension is "always"** cannot mean anything to you until you remember God's open Arms, and finally know **God's** open Mind. 3 Like **God,** <*you*> are "always." **You are** in **God's** Mind and with a mind like **God's Mind.** 4 In your open mind are your creations, in perfect communication born of perfect understanding. 5 Could you but accept one of **your creations,** you would not want anything the **dream world of your provisional reality** has to offer. 6 Everything else **in your dream world of provisional reality** would be totally meaningless. 7 God's meaning is incomplete without you, **His Creation,** and you are incomplete without your creations. 8 Accept your brother in this world and accept nothing else, for in **your brother** you will find your creations because **your brother** created **your creations** with you. 9 You will never know that you are co-creator with God until you learn that your brother is co-creator with you.

Note # 62: Since there is one mind, the Mind of God, all are a part of this One Mind. The Sonship and the Sonship's creations, like God the Father, are perfect, whole and complete; a Oneness of Everything. God is First Cause. We are the Effect of God. God knows Himself through His Effect. Although we are God's Effect, to know that we are the perfect extension of God, we too must have our effect. We are cause to our creations and our creations are our effect. In this way we know ourselves and know our Father. Cause and Effect are intertwined as One. Each completes the other and all become inseparable as part of the holographic Mind of God. Nothing is outside or apart from this Oneness of "All That Is." Our ego and its world of perception is the Sonship's joint creation made out of fear. It was our power of creativity that birthed this world of fear and it is our return to love that will correct our misperceptions of what we are and what we have made. When we claim ownership for our thoughts and no longer perceive our thoughts with fear and judgment, we will learn allowance, which is the bedrock to unconditional or real love. Love does not judge. Instead, love accepts and allows the object of its love the perfect freedom to be whatever it desires to be. Love only desires that the object of its love be happy and free. We are happy when we know that no action or thought that we may take could ever have any adverse effect on this flow of God's love toward us. With real love, the recipient of the love is unable to force the source of that love to withdraw its love. The recipient can deny that love is flowing its way, but it is powerless to stop or change the source of the flow of love. While in time, we are learning to remove the blocks that we have place between ourselves and love. When we allow all and judge not, we have responded lovingly. When we respond only with love, we will remember that we could never lose our divine inheritance. We will understand that an effect cannot change its cause. We will accept the Atonement for ourselves and acknowledge the Sonship's sinless and guiltless nature. By reclaiming our innocence, knowledge can be restored.

VII. The Two Evaluations

T-9.VII.1.God's Will is your salvation. 2 Would **God** not have given you the means to find **your salvation**? 3 If **God** wills you to have **your salvation**, **God** must have made **your salvation** possible and easy to obtain **your salvation**. 4 Your brothers are everywhere. 5 You do not have to seek far for salvation. 6 Every minute and every second gives you a chance to save yourself. 7 Do not lose these chances, not because **these chances** will not return, but because delay of joy is needless. 8 God wills you perfect happiness now. 9 Is it possible that **perfect happiness now** is not also your will? 10 And is it possible that **perfect happiness now** is not also the will of your brothers?

Note # 63: Salvation is only one choice away. When we decide to be only vigilant for God, we will awaken. Doing this means that we have made the decision to only follow the thought system of the Holy Spirit and "be" only love. We have decided to be happy rather than "right." This decision is the free choice to share the same purpose as God's Will. We have thus accepted that God's Will and our will are One.

T-9.VII.2.Consider, then, that in this joint will **for perfect happiness now,** you are all united, and **only in this joint will for perfect happiness now, are you all united.** 2 There may be disagreement on anything else, but not on this **joint will for perfect happiness now**. 3 This **joint will for perfect happiness now**, then, is where peace abides. 4 And you abide in peace when you so decide. 5 Yet you cannot abide in peace unless you accept the Atonement, because the Atonement <*is*> the way to peace. 6 The reason **that the Atonement <*is*> the way to peace** is very simple, and so obvious that **the reason** is often overlooked. 7 The ego is afraid of the obvious, since obviousness is the essential characteristic of reality. 8 Yet <*you*> cannot overlook **the obvious** unless you are not looking **for the obvious**.

Note # 64: Our goal is perfect happiness now because perfect happiness is what God has willed for us. Our brother's goal is perfect happiness now. Everything's goal is perfect happiness now. Perfect happiness now is the joint will of everything. It is in this single purpose that we are joined. Form cannot be shared. It requires one person who originally had the totality of the object to now share that object with another. Sharing of a form requires at least one party to sacrifice. Yet, my goal of being perfectly happy now is an idea that can be shared. If I shared this goal with you and you accept it as your own goal, the idea is strengthened. No one loses when you share an idea.

T-9.VII.3.It is perfectly obvious that if the Holy Spirit looks with love on all **that the Holy Spirit** perceives, **the Holy Spirit** looks with love on you. 2 **The Holy Spirit's** evaluation of you is based on **the Holy Spirit's knowledge** of what you are, and so **the Holy Spirit** evaluates you truly. 3 And this evaluation must be in your mind, because **the Holy Spirit** is **in your mind**. 4 The ego is also in your mind, because you have accepted **the ego** there **and put the ego into your mind**. 5 **The ego's** evaluation of you, however, is the exact opposite of the Holy Spirit's, because the ego does not love you. 6 **The ego** is unaware of what you are, and wholly mistrustful of everything **the ego** perceives because **the ego's** perceptions are so shifting. 7 The ego is therefore capable of suspiciousness at best and viciousness at worst. 8 **Suspiciousness and viciousness** is **the ego's** range **of capabilities.** 9 **The ego** cannot exceed **the range of suspiciousness and viciousness** because of **the ego's** uncertainty. 10 And **the ego** can never go beyond **the range of suspiciousness and viciousness** because **the ego** can never <be> certain.

Note # 65: Because the ego's world is based on perceptions, the ego's "world" of provisional reality is always uncertain. Perception, which is not knowledge, changes with time. Time does not exist in eternity since eternity is "always" and thus, changeless. Change and time are an integral part of your ego's world of provisional reality. Time is not in the Mind of God since time is the measures of change and God is changeless.

The ego is in your split-mind only because you have placed the ego there. The ego does not exist without your permission. The ego serves at your mind's command yet the ego has attempted to usurp the power of your mind which resides as your Big "S" Self. In this way, the ego is the "authority problem." The "authority problem" is our claim that we can usurp God's Will. It states that we, God's Effect, can somehow change its Cause, which is God. The ego also claims that the ego, which is our mind's effect, can change its cause, which is our mind. The ego claims that it has become causative over our mind, when in actuality, all the ego's power comes from our mind. Our world of perception and provisional reality was "made" by our mind so that we could act in and play the game of the "authority problem." Another name for this game is "What Am I?" The "authority problem game" must end when all the players discover that an effect cannot change its cause and that cause and effect are intertwined and inseparable. Each is needed to complete the other.

T-9.VII.4.You, then, have two conflicting evaluations of yourself in your mind, and **the ego's and the Holy Spirit's evaluations** cannot both be true. 2 You do not yet realize how completely different these evaluations **of the ego's and the Holy Spirit's** are, because you do not understand how lofty the Holy Spirit's perception of you really is. 3 **The Holy Spirit** is not deceived by anything you do, because **the Holy Spirit** never forgets what you are **as the Son of God**. 4 The ego is deceived by everything you do, especially when you respond to the Holy Spirit, because at such times **the ego's** confusion increases. 5 The ego is, therefore, particularly likely to attack you when you react lovingly, because **the ego** has evaluated you as unloving and you are going against **the ego's** judgment. 6 The ego will attack your motives as soon as **your motives** become clearly out of accord with **the ego's** perception of you. 7 This is when **the ego** will shift abruptly from suspiciousness to viciousness, since **the ego's** uncertainty is increased. 8 Yet it is surely pointless to attack **the ego** in return. 9 What can **the attacking of the ego by you, our Big "S" Self,** mean except that you are agreeing with the ego's evaluation of what you are, **which is the ego's belief that you are a vulnerable, unloving, limited being**?

Note # 66: If you attack the ego, you are demonstrating that you are a body and, therefore, something separate that can attack. Only something that is not a Oneness or not everything can attack. Spirit does not attack.

Again note the parallels between the "authority problem" between God and His Son and our mind and our own "child," which is our ego. How we respond to God and how the ego responds to our mind, our Big "S" Self, are the same. Both make up a fearful and unloving creator. Also, how God responds to His Son's belief in the separation and how Jesus is telling us our Big "S" Self responds to the ego's insane idea of the authority problem is the same. The Big "S" Self or Holy Spirit does not acknowledge or attack its creation but merely realizes that anything that the ego does has no ability to change its source or to change the truth. The ego is only playing a game of separation, and the child's game is powerless to change the will of the Big "S" Self, which is the ego's cause. The ego is the thoughts we hold about ourselves. When we remember that our Big "S" Self knows that its true will is God's Will and that God wills us to be happy, we will not judge our thoughts. Instead, we will just allow, knowing that our thoughts have no consequences and are powerless to change our reality. The law of extension states that an effect must be like its cause. Thus, being love, we can only extend love's freedom, joy and peace. Being happy now is the common purpose that joins and binds "All That Is" into the One Self. The Holy Spirit and Big "S" Self know that its creations must be like Its Father's creation. Both must be perfect, whole and complete since that is the nature of their Source, which is the holographic Mind of God. The Holy Spirit will teach the ego, which is our creation, the truth about itself. Our ego will come to know that it, like its Father, our Big "S" Self, is only love. This realization completes the Sonship and extends the Mind of God. The Sonship, our Big "S" Self, and its child, our ego, join as one mind and the ego knows that its will and our Big "S" Self's will is One. Whole-mindedness has returned to the Sonship's split mind. The Sonship, like God, has created the perfect child, who is only the reflection of Love. This is the act of creation. This is the joy of being happy now. This is the One shared Will of God.

It is not the idea of the separation that was the problem. The problem was that we took seriously the idea that our thoughts could somehow change what we eternally are. We thought an effect could change its source and thus, change God, Itself. When we forgot to laugh, we took our playful thought of what it would be like to be other than God, and transformed this thought into a real monster in our imagination. Now rather than allow and experience, we judged, fragmented and were afraid. Our play world became an image of sin, guilt and fear. Our ego, perception, time and space all took on a perceived reality of their own.

T-9.VII.5. If you choose to see yourself as unloving, you will not be happy. 2 You are condemning yourself and must, therefore, regard yourself as inadequate. 3 Would you look to the ego to help you escape from a sense of inadequacy **that the ego** has produced, and **that the ego** must maintain for **the ego's** existence? 4 Can you escape from **the ego's** evaluation of you by using **the ego's** methods for keeping this picture **of regarding yourself as inadequate** intact?

<u>Note # 67:</u> We cannot buy into the idea that the ego can change what we are. Our deluded mind is the cause of the ego. Our Big "S" Self knows our true creation can only be the extension of love. We cannot let our true Self believe that an effect can change its cause. To do so would be to make the separation appear real.

T-9.VII.6. You cannot evaluate an insane belief system from within **an insane belief system**. 2 **An insane belief system's** range precludes **the evaluating an insane belief system from within the insane system. The ego's range of capabilities is limited and goes from suspiciousness to viciousness.** 3 You can only go beyond **the insane belief system by looking** back from a point where sanity exists and <*see the contrast*>**between sanity and insanity.** 4 Only by this contrast **between sanity and insanity** can insanity be judged as insane. 5 With the grandeur of God in you, you have chosen to be little and to lament your littleness. 6 Within the **ego's thought** system that dictated this choice **to choose to be little**

instead of choosing the grandeur of God within you, is the lament inevitable. 7 Your littleness is taken for granted there within the ego's thought system, and you do not ask, "Who granted my littleness?" 8 The question of "Who granted my littleness?" is meaningless within the ego's thought system, because the question would open the whole thought system to question.

Note # 68: To correct or even realize that something is illogical, you need to go outside that something to see the error. You cannot discover that the world is round by standing still and refusing to look beyond the apparent flatness of the surface. You need to rise above the planet to see its true shape.

T-9.VII.7.I have said that the ego does not know what a real question is. 2 Lack of knowledge of any kind is always associated with unwillingness to know, and this unwillingness to know, produces a total lack of knowledge simply because knowledge is total. 3 Not to question your littleness therefore is to deny all knowledge, and keep the ego's whole thought system intact. 4 You cannot retain part of a thought system, because a thought system can be questioned only at a thought system's foundation. 5 And this thought system's foundation must be questioned from beyond the thought system, because within the thought system, the thought system's foundation does stand. 6 The Holy Spirit judges against the reality of the ego's thought system merely because the Holy Spirit knows the ego's thought system's foundation is not true. 7 Therefore, nothing that arises from the ego's thought system means anything. 8 The Holy Spirit judges every belief you hold in terms of where the belief comes from. 9 If the belief comes from God, the Holy Spirit knows the belief to be true. 10 If the belief does not come from God, the Holy Spirit knows that the belief is meaningless.

Note # 69: You cannot build an accurate thought system if its foundation rests on lies. The false cannot become the truth.

T-9.VII.8.Whenever you question your value, say:

2 *God Himself is incomplete without me.*

3 Remember this, that "*God Himself is incomplete without you*" when the ego speaks, and you will not hear the ego speak. 4 The truth about you is so lofty that nothing unworthy of God is worthy of you. 5 Choose, then, what you want in these terms, that the grandeur of God is within you and the truth about you is so lofty that nothing unworthy of God is worthy of you, and accept nothing that you would not offer to God as wholly fitting for God. 6 You do not want anything else but the grandeur of God that is within you. 7 Return your part to God, and God will give you all of Himself in exchange for the return of what belongs to God and renders God complete.

Note # 70: God is Cause and we are God's Effect. Together we are inseparable. If God is only love, we must also be only love. If God is a creator, so must His Child be a creator. We complete God by extending love to our creations. Our creations complete us by extending only love. When the ego learns that it is only love, the Sonship is complete and we are returned to whole-mindedness. We have experienced the joy of co-creating with God. Our will, our creations' will and God's Will are One. They are joined in one goal and one common purpose, which is "to be happy now."

VIII. Grandeur versus Grandiosity

T-9.VIII.1.Grandeur is of God, and only of **God**. 2 **Because grandeur is of God, and only of God**, therefore **grandeur** is in you. 3 Whenever you become aware of **the grandeur that is in you,** however dimly, you abandon the ego automatically, because in the presence of the grandeur of God the meaninglessness of the ego becomes perfectly apparent. 4 When **the meaninglessness of the ego becomes perfectly apparent** occurs, **you become aware that God's grandeur is in you**, even though **the ego** does not understand **your grandeur**, the ego believes that **the ego's** "enemy" has struck, and **the ego** attempts to offer gifts to induce you to return to **the ego's** "protection." 5 Self-inflation is the only offering **the ego** can make. 6 The grandiosity of the ego, **which is self-inflation,** is **the ego's** alternative to the grandeur of God. 7 Which will you choose? **Your choice is between the ego's grandiosity of self-inflation or the grandeur of God?**

Note # 71: The ego's grandiosity of self-inflation claims that you are separate, different and more importantly special. Unfortunately, what being special means is to argue for egoic littleness when you are already the grandeur of God. Instead, of claiming the truth that we are one with "All That Is," we argue for egoic specialness, which is the equivalent to littleness.

T-9.VIII.2.Grandiosity is always a cover for despair. 2 **Grandiosity** is without hope because **grandiosity** is not real. 3 **The ego's grandiosity** is an attempt to counteract your littleness, based on the belief that the littleness is real. 4 Without this belief **that the littleness is real,** grandiosity is meaningless, and you could not possibly want **the ego's grandiosity**. 5 The essence of grandiosity is competitiveness, because **the ego's grandiosity** always involves attack. 6 **Grandiosity** is a delusional attempt to outdo, but not to undo. 7 We said before that the ego vacillates between suspiciousness and viciousness. 8 **The ego** remains suspicious as long as you despair of yourself. 9 **The ego** shifts to viciousness when you decide not to tolerate self-abasement and seek relief. 10 Then **the ego** offers you the illusion of attack as a "solution" **when you decide not to tolerate self-abasement and seek relief.**

Note # 72: Due to the ego's belief in separateness, competition is born. You are no longer a Oneness of Everything. Now you have needs. The ego claims that you are a limited ego-body in competition with other ego-bodies. Competition fosters the attempt to outdo the "other side." Yet, the ego refuses to look at the source of the competition problem, which is your belief in separation and lack. Rather than undo the error at its source, you accept the need for competition. Competition confirms your belief in the separation and that you are a body. To the ego, the body's purpose and function is to compete, attack and defend.

T-9.VIII.3.The ego does not understand the difference between grandeur and grandiosity, because **the ego** sees no difference between miracle impulses and ego-alien beliefs of **the ego's own belief system.** 2 I told you that the ego is aware of threat to **the ego's** existence, but **the ego** makes no distinctions between these two very different kinds of threat, **(between miracle impulses of grandeur and ego-alien beliefs of grandiosity).** 3 **The ego's** profound sense of vulnerability renders **the ego** incapable of judgment except in terms of attack. 4 When the ego experiences threat, **the ego's** only decision is whether to attack now or to withdraw to attack later. 5 If you accept **the ego's** offer of grandiosity, **which is self-inflation to cover the ego's belief in "littleness,"** the ego will attack immediately. 6 If you do not **accept the ego's offer of grandiosity, the ego** will wait **to attack.**

Note # 73: Miracle impulses of grandeur would foster healing, joining and sharing of wholeness. Ego-alien beliefs of grandiosity foster the idea of separateness, competition and attack. The ego's grandiosity is surrounded by the ego's need to be right. The ego will defend its right to be right and attack whenever it feels threatened. When your ego feels it has been wronged, it will eventually retaliate and attack. The timing of this attack may not be immediate but it will come.

T-9.VIII.4. The ego is immobilized in the presence of God's grandeur, because **God's** grandeur establishes your freedom. 2 Even the faintest hint of your reality literally drives the ego from your mind, because you will give up all investment in **the ego**. 3 Grandeur is totally without illusions, and because **grandeur** is real **grandeur** is compellingly convincing. 4 Yet the conviction of reality will not remain with you unless you do not allow the ego to attack **your conviction of reality and its grandeur**. 5 The ego will make every effort to recover and mobilize **the ego's** energies against your release **from the ego's illusions to the reality of your grandeur**. 6 **The ego** will tell you that you are insane, and argue that grandeur cannot be a real part of you because of the littleness in which **the ego** believes **you are**. 7 Yet your grandeur is not delusional because you did not make **your grandeur. God did.** 8 You made **egoic** grandiosity and are afraid of **grandiosity** because **grandiosity** is a form of attack, but your grandeur is of God, Who created **your grandeur** out of **God's** Love.

Note # 74: We made the belief in our littleness when our mind created our ego. Grandiosity is of our making since it is made based on our false notion that we are a limited and separate body. God created our grandeur, since grandeur is a part of the creative process, which is extension of God. God's grandeur is our shared reality and truth.

T-9.VIII.5. From your grandeur you can only bless, because your grandeur is your abundance. 2 By blessing you hold **your grandeur** in your mind, protecting **your grandeur** from illusions and keeping yourself in the Mind of God. 3 Remember always that you cannot be anywhere except in the Mind of God. 4 When you forget **you are in the Mind of God,** you <*will*> despair and you <*will*> attack.

Note # 75: Despair is covered up by the ego's grandiosity. The ego's grandiosity is made from lack and represents our little "s" self. God's grandeur is the extension of abundance and is represented by our Big "S" Self.

T-9.VIII.6. The ego depends solely on your willingness to tolerate **the ego.** 2 If you are willing to look upon your grandeur you cannot despair, and therefore you cannot want the ego. 3 Your grandeur is God's answer to the ego, because **your grandeur** is true. 4 Littleness and grandeur cannot coexist, nor is it possible for **littleness and grandeur** to alternate. 5 Littleness and grandiosity can and must alternate, since both are untrue and are therefore **both littleness and grandiosity are** on the same level, **which is the ego's world of provisional reality**. 6 Being the level of shift, **littleness and grandiosity** is experienced as shifting and extremes. **Shifting and extremes** are **littleness and grandiosity's** essential characteristic.

Note # 76: The world of perception is a world of shifts and changes. The world of perception is unstable since we are constantly shifting our beliefs about ourselves and it is our belief's that "make' the world we perceive. One moment we argue for our importance and insist on why we are right. The next moment we may think we are unworthy and guilty of sin. In either case, we are confirming our belief in separation, specialness and littleness.

T-9.VIII.7. Truth and littleness are denials of each other because grandeur is truth. 2 Truth does not vacillate; **truth** is always true. 3 When grandeur slips away from you, you have replaced **grandeur** with something you have made. 4 Perhaps **the replacement for grandeur** is the belief in littleness; perhaps the replacement for grandeur is the belief in grandiosity. 5 Yet **the replacement for grandeur** must be insane because **the replacement for grandeur** is not true. 6 Your grandeur will never deceive you, but your illusions always will **deceive you**. 7 Illusions are deceptions. 8 You cannot triumph, but you <*are*> exalted. 9 And in your exalted state you seek others like you and rejoice with **the others like you**.

Note # 77: We exalt when we believe we are egoically right. We exalt even more when we can get others of "littleness" to agree with our "correct" misperceptions and beliefs. An insane person agreeing with other insane people does not make their fantasies true.

T-9.VIII.8. It is easy to distinguish grandeur from grandiosity, because **with grandeur** love is returned and pride is not. 2 Pride will not produce miracles, and will therefore deprive you of the true witnesses to your reality. 3 Truth is not obscure nor **is truth** hidden, but **truth's** obviousness to you lies in the joy you bring to **truth's** witnesses, who show **truth** to you. 4 **The witnesses for truth** attest to your grandeur, but **the witnesses for truth** cannot attest to pride because pride is not shared. 5 God wants you to behold what **God** created because **what God created** is **God's** joy.

Note # 78: Pride is an exaggerated belief in your worth or importance. It is exaggerated because you do not possess the characteristic in the quantity or quality that you claim to have. To express what you actually possess is not pride; it is simply the expression of the truth.

T-9.VIII.9. Can your grandeur be arrogant when God Himself witnesses to **your grandeur**? 2 And what can be real that has no witnesses? 3 What good can come of **what has no witnesses**? 4 And if no good can come of **what has no witnesses** the Holy Spirit cannot use **what has no witnesses**. 5 What **the Holy Spirit** cannot transform to the Will of God does not exist at all. 6 Grandiosity is delusional, because **grandiosity** is used to replace your grandeur. 7 Yet what God has created, **your grandeur** cannot be replaced. 8 God is incomplete without you because **God's** grandeur is total, and you cannot be missing from **God's grandeur**.

Note # 79: The Holy Spirit cannot take the illusion of littleness and make it real. Instead, It awakens the sleeping mind to the Son's true reality as God's grand completion. God's Creations are the Grandeur of God.

T-9.VIII.10. You are altogether irreplaceable in the Mind of God. 2 No one else can fill your part in **the Mind of God**, and while you leave your part of **the Mind of God** empty, your eternal place merely waits for your return. 3 God, through His Voice, **the Holy Spirit,** reminds you of **your part in the Mind of God**, and God Himself keeps your extensions safe within **your part in the Mind of God**. 4 Yet you do not know **your extensions** until you return to **your extensions or creations**. 5 You cannot replace the Kingdom, and you cannot replace yourself. 6 God, Who knows your value, would not have **you replace yourself nor the Kingdom**, and so **to replace yourself or the Kingdom** is not so. 7 Your value is in God's Mind, and therefore not in **your mind** alone. 8 To accept yourself as God created you cannot be arrogance, because **to accept yourself as God created you** is the denial of arrogance. 9 To accept your littleness <*is*> arrogant, because **to accept your littleness** means that you believe your evaluation of yourself is truer than God's.

Note # 80: Arrogance is the denial of the truth. God knows us as He created us, perfect, whole and complete. To argue for our littleness is arrogant indeed. To claim that we are God's perfect Child is not pride. It is merely a statement of fact. To argue that God does not know what He created is arrogance at the highest level.

T-9.VIII.11. Yet if truth is indivisible, your evaluation of yourself must <*be*> God's evaluation of yourself. 2 You did not establish your value and **your value** needs no defense. 3 Nothing can attack **your value** nor prevail over **your value**. 4 **Your value** does not vary. 5 **Your value** merely <*is.*> 6 Ask the Holy Spirit what **your value** is and **the Holy Spirit** will tell you, but do not be afraid of **the Holy Spirit's** answer, because **the Holy Spirit's answer** comes from God. 7 **The Holy Spirit's answer** is an exalted answer because of **the answer's** Source, but the Source is true and so is **the Source**'s answer. 8 Listen and do not question what you hear, for God does not deceive. 9 **God** would have you replace the ego's belief in littleness with **God's** Own exalted Answer to what you are, so that you can cease to question **what you are** and know **what you are** for what it is.

Note # 81: What you are comes from God and is unchangeable because this is God's Will. To believe you could be something other than how God created you is the height of arrogance since you would be claiming that your evaluation of yourself would be "truer" than God's knowledge of what you are.

A good prayer would be. "God let me accept the reality of my being no matter how much more beautiful it is than I could ever imagine I could be." We cannot imagine the magnificence of the truth of what we are.

Chapter 10. THE IDOLS OF SICKNESS

Introduction

T-10.in.1. Nothing beyond yourself can make you fearful or loving, because nothing <*is*> beyond you. 2 Time and eternity are both in your mind and **time and eternity** will conflict until you perceive time solely as a means to regain eternity. 3 You cannot **perceive time solely as a means to regain eternity** as long as you believe that anything happening to you is caused by factors outside yourself. 4 You must learn that time is solely at your disposal, and that nothing in the world can take this responsibility **that time is solely at your disposal** from you. 5 You can violate God's laws in your imagination, but you cannot escape from **God's laws**. 6 **God's laws** were established for your protection and **God's laws** are as inviolate as your safety.

Note # 1: Nothing is beyond us because God gave us everything. We are the creators of what we perceive and we need to take sole responsibility for our own provisional reality. We alone decide which of the endless possibilities that are available within the "All That Is" that we wish to call into our experience. We do this by choosing which part of the "All That Is" that we will focus our awareness upon. We are the decision-maker, scriptwriter and producer of our moment-to-moment experience within the Oneness. If we wish to experience our imagined separation or the totality of the Oneness, it is our choice. Ultimately, however, once we remember or reclaim what we are, we will accept and embrace the fact that we are unlimited Spirit. Our split mind will once again know and be a Oneness with Our Father. There is only one Law and one Will and that is the Law and Will of the Father. In the Kingdom, God's Will and our will are the same.

T-10.in.2. God created nothing beside you and nothing beside you exists, for you are part of **God**. 2 What except **God** can exist? 3 Nothing beyond **God** can happen, because nothing except **God** is real. 4 Your creations add to **God,** as you **add to God,** but nothing is added that is different **to God** because everything has always been. 5 What can upset you except the ephemeral, and how can the ephemeral be real if you are God's only creation and **God** created you eternal? 6 Your holy mind establishes everything that happens to you. 7 Every response you make to everything you perceive is up to you, because your mind determines your perception of **everything you perceive**.

Note # 2: You are the decision-maker for everything you perceive. You can either perceive under the guidance of the Holy Spirit or the ego. The guide you choose to follow is up to you. This Course's goal is to reawaken your ability to act as the decision-maker and choose again. This time, choose the Holy Spirit to guide you out of your egoic world of perception, space and time.

God is only love. Love does not limit. Love does not judge but instead allows us the freedom to be and experience whatever we wish. Love's goal is that we be happy. God's love allows His Creation the absolute freedom to create and be, with the totality of God supporting you, loving you and delighting in that which His Child creates or makes. Nothing the Child creates or imagines (makes) can be wrong, a sin or inappropriate for there is only freedom and no judgment. Happiness is perfect freedom to be what you are with the totality of the universe supporting your desires and decisions.

T-10.in.3. God does not change **God's** Mind about you, for **God** is not uncertain of Himself. 2 And what **God** knows can be known, because **God** does not know **God's Mind** only for Himself. 3 **God** created you for Himself, but **God** gave you the power to create for yourself so you would be like **God Who created you like Himself.** 4 **Because God created you like Himself,** that is why your mind is holy. 5 Can anything exceed the Love of God? 6 Can anything, then, exceed your will? 7 Nothing can reach you from beyond **your will** because, being in God, you encompass everything. 8 Believe this, **that being in God, you encompass everything,** and you will realize how much is up to you. 9 When anything threatens your peace of mind, ask yourself, "Has God changed **God's** Mind about me?" 10 Then accept **God's** decision, for **God's decision** is indeed changeless, and **then** refuse to change your mind about yourself. 11 God will never decide against you, or **God** would be deciding against Himself.

Note # 3: God gave us the power to create so we would be like Our Father. God has given this power and everything God "is" because that is how creation occurs. Extension is sharing all. God gives all (everything) to all, (the Sonship) and this is God's Being. God knows His creation as Himself, perfect, whole and complete. This is our changeless reality because this is God's Will. We can imagine we are not God's Effect but we cannot change being God's Effect.

I. At Home in God

T-10.I.1. You do not know your creations simply because you would decide against **your creations** as long as your mind is split, and to attack what you have created is impossible. 2 But remember that <*it is as impossible for God* **to attack what has been created**.> 3 The law of creation is that you love your creations as yourself, because **your creations** are part of you. 4 Everything that was created is therefore perfectly safe, because the laws of God protect **everything that was created** by **God's** Love. 5 Any part of your mind that does not know **everything that was created by God's Love is perfectly safe and protected by the laws of God** has banished itself, **which is your egoic mind,** from knowledge, because **your split-mind** has not met **knowledge's** conditions. 6 Who could have done this but you? 7 Recognize **that you have done this to yourself** gladly, for in this recognition lies the realization that your banishment is not of God, and therefore does not exist.

Note # 4: You have dreamed that you could do something contradictory to God's Will. God's Will is changeless. Only in your dream world of provisional reality does time and space "exist." This world is only in your mind. You imagined that you could create from a source other than that of love. Coming from fear, you do not know that the Law of God protects all of creation from attack. Making is only an imagined dreamed. You can choose to reawaken to reality whenever you choose to follow God's Laws for creation.

T-10.I.2. You are at home in God, dreaming of exile but perfectly capable of awakening to reality. 2 Is it your decision to do so? **(To reawaken?)** 3 You recognize from your own experience that what you see in dreams you think is real while you are asleep. 4 Yet the instant you waken you realize that everything that seemed to happen in the dream did not happen at all. 5 You do not think this strange **that what seemed to happen in the dream did not happen at all** even though all the laws of what you awaken to were violated while you slept. 6 Is it not possible that you merely shifted from one dream to another, without really waking?

Note # 5: This dream world is our provisional reality. It is a pretend world in which we image that we do not know what we are. It is a world in which time and space appear to have reality. This whole dream appears to have reality to the dreamer while the dreamer is asleep. Provisional reality is your dream state of separation. It includes all the "time" your mind believed that it was separate from God. This includes our waking and sleeping moments on this earth plane. It also includes our moments when we are not on this earth plane (when we are "dead"). It is any time we perceive that we are not a Oneness with God; any time we do not remember what we are. Throughout this state of not remembering our true reality of our Big "S" Self, we still remain safe in the Oneness of the Mind of God. Our dream state does not change the truth that we are eternally God's Effect.

T-10.I.3. Would you bother to reconcile what happened in conflicting dreams, or would you dismiss both **conflicting dreams** together if you discovered that reality is in accord with neither **conflicting dream**? 2 You do not remember being awake. 3 When you hear the Holy Spirit you may feel better because loving then seems possible to you, but you do not remember yet that **loving** once was so. 4 And it is in this remembering **that loving once was so,** that you will know **loving** can be so again. 5 What is possible has not yet been accomplished. 6 Yet what has once been is so now, **if what has once been** is eternal. 7 When you remember **what has once been**, you will know that what you remember is eternal, and therefore **what you remember** is now.

Note # 6: The Holy Spirit does not teach us to love; rather It assists us in removing all the blocks that we have placed in order to hide the love that we are. We were created as love and thus, we need only to remember that we are to once again allow our love to shine forth.

T-10.I.4. You will remember everything the instant you desire **to remember everything** wholly, for if to desire wholly is to create, you will have willed away the separation, returning your mind simultaneously to your Creator and your creations. 2 Knowing **your Creator and your creations** you will have no wish to sleep, but only the desire to waken and be glad. 3 Dreams will be impossible because you will want only truth, and being at last your will, **truth** will be yours.

Note # 7: The dream of separation was our choice. The dream of separation will end when we no longer value anything that we believe the dream represents.

II. The Decision to Forget

T-10.II.1. Unless you first know something you cannot dissociate **from that something**. 2 Knowledge must precede dissociation, so that dissociation is nothing more than a decision to forget **knowledge**. 3 What has been forgotten then appears to be fearful, but only because the dissociation **from your decision to forget knowledge** is an attack on truth. 4 You are fearful <because> you have forgotten **you decided not to remember knowledge**. 5 And you have replaced your knowledge by an awareness of dreams because you are afraid of your dissociation **from your decision to forget knowledge. You are not afraid** of what you have dissociated, **which is knowledge.** 6 When what you have dissociated is accepted **you remember knowledge and what you have dissociated** ceases to be fearful.

Note # 8: It is fear of the unknown, not the truth itself that frightens us. When you know the truth that you are the Oneness of "All That is," you realize there is nothing to fear. We chose to forget this truth and now fear what the truth might be. The laws of God protect everything that was created by God's Love. Thus, there is nothing to fear, yet we have banished this knowledge of God's laws from our own mind.

T-10.II.2. Yet to give up the dissociation of reality, **which is the remembrance of the knowledge of God's Kingdom,** brings more than merely lack of fear. 2 In this decision **to remember the knowledge of reality** lie joy and peace and the glory of creation. 3 Offer the Holy Spirit only your willingness to remember, for **the Holy Spirit** retains the knowledge of God and of yourself for you, waiting for your acceptance. 4 Give up gladly everything that would stand in the way of your remembering **God and yourself**, for God is in your memory. 5 **The Holy Spirit, God's** Voice will tell you that you are part of **God** when you are willing to remember **God** and know your own reality again. 6 Let nothing in y**our dream** world **of perception, time and space** delay your remembering of **God**, for in this remembering **of God** is the knowledge of yourself.

Note # 9: When we questioned and rejected the truth about ourselves, we denied all the benefits associated with that fact. Happiness, peace joy and the creation process also were forgotten. When we valued our specialness more than the oneness, we obtained the entire package of the egoic thought system. Along with specialness, we also received sin, guilt and fear.

T-10.II.3. To remember is merely to restore to your mind <*what is already there.*> 2 You do not make what you remember; you merely accept again what is already there, but was rejected. 3 The ability to accept truth in this world, **your dream world of provisional reality,** is the perceptual counterpart of creating in the Kingdom. 4 God will do **God's** part if you will do **your part**, and **God's** return in exchange for yours is the exchange of knowledge for perception. 5 Nothing is beyond **God's** Will for you. 6 But signify your will to remember **God,** and behold! 7 **God** will give you everything but for the asking.

Note # 10: When we chose to forget the truth of our Oneness with God's Will, we also lost our remembrance of the Kingdom, which is the real world of knowledge. We gave up knowledge in exchange for perception. Our split mind then projected the image of a world of perception, time and space. This projection became our dream world of provisional reality. To access knowledge again, we must demonstrate our willingness to do our part toward our remembrance of God by simply asking for and then following the thought system of the Holy Spirit. The Holy Spirit reinterprets our misperceptions into correct perceptions that support and align with the truth of the Kingdom. When we accept the Atonement for ourselves, God, our Father, exchanges perception for the return to knowledge.

T-10.II.4. When you attack, you are denying yourself. 2 You are specifically teaching yourself that you are not what you are. 3 Your denial of reality precludes the acceptance of God's gift, because you have accepted something else in **the place of God's gift of your Oneness**. 4 If you understand that this **acceptance of something else in the place of God's gift** is always an attack on truth, and truth is God, you will realize why **the acceptance of something else in the place of God's gift of your Oneness** is always fearful. 5 If you further recognize that you are part of God, you will understand why it is that you always attack yourself first.

Note # 11: Some of God's gifts are love, truth, joy, happiness, freedom and peace. Being a Oneness of Everything, to deny the truth is to deny our divine inheritance. We exchange the happiness of everything for the promise of specialness. The quest for specialness rewards us with limitation, competition, lack, loneliness, guilt and fear.

T-10.II.5. All attack is Self attack. 2 **Attack** cannot be anything else **than attack upon your Big "S" Self**. 3 Arising from your own decision not to be what you are, it is an attack on your identification **as your Big "S" Self and your Oneness**. 4 Attack is thus the way in which your identification is lost, because when you attack, you must have forgotten what you are. 5 And if your reality is God's, when you attack you are not remembering **God**. 6 This **not remembering God** is not because **God** is gone, but because you are actively choosing not to remember **God**.

Note # 12: Knowledge was not taken away from us. Instead it was our own free choice to forget the truth of what we are. We wondered what it would be like to be something other than God. Once we imagined it, we took the illusion seriously enough to become frightened. We forgot to laugh; let fear and uncertainty enter our now split-mind and made the dream of separation appear real within the mind of the dreamer. We identified ourselves as something other than the Oneness of all. Now there was an observer and something outside the observer to observe. Perception was born and knowledge forgotten.

T-10.II.6. If you realized the complete havoc this **not remembering God** makes of your peace of mind you could not make such an insane decision. 2 You make **the insane decision to not remember God** only because you still believe **that not remembering God** can get you something you want. 3 It follows, then, that you want something other than peace of mind, but you have not considered what **that something other than peace of mind that you want** must be. 4 Yet the logical outcome of your decision is perfectly clear, if you will only look at **the logical outcome of your decision**. 5 By deciding against your reality, you have made yourself vigilant <*against*> God and **God's** Kingdom. 6 And **by deciding against your reality,** it is this vigilance **against God** that makes you afraid to remember **God**.

Note # 13: All attack is attack against your true reality which is Self attack against the Son of God. We attack our real identification as the Big "S" Self. Since we are part of God, any attack on our Big "S" Self is an attack on our Father. When we remember God, we also remember what we are and accept our true nature as God's Creation. We have exchanged our peace and happiness for the specialness of our egoic little "s' self. We cling to our ego's decision to declare that we are right even when we are "dead" wrong.

III. The God of Sickness

T-10.III.1. You have not attacked God and you do love **God**. 2 Can you change your reality? 3 No one can will to destroy himself. 4 When you think you are attacking yourself, **this attack on yourself** is a sure sign that you hate what you <*think*> you are. 5 And **what you <*think*> you are** and only **what you <*think*> you are**, can be attacked by you. 6 What you think you are can be very hateful, and what this strange image **of what you <*think*> you are** makes you do can be very destructive. 7 Yet the destruction is no more real than the image **of what you <*think*> you are**, although those who make idols do worship **the idols of their imaginations**. 8 The idols are nothing, but their worshippers are the Sons of God in sickness. 9 God would have **these sick Sons of God who worship the idols of their imagination** released from their sickness and returned to **God's** Mind. 10 **God** will not limit your power to help **these sick Sons of God who worship the idols of their imagination** because **God** has given you **the power to help your sick brothers**. 11 Do not be afraid of **the power to help your sick brothers** because **the power to help your sick brothers** is your salvation.

Note # 14: You cannot attack what you really are because what God created is changeless and eternal. You can attack what you imagine yourself to be in your dream world of provisional reality. Since God created you like Himself, your mind has been given the power to remember the wholeness of the Sonship. That is what we really are, a Oneness. Your Big "S" Self coupled with the Holy Spirit can heal and reunite the Sonship and return It to right or whole-mindedness.

T-10.III.2. What Comforter can there be for the sick children of God except **God's** power through you? 2 Remember that it does not matter where in the Sonship **God** is accepted. 3 **God** is always accepted for all, and when your mind receives **God** the remembrance of **God** awakens throughout the Sonship. 4 Heal your brothers simply by accepting God for **your brothers**. 5 **You and your brother's** minds are not separate, and God has only one channel for healing because **God** has but one Son. 6 God's remaining Communication Link with all **God's** children joins **all God's children** together, and **all God's children** to **God**. 7 To be aware of this **joining all God's children together through this Communication Link** is to heal **all God's children** because it is the awareness that no one is separate, and so no one is sick.

Note # 15: We are all united in the Sonship since the Sonship is all that the Father created. To heal any part of the Sonship is to heal the totality. The Comforter is the Holy Spirit.

T-10.III.3. To believe that a Son of God can be sick is to believe that part of God can suffer. 2 Love cannot suffer, because **love** cannot attack. 3 The remembrance of love therefore brings invulnerability with **love**. 4 Do not side with sickness in the presence of a Son of God even if **a Son of God** believes in **sickness**, for your acceptance of God in **a Son of God** acknowledges the Love of God **that a sick Son of God** has forgotten. 5 Your recognition of **a Son of God** as part of God reminds **a Son of God** of the truth about himself, which **a sick Son of God** is denying. 6 Would you strengthen **a sick Son of God's** denial of God and thus lose sight of yourself? 7 Or would you remind **a sick Son of God** of his wholeness and remember your Creator with **a sick Son of God?**

Note # 16: By seeing a Son of God as "sick," you are accepting the belief in limitation and that there can be something other than the Will of God. This reinforces both his and your own belief that the separation is real. This does not lead to healing and correction of the fundamental error that a sick person is not remembering what they are. To acknowledge the false in another, which is the belief that they are sick, is to accept the false as real. We have raised the false to the status of truth. We can choose to either share the truth or the false with our brother. Whichever we share, we strengthen. ACIM states that we should deny the existence of the false and accept and share the reality of the truth. This is how we assist the Holy Spirit in His healing of the split-minded Sonship.

T-10.III.4. To believe a Son of God is sick is to worship the same idol **a sick Son of God** does. 2 God created love, not idolatry. 3 All forms of idolatry are caricatures of creation, taught by sick minds too divided to know that creation shares power and never usurps **power**. 4 Sickness is idolatry, because **sickness** is the belief that power can be taken from you. 5 Yet **the belief that power can be taken from you** is impossible, because you are part of God, Who is all power. 6 A sick god must be an idol, made in the image of what its **sick** maker thinks the **sick** maker, himself, is. 7 And that **idol to a sick god** is exactly what the ego does perceive in a Son of God; a sick god, self-created, self-sufficient, very vicious and very vulnerable. 8 Is this the idol you would worship? 9 Is this **idol to a sick god** the image you would be vigilant to save? 10 Are you really afraid of losing this? **(Losing this idol of a sick Son of God, which is a sick god, egoically self-created, self-sufficient, very vicious and very vulnerable)**

Note # 17: What we value, we will protect and defend. What we value, we perceive and project into our dream world. What we choose to believe, we will choose to perceive. Your perception follows your purpose. We value our littleness more than we value the Oneness that is the Love of God. Our sick minds have created an image of a false egoic god made in the likeness of our own egoic image of ourselves.

T-10.III.5. Look calmly at the logical conclusion of the ego's thought system and judge whether **the ego's thought system's** offering is really what you want, for this **image of a sick Son of God** <*is*> what **the ego's thought system** offers you. 2 To obtain this **logical conclusion of the ego's thought system's image of a sick Son of God,** you are willing to attack the Divinity of your brothers, and thus lose sight of **your divinity**. 3 And you are willing to keep **your divinity** hidden, to protect an idol you think will save you from the dangers for which **the idol** stands, but which **the idol's dangers** do not exist **since a sick Son of God is only imagined in a deluded mind**.

Note # 18: Not remembering what we are, we fear losing the false protection that our idols to littleness offer us against the unknown. The unknown is our forgetting the truth of what we are. The ego's thought system warns us that in a world of lack, we must compete against our brother's if we are to survive. Attack becomes a way of life. The ego tells us this world is a zero sun-game and that we need the help of outside powers or idols if we are to survive, let alone be happy.

T-10.III.6. There are no idolaters in the Kingdom, but there is great appreciation for everything that God created, because of the calm knowledge that each one **of the aspects that God created** is part of **God**. 2 God's Son, **the Big "S" Self,** knows no idols, but **the Big "S" Self** does know his Father. 3 Health in this world is the counterpart of value in Heaven. 4 It is not my merit that I contribute to you but my love, for you do not value yourself. 5 When you do not value yourself you become sick, but my value of you can heal you, because the value of God's Son is one. 6 When I said, "My peace I give unto you," I meant it. 7 Peace comes from God through me to you. 8 **Peace** is for you although you may not ask for **peace**.

Note # 19: Thoughts never leave the mind of the thinker. What we give, we receive. If we are willing to receive the peace of God, we will also share that same peace with our brother. Extension is the sharing of thoughts which strengthens the thought.

T-10.III.7. When a brother is sick it is because he is not asking for peace, and therefore does not know he has **peace**. 2 The acceptance of peace is the denial of illusion, and sickness <*is*> an illusion. 3 Yet every Son of God has the power to deny illusions anywhere in the Kingdom, merely by denying **illusions** completely in himself. 4 I can heal you because I know you. 5 I know your value for you, and it is this value that makes you whole. 6 A whole mind is not idolatrous, and does not know of conflicting laws. 7 I will heal you merely because I have only one message, **which is "My peace I give unto you,"** and **this one message** is true. 8 Your faith in **this one message, which is "My peace I give unto you,"** will make you whole when you have faith in me.

Note # 20: The peace of God is the acceptance of what you are. The illusion of the provisional reality of limitations and separateness fades away upon the reawakening and reclaiming our divine birthright as the Son of God. The Peace of God is our destiny. The acceptance of the Atonement for ourselves is the denial of all illusions. The Atonement is healing and salvation.

T-10.III.8.I do not bring God's message with deception, and you will learn **God's message** as you learn that you always receive as much as you accept. 2 You could accept peace now for everyone, and offer **everyone** perfect freedom from all illusions because you heard **God's** Voice. 3 But have no other gods before **God, your Father,** or you will not hear **God's Voice, which is the Holy Spirit.** 4 God is not jealous of the gods you make, but you are **jealous of the gods you make.** 5 You would save **the gods you make** and serve **the gods you make,** because you believe that **the gods you make** made you. 6 You think **the gods you make** are your father, because you are projecting onto, **the gods you make** the fearful fact that you made **these false gods** to replace God, **Your Father.** 7 Yet when **these false gods you made** seem to speak to you, remember that nothing can replace God, **Your Father,** and whatever replacements you have attempted are nothing.

Note # 21: This replacement of Our Creator with idols is the "Authority Problem." The ego would have you believe that you fathered yourself, and that God, Our Father, either does not exist, or has somehow lost His Power, or perhaps even has been destroyed by you. The ego claims that an effect can change its cause. It claims that you have a will that can be different from the Will of God. Since there is only the Will of God, the images or dreams of the "sick" or "split-minded," are only false imaginings. They are dreams that disappear once we choose to remember the truth. Outside the insane mind of the dreamer these magical fantasies are nothing. Thus, within the Mind of God, our dream world of idols, sin, guilt and fear are nothing since they are not real. The imaginings of an insane mind cannot change reality. The false cannot change the truth. God, as First Cause, will always have His Effect as He caused it.

T-10.III.9. Very simply, then, you may believe you are afraid of nothingness, but you are really afraid of nothing. 2 And in that awareness **that the ego's world of false gods and idols is only imagined and not real, you realize you were afraid of nothing and thus,** you are healed. 3 You will hear the god you listen to. **This voice will be either the ego's thought system or the thought system of the Holy Spirit.** 4 You made the god of sickness, and by making **the god of sickness** you made yourself able to hear **the god of sickness, which symbolizes the ego's thought system.** . 5 Yet you did not create **the god of sickness,** because he, **the god of sickness, which symbolizes the ego's thought system,** is not the Will of the Father. 6 **The god of sickness, which symbolizes the ego's thought system,** is therefore not eternal and will be unmade for you the instant you signify your willingness to accept only the eternal.

Note # 22: We did not create the god of sickness, because to create is the extension of the Mind of God. We "make" when we deny our Big "S" Self and believe in limitation and fear. Sickness is not a part of the Mind of God. We did "make" the god of sickness "real" in our imagined dream world of provisional reality. Our provisional reality is based on our perception. If we give our perception to the Holy Spirit, He will reinterpret our misperceptions as a learning device to bring us back of the remembrance of God.

T-10.III.10. If God has but one Son, there is but one God. 2 You share reality with **God,** because reality is not divided. 3 To accept other gods before **God** is to place other images before yourself. 4 You do not realize how much you listen to your gods, **the ego's thought system,** and how vigilant you are on **your imagined gods'** behalf. 5 Yet **your imagined gods** exist only because you honor **your imagined gods.** 6 Place honor where **honor** is due and peace will be yours. 7 **Peace** is your inheritance from your real Father. 8 You cannot make your Father, and the father you made, **your ego's thought system with its false gods,** did not make you. 9 Honor is not due to illusions, for to honor **your imagined gods** is to honor nothing. 10 Yet fear is not due **your imagined gods** either, for nothing, **which is what your imagined gods are,** cannot be fearful. 11 You have chosen to fear love because of **love's** perfect harmlessness, and because of this fear **of love** you have been willing to give up your own perfect helpfulness and your own perfect Help, **which is the Love of God**.

Note # 23: What we value, we will choose to perceive. When we no longer value the egoic specialness, we will be willing to give up the illusion of littleness and turn to the thought system of the Holy Spirit. By asking and accepting God's Guide, we will be led back to the remembrance of knowledge.

T-10.III.11. Only at the altar of God will you find peace. 2 And this altar **of God** is in you because God put it there **in you**. 3 **God's** Voice, **the Holy Spirit,** still calls you to return, and **the Holy Spirit** will be heard when you place no other gods before **God, your Father**. 4 You can give up the god of sickness for your brothers; in fact, you would have to do so if you give **the god of sickness** up for yourself. 5 For if you see the god of sickness anywhere, you have accepted **the god of sickness**. 6 And if you accept **the god of sickness** you will bow down and worship **the god of sickness**, because **the god of sickness** was made as God's replacement. 7 **The god of sickness** is the belief that you can choose which god is real. 8 Although **the belief that you can choose which god is real** is clear this has nothing to do with reality. It is equally clear that **the belief that you can choose which god is real** has everything to do with reality as you perceive **reality within your split mind**.

Note # 24: How we choose to view reality depends on which thought system we follow. Follow the ego and you will see yourself as a limited ego body. A world of limitation and competition will become your provisional reality. Follow the Holy Spirit, and you will see that you are unlimited Spirit and one with the Mind of God; that your will and God's Will are the same since you are part of a Oneness. You are the decision-maker and the Holy Spirit invites you to choose again. When you make the choice, you choose for the entire Sonship. If you choose to exclude one brother from healing, you exclude the entire Sonship from healing. Healing is an all or nothing proposition.

The thought system of the ego claims that you are separate and the arbitrator of truth. It claims that you decide what will be the truth and when it will be true. What you declare to be your "truth" will form the foundation for your imagination to create a false dream world dedicated to these imagined "truths." This belief that each is the arbitrator of truth birthed the world of perception from which each made their own private world of provisional reality. Your provisional reality is a world of personal delusion that you alone created. It only exists within your mind's imagination yet it appears to be real because you choose to believe that it is "true." Due to the power of our mind's beliefs, the dimensions of time and space becomes the game board upon which the game of separation can be play out. Yet, childhood games of make believe cannot change the reality of the truth which remains eternally fixed in the Mind of God.

IV. The End of Sickness

T-10.IV.1. All magic is an attempt at reconciling the irreconcilable. 2 All religion is the recognition that the irreconcilable cannot be reconciled. 3 Sickness and perfection are irreconcilable. 4 If God created you perfect, you <are> perfect. 5 If you believe you can be sick, you have placed other gods before **God, our Father**. 6 God is not at war with the god of sickness you made, but you are **at war with the god of sickness**. 7 **The god of sickness** is the symbol of deciding against God, and you are afraid of **the god of sickness** because **the god of sickness** cannot be reconciled with God's Will. 8 If you attack **the**

god of sickness, you will make **the god of sickness** real to you. 9 But if you refuse to worship **the god of sickness** in whatever form **the god of sickness** may appear to you, and wherever you think you see him, **the god of sickness** will disappear into the nothingness out of which **the god of sickness** was made.

Note # 25: Truth cannot be reconciled with the false. Truth calls for the denial of the false, which leaves the truth remaining. The proper use of denial does not attack, it just acknowledges the fact that what is false is nothing and can have no impact or power over the truth. The Truth just is. When we choose to attack the false, we uplift the false illusion and give it an imagined power to attack and oppose the truth that it does not possess. When we defend the truth by attacking the false, we make the game of separation appear real within the mind of those who are uncertain of what they are. We took the imagined threat seriously and forgot to laugh. We allowed doubt into the Kingdom and thus, forgot knowledge. Perception took the place of knowledge and "paradise" was forgotten but not lost.

T-10.IV.2. Reality can dawn only on an unclouded mind. 2 **Reality** is always there to be accepted, but **reality's** acceptance depends on your willingness to have **reality**. 3 To know reality must involve the willingness to judge unreality for what **unreality** is. 4 To overlook nothingness is merely to judge **nothingness** correctly, and because of your ability to evaluate **nothingness** truly, to let **nothingness** go. 5 Knowledge cannot dawn on a mind full of illusions, because truth and illusions are irreconcilable. 6 Truth is whole, and cannot be known by part of a mind.

Note # 26: Recognizing the false as the nothing that it is, allows us to dismiss the false into the nothingness from which it arose. The false is powerless to change the truth. By the simple denial of the existence of the false, the false fades away. We cannot know the truth as long as we cling to the ego's claim that we, not God, can determine what is to be the truth. Give all perception over to the Guidance of the Holy Spirit Who knows the difference between the true and false. The Holy Spirit will help you heal your split-mind and return it to right-mindedness. You cannot do this alone.

T-10.IV.3. The Sonship cannot be perceived as partly sick, because to perceive **the Sonship as partly sick** is not to perceive **the Sonship** at all. 2 If the Sonship is One, **the Sonship** is One in all respects. 3 Oneness cannot be divided. 4 If you perceive other gods your mind is split, and you will not be able to limit the split, because a **split mind** is the sign that you have removed part of your mind from God's Will. 5 This means a **split mind** is out of control. 6 To be out of control is to be out of reason, and then the mind does become unreasonable. 7 By defining the mind wrongly, you perceive **the mind** as functioning wrongly.

Note # 27: We cannot be a "little insane." To be deluded about what you are is to be insane. There is no such thing as a partial Oneness. It is a contradiction of terms and to accept a partial Oneness as your reality demonstrates that your mind is insane.

T-10.IV.4. God's laws will keep your mind at peace because peace is **God's** Will, and **God's** laws are established to uphold **your mind at peace, which is God's Will for you**. 2 **God's laws** are the laws of freedom, but **your laws** are the laws of bondage. 3 Since freedom and bondage are irreconcilable, **God's laws and your** laws cannot be understood together. 4 The laws of God work only for your good, and there are no other laws beside **God's Laws**. 5 Everything else **that is not based on God's laws, are** merely lawless and therefore chaotic. 6 Yet God Himself has protected everything **God** created by **God's** laws. 7 Everything that is not under **God's laws** does not exist. 8 "Laws of chaos," **which are your egoic laws,** is a meaningless term. 9 Creation is perfectly lawful, and the chaotic is without meaning because **the chaotic** is without God. 10 You have "given" your peace to the gods **of sickness**

that you made, but **the gods that you made** are not there to take **your peace** from you **for they are not real.** And you cannot give **your peace** to **these false gods that you believe you have made**.

<u>Note # 28:</u> You cannot give your peace to the gods that you made for two basic reasons. The first is that this is not the Will of God. God wills you the Peace of God. Nothing can take your Peace of God away from you, but you can choose to "forget" this during your dream state of provisional reality, which is your denial of truth. The second reason is basically a corollary to the first, which is that it was not God's Will. Anything that is not shared with the Will of God is not real and, therefore, does not exist. The gods you "made" can only exist in your illusionary world of provisional reality. These false idols appear "true" to the dreamer, but will disappear when the dreamer reawakens.

This section makes it clear that the two thought systems of the ego and the Holy Spirit are irreconcilable. Only one can be correct. They can never co-exist. You must choose which thought system you will give your allegiance to. This decision to follow either thought system is a choice that the decision-making part of your mind must freely make. Ultimately, the thought system of the Holy Spirit will be freely chosen by the Son of God, because that is the Will of God which must also be His Son's will. One mind can have only one will.

T-10.IV.5. You are not free to give up freedom, but only to deny **freedom**. 2 You cannot do what God did not intend, because what **God** did not intend does not happen. 3 Your gods do not bring chaos; you are endowing **the god's you made** with chaos, and accepting **chaos** of **the god's you made**. 4 All this has never been**, because what God did not intend does not happen. This has only appeared to happen in the imagination of the split-minded.** 5 Nothing but the laws of God has ever been, and nothing but **God's** Will will ever be. 6 You were created through **God's** laws and by **God's** Will, and the manner of your creation established you a creator. 7 What you have made is so unworthy of you that you could hardly want **what you have made**, if you were willing to see **what you have made** as it is. 8 You will see nothing at all **when you look with true vision on what you have made.** 9 And your vision will automatically look beyond **what you have made**, to what is in you and all around you. 10 Reality cannot break through the obstructions you interpose, but **reality** will envelop you completely when you let **what you have made** go.

<u>Note # 29:</u> Because you have free will, you can choose to be what you are or pretend that you are something that you are not. God is Love and love allows Its creations total freedom to experience anything that they wish to call into their awareness without God's judgment or condemnation. God's love insures us that our birthright of perfect freedom will be preserved for us because it is God's Truth. We can deny God's love but our denial cannot change God's Love. Eventually, we will freely choose to accept, extend and be love. This is inevitable because it is our Cause's Will for His Effect.

What you have made is your dream world of provisional reality. When you choose to reawaken from your dream, you will realize that your dream was never real and that your dream had no affect on reality since your dream was not part of the Mind of God. Creation, unlike making, is shared. Your world of provisional reality is a private world. It is not shared and, therefore, it was never created in the Mind of God. The Mind of God shares and gives all, to all. Your "making" shares nothing with anyone, not even our own split mind.

T-10.IV.6. When you have experienced the protection of God, the making of idols becomes inconceivable. 2 There are no strange images in the Mind of God, and what is not in **God's** Mind cannot be in **your mind**, because you are of one mind and that mind belongs to **God**. 3 **The Mind of God** is **your mind** <*because*> **the Mind of God** belongs to **God**, for to **God** ownership is sharing. 4 And if it is so for **God that ownership is sharing**, it is so for you. 5 **God's** definitions <*are*> **God's** laws, for by **God's laws, God** established the universe as what **the universe** is. 6 No false gods you attempt to interpose between yourself and your reality affect truth at all. 7 Peace is yours because God created you. 8 And **God** created nothing else.

Note # 30: Our perceived world of provisional reality has no effect on true reality, which is synonymous with God's Will. Reality is changeless and eternal because that is God's Will.

T-10.IV.7. The miracle is the act of a Son of God who has laid aside all false gods, and calls on his brothers to do likewise **and laid aside all the brothers' false gods.** 2 **The miracle** is an act of faith, because **the miracle** is the recognition that his brother can **also lay aside all his false gods.** 3 **The miracle** is a call to the Holy Spirit in **the miracle worker's** mind, a call that is strengthened by joining. 4 Because the miracle worker has heard God's Voice, **the miracle worker** strengthens **God's Voice** in a sick brother by weakening **a sick brother's** belief in sickness, which **the miracle worker** does not share. 5 The power of one mind can shine into another **mind,** because all the lamps of God were lit by the same spark. 6 **That spark from God** is everywhere and **the spark** is eternal.

Note # 31: The miracle is a process of rejoining perceived individualized aspects of the whole into the realization that they are joined together as part of a Oneness. The "Mind" of a Oneness is connected to all parts which are truly inseparable because there is only one mind. In a hologram all parts contain the whole and the whole is in all parts.

T-10.IV.8. In many only the spark remains, for the Great Rays are obscured. 2 Yet God has kept the spark alive so that the Rays can never be completely forgotten. 3 If you but see the little spark you will learn of the greater light, for the Rays are there unseen. 4 Perceiving the spark will heal, but knowing the light will create. 5 Yet in the returning the little light must be acknowledged first, for the separation was a descent from magnitude to littleness. 6 But the spark is still as pure as the Great Light, because **the spark** is the remaining call of creation. 7 Put all your faith in **the spark, which is the remaining call of creation** and God Himself will answer you.

Note # 32: This spark is the reality of our Big "S" Self or Christ consciousness which was never lost. This spark lies hidden behind the veil of the body. We need to look past our brother's bodily form that obscures this light and "see" the Christ that is his reality. By sharing this vision with our brothers, our light and minds are joined and healed.
Perceiving the spark is an individual act that is shared with a brother but unlike knowing is subject to change. Perception is in the realm of provisional reality. Knowing or knowledge is in the realm of the Mind of God. All creation comes from sharing, extending, or giving all, to the creation. Creation includes and nothing is held back.

V. The Denial of God

T-10.V.1. The rituals of the god of sickness are strange and very demanding. 2 Joy is never permitted, for depression is the sign of allegiance to **the god of sickness.** 3 Depression means that you have forsworn God. 4 Many are afraid of blasphemy, but they do not understand what **blasphemy** means. 5 **The many who are afraid of blasphemy** do not realize that to deny God is to deny their own Identity, and in this sense the wages of sin <*is*> death. 6 The sense is very literal; denial of life perceives its opposite, **which is death,** as all forms of denial replace what is with what is not. 7 No one can really do this, **replace what is with what is not,** but that you can think you can **replace what is with what is not** and **then** believe **that** you have **done this** is beyond dispute.

Note # 33: God is Truth. Within the mind of the person that chooses to deny the truth, his denial becomes his perceived reality. Denying the truth cannot change the truth's reality in the Kingdom of the real world, but it does affect how the insane relates to his imagined world of delusion. Since we are a part of the shared Oneness that is the Mind of God, when we deny the truth, we deny the identity of both God and Our Big "S" Self.

T-10.V.2. Do not forget, however, that to deny God will inevitably result in projection, and **due to your own projections** you will believe that others and not yourself have done this **denial of God** to you. 2 You must receive the message you give because **the message you give** is the message you want. 3 You may believe that you judge your brothers by the messages **your brothers** give you, but you have judged **your brothers** by the message you give to **your brothers**. 4 Do not attribute your denial of joy to **your brothers**, or you cannot see the spark in **your brothers** that would bring joy to you. 5 It is the denial of the spark that brings depression, for whenever you see your brothers without **the spark** you are denying God.

Note # 34: What we perceive in another mirrors our own beliefs about ourselves. This is how projection works. Deny our brother his divinity and we deny our own divinity for what we receive is what we have given.

T-10.V.3. Allegiance to the denial of God is the ego's religion. 2 The god of sickness obviously demands the denial of health, because health is in direct opposition to **the god of sickness'** own survival. 3 But consider what this **denial of health** means to you. 4 Unless you are sick you cannot keep the gods you made, for only in sickness could you possibly want **the god of sickness**. 5 Blasphemy, then, is <*self-destructive,*> not God-destructive. 6 This **blasphemy of the denial of your health** means that you are willing not to know yourself in order to be sick. 7 This **blasphemy of not to know yourself in order to be sick,** is the offering your god **of sickness** demands because, having made **your god of sickness** out of your insanity, **your god of sickness** is an insane idea. 8 **Your god of sickness** has many forms, but although **your god of sickness** may seem to be many different things **your god of sickness** is but one idea;–the denial of God.

Note # 35: In order to deny God, you must deny your own identity. This denying of what you truly are is the denial of what God truly is. Your denial of yourself, of course, does not change the reality of what you are as God created you. God's Will is unalterable.
Sickness is not just lack of bodily health. Sickness is any denial of your own Big "S" Self's divinity. Anytime you believe yourself to be something other than perfect, whole and complete as God created you, you are suffering from the delusions of a sick mind.

T-10.V.4. Sickness and death seemed to enter the mind of God's Son against **God's** Will. 2 The "attack on God" made His Son think he was Fatherless, and out of his depression he, **God's Son,** made the god of depression. 3 This was his alternative to joy, because he, **God's Son,** would not accept the fact that, although he was a creator, he, **being God's Son,** had been created **by God**. 4 Yet the Son <*is*> helpless without the Father, Who alone is **God's Son's** Help.

Note # 36: This is the authority problem. The ego tells us that we are self-created. All our power, whether it is used to create or misused to make, comes from being an extension of the Mind of God.

Without God as our Cause, we are powerless.

T-10.V.5.I said before that of yourself you can do nothing, but you are not <*of*> yourself. 2 If you were **of yourself, the illusion of** what you have made would be true, and you could never escape **the illusion**. 3 It is because you did not make yourself that you need be troubled over nothing. 4 Your gods are nothing, because your Father did not create **your gods of sickness that you made up**. 5 You cannot make creators who are unlike your Creator, any more than **God, Your Father,** could have created a Son who was unlike **God, Your Father.** 6 If creation is sharing, **creation** cannot create what is unlike itself. 7 **Creation** can share only what it is. 8 Depression is isolation, and so **depression** could not have been created.

Note # 37: Since creation is defined as extension, the only thing that can be created is a "carbon copy" of the original. Extension is sharing everything that the creator is with his creation. Since God, the Father, is our creator, only the attributes that are God-like can be real. God is unconditional Love and Truth. Because God is Love, attributes like hate, sickness and depression cannot exist. They are not part of the Mind of God. Attributes like sickness and depression can only exist in the illusions of the mind of the small "s" self, which is the dream world of provisional reality and misperception. God's Child is never alone. Even in the split-minded the Big "S" Self remains as the home of the Holy Spirit. The small "s" self will claim that it is home alone, but our Big "S" Self has not deserted us. We have just chosen to forget to listen.

T-10.V.6. Son of God, you have not sinned, but you have been much mistaken. 2 Yet this **mistake** can be corrected and God will help you, knowing that you could not sin against **God**. 3 You denied **God** because you loved **God**, knowing that if you recognized your love for **God**, you could not deny **God**. 4 Your denial of **God** therefore means that you love **God**, and that you know **God** loves you. 5 Remember that what you deny you must have once known. 6 And if you accept denial, you can accept **the undoing of your denial of God.**

Note # 38: Your Big "S" Self, has never lost its remembrance of God and the Truth of its Oneness. Our egoic denial is blocking the hearing of the Voice for God but it cannot remove it totally from your insane mind. Everyone hears the Voice for Truth sporadically throughout his or her current physical existence. The only question is when will we stop and listen. Our mind has denied our love for God. However, that same mind, under the guidance of the Holy Spirit, can correct this mistake.

T-10.V.7. God, Your Father has not denied you. 2 **God** does not retaliate, but **God** does call to you to return. 3 When you think **God** has not answered your call, you have not answered **God's call**. 4 **God** calls to you from every part of the Sonship, because of **God's** Love for His Son. 5 If you hear **God's** message **God** has answered you, and you will learn of **God** if you hear aright. 6 The Love of God is in everything **God** created, for **God's** Son is everywhere. 7 Look with peace upon your brothers, and God will come rushing into your heart in gratitude for your gift to **God**.

Note # 39: The Sonship is all God created. You and your brother are all a part of this Sonship. Every time you look upon any part of the Sonship with true Christ Vision, you look upon the Face of God. God is unconditional love. Love allows you the freedom to create or imagine anything you like. God does not condemn or judge. God knows His Creation as an extension of His Love, perfect whole and complete in the shared Oneness that is their Creator.

T-10.V.8. Do not look to the god of sickness for healing but only to the God of love, for healing is the acknowledgment of **God, Your Father.** 2 When you acknowledge **God** you will know that **God** has never ceased to acknowledge you, and that in **God's** acknowledgment of you lies your being. 3 You are not sick and you cannot die. 4 But you can confuse yourself with things that do **become sick and die.** 5 Remember, though, that to do this **denial of what you truly are and your belief that you can be sick** is blasphemy, for **this denial** means that you are looking without love on God and **God's** creation, from which **God** cannot be separated.

Note # 40: Our sickness, like all parts of a dream, has no reality outside the dream itself. Any perceived sickness of our small "s" self was just a part of the egoic dream for littleness. It never had any reality and thus, always remained powerless to affect any change in our Big "S" Self.

T-10.V.9. Only the eternal can be loved, for love does not die. 2 What is of God is **God's** forever, and you are of God. 3 Would **God** allow Himself to suffer? 4 And would **God** offer His Son anything that is not acceptable to **God**? 5 If you will accept yourself as God created you, you will be incapable of suffering. 6 Yet to accept yourself as God created you, you must acknowledge **God** as your Creator. 7 This **acknowledgment of God as your Creator** is not because you will be punished otherwise. 8 It is merely because your acknowledgment of your Father is the acknowledgment of yourself as you are. 9 Your Father created you wholly without sin, wholly without pain and wholly without suffering of any kind. 10 If you deny **your Father,** you bring sin, pain and suffering into your own mind because of the power **your Father** gave **your own mind.** 11 Your mind is capable of creating worlds, but **your own mind** can also deny what **your own mind** creates because **your own mind** is free.

Note # 41: Because God has given us the power to create, our mind is powerful. In our dream world of provisional reality, we can "use" this power of the mind to make or "miscreate." When we attempt to create from the false belief in lack and fear, we make a private dream world that is designed to bear witness to our false belief that we are separate from the Oneness. This delusional world is not shared and it is an attempt to exclude and fragment the One Self. The denial of what we truly are, Sons of our Father, is the cause of our inability to create like our Father created us. Because we view ourselves as limited and separate, we are unwilling to share ourselves completely. The Law of Creation is extension. To have and be all, we must give all, to all. By sharing ourselves completely, we become creators. This co-creation process is the completion of God.

T-10.V.10. You do not realize how much you have denied yourself, and how much God, in **God's** Love, would not have **you denied yourself** so. 2 Yet **God** would not interfere with you, because **God** would not know His Son if **His Son** were not free. 3 To interfere with you would be to attack Himself, and God is not insane. 4 When you deny **God** <*you*> are insane. 5 Would you have **God** share your insanity? 6 God will never cease to love His Son, and **God's** Son will never cease to love **God.** 7 **This mutual exchange of love between Father and Son** was the condition of **God's** Son's creation, fixed forever in the Mind of God. 8 To know that **God's Son will never cease to love God and God will never cease to love His Son** is **to know** sanity. 9 To deny **that God's Son will never cease to love God and God will never cease to love His Son** is insanity. 10 God gave Himself to you in your creation, and **God's** gifts are eternal. 11 Would you deny yourself to **God?**

Note # 42: Like God, we have been given freedom. Our free will does not give us the power to do anything outside the Mind of God since our will is the same as our Father's Will. Free will does give us the power to temporarily deny the truth. In the illusionary world of time and space, we get to decide when we will choose to reawaken from our dream of separation. Until we freely choose to awaken, we are free to imagine anything that we want. We can even pretend what it would be like to experience something other than God's love. What we are, our Big "S" Self, is eternal and always remains safe in the Kingdom, which is the Oneness of the Mind of God.

T-10.V.11. Out of your gifts to **God** the Kingdom will be restored to **God's** Son. 2 His Son removed himself from **God's** gift by refusing to accept what had been created for him, and what he, **God's Son,** had created in the Name of his Father. 3 Heaven waits for **God's Son's** return, for **the Kingdom, or Heaven,** was created as the dwelling place of God's Son. 4 You are not at home anywhere else, or in any other condition. 5 Do not deny yourself the joy that was created for you for the misery you have made for yourself. 6 God has given you the means for undoing what you have made. 7 Listen, and you will learn how to remember what you are.

Note # 43: By following the guidance of the Holy Spirit, we can escape from the world of perception and our provisional reality and go back to the Kingdom. This is God's means with which the Sonship's sanity is restored. By our acceptance of the Atonement for ourselves, we reject the false and embrace the truth. The Kingdom rests only on the knowledge of God. Illusion rests on the ego's perception of separateness.

T-10.V.12. If God knows His children as wholly sinless, it is blasphemous to perceive **God's children** as guilty. 2 If God knows His children as wholly without pain, it is blasphemous to perceive suffering anywhere. 3 If God knows His children to be wholly joyous, it is blasphemous to feel depressed. 4 All of these illusions, and the many other forms that blasphemy may take, are refusals to accept creation as it is. 5 If God created His Son perfect, that is how you must learn to see **His Son** to learn of **His Son's perfect** reality. 6 And as part of the Sonship, that **perfection** is how you must see yourself to learn of **your perfect reality.**

Note # 44: When we perceive the littleness of another or ourselves, we make the illusion appear real within our own split mind. All attempts at raising body thoughts to the level of mind are an attack on both God and our reality. Sin is any belief in lack and God, the Oneness of Everything, lacks for nothing. Give our brother his "Christness" and our brother returns you to your Big "S" Self. We can only give what we possess and what we give we receive.

T-10.V.13. Do not perceive anything God did not create or you are denying **God**. 2 **God** is the only Fatherhood, and **fatherhood** is yours only because **God** has given **fatherhood** to you. 3 Your gifts to yourself are meaningless, but your gifts to your creations are like **God's gifts to His creations,** because they are given in **God's** Name. 4 That is why your creations are as real as **God's creations**. 5 Yet the real Fatherhood must be acknowledged if the real Son is to be known. 6 You believe that the sick things you have made are your real creations, because you believe that the sick images you perceive are the Sons of God. 7 Only if you accept the Fatherhood of God will you have anything, because **God's** Fatherhood gave you everything. 8 That is why to deny **God** is to deny yourself.

Note # 45: Our purpose as God's Son is to create like our Father. Because we believe that we are separated and, therefore, limited, we cannot create like our Father. We can only make, because we fail to understand the Law of Creation, which states that creation is giving or sharing. When we stop denying our divine birthright, we automatically recover our full creative powers. When we deny God's Fatherhood, we deny that we are the extension of our Father. We claim that we are limited and, therefore, can only believe that we have littleness to give to our own creations. God knows that His Child is as unlimited as Himself and that creation is only the extension of the Oneness of Everything. When we remember God's Fatherhood, we will reawaken to the truth about our own fatherhood. We, like our Father, only extended the perfect, the whole and the complete.

T-10.V.14. Arrogance is the denial of love, because love shares and arrogance withholds. 2 As long as both **the denial and the sharing of love** appear to you to be desirable the concept of choice, which is not of God, will remain with you. 3 While this **concept of choice** is not true in eternity **the concept of choice** <*is*> true in time, so that while time lasts in your mind there will be choices. 4 Time itself is your choice. 5 If you would remember eternity, you must look only on the eternal. 6 If you allow yourself to become preoccupied with the temporal, you are living in time. 7 As always, your choice is determined by what you value. 8 Time and eternity cannot both be real, because **time and eternity** contradict each other. 9 If you will accept only what is timeless as real, you will begin to understand eternity and make **eternity** yours.

Note # 46: Prior to the separation, there was no choice. What can a Oneness of Everything choose between? God is love and so there was only love. With our egoic belief that God's love could be denied, choice appeared to be possible. Love and love's denial, which is fear, now appeared to be possible choices. Now we had the choice for truth, which is love or the false, which is fear. Choice cannot exist in eternity since truth has no opposites. Choice is only possible where there is the belief in separation. Choice exists in the world of perception, or provisional reality, because we believe that we are separate. Prior to the belief in separation, there was nothing outside ourselves to perceive since we were everything. Once we believed that there was something outside ourselves, time and space came into being. Time and space allow for the measure of change which results from making different choices. Perception and provisional reality were birthed because now there was something to differentiate. All parts were not perceived as equal. Time, space, perception and choice all hinge on your mistaken belief in the "authority problem." We believe we could be self-created instead of God-created. This mistaken belief made the world of separation appear real. Since these items are only mistaken beliefs in our deluded mind, we need only to reawaken from our insane dream to return to the wholeness of the Mind of God. Sin, guilt and fear are denials of love's truth and do not exist in the Mind of God.

Chapter 11. GOD OR THE EGO

Introduction

T-11.in.1. Either God or the ego is insane. 2 If you will examine the evidence on both sides fairly, you will realize **that either God or the ego is insane** and this must be true. 3 Neither God nor the ego proposes a partial thought system. 4 Each **thought system** is internally consistent, but **each thought system is** diametrically opposed in all respects so that partial allegiance is impossible. 5 Remember, too, that **each thought system's** results are as different as **each thought system's** foundations, and **each thought system's** fundamentally irreconcilable natures cannot be reconciled by vacillations between **the two thought systems**. 6 Nothing alive is Fatherless, for life is creation. 7 Therefore, your decision is always an answer to the question, "Who is my father?" 8 And you will be faithful to the father you choose

Note # 1: ACIM ask you to choose between the thought system of either God's, which is represented by the Holy Spirit, or the thought system of the little "s" self, which is represented by the ego. The ego claims that you are egoically self-created and, therefore, different from God. The Holy Spirit states that you are God's effect and, therefore, are the perfect extension of God. Due to each system's different major premise, they give opposite answers to every question asked. Both cannot be right. ACIM states that our decision-maker must choose only one.

T-11.in.2. Yet what would you say to someone who believed this question, **"Who is my father?"** really involves conflict? 2 If you made the ego, how can the ego have made you? 3 The authority problem, **which asks, "Who is my father?"** is still the only source of conflict, because the ego was made out of the wish of God's Son to father **God**. 4 The ego, then, is nothing more than a delusional system in which you made your own father. 5 Make no mistake about this **that the ego, then, is nothing more than a delusional system in which you made your own father.** 6 It sounds insane when **the ego that you made claims also to be your own father. Yet when you look at it** with perfect honesty, **this is what the ego is claiming. Because of this** the ego never looks on what **the ego** does with perfect honesty. 7 Yet that is **the ego's** insane premise **of the fatherhood of you,** which is carefully hidden in the dark cornerstone of **the ego's** thought system. 8 And either the ego, which you made, <*is*> your father, or **the ego's** whole thought system will not stand.

Note # 2: The authority problem forms the basis for the ego's thought system. It claims that you are your own creator. Being egoically self-created, the ego claims that it also will create a god in its own image. This god of the ego is a god of fear, limitation and judgment. If the ego's thought system's first premise is wrong, everything that follows logically will also be incorrect. ACIM points out that our mind made our ego and, therefore, our ego could not create our mind. Both beliefs are in conflict, which means that the egoic thought system must leave us fatherless.

T-11.in.3. You make by projection, but God creates by extension. 2 The cornerstone of God's creation is you, for **God's** thought system is light. 3 Remember the Rays that are there unseen. 4 The more you approach the center of **God's** thought system, the clearer the light becomes. 5 The closer you come to the foundation of the ego's thought system; the darker and more obscure becomes the way. 6 Yet even the little spark in your mind is enough to lighten **your mind to the way**. 7 Bring this light fearlessly with you, and bravely hold **this light** up to the foundation of the ego's thought system. 8 Be willing to judge **the ego's thought system** with perfect honesty. 9 Open the dark cornerstone of terror on which **the ego's thought system** rests, and bring **the ego's thought system** out into the light. 10 There you will see that **the ego's thought system** rested on meaninglessness, and that everything of which you have been afraid was based on nothing.

Note # 3: Projection's goal is exclusion. Creation or extension is inclusion. Creation is the process of extending all that you are to our creation. This is sharing and the extension of the Oneness. Projection is the process of trying to get rid of something you do not want. This is exclusion.
ACIM states that we need to be vigilant for God, which is truth. When we examine the thought system of the ego before the light of truth, we will discover that the ego's thought system is fundamentally flawed and needs to be discarded.

T-11.in.4. My brother, you are part of God and part of me. 2 When you have at last looked at the ego's foundation without shrinking you will also have looked upon our **foundation of your little "s" self**. 3 I come to you from our Father to offer you everything again. 4 Do not refuse **everything again** in order to keep a dark cornerstone hidden, for **the** protection **of this dark cornerstone of the ego's thought system** will not save you. 5 I give you the lamp and I will go with you. 6 You will not take this journey alone. 7 I will lead you to your true Father, Who hath need of you, as I have. 8 Will you not answer the call of love with joy?

Note # 4: Jesus asks that we follow him and the thought system of the Holy Spirit, which offers us everything. The ego's thought system promises us specialness but gives us only the false. Instead of love, we get loves opposites of sin, guilt and fear. How can we sanely perceive this exchange of our happiness for the ego's gifts as being a "good trade?"

I. The Gifts of Fatherhood

T-11.I.1.You have learned your need of healing. 2 Would you bring anything else **but healing** to the Sonship, recognizing your need of healing for yourself? 3 For in this **healing** lies the beginning of the return to knowledge. **Healing is** the foundation on which God will help build again the thought system you share with **God**. 4 Not one stone you place upon **the thought system you share with God** but will be blessed by **God**, for you will be restoring the holy dwelling place of His Son, where **God** wills His Son to be and where **His Son** is. 5 In whatever part of the mind of God's Son you restore this reality, you restore **this reality** to yourself. 6 You dwell in the Mind of God with your brother, for God Himself did not will to be alone.

Note # 5: We share the mind of the Sonship with all our brothers. If a brother and we jointly heal our fragmented split-mind, all the Sonship benefits. Healing is accomplished by choosing to follow the guidance of the Holy Spirit. Our egoic misperceptions and judgment are converted into correct perception.

T-11.I.2. To be alone is to be separated from infinity, but how can **you be separated from infinity** if infinity has no end? 2 No one can be beyond the limitless, because what has no limits must be everywhere. 3 There are no beginnings and no endings in God, Whose universe is Himself. 4 Can you exclude yourself from the universe, or from God Who <*is*> the universe? 5 I and my Father are one with you, for you are part of Us. 6 Do you really believe that part of God can be missing or lost to **God**?

Note # 6: Since God is the Oneness of everything, where could we be except in God? In a hologram, the whole is contained in each part. Because we are part of God's Oneness, we must be part of the whole. This is why the return to knowledge is based on our healing which is part of the healing of the entire Sonship. All are connect to the Oneness that is the web of life that is the Mind of God.

T-11.I.3. If you were not part of God, **God's** Will would not be unified. 2 Is this conceivable **that God's Will would not be unified**? 3 Can part of **God's** Mind contain nothing? 4 If your place in **God's** Mind cannot be filled by anyone except you, and your filling **God's Mind** was your creation, without you there would be an empty place in God's Mind. 5 Extension cannot be blocked, and **extension and God's Mind** has no voids. 5 **The extension of God's Mind** continues forever, however much **the extension of God's Mind** is denied. 7 Your denial of **the** reality of the **extension of God's Mind** may arrest **the extension of God's Mind** in time, but not in eternity. 8 That is why your creations have not ceased to be extended, and why so much is waiting for your return.

Note # 7: In time, our creations await our return to whole-mindedness. Our denial of our Oneness does not change the truth, it merely limits our total recognition of the truth. Our Big "S" Self continues to co-create while our egoic mind chooses to make images of the false. In eternity, there can be nothing missing from the Oneness of Everything since that would be a contradiction in terms. In time, we can perceive the false and imagine a void in the Oneness. Our imagination cannot make the void real. In time, we can believe something that is not true. Yet, our erroneous belief is powerless to change reality.

T-11.I.4. Waiting is possible only in time, but time has no meaning. 2 You who made delay can leave time behind simply by recognizing that neither beginnings nor endings were created by the Eternal. **God** placed no limits on His creation or upon those who create like **God.** 3 You do not know this simply because you have tried to limit what **God** created, and so you believe that all creation is limited. 4 How, then, could you know your creations, having denied infinity?

Note # 8: Time is needed until we decide to be vigilant only for truth. Time exists to allow us to imagine what it would be like to be something other than as God created us. Until we make the decision to be only love, we will continue to miscreate out of fear. Creation is extension. God's Law of Creation is to have all, give all, to all. Since we believe that we are limited, we cannot create. Making is the attempt to exclude. Extension always is inclusive. Making attempts to confirm that there is something outside of you and that it is different. Creation always includes everything since that is what the creator is. You can only extend what you are. Making attempts to give something, which you are not. This something is the belief in the separation due to your belief that you are limited. When we accept the truth of the Atonement for ourselves, we will no longer value anything that time appears to offer. Placing no value in egoic littleness, time will become functionless and disappear.

T-11.I.5. The laws of the universe do not permit contradiction. 2 What holds for God holds for you. 3 If you believe you are absent from God, you will believe that **God** is absent from you. 4 Infinity is meaningless without you, and you are meaningless without God. 5 There is no end to God and His Son, for we <are> the universe. 6 God is not incomplete, and **God** is not childless. 7 Because **God** did not will to be alone, **God** created a Son like Himself. 8 Do not deny **God** His Son, for your unwillingness to accept **God's** Fatherhood has denied you **your fatherhood**. 9 See **God's** creations as His Son, for your **creations** were created in honor of **God**. 10 The universe of love does not stop because you do not see **the universe of love**, nor have your closed eyes lost the ability to see. 11 Look upon the glory of **God's** creation, and you will learn what God has kept for you.

Note # 9: God has preserved our birthright for us. Although we can deny our birthright, we can never lose it. Our Big "S" Self, God, Our Creator, and the Holy Spirit all know the eternal truth of what we are. We can never be separate for our Source. Cause and Effect remain eternally intertwined as one Oneness of "All That Is."

T-11.I.6. God has given you a place in **God's** Mind that is yours forever. 2 Yet you can keep **your place in God's Mind** only by giving it, as **your place in God's Mind** was given you, **which is forever**. 3 Could you be alone there, when **your place in God's Mind** was given you because God did not will to be alone? 4 God's Mind cannot be lessened. 5 **God's Mind** can only be increased, for everything **God** creates has the function of creating. 6 Love does not limit, and what **love** creates is not limited. 7 To give without limit is God's Will for you, because only **to give without limit** can bring you the joy that is **God's** and that **God** wills to share with you. 8 Your love is as boundless as **God's** because **your love** <is> **God's Love**.

Note # 10: Your function is to create or extend like God, since the Sonship is created in God's exact image. We cannot be happy unless we are fulfilling our function as co-creators with God. Creation is being and thus, extending only love.

T-11.I.7. Could any part of God be without **God's** Love, and could any part of **God's** Love be contained? 2 God is your heritage, because **God's** one gift is Himself. 3 How can you give except like **God** if you would know **God's** gift to you? 4 Give, then, without limit and without end, to learn how much **God** has given you. 5 Your ability to accept **God** depends on your willingness to give as **God** gives. 6 Your fatherhood and your Father are One. 7 God wills to create, and your will is **God's Will**. 8 It follows, then, that you will to create, since your will follows from **God's Will**. 9 And being an extension of **God's** Will, your **will** must be the same **as God's Will**.

Note # 11: Only by giving all, do we experience that we have all. If we decide to accept God's love, we also have decided to give God's love. Giving and receiving are two sides of the same coin. You cannot have a one sided coin. Each half completes the other and creates a whole. Through our creation, we know ourselves to be complete and with this being a co-creator with our Father, we complete each other. Cause must have its effect and God's creations are not causeless. The only difference between the Father and Son is that God is First Cause. After this there is no difference. There is just the extension of the Oneness of "All That Is."

T-11.I.8. Yet what you will you do not know. 2 This **idea of not knowing what you will** is not strange when you realize that to deny is to "not know." 3 God's Will is that you are His Son. 4 By denying **that you are His Son,** you deny your own will, and therefore do not know what **your own will** is. 5 You must ask what God's Will is in everything, because **God's Will** is **your will**. 6 You do not know what **your will** is, but the Holy Spirit remembers **your will** for you. 7 Ask **the Holy Spirit**, therefore, what God's Will is for you, and **the Holy Spirit** will tell you your will. 8 It cannot be too often repeated that you do not know **your will is God's Will**. 9 Whenever what the Holy Spirit tells you appears to be coercive, it is only because you have not recognized your will.

Note # 12: ACIM suggests that you ask the Holy Spirit's advice, rather than asking the ego's thought system. Only the Holy Spirit knows both your illusion of limitation and the truth about the Oneness that you really are. The Holy Spirit's advice will always align your will, which is your Big "S" Self's will, with God's Will, for they are One and the same.

T-11.I.9. The projection of the ego makes it appear as if God's Will is outside yourself, and therefore **that God's Will** is not **your will**. 2 In this interpretation **of separate wills,** it seems possible for God's Will and **your will** to conflict. 3 God, then, may seem to demand of you what you do not want to give, and thus **God may seem to** deprive you of what you want. 4 Would God, Who wants only your will, be capable of this **desire to deprive you**? 5 Your will is **God's** life, which **God** has given to you. 6 Even in time you cannot live apart from **God**. 7 Sleep is not death. 8 What **God** created can sleep, but **what God created** cannot die. 9 Immortality is **God's** Will for His Son, and His Son's will for himself. 10 God's Son cannot will death for himself because his Father is life, and His Son is like **His Father**. 11 Creation is your will *<because>* **creation** is **God's Will**.

Note # 13: The ego's thought system is based on the concept of separation. It has made an entire illusionary world to entrap your mind into the belief that you are a limited ego-body. The ego will always claim that you are separate from your Father because the ego claims you are self-created and that what you created, your little "s" self, somehow could create you. The ego claims that somehow the child can create its father. Littleness cannot be the will of the Big "S" Self, which is the extension of the Creator's Will. Creation, not making, is the Sonship's will.

T-11.I.10. You cannot be happy unless you do what you will truly, and you cannot change this because **to be happy you must do your true will for this fact** is immutable. 2 **To be happy you must do your true will** is immutable by God's Will and **your will,** for otherwise **God's** Will would not be extended. 3 You are afraid to know God's Will, because you believe **God's Will** is not **your will**. 4 This belief **that God's Will is not your will** is your whole sickness and your whole fear. 5 Every symptom of sickness and fear arises **from this belief that God's Will is not your will**, because this **belief that God's Will is not your will** is the belief that makes you *<want>* not to know. 6 Believing this **belief that God's Will is not your will,** you hide in darkness, denying that the light is in you.

Note # 14: God's will is only that His Creation be happy. How can we deny that this is not our own will? The ego sacrifices our happiness so that we can pretend to be right. This is not the will of our Big "S" Self.
Sickness is any belief that we are not as God created us to be. ACIM states clearly that our belief in sickness and fear arises from our wish to deny that our will and God's Will are the same. This claim arises from our belief that we are separate and, therefore, different from how God created us. The ego claims that we could deny the Will of God, which is only that we be happy. The ego argues that the changeless and eternal could be changed. It argues for our littleness and that we could be something other than perfect, whole and complete. How can this claim for littleness make you happy? Would you rather be happy or "right?"

T-11.I.11. You are asked to trust the Holy Spirit only because **the Holy Spirit** speaks for you. 2 **The Holy Spirit** is the Voice for God, but never forget that God did not will to be alone. 3 **God** shares His Will with you; **God** does not thrust **His Will** upon you. 4 Always remember that what **God** gives **God** keeps, so that nothing **God** gives can contradict **God**. 5 You who share **God's** life must share **God's**

Will to know **God's life**, for sharing *<is>* knowing. 6 Blessed are you who learn that to hear the Will of your Father is to know your own **will**. 7 For it is your will to be like **God**, Whose Will it is that it be so **that you are like your Father**. 8 God's Will is that His Son be One, and united with Him in His Oneness. 9 That is why healing is the beginning of the recognition that your will is **God's Will**.

Note # 15: To know is to be. This world of separation was made to keep God's love out. The Holy Spirit has transformed the world of perception into a learning device in which we relearn what we really are. Here in time and space, we can reawaken to what it feels like to be only love. Since the world of perception allows for both love and the illusion of fear to exist side by side, it allows our decision-maker the choice of freely choosing between love and fear. The choice for love is the decision to create. The decision for fear only miscreates or makes. We remember God when we choose to co-create like and with Him. To be like your Father is to create like the Father. The only difference between the Sonship and the Father is that the Father came first. We, as God's Children, can create our own "children," who in turn can create their own "children." In this way we are like the Father, but we cannot be father to ourselves. This egoic idea in self-creation is the underlying belief that results in the "authority problem." It states that somehow a child can create or be his own parent.

II. The Invitation to Healing

T-11.II.1. If sickness is separation, the decision to heal and to be healed is the first step toward recognizing what you truly want, **which is to be one will with God's Will**. 2 Every attack is a step away from **what you truly want**, and every healing thought brings **what you truly want** closer. 3 The Son of God *<has>* both Father and Son, because **the Son of God** *<is>* both Father and Son. 4 To unite *<having>* and *<being>* is to unite your will with **God's Will**, for **God** wills you Himself. 5 And you will yourself to **God** because, in your perfect understanding of **God**, you know there is but one Will. 6 Yet when you attack any part of God and His Kingdom your understanding is not perfect, and what you really want is therefore lost to you.

Note # 16: Sickness is any belief that we are not one with God. Anytime we have thoughts that contradict the truth that we are perfect, whole and complete, our mind is in need of healing. It has slipped into fear-based thoughts and doubts about our own nature as unlimited spirit. Whole-mindedness is not intellectual egoic thinking that we are one. Instead, whole-mindedness is being One. It is being a co-participant with God in the dance of creation. It is our being a conduit for only love.

T-11.II.2. Healing thus becomes a lesson in understanding, and the more you practice **healing** the better teacher and learner you become. 2 If you have denied truth, what better witnesses to **truth's** reality could you have than those who have been healed by **truth's reality**? 3 But be sure to count yourself among **the healed**, for in your willingness to join **the healed** is your healing accomplished. 4 Every miracle that you accomplish speaks to you of the Fatherhood of God. 5 Every healing thought that you accept, either from your brother or in your own mind, teaches you that you are God's Son. 6 In every hurtful thought you hold, wherever you perceive **a hurtful thought,** lies the denial of God's Fatherhood and of your Sonship.

Note # 17: To heal is to accept the truth that God is the First Cause and that we are His Effect. An effect cannot change its cause and Cause and Effect are inseparable, forever joined as one. We also need to be clear that like begets like and thus, being God's creation we must also replicate God's creation, which is the extension of the Oneness of the Mind of God. Creation is extension. We, God's Effect, complete our Cause when we freely join in the co-creative process with God. Creating like Our Father is the demonstration that extension, not separation, of the Oneness is the only reality within the Oneness of the Mind of God.

T-11.II.3. And denial is as total as love. 2 You cannot deny part of yourself, because the rest **of yourself** will seem to be separate and therefore without meaning. 3 And **the rest of yourself** being without meaning to you, you will not understand **yourself**. 4 To deny meaning is to fail to understand. 5 You can heal only yourself, for only God's Son needs healing. 6 You need **healing** because you do not understand yourself, and therefore know not what you do. 7 Having forgotten your will, you do not know what you really want.

Note # 18: The split-minded have moved into a state of doubt. Our Big "S" Self knows what it is. It operates from an "I AM" State of consciousness. The egoic little "s" self has moved into the questioning state. Instead of just being the "I AM" State, the ego is in the "What AM I?" state. The ego is the state of mind that claims it does not know that your will and God's will are the same. Since the split-minded have forgotten that they are the Effect of their Creator, they fail to remember their true Source and deny their shared Oneness in the holographic Mind of God.

T-11.II.4. Healing is a sign that you want to make whole. 2 And this willingness **to make whole** opens your ears to the Voice of the Holy Spirit, Whose message is wholeness. 3 **The Voice of the Holy Spirit** will enable you to go far beyond the healing you would undertake, for beside your small willingness to make whole **the Voice of the Holy Spirit** will lay **the Holy Spirit's** Own complete Will and make **your will** whole. 4 What can the Son of God not accomplish with the Fatherhood of God in him? 5 And yet the invitation **to invite the Fatherhood of God back in him** must come from you, for you have surely learned that whom you invite as your guest will abide with you.

Note # 19: The Holy Spirit will help you heal your split-mind and return it to wholeness or right-mindedness. The Holy Spirit cannot do this task alone. It requires that you ask or invite Its assistance. Once invited to be your guide, the Holy Spirit cannot fail in Its mission for that is the One Will that we share with our Father.

T-11.II.5. The Holy Spirit cannot speak to an unwelcoming host, because **the Holy Spirit** will not be heard. 2 The Eternal Guest remains, but **the Holy Spirit's** Voice grows faint in alien company. 3 **The Holy Spirit** needs your protection, only because your care is a sign that you want **the Holy Spirit**. 4 Think like **the Holy Spirit** ever so slightly, and the little spark becomes a blazing light that fills your mind so that **the Holy Spirit** becomes your only Guest. 5 Whenever you ask the ego to enter, you lessen **the Holy Spirit's** welcome. 6 **The Holy Spirit** will remain, but you have allied yourself against **the Holy Spirit**. 7 Whatever journey you choose to take, **the Holy Spirit** will go with you, waiting. 8 You can safely trust **the Holy Spirit's** patience, for **the Holy Spirit** cannot leave a part of God. 9 Yet you need far more than patience.

Note # 20: The Holy Spirit always remains a part of you, but you must ask for His guidance and then silence the voice for the ego. Without quieting the voice of the ego, we will not hear or heed the wisdom of the Holy Spirit. The Holy Spirit's home is our Big "S" Self and It will not and cannot leave Its host, our Christ Self. Being only part of the indivisible Oneness, where could It go? The Holy Spirit will wait patiently until the split-minded are tired of their game of separation and ask to be returned and reawakened in their home, which is the Kingdom. Upon awakening, the now whole-minded will realize that they had never left their home, which is the shared Oneness of the Mind of God.

T-11.II.6. You will never rest until you know your function and fulfill **your function**, for only in **knowing your function** can your will and your Father's **Will** be wholly joined. 2 To have **God** is to be like **God**, and **God** has given Himself to you. 3 You who have God must be as God, for **God's** function became yours with **God's** gift. 4 Invite this knowledge back into your mind, and let nothing that obscures **knowing your function** enter **your mind**. 5 The Guest Whom God sent you will teach you how to do this, if you but recognize the little spark and are willing to let **the little spark** grow. 6 Your willingness need not be perfect, **because God's witness, the Holy Spirit**, is **perfect**. 7 If you will merely offer **the Holy Spirit** a little place, **the Holy Spirit** will lighten **this little place** so much that you will gladly let **this little place** be increased. 8 And by this increase, you will begin to remember creation.

<u>Note # 21:</u> Being an extension of God, we must fulfill our now shared function with God. This shared function is to co-create with God. The Holy Spirit will heal the split-minded so that the Sonship will know Himself and resume His rightful place as a conduit for love. By extending what we are, which is only love; we partake in the creative process.

T-11.II.7. Would you be hostage to the ego or host to God? 2 You will accept only whom you invite. 3 You are free to determine who shall be your guest, and how long he shall remain with you. 4 Yet this **freedom to determine who shall be your guest and for how long** is not real freedom, for **who shall be your guest** still depends on how you see it. 5 The Holy Spirit is there, although **the Holy Spirit** cannot help you without your invitation. 6 And the ego is nothing, whether you invite **the ego** in or not. 7 Real freedom depends on welcoming reality, and of your guests only the Holy Spirit is real. 8 Know, then, **the Holy Spirit** Who abides with you merely by recognizing what is there already, and do not be satisfied with imaginary comforters **like the ego**, for the Comforter of God is in you.

<u>Note # 22:</u> Only the Holy Spirit is real and, therefore, the only real choice you can ultimately make is to choose reality. The choice to follow the thought system of the ego is a choice for illusion and thus, is not a real choice. Any choice for an illusion is no choice since an illusion is powerless to change reality. Since illusions are nothing and not real, the choice to maintain an illusion is a choice for nothing. Nothingness is not a replacement for the truth of reality. Reality is everything since it is truth. The Holy Spirit, not an illusion, is real.

III. From Darkness to Light

T-11.III.1. When you are weary, remember you have hurt yourself. 2 Your Comforter, **the Holy Spirit**, will rest you, but you cannot **rest yourself**. 3 You do not know how **to rest**, for if you did **know how**, you could never have grown weary. 4 Unless you hurt yourself you could never suffer in any way, for that **you be hurt** is not God's Will for His Son. 5 Pain is not of **God**, for **God** knows no attack and **God's** peace surrounds you silently. 6 God is very quiet, for there is no conflict in **God**. 7 Conflict is the root of all evil, for being blind **conflict** does not see whom **conflict** attacks, **which is truth and our Big "S" Self**. 8 Yet **conflict** always attacks the Son of God, and the Son of God is you.

Note # 23: Conflict is failing to align our split mind's thoughts with our shared will with God's. Conflict is the result of this misalignment and is the source of all "evil." When we fail to be our true Big "S" Self's will, we attack ourselves. We are out of alignment with our true spiritual nature of what we are. An attack on any brother is an attack upon both ourselves and the entire oneness of the Sonship.

T-11.III.2. God's Son is indeed in need of comfort, for **God's Son** knows not what **God's Son** does, believing **God's Son's** will is not his own. 2 The Kingdom is **the Son of God's kingdom**, and yet **God's Son** wanders homeless. 3 At home in God, **God's Son** is lonely, and amid all his brothers **God's Son** is friendless. 4 Would God let His Son **be lonely and could** this be real, when **God** did not will to be alone Himself? 5 And if your will is **God's Will, to be alone** cannot be true of you, because **to be alone** is not true of **God**.

Note # 24: We are not at home in the world of time, space and perception. It is not God's will that we should attempt to hide from our Creator. God asks his prodigal Son to return to the knowledge of the Oneness of all there is.

T-11.III.3.O my child, if you knew what God wills for you, your joy would be complete! 2 And what **God** wills has happened, for **God's Will** was always true. 3 When the light comes and you have said, "God's Will is mine." you will see such beauty that you will know **the light** is not of you. 4 Out of your joy you will create beauty in **God's** Name, for your joy could no more be contained than **God's joy.** 5 The bleak little world will vanish into nothingness, and your heart will be so filled with joy that **your heart** will leap into Heaven, and into the Presence of God. 6 I cannot tell you what this will be like, for your heart is not ready. 7 Yet I can tell you, and remind you often, that what God wills for Himself **God** wills for you, and what **God** wills for you is your **will**.

Note # 25: The "light is not of you" means that the light does not come from your limited ego, but rather your shared Oneness with the Creator. All of our powers flow from our Source.

T-11.III.4. The way is not hard, but **the way** <is> very different. 2 Yours is the way of pain, of which God knows nothing 3 That way, **your way of pain**, is hard indeed, and very lonely. 4 Fear and grief are your guests, and **fear and grief** go with you and abide with you on the way. 5 But the dark journey is not the way of God's Son. 6 Walk in light and do not see the dark companions **of fear and grief**, for **fear and grief** are not fit companions for the Son of God, who was created <of> light and <in> light. 7 The Great Light always surrounds you and shines out from you. 8 How can you see the dark companions **of fear and grief** in a light such as this? 9 If you see **fear and grief**, it is only because you are denying the light. 10 But deny **fear and grief** instead, for the light is here and the way is clear.

Note # 26: We walk with our brother on our journey home. The direction in which we walk depends on which thought system we choose to follow. Do we value the light of truth or the darkness of fear and the false?

T-11.III.5. God hides nothing from His Son, even though His Son would hide himself. 2 Yet the Son of God cannot hide his glory, for God wills **His Son** to be glorious, and gave **His Son** the light that shines in **His Son**. 3 You will never lose your way, for God leads you. 4 When you wander, you but undertake a journey that is not real. 5 The dark companions **of fear and grief, this** dark way **you wander alone**, are all illusions. 6 Turn toward the light, for the little spark in you is part of a light so great that this **little spark of light in you** can sweep you out of all darkness forever. 7 For your Father <is> your Creator, and you <are> like **your Father**.

Note # 27: We can choose to follow our Big "S" Self and the guidance of the Holy Spirit. By following the Voice for God, the darkness of our egoic world of fear and illusions will fade away. Darkness fades way before the light of truth. Our Big "S" Self represents this truth about what we are.

T-11.III.6. The children of light cannot abide in darkness, for darkness is not in **God's children**. 2 Do not be deceived by the dark comforters **of fear and grief**, and never let **fear and grief** enter the mind of God's Son, for **fear and grief** have no place in **God's** temple. 3 When you are tempted to deny **God** remember that there <*are*> no other gods to place before **God**, and accept **God's** Will for you in peace. 4 For you cannot accept **God's Will for you** otherwise. **For God's Will for you comes only in your own peace.**

Note # 28: God's temple is you, the Sonship, as God created it, perfect, whole and complete. Fear and grief are cornerstones of the egoic thought system. When we follow our ego, we lose our inner peace because our split-mind is in conflict.

T-11.III.7. Only God's Comforter, **the Holy Spirit**, can comfort you. 2 In the quiet of God's temple, **the Holy Spirit** waits to give you the peace that is yours. 3 Give **the Holy Spirit's** peace, that you may enter the temple and find **God's peace** waiting for you. 4 But be holy in the Presence of God, or you will not know that you are there **in God's temple**. 5 For what is unlike God cannot enter **God's** Mind, because **what is unlike God** was not **God's** Thought and therefore does not belong to **God's Mind**. 6 And your mind must be as pure as **God's Mind**, if you would know what belongs to you. 7 Guard carefully **God's** temple, for **God** Himself dwells there and abides in peace. 8 You cannot enter God's Presence with the dark companions **of fear and grief** beside you, but you also cannot enter alone. 9 All your brothers must enter with you, for until you have accepted **all your brothers** <*you*> cannot enter **God's temple**. 10 For you cannot understand wholeness unless you are whole, and no part of the Son can be excluded if he would know the Wholeness of his Father.

Note # 29: We need to forgive our brothers and view all parts of the Sonship as perfect if we are to know our own wholeness. To be holy is to be whole, for that is how God creates. Creation is extension. God created us in His image, therefore, like our Father, all the Sonship is perfect, whole and complete. God's temple is His creation. We are God's temple. When we believe that we are separate from God's Will, we place the false idols of our ego into our split-mind. Our split-mind becomes the home for the false egoic gods we chose to worship.

God's Temple and our temple are not places. Like everything else that is real, the term temple refers back to mind. God's creation is God's thoughts. Only ideas, not form, can be shared. The Holy Spirit is also a thought of God. The Holy Spirit is the thought within our mind that remembers God's thoughts. God's thoughts are only love, joy, peace and Oneness. The Mind of God is our temple as it is the Home of God and the Holy Spirit. Where else could thoughts be at home except in the mind that thinks them? When we have thoughts other than God's thoughts, we are in conflict, pain and separation. Due to our free will, we have chosen to place blocks before the thoughts of God. These blocks are the thought system of the egoic separation. Remember, although we speak of the ego like it is a "bad thing," the ego is only a group of thoughts that we currently utilize in time and space to define how we perceive ourselves. When we choose to define ourselves based on the thought system of the Holy Spirit, our "ego" does not really "disappear." Instead, we choose to define ourselves as God knows us, which is only love, joy, peace and Oneness. As long as perception exists, our decision-maker will determine what thoughts we will call into our awareness. When we are vigilant only for God, we only hold thoughts of love, joy, peace and oneness in our mind's awareness. This is the happy dream. From this state of mind, God will take the final step and return the Sonship to knowledge. Knowledge is certain. It is beyond perception since it does not involve thinking and choice. There is no conflict since knowledge just knows what is. Our mind and God's mind are One Will and One Mind.

T-11.III.8. In your mind you can accept the whole Sonship and bless **the whole Sonship** with the light your Father gave **the whole Sonship**. 2 Then you will be worthy to dwell in the temple with God, because it is your will not to be alone. 3 God blessed His Son forever. 4 If you will bless **the whole Sonship** in time, you will be in eternity. 5 Time cannot separate you from God if you use **time** on behalf of the eternal.

<u>Note # 30:</u> We bless our brothers when we drop all our grievances and forgive our brothers of any wrong that we believe they have done to us. By utilizing time to grant forgiveness to our brothers, we also grant forgiveness to ourselves. By granting forgiveness to all, we remember that we are eternally One, created perfect, whole and complete. In this remembering of our true nature, we remember God and time has served its purpose. We recall that we are God's temple and thus, reclaim our birthright as a Child of God. We return to the Oneness of God, which is our eternal reality. In the Mind of God, we have never left the Oneness. Our little "s" self has merely dreamed that our oneness had been shattered when it imagined that God's Son had denied God's Love. This dream of separation arose from our decision to experience thoughts that were not of God. We chose to believe that conflict, pain and separation were possible and thus, made them real within our now perceived split-mind. Since these thoughts are not of the Mind of God, they are only thoughts held in our imaginations. These fear-based thoughts are not shared with God and thus, are not real. We need to drop all fears and judgments and reawaken from our illusionary world of provisional reality and enter into the truth of the Kingdom. In truth, the Sonship stands united with the Oneness we call the Mind of God.

IV. The Inheritance of God's Son

T-11.IV.1. Never forget that the Sonship is your salvation, for the Sonship is your **Big "S" Self**. 2 As God's creation, **the Sonship, your Big "S" Self and salvation** is yours, and belonging to you. **The Sonship, your Big "S" Self and salvation** is **God, the One Self**. 3 Your **Big "S"** Self does not need salvation, but your mind needs to learn what salvation is. 4 You are not saved <*from*> anything, but you are saved <*for*> glory. 5 Glory is your inheritance, given you by your Creator that you might extend **glory**. 6 Yet if you hate part of your Self all your understanding is lost, because you are looking on what God created as yourself without love. 7 And since what **God** created is part of **God**, you are denying **God** His place in **God's** Own altar.

<u>Note # 31:</u> There is but One Self. This is the oneness of "All That Is." This One Self is the united Sonship. It is our Christ or Big "S" Self. It is the face of God. They are One Self, indivisible and never changing. All parts once perceived as separate are now known as One. Because we perceive ourselves to exist in a dualistic world, ACIM must refer to them as if they are separate but this is only to aid in our understanding. In the Kingdom, there is but truth and that truth is the One Self and we are that One. Nothing exists outside or beyond the One Self for It is everywhere and everything.

T-11.IV.2. Could you try to make God homeless and know that you are at home? 2 Can the Son deny the Father without believing that the Father has denied **the Son**? 3 God's laws hold only for your protection, and **God's laws** never hold in vain. 4 What you experience when you deny your Father is still for your protection, for the power of your will cannot be lessened without the intervention of God against **your will**, and any limitation on your power is not the Will of God. 5 Therefore, look only to the power that God gave to save you, remembering that **the power that God gave to save you** is yours <*because*> **the power that God gave to save you** is **God's power**, and join with your brothers in **God's** peace.

Note # 32: God's Will protects us even when we appear to be trapped in our dream world of provisional reality. God has insured that we will reawaken by placing the call of the Holy Spirit's thought system in our split mind. The acceptance of the Atonement for ourselves is the means in which we recover what we really are, a capital "S" Self.

Our denial of God made our imagined world of provisional reality real to us. Even in this illusion of suffering, pain and separation, we are protected by our Father's Will. By allowing us to play our game of separation, God has protected our absolute freedom. God does not allow the illusion to become real in His Mind so He has protected our divine birthright. If God's Will had not "trumped" our own desire, we would have made the illusion of separation real and condemned ourselves into everlasting limitation. God did not take our illusion seriously and, therefore, we could not share the illusion with God and make it real. Due to God's Laws or God's Will, ideas that remain unshared are not real and thus, are not so. The error in thinking that we could be different from our Cause was not allowed to be raised to the level of reality or knowledge. If this error had been accepted as part of the Mind of God, the error would have been elevated to the status of knowledge and thus, it would have made sin real. The error of our mistaken identity occurred only at the level of perception. It remained only an error that is only a mistake and just requires correction in the mind of the thinker. The Holy Spirit, God's Voice, simply asks the thinking Sonship to choose again thus, correcting their erroneous thought. Because of this, in God's Mind there was no harm and therefore, no foul. God's Creation remains sinless and guiltless.

T-11.IV.3. Your peace lies in **your Big "S" Self's** limitlessness. 2 Limit the peace you share, and your **Big "S"** Self must be unknown to you. 3 Every altar to God is part of you, because the light **God** created is one with **God**. 4 Would you cut off a brother from the light that is yours? 5 You would not do so if you realized that you can darken only your own mind. 6 As you bring **a brother** back **to the light**, so will you return **to the light that is yours.** 7 That is the law of God, for the protection of the Wholeness of His Son.

Note # 33: The law of God is that what you give, you will receive. Give forgiveness to your brother and you get forgiveness for yourself. All of the parts of the Sonship are connected. Just as the Sonship is One with the Father, we are united as one with the Sonship. There is just the One Self.

T-11.IV.4. <*Only you can deprive yourself of anything.*> 2 Do not oppose this realization **that** *only you* **can deprive yourself of anything**, for **this realization that only you can deprive yourself of anything** is truly the beginning of the dawn of light. 3 Remember also that the denial of this simple fact that **only you can deprive yourself of anything** takes many forms, and these **many forms** you must learn to recognize and to oppose steadfastly, without exception. 4 **Your steadfast opposition of any form of denial that only you can deprive yourself of anything** is a crucial step in the reawakening. 5 The beginning phases of this reversal **and the realization that you are the source of all you experience** are often quite painful, for as blame is withdrawn from without, there is a strong tendency to harbor **blame** within. 6 It is difficult at first to realize that this is exactly the same thing, for there is no distinction between **blame** within and **blame** without.

Note # 34: Reclaiming the realization that you have the power to project your thoughts outside yourself and into your own illusionary world of provisional reality is critical for remembering who you are. Until you accept responsibility for your world of provisional reality, you believe that you are a victim of some outside force beyond your control. Only by reclaiming the mind's decision-making ability can you move out of victim consciousness, which is where the ego's thought system is designed to entrap you. When you do finally realize that only you can deprive yourself of anything, you will need to guard against shifting the guilt you normally associate with being limited, which is defined as sin, from someone outside you, to yourself. As long as you believe guilt must be associated with your experiences, you will remain trapped in the ego's world of victim consciousness. All blame must disappear if we are to reclaim our unlimited power that God gave to us.

Because of our belief that we have sinned against God, we use egoic projection to get rid of our own guilt and blame it on our brother. Blaming another is less painful to the split-minded than blaming ourselves. When you realize that you are 100% responsible for all that you call into your experience, blaming another becomes impossible. Yet, since you still believe you have sinned, you now must turn upon yourself and place the blame upon yourself. The blame you felt for another now becomes the guilt you feel towards yourself. This blaming yourself will feel worse than blaming your brother. You cannot escape this guilt until you accept the fact that you are not a body and that your belief in sin is not justified since the body is not real. When you disassociate your experience from all judgments of good and bad, sin no longer has any basis for reality. This is why sin is a preeminent player in the thought system of the ego and is nonexistent in the thought system of the Holy Spirit.

T-11.IV.5. If your brothers are part of you and you blame **your brothers** for your deprivation, you are blaming yourself. 2 And you cannot blame yourself without blaming **your brothers**. 3 That is why blame must be undone, not seen elsewhere. 4 Lay **blame upon** yourself and you cannot know yourself, for only the ego blames at all. 5 Self-blame is therefore ego identification, **and, therefore, self-blame is** as much an ego defense as blaming others. 6 <*You cannot enter God's Presence if you attack His Son.*> 7 When His Son lifts his voice in praise of his Creator, he will hear the Voice for his Father. 8 Yet the Creator cannot be praised without His Son, for Their glory is shared and **Father and Son** are glorified together.

Note # 35: When we place blame on our brother or ourselves, we are placing our allegiance with the ego's thought system. We are denying our divine birthright and, therefore, claiming that our Father was not our Creator. Any blame or guilt is a denial of our unlimited nature. Blame is associated with sin and if sin is real, it requires punishment for someone must judge and demand retribution. God and the thought system of the Holy Spirit deny the existence of sin. Without sin there is no blame.

T-11.IV.6. Christ, **your Big "S" Self**, is at God's altar, waiting to welcome His Son. 2 But come wholly without condemnation, for otherwise you will believe that the door is barred and you cannot enter. 3 The door is not barred, and it is impossible that you cannot enter the place where God would have you be. 4 But love yourself with the Love of Christ, for so does your Father love you. 5 You can refuse to enter **God's altar**, but you cannot bar the door that Christ holds open. 6 Come unto me who holds **the door to God's altar** open for you, for while I live **the door to God's altar** cannot be shut, and I live forever. 7 God is my life and yours, and nothing is denied by God to His Son.

Note # 36: God's altar is the Christ in you. The Sonship is God's creation, as God created It. We are the One Self and can do nothing to change that truth. When following our ego, we can and do deny the Christ within us. This denial takes the form of condemnation of any part of the Sonship. Deny the Christ in anyone and you deny it in yourself. This means that you have refused to accept the Atonement for yourself.

T-11.IV.7. At God's altar Christ waits for the restoration of Himself in you. 2 God knows His Son as wholly blameless as Himself, and **God and the Christ** is approached through the appreciation of His Son. 3 Christ waits for your acceptance of Him as yourself, and of Christ's Wholeness as yours. 4 For Christ is the Son of God, Who lives in His Creator and shines with **God's** glory. 5 Christ is the extension of the Love and the loveliness of God, as perfect as His Creator and at peace with Him.

Note # 37: We, the Big "S" Self, are the Christ, which is one with the Father. We share in all the Father's attributes since extension of the totality of God, Himself, is the law of creation. We can deny we are this Oneness, but our denial can never change the truth. We remain eternally as God created us. Accepting the Atonement for ourselves is all we need do to reclaim our Oneness. Blame, sin guilt and fear are all removed by this acceptance. We reclaim our divine birthright as the One Self.

T-11.IV.8. Blessed is the Son of God whose radiance is of his Father, and whose glory he wills to share as his Father shares **glory** with him. 2 There is no condemnation in the Son, for there is no condemnation in the Father. 3 Sharing the perfect Love of the Father the Son must share what belongs to Him, for otherwise he will not know the Father or the Son. 4 Peace be unto you who rest in God, and in whom the whole Sonship rests.

Note # 38: There is no condemnation in the Father since the Father only knows His Son as perfect, whole and complete. The Sonship is God's creation and always remains eternally perfect as God created Him. When we accept the Atonement for ourselves, we grant the Atonement to all the Sonship. We share the Atonement with our brother. Loving thoughts can be shared with God and our brother. This is extension or co-creation with God. To have all, we must give all to all. This is the fulfilling of our function as co-creator and the achieving of our destiny, which is the peace of God.

V. The "Dynamics" of the Ego

T-11.V.1. No one can escape from illusions unless he looks at **illusions,** for not looking **at illusions** is the way **illusions** are protected. 2 There is no need to shrink from illusions, for **illusions** cannot be dangerous. 3 We are ready to look more closely at the ego's thought system because together we have the lamp that will dispel **the illusions of the ego's thought system.** And since you realize you do not want **the ego's thought system,** you must be ready. 4 Let us be very calm **in looking at the ego's thought system since** in doing this, for we are merely looking honestly for truth. 5 The "dynamics" of the ego will be our lesson for a while, for we must look first at **the "dynamics" of the ego** to see beyond **the ego,** since you have made **the ego** real. 6 We will undo this error **of making the ego real** quietly together, and then look beyond **this error of making the ego real** to **the** truth.

Note # 39: If we refuse to examine the validity of our beliefs, we will never be able to move beyond them. Jesus asks that together we examine the beliefs of the egoic thought system objectively without first assuming that what we are to examine must be true. We will examine it under the light of Truth and see if it can stand up to cross-examination from Jesus.

T-11.V.2. What is healing but the removal of all that stands in the way of knowledge? 2 And how else can one dispel illusions except by looking at **illusions** directly, without protecting **illusions**? 3 Be not afraid, therefore, for what you will be looking at **in an illusion** is the source of fear, and you are beginning to learn that fear is not real **for fear is based on only illusions**. 4 You are also learning that

fear's effects can be dispelled merely by denying **the illusion's** reality. 5 The next step is obviously to recognize that what has no effects does not exist. 6 Laws do not operate in a vacuum, and what leads to nothing has not happened. 7 If reality is recognized by **reality's** extension, what leads to nothing could not be real. 8 Do not be afraid, then, to look upon fear, for **illusions** cannot be seen. 9 Clarity undoes confusion by definition, and to look upon darkness through light must dispel **confusion.**

Note # 40: Jesus states that we must not be afraid to look upon our fears. Fear arises from lack of knowledge and our raising of false beliefs into misperceptions of reality. Illusions are not real since they have no effect on the reality of truth. Examine your fears with the knowledge that you are unlimited, invulnerable spirit and your fears will be dispelled. If they disappear when confronted by Truth, they are powerless and, thus, must be nothing.

T-11.V.3. Let us begin this lesson in "ego dynamics" by understanding that the term, **"ego dynamics,"** itself does not mean anything. 2 **"Ego dynamics"** contains the very contradiction in terms that makes it meaningless. 3 "Dynamics" implies the power to do something, and the whole separation fallacy lies in the belief that the ego <*has*> the power to do anything. 4 The ego is fearful to you because you believe **in the fallacy that the ego <has> the power to do something.** 5 Yet the truth is very simple:

6 *All power is of God.*
7 *What is not of* **God** *has no power to do anything.*

Note # 41: Since God did not create the ego the ego is powerless. We made the ego rather than created the ego. The egoic little "s" self was made out of fear born from our belief that we were separate and limited. Thus, the ego rests upon the false premise of separation and can only be a witness to the false. The false cannot be real and is powerless to change the Truth. The ego is a symbol for this fallacy that we have made up about ourselves. It can have no reality except in the mind of the insane who claim they do not know what they are.

T-11.V.4. When we look at the ego, then, we are not considering dynamics but delusions. 2 You can surely regard a delusional system without fear, for a **delusional system** cannot have any effects if **the delusional system's** source is not real. **The ego's delusional system cannot be real since the egoic little "s" self is not real.** 3 Fear becomes more obviously inappropriate if you recognize the ego's goal, which is so clearly senseless that any effort on **the egoic goal's** behalf is necessarily expended on nothing. 4 The ego's goal is quite explicitly ego autonomy. 5 From the beginning, then, **the ego's** purpose is to be separate, sufficient unto itself and independent of any power except **the ego's** own. 6 This is why **the ego** is the symbol of separation.

Note # 42: Ego autonomy is the belief that the ego is self-created and has power independent of God. It is the belief that the ego, rather than God, is the source of our power. It is the belief that the ego, which was made by your own mind, has power over its own source. Ego autonomy is part of the authority problem. The ego, our mind's effect, claims that it is self-created and that the mind's effect, which is the ego, now controls its maker. Ego autonomy claims that the effect has somehow usurped the power of its creator and that the effect now is the creator of its cause. The ego claims that effect is now cause and cause, your mind, is now the ego's effect.

T-11.V.5. Every idea has a purpose, and **every idea's** purpose is always the natural outcome of what **the idea** is. 2 Everything that stems from the ego is the natural outcome of **the ego's** central belief **of ego autonomy.** The way to undo **the** results **in the ego's central belief of ego autonomy** is merely to recognize that **the source of the belief, the ego,** is not natural, being out of accord with your true nature.

3 I said before that to will contrary to God is wishful thinking and **is** not real willing. 4 **God's** Will is One <*because*> the extension of **God's** Will cannot be unlike itself. 5 The real conflict you experience, then, is between the ego's idle wishes and the Will of God, which you share. 6 Can **an idle wish of the unreal ego** be a real conflict **to the Will of God**?

Note # 43: ACIM states that since ego autonomy is based off the false premise that the ego has the power of self-creation, it is an illusion that can have no effect on realty. Ego autonomy defies our spiritual nature. The fantasy of ego autonomy is an illusion of nothing and cannot oppose God's Will. Since it is not real, ego autonomy cannot conflict with God's will and should not be perceived as fearful, but rather laughable. The thought of separation was not a problem. The problem arose when God's Son took the illusion seriously and forgot to laugh. When we forgot to laugh, we made the illusion real within our mind and fear was birthed.

T-11.V.6.Your will is the independence of creation, not of autonomy. 2 Your whole creative function lies in your complete dependence on God, Whose function **God** shares with you. 3 By **God's** willingness to share **His function of creation with you, God** became as dependent on you as you are on **God**. 4 Do not ascribe the ego's arrogance to **God** Who wills not to be independent of you. 5 **God** has included you in **God's** Autonomy. 6 Can you believe that autonomy is meaningful apart from **God**? 7 The belief in ego autonomy is costing you the knowledge of your dependence on God, in which your freedom lies. 8 The ego sees all dependency as threatening, and has twisted even your longing for God into a means of establishing itself. 9 But do not be deceived by **the ego's** interpretation of your conflict.

Note # 44: The undoing of the ego's thought system rests on our reclaiming our divine birthright of what we are, God's perfect creation, a Oneness with our Father. We need to realize that we are God-created and not self-created. By claiming our birthright, we reclaim all the power that resides in our Source. God, being real and "All That Is," is the true source of all power. Since creation is the extension of God, we have become one with our Source. To deny our Cause is to render our mind powerless to create since by our denial of our spirit nature, we refuse to give all to all. The ego is nothing. Being nothing, the ego can only give nothing. The attempt to "share" nothing cannot be creation. It can only be nothing.

T-11.V.7. The ego always attacks on behalf of separation. 2 Believing **the ego** has the power to do this **the ego** does nothing else **but attack on behalf of separation**, because **the ego's** goal of autonomy <*is*> nothing else **but an attack on behalf of separation**. 3 The ego is totally confused about reality, but **the ego** does not lose sight of **the ego's** goal **of ego autonomy**. 4 **The ego** is much more vigilant than you are, because **the ego** is perfectly certain of **the ego's** purpose **of separation by obtaining ego autonomy**. 5 You are confused because you do not recognize your **purpose is to be a creator, like your Father**.

Note # 45: The ego is single minded about its purpose. It understands that its existence rests on convincing its creator, your own mind, that the ego is the controller of your mind. If we accept the belief in egoic autonomy, we fail to maintain our One Self's goal of co-creation, which is "to make happy." We confuse our Big "S" Self's purpose with the ego's purpose of separation. The ego's goal and purpose is to claim the correctness of ego autonomy. Now within our split mind, we have two conflicting purposes. Our Big "S" Self wants to be happy and our split-minded egoic side demands to be right in its claim of egoic autonomy.

T-11.V.8. You must recognize that the last thing the ego wishes you to realize is that you are afraid of **the ego**. 2 For if the ego could give rise to fear, **fear** would diminish your independence and weaken your power. 3 Yet **the ego's** one claim to your allegiance is that **the ego** can give power to you. 4 Without this belief **that the ego can give power to you**, you would not listen to **the ego** at all. 5 How, then, can **the ego's** existence continue if you realize that, by accepting **the ego**, you are belittling yourself and depriving yourself of power?

Note # 46: Sin, guilt and fear are the "unholy trinity" which keeps the ego's thought system in power. The ego would "lose" its control over us if we realized that all three concepts are based on the fallacy of our belief in egoic separation. The goal of the ego is to advise its follower that sin, guilt and fear are not of the ego's making but that the ego has a plan that allows its followers to escape from them. Projection is one of the chief tools used by the ego to attempt to "save" us from the egoic sin, guilt and fear.

T-11.V.9. The ego can and does allow you to regard yourself as supercilious, unbelieving, "lighthearted," distant, emotionally shallow, callous, uninvolved and even desperate, but not really afraid. 2 Minimizing fear, but not **the undoing of fear**, is the ego's constant effort, and is indeed a skill at which **the ego** is very ingenious. 3 How can **the ego** preach separation without upholding **separation** through fear, and would you listen to **the ego** if you recognized **upholding separation through fear** is what **the ego** is doing?

Note # 47: Without the belief in the separation, the entire egoic thought system would fall apart along with the ego. A Oneness of everything has nothing to fear. Fear needs something outside itself to be afraid of. Since there is nothing outside the Oneness, the split-mind makes an illusionary world based on sin, guilt and fear. We fear because we believe that we lack something. The ego's plan is to help you manage your fear but not eliminate fear totally. If fear were eliminated, only the truth of our wholeness would remain. Realizing that we are unlimited and invulnerable spirit, the ego would disappear.

T-11.V.10. Your recognition that whatever seems to separate you from God is only fear, regardless of the form **the ego's idea of separation** takes and quite apart from how the ego wants you to experience **the idea of separation. Our realization that only fear separates us from God** is therefore the basic ego threat. 2 **The ego's** dream of autonomy is shaken to its foundation by this awareness **that only fear separates us from God.** 3 For though you may countenance a false idea of independence, you will not accept the cost of fear if you recognize **the price the false idea of independence brings.** 4 Yet **fear** is the cost, and the ego cannot minimize **this cost.** 5 If you overlook love you are overlooking yourself, and you, **who have overlooked God's love**, must fear unreality <because> you have denied yourself, **which is love.** 6 By believing that you have successfully attacked truth, you are believing that attack has power. 7 Very simply, then, you have become afraid of yourself, **which is love.** 8 And no one wants to find what he believes would destroy him.

Note # 48: Our belief in the ego is the result of the desire to be separate from the Oneness. It is a rejection of our true nature, which is the love that we share with our Creator. Our belief in sin, which has been defined as the lack of love, is a founding member for the rise of the ego to predominance. The ego's thought system is based on the belief in sin, which is immediately accompanied by guilt and fear. We have replace God's love, with the ego's belief that God will seek His revenge upon us. Now the true God of Love has become the ego's god of fear.
Our false belief in ego autonomy has birthed fear at the price of our true nature, which is love. The ego's goal is to keeps us from remembering our true nature. When we rediscover our true nature, we will remember our true Creator. This would result in the undoing to the ego. It is our acceptance of the ego's vision of what god is that keeps us afraid to seek God's help. When we understand that only love is real and God is love, we realize there is nothing to fear.

T-11.V.11. If the ego's goal of autonomy could be accomplished, God's purpose could be defeated, and this is impossible. 2 Only by learning what fear is can you finally learn to distinguish the possible from the impossible and the false from the true. 3 According to the ego's teaching, <*the ego's*> goal can be accomplished and God's purpose can <*not.*> 4 According to the Holy Spirit's teaching, <*only*> God's purpose can be accomplished, and **God's purpose** is accomplished already.

Note # 49: In eternity, we have never left the Mind of God. Only in the false world of provisional reality do we dream that we are separate ego-bodies. The Holy Spirit is God's representative for truth while God's Child sleeps.

T-11.V.12. God is as dependent on you as you are on **God**, because **God's** Autonomy encompasses **your autonomy**, and is therefore incomplete without **your autonomy**. 2 You can only establish your autonomy by identifying with **God,** and fulfilling your function as **your function** exists in truth. 3 The ego believes that to accomplish **the ego's** goal is happiness. 4 But it is given you to know that God's function, **which is love demonstrated in his creation, the Sonship**, is **also your function**, and happiness cannot be found apart from Your joint Will. 5 Recognize only that the ego's goal, which you have pursued so diligently, has merely brought you fear, and it becomes difficult to maintain that fear is happiness. 6 Upheld by fear, this is what the ego would have you believe. 7 Yet God's Son is not insane, and cannot believe **that fear is happiness**. 8 Let **God's Son** but recognize **that the ego's goal has brought you fear**, and **God's Son** will not accept **the ego's goal**. 9 For only the insane would choose fear in place of love, and only the insane could believe that love can be gained by attack. 10 But the sane realize that only attack could produce fear, from which the Love of God completely protects them.

Note # 50: Our safety lies in the Will of God, which protects us from our delusions about ourselves. God wills only happiness for His Son. We need to honestly examine what our years of following the egoic thought system have brought us. Has it brought us happiness and love or fear and guilt? If we are dissatisfied with the results, the Holy Spirit advises us to drop all judgment and blame, and simply choose again.

T-11.V.13. The ego analyzes; the Holy Spirit accepts. 2 The appreciation of wholeness comes only through acceptance, for to analyze means to break down or to separate out. 3 The attempt to understand totality by breaking **totality** down is clearly the characteristically contradictory approach of the ego to everything. 4 The ego believes that power, understanding and truth lie in separation, and to establish this belief **of the separation, the ego** must attack. 5 Unaware that the belief **of the separation** cannot be established, and obsessed with the conviction that separation is salvation, the ego attacks everything it perceives by breaking **everything it perceives** into small, disconnected parts, without meaningful relationships and therefore without meaning. 6 The ego will always substitute chaos for meaning, for if separation is salvation, harmony is threat.

Note # 51: The ego divides and separates to prove that the Oneness does not exist. To the ego, a whole can be broken into distinct parts that are not equal. Separation and littleness is the law of the illusionary world of the ego. Yet, the Holy Spirit knows that hidden beneath the body-form is the content of what we truly are, which is the shared Oneness of the Mind of God. Mind is thought, not form, and thus, can be shared. By sharing thought, the thought is strengthened and is extended. When thought is shared and accepted as one's own, the thought becomes one with that mind. True sharing excludes nothing and is given to all. We extend or co-create with God when we share God's thoughts. God's thoughts are love, joy, peace and Oneness. Mind is holographic in nature. In a hologram, each indivisible part contains the whole and the whole contains all parts. Indivisible wholeness is the Law of God. All God's thoughts are shared completely and thus, all parts contain the whole of God and each part is the whole of God. There is no separation. There is only the extension of the One Mind of God.

T-11.V.14. The ego's interpretations of the laws of perception are, and would have to be, the exact opposite of the Holy Spirit's **interpretations**. 2 The ego focuses on error and overlooks truth. 3 **The ego** makes real every mistake **the ego** perceives, and with characteristically circular reasoning concludes that because of the **ego's** mistake consistent truth must be meaningless. 4 The next step **the ego takes**, then, is obvious. 5 If consistent truth is meaningless, inconsistency must be true. 6 Holding error clearly in mind, and protecting what **the ego** has made real, the ego proceeds to the next step in its thought system: Error is real and truth is error.

Note # 52: The idea that error is real and that Truth is error, demonstrates the insanity of the ego's thought system. To the ego, Truth is not changeless but rather something that is arbitrarily determined by you based on your current desires and beliefs. It is the ego's mistaken belief system that results in egoic misperception that the false is true and the true is false. The entire erroneous egoic thought system needs to be discarded. Truth cannot be found within a thought system, which is built upon the false. The ego would have us believe that truth is a "sometimes thing." Sometimes truth is true and sometimes truth is false. Truth just is. Neither the ego nor we can be the arbitrators of truth. Truth belongs to God and is God.

T-11.V.15. The ego makes no attempt to understand this **insane logic that "error is real and truth is error." This insane logic** is clearly not understandable, but the ego does make every attempt to demonstrate **this insane logic that "error is real and truth is error." This attempt to demonstrate that the false is true the ego** does constantly. 2 Analyzing to attack meaning, the ego succeeds in overlooking **totality** and is left with a series of fragmented perceptions which **the ego** unifies on behalf of itself. 3 **These fragmented perceptions, which the ego unifies on behalf of itself**, then, becomes the universe **the ego** perceives. 4 And it is this **fragmented** universe which, in turn, becomes **the ego's** demonstration of its own reality.

Note # 53: By ignoring the totality of the Oneness, perception is born. Perception requires separation since there must be a perceiver and something outside to perceive. This gives rise to the birth of the ego, and the world of provisional reality. The physical world and the body are both examples of the use of form to bear "false witness" on behalf of the egoic belief that the separation is real. Provisional reality is a world in which error is made to appear real in the mind of the perceiver, while the Truth of the Oneness is now perceived as error. We misperceive ourselves as separate bodies and fail to see our true content, which is that we exist as unlimited spirit that is of One Mind. We are the thought of God, not some body-form. Thought is the content. Form is only the wrapping paper for the gift, which is the content that is inside

T-11.V.16. Do not underestimate the appeal of the ego's demonstrations to those who would listen. 2 Selective perception chooses its witnesses carefully, and **the ego's** witnesses are consistent. 3 The case for insanity is strong to the insane. 4 For reasoning ends at its beginning, and no thought system transcends its source 5 Yet reasoning without meaning cannot demonstrate anything, and those who are convinced by **reasoning without meaning** must be deluded. 6 Can the ego teach truly when **the ego** overlooks truth? 7 Can **the ego** perceive what it has denied? 8 **The ego's** witnesses do attest to its denial, but hardly to what it has denied. 9 The ego looks straight at the Father and does not see Him, for **the ego** has denied His Son.

Note # 54: The ego's major premise is the false belief in the separation and self-creation. If its major premise is false, any other conclusion that would be based on the major premise would not necessarily be true. If at the beginning of a system of logic, the original premise is false, we need to disregard the entire thought system that follows. The ego's thought system is false because the major premise upon which it is based is false. The ego denies both the truth of what God is and what God's creation is. Thus, the ego will never see that They are One. Cause and Effect cannot be separated yet; the ego denies that you are God's Effect. The ego fragments, separates than judges a part that is inseparable from the whole. The ego attempts to separate Cause from Effect. Each cannot be understood without the other for each completes the other. They form different sides of the same coin. Yet, you cannot have one without the other. There are inseparable in their wholeness and oneness.

T-11.V.17. Would *<you>* remember the Father? 2 Accept **God's** Son and you will remember **the Father**. 3 Nothing can demonstrate that **God's** Son is unworthy, for nothing can prove that a lie is true. 4 What you see of **God's** Son through the eyes of the ego is a demonstration that **God's** Son does not exist, yet where the Son is the Father must be. 5 Accept what God does not deny, and it will demonstrate its truth. 6 The witnesses for God stand in **the Son of God's** light and behold what **God** created. 7 Their silence is the sign that **the witnesses for God** have beheld God's Son, and in the Presence of Christ they need demonstrate nothing, for Christ speaks to **the witnesses for God** of Himself and of His Father. 8 **The witnesses for God** are silent because Christ speaks to them, and it is His words they speak.

Note # 55: The true witness for the Son of God knows and recognizes the Christ that is the very essence of the Sonship. The Holy Spirit is the bridge that is aware of our dream world of provisional reality and also, that of our true nature is mind or spirit. This is why it is important to request guidance from the Holy Spirit to reinterpret the "event" that occurred in our dream world of provisional reality. Without Its assistance, we would believe the false witness of the ego's thought system. The Christ or the Holy Spirit does not attack the ego's witnesses, for to attack is to make real. Instead, They merely deny and look past the ego's misperception of form and observe the content. They know that only love is real and, therefore, ask, "What would love have me do?" Love extends and thus, co-creates with God.

T-11.V.18. Every brother you meet becomes a witness for Christ or for the ego, depending on what you perceive in **your brother**. 2 Everyone convinces you of what you want to perceive, and of the reality of the kingdom you have chosen for your vigilance. 3 Everything you perceive is a witness to the thought system **that** you want to be true. 4 Every brother has the power to release you, if you choose to be free. 5 You cannot accept false witness of **your brother** unless you have evoked false witnesses against **your brother**. 6 If **your brother** speaks not of Christ to you, you spoke not of Christ to **your brother**. 7 You hear but your own voice, and if Christ speaks through you, you will hear **Christ**.

Note # 56: Which thought system we value will determine how we perceive another's testimony. Our purpose will determine what we are willing to perceive. Each event and witness will give testimony to support the belief system with which we choose to align ourselves. Either, the ego's or the Holy Spirit's belief in what you are, will determine what you are willing to allow into your world of provisional reality.

VI. Waking to Redemption

T-11.VI.1. It is impossible not to believe what you see, but it is equally impossible to see what you do not believe. 2 Perceptions are built up on the basis of experience, and experience leads to beliefs. 3 It is not until beliefs are fixed that perceptions stabilize. 4 In effect, then, what you believe you <do> see. 5 That is what I meant when I said, "Blessed are ye who have not seen and still believe," for those who believe in the resurrection will see **the resurrection**. 6 The resurrection is the complete triumph of Christ over the ego, not by attack but by transcendence. 7 For Christ does rise above the ego and all **the ego's** works, and ascends to the Father and His Kingdom.

Note # 57: You see what you believe. Perception is based on your beliefs. Once you have determined what you wish to believe, you will then project out the thought pattern that you wish to see. Thus "seeing" becomes your predetermined verification or witness to what you already believe. The resurrection is the complete triumph of the Christ mind over the ego. This is a triumph of Truth over error or misperception. The Christ Mind denies the false and correctly perceives what aligns with God's Truth. ACIM makes the distinction between "seeing" and "vision." Vision records the Truth about reality. Vision bypasses the nothingness of the false and only looks upon the truth that remains. Seeing only verifies your preconceived beliefs. Your perceptions are based only on what you choose to experience.

We have been given the power to extend the real or pretend to make the unreal. The unreal exists only in the unshared imagination of the dreamer. It is not shared with the totality that is the Mind of God. If you choose to experience yourself as a limited-ego body in your world of provisional reality, you will allow yourself to perceive experiences that only witness to your belief that you are a limited ego-body. Once your beliefs become fixed, how you perceive yourself will also become more ridged, fixed and stable. Since you falsely believe you are a body, you will perceive by utilizing the tool for making, which is projection. Projection is based on your belief in lack and limitation. You will make and project false witnesses that confirm your erroneous belief that your illusionary world of provisional reality is "true." Therefore, you "see" what you believe and you believe what you see. But, it is the thought that always comes first.

T-11.VI.2. Would you join in the resurrection or the crucifixion? 2 Would you condemn your brothers or free **your brothers**? 3 Would you transcend your prison and ascend to the Father? 4 These questions are all the same, and are answered together. 5 There has been much confusion about what perception means, because the word, **perception,** is used both for awareness and for the interpretation of awareness. 6 Yet you cannot be aware without interpretation, for what you perceive <is> your interpretation.

Note # 58: Perception is your viewpoint, which is your interpretation. Perception is not based on truth, which would be associated with knowledge. We lost knowledge when we fell under the spell of the ego's belief or thought system, which claimed that the separation was real. Now that which we choose to call into our awareness is based on our beliefs, which predetermine what we are willing to allow into our experience. Our viewpoint or interpretation shapes what we perceive. This is why, when we change our viewpoint; we automatically change how we perceive our world.

T-11.VI.3. This course is perfectly clear. 2 If you do not see **this course** clearly, it is because you are interpreting against **this course**, and therefore do not believe **this course**. 3 And since belief determines perception, you do not perceive what **this course** means and therefore do not accept **this course**. 4 Yet different experiences lead to different beliefs, and with **different beliefs you get** different perceptions. 5 For perceptions are learned <with> beliefs, and experience does teach **beliefs**. 6 I am leading you to a new kind of experience that you will become less and less willing to deny. 7 Learning of Christ is easy, for to perceive with **Christ** involves no strain at all. 8 **Christ's** perceptions are your natural awareness, and it is only the distortions you introduce that tire you. 9 Let the Christ in you interpret for you, and do not try to limit what you see by narrow little beliefs that are unworthy of God's Son. 10 For until Christ comes into His Own, the Son of God will see himself as Fatherless.

Note # 59: The Christ in you is the home of the Holy Spirit. By perceiving through the vision of Christ, you are operating under the thought system of the Holy Spirit and allowing your Big "S" Self to act as the interpreter of your experience. By your willingness to choose again, you are allowing the Holy Spirit to reinterpret the same experience through the viewpoint of correct perception. This reinterpretation gives us a "new experience" from the old one and helps reform past beliefs. Beliefs can be changed since beliefs are based on our experience. When we choose to reinterpret the same experience differently, our beliefs are slowly realigned to correspond with our new interpretation.

T-11.VI.4.I am <your> resurrection and <your> life. 2 You live in me because you live in God. 3 And everyone lives in you, as you live in everyone. 4 Can you, then, perceive unworthiness in a brother and not perceive **unworthiness** in yourself? 5 And can you perceive **unworthiness** in yourself and not perceive **unworthiness** in God? 6 Believe in the resurrection because **the resurrection, which is the triumph of truth over the fallacies of the ego's thought system,** has been accomplished, and **the resurrection** has been accomplished in you. 7 **That the resurrection has been accomplished in you** is as true now as it will ever be, for the resurrection is the Will of God, which knows no time and no exceptions. 8 But make no exceptions yourself, or you will not perceive what has been accomplished for you, **which is the triumph of truth, which is the resurrection**. 9 For we ascend unto the Father together, as it was in the beginning, is now and ever shall be, for such is the nature of God's Son as his Father created him.

Note # 60: Only our false belief in our true nature, limits us. When we correct our belief in "littleness," we accept the resurrection of our divine birthright. We accept the truth that we are made like our Father to extend or co-create like our Father. Only in time, could we choose to perceive ourselves as separate and different from the Oneness of Everything that is the holographic Mind of God. In eternity, our Christ, the One Self, always knows the changeless truth.

T-11.VI.5. Do not underestimate the power of the devotion of God's Son, nor the power the god he worships has over him. 2 For **God's Son** places himself at the altar of his god, whether it be the god he made or the God Who created him. 3 That is why his slavery is as complete as his freedom, for **God's Son** will obey only the god he accepts. 4 The god of crucifixion, **which is the gods of the ego's thought system**, demands that he crucify, and his worshippers obey. 5 In **the gods of the ego's thought system's** name they crucify themselves, believing that the power of the Son of God is born of sacrifice and pain. 6 The God of resurrection demands nothing, for **the God of resurrection** does not will to take away. 7 **The God of resurrection** does not require obedience, for obedience implies submission. 8 **The God of resurrection** would only have you learn your will and follow **your will**, not in the spirit of sacrifice and submission, but in the gladness of freedom.

Note # 61: When we believe that we are separate and self-created, we worship the false fearful gods of the ego's belief system. If we believe we are as God created us, we will follow God's Loving Will.
The ego's gods always demand sacrifice and suffering because this is what the ego and its gods represent. The ego says we lack and are not perfect, whole and complete. The idols of the ego represent what we believe we need to complete our imperfect little "s" self. The God of the resurrection is Our Creator. Our Creator knows His Son as only perfect, whole and complete. Our Father wants us only to be happy. Our Father, being everything, gives everything to His Creations. Our Father, being everything, has no desire to remove anything from the Oneness since to do so would be to place limits on Himself.

T-11.VI.6. Resurrection must compel your allegiance gladly, because **the resurrection** is the symbol of joy. 2 **The resurrection's** whole compelling power lies in the fact that **the resurrection** represents what you want to be. 3 The freedom to leave behind everything that hurts you and humbles you and frightens you cannot be thrust upon you, but **this freedom to leave behind everything that hurts you** can be offered you through the grace of God. 4 And you can accept **this freedom to leave behind everything that hurts you** by God's grace, for God is gracious to His Son, accepting him without question as **God's** Own. 5 Who, then, is <*your*> own? 6 The Father has given you all that is His, and **God** Himself is yours with **all that is His.** 7 Guard **all that is His** in their resurrection, for otherwise you will not awake in God, safely surrounded by what is yours forever.

Note # 62: All that is His or God's is everything. God is truth. God's Will is that we, His creation, know the Truth about ourselves. We are not limited, but rather, part of the Oneness of everything. With our brother, we share the Oneness that is part of the Sonship. God's creation, the Sonship, is the extension of all that God is. The resurrection is the reclaiming of the truth about the Sonship's divine birthright. If we attempt to exclude part of the Sonship from the Oneness, we are also attempting to limit our Creator and ourselves. God cannot be limited since part of the definition of God is unlimitedness. Since creation is extension, we too must be unlimited, like our Father.

T-11.VI.7. You will not find peace until you have removed the nails from the hands of God's Son, and taken the last thorn from his forehead. 2 The Love of God surrounds His Son whom the god of crucifixion condemns. 3 Teach not that I died in vain. 4 Teach rather that I did not die by demonstrating that I live in you. 5 For the undoing of the crucifixion of God's Son is the work of the redemption, in which everyone has a part of equal value. 6 God does not judge His guiltless Son. 7 **God,** having given Himself to him, how could it be otherwise?

Note # 63: Jesus' resurrection proved that we are not a limited ego-body. God only sees us as perfect, whole and complete. Jesus' resurrection is the overthrowing of the ego's thought system and the acceptance of the truth of what we are. Like Jesus, we who are part of the Sonship, share in this triumph of Truth over falseness. Jesus demonstrated that he knows that he is the Christ by accepting the Atonement for himself. Being part of the united Sonship, Jesus lives in us. By our acceptance of this universal fact of the interconnectedness of Mind, we benefit from Jesus' experience and belief. How could Jesus not be part of our shared oneness, which is the Mind of God? We need only accept the Atonement for ourselves, to acknowledge the return of the Sonship to the knowing found in eternity.

T-11.VI.8. You have nailed yourself to a cross, and placed a crown of thorns upon your own head. 2 Yet you cannot crucify God's Son, for the Will of God cannot die. 3 His Son has been redeemed from his own crucifixion, and you cannot assign to death whom God has given eternal life. 4 The dream of crucifixion still lies heavy on your eyes, but what you see in dreams is not reality. 5 While you perceive the Son of God as crucified, you are asleep. 6 And as long as you believe that you can crucify him, **the Son of God,** you are only having nightmares. 7 You who are beginning to wake are still aware of dreams, and have not yet forgotten **these dreams of separation and crucifixion.** 8 The forgetting of dreams and the awareness of Christ come with the awakening of others to share your redemption.

Note # 64: Due to our belief in littleness, we perceive ourselves as something we are not. As long as we perceive ourselves to be separate from our brother or God, we will continue to crucify our brother, our God, and ourselves. Forgiveness will lead us back up the path to right-mindedness and the acceptance of truth. Giving is receiving and in order to forget, we must forgive all past egoic beliefs in littleness. We are our own crucifier.

T-11.VI.9. You will awaken to your own call, for the Call to awake is within you. 2 If I live in you, you are awake. 3 Yet you must see the works I do through you, or you will not perceive that I have done **these works** unto you. 4 Do not set limits on what you believe I can do through you, or you will not accept what I can do <for> you. 5 Yet **these works I do through you are** done already, and unless you give all that you have received you will not know that your redeemer liveth, and that you have awakened with **your redeemer**. 6 Redemption is recognized only by sharing **redemption**.

Note # 65: Our beliefs determine what we are willing to experience. Until we are willing to believe that we are guiltless and sinless, we will refuse to accept our true spiritual magnificence as the One Self. To give is to receive and you cannot give what you believe you do not possess. Unless we share or give, we cannot receive. God gives all, because God is all. To reclaim the Truth about ourselves, we must share this Truth with all our brothers. Through the tool of forgiveness, we reawaken to the Oneness that we share. To share involves sharing the truth with another. By sharing the idea, it becomes the other person's truth and both remain complete. When we share, it is inclusive and a joining. There is no one that we would withhold the truth from. Until we truly see the Christ in our brother, we cannot find the Christ in us. The Christ has always remained in us since this is God's changeless Will.

T-11.VI.10. God's Son <is> saved. 2 Bring only this awareness **that God's Son <is> saved** to the Sonship, and you will have a part in the redemption as valuable as mine. 3 For your part must be like mine if you learn **your part** of me. 4 If you believe that **your part** is limited, you are limiting **my part**. 5 There is no order of difficulty in miracles because all of God's Sons are of equal value, and their equality is their oneness. 6 The whole power of God is in every part of Him, and nothing contradictory to His Will is either great or small. 7 What does not exist has no size and no measure. 8 To God all things are possible. 9 And to Christ it is given to be like the Father.

Note # 66: The Mind of God is holographic. All parts are indivisible yet, each part contains the whole. The only limitation that can be placed on the Oneness is in the split-mind that temporarily chooses to deny the truth that he is a part of this One Self. This denial cannot affect the truth but it can change how that part of the mind perceives its "reality." The illusion can be accepted as the provisional "truth" in this deluded mind until it chooses to reawaken to the Truth of its unlimited nature.
Being part of the Oneness of God, any part of the Sonship must share equally in the total power that is God. Extension is creating in the exact image. God holds nothing back. The only difference between God, the Father, and the Sonship is that the Father came first. Our will is the Will of the Father, and, therefore, nothing contradicts God's Will since we share this same Mind of God.

VII. The Condition of Reality

T-11.VII.1. The world as you perceive **the world** cannot have been created by the Father, for the world is not as you see **the world**. 2 God created only the eternal, and everything you see is perishable. 3 Therefore, there must be another world that you do not see. **This is the eternal world of God, which is the Kingdom or Heaven.** 4 The Bible speaks of a new Heaven and a new earth, yet this cannot be literally true, for the eternal are not re-created. 5 To perceive anew is merely to perceive again, implying that before, or in the interval between, you were not perceiving at all. 6 What, then, is the world that awaits your perception when you see it?

Note # 67: Our illusionary world of egoic misperception has hidden the real world from our awareness. This veil has not changed eternity but it prevents the insane from being willing to allow the truth into their experience. Our refusal to look upon the Truth was a free will choice involving a decision in which we desired to experience something other than God's Love. In this egoic world of individual perception, we have chosen to focus on the experience of imagining what it would be like to be something other than the Oneness of God. Our free will allows us to drop imagining limitation and return to being co-creator with God, whenever we decide to only value the Truth. The decision to be vigilant only for God is just one decision away. To be vigilant for God is to allow and desire only the thoughts of God into our awareness. The thoughts of God are love, joy, peace and oneness. Heaven is but one decision away.

T-11.VII.2. Every loving thought that the Son of God ever had is eternal. 2 The loving thoughts his mind perceives in this world are the world's only reality. 3 **The loving thoughts** are still perceptions, because he still believes that he is separate. 4 Yet **the loving thoughts** are eternal because **the loving thoughts are loving.** 5 And being loving **these loving thoughts** are like the Father, and therefore **are eternal and** cannot die. 6 The real world can actually be perceived. 7 All that is necessary is a willingness to perceive nothing else **but the real world.** 8 For if you perceive both good and evil, you are accepting both the false and the true and making no distinction between **good and evil.**

Note # 68: You cannot perceive correctly if you are aware of both good and evil. To "know" both good and evil implies that you still believe that there is something that opposes the Truth. This belief, that there is something that must be opposed, makes the separation appear real within your own mind. To perceive the real world, the Kingdom, you can only perceive what Truth is. Truth aligns with the Will of God. The false is simply denied since it is nothing. Truth is the reality of the Mind of God and is eternal, perfect, whole and complete as God created it. Truth is Thoughts of God. Truth is love, joy, peace and oneness.

T-11.VII.3. The ego may see some good, but never only **sees** good. 2 That is why **the ego's** perceptions are so variable. 3 **The ego's perceptions do** not reject goodness entirely, for that you could not accept. 4 But **the ego's perception always adds** something that is not real to the real, thus confusing illusion and reality. 5 For perceptions cannot be partly true. 6 If you believe in truth and illusion, you cannot tell which is true. 7 To establish your personal autonomy you tried to create unlike your Father, believing that what you made is capable of being unlike **your Father.** 8 Yet everything true <*is*> like **your Father.** 9 Perceiving only the real world will lead you to the real Heaven, because **perceiving only the real world** will make you capable of understanding **the real world.**

Note # 69: By adding any untruth to the ego's perception, the entire perception becomes wrong. This misperception of conditional or partial truth once again supports the notion that there is separation. Truth cannot be compromised by attempting to join truth with illusion. This is why we need to be vigilant only for God, which is Truth. To see the real world we must have correct perception. Heaven is different from the real world in which love is only perceived. In Heaven, knowledge has replaced perception. Perception requires both an observer and something to observe. In correct perception, the observer observes the Oneness in all that is. Knowledge just knows that it is just the One Self. No interpretation or thinking is involved. The condition of knowledge requires awareness that there is nothing real that ever existed which could oppose the goodness of truth. Only in fantasies can it appear as if something opposes truth's reality. Wake up and the fantasy is gone.

T-11.VII.4. The perception of goodness is not knowledge, but the denial of the opposite of goodness enables you to recognize a condition in which opposites do not exist. 2 And this denial **of the existence**

of anything that could oppose goodness <is> the condition of knowledge. 3 Without this awareness **of the denial of the existence of anything that could oppose goodness,** you have not met **knowledge's** conditions, and until you do, you will not know **knowledge** is yours already. 4 You have made many ideas that you have placed between yourself and your Creator, and these beliefs are the world as you perceive **to be your illusionary world of provisional reality**. 5 Truth is not absent here, but **truth** is obscure. 6 You do not know the difference between what you have made and what God created, and so you do not know the difference between what you have made and what <you> have created. 7 To believe that you can perceive the real world is to believe that you can know yourself. 8 You can know God because **to know God** is **God's** Will to be known. 9 The real world is all that the Holy Spirit has saved for you out of what you have made, and to perceive only this is salvation, because it is the recognition that reality is only what is true.

Note # 70: True loving thoughts can and are shared with the entire holographic Mind of God. They are real extensions of a co-creation with the Father. The Holy Spirit saves our creations which arise out of love and forgiveness. Anything that we make to defend the thought system of the ego is not preserved or saved by the Holy Spirit. These defenses are fear based attack thoughts that are not real and, therefore, are not eternal. Making arises from projection, which is exclusion. Creation is extension, which is sharing. Love and forgiveness can be shared because they are co-creative thoughts. They are part of the real world and are our true creations.

VIII. The Problem and the Answer

T-11.VIII.1. This is a very simple course. 2 Perhaps you do not feel you need a course which, in the end, teaches that only reality is true. 3 But do you believe **that only reality is true**? 4 When you perceive the real world, you will recognize that you did not believe **that only reality is true**. 5 Yet the swiftness with which your new and only real perception will be translated into knowledge will leave you but an instant to realize that this alone **(that only reality is true)** is true. 6 And then everything you made will be forgotten; the good and the bad, the false and the true. 7 For as Heaven and earth become one, even the real world will vanish from your sight. 8 The end of the world is not its destruction, but its translation into Heaven. 9 The reinterpretation of the world is the transfer of all perception to knowledge.

Note # 71: ACIM is a simple course since it involves only black and white. There is no gray in ACIM. Everything is either true or false. There is no sometimes. Our problem is that we have been taught by the ego that change is possible and that both maybe and sometimes do exist. Truth, false, maybe and sometimes all appear to exist in the dream world of time and perception but they have no reality in changeless eternity. ACIM states simply what is not truth is false and that the false does not exist.
Everything you have made will be forgotten because to make is to exclude. Projection, which is always making comes from the belief that you lack something. This is why all projected thoughts, both "good and bad," will be forgotten. The belief that there could be something outside of the Oneness is the belief in separation. Perception arises from the viewpoint that there is something you lack. Therefore, you identify yourself as something other than as God created you, which is perfect, whole and complete.
 Even "true or correct" perception "confirms" that there is something observable outside of you that you then recognize as part of the your One Self. Perception involves thinking and is not part of knowledge. Knowledge just knows.

T-11.VIII.2. The Bible tells you to become as little children. 2 Little children recognize that they do not understand what they perceive, and so **little children** ask what **they do not understand** means. 3 Do not make the mistake of believing that you understand what you perceive, for **the** meaning **of what you perceive has been** lost to you. 4 Yet the Holy Spirit has saved **the true** meaning **of what you perceive** for you, and if you will let **the Holy Spirit** interpret **what you perceived, the Holy Spirit** will restore to you what you have thrown away. 5 Yet while you think you know **what your perceived** meaning **is,** you will see no need to ask **for reinterpretation by the Holy Spirit.**

Note # 72: We need to ask the Holy Spirit to reinterpret our perceived experiences since only the Holy Spirit is aware of both our illusions and the truth about ourselves. Only the Holy Spirit is aware of all the facts of God's Plan for salvation and, therefore, is the only one that is capable of judging the experience correctly. The only judgment we need make is to realize that due to our belief in the separation, our mind is "split" and, therefore, we are incapable of judging correctly. Correct judgment requires knowledge that we have chosen to forget. We need to ask for the Holy Spirit's guidance in our world of perception, so that we can regain knowledge of the Kingdom.

T-11.VIII.3. You do not know the meaning of anything you perceive. 2 Not one thought you hold is wholly true. 3 The recognition **that not one thought you hold is wholly true** is your firm beginning. 4 You are not misguided; you have accepted no guide at all. **The Holy Spirit is the guide you seek.** 5 Instruction in perception is your great need, for you understand nothing. 6 Recognize **that you understand nothing** but do not accept **that you understand nothing,** for understanding is your inheritance. 7 Perceptions are learned, and you are not without a Teacher, **which is the Holy Spirit.** 8 Yet your willingness to learn of **the Holy Spirit as your Teacher** depends on your willingness to question everything you learned of yourself, **(your ego small "s" self)** for you who learned amiss should not be your own teacher.

Note # 73: Perception is based on values and beliefs. What you choose to value and believe can be changed by a simple decision. By adopting a new teacher with different beliefs, we can relearn about the truth of our Big "S" Self. If we attempt to keep both teachers, we will remain confused and in conflict.

T-11.VIII.4. No one can withhold truth except from himself. 2 Yet God will not refuse you the Answer **God** gave. 3 Ask, then, for what is yours, but which you did not make, and do not defend yourself against truth. 4 You made the problem God has answered. 5 Ask yourself, therefore, but one simple question:

6 *Do I want the problem or do I want the answer?*

7 Decide for the answer and you will have **the answer,** for you will see **the problem** as it is, and **the answer** is yours already.

Note # 74: The problem is our denial of the truth. It is our claim to be something other than as God made us. It is our desire to be a separate, special individual at the cost of our Oneness of Everything. The problem is the claim for self-creation that births the illusion of "littleness." God's answer is the truth. The truth never ceased to be, we have just refused to listen. The acceptance of the Atonement is the acceptance of the Truth about us. To want the answer, is to want to know the truth about what we are. We are and remain sinless and guiltless, God's perfect creation. The only thing that can keep the answer from our awareness is our own egoic desire not to want to hear the answer.

T-11.VIII.5. You may complain that this course is not sufficiently specific for you to understand and use. 2 Yet perhaps you have not done what **this course** specifically advocates. 3 This is not a course in the play of ideas, but in their practical application **of these ideas**. 4 Nothing could be more specific than to be told that if you ask you will receive. 5 The Holy Spirit will answer every specific problem as long as you believe that problems are specific. 6 **The Holy Spirit's** answer is both many and one, as long as you believe that the one is many. 7 You may be afraid of **the Holy Spirit's** specificity, for fear of what you think **the Holy Spirit's specificity** will demand of you. 8 Yet only by asking will you learn that nothing of God demands anything of you. 9 God gives; He does not take. 10 When you refuse to ask, it is because you believe that asking is taking rather than sharing.

<u>Note # 75:</u> The Holy Spirit will answer all questions asked. We believe that we have specific problems that vary from place to place. We believe that if the form that the problem appears in is different from another form of the same problem the solution must be different. All problems are the same. They are all different forms of the "authority problem." The ego tells us that we are the arbitrators of truth; that we are self-created. To correct all forms of the same and only problem is simply to accept the truth. When we accept the Atonement for ourselves, we accept the truth and all forms of the one common problem disappear. Accept the truth that our will and God's will are the same.
God is everything because God is everything. There is nothing else. God creates by extension. To be everything, God gives everything to everything. This is God's Law of Creation or Sharing. God demands nothing since God shares all that He is. By sharing thought, there is no diminishment and the idea is strengthened. This sharing is the extension of the Mind of God. Because we have identified with the ego-body, we have made a world of form. Form cannot be shared, since to share form would result in diminishment to the original "owner" and giver of the form. Sharing requires no sacrifice. Thoughts of love and forgiveness can be shared and, therefore, they are real. Ask for the Holy Spirit's guidance, and He will reinterpret your misperceptions into thoughts of love and forgiveness.

T-11.VIII.6. The Holy Spirit will give you only what is yours, and will take nothing in return. 2 For what is yours is everything, and you share **everything** with God. 3 That is its reality. 4 Would the Holy Spirit, Who wills only to restore, be capable of misinterpreting the question you must ask to learn **the Holy Spirit's** answer? 5 You <have> heard the answer, but you have misunderstood the question. 6 You believe that to ask for guidance of the Holy Spirit is to ask for deprivation.

<u>Note # 76:</u> Since we identify, with the body, we believe that we "live" in a world of form. Form cannot be shared since the giver would have less after he gave. Because we believe we live in a world of form, lack and separation, we think to give is not the same as to receive. We fail to understand God's basic law that to give is to receive. Because of the ego's belief in the need for sacrifice, we refuse to hear the true answer from the Holy Spirit. We are afraid to ask for the Holy Spirit's guidance. We fear that the Holy Spirit's answer will require that we sacrifice something that we value. The Holy Spirit knows that we are not the body and that form is of no value to unlimited spirit. Form attempts to limit, imprison and bind. The Holy Spirit's criterion is "How would love respond?" Only love and forgiveness is the proper response to a perceived problem since only love and forgiveness can be shared and by sharing both parties are strengthened. No sacrifice is required when thoughts are shared.

T-11.VIII.7. Little child of God, you do not understand your Father. 2 You believe in a world that takes, because you believe that you can get by taking. 3 And by that perception you have lost sight of the real world. 4 You are afraid of the world as you see **the world**, but the real world is still yours for the asking. 5 Do not deny **the real world** to yourself, for **the real world** can only free you. 6 Nothing of God will enslave His Son whom **God** created free and whose freedom is protected by **God's** Being. 7 Blessed are you who are willing to ask the truth of God without fear, for only thus **by asking the truth of God**

without fear can you learn that **God's** answer is the release from fear.

Note # 77: God's Will is that we be happy. By not asking for and claiming our divine birthright, we choose to deny ourselves the happiness that is the peace of God. A Oneness has no wants and no fears.

T-11.VIII.8. Beautiful child of God, you are asking only for what I promised you. 2 Do you believe I would deceive you? 3 The Kingdom of Heaven <*is*> within you. 4 Believe that the truth is in me, for I know that **the truth is** in you. 5 God's Sons have nothing they do not share. 6 Ask for truth of any Son of God, and you have asked **the truth** of me. 7 Not one of us, **any Son of God,** but has the answer in him, to give to anyone who asks **the truth** of him.

Note # 78: The answer to the question of "What are we?" is found within us. It is arrogance to claim that you do not know what you are or that you are something that you are not. All mystic traditions say the same thing. They advise their devotee to go within. God is everything, everywhere and every when. If we wish to find God, we need only look within ourselves. ACIM is no different. If there is only a Oneness of which we are part, God must be within us and our brother. Deny not the truth in your brother and he will not deny that same truth in you. God must be in all that is real and we all are that One Self. The ego tells us to look outside ourselves to find wholeness and completeness. What could we expect to find outside a Oneness of All that Is? There can only be the false illusions of nothingness outside the Oneness of Everything.

T-11.VIII.9. Ask anything of God's Son and his Father will answer you, for Christ is not deceived in His Father and His Father is not deceived in **God's Son**. 2 Do not, then, be deceived in your brother, and see only **your brother's** loving thoughts as **your brother's** reality, for by denying that **your brother's** mind is split you will heal **your own mind**. 3 Accept **your brother** as his Father accepts **your brother** and heal **your brother** unto Christ, for Christ is **your brother's** healing and **your own healing**. 4 Christ is the Son of God Who is in no way separate from His Father, Whose every thought is as loving as the Thought of His Father by which **the Son of God** was created. 5 Be not deceived in God's Son, for thereby you must be deceived in yourself. 6 And being deceived in yourself you are deceived in your Father, in Whom no deceit is possible.

Note # 79: Your brother's true self, like you, is the Christ consciousness or Big "S" Self. Look past the body form and egoic littleness to your brother's spiritual essence. We are not an ego-body in competition with only limited ego-bodies. We are Mind, the shared Thought of God, our Creator. Deny your brother's illusion of his own littleness and only acknowledge his Big "S" Self. By granting your brother this truth, he will share that same truth with you. Truth can be shared. The false is impossible to share since it is nothing.

T-11.VIII.10. In the real world there is no sickness, for there is no separation and no division. 2 Only loving thoughts are recognized, and because no one is without your help, the Help of God goes with you everywhere. 3 As you become willing to accept this Help **from the Holy Spirit** by asking for **this Help**, you will give **this Help** because you want **this Help from the Holy Spirit**. 4 Nothing will be beyond your healing power, because nothing will be denied your simple request. 5 What problems will not disappear in the Presence of God's Answer, **which is the Holy Spirit's correct perception and the Atonement**? 6 Ask, then, to learn of the reality of your brother, because **the reality of your brother** is what you will perceive in **your brother**, and you will see your beauty reflected in **your brother's beauty**.

Note # 80: Because of our shared Oneness with our brother and God, anything we do to or for our brother, we do onto our Father and ourselves. To heal our split mind, we must not perceive our brother's mind as split. To aid in the healing of our brother's mind is to heal our own.

T-11.VIII.11. Do not accept your brother's variable perception of himself for his split mind is your **split mind**, and you will not accept your healing without his **healing**. 2 For you share the real world as you share Heaven, and his healing is **your healing**. 3 To love yourself is to heal yourself, and you cannot perceive part of you as sick and achieve your goal **of healing your split mind**. 4 Brother, we heal together as we live together and love together. 5 Be not deceived in God's Son, for **God's Son** is one with himself and one with his Father. 6 Love **God's Son** who is beloved of his Father, and you will learn of the Father's Love for you.

Note # 81: We are all connected. There is one Sonship, which is all God created as God created it. You cannot deny a brother his divine nature without denying it to all the Sonship. There is only one will and one mind and that is the shared indivisible holographic Mind of God.

T-11.VIII.12. If you perceive offense in a brother pluck the offense from your mind, for you are offended by Christ and are deceived in **your perception of the Christ that is your brother**. 2 Heal in Christ and be not offended by **the Christ that is your brother**, for there is no offense in Him, **the Christ that is your brother**. 3 If what you perceive offends you, you are offended in yourself and are condemning God's Son whom God condemneth not. 4 Let the Holy Spirit remove all offenses of God's Son against himself and perceive no one but through **the Holy Spirit's** guidance, for **the Holy Spirit** would save you from all condemnation. 5 Accept **the Holy Spirit's** healing power and use **the Holy Spirit's healing power** for all **the Holy Spirit** sends you, for **the Holy Spirit** wills to heal the Son of God, in whom **the Holy Spirit** is not deceived.

Note # 82: When we condemn another, we condemn ourselves. Only the egoic thought system condemns because it judges what it does not know. The Holy Spirit condemns nothing for the Holy Spirit knows that God's Child is sinless and guiltless. Give all our perception over to the Holy Spirit, Who will heal them with His correct perception.

T-11.VIII.13. Children perceive frightening ghosts and monsters and dragons, and **these children** are terrified. 2 Yet if **these frightened children** ask someone **these children** trust for the meaning of what they perceive, and are willing to let their own **frightening** interpretations go in favor of reality, their fear goes with them. 3 When a child is helped to translate his "ghost" into a curtain, his "monster" into a shadow, and his "dragon" into a dream **the child** is no longer afraid, and laughs happily at his own fear.

Note # 83: By asking for the Holy Spirit's guidance, we will be told the truth about our egoic misperception. We will be told that we are unlimited invulnerable spirit that is part of the indivisible shared Oneness of the Mind of God. We will understand this truth and join with our brothers and once again choose to remember to laugh at the illusion of separation.

T-11.VIII.14. You, my child, are afraid of your brothers and of your Father and of yourself. 2 But you are merely deceived in **your brothers, your Father and yourself**. 3 Ask what **your brothers, your Father and you** are of the Teacher of reality, **which is the Holy Spirit**, and hearing **the Holy Spirit's** answer, you too will laugh at your fears and replace **your fears** with peace. 4 For fear lies not in reality, but in the minds of children who do not understand reality. 5 It is only their lack of understanding that frightens **the child**, and when **the child learns** to perceive truly **of reality the child is** not afraid. 6 And because of this **perceiving the truth about reality, the child** will ask for truth again when **the child is** frightened. 7 It is not the reality of your brothers or your Father or yourself that frightens you. **It is your**

misperception of what they are. 8 You do not know what **your brother, your Father or you** are, and so you perceive them as ghosts and monsters and dragons. 9 Ask what **your brother, your Father or your** reality is from the One, **the Holy Spirit,** knows **their true reality** and **the Holy Spirit** will tell you what they **really** are. 10 For you do not understand **your brothers, your Father or yourself**, and because you are deceived by what you see you need reality to dispel your fears.

Note # 84: Ask the Holy Spirit for His guidance, and the Holy Spirit will correct your misperceptions that you hold in your split mind. Only the Holy Spirit is capable of doing this, for only the Holy Spirit is aware of your illusionary misperception about the world and the reality of what you really are. It is our belief that our illusion of separation is real that is frightening. By learning the truth of our Oneness, we understand that we were just pretending to play the "game of separation." This game was not to be taken seriously and had no effect of the reality of what we are or the Mind of God. We learn that we are the dreamer and as such, we can choose to awaken whenever we wish. Dreams lose their ability to frighten when we understand they are not real.

T-11.VIII.15. Would you not exchange your fears for truth, if the exchange **from fear to truth** is yours for the asking? 2 For if God is not deceived in you, you can be deceived only in yourself. 3 Yet you can learn the truth about yourself from the Holy Spirit, Who will teach you that **since you are** part of God, deceit in you is **also** impossible. 4 When you perceive yourself without deceit, you will accept the real world in place of the false **world** you have made **through your own misperception**. 5 And then your Father will lean down to you and take the last step for you, by raising you unto Himself.

Note # 85: We are the wardens of our own prison. Only we have the power to free ourselves from our own self-imprisonment for we alone condemned and then made our prison. When we no longer value egoic specialness, we will freely ask for the Holy Spirit's guidance and accelerate our journey back to the truth. Once you have accepted the correction of all of your own misperceptions, God, the Father, will take the final step in returning you to the knowledge of the Kingdom. The Holy Spirit prepares you for this remembrance of God through the use of the tools of forgiveness and love. Unless we relearn the reality of our Oneness with our brother, we cannot remember our Oneness with our Father. By accepting the Atonement for ourselves, the Sonship is healed.

Chapter 12. THE HOLY SPIRIT'S CURRICULUM

I. The Judgment of the Holy Spirit

T-12.I.1. You have been told not to make error real, and the way to **not make error real** is very simple. 2 If you want to believe in error, you would have to make **error** real because **error** is not true. 3 But truth is real in **truth's** own right, and to believe in truth <*you do not have to do anything*>. 4 Understand that you do not respond to anything directly, but to your interpretation of **that something**. 5 Your interpretation thus becomes the justification for the response. 6 That is why analyzing the motives of others is hazardous to you. 7 If you decide that someone is really trying to attack you or desert you or enslave you, you will respond as if he had actually done so, having made his error real to you. 8 To interpret error is to give **error** power, and having **given error power**, you will overlook truth.

Note # 1: Our individual interpretation does not correspond to the truth, but rather, to how we perceive something. Based on how we perceive something, this interpretation becomes our individual "truth." Our belief, however, has no impact on truth. Truth is eternal and changeless. Our perception is unstable and subject to change. Since our interpretation is changeable, it is not fixed. If we wish to, we can utilize the learning experience to decide to choose again and follow the thought system of the Holy Spirit instead of the ego's.

T-12.I.2. The analysis of ego motivation is very complicated, very obscuring, and never without your own ego involvement. 2 The whole process of **the analysis of ego motivation** represents a clear-cut attempt to demonstrate your own ability to understand what you perceive. 3 This **demonstration of your own ability to understand what you perceive** is shown by the fact that you react to your interpretations as if **your interpretations** were correct. 4 You may then control your reactions behaviorally, but not emotionally. 5 This **ability to control your reactions behaviorally, but not emotionally** would obviously be a split or an attack on the integrity of your mind, pitting one level within **your mind** against another.

Note # 2: This ability to control your reactions behaviorally, but not emotionally, demonstrates the conflict within your mind itself. This is an attack against your right-mindedness. The body takes orders from our mind. Our emotions are the result of conflict within our mind. If part of our mind erroneously believes that it is a body, it will respond with attack which is out of alignment with our Big "S" Self that knows that we are one unlimited spirit. Actions inappropriate to our Big "S" Self's truth will ultimately result in our loss of peace.

T-12.I.3. There is but one interpretation of motivation that makes any sense. 2 And because **the one interpretation of motivation that makes any sense** is the Holy Spirit's judgment **this interpretation**

requires no effort at all on your part. 3 Every loving thought is true. 4 Everything else **that is not a loving thought** is an appeal for healing and help, regardless of the form **everything else** takes. 5 Can anyone be justified in responding with anger to a brother's plea for help? 6 No response **to a brother's plea for help** can be appropriate except the willingness to give **help** to him, for **help** and only **help** is what **the brother** is asking for. 7 Offer **the brother** anything else **to a brother's plea for help** and you are assuming the right to attack **your brother's** reality by interpreting **your brother's reality** as you see fit. 8 Perhaps the danger of this **interpreting your brother's reality as you see fit** to your own mind is not yet fully apparent. 9 If you believe that an appeal for help is something else you will react to something else. 10 Your response will therefore be inappropriate to reality as it is, but not to your perception of **what you believe your brother's reality might be, which you have misinterpreted to be something other than a plea for help.**

Note # 3: Because we fail to interpret correctly, our response to any situation may not be what is really justified. If we knew the truth about our brother's or our own situation, our response would be different. If we perceive a brother's cry for help and love as an attack, we will respond with a counterattack instead of with loving help. Only the Holy Spirit has the ability to "judge" correctly and thus, guide us to the appropriate response.

T-12.I.4. There is nothing to prevent you from recognizing all calls for help as exactly what they are, **which is a brother's call for help,** except your own imagined need to attack. 2 It is only **your own imagined need to attack** that makes you willing to engage in endless "battles" with reality, in which you deny the reality of the need for healing by making **the need for healing** unreal. 3 You would not **attack your brother** except for your unwillingness to accept reality as it is, and which you therefore withhold from yourself **the reality of what you really are.**

Note # 4: Because we misperceive our oneness with our brother, we fail to recognize our brother's cry for help. Since we believe that we are a body-form, we also believe that to help our brother would require sacrifice on our part. We believe that we are not everything and, therefore, answer our brother's cry for help and love as if it were a personal attack. Because we perceive ourselves as different and separate from our brother, we believe that we will be diminished if we aid our brother. This belief in diminishment and sacrifice is true only if we believe that we are separate limited ego-bodies. If we see ourselves as one mind, we understand that there can be no diminishment. Thoughts can be shared and by sharing our own thoughts are strengthened. This sharing of our mind with our brother returns us to the reality of what we are, one mind. We are joined together in the shared, unlimited Oneness of the Mind of God.

T-12.I.5. It is surely good advice to tell you not to judge what you do not understand. 2 No one with a personal investment is a reliable witness, for truth to him has become what he wants **truth** to be. 3 If you are unwilling to perceive an appeal for help as what **the appeal for help** is, it is because you are unwilling to give help and to receive **help.** 4 To fail to recognize a call for help is to refuse help. 5 Would you maintain that you do not need **help?** 6 Yet this **claim that you do not need help** is what you are maintaining when you refuse to recognize a brother's appeal, for only by answering his appeal <can> you be helped. 7 Deny **your brother** your help and you will not recognize God's Answer to you, **which is the Atonement.** 8 The Holy Spirit does not need your help in interpreting motivation, but you do need **the Holy Spirit's help in interpreting a brother's motivation.**

Note # 5: The ego always misperceives and will interpret our brother's call for help as an attack. If we do not understand this error in thinking, we will fail to ask for the guidance of the Holy Spirit. We will respond to our brother's cry for help by attacking him and thus, making this misperception real in the minds of both parties. By following the thought system of the ego, we fail to ask for higher guidance and deny our brother and ourselves the Holy Spirit's help.

T-12.I.6. Only appreciation is an appropriate response to your brother. 2 Gratitude is due **your brother** for both **your brother's** loving thoughts and **your brother's** appeals for help, for both are capable of bringing love into your awareness if you perceive **both your brother's loving thoughts and your brother's appeals for help** truly **as they are.** 3 And all your sense of strain comes from your attempts not to **appropriately respond to your brother's loving thoughts and appeals.** 4 How simple, then, is God's plan for salvation. 5 There is but one response to reality, for reality evokes no conflict at all. **Reality knows only the truth.** 6 There is but one Teacher of reality, **the Holy Spirit Who** understands what **reality** is. 7 **The Holy Spirit** does not change His Mind about reality because reality does not change. 8 Although your interpretations of reality are meaningless in your divided state, **the Holy Spirit's interpretations of reality** remain consistently true. 9 **The Holy Spirit** gives **His interpretation of reality** to you because **the Holy Spirit's interpretation of reality is** <*for*> you. 10 Do not attempt to "help" in your way, for you cannot help yourself. 11 But hear **a brother's** call for the Help of God, and you will recognize your own need for the Father.

<u>Note # 6:</u> All our sense of strain and conflict comes from our inappropriate response to our brother's loving thoughts and appeals for help. Because we believe that we are the body, we generally follow the thought system of the ego. Our egoic little "s" self responds to our brother's actions as an attack upon our perceived, vulnerable ego-body This egoic response conflicts with the proper response that both our Big "S" Self and the Holy Spirit knows is correct. This conflict between the two parts of our split-mind represents misalignment and is associated emotionally with our loss of peace. Any misalignment between our behavior and our Big "S" Self's reality and truth is felt emotionally as a bad felling and results in our loss of inner peace. Thus, our emotional feelings help monitor and gage our alignment of the spilt mind with the thought system of the Holy Spirit. When we feel true joy, our behavior and our thoughts are in alignment with our Big "S" Self. When we feel bad, angry, and guilty or have lost our inner peace, we can rest assured that we are in misalignment with the true loving nature of our One Self.

T-12.I.7. Your interpretations of your brother's needs are your interpretation of **your needs**. 2 By giving help you are asking for **help**, and if you perceive but one need in yourself you will be healed. 3 For you will recognize God's Answer as you want **God's Answer** to be, and if you want **God's Answer** in truth, **God's Answer** will be truly yours. 4 Every appeal you answer in the Name of Christ brings the remembrance of your Father closer to your awareness. 5 For the sake of your need, then, hear every call for help as what it is, **which is a cry for help** so God can answer <*you.*> **God's answer is the Atonement.**

<u>Note # 7:</u> Our one need is the remembrance of God. When we choose to remember God, we reclaim the Sonship's divine birthright. We realize the Atonement principle's truth of the sinless and guiltless reality of God's Son. God's Law states that by giving help, we receive help.

T-12.I.8. By applying the Holy Spirit's interpretation of the reactions of others more and more consistently, you will gain an increasing awareness that **the Holy Spirit's** criteria are equally applicable to you. 2 For to recognize fear is not enough to escape from **fear**, although the recognition is necessary to demonstrate the need for **the** escape **from fear**. 3 The Holy Spirit must still translate the fear into truth. 4 If you were left with the fear, once you had recognized **fear**, you would have taken a step away from reality, not towards **reality**. 5 Yet we have repeatedly emphasized the need to recognize fear and face **fear** without disguise as a crucial step in the undoing of the ego. 6 Consider how well the Holy Spirit's interpretation of the motives of others will serve you then. 7 **The Holy Spirit's interpretation**

of the motives of others will have taught you to accept only loving thoughts in others and to regard everything else as an appeal for help. **The Holy Spirit's interpretation of the motives of others** has taught you that fear itself is an appeal for help. 8 This is what recognizing fear really means. 9 If you do not protect **fear, the Holy Spirit** will reinterpret **fear as a cry for help.** 10 That is the ultimate value in learning to perceive attack as a call for love. 11 We have already learned that fear and attack are inevitably associated. 12 If only attack produces fear, and if you see attack as the call for help that it is, the unreality of fear must dawn on you. 13 For fear <*is*> a call for love, in unconscious recognition of what has been denied, **which is love.**

Note # 8: The idea of the separation is our denial of God's unconditional love toward us, God's Creation. This belief that we are other than God's Effect has led us into fear. If we follow the Holy Spirit's thought system and perceive any experience as either love or a cry for love, we no longer move into "fear-mode." We can transform fear into truth. The Holy Spirit will only respond to any situation with truth. When we perceive fear in another as only a cry for love, we will not respond by egoically attacking our brother. When we are in fear, we move into attack-mode. This results in misalignment and conflict between our split-mind. By controlling our fear and asking for the guidance of the Holy Spirit, we can move back into realignment with our One Self and regain our inner peace.

T-12.I.9. Fear is a symptom of your own deep sense of loss. 2 If when you perceive a **sense of loss** in others you learn to supply the loss, the basic cause of fear is removed. 3 Thereby you teach yourself that fear does not exist in you. 4 The means for removing **the sense of loss caused by fear** is in yourself, and you have demonstrated this by giving **love, which removes fear.** 5 Fear and love are the only emotions of which you are capable. 6 **Fear** is false, for **fear** was made out of denial; and denial depends on the belief in what is denied for its own existence. 7 By interpreting fear correctly as a positive affirmation of the underlying belief **that fear** masks, you are undermining **fear's** perceived usefulness by rendering **fear** useless. 8 Defenses that do not work at all are automatically discarded. 9 If you raise **love, which is** what fear conceals, to clear-cut unequivocal predominance, fear becomes meaningless. 10 You have denied **fear's** power to conceal love, which was **fear's** only purpose. 11 **Fear**, the veil that you have drawn across the face of love has disappeared.

Note # 9: There are only two emotions of which we are capable; either love or fear. In the world of perception, both fear and love seem possible. In eternity, only love is real. When we follow the thought system of the ego, we are operating out of fear. The Holy Spirit's thought system is the path to love. The little "s" self believes that both fear and love are viable choices. The Big "S" Self knows that the only real choice is love. When our behavior and thoughts align with fear, we feel stressed and conflicted because we are not following the true nature of our Big "S" Self. When we control our fears, we are able to ask for guidance. The Holy Spirit will bring truth to fear and fear will dissipate.
Fear is removed by the realization that you are truly one with the Love of God. Being love, you can only give love. Fear disappears, since fear only existed in your split-mind. It is our fear from our sense of loss of God's love that makes the illusion of separation appear real within our split-mind.

T-12.I.10. If you would look upon love, which <*is*> the world's reality, how could you do better than to recognize, in every defense against **love,** the underlying appeal <*for*> love? 2 And how could you better learn of **love's** reality than by answering the appeal for **love** by giving **love?** 3 The Holy Spirit's interpretation of fear does dispel **fear,** for the awareness of truth cannot be denied. 4 Thus does the Holy Spirit replace fear with love and translate **the** error **of fear** into truth. 5 And thus will you learn of **the Holy Spirit** how to replace your dream of separation with the fact of unity. 6 For the separation is only the denial of union, and correctly interpreted, attests to your eternal knowledge that union is true.

Note # 10: Fear arises out of the denial of truth. The belief in the separation results in fear since the separation is the denial of God's love for the Sonship. If we recognize that fear arises only from our belief in our lack of love, we can utilize any thought of fear, as a triggering mechanism to remind us to ask for the Holy Spirit's help. The Holy Spirit will reinterpret our fearful perception into a tool for forgiveness, unity and love. This reinterpretation of our fearful perception will help us remember the truth that we are united with the Oneness of our Father.

II. The Way to Remember God

T-12.II.1. Miracles are merely the translation of denial into truth. 2 If to love oneself is to heal oneself, those who are sick do not love themselves. 3 Therefore, **those who are sick** are asking for the love that would heal them, but which **those who are sick** are denying to themselves. 4 If **those who are sick** knew the truth about themselves **those who are sick** could not be sick. 5 The task of the miracle worker thus becomes <*to deny the denial of truth.*> 6 The sick must heal themselves, for the truth is in them, **the sick person**. 7 Yet having obscured **the denial of truth in themselves**, the light in another mind must shine into **the sick person's mind** because that light **of the miracle worker** <*is*> also the light of the sick person.

Note # 11: The miracle worker translates the denial of truth in their brother back into the truth. The miracle worker observes the Christ, rather than the little "s' self in his brother. In the miracle, the miracle worker refuses to see any limitation in his brother and looks past the apparent form that "sickness" has taken within their brother. When given this correct perception of himself by the miracle worker, the sick brother may be able to accept the truth about himself and thus, heal himself. Only the sick person can heal himself or herself. The miracle takes place within the individual's own mind and is merely a change from wrong perception to correct perception.

T-12.II.2. The light in **the sick person** shines as brightly regardless of the density of the fog that obscures **the sick person's light**. 2 If you give no power to the fog to obscure the light, the fog, **which arose by the denial of the truth**, has **no power**. 3 For **the fog, which arose by the denial of the truth**, has power only if the Son of God gives power to **the denial of the truth**. 4 **The Son of God** must himself withdraw that power **that he gave the denial of the truth**, remembering that all power is of God. 5 You can remember **that all power is of God** for all the Sonship. 6 Do not allow your brother not to remember **that all power is of God**, for **our brother's** forgetfulness is your **forgetfulness**. 7 But your remembering is **our brother's remembering**, for God cannot be remembered alone. 8 <*Because if you try to remember alone, you have forgotten that God cannot be remembered alone and this is what you have forgotten.*> 9 To perceive the healing of your brother as the healing of yourself is thus the way to remember God. 10 For **when** you forgot your brothers **you forgot** God **also,** and God's Answer to your forgetting is but the way to remember **the truth about your brother and God.**

Note # 12: Healing is realizing the Oneness that we share with all God's creations because we live in the one Mind of God. It is only by our abdicating to the ego our own mind's power as decision-maker that makes the illusion appear real. All egoic power comes from our own mind. Thus, we imagine that we have given to the ego creative powers that belong only to our mind. This transfer of our creative power is what gives the illusion a life of its own. When we choose to forget the truth about our brother or ourselves, we perceive both our brother and ourselves as a little "s" self. This also transforms the God of Love into an idol to fear. We need to deny the false and thus, observe the truth, which is all that remains.

T-12.II.3.Perceive in sickness but another call for love, and offer your brother what **your brother** believes he cannot offer himself, **which is the truth about himself that he is only love's Big "S" Self.** 2 Whatever the sickness, there is but one remedy. 3 You will be made whole as you make whole, for to perceive in sickness the appeal for health is to recognize in hatred the call for love. 4 And to give a brother what he really wants is to offer **what he really wants, which is love,** unto yourself, for your Father wills you to know your brother as yourself. 5 Answer his call for love, and your **call for love** is answered. 6 Healing is the Love of Christ for His Father and for Himself.

<u>Note # 13:</u> Sickness is a form of self-hatred, which is a denial of God's love. Love, which is all we are and is all that is real, heals all illusions. When the false is brought into the light of truth, the false fades into the nothingness from which it arose.

T-12.II.4.Remember what was said about the frightening perceptions of little children, which terrify them because **the little children** do not understand **their frightening perceptions.** 2 If **the little children** ask for enlightenment and accept **enlightenment,** their fears vanish. 3 But if **the little children** hide their nightmares, **the little children** will keep **their nightmares.** 4 It is easy to help an uncertain child, for **an uncertain child** recognizes that he does not understand what his perceptions mean. 5 Yet you believe that you do understand **what your perceptions mean.** 6 Little child, you are hiding your head under the cover of the heavy blankets you have laid upon yourself. 7 You are hiding your nightmares in the darkness of your own false certainty, and refusing to open your eyes and look at **your nightmares**.

<u>Note # 14:</u> By misinterpreting our perception, we fail to realize that we need outside guidance to understand our problems. Because we believe that we understand the source of our problems, we fail to ask for the guidance of the Holy Spirit. Only the Holy Spirit knows the truth about what we are and what we perceive ourselves to be. Therefore, only the Holy Spirit is capable of judging correctly. The ego is the problem. We cannot expect to find the solution to the problem of not knowing our divine nature by asking the ego for an answer that the ego refuses to hear and accept.

T-12.II.5.Let us not save nightmares, for **our nightmares** are not fitting offerings for Christ, and so **our nightmares** are not fit gifts for you. 2 Take off the covers and look at what you are afraid of. 3 Only the anticipation will frighten you, for the reality of nothingness cannot be frightening. 4 Let us not delay this **looking at what you are afraid of,** for your dream of hatred will not leave you without help, and Help, **in the form of the Holy Spirit,** is here. 5 Learn to be quiet in the midst of turmoil, for quietness is the end of strife and this **quietness that ends strife** is the journey to peace. 6 Look straight at every image that rises to delay you, for the goal is inevitable because **peace** is eternal. 7 The goal of love is but your right, and **love** belongs to you despite your dreams.

<u>Note # 15:</u> The ego will always tell you why it is right and why you are justified in your fear, anger, hurt and ultimate attack. Quiet your egoic chatter and ask for the guidance of the Holy Spirit. Only the Holy Spirit knows how to regain your inner peace.

T-12.II.6.You still want what God wills, and no nightmare can defeat a child of God in his purpose. **What both God and you will is love. This is your purpose**. 2 For your purpose was given you by God, and you must accomplish **your purpose** because **your purpose** is **God's** Will. 3 Awake and remember your purpose **of love,** for it is your will to do so. 4 What has been accomplished for you must be yours. 5

Do not let your hatred stand in the way of love, for nothing can withstand the Love of Christ for His Father, or His Father's Love for Him, **the Christ**.

Note # 16: Our Father, our Big "S" Self and the Holy Spirit all know the truth; our Will is one for we are the One Self. A false illusion of the nothingness of separation can have no affect upon the holographic Mind of God. Our little "s" self's reawakening is inevitable for God's Will is not mocked.

T-12.II.7.A little while and you will see me, for I am not hidden because <you> are hiding. 2 I will awaken you as surely as I awakened myself, for I awoke for you. 3 In my resurrection is your release. 4 Our mission is to escape from crucifixion, not **to escape** from redemption. 5 Trust in my help, for I did not walk alone, and I will walk with you as our Father walked with me. 6 Do you not know that I walked with **our Father** in peace? 7 And does not that mean that peace goes with <us> on the journey?

Note # 17: Jesus has already shown the way and will continue to do so until we too arrive in the knowing of the peace of God. We, not Jesus, are the ones that are currently choosing to deny our truth under the veil of egoic littleness.

T-12.II.8. There is no fear in perfect love. 2 We will but be making perfect to you what is already perfect in you. 3 You do not fear the unknown, **which is the perfection of your Big "S" Self,** but **you do fear** the known, **which is the false image of your egoic little "s" self.** 4 You will not fail in your mission because I did not fail in **my mission of the return to truth and love.** 5 Give me but a little trust in the name of the complete trust I have in you, and we will easily accomplish the goal of perfection together. 6 For perfection <is,> and cannot be denied. 7 To deny the denial of perfection is not so difficult as to deny truth, and what we can accomplish together will be believed when you see **truth's perfection** as accomplished.

Note # 18: Truth just is. It is the false that must be made to cover-up the truth. To maintain the illusion of separation requires work and a great deal of effort. This is why the aim of ACIM is not to teach love, but instead to remove all the blocks that we have placed in front of love. We cannot be taught how to love because love is our natural state of being.

T-12.II.9. You who have tried to banish love have not succeeded, but you who choose to banish fear must succeed. 2 The Lord is with you, but you know not **that the Lord is with you.** 3 Yet your Redeemer liveth, and abideth in you in the peace out of which your Redeemer, **the Christ in you**, was created. 4 Would you not exchange this awareness **of perfect love** for the awareness of fear? 5 When we have overcome fear–not by hiding **fear**, not by minimizing **fear**, and not by denying **fear's** full import in any way–this, **perfect love,** is what you will really see. 6 You cannot lay aside the obstacles to real vision without looking upon **the obstacles to real vision**, for to lay aside means to judge against. 7 If you will look, the Holy Spirit will judge, and **the Holy Spirit** will judge truly. 8 Yet **the Holy Spirit** cannot shine away what you keep hidden, for you have not offered **what you keep hidden** to **the Holy Spirit** and **the Holy Spirit** cannot take **what you keep hidden** from you.

Note # 19: Because we have free will, we must make the conscious choice of asking for the Holy Spirit's guidance. Only we have the power to overcome our fears. We must control our fears and then turn them over to the truth of the Holy Spirit. Neither Jesus nor the Holy Spirit can remove our fears, for the source of fear is in your own mind. The Holy Spirit will guide us to the truth about our nightmares but we alone must choose for truth over illusions.

T-12.II.10. We are therefore embarking on an organized, well-structured and carefully planned program aimed at learning how to offer to the Holy Spirit everything you do not want. 2 **The Holy Spirit** knows what to do with **everything you do not want**. 3 You do not understand how to use what **the Holy Spirit** knows. 4 Whatever is given **the Holy Spirit** that is not of God is gone. 5 Yet you must look at **what the Holy Spirit knows within** yourself in perfect willingness, for otherwise **the Holy Spirit's** knowledge remains useless to you. 6 Surely **the Holy Spirit** will not fail to help you, since help is **the Holy Spirit's** only purpose. 7 Do you not have greater reason for fearing the world as you perceive **the world**, than for looking at the cause of fear and letting **fear** go forever?

Note # 20: The cause of fear is the result of the guilt we feel for our belief that we have "sinned" against the Will of God. This belief of sin, guilt and fear arose from the belief of the separation. The Holy Spirit was placed inside our minds to provide guidance for our remembrance of the truth about our Father and ourselves. The purpose of the Holy Spirit is to assist in the healing of our split mind. This healing is our reawakening into the One Self that is the holographic Mind of God.

III. The Investment in Reality

T-12.III.1.I once asked you to sell all you have and give to the poor and follow me. 2 This is what I meant: If you have no investment in anything in this world, you can teach the poor where their treasure is. 3 The poor are merely those who have invested wrongly, **believing that in this world of illusion, they will find the treasure they seek** and, **therefore,** they are poor indeed! 4 Because **the poor** are in need it is given you to help **the poor,** since you are among **the poor.** 5 Consider how perfectly your lesson would be learned if you were unwilling to share their poverty, **which is their belief in lack of love.** 6 For poverty is lack **of love,** and there is but one lack since there is but one need.

Note # 21: A person's perceptions follow what that person values. We are poor when we give value to the nothingness of the illusion of fear and separation. We are poor when we value the idols of egoic specialness. We need to accept the Atonement for ourselves. The Atonement is the denial of the false and the acceptance of the true. It is the healing of the split mind. When we look past the littleness of the ego and look upon the Christ in our brother, we receive and see the Christ within us. Love replaces fear and God, which is love, is remembered.

T-12.III.2. Suppose a brother insists on having you do something you think you do not want to do. 2 **A brother's** very insistence should tell you that **this brother** believes salvation lies in **you doing something that he wants.** 3 If you insist on refusing and experience a quick response of opposition, you are believing that your salvation lies in <not> doing **something that he wants.** 4 You, then, are making the same mistake **this brother** is, and are making **this brother's** error real to both of you. 5 Insistence means investment, and what you invest in is always related to your notion of salvation. 6 The question is always twofold; first, <what> is to be saved? 7 And second, <how> can it be saved?

Note # 22: When we insist upon something in this world of nothingness, we are saying that our salvation rests upon doing something. We have placed value on the worthless. God's love is freely given and requires nothing of us. Love allows; it does not demand someone get "fixed." We are arguing for our ego's rightness over our brother's. Our happiness rests on being love, not in being egoically right. By requiring that we fix our brother, we make his belief in his sickness and lack real. Since to give is to receive, we acknowledge our own lack.

What we insist on is related to where and what we believe is needed to make us happy. Do we believe that our salvation must come from something outside ourselves, that we lack something or that we must do something? We need do nothing. All we need do is to be as God created us. This requires no effort. Yet, to attempt to be something that we are not does require effort. The idea that something outside ourselves must take place in order for us to be fulfilled indicates that we have accepted the idea that we are a limited, ego-body. This insistence that we are not perfect, whole and complete makes your illusionary world of provisional reality real for us. We perceive that we lack. Perceive our brother's belief in lack and you confirm your own belief that you need something to happen for you to be "saved." This is an affirmation that you are not whole yourself. When you argue for your limitations, you get to keep them.

T-12.III.3. Whenever you become angry with a brother, for whatever reason, you are believing that the ego is to be saved, and to be saved by attack. 2 If **a brother** attacks, you are agreeing with this belief **that the ego is to be saved by attack**; and if you attack, you are reinforcing **this belief that the ego is to be saved by attack since there is lack**. 3 <Remember that those who attack are poor.> 4 Their poverty asks for gifts, not for further impoverishment. 5 You who could help **those who attack** are surely acting destructively if you accept their poverty as yours. 6 If you had not invested **in the treasures of illusions** as **those who attack** had, it would never occur to you to overlook their need.

Note # 23: The world of illusion is not real. There is nothing of value in the unreal. Our salvation and happiness cannot be found in the unreal. If we substitute an illusion for the truth about ourselves, we will never escape the dream world. Our insistence that something outside ourselves is needed for us to be loved and to love is the insistence that we lack love. Defense and attack both act as false witnesses for our vulnerability as a limited ego-body. Attack is never justified. The proper response to a brother's cry for help is love. Only through the eyes of love will we properly perceive our brother. If we look with fear, we will respond with attack in the name of egoic self-defense.

T-12.III.4. <Recognize what does not matter,> and if your brothers ask you for something "outrageous," do **the "outrageous," for your brother** <because> it does not matter. 2 Refuse **a brother's "outrageous" request**, and your opposition establishes that it does matter to you. 3 It is only you, therefore, who have made the request outrageous, and every request of a brother is for you. 4 Why would you insist in denying **a brother's request**? 5 For to do so is to deny yourself and impoverish both. 6 **A brother** is asking for salvation, as you are **asking for salvation**. 7 Poverty is of the ego, and never of God. 8 No "outrageous" requests can be made of one who recognizes what is valuable and wants to accept nothing else.

Note # 24: Nothing of this dream world is real and, therefore, of value. Only love is real. The only value this dream world can provide is as a learning device for reawakening from this dream to the realization that we are only love and invulnerable to the false. We are the One Self. By learning forgiveness and love for our brother, we give this to ourselves. This leads us back up the path of remembering God and thus, reclaiming our divine birthright.

T-12.III.5. Salvation is for the mind, and **salvation** is attained through peace **that arises out of love**. 2 **The mind** is the only thing that can be saved and the only way to save **the mind is through the attainment of the peace of God**. 3 Any response other than love arises from a confusion about the "what" and the "how" of **obtaining** salvation, and this, **love**, is the only answer. 4 Never lose sight **that salvation is found in love**, and never allow yourself to believe, even for an instant, that there is another answer **than love.** 5 For you will surely place yourself among the poor, who do not understand that they,

who believe they are poor actually dwell in abundance and that salvation is come.

Note # 25: We can deny reality, but our erroneous belief cannot change the truth. We remain always as God created us, for in reality we have never left the Mind of God. There has never been a time that God did not love His Son unconditionally. We alone have chosen to deny this truth. What we value becomes what we perceive as our "truth." Discard fear and value only love, which is the truth that is the peace of God.

T-12.III.6.To identify with the ego is to attack yourself and make yourself poor. 2 That is why everyone who identifies with the ego feels deprived. 3 What he experiences **by identifying with the ego** then is depression or anger, because what he did **by identifying with the ego** was to exchange Self-love for self-hate, making him afraid of himself. 4 He, **who identifies with the ego,** does not realize **he has exchanged Self-love for self-hate.** 5 Even if he is fully aware of anxiety he does not perceive **anxiety's** source as his own ego identification, and he always tries to handle this **anxiety that result from ego identification** by making some sort of insane "arrangement" with the world. 6 He always perceives this world as outside himself, for this is crucial to his adjustment. 7 He does not realize that he makes this world, for there is no world outside of him.

Note # 26: When we identify with the ego, we fall into a state of victim consciousness. Playing the role of victim, we abdicate responsibility for the events in our life. We fail to see ourselves as the source or creator of the dream and, instead, hope something outside ourselves will arrive and make us complete and thus, "save" us. We cannot find the truth about ourselves in an unreal illusion. Only by reclaiming our decision making ability can we choose for the Holy Spirit and against the thought system of the ego. It is our choice to follow the thought system of the ego that transports us into the dream world of ego identification.

When we identify with the ego, we have moved out of alignment with our Big "S" Self. Our mind is split in its allegiance and this results in conflict and stress. Self-love and self-hate cannot co-exist. When we feel bad, our Big "S" Self is attempting to signal that we are out of balance with our true nature. Feelings of blame, fear, anger, frustration and depression all tell us that our behavior is not in alignment with love's correct response. We will have lost our joy and inner peace. Treat any bad feeling as a warning to stop thinking egoically and ask for the guidance of the Holy Spirit. Only the Holy Spirit knows the way back to the inner peace of the One Self.

T-12.III.7.If only the loving thoughts of God's Son are the world's reality, the real world must be in his mind. 2 **The split-mind's** insane thoughts, too, must be in his mind, but an internal conflict of this magnitude **within the son's mind** cannot tolerate. 3 A split mind is endangered **in God's Son,** and the recognition that **the split mind** encompasses completely opposed thoughts within itself is intolerable. 4 Therefore the mind projects the split, not the reality. 5 Everything you perceive as the outside world is merely your **split-mind's** attempt to maintain your ego identification, for everyone believes that identification **with the ego** is salvation. 6 Yet consider what has happened **when you identify with the ego,** for thoughts do have consequences to the thinker. 7 You have become at odds with the world as you perceive **the world,** because you think **that your perceived world** is antagonistic to you. 8 This is a necessary consequence of what you have done. 9 You have projected outward what is antagonistic to what is inward, **in your own split mind,** and therefore you would have to perceive **your outside world as antagonistic to you in** this way. 10 That is why you must realize that your hatred is in your mind and not outside **your mind** before you can get rid of **your hatred**; and why you must get rid of **your hatred** before you can perceive the world as **the world** really is.

Note # 27: This viewpoint of the antagonistic outside world is the natural outcome of projection. In projection, we take something inside our mind and project it outside ourselves in an attempt to get rid of it. This results in our denial of ourselves as the source of the item that is actually found in our mind. All thoughts must originate from mind.

T-12.III.8.I said before that God so loved the world that **God** gave **the real world** to **God's** only begotten Son. 2 God does love the real world, and those who perceive **the real world's** reality cannot see the world of death. 3 For death is not of the real world, in which everything reflects the eternal. 4 God gave you the real world in exchange for the **world** you **perceive that you** made out of your split mind. **The world you perceive that you made out of your split mind** is the symbol of death. 5 For if you could really separate yourself from the Mind of God you would die.

<u>Note # 28:</u> The real world is the Kingdom or Heaven, which is only love. Heaven is not a place but a state of mind in which only love is real. Our Big "S" Self knows this truth that only love is real. Our split minded ego believes that both love and fear are possible. The split-mind has made an illusionary world so that it can play the game of separation until it has relearned the truth about itself.

T-12.III.9. The world you perceive is a world of separation. 2 Perhaps you are willing to accept even death to deny your Father. 3 Yet **God** would not have **you die**, and so **your death cannot be** so. 4 You still cannot will against **God**, and **because you cannot will against God this** is why you have no control over the world you made. 5 It is not a world of will because **the world you made** is governed by the desire to be unlike God, and this desire is not will. 6 The world you made is therefore totally chaotic, governed by arbitrary and senseless "laws," and without meaning of any kind. 7 For **the world you made** is made out of what you do not want, projected from your mind because you are afraid of **what you do not want**. 8 Yet this world is only in the **split** mind of its maker, along with his real salvation. 9 Do not believe **the world you made** is outside of yourself, for only by recognizing where **the world you made** is will you gain control over **the world you made within your mind**. 10 For you do have control over your mind, since the mind is the mechanism of decision.

<u>Note # 29:</u> Only in the mind of the dreamer can the dream be undone. The nightmare can only be stopped at its source, which is the insane mind that is the thought projector. If we reclaim our mind's decision-making ability and realize that we are the dreamer of the dream of separation, we can chose again. By remembering what we are, we will remember God, Whose love we have never lost.

T-12.III.10. If you will recognize that all the attack you perceive is in your own mind and nowhere else, you will at last have placed **the** source **of the attack**, and where **the attack** begins **the attack** must end. 2 For in this same place, **which is your mind, there** also lies salvation. 3 The altar of God where Christ abideth is there **in your mind**. 4 You have defiled the altar, but not the **real** world. 5 Yet Christ has placed the Atonement on the altar for you. 6 Bring your perceptions of the world to this altar, **for Christ's altar which holds the Atonement** is the altar to truth. 7 There you will see your vision changed, and there you will learn to see truly. 8 From this place, where God and His Son dwell in peace and where you are welcome, you will look out in peace and behold the world truly. 9 Yet to find the place, you must relinquish your investment in the world as you project it, allowing the Holy Spirit to extend the real world to you from the altar of God.

<u>Note # 30:</u> By accepting the Atonement for ourselves, we reclaim the remembrance of God and what we are. The Atonement principle undoes all misperception with the truth. The Atonement principle states that what we perceived in our dreams was never real since it was not in the Mind of God. The dream world of provisional reality is only a dream. Therefore, God demands no sacrifice or punishment from us since we have never "sinned." To God, we will always be perfect as He created us. God's Son

remains eternally sinless and guiltless. This is our reality and our birthright. By accepting the Atonement for ourselves, we cease to deny God's Fatherhood and accept our divine birthright. We reawaken to the Kingdom, which is the real world from which we have never left. We have always been and always will remain part of the Mind of God for we are eternal.

IV. Seeking and Finding

T-12.IV.1. The ego is certain that love is dangerous, and **that love is dangerous** is always **the ego's** central teaching. 2**The ego** never puts it this way **that love is dangerous**; on the contrary, everyone who believes that the ego is salvation seems to be intensely engaged in the search for love. 3 Yet the ego, though encouraging the search for love very actively, makes one proviso; do not find **love**. 4 **The ego's** dictates, then, can be summed up simply as: "Seek and do <*not*> find **love**." 5 **"Seek and do <*not*> find love."** is the one promise the ego holds out to you, and the one promise **the ego** will keep. 6 For the ego pursues **the ego's** goal with fanatic insistence, and **the ego's** judgment, though severely impaired, is completely consistent.

Note # 31: The ego does not understand what love is and, therefore, views it as dangerous. True love is dangerous to something that opposes the truth. What the ego would term love is not true love, but rather conditional love. Conditional love is acceptable to the ego because conditional love only gives to get. Conditional love confirms that the giver is not perfect, whole and complete. The giver is in need of "something" from outside itself to make it better. If this "something" is not forthcoming, the "giver" is free to take their sacrifice to another in search of a better trade. Thus, the ego's goal and motto is "Seek and do <not> find love." The ego is very diligent and single minded in working to achieve its goal.

T-12.IV.2. The search the ego undertakes is therefore bound to be defeated. 2 And since **the ego** also teaches that **the ego** is your identification, **the ego's** guidance leads you to a journey which must end in perceived self-defeat. 3 For the ego cannot love, and in **the ego's** frantic search for love **the ego** is seeking what **the ego** is afraid to find, **which is love.** 4 The **ego's** search, **which is "seek and do <not> find love,"** is inevitable because the ego is part of your mind, and because of **the ego's** source, **which is the mind,** the ego is not wholly split off, or **the ego** could not be believed at all. 5 For it is your mind that believes in **the ego** and gives existence to **the ego**. 6 Yet it is also your mind that has the power to deny the ego's existence, and you will surely do so when you realize exactly what the journey is on which the ego sets you.

Note # 32: Because the ego's goal is "seek and do <not> find love." the ego wants to hide this goal from your mind. If you realized that never finding love was the true goal of the ego, you would not want to play the ego's game of "let's hide and never find God's Love." The goal of the ego is to bring you pain; yet, the ego constantly holds out to you the idea that love is just around the corner. Once we obtain what the ego claims would bring us love, we realize that we are still unhappy. The ego then changes its story and tells us that although we failed to find love in the achievement of this item or goal, something else will bring us love. **Example:** First, the ego tells us that we will be happy when we get married. Once married, the ego tells us that we will be happy when we get a divorce. And so it goes, on and on. We are constantly seeking things outside ourselves only to find that once obtained, they do not bring us happiness. By this constant seeking outside yourself, the ego confirms that you are not perfect, whole and complete. This guarantees that you will continue your false belief in the separation. This "seek and do <not> find" motto is what makes the ego's thought system so insidious and insane. As long as the ego can keep our mind, which is the true source of the ego's alleged power, in victim consciousness, our mind will never realize that the mind has the ability to choose again. Our mind will continue to believe that it is powerless and that its fate is controlled by everything outside of it. Therefore, our mind can continue to claim that it is not responsible for the "bad luck" which so often brings pain.

T-12.IV.3. It is surely obvious that no one wants to find what would utterly defeat him. 2 Being unable to love, the ego would be totally inadequate in love's presence, for **the ego** could not respond at all **to love**. 3 Then, you would have to abandon the ego's guidance, for it would be quite apparent that **the ego** had not taught you the response you need **to obtain and be love**. 4 The ego will therefore distort love, and teach you that love really calls forth the responses the ego <can> teach. 5 Follow **the ego's** teaching, then, and you will search for love, but will not recognize **love**.

Note # 33: The ego teaches that love is always conditional. Conditional love, which is not to be confused with true love, only gives in order to get something of greater value in return. Egoic, conditional love is based on separation and demands sacrifice. Each party only "gives to get." This insures that you will always be lacking something and that the return to whole-mindedness will not be achieved. If we can find a "better trade," we quickly leave the old relationship in search of greener pastures.

T-12.IV.4. Do you realize that the ego must set you on a journey **of "seek and do <not> find love,"** which cannot but lead to a sense of futility and depression? 2 To seek and not to find is hardly joyous. 3 Is this the promise you would keep? 4 The Holy Spirit offers you another promise, and **the Holy Spirit's promise is** one that will lead to joy. 5 For **the Holy Spirit's** promise is always, "Seek and you <will> find **Love,"** and under **the Holy Spirit's** guidance you cannot be defeated. 6 **The Holy Spirit's promise** is the journey to accomplishment, and the goal **the Holy Spirit** sets before you **the Holy Spirit** will give you. 7 For **the Holy Spirit** will never deceive God's Son whom **the Holy Spirit** loves with the Love of the Father.

Note # 34: The goal of the Holy Spirit is to guide you to your return to God and the remembrance of who you really are, which, like your Father, is perfect love. The Holy Spirit's promise of "Seek and you <will> find Love," must be achieved since this is God's Will.

T-12.IV.5. You <will> undertake a journey because you are not at home in this **illusionary** world **of your own misperception**. 2 And you <will> search for your home whether you realize where **your home** is or not. 3 If you believe **your home** is outside you the search will be futile, for you will be seeking **your home** where it is not **in your illusionary world of provisional reality**. 4 You do not remember how to look within for you do not believe your home is there **within you**. 5 Yet the Holy Spirit remembers **where your home is** for you, and **the Holy Spirit** will guide you to your home **within you** because that is **the Holy Spirit's** mission. 6 As **the Holy Spirit** fulfills His mission **the Holy Spirit** will teach you your **mission**, for your mission is the same as **the Holy Spirit's mission, which is to return to your home in the Mind of God.** 7 By guiding your brothers home you are but following **the Holy Spirit's mission**.

Note # 35: Your home is your source. Your source is the Mind of God. Although in reality you never left your Source, due to our free will, we can temporarily deny the truth about ourselves and pretend that we live in our illusionary world of perception.
If you lost your keys in the United States, it is futile to seek them in Brazil. You need to seek your keys

in the place you lost them. We lost our knowledge of love in our mind. That is where we will find it. To look outside our mind is a futile waste of time.

T-12.IV.6. Behold **the Holy Spirit,** the Guide your Father gave you, that you might learn you have eternal life. 2 For death is not your Father's Will nor **your will** and whatever is true is the Will of the Father. 3 You pay no price for life for **eternal life** was given you, but you do pay a price for death, and a very heavy one. 4 If death is your treasure, you will sell everything else to purchase **death**. 5 And you will believe that you have purchased **death**, because you have sold everything else **to obtain your treasure of death**. 6 Yet you cannot sell the Kingdom of Heaven. 7 Your inheritance, **which is the Kingdom of Heaven,** can neither be bought nor sold. 8 There can be no disinherited parts of the Sonship, for God is whole and all **God's** extensions are like **God**.

Note # 36: Since creation is extension, we are exactly like our Father. We share all the attributes of the Father because we share one mind, which is the Mind of God. Free will allows us to deny the truth but denial cannot change truth's reality. Since our will is God's Will, eventually, we will freely decide to choose the truth and be that Love.

T-12.IV.7. The Atonement is not the price of your wholeness, but **the Atonement** <*is*> the price of your awareness of your wholeness. 2 For what you chose to "sell" had to be kept for you, since you could not "buy" **what you chose to "sell"** back, **which was your divine inheritance of eternal life**. 3 Yet you must invest in **what you chose to "sell,"** not with money but with spirit. 4 For spirit is will, and will is the "price" of the Kingdom. 5 Your inheritance awaits only the recognition that you have been redeemed. 6 The Holy Spirit guides you into life eternal, but you must relinquish your investment in death, or you will not see life though **eternal life** is all around you.

Note # 37: We must accept the Atonement for ourselves. The Atonement is our healing since it is the acceptance to the truth that God's Son is guiltless and sinless. The Holy Spirit will show us the way but the ultimate choice to recognize the Holy Spirit's thought system as our only thought system is a choice we must freely make. To freely realize that our will is the same as the Father's Will, will bring us home to the remembrance of God and our true spiritual nature. We will reclaim our divine inheritance.

V. The Sane Curriculum

T-12.V.1. Only love is strong because **love** is undivided. 2 The strong do not attack because **the strong** see no need to **attack**. 3 Before the idea of attack can enter your mind, you must have perceived yourself as weak. 4 Because you attacked yourself and believed that the attack was effective, you behold yourself as weakened. 5 No longer perceiving yourself and your brothers as equal, and regarding yourself as weaker, you attempt to "equalize" the situation you made. 6 You use attack **to attempt to "equalize" the situation you made of being unequal in the strength with your brother** because you believe that attack was successful in weakening you.

Note # 38: When we perceive ourselves as limited ego-body, we adopt the belief that we are vulnerable and can be hurt. The world of perception becomes a fearful place that is predicated on limited resources and lack. Life becomes a competitive "zero-sum game." If I am to win, someone must lose. Self-defense is required to maintain what you have and the best defense is a good offense. To insure your body's survival "preemptive strikes" becomes a way of life.

T-12.V.2.Because you believe that attack was successful in weakening you, this is why the recognition of your own invulnerability is so important to the restoration of your sanity. 2 For if you accept your invulnerability, you are recognizing that attack has no effect **and, therefore, you remain strong**. 3 Although you have attacked yourself, you will be demonstrating that nothing really happened **since you recognize that you are invulnerable**. 4 Therefore, by attacking you have not done anything. 5 Once you realize **that by attacking you have not done anything**, you will no longer see any sense in attack, for **attack** manifestly does not work and cannot protect you. 6 Yet the recognition of your invulnerability has more than negative value. 7 If your attacks on yourself have failed to weaken you, you are still strong. 8 You therefore have no need to "equalize" the situation to establish your strength **by attacking your brother.**

Note # 39: Unlimited spirit is invulnerable. Only when you perceive yourself as an ego-body, do you believe you are vulnerable to attack. We are not self-created. Since God is love and you are an extension of God, you must be love. Unconditional love is invulnerable and comes from strength. Attack cannot weaken it and love does not attack. Any attack on the one you love unconditionally would be an attack on yourself. The love of God gives all to all and the Christ in us is the expression of God's love. We are the One Self. A Oneness knows there can be nothing outside itself to attack.

T-12.V.3. You will never realize the utter uselessness of attack except by recognizing that your attack on yourself has no effects. 2 For others do react to attack if they perceive **an attack**, and if you are trying to attack **another** you will be unable to avoid interpreting this **attack on another** as reinforcement **to the idea that attack has no effect since your brother will react to your attack.** 3 The only place you can cancel out all reinforcement **for the idea that attack produces no effects** is in yourself. 4 For you are always the first point of your attack, and if this has never been, **attack** has no consequences.

Note # 40: The Laws of God state that what we give, we will receive. Only when we perceive ourselves as a body, do we believe that we are vulnerable to attack. It is this belief that we can be hurt that leads us to believe that "preemptive strikes" are a means of self-defense. If you realize that you are spirit, the One Self, you will understand that love and forgiveness are your function. Being a Oneness, you will see no gain in attack since all attack is a form of self-attack and self-hatred.

T-12.V.4. The Holy Spirit's Love is your strength, for **your strength** is divided and therefore not real. 2 You cannot trust your own love when you attack **your own love**. 3 You cannot learn of perfect love with a split mind, because a split mind has made itself a poor learner. 4 You tried to make the separation eternal, because you wanted to retain the characteristics of creation, but with your own content. 5 Yet creation is not of you, and poor learners do need special teaching.

Note # 41: Believing that we could be separate from God, we wanted to be able to make something other than an extension of our Big "S" Selves. We wanted to "create" based on limitation and specialness. Unlike God, Who gives everything of Himself, we wished to give selectively. We wished to exclude rather than include and thus, maintain our claim to a unique, individual separateness that we perceive to be our little "s" self. This egoic mindset of making is an attack on our Big "S" Self. Special or conditional love is not the Love of God. The split mind is divided and cannot learn two opposing concepts of love. We need the Holy Spirit's guidance.

T-12.V.5. You have learning handicaps in a very literal sense. 2 There are areas in your learning skills that are so impaired that you can progress only under constant, clear-cut direction, provided by a Teacher Who can transcend your limited resources. 3 **The Holy Spirit** becomes your Resource because of yourself you cannot learn. 4 The learning situation in which you placed yourself is impossible, and in this situation you clearly require a special Teacher, **who is the Holy Spirit,** and a special curriculum. 5 Poor learners are not good choices as teachers, either for themselves or for anyone else. 6 You would hardly turn to **poor learners** to establish the curriculum by which **the poor learners** can escape from their limitations. 7 If **the poor learners** understood what is beyond them, **the poor learners** would not be handicapped.

Note # 42: Someone who does not know the truth can neither teach the truth nor establish its curriculum. They lack the basic knowledge to achieve the desired results. The split-minded do not know the truth. The egoic thought system cannot teach what it does not know. Only the Holy Spirit knows the truth and thus, can teach it.

T-12.V.6. You do not know the meaning of love, and that is your handicap. 2 Do not attempt to teach yourself what you do not understand, and do not try to set up curriculum goals where yours have clearly failed. 3 Your learning goal **of the meaning of love** has been <*not*> to learn, and this cannot lead to successful learning **of love.** 4 You cannot transfer what you have not learned, and the impairment of the ability to generalize is a crucial learning failure. 5 Would you ask those who have failed to learn what learning aids are for? 6 **Those who have failed to learn** do not know **what learning aids are for.** 7 If **those who have failed to learn** could interpret the aids correctly, they would have learned from **the learning aids**.

Note # 43: The ego's goal is for us to "Seek and never find love." To the ego, the body is a device for separation. The body has become a tool of attack and vulnerability. To the Holy Spirit the body is a communication device that the Holy Spirit can utilize to teach us that we are that One Self.

T-12.V.7. I have said that the ego's rule is, "Seek and do not find." 2 Translated into curricular terms this means, "Try to learn but do not succeed." 3 The result of **the ego's** curriculum goal is obvious. 4 Every legitimate teaching aid, every real instruction, and every sensible guide to learning will be misinterpreted, since they are all for facilitating the learning this strange curriculum is against. 5 If you are trying to learn how not to learn, and the aim of your teaching is to defeat itself, what can you expect but confusion? 6 Such a curriculum as **"Try to learn but do not succeed,"** does not make sense. 7 This attempt at "learning" has so weakened your mind that you cannot love, for the curriculum you have chosen is against love, and amounts to a course in how to attack yourself. 8 A supplementary goal in **the ego's** curriculum **of "Try to learn but do not succeed,"** is learning how <*not*> to overcome the split that makes **the ego's** primary aim, **the belief in the separation,** believable. 9 And you will not overcome the split in **the ego's** curriculum, for all your learning will be on **the ego's** behalf. 10 Yet your mind, **our Big "S" Self,** speaks against your **egoic** learning as your **egoic** learning speaks against your **mind's Big "S" Self,** and so you fight against all learning and succeed, for that is what you want. 11 But perhaps you do not realize, even yet, that there is something you want to learn, and that you can learn it because **to learn what you really want to learn** <*is*> your choice to do so.

Note # 44: The ego does not know love or how to love and, therefore, cannot teach love. Love is inclusive and the ego teaches exclusion. As long as we follow the instructions of the ego, we will fail to learn about love. The ego can only teach what it knows, which is the belief in separation. We need to change our teacher if we wish to learn about love. The Holy Spirit, which is love, is the only logical choice to teach us how to remove all the blocks that we place before love. Until we make the choice for this new teacher, our "two selves" will continue to be in conflict and whole-mindedness cannot return.

T-12.V.8. You who have tried to learn what you do not want should take heart, for although the curriculum you set yourself is depressing indeed, it is merely ridiculous if you look at **the curriculum you set yourself, which was, "Try to learn but do not succeed."** 2 Is it possible that the way to achieve a goal is not to attain **the goal**? 3 Resign now as your own teacher. 4 This resignation will not lead to depression. 5 **Your resignation as your own teacher** is merely the result of an honest appraisal of what you have taught yourself, and of the learning outcomes that have resulted. 6 Under the proper learning conditions, which you can neither provide nor understand, you will become an excellent learner and an excellent teacher. 7 But **the proper learning conditions are** not so yet, and will not be so until the whole learning situation as you have set it up is reversed.

Note # 45: As long as we believe and value the egoic thought system, we will not be willing to change teachers. ACIM asks us to look at the results of our ego's curriculum and honestly ask if we are pleased with our progress toward our goal of love and happiness. If we are not, we need to realize we cannot self-teach what we do not know. Yet, under the tutelage of the Holy Spirit, we will become both an excellent student and teacher.

T-12.V.9. Your learning potential, properly understood, is limitless because **your learning potential will lead you to God.** 2 You can teach the way to **God** and learn **the way to God,** if you follow the Teacher, **the Holy Spirit**, Who knows the way to **God** and understands His curriculum for learning **the way to God.** 3 The curriculum is totally unambiguous, because the goal is not divided and the means and the end are in complete accord. 4 You need offer only undivided attention. 5 Everything else will be given you. 6 For you really want to learn aright, and nothing can oppose the decision of God's Son **to learn.** 7 **God's Son's** learning is as unlimited as he is.

Note # 46: We have truly only wanted to experience love, extend love and thus, be love. This is our goal. When we follow the thought system of the Holy Spirit, both the means to achieve the goal of being only love and the goal of love are in alignment. The Holy Spirit's curriculum is designed to teach the remembrance of love. Since the means and the goal are in alignment, our learning will be quick and easy. When we follow the egoic little "s" self, the curriculum's goal is never to obtain love and thus, we could not learn to be love.

VI. The Vision of Christ

T-12.VI.1. The ego is trying to teach you how to gain the whole world and lose your own soul. 2 The Holy Spirit teaches that you cannot lose your soul and there is no gain in the world, **for of itself to gain the whole world and lose your own soul, you** profit nothing. 3 To invest without profit is surely to impoverish yourself, and the overhead is high. 4 Not only is there no profit in the investment **to gain this illusionary world** but the cost to you is enormous. 5 For this investment costs you the **real** world's reality by denying **your divine birthright**, and gives you nothing in return. 6 You cannot sell your soul, but you can sell your awareness of **your soul.** 7 You cannot perceive your soul, but you will not know **your soul** while you perceive something else as more valuable.

Note # 47: Since this world of perception is not of the Mind of God, it is unreal. A fantasy world is nothing in eternity; therefore, to attain an illusionary dream world would be to gain nothing. Yet, when we believe in and value an illusionary world of nothing, we deny your divine birthright as unlimited spirit. If you value your false belief in individuality, specialness and separation over the reality of your Oneness in the Mind of God, you deny the truth and prefer a false illusion. The decision to cast this vote comes from the egoic belief in the reality of the separation and is your attempt to make the dream real. What you value, you will choose to perceive for perception flows from your beliefs. The value you place on specialness is greater than the value you place on the truth that you are that One Self. Truth can be denied, but your denial of truth will never affect the truth in eternity. You are not a body. You are unlimited spirit. You are the Christ.

T-12.VI.2.The Holy Spirit is your strength because **the Holy Spirit** knows nothing but the spirit as you. 2 **The Holy Spirit** is perfectly aware that you do not know yourself, and perfectly aware of how to teach you to remember what you are. 3 Because **the Holy Spirit** loves you, **the Holy Spirit** will gladly teach you what **the Holy Spirit** loves, for **the Holy Spirit** wills to share **His knowledge of what you truly are with you**. 4 Remembering you always, **the Holy Spirit** cannot let you forget your worth. 5 For the Father never ceases to remind **the Holy Spirit** of **the Father's** Son, and **the Holy Spirit** never ceases to remind **God's** Son of the Father. 6 God is in your memory because of **the Holy Spirit**. 7 You chose to forget your Father but you do not really want to do so, and therefore you can decide otherwise. 8 As it was my decision **not to forget my Father**, so is it **your decision not to forget your Father.**

Note # 48: The Holy Spirit knows the truth that you are the Christ, the One Self and will teach you to rediscover your divine birthright. When the idea of the separation occurred, God placed the Holy Spirit within the split mind of the Sonship so that His Son would eternally remain safe and always be able to find his way home. The Christ in you is the home of the Holy Spirit and is your remembrance of God. Your return home is guaranteed. In eternity, the separation never occurred but in time the guidance of the Holy Spirit is needed to reawaken God's Son and return him to the Kingdom. Time arose in order to allow for the correction of this mad idea of the separation. Time allows us to play the "game of forgetfulness" in perfect safety. Time exists only in the world of perception and will disappear along with the dream of the "game of forgetfulness" when knowledge returns to God's Son.

T-12.VI.3.You do not want the world **of perception**. 2 The only thing of value in **the world of perception** is whatever part of **the world of perception** you look upon with love. 3 **Your loving thoughts** gives **the world of perception** the only reality **the world of perception** will ever have. 4 **The world of perception's** value is not in itself, but your **value** is in you. 5 As self-value comes from self-extension, so does the perception of self-value come from the extension of loving thoughts outward. 6 Make the world real unto yourself, for the real world is the gift of the Holy Spirit, and so **the real world** belongs to you.

Note # 49: Even in the "game of forgetfulness," we have the power to create. We create whenever we respond to any experience with only loving thoughts. Being the One Self, loving thoughts are really self-love. If we respond out of fear, the Holy Spirit only asks for us to choose again. In this way, we relearn the truth that only love is real and we are only love. Creation is extension. Only by the sharing of love, which is what you are, does creation occur. Creation does not exclude but only gives what it truly is. Being love, only loving thoughts can create and are part of the Mind of God.

T-12.VI.4.Correction is for all who cannot see. 2 To open the eyes of the blind is the Holy Spirit's mission, for **the Holy Spirit** knows that **all who cannot see** have not lost their vision, but **all who cannot see** merely sleep. 3 **The Holy Spirit** would awaken **all who cannot see** from the sleep of forgetting to the remembering of God. 4 Christ's eyes are open, and **Christ** will look upon whatever you see with love if you accept **Christ's** vision as **your vision**. 5 The Holy Spirit keeps the vision of Christ for every Son of God who sleeps. 6 In **the Holy Spirit's** sight the Son of God is perfect, and **the Holy Spirit** longs to share **Christ's** vision with you. 7 **The Holy Spirit** will show you the real world because God gave you Heaven. 8 Through **the Holy Spirit** your Father calls His Son to remember. 9 The awakening of His Son begins with **His Son**'s investment in the real world, and by this he will learn to re-invest in himself. 10 For reality is one with the Father and the Son, and the Holy Spirit blesses the real world in Their Name.

Note # 50: By following the guidance of the ego's thought system, you block the vision of Christ. By asking for the Holy Spirit's guidance, the vision of Christ overcomes this "egoic way of seeing," The Christ represents the right-minded part of the split-minded son's mind. The Christ is your remembrance of God and what you are. It is the home of the Holy Spirit. Your Christ consciousness can never be lost, but you can refuse to hear it.

T-12.VI.5. When you have seen this real world, as you will surely do, you will remember Us, **the Christ, Jesus and the Holy Spirit**. 2 Yet you must learn the cost of sleeping, **which is the forgetting of your divine birthright,** and refuse to pay **this cost.** 3 Only **when you refuse to pay the cost of your divine birthright** will you decide to awaken. 4 And then the real world will spring to your sight, for Christ has never slept. 5 **Christ** is waiting to be seen, for **Christ** has never lost sight of you. 6 **Christ** looks quietly on the real world, which **Christ** would share with you because **Christ** knows of the Father's Love for **His Son.** 7 And knowing **the Father's Love for His Son, Christ** would give you what is yours. 8 In perfect peace **Christ** waits for you at His Father's altar, holding out the Father's Love to you in the quiet light of the Holy Spirit's blessing. 9 For the Holy Spirit will lead everyone home to his Father, where Christ waits as his **Big "S"** Self.

Note # 51: When we choose to play the "game of forgetfulness," the price that we pay to play this game is the forgetting of our divine birthright. This game ends when we no longer value anything but the Oneness of the Mind of God. We are no longer willing to continue paying the painful price of our birthright in order to play this game of "What AM I?" We choose to be love and, therefore, transcend the world of perception and reawaken back into the real world of the loving One Self. Christ is the Big "S" Self. The Christ has never lost the truth of what you are. The ego's thought system represents the small or little "s" self.

T-12.VI.6. Every child of God is one in Christ, for his being is in Christ as Christ's is in God. 2 Christ's Love for you is **Christ's** Love for His Father, which **Christ** knows because **Christ** knows His Father's Love for Him, **the Christ**. 3 When the Holy Spirit has at last led you to Christ at the altar to His Father, perception fuses into knowledge because perception has become so holy that **perception's** transfer to holiness is merely **perception's** natural extension. 4 Love transfers to love without any interference, for the two, **holiness and knowledge**, are one. 5 As you perceive more and more common elements in all situations, the transfer of training under the Holy Spirit's guidance increases and becomes generalized. 6 Gradually you learn to apply **the Holy Spirit's guidance** to everyone and everything, for **the Holy Spirit's guidance** applicability is universal. 7 When this has been accomplished, **this holy** perception and knowledge have become so similar that they share the unification of the laws of God.

Note # 52: The Holy Spirit will reinterpret your misperceptions into correct perceptions. This occurs through the tool of forgiveness and love. The Holy Spirit's thought system comes from the knowledge that we are joined in the Mind of God and, therefore, what we do to our brother, we do onto ourselves. By forgiving our brother, we forgive ourselves and realize our shared oneness with God's Will. Correct perception aligns with the truth. When we ask for the guidance of the Holy Spirit, egoic misperception is replaced with correct perception. When we choose to exclusively follow the Holy Spirit's thought system, we perceive only with the eyes of Christ and our perception becomes holy perception that is easily transformed into knowledge. When we are vigilant only for God, God will return His Son to knowledge.

T-12.VI.7. What is one cannot be perceived as separate, and the denial of the separation is the reinstatement of knowledge. 2 At the altar of God, the holy perception of God's Son becomes so enlightened that light streams into **the altar of God**, and the spirit of God's Son shines in the Mind of the Father and becomes one with **the altar of God**. 3 Very gently does God shine upon Himself, loving the extension of Himself that is His Son. 4 The world has no purpose as **the world** blends into the purpose of God. 5 For the real world has slipped quietly into Heaven, where everything eternal in **the real world** has always been. 6 There the Redeemer and the redeemed join in perfect love of God and of each other. 7 Heaven is your home, and being in God, **heaven** must also be in you.

Note # 53: When we share the same goal and purpose of love's extension, we realize that we are one. When our holy perception mirrors the knowledge of God, the Father takes the final step to raise the Son back to the return to knowledge. Our total denial of the belief that the separation was real is needed to return our split minds to whole-mindedness. With this denial of the false, our world of provisional reality and individual perception will disappear. The Sonship will return to the Kingdom, which is the Oneness of the Mind of God. The Father, the Holy Spirit, the Sonship and the Son's Creation will continue to extend the wholeness of this One Self throughout eternity. The unified Mind of God, perfect, whole and complete, will continue to know Itself by extending itself to all of Itself. This is the co-creative process that we call love.

VII. Looking Within

T-12.VII.1. Miracles demonstrate that learning has occurred under the right guidance **of the Holy Spirit,** for learning is invisible and what has been learned can be recognized only by **learning's** results. 2 The generalization **of the Holy Spirit's learning** is demonstrated as you use **the Holy Spirit's guidance** in more and more situations. 3 You will recognize that you have learned there is no order of difficulty in miracles when you apply **the Holy Spirit's guidance** to all situations. 4 There is no situation to which miracles do not apply, and by applying **the Holy Spirit's guidance** to all situations you will gain the real world. 5 For in this holy perception **under the Holy Spirit's guidance** you will be made whole, and the Atonement will radiate from your acceptance of **the Atonement** for yourself to everyone the Holy Spirit sends you for your blessing. 6 In every child of God, **God's** blessing lies, and in your blessing of the children of God is **God's** blessing to you.

Note # 54: Miracles are natural when we follow the thought system of the Holy Spirit instead of the ego's system. The Holy Spirit applies the Atonement principle to all that we perceive. Our alignment of perception with the truth becomes the basis for miracle mindedness.

T-12.VII.2. Everyone in the world must play his part in **the world's** redemption, in order to recognize that the world has been redeemed. 2 You cannot see the invisible. 3 Yet if you see **the invisible's** effects **upon the world's redemption** you know **the invisible** must be there. 4 By perceiving what **the**

invisible's effect does, you recognize **the invisible's** being. 5 And by what **the invisible's effect** does, you learn what **the invisible** is. 6 You cannot see your strengths, but you gain confidence in **your strengths'** existence as **your invisible strengths** enable you to act. 7 And the results of your actions you <can> see.

Note # 55: You will know the effects of anything by observing their results. If the effect is there, you assume the effect's cause was also present. You learn that you exist as a Oneness by Its effects. You learn that the Holy Spirit exists in you by Its effects. If the results do not bring you peace, the Holy Spirit asks that you choose again. All parts have a role to play in the return to knowledge. No one can be left out.

T-12.VII.3. The Holy Spirit is invisible, but you can see the results of **the Holy Spirit's** Presence, and through **the results of the Holy Spirit's Presence** you will learn that **the Holy Spirit** is there. 2 What **the Holy Spirit** enables you to do is clearly not of this world, for miracles violate every law of reality as this world judges **reality**. 3 Every law of time and space, of magnitude and mass is transcended **by miracles,** for what the Holy Spirit enables you to do is clearly beyond **all of the laws of time and space, of magnitude and mass.** 4 Perceiving **the Holy Spirit's** results, you will understand where **the Holy Spirit** must be, and finally know what **the Holy Spirit** is.

Note # 56: Although invisible, the result of the Holy Spirit's thought system is obvious to the follower because the results bring the follower peace. The miracle follows the Laws of God, not the laws of time and space.

T-12.VII.4. You cannot see the Holy Spirit, but you can see **the Holy Spirit's** manifestations. 2 And unless you do **see the Holy Spirit's manifestations,** you will not realize **the Holy Spirit** is there. 3 Miracles are **the Holy Spirit's** witnesses, and speak for **the Holy Spirit's** Presence. 4 What you cannot see becomes real to you only through the witnesses that speak for **what you cannot see.** 5 For you can be aware of what you cannot see, and **what you cannot see** can become compellingly real to you as **the** presence **of what you cannot see** becomes manifest through you. 6 Do the Holy Spirit's work, for you share in **the Holy Spirit's** function. 7 As your function in Heaven is creation, so your function on earth is healing. 8 God shares the **Father's** function with you in Heaven, and the Holy Spirit shares **the Holy Spirit's function of healing** with you on earth. 9 As long as you believe **that you have other functions than creation in heaven or healing on earth,** so long will you need correction. 10 For this belief **that you have other functions than creation in heaven or healing on earth** is the destruction of peace. **The destruction of peace is** a goal in direct opposition to the Holy Spirit's purpose, **which is to return God's Son to peace thought healing of the Son's split mind.**

Note # 57: In the real world of the Kingdom, we share God's function and co-create with our Father. In our present split-minded state that resulted from our belief in separation, we currently share the function of the Holy Spirit, which is the healing of the Sonship's split mind. The Father is unaware of our belief in the separation and, therefore, never sees His Creation as anything but perfect, whole and complete. The function of the Holy Spirit is healing since the Holy Spirit is aware of both our true nature and our misperception that we are a limited ego-body. Forgiveness is the major tool that the Holy Spirit uses to teach the sleeping child to reawaken to whole-mindedness. While we participate in the dream of separation, our purpose becomes healing of both our brother's mind and our own mind.

T-12.VII.5. You see what you expect, and you expect what you **invite**. 2 Your perception is the result of your invitation. **Your perception comes** to you as you sent for it, **based on what you expected.** 3 Whose manifestations would you see? 4 Of whose presence would you be convinced? 5 For you will believe in what you manifest, and as you look out so will you see in **what you believe**. 6 Two ways of looking at the world are in your mind, and your perception will reflect the guidance you have chosen.

Note # 58: Our perception follows our purpose or intention. Because thoughts are causative and what we become aware of is the effect of the causative thought, what we think becomes important. Our thoughts become our perceived reality. If we follow the thought system of the ego, what we choose to manifest into our awareness will confirm the idea that the separation was real. If we follow the thought system of the Holy Spirit, we will manifest into our awareness the unity and oneness with our brother. There are only two thought systems and, therefore, only two choices are available for the decision-maker.

T-12.VII.6.I, **Jesus**, am the manifestation of the Holy Spirit, and when you see me it will be because you have invited **the Holy Spirit**. 2 For **the Holy Spirit** will send you **the Holy Spirit's** witnesses if you will but look upon **the Holy Spirit's witnesses**. 3 Remember always that you see what you seek, for what you seek you will find. 4 The ego finds what **the ego** seeks, and only **what the ego seeks**. 5 **The ego** does not find love, for **love** is not what **the ego** is seeking. 6 Yet seeking and finding are the same, and if you seek for two goals you will find **both goals**, but you will recognize neither **goal**. 7 You will think **both goals** are the same because you want both of them. 8 The mind always strives for integration, and if **the mind** is split and wants to keep the split, **the split mind** will still believe **the split mind** has one goal by making **both goals** seem to be one **goal**.

Note # 59: We cannot follow both thought systems and expect to achieve the goal of either since we will always be in conflict. We cannot serve two conflicting masters and be at peace. The ego's thought system teaches and brings all the obstacles to block love and peace. The Holy Spirit's thought system will bring love and inner peace by healing our split mind. We must be only vigilant for God if we wish to return to the peace of God.

T-12.VII.7.I said before that what you project or extend is up to you, but you must do one or the other, **(project or extend),** for that, **(to project or extend),** is a law of mind, and you must look in before you look out. 2 As you look in, you choose **either the ego or the Holy Spirit as** the guide for seeing. 3 And then you look out and behold **your chosen guide's** witnesses. 4 This is why you find what you seek. 5 What you want in yourself you will make manifest, and you will accept **what you want in yourself** from the world because you put **what you want in the world** by wanting **what you want in yourself**. 6 When you think you are projecting what you do not want, it is still because you <do> want **what you believe that you do not want**. 7 This leads directly to dissociation, for **wanting what you believe you do not want** represents the acceptance of two goals, each perceived in a different place; separated from each other because you made **each goal** different. 8 The mind then sees a divided world outside itself, but not within **its own mind**. 9 This gives **the split mind** an illusion of integrity, and enables **the split mind** to believe that **the split mind** is pursuing one goal. 10 Yet as long as you perceive the world as split, you are not healed. 11 For to be healed is to pursue one goal, because you have accepted only one and want but one.

Note # 60: Whether we project or extend is contingent on whether we are coming from fear or love. Due to the creative power of the mind, we always manifest our thoughts. However, we are often not aware of what we are actually thinking in our subconscious mind. What we say we want and what we actually want are often at opposite ends of the same pole. We will manifest what we actually want. No decision is a decision.

Both the ego and the Holy Spirit claim their goal is that we are happy and find love. Yet, because of opposing beliefs as to what we are, they seek different results. When we first look within mind to choose our guide, we will be making this choice based on what we value the most. Will it be egoic specialness or the Holy Spirit's truth of our One Self?

T-12.VII.8. When you want only love you will see nothing else. 2 The contradictory nature of the witnesses you perceive is merely the reflection of your conflicting invitations **to both the Holy Spirit and the ego.** 3 You have looked upon your mind and accepted opposition there, having sought **conflicting goals of both the Holy Spirit and the ego** there **in your split mind.** 4 But do not then believe that the witnesses for opposition, **the ego's,** are true, for **the egoic witnesses for opposition** attest only to your decision about reality, returning to you the messages you gave them **about your individualized provisional reality of separation.** 5 Love, too, is recognized by its messengers, **which come from the Holy Spirit.** 6 If you make love manifest, **the Holy Spirit's** messengers will come to you because you invited **the Holy Spirit's messengers.**

Note # 61: You cannot have love if you want exclusion. The thought system of the ego requires specialness, which is based of exclusion. Love requires sharing. Our Big "S" Self always seeks only love. It is our little "s" self that believes it has a choice between love and fear, inclusion and exclusion. When we choose for fear, we will feel conflicted and lose our peace. Individualization or specialness requires the belief in inequality.

T-12.VII.9. The power of decision is your one remaining freedom as a prisoner of this world **of perception or your provisional reality.** 2 You can decide to see **the world of perception** right. 3 What you made of **the world of perception** is not its reality, for **the world of perception's** reality is only what you give it. 4 You cannot really give anything but love to anyone or anything, nor can you really receive anything but love from **anyone or anything.** 5 If you think you have received anything else **but love,** it is because you have looked within **your mind** and thought you saw the power to give something else within yourself **other than love.** 6 It was only this decision **of what you wish to project** that determined what you found, for it was the decision for what you sought.

Note # 62: Although we are only love, in our dream world, we can believe we are something other than as God created us. This incorrect remembering of what we are leads us to the thought that we can be something that we are not. Projection comes from exclusion and the belief in limitation. Creation comes from inclusion, which is sharing. Whatever we value the most will determine whether we project (fear based) or extend (love based). Whichever thought system we value will determine the witnesses we choose to perceive.

T-12.VII.10. You are afraid of me because you looked within and are afraid of what you saw. 2 Yet you could not have seen reality, for the reality of your mind is the loveliest of God's creations. 3 Coming only from God, **your mind's true** power and grandeur could only bring you peace <*if you really looked upon your true mind.*> 4 If you are afraid, it is because you saw something that is not there **in your true mind.** 5 Yet in that same place **with your true Big "S" Self's mind,** you could have looked upon me and all your brothers, in the perfect safety of the Mind which created us, **which is the Mind of God.** 6 For we are there **in your true Big "S" Self's mind** in the peace of the Father, Who wills to extend **the Father's** peace through you.

Note # 63: If we are afraid to look within our mind, it is because we once misperceived what we were. We saw the split mind of the ego, not our Big "S" Self's mind, which is the Christ. We all share in the Oneness of the Mind of God. We are all that One Self.

T-12.VII.11. When you have accepted your mission to extend peace you will find peace, for by making

your mission the extension of peace, peace's manifest you will see. 2 **Peace's** holy witnesses will surround you because you called upon **peace's holy witnesses**, and **peace's holy witnesses** will come to you. 3 I have heard your call and I have answered **your call**, but you will not look upon me nor hear the answer that you sought. 4 That is because you do not yet want <*only*> **the extension of peace**. 5 Yet as I become more real to you, you will learn that you do want only **the extension of peace**. 6 And you will see me as you look within **your mind**, and we will look upon the real world together. 7 Through the eyes of Christ, only the real world exists and only the real world can be seen. 8 As you decide so will you see. 9 And all that you see but witnesses to your decision **of which thought system you will follow.**

Note # 64: We will vacillate between the two thought systems for a while. If our goal is the extension of peace then when we compare the differing results, we will tend to decide more and more in favor of the guidance of the Holy Spirit.

T-12.VII.12. When you look within and see me, it will be because you have decided to manifest truth. 2 And as you manifest **truth** you will see **truth** both without and within **your mind**. 3 You will see **truth** without <*because*> you saw **truth** first within **your mind**. 4 Everything you behold without is a judgment of what you beheld within **your mind**. 5 If **what you beheld within your mind** is your **egoic** judgment **your judgment** will be wrong, for judgment is not your function. 6 If **what you beheld within your mind** is the judgment of the Holy Spirit **the judgment** will be right, for judgment <*is*> the **Holy Spirit's** function. 7 You share **the Holy Spirit's** function only by judging as **the Holy Spirit** does, reserving no judgment at all for **your egoic self**. 8 You will judge against yourself, but **the Holy Spirit** will judge <*for*> you.

Note # 65: Because we have forgotten what we are, we are incapable of judging correctly. We lack knowledge because our mind is split. The only judgment that we should make is to accept the fact that we are incapable of judging correctly and, therefore, ask the Holy Spirit to replace our judgment with His. Only the Holy Spirit is capable of judging correctly because He knows both the truth about what we are and is also, aware that we have fallen asleep. The Holy Spirit's judgment comes from knowledge, not perception.

T-12.VII.13. Remember, then, that whenever you look without and react unfavorably to what you see, you have judged yourself unworthy and have condemned yourself to death. 2 The death penalty is the ego's ultimate goal, for **the ego** fully believes that you are a criminal, as deserving of death as God knows you are deserving of life. 3 The death penalty never leaves the ego's mind, for **the death penalty** is what **the ego** always reserves for you in the end. 4 Wanting to kill you as the final expression of **the ego's** feeling for you, **the ego** lets you live but to await death. 5 **The ego** will torment you while you live, but **the ego's** hatred is not satisfied until you die. 6 For your destruction is the one end toward which **the ego** works, and **your destruction is** the only end with which **the ego** will be satisfied.

Note # 66: The ego's thought system requires your destruction because your death is the ultimate proof that you are not created by God. Death is the ego's ultimate proof that you are an individual, separate from God. Ego autonomy is the goal of the ego and this can only be achieved by the denial of the Oneness that you share in the Mind of God. Your belief and participation in death confirms to your split mind that you are a body, not spirit and, therefore can and must die.

T-12.VII.14. The ego is not a traitor to God, to Whom treachery is impossible. 2 But **the ego** is a traitor to you who believe that you have been treacherous to your Father. 3 That is why the undoing of guilt is an essential part of the Holy Spirit's teaching. 4 For as long as you feel guilty **because you believe that you have been treacherous to your Father**, you are listening to the voice of the ego, which tells you that you have been treacherous to God and therefore deserve death. 5 You will think that death comes from God and not from the ego because, by confusing yourself with the ego, you believe that you want death. 6 And from what you want God does not save you.

Note # 67: When we believe that we are a body, we identify with the thought system of the ego. We believe that we are the ego and not God's Son. Because we have free will, God will not prevent us from exercising our ability to choose for the ego's thought system. If God were to prevent us from choosing for the ego and thus, save us from ourselves, God would be giving reality to our illusion of the separation. God would be acknowledging that His Son is flawed. God knows us to always be perfect as God created us. It is the task of the Holy Spirit to gently reawaken God's Son to the Sonship's own spiritual magnificent. The Son will do this freely by relearning what he is and thus, freely choosing for the remembrance of God and whole-mindedness. Reality will be restored in the healed mind of the Son. This is why healing is the function of the Holy Spirit. Healing is also our function as long as we choose to believe that we are split minded and thus, in need of healing.

T-12.VII.15. When you are tempted to yield to the desire for death, <*remember that I did not die.*> 2 You will realize that this is true when you look within **your mind** and <*see*> me. 3 Would I have overcome death for myself alone? 4 And would eternal life have been given me of the Father unless **the Father** had also given **eternal life** to you? 5 When you learn to make me manifest, you will never see death. 6 For you will have looked upon the deathless in yourself, and you will see only the eternal as you look out upon a world that cannot die.

Note # 68: When you see with the Vision of Christ, you will be aware of the eternal truth of reality. You will see the great rays in your brother, not his physical body. This truth never left your Christ consciousness, which is the home of the Holy Spirit. You will reawaken to the Kingdom when you accept the Atonement for yourself.

VIII. The Attraction of Love for Love

T-12.VIII.1. Do you really believe that you can kill the Son of God? 2 The Father has hidden His Son safely within Himself, and kept **His Son** far away from your destructive thoughts, but you know neither the Father nor the Son because of **your destructive thoughts**. 3 You attack the real world every day and every hour and every minute, and yet you are surprised that you cannot see **the real world**. 4 If you seek love in order to attack **love**, you will never find **love**. 5 For if love is sharing, how can you find **love** except through itself? 6 Offer **love** and **love** will come to you, because **love** is drawn to itself. 7 But offer attack and love will remain hidden, for **love** can live only in peace.

Note # 69: Because perception follows our purpose, we will see love only when love is our purpose. The real world of the Kingdom remains safe from any egoic fear-based thoughts since fear is not part of love's reality, which is the Kingdom.

T-12.VIII.2. God's Son is as safe as his Father, for the Son knows his Father's protection and cannot fear. 2 His Father's Love holds **God's Son** in perfect peace, and needing nothing, **God's Son** asks for nothing. 3 Yet **God's Son** is far from you whose Self, **God's Son** is, for you chose to attack **God's Son** and

God's Son disappeared from your sight into his Father. 4 **God's Son** did not change, but you did. 5 For a split mind and all **a split mind's** works were not created by the Father, and could not live in the knowledge of the **Father**.

<u>Note # 70:</u> In the split mind of someone who is under the ego's thought system, God's Son appears to have disappeared. Yet, this is not true in reality. God's Son, our Big "S" Self, remains within our mind as the Christ consciousness part of our split mind. The Christ appears to be asleep because the Voice for God, the Holy Spirit, is not being listened to. We cannot hear the Voice for God because we have chosen to follow the ego's thought system. Our split mind has chosen to believe that we are a limited ego-body rather than unlimited spirit.

T-12.VIII.3. When you made visible what is not true, **which was your illusionary world of provisional reality,** what <*is*> true, **the Kingdom, which is reality,** became invisible to you. 2 Yet **the Kingdom, which is reality,** cannot be invisible in itself, for the Holy Spirit sees **the Kingdom, which is the real world,** with perfect clarity. 3 **The Kingdom, which is the real world,** is invisible to you because you are looking at something else **which is your illusionary world of provisional reality.** 4 Yet it is no more up to you to decide what is visible and what is invisible, than it is up to you to decide what reality is. 5 What can be seen is what the Holy Spirit sees. 6 The definition of reality is God's, not yours. 7 **God** created **what reality is,** and **God** knows what **reality** is. 8 You who knew have forgotten **what reality is,** and unless **God** had given you a way to remember **what reality is,** you would have condemned yourself to oblivion, **which is your illusionary world of provisional reality.**

<u>Note # 71:</u> The ego tells us that we are the arbitrators of truth. If we can decide what truth is for us, it also follows that egoic thought would claim that we are the arbitrators or creators of our own reality. We can deny reality; yet, our denial does not change the truth of what reality is. Yet, within our split mind, our denial does result in our belief that our illusionary world of misperception is real. Because of this denial by the split-minded, the false has replaced the real and become our provisional reality.

T-12.VIII.4. Because of your Father's Love you can never forget **your Father,** for no one can forget what God Himself placed in his memory. 2 You can deny **what God placed in your memory,** but you cannot lose **what God placed in your memory.** 3 A Voice, **which is the Holy Spirit's,** will answer every question you ask, and a vision, **which is the Vision of Christ,** will correct the perception of everything you see. 4 For what you have made invisible is the only truth, and what you have not heard is the only Answer. 5 God would reunite you with yourself, and did not abandon you in your distress. 6 You are waiting only for **God,** and do not know **you are waiting only for God.** 7 Yet **God's** memory shines in your mind and **God's memory** cannot be obliterated. 8 **God's memory** is no more past than future, being forever always.

<u>Note # 72:</u> The Christ consciousness always remembers God even when we are unaware of Christ's presence. This "forgetfulness" is due to our mind's erroneous belief in the separation. Yet, our denial is powerless to change the Will of God.

T-12.VIII.5. You have but to ask for this memory **of God,** and you will remember. 2 Yet the memory of God cannot shine in a mind that has obliterated **this memory of God** and wants to keep **this memory of God in oblivion.** 3 For the memory of God can dawn only in a mind that chooses to remember, and that has relinquished the insane desire to control reality. 4 You who cannot even control yourself should hardly aspire to control the universe. 5 But look upon what you have made of **your world of provisional reality,** and rejoice that **your world of provisional reality** is not so.

<u>Note # 73:</u> Because we have free will, we must freely request the guidance of the Holy Spirit. With His guidance, we can freely choose to align our will with the Will of God. When we do this, we understand that God's Will and our will are one. The memory of God is in our Christ consciousness and is reawakened in God's sleeping Son through the guidance of the Holy Spirit.

T-12.VIII.6. Son of God, be not content with nothing, **which is what your illusionary world of provisional reality is**! 2 What is not real cannot be seen and has no value. 3 God could not offer His Son what has no value, nor could His Son receive **what has no value**. 4 You were redeemed the instant you thought you had deserted **God**. 5 Everything you made has never been, and is invisible because the Holy Spirit does not see **every illusion that you made in your dream world as real**. 6 Yet what **the Holy Spirit** does see is yours to behold, and through **the Holy Spirit's** vision your perception is healed. 7 You have made invisible the only truth that this world holds. 8 Valuing nothing, you have sought nothing. 9 By making nothing real to you, you have seen **nothing that was real**. 10 <*But what you wrongly thought and saw as real is not there.*> 11 And Christ is invisible to you because of what you have made visible to yourself, **which is your belief that you are a limited ego-body.**

<u>Note # 74:</u> We allow ourselves to "see" only what we choose to value. Our perception always follows our purpose. Our dream world of perception is not real and is worthless since it is nothing. The world of perception was made by our egoic selves for the purpose of hiding the truth about our spiritual nature from us. This world was made by us as a place to keep out God's love so that we could pretend that we were separate from God and could do something other than God's Will. We wanted to be special individuals, not an equal Oneness of Everything. Whenever we attempt to deny our divine birthright, our inheritance remains safe in the Mind of God. The Holy Spirit will guide God's prodigal Son back home.

T-12.VIII.7. Yet it does not matter how much distance you have tried to interpose between your awareness and truth. 2 God's Son, **the Christ**, can be seen because his **Christ** vision is shared. 3 The Holy Spirit looks upon him, and sees nothing else in you, **but God's Son**. 4 What is invisible to you is perfect in **the Holy Spirit and Christ's** sight, and encompasses all of **what is invisible to you**. 5 **The Holy Spirit and the Christ** has remembered you because **Christ** forgot not the Father. 6 You looked upon the unreal and found despair. 7 Yet by seeking the unreal, what else could you find **but despair**? 8 The unreal world <*is*> a thing of despair, for **the unreal world** can never be. 9 And you who share God's Being with **God** could never be content without reality. 10 What God did not give you has no power over you, and the attraction of love for love remains irresistible. 11 For it is the function of love to unite all things unto itself, and to hold all things together by extending **love's** wholeness.

<u>Note # 75:</u> The Holy Spirit helps reawaken your split mind to the truth that you are the Christ, God's Son. This knowledge of what you are has never been lost to the Christ conscious part of our split mind. We just choose to ignore Its voice and, therefore, to the split-minded, the Christ consciousness mind appears to have fallen asleep. Thus the split-minded only chose to listen to the egoic thought system's version of "reality" and "truth."

T-12.VIII.8. The real world was given you by God in loving exchange for the world **of illusion** you made and the world **of illusion** you see. 2 Only take **the real world, which is the Kingdom,** from the hand of Christ and look upon **the real world**. 3 **The real world's** reality will make everything else invisible, for beholding **the real world** is total perception. 4 And as you look upon **the real world** you will remember that **the real world** was always so. 5 Nothingness will become invisible, for you will at last have seen truly. 6 Redeemed perception is easily translated into knowledge, for only perception is capable of error and perception has never been. 7 Being corrected **perception** gives place to knowledge, which is forever the only reality. 8 The Atonement is but the way back to what was never lost. 9 Your Father could not cease to love His Son.

Note # 76: When we no longer value any part of the illusion of perception, we will freely exchange our egoic misperception and judgments for the Holy Spirit's correct perception and correct judgment. When we ask for only the Holy Spirit's guidance, the light of truth will dissolve all illusion of the false. Misperception will be replaced with correct perception. This is the acceptance of the Atonement for ourselves. The Atonement is the realization that the separation never happened and we remain sinless and guiltless. All illusions are undone and fade away into the nothingness from which they arose. Sin, which can be defined as belief in lack, never occurred in the Mind of God. God is unconditional love. Being Love, God gives Love totally to His Creation. God created by extending Himself completely to the Sonship. There can never be a moment when God's Love for His Son is not total and perfect. God's Son has never lacked God's love and thus, could never lack for anything. The split-minded, however, have chosen to deny God's love for His Son. This denial is a mistake, not a sin. By accepting the Atonement for ourselves, this mistake is corrected and the split-minded are returned to the sanity of whole-mindedness. Illusions are dispelled and the real world reappears.

Chapter 13. THE GUILTLESS WORLD

Introduction

T-13.in.1. If you did not feel guilty you could not attack, for condemnation is the root of attack. 2 **Condemnation** is the judgment of one mind by another as unworthy of love and deserving of punishment. 3 But **this condemnation of another as unworthy of love and deserving of punishment is caused by the belief in separation and** herein lies the split **of your mind.** 4 For the mind that judges perceives itself as separate from the mind being judged, believing that by punishing another, **the mind that judges** will escape punishment. 5 All this **condemnation and judgment of another** is but the delusional attempt of the mind to deny itself, and escape the penalty of denial. 6 **This condemnation and judgment of another** is not an attempt to relinquish denial, but to hold on to **denial.** 7 For **denial of another as being worthy of love** is **the** guilt that has obscured the Father to you and **this denial of another as being worthy of love** is **the** guilt that has driven you insane.

<u>Note #1:</u> ACIM defines **Condemnation** as the judgment of one mind by another as unworthy of love and deserving of punishment. Condemnation is caused by the belief in separation. Perceiving our brother as separate from our own mind, we believe that by condemning another we can escape our own condemnation and our feelings of guilt within our own split mind. We first project our guilt upon another and then see our brother as guilty and as being unworthy of our love. Since thoughts never leave the mind of the thinker, our mind still harbors the projected thought and also the guilt and the condemnation that we have placed upon our brother. We deny both our brother's and our own Big "S" Selves and strengthen our split mind's belief that we are separate and unworthy of God's love.

T-13.in.2. The acceptance of guilt into the mind of God's Son was the beginning of the separation, as the acceptance of the Atonement is **the separation's** end. 2 The world you see is the delusional system of those made mad by guilt. 3 Look carefully at this world **that was born from your guilt**, and you will realize that this is so. 4 For this world **of your misperception** is the symbol of punishment, and all the laws that seem to govern **your dream world of provisional reality** are the laws of death. 5 Children are born into **this world that was made from your guilt** through pain and in pain. 6 **The children's** growth is attended by suffering, and **the children** learn of sorrow and separation and death. 7 **The children's** minds seem to be trapped in their brain, and **the mind's** powers **seem** to decline if their bodies are hurt. 8 **The children** seem to love, yet they desert and are deserted. 9 **The children** appear to lose what they love, perhaps the most insane belief of all. 10 And **the children's** bodies wither and gasp and are laid in the ground, and are no more. 11 Not one of **the children** but has thought that God is cruel.

<u>Note # 2:</u> When the Sonship accepted the idea that it could be guilty of something, the separation began.

The Sonship, not God, made this world from its split-mind. The Sonship's mind appeared to split into two separate parts when it forgot to laugh and took seriously the imagined game of being something other than God. The Sonship insanely claimed it did not know that it was God's perfect Creation. Sin, guilt and fear are related. They are "kissing cousins" that arose out of the belief in the separation. Out of these three, the split-minded Sonship birthed the dream world of provisional reality and the egoic thought system upon which it rests. This world of illusion was an attempt to keep God and God's love away from God's Son. It was our self-inflected punishment caused from the guilt the Sonship felt from the denial of our divine birthright. Guilt is the feeling that results in our mind when we attack our innocence. Due to our self-inflected punishment, we, the fragmented Sonship, all perceive God as cruel. Our ego projects our own actions of self-inflected punishment upon God and then blames God and calls Him cruel.

T-13.in.3. If this **world, which was actually born or made from your own guilt,** were the real world, God <*would*> be cruel. 2 For no Father could subject His children to **this world of punishment** as the price of salvation and <*be*> loving. 3 <*Love does not kill to save.*> 4 If **love** did **kill to save,** attack would be salvation, and this is the ego's interpretation, not God's **interpretation.** 5 Only the world of guilt could demand this **killing to save,** for only the guilty could conceive **that killing to save could bring salvation.** 6 Adam's "sin" could have touched no one, had **Adam** not believed it was the Father Who drove **Adam** out of Paradise. 7 For in that belief **that God drove Adam out of Paradise,** the knowledge of the Father was lost, since only those who do not understand **the Father** could believe **a God of love would do such a cruel thing**.

<u>Note #3:</u> A classic example of projection occurred when Adam claimed that God drove him from paradise. Adam attempted to get rid of his own guilt by blaming it on someone else, in this case, God. Thus, Adam denied that he was the source of his own made-up dream. This denial of sourceness makes the belief in separation real; for now rather than a Oneness, there is something outside itself. We have lost or denied knowledge of what God is and that we are an extension of that One Self. God did not make this world. We did. This world of perception is not part of the Mind of God. Therefore, it is neither eternal nor real. The illusion of separation has no reality outside the mind of the dreamer who is dreaming that this world of guilt and punishment is real.

T-13.in.4.This world **born of our guilt** <*is*> a picture of the crucifixion of God's Son. 2 And until you realize that God's Son cannot be crucified, this is the world you will see. 3 Yet you will not realize **that God's Son cannot be crucified** until you accept the eternal fact that God's Son is not guilty. 4 **God's Son** deserves only love because he has given only love. 5 **God's Son** cannot be condemned because he has never **been** condemned **by His Father.** 6 The Atonement is the final lesson **God's Son** need learn, for **the Atonement** teaches **God's Son** that, never having sinned, **God's Son** has no need of salvation.

<u>Note # 4:</u> The Atonement principle states that the separation never was real. The illusion of separation is not part of the Mind of God and thus, we have not done anything wrong. We merely dreamed a nightmare. Dreams are not punishable for they never happened. The Atonement is the acknowledgment of the fact that God's Creation remains sinless and guiltless. The Atonement must be accepted for oneself since the belief in the separation is only in the deluded mind of the dreamer.

I. Guiltlessness and Invulnerability

T-13.I.1.Earlier, I said that the Holy Spirit shares the goal of all good teachers, whose ultimate aim is to make **the teacher** unnecessary by teaching their pupils all **that the teacher** knows. 2 The Holy Spirit wants only **that we learn the truth about ourselves**, for sharing the Father's Love for His Son, **the Holy Spirit** seeks to remove all guilt from **the pupil's** mind that **the Son of God** may remember his Father in peace. 3 Peace and guilt are antithetical, and the Father can be remembered only in peace. 4 Love and guilt cannot coexist, and to accept **love and guilt** is to deny the other. 5 Guilt hides Christ from your sight, for **guilt** is the denial of the blamelessness of God's Son.

Note # 5: The Holy Spirit's function is to gently reawaken the split-minded into remembering and reawakening to their divine birthright. This birthright was never lost, it was only forgotten.

T-13.I.2.In the strange world that you have made the Son of God <*has*> sinned. 2 How could you see him, then? 3 By making him invisible, the world of retribution rose in the black cloud of guilt that you accepted, and you hold **this cloud of guilt and world of retribution you made** dear **to your little "s" self**. 4 For the blamelessness of Christ is the proof that the ego never was, and can never be. 5 Without guilt the ego has no life, and God's Son <*is*> without guilt.

Note # 6: It is our own self-denial of the Christ, our Big "S" Self, that resulted in our making a world that is absent from God's love. Our ego's guilt requires that we believe in our personal littleness, rather than the great Oneness that we are. The ego's thought system is based on the belief in sin, guilt and fear. The Holy Spirit's thought system is based on the idea that we are as God created us, always perfect, whole and complete.

T-13.I.3.As you look upon yourself and judge what you do honestly, you may be tempted to wonder how you can be guiltless. 2 Yet consider this: You are not guiltless in time, but in eternity. 3 You have "sinned" in the past, but there is no past. 4 Always has no direction. 5 Time seems to go in one direction, but when you reach **time's** end **time** will roll up like a long carpet spread along the past behind you, and **time** will disappear. 6 As long as you believe the Son of God is guilty you will walk along this carpet **of time**, believing that **time** leads to death. 7 And the journey will seem long and cruel and senseless, for so **this journey** is **senseless**.

Note # 7: Time is a concept that became necessary due to our belief that the separation was real. Since reality is changeless, time does not exist in the Kingdom. Time, however, is required in our dream world of illusion. Time measures the rate of change. Only in the world of perception is there any change. Time measures the rate of change in our perceptual viewpoints. As our misperceptions and beliefs about what we are change, time moves "forward." Learning is the change of our misperceptions into correct perceptions. The more often our decision-maker "chooses again," the faster time moves. When we refuse to "choose again," time stands still. When we are returned to knowledge, time will disappear since there is no change occurring. The eternal is changeless by definition. Only in the dream world of perception is change possible. Only in the dream world of illusion can you perceive God's Child as sinful and guilty.

T-13.I.4.The journey the Son of God has set himself is useless indeed, but the journey on which his Father sets him is one of release and joy. 2 The Father is not cruel, and His Son cannot hurt himself. 3 The retaliation that **the son** fears and that **the son** sees will never touch **the son**, for although **the son** believes in **God's retaliation** the Holy Spirit knows it is not true. 4 The Holy Spirit stands at the end of time, where you must be because **the Holy Spirit** is with you. 5 **The Holy Spirit** has already undone everything unworthy of the Son of God, for such was **the Holy Spirit's** mission, given **the Holy Spirit** by God. 6 And what God gives has always been.

Note # 8: The journey that the split-minded have set for themselves is useless since it is a journey into madness and the false. For to deny what you truly are is madness. This journey is also impossible to achieve because we remain changeless as our Father created us. We can deny the truth but our denial of the truth will not change the truth. The truth will always remain in the Mind of God and, therefore, we will remain in eternity as perfect, whole and complete. If this were not so, our imperfection would also make God imperfect. The journey on which God sends his split-minded son is one that releases God's Son from the son's own egoic journey into the illusion of separation. This journey ends in joy with the return of the prodigal son to knowledge and the Kingdom. This second journey back to God was only made necessary due to our taking the illusion of separation seriously and responding to this false illusion with fear.

T-13.I.5. You will see me, **the Christ consciousness,** as you learn the Son of God is guiltless. 2 **The Son of God** has always sought his guiltlessness, and **the Son of God** has found it. 3 For everyone is seeking to escape from the prison he has made, and the way to find release is not denied **the Son of God**. 4 Being in him, he has found **the way to find release from the prison he has made for himself.** 5 <When> he finds **his release from his self-imposed prison** is only a matter of time, and time is but an illusion. 6 For the Son of God is guiltless now, and the brightness of his purity shines untouched forever in God's Mind. 7 God's Son will always be as he was created. 8 Deny your **egoic** world and judge **the Son of God** not, for his eternal guiltlessness is in the Mind of his Father, and protects **the Son of God** forever.

Note # 9: By accepting the Atonement for ourselves, we accept guiltlessness for all the Sonship and ourselves.

T-13.I.6. When you have accepted the Atonement for yourself, you will realize there is no guilt in God's Son. 2 And only as you look upon him as guiltless can you understand **the** oneness **of God's Son.** 3 For the idea of guilt brings a belief in condemnation of one by another, projecting separation in place of unity. 4 **Because you are a oneness, y**ou can condemn only yourself, and by **condemning yourself,** you cannot know that you are God's Son. 5 You have denied the condition of **God's Son's** being, which is his perfect blamelessness. 6 Out of love **God's Son's** was created, and in love **God's Son's** abides. 7 Goodness and mercy have always followed **God's Son**, for **God's Son** has always extended the Love of his Father.

Note # 10: Being an extension of the Father, we also have been given the power to create like Him. Love creates, for love is sharing. When we create, we extend our true Big "S" Self onto our creation. There is no diminishment for creation is based on inclusion. When we make, we exclude, which confirms our belief in separation. Guilt and condemnation imply separateness. Since we are a Oneness, to give is to receive.

T-13.I.7. As you perceive the holy companions who travel with you, you will realize that there is no journey, but only an awakening. 2 The Son of God, who sleepeth not, **which is the Christ consciousness in you**, has kept faith with his Father for you. 3 There is no road to travel on, and no time to travel through. 4 For God waits not for His Son in time, being forever unwilling to be without **His Son.** 5 And so it has always been **that God's Son has never left His Father**. 6 Let the holiness of God's

Son, **the Christ consciousness in you,** shine away the cloud of guilt that darkens your mind, and by accepting **Christ's** purity as yours, learn of **the Christ consciousness** that it <*is*> yours.

Note # 11: Within our split mind, the Christ consciousness has always remained. The Christ consciousness is the home of right-mindedness and also the home of the Holy Spirit. In eternity, It has never left the Mind of God. While the son listens to the voice of the ego, the Voice for Christ falls on the deaf ears of the split-minded. Yet, our Big "S" Self and the Father remain united together through and with the Holy Spirit. We are that One Self.

T-13.I.8. You are invulnerable because you are guiltless. 2 You can hold on to the past only through guilt. 3 For guilt establishes that you will be punished for what you have done, and thus depends on one-dimensional time, proceeding from past to future. 4 No one who believes in one-dimensional time, which proceeded from past to future, can understand what "always" means, and therefore guilt must deprive you of the appreciation of eternity. 5 You are immortal because you are eternal, and "always" must be now. 6 Guilt, then, is a way of holding past and future in your mind to ensure the ego's continuity. 7 For if what has been will be punished, the ego's continuity is guaranteed. 8 Yet the guarantee of your continuity is God's, not the ego's **guarantee.** 9 And immortality is the opposite of time, for time passes away, while immortality is constant.

Note # 12: Because of the ego's belief in sin, guilt and fear, all "sin" must be punished some time in the future. The need for time arises in the thought system of the ego since time measure rates of change. The sinful must be punished to make amends for their sinful ways. To the ego, change is required because you are imperfect. If you were perfect, whole and complete, you would be changeless. In the world of perception, time has a purpose and is needed. Time allows for learning to occur. In the eternal changeless Kingdom there is no change to measure and, therefore, time serves no purpose. Time, being functionless in eternity, disappears.

T-13.I.9. Accepting the Atonement teaches you what immortality is, for by accepting your guiltlessness you learn that the past has never been, and so the future is needless and will not be. 2 The future, in time, is always associated with expiation, and only guilt could induce a sense of a need for expiation. 3 Accepting the guiltlessness of the Son of God as **your guiltlessness** is therefore God's way of reminding you of His Son, **the Christ,** and what **His Son, the Christ,** is in truth. 4 For God has never condemned His Son, and being guiltless he is eternal.

Note # 13: Expiation is the removal of guilt by suffering punishment.
 It is only in our split-mind's illusionary world that the belief that we could do something other than God's Will is possible. God, however, always knew His Son as perfect and, therefore, guiltless. By accepting the Atonement, which is the truth of the Sonship's sinlessness and guiltlessness, our need to suffer punishment in the future is gone. Being both sinless in the past and guiltless in the future, our need for time is no longer necessary. We can be in the changeless now that is the "always" of eternity.

T-13.I.10. You cannot dispel guilt by making **guilt** real, and then atoning for **guilt.** 2 **Making guilt real and then atoning for the guilt** is the ego's plan, which **the ego** offers instead of dispelling **guilt.** 3 The ego believes in atonement through attack, **since the ego is** fully committed to the insane notion that attack is salvation. 4 And you who cherish guilt must also believe **that attack is salvation,** for how else but by identifying with the ego could you hold dear what you do not want, **which is guilt?**

Note # 14: If we make guilt real, we are required to do some sort of penance for our sins which we believe that we have committed. We are making both sin and guilt real within our split-mind. By making them real, we get to keep both sin and guilt in our deluded mind. If sin is real, we are not perfect, whole and complete. The ego wants our decision-maker to agree with its egoic logic since this confirms that the separation actually occurred. The Atonement rejects the idea of sin since we are eternally perfect as God created us. Any illusion in which we believe that we have sinned does not require punishment because it is only an error in our deluded mind. The dreamer needs to only awaken to the truth. Therefore, there is no sin to forgive and nothing that requires punishment now or in the future. The Atonement just reawakens the sleepy child to His divine birthright.

T-13.I.11.The ego teaches you to attack yourself because you are guilty, and this **self-attack** must increase the guilt, for guilt is the result of attack. 2 In the ego's teaching, then, there is no escape from guilt. 3 For attack makes guilt real, and if **guilt** is real there <*is*> no way to overcome **guilt**. 4 The Holy Spirit dispels **guilt** simply through the calm recognition that **both sin and guilt have** never been. 5 As **the Holy Spirit** looks upon the guiltless Son of God, **the guiltless Son of God** knows that this is true. 6 And being true for you, you cannot attack yourself, for without guilt attack is impossible. 7 You, then, are saved because God's Son is guiltless. 8 And being wholly pure, you are invulnerable

Note # 15: To accept the Atonement for oneself, all attacks on any brother or yourself must cease. Attack is the tool of the ego and strengthens both our belief in sin and guilt's reality within our deluded mind. What we attack, we must fear. This perpetuates our belief in separation.

II. The Guiltless Son of God

T-13.II.1.The ultimate purpose of projection is always to get rid of guilt. 2 Yet, characteristically, the ego attempts to get rid of guilt from **the ego's** viewpoint only, for much as the ego wants to retain guilt <*you*> find **guilt** intolerable, since guilt stands in the way of your remembering God, Whose pull is so strong that you cannot resist **the pull to remember God**. 3 On this issue **of guilt versus the pull to remember God,** then, the deepest split of all occurs, for if you are to retain guilt, as the ego insists, <*you cannot be you who desires to remember God.* > 4 Only by persuading you that the **ego** is you could the ego possibly induce you to project guilt, and thereby keep **guilt** in your mind.

Note # 16: The ego's thought system is predicated on sin, guilt and fear. The Holy Spirit's is based on the remembrance of God. If the ego can convince you that you are the ego, you will place your faith in its thought system and choose guilt over the remembrance of God. Your decision-maker will abdicate it rights to the ego and you will identify your mind as the ego. The ego's goal is for you to believe that you exist as a limited ego-body, rather than believe you are an unlimited spirit. You will deny our Big "S" Self's existence in our split mind. It is the Big "S" Self that remembers God and your reality. This difference in beliefs results in misalignment with God's will. Misalignment will be felt as conflict, stress and loss of inner peace. Only by our asking for the guidance of the Holy Spirit can our peace be recovered.

T-13.II.2.Yet consider how strange a solution the ego's arrangement is. 2 You project guilt to get rid of **guilt**, but you are actually merely concealing **guilt**. 3 You do experience the guilt, but you have no idea why **you still experience the guilt**. 4 On the contrary, you associate **guilt** with a weird assortment of "ego ideals," which the ego claims you have failed. 5 Yet you have no idea that you are failing the Son of God by seeing **the Son of God** as guilty. 6 Believing you are no longer you, you do not realize that you are failing yourself.

<u>Note # 17:</u> If you forget what you are, the Son of God, you will believe you are powerless to resist the ego's thought system. Being powerless you become an innocent victim of the world around you. You lose your ability to be source or the cause of the events surrounding you.

Projection is a useful tool for the giving and receiving of egoic guilt. We project our guilt upon another in the hope of getting rid of this guilt within ourselves. Since ideas never leave their source, they remain hidden deep within our mind and we are powerless to change them for we have forgotten that we are the source of the guilt. Thus, projection insures that we retain our feelings of deep-seated guilt.

T-13.II.3. The darkest of your hidden cornerstones holds your belief in guilt from your awareness. 2 For in that dark and secret place is the realization that you have betrayed God's Son by condemning **God's Son** to death. 3 You do not even suspect this murderous but insane idea **of you condemning God's Son to death** lies hidden there **as a cornerstone in your belief in guilt**, for the ego's destructive urge is so intense that nothing short of the crucifixion of God's Son can ultimately satisfy **the ego**. 4 **The ego** does not know who the Son of God is because **the ego** is blind. 5 Yet let **the ego** perceive guiltlessness anywhere, and **the ego** will try to destroy **guiltlessness** because **the ego** is afraid **of guiltlessness**.

<u>Note # 18:</u> The ego is afraid of guiltlessness because without your belief that you are guilty, you will regain your ability as decision-maker and choose again. This time your decision-maker would choose the Holy Spirit's thought system that leads to the remembrance of God. Your belief in guilt helps your ego keep you in victim consciousness thus, keeping you under its sin, guilt and fear-based thought system.

T-13.II.4. Much of the ego's strange behavior is directly attributable to **the ego's** definition of guilt. 2 To the ego, *<the guiltless are guilty.>* 3 Those who do not attack are **the ego's** "enemies" because, by not valuing **the ego's** interpretation of salvation, they, **the guiltless**, are in an excellent position to let go **of the ego and the ego's insane interpretation of salvation which rests on the belief that you have killed the Son of God and, therefore, are no longer your real Christed Self.** 4 **The guiltless** have approached the darkest and deepest cornerstone in the ego's foundation, and while the ego can withstand your raising all else to question, **the ego** guards this one secret **about guilt** with **the ego's** life, for **the ego's** existence depends on keeping this secret, **that to the ego** *<the guiltless are guilty. >* 5 So it is this secret **that to the ego** *<the guiltless are guilty>* that we must look upon, for the ego cannot protect you against truth, and in **truth's** presence the ego is dispelled.

<u>Note # 19:</u> According to the ego, if your decision-maker is to side with the ego's insane thought system, truth must be made false and the false made true. This is why to the ego's secret that <the guiltless are guilty> must be kept from you. For if you understood that this is what the ego's thought system is based upon, who could believe it? The teaching that <the guiltless are guilty> is self-contradictory.

T-13.II.5. In the calm light of truth, let us recognize that you believe you have crucified God's Son. 2 You have not admitted to this "terrible" secret **that you believe you have crucified God's Son** because you would still wish to crucify him if you could find him. 3 Yet the wish has hidden **God's Son** from you because **this wish** is very fearful, and so you are afraid to find **God's Son**. 4 You have handled this wish to kill yourself by not knowing who you are, and identifying **yourself** with something else, **who is the little "s" self ego-body**. 5 You have projected guilt blindly and indiscriminately, but you have not uncovered **guilt's** source. 6 For the ego does want to kill you, and if you identify with **the ego** you must believe **the ego's** goal is **your goal**.

Note # 20: To the ego, God's guiltless Son must be destroyed. Since the ego has no power in itself, you who have denied your existence as God's Son, must desire to kill yourself so that the ego can maintain its existence. Egoic projection is the tool in which you appear to get rid of your guilt by placing it upon another. With projection you forget your sourceness and make someone else your victimizer. Projection is the ego's tool that keeps you in victim consciousness. You have forgotten your Big "S" Self and instead have identified yourself as a limited ego-body.

T-13.II.6. I have said that the crucifixion is the symbol of the ego. 2 When **the ego** was confronted with the real guiltlessness of God's Son **the ego** did attempt to kill **God's Son**, and the reason **the ego** gave was that guiltlessness is blasphemous to God. 3 To the ego, the <*ego*> is God, and guiltlessness must be interpreted as the final guilt that fully justifies murder. 4 You do not yet understand that any fear you may experience in connection with this course stems ultimately from this interpretation, **that guiltlessness must be interpreted as the final guilt that fully justifies murder,** but if you will consider your reactions to **this interpretation that guiltlessness fully justifies murder,** you will become increasingly convinced **that any fear you may experience in connection with this course stems ultimately from this interpretation** that this is so.

Note # 21: The ego wants to usurp the power of God. What better way to usurp God's power than to replace God with the ego? To do this, the ego must destroy the Oneness of God by killing the Oneness that is God's Son. The separation represents this destruction of the Oneness. The egoic replacement of God is the natural result in our belief that the separation was real. Our belief in sin, guilt and fear has allowed the ego to substitute an egoic god of fear and retribution in place of the God of Love.

T-13.II.7. This course has explicitly stated that **this course's** goal for you is happiness and peace. 2 Yet you are afraid **of this course's goal of happiness and peace.** 3 You have been told again and again that **happiness and peace** will set you free, yet you sometimes react as if **happiness and peace** is trying to imprison you. 4 You often dismiss **happiness and peace** more readily than you dismiss the ego's thought system. 5 To some extent, then, you must believe that by not learning the course you are protecting yourself. 6 And you do not realize that it is only your guiltlessness that <*can*> protect you.

Note # 22: Truth's guiltlessness protects you because it comes from God, Himself. Your innocence comes from what you are, which is the perfect extension of God. All power has already been given to you by God. You need only to reclaim your divine birthright as His beloved Son. By accepting the Atonement for yourself, you reclaim your inheritance.

T-13.II.8. The Atonement has always been interpreted as the release from guilt, and this is correct if it is understood. 2 Yet even when I interpret **the Atonement** for you, you may reject **the Atonement** and do not accept **the Atonement** for yourself. 3 You have perhaps recognized the futility of the ego and **the ego's** offerings, but though you do not want **the ego's offerings,** you may not yet look upon the alternative **to the ego's offerings** with gladness. 4 In the extreme, you are afraid of redemption and you believe **redemption** will kill you. 5 Make no mistake about the depth of this fear **of redemption.** 6 For you believe that, in the presence of truth, you might turn on yourself and destroy yourself.

Note # 23: Although we do not want the guilt that is associated with the ego's belief system, we may still value some of its supposed gifts. We may still value egoic specialness and individuality. If we identify ourselves as the body, we get to be special. If we accept the Holy Spirit and "become" a Oneness with our brother, we fear that we are killing our specialness. We would like to get rid of the guilt, yet, keep our body and our perceived specialness. We like the ego's idea that we are the arbitrators for truth and can pick and choose the "truth for the day." We cannot keep some things outside the forgiveness of the Holy Spirit's thought system and claim that we have accepted the Atonement for ourselves. We must choose to be vigilant only for God.

T-13.II.9.Little child, this is not so. **You did not kill God's Son for you are, and always will be, God's perfect, guiltless Son.** 2 Your "guilty secret" is nothing, and if you will but bring **your "guilty secret"** to the light, the light will dispel **your "guilty secret."** 3 And then no dark cloud will remain between you and the remembrance of your Father, for you will remember His guiltless Son, who did not die because he is immortal. 4 And you will see that you were redeemed with him, and have never been separated from him, **God's guiltless Son.** 5 In this understanding lies your remembering, for **this understanding** is the recognition of love without fear. 6 There will be great joy in Heaven on your homecoming, and the joy will be yours. 7 For the redeemed son of man is the guiltless Son of God, and to recognize him, **the son of man, as the guiltless Son of God** <*is*> your redemption.

Note # 24: By seeing our brother as guiltless, we accept that same guiltlessness. For to give, is to receive. When we use only our Christ Vision, we recognize our brother's Big "S" Self, not his body, and we recognize the truth of our eternal Oneness that is the One Self that we share. We are back home.

III. The Fear of Redemption

T-13.III.1.You may wonder why it is so crucial that you look upon your hatred and realize **the** full extent **of your hatred**. 2 You may also think that it would be easy enough for the Holy Spirit to show **the full extent of your hatred** to you, and to dispel **the full extent of your hatred** without the need for you to raise it to awareness yourself. 3 Yet there is one more obstacle you have interposed between yourself and the Atonement. 4 We have said that no one will countenance fear if he recognizes **fear**. 5 Yet in your disordered state of mind you are not afraid of fear. 6 You do not like **fear**, but it is not your desire to attack that really frightens you. 7 You are not seriously disturbed by your hostility. 8 You keep **your hostility** hidden because you are more afraid of what **your hostility** covers. 9 You could look even upon the ego's darkest cornerstone without fear if you did not believe that, without the ego, you would find within yourself something you fear even more. 10 You are not really afraid of crucifixion. 11 Your real terror is of redemption.

Note # 25: We are afraid to look within because we fear what we may find. This is the fear of the unknown; our belief that we may discover something that is worse than our present state. Believing we are the ego-body, we fear we will lose what little we have. We fear that if we looked within our mind, our belief in specialness and separation that has become our identity may disappear and be destroyed. Not understanding what God's love is, we fear being returned to the equality of God's love.

T-13.III.2.Under the ego's dark foundation, **which is based on sin, guilt and fear,** is the memory of God, and it is of this **memory of God**, that you are really afraid. 2 For this memory **of God** would instantly restore you to your proper place, and it is this place **of the memory of God** that you have sought to leave. 3 Your fear of attack is nothing compared to your fear of love. 4 You would be willing to look even upon your savage wish to kill God's Son, if you did not believe that **your wish to kill God's Son** saves you from love. 5 For this wish **to leave the memory of God and God's love** caused the separation, and you have protected **this wish to forget the memory of God** because you do not want the separation healed. 6 You realize that, by removing the dark cloud that obscures **the memory of God**, your love for your Father would impel you to answer God's Call and leap into Heaven. 7 You believe that attack is salvation because **attack** would prevent you from **the memory of God and God's call for His Son's return to Heaven.** 8 For still deeper than the ego's foundation, and much stronger than **the ego's foundation** will ever be, is your intense and burning love of God, and **God's love** for you. 9 This **love for and from God** is what you really want to hide.

Note # 26: The ego cannot love and, therefore, it fears love. Since we are created in God's image, which is love, love is our divine birthright. The memory of God will return us to our true nature, which is only love. This would be returning to whole-mindedness and our Big "S" Self would act as the decision-maker and freely follow God's Will. To the ego, this would result in the disappearance and destruction of the "little s" self, which is the ego. Thus, the ego fears our return, or redemption to whole-mindedness. This healing would result in our Big "S" Self resuming total control as decision-maker over our split-minded egoic small "s" self.

T-13.III.3. In honesty, is it not harder for you to say "I love" than "I hate"? 2 You associate love with weakness and hatred with strength, and your own real power, **which is love,** seems to you as your real weakness. 3 For you could not control your joyous response to the call of love if you heard **the call of love**, and the whole world you thought you made would vanish. 4 The Holy Spirit, then, seems to be attacking your fortress, **which is your unloving world of provisional reality that you made to** shut out God, and **God** does not will to be excluded.

Note # 27: We made the world of perception based on our belief that the separation was real. This world is our attempt to exclude ourselves from the memory of God and God's love for his Son. We wanted to be special. Being a Oneness of Everything, it is impossible for the One Self to be torn away from perfection. Without this world of illusion, God's Call for His Son's return to sanity (right-mindedness) would be so strong that we would lose the specialness of separation that we value. We would return control of our decision-maker over to our Big "S" Self. We would return to our true home, which is Heaven. The Love of the Father for His Son and our love for the Father would be remembered. We would abandon the mad idea of the separation and return to the Oneness of the Mind of God, which is our only true reality.

T-13.III.4. You have built your whole insane belief system because you think you would be helpless in God's Presence, and you would save yourself from His Love because you think **God's Love** would crush you into nothingness. 2 You are afraid **God's Love** would sweep you away from yourself and make you little, because you believe that magnitude lies in defiance, and that attack is grandeur. 3 You think you have made a world God would destroy; and by loving **God**, which you do, you would throw this world **of the little "s" self** away, which you <*would.*> 4 Therefore, you have used the world to cover your love, and the deeper you go into the blackness of the ego's foundation, the closer you come to the Love that is hidden there **within you true Self, the Christ.** 5 <*And it is this **return to love,** that frightens you*>.

Note # 28: The return to the Christ in you is the return to right-mindedness. The ego fears the Christ within you, since that would lead to the ego's disappearance and your return to the Oneness of the Mind of God. The ego's goal is that your Big "S" Self would never regain control of your split mind. The ego does not want you to reclaim your decision-making power. As long as you remain in victim consciousness, you will never realize that you can choose again. The ego does not want you to know that there is another thought system that you can freely choose to follow. It does not want you to hear the voice for God. If the ego is to continue to exist, it cannot let you decide to remember God's love.

T-13.III.5. You can accept insanity because you made **insanity**, but you cannot accept love because you did not **make love**. 2 You would rather be a slave of the crucifixion than a Son of God in redemption. 3 Your individual death seems more valuable than your living oneness, for what is given you is not so dear as what you made. 4 You are more afraid of God than of the ego, and love cannot enter where **love** is not welcome. 5 But hatred can **enter your mind** for **hatred** enters of **hatred's** own volition and cares not for **your true volition, which is based on love.**

Note # 29: We value our egoic specialness and individuality over our true Big "S" Self. The ego's thought system is based on separation. We value the illusion of specialness over the truth of our Oneness. We prefer the ego's thought system since it alone promises the specialness that we desire. Believing that we are limited ego-bodies, we would rather die than lose our individuality. We like the idea of being separate and fear the return to the Oneness because we fear that this will cost us our individuality. The price that the ego demands for maintaining our belief in separation is pain, suffering and death. If we, the decision-maker, realized this cost, we would feely chose to return to the memory of God. Our little "s" self fears the restoration of love and the reawakening of the Sonship.

T-13.III.6. You must look upon your illusions and not keep **your illusions** hidden, because **your illusions** do not rest on their own foundation. 2 In concealment **your illusions** appear to **rest on their own foundation**, and thus **your illusions** seem to be self-sustained. 3 This **concealment of your illusions' foundation from yourself** is the fundamental illusion on which the others rest. 4 For beneath **your illusions,** and concealed as long as your **illusions' foundations** are hidden, is the loving mind that thought it made **your illusions** in anger. 5 And the pain in **your loving** mind is so apparent, when **the pain** is uncovered, that **your mind's** need of healing cannot be denied. 6 Not all the tricks and **egoic** games you offer **your loving mind** can heal **your mind**, for here is the real crucifixion of God's Son.

Note # 30: Our dream world of illusions hides our true loving nature. Being created by God's Love, we are love. We believed that we attacked and sinned against God when we denied God's Love. In our world of illusions, we can pretend that we are something other than what we are. We can pretend to hide from God's Love. We can even believe that we can do something other than the Will of God but our illusions have no affect on the truth of the One Self. We cannot change the divine inheritance of our Christ Mind.

T-13.III.7. And yet **God's Son** is not crucified. 2 Here **in the Son's illusionary dream world** is both **the Son of God's** pain and healing, for the Holy Spirit's vision is merciful and **the Holy Spirit's** remedy is quick. 3 Do not hide suffering from **the Holy Spirit's** sight, but bring **your suffering and pain, which are born in your illusions** gladly to **the Holy Spirit**. 4 Lay **all your hurts caused by your illusions and misperceptions** before **the Holy Spirit's** eternal sanity, and let **the Holy Spirit** heal you. 5 Do not leave any spot of pain hidden from **the Holy Spirit's** light, and search your mind carefully for any thoughts you may fear to uncover. 6 For **the Holy Spirit** will heal every little thought you have kept to hurt you and cleanse **these hurtful thoughts** of **their** littleness, restoring **your every thought** to the magnitude of God.

Note # 31: If we ask for the guidance of the Holy Spirit, He will reinterpret all our misperceptions. The

Holy Spirit's reinterpretation will allow us to recover the true nature of our Big "S" Self. The correcting mechanism that the Holy Spirit utilizes is the tool of forgiveness. We forgive our brother, which in turn results in our forgiving ourselves. Our fear-based thoughts are transformed into the Big "S" Self's relationships of love and forgiveness.

T-13.III.8. Beneath all the grandiosity you hold so dear is your real call for help. 2 For you call for love to your Father as your Father calls you to Himself. 3 In that place which you have hidden, **the Christ within your split mind,** you will only to unite with the Father, in loving remembrance of **the Father.** 4 You will find this place of truth as you see **this place of truth, the Christ consciousness,** in your brothers, for though **your brothers** may deceive themselves, like you, **your brothers** long for the grandeur that is in **themselves.** 5 And perceiving **the Christ consciousness in your brothers** you will welcome it, and **the Christ consciousness in your brothers** will be **your Christ consciousness.** 6 For grandeur is the right of God's Son, and no illusions can satisfy **God's Son** or save **God's Son** from what he is. 7 Only **the Son of God's** love is real, and **God's Son** will be content only with his reality.

Note # 32: Being like God, we have everything because we are everything. This is the natural result of God's extension of Himself. When God created the Sonship, God gave all of Himself, which was everything. When we realize that we are everything, why would we settle for anything less? Why would we give up everything for littleness? This choice for littleness demonstrates why anyone following of the ego's thought system must be insane.

T-13.III.9. Save **God's Son** from his illusions that you may accept the magnitude of your Father in peace and joy. 2 But exempt no one from your love, or you will be hiding a dark place in your mind where the Holy Spirit is not welcome. 3 And **by withholding love from a brother,** thus you will exempt yourself from **the Holy Spirit's** healing power, for by not offering total love you will not be healed completely. 4 Healing must be as complete as fear, for love cannot enter where there is one spot of fear to mar **love's** welcome.

Note # 33: We cannot withhold our love from any part of the Sonship if we wish to be completely healed. Healing can only be accomplished completely. We cannot be partially healed. The Sonship shares its Oneness with God. We cannot exclude a brother without denying our own Oneness. All minds are part of the shared reality of the Mind of God. Forgiveness is the tool that is utilized by the Holy Spirit to exchange our fears for our return to love.

T-13.III.10. You who prefer separation to sanity cannot obtain **separation** in your right mind. 2 You were at peace until you asked for special favor. 3 And God did not give **the special favor** for the request was alien to **God,** and you could not ask this **special favor** of a Father Who truly loved His Son. 4 Therefore you made of **God** an unloving father, demanding of **God** what only such **an unloving** father could give, **which would be to place limits on His Son.** 5 And the peace of God's Son was shattered, for **God's Son** no longer understood his Father. 6 **God's Son** feared what he had made, **which was an unloving father who would grant his child specialness at the cost of his child's unlimitedness. But** still more did **God's Son** fear his real Father, **since the son had** attacked his own glorious equality with **his true Father.**

Note # 34: God created us perfect, whole, and complete. As such, we are everything God is. When we ask for "a special favor," the only thing that we could be asking for is limitation. If God granted us limitation, God, Himself, would be limited for we share equally in the Mind of God. God cannot extend limitation because God is unlimited. In order to obtain specialness, we had to make-believe that God was something other than unconditional Love. Our Father, the God of Love, would not be willing to create something that was imperfect, not complete, and not whole. This idea could never be part of the Mind of a Loving God. Therefore, we denied our Father's Loving nature and substituted an egoic idol for separation, limitation and specialness. We made a god of limitation and littleness. We rejected the equality of the Oneness for the belief that we could be limited, which made us special. This was the birth of our belief that we had attacked God, our Father. We believed that we had usurped the power of God. We claimed that we, God's Effect, were now self-created.

T-13.III.11. In peace **God's Son** needed nothing and asked for nothing. 2 In war **God's split-minded Son** demanded everything and found nothing. 3 For how could the gentleness of love respond to **God's split-minded Son's** demands **for separation and limitation**, except by **love** departing in peace and returning to the Father? 4 If the Son did not wish to remain in peace, he could not remain at all. 5 For a darkened mind cannot live in the light, and **a darkened mind** must seek a place of darkness where **this darkened mind** can believe it is where **this darkened mind** is not. 6 God did not allow **His split-minded Son to leave the peace of the Mind of God. The Son leaving the Mind of God did not happen.** 7 Yet you, **the split minded child,** demanded that **you could leave the peace and Oneness of the Mind of God and that this could** happen, and therefore **you** believed **in your imaginings** that it was so. **In your imagination you believed that you could and actually did leave the Mind of God and thus, became separate from the Will of God. Although this could not happen in reality, God's love allows your free will to imagine anything you want**.

Note # 35: Since we are changeless, we could not change what we truly are and, therefore, we always remain perfect, whole and complete. Yet, we can choose to deny this truth of our perfection. Our world of provisional reality was birthed by the Sonship's collective denial of the truth. Although we remain part of the Mind of God, which is our Christ consciousness, the rest of our split mind appears to have forgotten our Oneness. We, the dreamer, have been caught up in our own dream, and believe that our dream is our reality. Our belief in our dream has no effect on the Mind of God since the Mind of God only deals with truth. Illusions are unknown to God, our Father.

T-13.III.12. To "single out" is to "make alone," and thus make lonely. 2 God did not do this to you. 3 Could **God** set you apart, knowing that your peace lies in **God's** Oneness? 4 **God** denied you only your request for pain, for suffering is not of **God's** creation. 5 Having given you creation, **God** could not take **creation** from you. 6 **God** could but answer your insane request with a sane answer that would abide with you in your insanity. 7 And this **God** did. 8 No one who hears **God's** answer but will give up insanity. 9 For **God's** answer is the reference point beyond illusions, from which you can look back on **illusions** and see **illusions** as insane. 10 But seek this place **beyond illusions** and you will find **this place**, for Love is in you and will lead you there.

Note # 36: Your Christ consciousness remains within your split mind. This is the home of the Holy Spirit who will guide you back to the remembrance of God and whole-mindedness. The Christ is the love in you and It is your true reality from which you never left the Mind of God. The Christ remains within the Peace of God. The acceptance of the Atonement for yourselves will return you to the Kingdom, which is eternal reality. We will remember that our will and God's Will are One since we shared this One Self that is the Mind of God.

IV. The Function of Time

T-13.IV.1. And now the reason why you are afraid of this course should be apparent. 2 For this is a course on love, because **this course** is about you. 3 You have been told that your function in this world **of perception** is healing, and your function in Heaven is creating. 4 The ego teaches that your function on earth is destruction, and you have no function at all in Heaven. 5 **The ego** would thus destroy you here **in this illusionary world of your perception** and bury you here **in this illusionary world of your perception**, leaving you no inheritance except the dust out of which **the ego** thinks you were made. 6 As long as **the ego** is reasonably satisfied with you, as **the ego's** reasoning goes, **the ego** offers you oblivion. 7 When **the ego** becomes overtly savage, **the ego** offers you hell.

<u>Note # 37:</u> It is important to remember our purpose under each thought system:

		Function of	
Level of Reality	Thought System of:	Holy Spirit	Ego
Level #1: Heaven		Co-creation	No Function
Level #2: World of Perception		Healing	Destruction

T-13.IV.2. Yet neither oblivion nor hell is as unacceptable to you as Heaven. 2 Your definition of Heaven <*is*> hell and oblivion, and the real Heaven is the greatest threat you think you could experience. 3 For hell and oblivion are ideas that you made up, and you are bent on demonstrating **the** reality **of ideas you made up, (hell and oblivion),** to establish **the reality that you wish yourself to be which is the littleness of specialness.** 4 If **the** reality **of ideas you made up, (hell and oblivion),** is questioned, you believe that **the reality that you wish yourself to be which is the littleness of specialness** is **questioned**. 5 For you believe that attack is your reality, and that your destruction is the final proof that you were right.

<u>Note # 38:</u> We fear Heaven for we believe it to be the destruction of our desire to be separate and special. The ego's thought system is determined to be right at all costs. The ego needs to be right since without your belief that you are the ego, the ego would disappear. The ego is powerless and any power it appears to have is abdicated from your own mind. Because of this dependence when you are following the ego's thought system, the ego insists that it is more important to be "right" than to be happy. This is why the ego would rather have you choose hell, the need to be right, over Heaven, the need to be happy. Being born as the unlimited Spirit of Oneness that is Everything, how can we be happy with "littleness?" When we believe in death, we are claiming that we are a little "s" self. Death is the ultimate proof that we are not eternal and separate from God. To the ego, our death "proves" that God is powerless to impose His will upon us. The ego has thus, usurped the power of life from the Living God of Love.

T-13.IV.3. Under the circumstances **that your death is required for you and the ego's thought system to be "right,"** would it not be more desirable to have been wrong, even apart from the fact that you were wrong? 2 While it could perhaps be argued that death suggests there <*was*> life, no one would claim that **death** proves there <*is*> life. 3 Even the past life that death might indicate, could only have been futile if **the past life** must come to **death**, and needs **death** to prove that **the past life** was **once alive** at all. 4 You question Heaven, but you do not question **the need to use death to prove that you live in your own world of littleness.** 5 Yet you could heal and be healed if you did question **that death is required to prove you live**. 6 And even though you know not Heaven, might **Heaven** not be more desirable than death? 7 You have been as selective in your questioning as in your perception. 8 An open mind is more honest than this **selective questioning and selective perception in which you have engaged.**

Note # 39: Your death is the ego's ultimate proof that you exist separate from God. ACIM suggest that we need to look very closely at a thought system that is demanding that we sacrifice our immortality and happiness, in order for the ego to be right. Why insist on our littleness when the Holy Spirit's thought system offers us Heaven. Heaven grants us everything including our happiness. To choose to claim that you are right, even when you are wrong, is a questionable philosophy. But the demand that you lose your divine birthright in order to be "right" is insanity. ACIM requests that you ask this question, "Would I rather be right, or happy?" If happiness is the answer, ACIM suggests that you too choose the Holy Spirit's thought system.

T-13.IV.4. The ego has a strange notion of time, and it is with this notion **of time** that your questioning might well begin. 2 The ego invests heavily in the past, and in the end believes that the past is the only aspect of time that is meaningful. 3 Remember that **the ego's** emphasis on guilt enables **the ego** to ensure **the ego's** continuity by making the future like the past, and thus avoiding the present. 4 By the notion of paying for the past in the future, the past becomes the determiner of the future, making **the past and the future** continuous without an intervening present. 5 For the ego regards the present only as a brief transition to the future, in which **the ego** brings the past to the future by interpreting the present in past terms.

Note # 40: Only when we are in the presence of the <now> can we make a different choice. The ego wants time to continue exactly like the past since in the past your mind was under the influence of the ego's thought system. In the past, you believed that you were an innocent victim of outside forces that were beyond your control. When you are in victim consciousness, you cannot reclaim your decision-making ability and choose again. If the ego can use the memory of the past to color or, more correctly, distort the present, you will continue to make the same misperceptions over and over again. Because you believe you are a victim, you believe that you are powerless to affect any change in your fate. Your future life experience will thus, remain the same as the past upon which it was based. When we fail to focus on the present, the<now>, we live in the past. This guarantees that the future will be a replica of the past. ACIM states that we should focus our awareness only upon the <now> and choose differently.

T-13.IV.5."Now" has no meaning to the ego. 2 The present merely reminds **the ego** of past hurts, and **the ego** reacts to the present as if **the present** <were> the past. 3 The ego cannot tolerate release from the past, and although the past is over, the ego tries to preserve **the past's** image by responding as if **the past** were present. 4 **The ego** dictates your reactions to those you meet in the present from a past reference point, obscuring **the** present reality **of those you meet.** 5 In effect, if you follow the ego's dictates you will react to your brother as though he were someone else **based on a reference point from your own past,** and this will surely prevent you from recognizing **your brother** as he is. 6 And you will receive messages from **your brother** out of your own past because, by making **your own past** real in the present, you are forbidding yourself to let **your own past** go. 7 You thus deny yourself the message of release that every brother offers you <now> **in the present because you choose to base your current perception on some past reference point.**

Note # 41: We live in our own private world of provisional reality. This is a world of perception. Perception is based on our current viewpoint. Change our viewpoint and we can change our perception. If we consistently use our past viewpoint to interpret our present experiences, we will obtain the same results in the present as we received from our past misperceptions. To reference and interpret the present based on the past, dooms us to having the past, present and future all be the same. The <now> does not appear in our awareness since we have chosen to live our present as a reenactment of the past. The ego has our minds under its current control, keeping us in victim consciousness which is exactly where the ego wants our decision-maker to remain. Thus, to the ego, the past is the most important element of time. If the ego can keep us referencing our past misperception about our private world, our future will be a copy of our past victimhood and we will continue to forget that we have the power to choose a different guide.

T-13.IV.6. The shadowy figures from the past are precisely what you must escape. 2 **The shadowy figures from the past** are not real, and have no hold over you unless you bring **these shadowy figures from the past** with you. 3 **The shadowy figures from the past** carry the spots of pain in your mind, directing you to attack in the present in retaliation for a past that is no more. 4 And this decision **to attack based on past misperception** is one of future pain. 5 Unless you learn that past pain is an illusion, you are choosing a future of illusions and losing the many opportunities you could find for release in the present. 6 The ego would preserve your nightmares, and prevent you from awakening and understanding **these current nightmares that require you to attack** are **based on your** past **misperceptions**. 7 Would you recognize a holy encounter if you are merely perceiving **a holy encounter** as a meeting with your own past? 8 For you would be meeting no one, and the sharing of salvation, which makes the encounter holy, would be excluded from your sight. 9 The Holy Spirit teaches that you always meet yourself, and the encounter is holy because you are **holy**. 10 The ego teaches that you always encounter your past, and because your dreams were not holy, the future cannot be **holy**, and the present is without meaning **since it is really the past repeating itself.**

Note # 42: The Holy Spirit always teaches that you are always meeting yourself in each encounter. This is true for a number of reasons. At its very basics, you are a Oneness and, therefore, there is nothing outside yourself to perceive. But more importantly, since we are dealing in the realm of provisional reality, our world is based on our own projections. We are constantly reinventing our private world based on our current projections. Projection is the process that we predetermine what we wish to perceive about a topic. We then project or send outside ourselves this same thought pattern that we wish to "see" confirmed by some "outside witness." Our senses then search out and find something that will confirm that what we thought was right. Thus, our senses have already prejudged what our "outside reality" will be. Based on projection, we choose to selectively "see" only what thought patterns we originally sent out. Because our selective "seeing" comes from projection, we always meet the thoughts we hold about ourselves. If we utilize our past misperception, which are based on the fact that we are sinners, our current interpretation of present events will be the same as our past misperceptions. The Holy Spirit knows the Sonship is only holy and that each encounter must be holy. To the Holy Spirit, the present is the only thing that is and each encounter becomes an opportunity to be transformed into a holy encounter if perceived correctly.

T-13.IV.7. It is evident that the Holy Spirit's perception of time is the exact opposite of the ego's. 2 The reason is equally clear, for **the ego and the Holy Spirit** perceive the goal of time as diametrically opposed. 3 The Holy Spirit interprets time's purpose as rendering the need for time unnecessary. 4 **The Holy Spirit** regards the function of time as temporary, serving only **the Holy Spirit's** teaching function, which is temporary by definition. 5 **The Holy Spirit's** emphasis is therefore on the only aspect of time that can extend to the infinite, for <*now*> is the closest approximation of eternity that this world offers. 6 It is in the reality of "now," without past or future, that the beginning of the appreciation of eternity lies. 7 For only "now" is here, and only "now" presents the opportunities for the holy encounters in which salvation can be found.

Note # 43: On Level #1, which is true reality of the Kingdom, there is only the eternal now. Time is the measure of change. Eternity is changeless; therefore, there is no change to measure. Only in the world of perception, which is predicated on the misperception that there is something outside you, is there anything that can change. The Holy Spirit places no value on past illusionary misperceptions that you have had since they must be false. The Holy Spirit's focus is on what is truly happening in your current dream state. By following the guidance and the correct perception of the Holy Spirit, any current experience can be transformed into a holy encounter.

T-13.IV.8. The ego, on the other hand, regards the function of time as one of extending itself, **the ego**, in place of eternity, for like the Holy Spirit, the ego interprets the goal of time as **the ego's** own **goal**. 2 The continuity of past and future, under **the ego's** direction, is the only purpose the ego perceives in time, and **the ego** closes over the present so that no gap in **the ego's** own continuity can occur. 3 **The ego's** continuity, then, would keep you in time, while the Holy Spirit would release you from **time**. 4 It is **the Holy Spirit's** interpretation of the means of salvation that you must learn to accept, if you would share **the Holy Spirit's** goal of salvation for you.

<u>Note # 44:</u> The ego only exists in time. Therefore, the ego requires time to continue to be under egoic control if the ego is to continue to exist.
The Holy Spirit's goal is to return you to the reality of what you are. Time is the means that is used to allow for our split mind to be returned to wholeness. Once this healing is achieved, time's purpose will have been served. The Sonship will have returned to the truth about Itself. Being eternal, perfect, whole and complete, we are changeless and time has no purpose or function in eternity.

T-13.IV.9. You, too, will interpret the function of time as you interpret **your own function**. 2 If you accept your function in the world of time as one of healing, you will emphasize only the aspect of time in which healing can occur, **which is the present of the <now>**. 3 Healing cannot be accomplished in the past. 4 **Healing** must be accomplished in the present to release the future. 5 This interpretation **of healing** ties the future to the present, and extends the present rather than the past. 6 But if you interpret your function as destruction, **which is the ego's function for you in the world of perception,** you will lose sight of the present and hold on to the past to ensure a destructive future. 7 And time will be as you interpret **time,** for of itself, **time,** is nothing.

<u>Note # 45:</u> Time is necessary only when we value the illusion of specialness and separation. Time, itself, has no reality in eternity. Time became necessary due to our belief that the separation was real. Time is needed only where change appears to be possible, which is the world of perception. How we perceive the present will depend on which thought system we choose to follow. We will either perceive the reality of the now or the misperceptions of our past. If we demand littleness and the need to pretend that we are right, we will choose to relive the past. If we choose happiness and the truth of our Big "S" Self, we will see the present as a <now> moment in which we can choose to live the present as a holy encounter. In a holy encounter, you would view the event with forgiving and loving eyes. This sharing might be directed at our brother, but since to give is to receive, the blessing of forgiveness and love will return to its source, which, of course, is our own mind.

V. The Two Emotions

T-13.V.1.I have said you have but two emotions, love and fear. 2 **Love** is changeless but continually exchanged, **love** being offered by the eternal to the eternal. 3 In this exchange **love** is extended, for **love** increases as **love** is given. 4 The other **emotion, fear,** has many forms, for the content of individual illusions differs greatly. 5 Yet **the many forms of the emotion of fear** have one thing in common; **the many forms of the emotion of fear** are all insane. 6 **The many forms of the emotion of fear** are made of sights that are not seen, and sounds that are not heard. 7 T**he many forms of the emotion of fear** make up a private world **of your provisional reality** that cannot be shared. 8 For **the illusionary forms of fear in your own private world of your provisional reality** are meaningful only to their maker, **you,** and so **the illusionary forms of fear** have no meaning at all. 9 In this **private** world their maker moves alone, for only **their maker** perceives **his illusions of fear.**

Note # 46: Your private world of provisional reality appears to be real to the maker, who is also the perceiver. Because we are projecting from our mind's viewpoint, what we wish to believe to be our provisional reality is projected from our mind's thoughts out into our "outside world." Our physical senses then confirm these same thoughts that we have projected into the world of perception. Whatever our egoic senses pick up have already been predetermined within the mind of the perceiver and, therefore, the senses only confirm your predetermined judgments. Because of projection, everyone who follows the ego's fear–based thought system makes up his or her own private world of provisional reality. Because everyone is projecting out from their own individual split mind's viewpoint, each person perceives their world differently. Projection is based on exclusion arising from fear. Projection is making. Creation or extension is sharing which comes from the emotion of love.

T-13.V.2. Each one peoples his world with figures from his individual past, and it is because of this **utilization of individualized past perceived experiences** that private worlds do differ. 2 Yet the figures that he sees were never real, for **these figures** are made up only of his reactions to his brothers, and do not include their reactions to him. 3 Therefore, he, **the maker,** does not see he made **these figures from his own past reactions and perceptions** and that **these figures** are not whole. 4 For these figures have no witnesses, being perceived in one separate mind only, **the mind of the maker.**

Note # 47: Perception is based on the individual viewpoint of the perceiver. The perceiver does not share his true perceptions with what is being observed. The perceiver is not concerned about how others actually view or react to him and the event. Therefore, the interpretation is one-sided. The other person is not allowed to even present their case or call any other witnesses that would support their side of the story. Because we lack knowledge, we lack all the facts. We are in no position to judge any event in the world of time. ACIM states the only judgment that we should make is that we are incapable of judging anything correctly. Because we identify ourselves as a limited ego-body, we need to ask the Holy Spirit to guide us. The function of the Holy Spirit is judgment and healing. Only the Holy Spirit can judge correctly, because only the Holy Spirit knows the truth about our Big "S" Self and is also aware of our temporary insanity in this illusionary world of littleness and limitation. If asked, the Holy Spirit will reinterpret our misperception so that we can choose correct perception.

T-13.V.3. It is through these strange and shadowy figures that the insane relate to their insane world. 2 For **the insane** see only those **shadowy figures** who remind **the insane** of these images, and it is to **these shadowy figures** that **the insane** relate. 3 Thus do **the insane** communicate with those **shadowy figures** who are not there, and it is **the insane,** who answer **for those shadowy figures that are not there.** 4 And no one else hears **those shadowy figures** answer save **the insane,** who called upon **his made-up shadowy figures to respond.** And **the insane** alone believes **his made-up shadowy figures have** answered him. 5 Projection makes perception, and you cannot see beyond **your self-induced projection.** 6 Again and again have you attacked your brother, because you saw in **your brother** a shadow figure in your private world. 7 And thus it is you must attack yourself first, for what you attack is not in others. 8 **For these shadowy figures that you make, perceive and attack in others do not exist. Their** only reality is in your own mind, and by attacking others you are literally attacking what is not there.

Note # 48: Our private world is produced by projection. The thoughts of the perceiver are being sent out; yet, these projected thoughts can never escape the mind of the projector. This private world is only seen as reality in the mind of the image-maker. This is why what we call "seeing" is actually "image making." We make up what we wish to "see" based on our past interpretation of previous experiences. By formulating judgments based on past misperceptions, we reincorporate the past into the present and future. In order to perceive the present correctly or even differently from the past, we have to be aware of the present. Unfortunately, since we have never released or forgiven ourselves from the judgments of our past, we shift into similar past reactive modes whenever we perceive current events. Rather than experience the now, we replay our past misperceptions. This constant modification of the present insures that we will continue to misperceive the present moment since we fail to be aware of what is really happening in the <now>. We remain in judgment and victim consciousness, constantly insuring that the future will replicate the past since our mind is never truly experiencing the now. Refusing to experience the now with another, we remain trapped in our own private world of provisional reality that cannot be shared. Our world of provisional reality is a private world no one else can enter because it only exists in the mind of the perceiver. The away to gain release from the past and this "private reality" is to ask the Holy Spirit to reinterpret the present correctly. Only the Holy Spirit is aware of truth and can judge the <now> correctly and transform the <now> into a holy encounter.

T-13.V.4.The delusional can be very destructive, for **the delusional insane** do not recognize **that the delusional insane** have condemned themselves. 2 **The delusional insane** do not wish to die, yet **the delusional insane** will not let condemnation go. 3 And so **the delusional insane** separate into their private worlds, where everything is disordered, and where what is within appears to be without. 4 Yet what is within **the delusional insane, which is their own imprisoned Big "S" Self,** they do not see, for the reality of their brothers' **Big "S" Self** they, **the delusional insane,** cannot recognize.

Note # 49: Projection is an egoic attempt to get rid of something the mind does not want. It is the source of our guilt. When we project something outside our mind, we are unaware that we are the source of the thought and, therefore, are the true director of everything we perceive. We believe that the source for what we are "observing" is from outside our own mind. Thus, not realizing that we are the actual generator of the image, we believe the outside world is acting as the independent source of what we perceive. We, the source of the projection, now claim that we are its effect and are being "done upon." These internal mirrors of projection help insure that we will never discover the source to the "problem." The ultimate source can be traced back to our own guilt. We will never find the source of our guilt out there because we have hidden the source of our guilt deep inside our minds. This is why the motto of the ego is "seek and never find." Looking outside ourselves, we blame everyone but ourselves. We refuse to accept the fact that the true source of guilt is our own mind. Projection is the main tool that allows the ego to remain in control of our thought system and keep us in victim consciousness. Being a victim, we believe that we are powerless to affect our world and incapable of choosing again.

 The Holy Spirit, if asked, will reinterpret our projection and correct our misperception. Through the use of the tool of forgiveness, the Holy Spirit returns us to the understanding that we have the power to decide again and choose for the truth of the One Self. The goal of the Holy Spirit is to gently reawaken the decision maker to right-mindedness. Right-mindedness is in the Christ consciousness part of our split mind.

Because your split mind is a mind in conflict, it holds two opposing viewpoints. These opposite beliefs of what you are results in constant warring within you. The split-minded see duality where only a oneness exists. You believe that you are both good and evil, loving and hating, mind and body. These are opposite and are not reconcilable. Only one is true. You cannot be both. Until you recognize that you can only be as God created you, you cannot heal your split mind and make it whole. The Holy Spirit knows you as your Big "S" Self. Yet, your egoic little "s" self believes that you are limited because it believes that you have a will other than Your Father's Will. The split-minded cannot reawaken to knowledge alone. They must have their brother beside them. Having lost knowledge, you live in your own private world of illusion. Since you fail to realize that you are the dreamer, you are incapable of correcting the problem. You have become so heavily involved in the dream that you are incapable of making a decision outside the dream to end it. You have forgotten that you are the dreamer. The solutions to the illusionary problems you experience in a dream cannot be corrected in the dream itself. The only away to correct this fictitious problem is to reawaken the mind so that the dreamer will know the illusion was never real. To seek an answer within the dream of separation is to give reality to the dream. This would only increase the dreamer's fears. The Holy Spirit will never do this, for the Holy Spirit will never do anything that would increase your fear. Fear is a cornerstone in the thought system of the ego. Therefore, to increase fear is contrary to the function and goal of the Holy Spirit, which is the healing of the split-minded.

T-13.V.5. You have but two emotions, **love and fear,** yet in your private world you react to each of them, **love and fear.** as though it were the other. 2 For love cannot abide in a world apart, where when **love** comes **love** is not recognized. 3 If you see your own hatred as your brother, you are not seeing **your brother but rather your own hatred.** 4 Everyone draws nigh unto what he loves, and recoils from what he fears. 5 And you react with fear to love, and draw away from **love.** 6 Yet fear attracts you, and believing **fear** is love, you call **fear** to yourself. 7 Your private world is filled with figures of fear you have invited into **your private world,** and all the love your brothers offer you, you do not see.

<u>Note # 50:</u> Following the ego's thought system, we made an up-side down world. The ego does not comprehend true love since the ego believes that you only give to get. Love becomes fear and fear love. Conditional love, which is based on fear, is accepted by the ego and is what the ego calls "love." Unconditional love is rejected and guarded against by the ego since it is viewed as a bad trade and a direct threat to egoic separation. Unconditional love is feared by the ego. This is insane and insures only unhappiness.
In the world of perception, there are only two emotions. Fear rules the ego's thought system; love rules the Holy Spirit's. In the real world of the Kingdom there is only love, for love is only real.

T-13.V.6. As you look with open eyes upon your **private** world **of perception**, it must occur to you that you have withdrawn into insanity. 2 **Within your own private world of provisional reality**, you see what is not there, and you hear what makes no sound. 3 Your manifestations of emotions are the opposite of what the emotions are. **Fear becomes love and love, fear.** 4 You communicate with no one, and you are as isolated from reality as if you were alone in all the universe. 5 In your madness you overlook reality completely, and you see only your own split mind everywhere you look. 6 God calls you and you do not hear, for you are preoccupied with your own **egoic** voice. 7 And the vision of Christ is not in your sight, for you look upon yourself alone.

<u>Note # 51:</u> Projection differs from creation or extension, since projection is based on exclusion, rather than inclusion. Extension is sharing and, therefore, inclusive. In creation, we are sharing what we truly are, which is thought, not form. In projection, a thought never truly leaves the mind of the projector. It is not shared. In projection, we are attempting to get rid of what we do not want. Although we believe that what we perceived was caused by someone other than us, the thought remains fixed in our own minds.

Because of the use of projection, we never see our brother's real Big "S" Self. We only see the image we have made of our brother as a little "s" self. It is not our brother's littleness that we see, but rather our own mind's little "s" self. We are not communicating with anybody real, since we have chosen to "talk" only to the shadowy figures that we have created within our own minds. This image-making allows us to replace the reality of Christ vision with the egoic "seeing.' Physical sight only "sees" the illusionary veils we have made to hide from the Mind of God. Christ vision is our only reality since it is part of the Mind of God and is the truth. Egoic seeing comes from fear because it was born from fear. Christ vision bears witness to love because it arises from love.

T-13.V.7. Little child, would you offer this **private world born out of your own fear** to your Father? 2 For if you offer **a world of fear** to yourself, you <are> offering **a world of fear** to **your Father**. 3 And **your Father** will not return **a world of fear**, for **a world of fear** is unworthy of you because **a world of fear** is unworthy of **your Father**. 4 Yet **your Father** would release you from **your world of fear** and set you free. 5 **Your Father's** sane Answer tells you what you have offered yourself, **your world of fear** is not true, but **your Father's** offering to you has never changed. 6 You who know not what you do can learn what insanity is, and look beyond **your private world of insanity and fear**. 7 It is given you to learn how to deny insanity, and come forth from your private world in peace. 8 You will see all that you denied in your brothers because you denied **these same things** in yourself. 9 For you will love **your brothers**, and by drawing nigh **(near or close to)** unto **your brothers** you will draw **your brothers** to yourself, perceiving **your brothers** as witnesses to the reality you share with God. 10 I am with **your brothers** as I am with you, and we will draw **your brothers** from their private worlds, for as we are united so would we unite with **your brothers**. 11 The Father welcomes all of us in gladness, and gladness is what we should offer **the Father**. 12 For every Son of God is given you to whom God gave Himself. 13 And it is God Whom you must offer **your brothers, who are Sons of God**, to recognize **God's** gift to you.

<u>Note # 52:</u> God's law states that to give is to receive. Being a Oneness, we can only give to ourselves. We cannot love God unless we love all of God. We, along with the entire Sonship, share in the unity of the Mind of God. Any withholding of love to any part of the Oneness is the rejecting of our Oneness and is not true unconditional love. This is why when God extended Himself, He gave everything to the Sonship because God is everything. God could not create except like Himself, perfect, whole and complete. We must freely decide to accept the unity for the entire Sonship and become that One Self. We cannot withhold our love from part of the indivisible Mind of God.

T-13.V.8. Vision depends on light. 2 You cannot see in darkness. 3 Yet in darkness, in the private world of sleep, you see in dreams although your eyes are closed. 4 And it is here **in the darkness of your private world** that what you see you made. 5 But let the darkness go and all you made you will no longer see, for sight of **what you made in the darkness of your own private world** depends upon denying vision. 6 Yet from denying vision it does not follow you cannot see. 7 But this is what denial does, for by **denying Christ's Vision** you accept insanity, believing you can make a private world and rule your own perception. 8 Yet for **your belief that you can make a private world and rule your own perception, the** light of Christ must be excluded. 9 Dreams disappear when light has come and you can see.

<u>Note # 53:</u> Light is an understanding of what you truly are. Light represents the truth. Christ vision, being of light, dispels the darkness so that your private delusionary world can fade away. With darkness gone, we can rediscover the reality of the One Self. This is our returning to the holographic oneness of whole-mindedness. With Christ vision, we look with the eyes of love and forgiveness upon all our brothers and ourselves.

T-13.V.9. Do not seek vision through your **egoic** eyes, for you made your way of seeing that you might see in darkness, and in this **way of seeing in darkness** you are deceived. 2 Beyond this darkness, and yet still within you, is the vision of Christ, Who looks on all in light. 3 Your **egoic** "vision" comes from fear, as **Christ vision comes** from love. 4 And **Christ** sees for you, as **Christ is** your witness to the real world. 5 **Christ** is the Holy Spirit's manifestation, looking always on the real world, and calling forth **the real world's** witnesses and drawing **the real world's witnesses** to you. 6 **The Holy Spirit** loves what **Christ** sees within you, and **Christ** would extend **what Christ truly sees within you**. 7 And **Christ** will not return unto the Father until **the Holy Spirit** has extended your perception even unto **the Father.** 8 And there perception is no more, for **the Holy Spirit** has returned you to the Father with **the Christ.**

<u>Note # 54:</u> Christ is the manifestation of the Holy Spirit. Although we speak of the Holy Trinity as being made up of three separate beings, the Father, Sonship, and Holy Spirit, they are part of the same Oneness and are not separate. They are the One Self. Because we are in the habit of dealing in a world of duality, we speak of things as being separate and distinct. The reality of the Oneness of God cannot be understood in language, which is limited. For the sake of discussion, the Holy Spirit and Christ could be used almost interchangeably. ACIM also states that the Christ is the home of the Holy Spirit. The Christ normally refers to the part of the split mind that has never lost the remembrance of God. The Holy Spirit is the bridge that reconnects the split-minded son and brings him back home to the Father.

T-13.V.10. You have but two emotions, and one you made, **which is the emotion of fear**, and one was given you **by God and is the emotion of love**. 2 Each **emotion** is a way of seeing, and different worlds arise from **love and fear's** different sights. 3 See through the vision **of love** that is given you, for through Christ's vision **Christ** beholds Himself, **the Sonship**. 4 And seeing what **Christ** is, **Christ** knows His Father. 5 Beyond your darkest dreams **Christ** sees God's guiltless Son within you, shining in perfect radiance that is undimmed by your dreams. 6 And this <*you*>, **God's guiltless Son**, will see as you look with **Christ**, for **Christ's** vision is **God's** gift of love to you, given **to the Son** of the Father for you.

<u>Note # 55:</u> You will decide on which thought system to follow based on what you value. With this choice, you will choose what you perceive yourself to be. The ego's thought system is based on sin, fear and guilt and, therefore, it breeds an illusionary world based on fear. The Holy Spirit's thought system is based on love and the truth about what you really are. It is the path that leads the insane back to the real world, Level #1, the Kingdom or Heaven, which is the remembrance of God.

T-13.V.11. The Holy Spirit is the light in which Christ stands revealed. 2 And all who would behold **Christ** can see **Christ**, for they have asked for light. 3 Nor will they, **who have asked for light**, see **Christ** alone, for **Christ** is no more alone than they are **who have asked for light.** 4 Because they, **who have asked for light,** saw the Son, they have risen in **the Son** to the Father. 5 And all this will they, **who have asked for light,** understand, because they looked within and saw beyond the darkness the Christ in them, **who have asked for light** and recognized **Christ.** 6 In the sanity of **Christ's** vision they, **who have asked for light,** looked upon themselves with love, seeing themselves as the Holy Spirit sees them. 7 And with this vision of the truth in them came all the beauty of the world to shine upon them, **who have asked for light and who now see with the Vision of Christ.**

<u>Note # 56:</u> When we ask for the guidance of the Holy Spirit, we are asking for the reinterpretation of our misperceptions into the Vision of Christ. With the Vision of Christ, we rediscover the truth about our brothers and ourselves. We "see" though the healing eyes of love and forgiveness.

VI. Finding the Present

T-13.VI.1. To perceive truly is to be aware of all reality through the awareness of your own **reality**. 2 But for this, **the ability to perceive truly**, no illusions can rise to meet your sight, for reality leaves no room for any error. 3 This means that you perceive a brother only as you see him <*now,* > **with no reference to the past.** 4 **A brother's** past has no reality in the present, so you cannot see **a brother's past in the present and perceive truly**. 5 Your past reactions to **a brother** are also not there, and if it is **there, it is** to **these past reactions to a brother** that you react, you see but an image of **your brother** that you made and cherish instead of **your brother's reality**. 6 In your questioning of illusions, ask yourself if it is really sane to perceive what was as now. 7 If you remember the past as you look upon your brother, you will be unable to perceive the reality that is now.

Note # 57: True perception allows for correct awareness of the whole through our correct awareness of our own reality. Each mirrors the other since they share the same Will of God. This is an example of "as above, so below." Knowledge and the Laws of God are universally applicable. Thus, we can go from a specific form of an example and generalize that same knowing to the abstract or general. If we allow our perception to be clouded by our past beliefs about our brother, we will not be able to accept the reality of the present. Old beliefs and judgments give rise to past misperceptions that we now project into the present. Thus, our viewpoints and perception remain the same as the past. Viewing the present from a past reference point dooms us to repeating our past perceived experiences as current events. This is why ACIM's goal is not to change the world, but rather change how you view your world. ACIM suggests that we need to replace all judgments with forgiveness if we are to rediscover what is the real truth about our Big "S" Self.

T-13.VI.2. You consider it "natural" to use your past experience as the reference point from which to judge the present. 2 Yet this is <*unnatural*> because **your past experiences were based on misperceptions and, therefore, this** is delusional. 3 When you have learned to look on everyone with no reference at all to the past, either his **past** or **your past** as you perceived **the past**, you will be able to learn from what you see <now.> 4 For the past can cast no shadow to darken the present, <*unless you are afraid of light.*> 5 And only if you are **afraid of light** would you choose to bring darkness with you, and by holding **the darkness from the past** in your mind, see **the <*now*>** as a dark cloud that shrouds your brothers and conceals their reality from your sight.

Note # 58: The dark thought system of the ego sees the past as the most important element of time. If the ego can keep your mind focused on the past, you will never see the present as an opportunity for your decision-maker to choose again. Thus, you remain in victim consciousness which insures the continued existence of your ego because the future will be interpreted as a reenactment of your past belief of separation and littleness.

T-13.VI.3. <*This darkness,* **which is caused by your past judgments and misperceptions,** *is in you.*> 2 The Christ as revealed to you now has no past, for **the Christ** is changeless, and in **the Christ's** changelessness lies your release. 3 For if **the Christ** is as **the Christ** was created, there is no guilt in **the Christ**. 4 No cloud of guilt has risen to obscure **the Christ**, and **the Christ** stands revealed in everyone you meet because you see **the Christ** through Himself. 5 To be born again is to let the past go, and look without condemnation upon the present. 6 The cloud that obscures God's Son to you <is> the past, and if you would have **the cloud** past and **be** gone, you must not see **any past cloud of misperceptions that obscures God's Son in the present, which is the** now. 7 If you see **any reference to the past** now in your **current** illusions, **these past misperceptions have** not gone from you, although **these past clouds are** not there **since they were reference points to an imagined past, which was an illusion and, therefore, never real**.

Note # 59: To be born again is to let the past go, and look without condemnation upon the present. This is how the vision of Christ functions. Its focus is only in the <now>.

T-13.VI.4. Time can release as well as imprison, depending on whose interpretation, **(the ego's or the Holy Spirit's)**, of **time** you use. 2 Past, present and future are not continuous, unless you force continuity on **the past, present and future**. 3 You can perceive **the past, present and future** as continuous, and **thus** make **time continuous** for you. 4 But do not be deceived, and then believe that this **continuousness of time** is how **time** is. 5 For to believe reality is what you would have **reality** be according to your use for **time** <is> delusional. 6 You would destroy time's continuity by breaking **time** into past, present and future for your own purposes. 7 You would anticipate the future on the basis of your past experience, and plan for **the future** accordingly. 8 Yet by doing so you are aligning past and future, and not allowing the miracle, which could intervene between **past and future in the presence of the** <now>, to free you to be born again. **Miracles are always in the now, the present.**

Note # 60: Time is not required to be linear. When we can accept the Holy Spirit's understanding of time, the focus on the past and future are dropped and we live in the now. Miracle-mindedness utilizes the time of <now>. The present and the future do not have to be based on the past. If we choose to believe that time is linear, then that is how we will perceive it to be. Time is always eternally <now>. Miracles are defined as a change in perception. In a miracle, we move from wrong perception to correct perception. The miracle is a decision to change the thought system we choose to follow. Since time arose out of a belief in the separation, time is a temporary tool required to facilitate the relearning process until the Sonship returns to whole-mindedness. When knowledge has returned, time will once again disappear. The closest thing that we currently can experience to aid us in our understanding of eternity is the <now>. The miracle compresses time. We believe that any change takes time. The miracle makes change happen instantaneously. Eternity is changeless; therefore, in eternity there is no change for time to measure. Unlike the thought system of the ego that utilizes the past to make the future, the Holy Spirit deals in the reality of the <now>. Any past reference points are laid aside so that nothing obscures the true light of the Christ we share. Forgiveness is the tool utilized by the Holy Spirit to remove these past reference points from our mind.

T-13.VI.5. The miracle enables you to see your brother without his past, and so perceive **your brother** as born again. 2 **Your brother's** errors are all past, and by perceiving **your brother** without **past errors** you are releasing **your brother**. 3 And since **your brother's** past is **your past**, you share in this release. 4 Let no dark cloud out of your past obscure **your brother** from you, for truth lies only in the present, and you will find **truth** if you seek **truth in the present**. 5 You have looked for **truth** where **truth** is not, and therefore have not found **truth**. 6 Learn, then, to seek **truth** where **truth** is, and **truth** will dawn on eyes that see 7 Your past was made in anger, and if you use your past to attack the present, you will not see the freedom that the present holds.

Note # 61: In utilizing the vision of Christ, we are aided by the Holy Spirit. We let the past go and look without condemnation upon the present. The miracle's focus is only on the <now>. Without past judgment, misperceptions are transformed into true or correct perception. The miracle is a change in perception that transcends time by eliminating the past. With the past gone, we can truly experience the <now> instead of reenacting our past misperceptions.

T-13.VI.6. Judgment and condemnation are behind you, and unless you bring **judgment and condemnation** with you, you will see that you are free of **judgment and condemnation.** 2 Look lovingly upon the present, for **the present** holds the only things that are forever true. 3 All healing lies within **the present** because **the present's** continuity is real. 4 **The present** extends to all aspects of the Sonship at the same time, and thus enables **all aspects of the Sonship** to reach each other. 5 The present is before time was, and will be when time is no more. 6 In **the present** are all things that are eternal, and **in the present all things** are one. 7 **The** continuity **of all things** is timeless and their communication is unbroken, for **all things** are not separated by the past. 8 Only the past can separate, and **the past** is nowhere.

<u>Note # 62:</u> In the real world of the Mind of God, there is only the eternal, which shares the Oneness of God's Will. In our world of perception, the Holy Spirit teaches us to be in the <now>. All healing and decisions to choose again only happen in the <now>. If your present moment's focus is referenced to the past or the future even though you perceive yourself to be in the present, you are not in the <now>. The <now> is a state of "being" in the present moment only. "Being," not "thinking," is required if one is to experience the <now>.

T-13.VI.7. The present offers you your brothers in the light that would unite you with **your brothers**, and free you from the past. 2 Would you, then, hold the past against **your brothers**? 3 For if you do **hold the past against your brothers**, you are choosing to remain in the darkness that is not there, and refusing to accept the light that is offered you. 4 For the light of perfect vision is freely given as **the light of perfect vision** is freely received, and **the light of perfect vision** can be accepted only without limit. 5 In this one, still dimension of time that does not change, and where there is no sight of what you were, you look at Christ and call **Christ's** witnesses to shine on you <*because you called **Christ's** witnesses forth.*> 6 And **Christ's witnesses** will not deny the truth in you, because you looked for **the truth** in **Christ's witnesses** and found **the truth** there.

<u>Note # 63:</u> The past binds and imprisons us to reenact these same past perceptions in present and future time frames. Instead of being in the <now> and choosing differently, we relive past illusions and misperception and continue to make the separation appear real in the present. In the <now> of a holy instant, we can drop all past judgments and be free to utilize the vision of Christ. The vision of Christ looks past all remnants of the false and observes correctly with the eyes of love and forgiveness. This heals and releases the Big "S" Self from the imprisonment of the egoic thought system.

T-13.VI.8. Now is the time of salvation, for now is the release from time. 2 Reach out to all your brothers, and touch **all your brothers** with the touch of Christ. 3 In timeless union with **all your brothers** is your continuity, unbroken because **your continuity** is wholly shared **with all your brothers**. 4 God's guiltless Son is only light. 5 There is no darkness in **God's guiltless Son** anywhere, for **God's guiltless Son** is whole. 6 Call all your brothers to witness to **God's guiltless Son's** wholeness, as I am calling you to join with me. 7 Each voice has a part in the song of redemption, the hymn of gladness and thanksgiving for the light to the Creator of light. 8 The holy light that shines forth from God's Son is the witness that **God's Son's** light is of his Father.

<u>Note # 64:</u> Only in the <now> can we make the decision to accept the Atonement for ourselves. This healing of the split-minded Sonship happens in the <now>. The <now> of correct perception mirrors the

truth of the changeless eternal One Self.

T-13.VI.9. Shine on your brothers in remembrance of your Creator, for you will remember **your Creator** as you call forth the witnesses to **your Creator's** creation. 2 Those whom you heal bear witness to your healing, for in their wholeness you will see your own **wholeness**. 3 And as your hymns of praise and gladness rise to your Creator, **your Creator** will return your thanks in **your Creator's** clear Answer to your call. 4 For it can never be that **God's** Son called upon **God** and **that the Son's call** remained unanswered. 5 **God's** Call to you is but your call to **God**. 6 And in **God** you are answered by **God's** peace.

Note # 65: God placed the Holy Spirit inside your Christ consciousness to insure the safety of your Big "S" Self during your temporary insanity while you dreamed the game of separation. The Holy Spirit is the Voice or Call for the Sonship's remembrance of God. The Atonement is God's answer to the belief that the separation is real.

T-13.VI.10. Child of Light, you know not that the light is in you. 2 Yet you will find **the light** through **the light's** witnesses, for having given light to them they, **your brothers,** will return **the light**. 3 Each one **of your brothers that** you see in light brings your light closer to your awareness. 4 Love always leads to love. 5 The sick, who ask for love, are grateful for **your love,** and in their joy **the sick, who ask for love,** shine with holy thanks. p252 6 And **it is** this **joy and love that the sick, who have received your love,** offer **back to** you who gave them joy. 7 The **sick, who have asked for love,** are your guides to joy, for having received **joy** of you they would keep it. 8 You have established **the sick, who have asked for love,** as guides to peace, for you have made **peace** manifest in them. 9 And seeing **peace manifest in them, the** beauty **of peace** calls you home.

Note # 66: Even though our goal is to accept the Atonement for ourselves, because of the unity of the Sonship in the shared Mind of God, all the Sonship shares the benefit. By correctly perceiving any experience as either an act of love or a cry for love, we move closer to our homecoming. By realizing that a supposed attack is merely a brother's cry for love, we can respond appropriately with loving and forgiving thoughts. Since what we give, we receive, our love and forgiveness to our brother is returned to ourselves. By seeing the Christ in our brother, we rediscover the Christ that was hidden in our own split-mind.

T-13.VI.11. There is a light that this **egoic** world cannot give. 2 Yet you can give **this light**, as **this light** was given you. 3 And as you give **this light**, **this light** shines forth to call you from the **egoic** world and follow **this light**. 4 For this light will attract you as nothing in this **egoic** world can do. 5 And you will lay aside the **egoic** world and find another **world**. 6 This other world is bright with love which you have given **this other world**. 7 And here **in this other world** will everything remind you of your Father and His holy Son. 8 Light is unlimited, and spreads across this world in quiet joy. 9 All those you brought with you will shine on you, and you will shine on them in gratitude because **all those you brought with you also** brought you here **to this world of light**. 10 Your light will join with theirs in power so compelling, that **this light** will draw the others out of darkness as you look on them.

Note # 67: Light is the Christ consciousness. Light is the understanding of what we really are, God's guiltless Son, perfect, whole and complete. We are spirit, not a bodily form. We are God's Thoughts, a Oneness in the holographic Mind of God that comprises the One Self.

T-13.VI.12. Awaking unto Christ is following the laws of love **out** of your **own** free will, and out of quiet recognition of the truth in **the laws of love**. 2 The attraction of light must draw you willingly, and willingness is signified by giving. 3 Those who accept love of you become your willing witnesses to the love you gave them, and it is they who hold **love freely** out to you. 4 In sleep you are alone, and your awareness is narrowed to yourself. 5 And that is why the nightmares come. 6 You dream of isolation because your eyes are closed. 7 You do not see your brothers, and in the darkness you cannot look upon the light you gave to **your bothers**.

Note # 68: The law of love is that love gives all that it is, for by giving love you receive love. Love must be given for its nature is one of sharing. In this sharing is the oneness of the Sonship reborn. Your free will determines when you will choose to accept the fact that your will is your Father's Will. God's Will is that His Son be happy. The awakening of the Christ is the reclaiming of your divine inheritance that comprises everything. We remain one with God, perfect, whole and complete.

T-13.VI.13. And yet the laws of love are not suspended because you sleep. 2 And you have followed **the laws of love** through all your nightmares, and have been faithful in your giving, for you were not alone. 3 Even in sleep has Christ protected you, ensuring the real world for you when you awake. 4 In your name **Christ** has given for you, and given you the gifts **Christ** gave. 5 God's Son is still as loving as his Father. 6 Continuous with his Father, he has no past apart from **his Father**. 7 So **God's Son, the Christ**, has never ceased to be his Father's witness and his own. 8 Although, **the split-minded son** slept, Christ's vision did not leave **the split-minded son**. 9 And so it is that **the split-minded son** can call unto himself the witnesses that teach him that he never slept.

Note # 69: Although we have forgotten our divine birthright due to our belief in the separation, our inheritance has been preserved in the Christ consciousness part of our mind. Our Big "S" Self has never forgotten the truth and remains aware of Its Oneness with the Mind of God. The light of Christ has shone continuously. It has been obscured by the ego's thought system, but it has never dimmed. Even during the illusion of separation, the Holy Spirit has continued to preserve any loving thoughts and will restore these creations to our awareness in eternity.

VII. Attainment of the Real World

T-13.VII.1. Sit quietly and look upon the world you see, and tell yourself: "The real world is not like **the egoic world I see**. 2 **The real world** has no buildings and there are no streets where people walk alone and separate. 3 **In the real world** there are no stores where people buy an endless list of things they do not need. 4 **The real world** is not lit with artificial light, and night comes not upon **the real world**. 5 **In the real world** there is no day that brightens and grows dim. 6 **In the real world** there is no loss. 7 **In the real world** nothing is there but shines, and shines forever."

Note # 70: The real world is based on truth. It is not a place or location set in time. It is a state of being. When we lost knowledge, we lost "sight" in the real world. We replaced truth with a world based on perception. Perception is not knowledge and our perception changes as our viewpoints shift. The real world is changeless and, therefore, eternal. The world of perception is an unstable, changeable world that becomes our private world of provisional reality. The world of perception was made by the split-minded to maintain the belief that our will could be separate from our Source. The Holy Spirit will use this same world of perception as a learning device to teach us that we are love and that only love is real.

When we have relearned this lesson, we will be ready to accept the Atonement for ourselves and return to the real world.

T-13.VII.2. The world you see must be denied, for sight of **the world you see** is costing you a different kind of vision, **the vision of Christ.** 2 *<You cannot see both worlds,>* for each of **these worlds** involves a different kind of seeing, and depends on what you cherish. **Do you cherish oneness or specialness born from the belief in separation? Do you cherish truth, or false illusions?** 3 The sight of one is possible because you have denied the other. 4 Both **worlds** are not true, yet either one will seem as real to you as the amount to which you hold **that one world** dear. 5 And yet **the** powers **of these two worlds are** not the same, because their real attraction to you is unequal.

Note # 71: The world we "see" will be based in where we, as decision-makers, place our allegiance. If we side with the thought system of the ego, we see a world of form based on our belief in separateness, specialness and limitation. Since we perceive ourselves as an ego-body, we project out of our mind a world that conforms to and bears witness to our belief that the separation is real. If we side with the Holy Spirit's thought system, our world of provisional reality will be reinterpret to become a learning tool that will lead us back to the reality of the real world. The real world is based on truth, and truth was something that was lost when we chose littleness or specialness, over our Big "S" Self. These denials of truth led us to project and make an imaginary world based on sin, guilt and fear. This world we made is our egoic attempt to keep out God and God's love.

T-13.VII.3. You do not really want the world you see, for **the world you see** has disappointed you since time began. 2 The homes you built have never sheltered you. 3 The roads you made have led you nowhere, and no city that you built has withstood the crumbling assault of time. 4 Nothing you made but has the mark of death upon it. 5 Hold **the world you made and see it** not dear, for **the world you made and see** is old and tired and ready to return to dust even as you made it. 6 This aching world has not the power to touch the living world at all. 7 You could not give **the world you made the power to be real**, and so although you turn in sadness from **the world you made**, you cannot find in **the world you made** the road that leads away from **the world you made** into another world, **which is real and eternal.**

Note # 72: This passage in ACIM clearly states that we, not God, made our private world of provisional reality which is based on our shifting perception. This world we made is not real because we made it. It is important to realize that the word "make" is different from "create." When we made this world, we failed to extend all that we are, which is unlimited spirit. Instead, we chose to limit or exclude something. Creation is extension. When God creates, being everything, God gives everything to His creations. It is not that we, as Sons of God, do not have the ability to create like God, but rather that when we made this world, we believed that we were something less than what God created. Believing that we were limited, imperfect and incomplete, the world we made was also limited, imperfect and incomplete. Creation is born out of love, which is sharing. Our world of perception was born out of fear, which is exclusion. The world of perception is Level # 2. The real world, the Kingdom or Heaven, is Level # 1. These two levels are parallel lines. They never met. We cannot find Heaven, Level #1, by looking in Level # 2's illusions. The Holy Spirit acts as the bridge between these two worlds. Only the Holy Spirit is aware of both the world of truth and the world of illusion. For ACIM purposes, nothing is real in the world of perception, for a dream, by its very definition is an illusion and, therefore, a fantasy. Salvation cannot be found in a dream. It can only be found by reawakening to the truth.

T-13.VII.4. Yet the real world has the power to touch you even here, because you love **the real world.** 2 And what you call with love will come to you. 3 Love always answers, being unable to deny a call for help, or not to hear the cries of pain that rise to **love's awareness** from every part of this strange world you made but do not want. 4 All that you need to give this world **of illusion** away in glad exchange for what you did not make, **which is the real world of the Kingdom,** is willingness to learn the one you made, **the illusionary world of perception,** is false.

Note # 73: The world of perception exists only in the mind of the perceiver. It has no real impact on truth. If we realize that we are the dreamer, we can choose to reawaken to the truth. The dream will fade away into the nothingness from which it arose. The Christ consciousness remembers the reality of what you are. It is your Big "S" Self that feels love's pull for you to rejoin the Kingdom.

T-13.VII.5. You have been wrong about the world because you have misjudged yourself **and believed yourself limited.** 2 From such a twisted reference point, what could you see? 3 All seeing starts with the perceiver, who judges what is true and what is false. 4 And what **the perceiver** judges false **the perceiver** does not see. 5 You who would judge reality cannot see **reality**, for whenever judgment enters reality has slipped away. 6 The out of mind <*is*> out of sight, because what is denied is there but is not recognized. 7 Christ is still there, although you know **Christ** not. 8 **Christ's** Being does not depend upon your recognition. 9 **Christ** lives within you in the quiet present, and waits for you to leave the past behind and enter into the world **Christ** holds out to you in love.

Note # 74: Christ has never left our mind. We have just refused to hear His Voice for God and the Truth. Christ is eternally in our mind since that is truth's reality. The changeless eternal has no past. The eternal is the "always." In perception, time, which arose to accommodate our belief that the separation was real, does appear to have a past, present and future. The ego wants us to remain tied to our past illusion so that we will continue to misperceive ourselves as limited and separate small "s" selves.

T-13.VII.6. No one in this distracted world but has seen some glimpses of the other world about him. 2 Yet while he still lays value on his own **private world of specialness**, he will deny the vision of the other **real world**, maintaining that he loves what he loves not, and following not the road that love points out. **He, the split-minded claims he loves his private world of specialness over the world of truth.** 3 Love leads so gladly! 4 As you follow **Christ**, you will rejoice that you have found **Christ's** company, and learned of **Christ** the joyful journey home. 5 You wait but for yourself. 6 To give this sad world over and exchange your errors for the peace of God is but <*your*> will. 7 And Christ will always offer you the Will of God, in recognition that you share **the Will of God** with **Christ.**

Note # 75: We will continue to perceive the world that we value. The egoic split-mind values separation, specialness and littleness. The Big "S" Self values the wholeness of Love's One Self. The Christ is the part of the split-mind that is the home of whole or right-mindedness. The Christ is also the home of the Holy Spirit. The Christ resides in the truth that you are the One Self of the Mind of God.

T-13.VII.7. It is God's Will that nothing touch His Son except Himself, and nothing else comes nigh unto him. 2 **Christ, God's Son,** is as safe from pain as God Himself, Who watches over him in everything. 3 The world about **Christ, God's Son,** shines with love because God placed him in God, Himself, where pain is not, and love surrounds him without end or flaw. 4 Disturbance of his peace can never be. 5 In perfect sanity **God's Son** looks on love, for **love** is all about him and within him. 6 **God's Son** must deny the world of pain the instant he perceives the arms of love around him. 7 And from this point of safety **Christ, God's Son,** looks quietly about him and recognizes that the world is one with him.

Note # 76: We are part of the Mind of God. As such, we have never left the Love of the Father and continue to abide in the Mind of God. This is the Christ in us. There is nothing outside the Mind of God since God is everything. Again ACIM describes the oneness that exists between God and His Creation. The Cause and Its Effect are intertwined until They are the inseparable One Self.

T-13.VII.8. The peace of God passeth your understanding only in the past. 2 Yet here **the peace of God** <*is*>, and you can understand **the peace of God** <*now.*> 3 God loves His Son forever, and His Son returns his Father's Love forever. 4 The real world is the way that leads you to remembrance of the one thing that is wholly true and wholly yours, **which is God's Love.** 5 For all else you have lent yourself in time, and **time** will fade. 6 But this one thing, **God's Love,** is always yours, being the gift of God unto His Son. 7 Your one reality, **God's Love,** was given you, and by **God's Love,** God created you as one with **God**

Note # 77: Being changeless, we can never lose God's Love for this is not part of God's Will. Only in time can we pretend to lack God's Love. Time exists only in the illusionary dream state in which the false appears to exist along with the truth. When we forgot knowledge, we denied the peace of God. Time allows us to correct our misperception that arose from our belief in the separation. With our reawakening, time will disappear along with the dream of separation. God's peace will be remembered.

T-13.VII.9. You will first dream of peace, and then awaken to **peace.** 2 Your first exchange of what you made for what you want is the exchange of nightmares for the happy dreams of love. 3 In these **happy dreams of love**, lie your true perceptions, for the Holy Spirit corrects the world of dreams, where all perception is. 4 Knowledge needs no correction. 5 Yet the dreams of love lead unto knowledge. 6 In **the happy dreams of love** you see nothing fearful, and because of this **the happy dreams of love** are the welcome that you offer knowledge. 7 Love waits on welcome, not on time, and the real world is but your welcome of what always was. 8 Therefore the call of joy is in **the happy dreams of love**, and your glad response is your awakening to what you have not lost.

Note # 78: Even the happy dream of love is still an illusion. But within this illusion, we begin to recognize the truth. The happy dream of love is as close as we can come to the return to the knowledge of Level # 1, while still within the world of perception, which is Level # 2. Knowledge and even correct perception is not the same. Knowledge is just being; it requires no thought. Since Level # 1 and # 2 never meet, God will take the final step to return His Son to the state of knowledge. Knowledge is the return to the Kingdom, which is the real world of Level # 1.

T-13.VII.10. Praise, then, the Father for the perfect sanity of His most holy Son. 2 Your Father knoweth that you have need of nothing. 3 In Heaven this is so **that you have need of nothing,** for what could you need in eternity? 4 In your world **of perception, born out of the belief in limitation** you do need things. 5 **Your world of perception** is a world of scarcity in which you find yourself <*because*> you are lacking. 6 Yet can you find **and rediscover** yourself, **your Big "S" Self,** in such a world? **Can you rediscover what you really are in the world of illusion?** 7 Without the Holy Spirit the answer would be no. 8 Yet because of **the Holy Spirit** the answer is a joyous <*yes!*> 9 As Mediator, **the Holy Spirit, is** between the two worlds, **the Holy Spirit** knows what you have need of and what will not hurt you. 10 Ownership is a dangerous concept if **ownership of your true needs were** left to you. 11 The ego wants to have things for salvation, for possession is **the ego's** law. 12 Possession for **possession's** own sake is the ego's fundamental creed, a basic cornerstone in the churches **the ego** builds to itself. 13 And at **the ego's** altar **the ego** demands you lay all of the things **the ego** bids you get, leaving you no joy in **all of the things you got**.

Note # 79: The ego's thought system is based on limitation and on you not being a oneness. Form is one of the best "proofs" that the ego has to verify that you are not everything. The ego then tells us that we will be saved when we collect something special from outside ourselves. The ego always places our happiness outside of our control because the ego does not want us to be the source for our own happiness. We learn to place value on the worthless changing world of form and thus, misperceiving our needs. When we request the aid of the Holy Spirit, the Holy Spirit will reinterpret the events that we misperceived into holy experiences. The tool of forgiveness is the major transformational weapon against the ego's thought system. Misperception is converted into correct perception through the Holy Spirit's guidance. The Holy Spirit knows that our only true need is to follow God's Will and thus, be happy.

T-13.VII.11. Everything the ego tells you that you need will hurt you. 2 For although the ego urges you again and again to get, **the ego** leaves you nothing, for what you get **the ego** will demand of you. 3 And even from the very hands that grasped **what the ego said you needed, the item** will be wrenched **from you by the ego** and hurled into the dust. 4 For where the ego sees salvation **the ego** sees separation, and so you lose whatever you have gotten in **the ego's** name. 5 Therefore ask not of yourself what you need, for you do not know **what you need**, and your advice to yourself will hurt you. 6 For what you think you need will merely serve to tighten up your world against the light, and render you unwilling to question the value that this world **of illusion** can really hold for you.

Note # 80: The ego teaches that we are limited forms. Believing that we are limited ego bodies, we perceive that we need something outside ourselves. This helps the ego convince us that we are lacking and are not whole. This strengthens our belief that the separation was real and reinforces the ego's thought system. Needs are things that we value. We believe that without these things, we will either die or remain incomplete. Until we are willing to give all our perception of vulnerability over to the Holy Spirit's correct perception, we will remain bound in the egoic world of lack and limitation. The Holy Spirit will provide everything you truly need in time, for the Holy Spirit will do nothing that would increase your fear. We cannot be unlimited spirit while we cling to a body-form. We only need God's love but God's love is impossible to either lose or earn. God's love is freely given because it is the unconditional Love of God for His One Self.

T-13.VII.12. Only the Holy Spirit knows what you need. 2 For **the Holy Spirit** will give you all things that do not block the way to light. 3 And what else could you need? 4 In time, **the Holy Spirit** gives you all the things that you need **to have in the illusionary world of time**, and will renew **all the things that you need to have in the illusionary world of time** as long as you have need of them. 5 **The Holy Spirit** will take nothing from you as long as you have any need of it. 6 And yet **the Holy Spirit** knows that everything you need is temporary, and will but last until you step aside from all your needs and realize that all of **your needs** have been fulfilled. 7 Therefore **the Holy Spirit** has no investment in the things that **the Holy Spirit** supplies, except to make certain that you will not use them on behalf of lingering in time. 8 **The Holy Spirit** knows that you are not at home there **in the illusionary world of time**, and **the Holy Spirit** wills no delay to wait upon your joyous homecoming.

Note # 81: Because we have lost knowledge, we are trapped in our illusionary world of time and perception, which arises out of the projection of our belief in sin, guilt and fear. Since we believe that we are separate, the concept of time was needed temporarily until we reawaken to the reality of the Oneness. We need the experiences of the dream world of perception so that we can freely choose to accept God's Will as our own will. The Holy Spirit, if asked, will reinterpret our misperception into correct perception. Our misperceptions are born out of fear. Correct perceptions arise from forgiveness, love and the realization of our common oneness with our brother. The Holy Spirit will not do anything that would increase our fear for that would drag us deeper into the unreality of the illusions. The Holy Spirit insures that we gently reawaken to the truth of our Big "S" Self's Oneness with God.

T-13.VII.13. Leave, then, your needs to **the Holy Spirit**. 2 **The Holy Spirit** will supply **your needs** with no emphasis at all upon **your needs**. 3 What comes to you of **the Holy Spirit** comes safely, for **the Holy Spirit** will ensure **that what comes to you of the Holy Spirit** never can become a dark spot, hidden in your mind and kept to hurt you. 4 Under **the Holy Spirit's** guidance you will travel light and journey lightly, for **the Holy Spirit's** sight is ever on the journey's end, which is **the Holy Spirit's** goal. 5 God's Son is not a traveller through outer worlds. 6 However holy his perception may become, no world outside himself holds **the Son of God's** inheritance. 7 Within himself **God's Son** has no needs, for light needs nothing but to shine in peace, and from itself to let the rays extend in quiet to infinity.

Note # 82: Being an extension of God, we need nothing for we, like Our Creator, are everything. We need do nothing, for the truth about what we really are is unalterable.

T-13.VII.14. Whenever you are tempted to undertake a useless journey that would lead away from light, remember what you really want, and say:

2 *The Holy Spirit leads me unto Christ, and where else would I go? 3 What need have I but to awake in* ***Christ***?

Note # 83: Always be willing to ask for the Holy Spirit's guidance since He speaks on behalf of your Big "S" Self.

T-13.VII.15. Then follow **the Holy Spirit** in joy, with faith that **the Holy Spirit** will lead you safely through all dangers to your peace of mind this world **of perception** may set before you. 2 Kneel not before the altars to sacrifice **to the false gods of the ego's thought system, and seek** not what you will surely lose. 3 Content yourself with what you will as surely keep, and be not restless, for you undertake a quiet journey to the peace of God, where **God** would have you be in quietness.

Note # 84: The Holy Spirit's thought system will return you home. Home cannot be found in the world of perception for illusions are nothing in the real world. The Holy Spirit's thought system will reinterpret all your misperceptions and return you to the Christ consciousness thus, healing your split-mind so that you can reawaken to the real world of knowledge. Christ never lost His place in the Mind of God. Anytime we lose our peace of mind, we can rest assured that our current thinking is out of alignment with your Big "S" Self. Use this loss of peace as a warning signal to ask for guidance and then choose again. Only the Holy Spirit knows the fastest return journey to the peace of God.

T-13.VII.16. In me, **Jesus, who along with you share the Christ consciousness that is a part of every brother**, you have already overcome every temptation that would hold you back. 2 We walk together on the way to quietness that is the gift of God. 3 Hold me dear, for what except your brothers can you need? 4 We, **your brothers,** will restore to you the peace of mind that we must find together. 5 The Holy Spirit will teach you to awaken unto us, **your brothers,** and to yourself **the Christ that we share.** 6 This, **the peace of God, which is the Christ,** is the only real need to be fulfilled in time. 7 Salvation from the world lies only here. 8 My peace I give you. 9 Take **the peace of God, which is the Christ,** of me in glad exchange for all the world has offered but to take away. 10 And we will spread **the peace of God** like a veil of light across the world's sad face, in which we hide our brothers from **this sad** world, and the world**'s sad face** from **our brothers' peace of God.**

Note # 85: Because Jesus has already overcome all temptations that could hold us from the peace of God, we all have shared this experience. We all share the same mind; we need only to freely accept the gifts that Jesus offers us. Jesus and the Christ, which is in all of the Sonship, knows the peace of God. It is this peace of God that is offered to all the Sonship. Being united, we all share equally in the accomplishments of any part of the Sonship. We are the Christ. The resurrection has already been achieved long ago. We need merely to remove all our past reference points to sin, guilt and fear and time, itself, will disappear.

T-13.VII.17. We cannot sing redemption's hymn alone. 2 My task is not completed until I have lifted every voice with mine. 3 And yet **redemption's hymn** is not mine, for as **redemption's hymn** is my gift to you, so was **redemption's hymn** the Father's gift to me, given me through His Spirit. 4 The sound of **redemption's hymn** will banish sorrow from the mind of God's most holy Son, where **sorrow** cannot abide. 5 Healing in time is needed, for joy cannot establish **joy's** eternal reign where sorrow dwells. 6 You dwell not here, in an illusionary world of fear, but in eternity. 7 You travel but in dreams, while **you remain** safe at home. 8 Give thanks to every part of you that you have taught how to remember you. 9 Thus does the Son of God give thanks unto his Father for his purity.

<u>Note # 86</u>: Redemption's hymn is God's Call for His Son's remembrance of what God's Son is. This is the remembrance of God and our freely choosing God's Will as our will. Salvation's healing is our only function here in the illusionary dream world of separation. God is and will always be only Love. This world of fear, which we made, is not God's Will. We are asked to set aside all our self-made fears and know ourselves as love, which has no opposites in us. We must freely choose to be no other self than the Big "S" Self God created us to be. The acceptance of this is our salvation or redemption. This is the acceptance of the Atonement for ourselves. By our acceptance of the Atonement, all the Sonship benefits because we are all connected in the Mind of God that is the One Self.

VIII. From Perception to Knowledge

T-13.VIII.1. All healing is release from the past. 2 That is why the Holy Spirit is the only Healer. 3 **The Holy Spirit** teaches that the past does not exist, a fact which belongs to the sphere of knowledge, and which therefore no one in the world can know. 4 It would indeed be impossible to be in the world with this knowledge **that the past does not exist.** 5 For the mind that knows **that the past does not exist** unequivocally knows also it, **the mind that knows that the past does not exist,** dwells in eternity, and utilizes no perception at all. 6 **The mind that knows that the past does not exist,** therefore does not consider where it is, because the concept "where" does not mean anything to **the mind that knows that the past does not exist.** 7 **The mind that knows that the past does not exist,** knows that it is everywhere, just as it has everything, and forever.

<u>Note # 87:</u> The Holy Spirit is the only one that is aware of both the truth and our perceptions that create our dream world of provisional reality. We, the dreamer, are unaware of our true nature when we believe we are part of the dream. Because of this, only the Holy Spirit can correctly interpret the proper use of time, which is the healing of the belief in separation.

T-13.VIII.2. The very real difference between perception and knowledge becomes quite apparent if you consider this: There is nothing partial about knowledge. 2 Every aspect is whole, and therefore no aspect **of knowledge** is separate. 3 You are an aspect of knowledge, being in the Mind of God, Who knows you. 4 All knowledge must be yours, for in you is all knowledge. 5 Perception, at **perception's** loftiest, is never complete. 6 Even the perception of the Holy Spirit, as perfect as perception can be, is without meaning in Heaven. 7 Perception can reach everywhere under **the Holy Spirit's** guidance, for the vision of Christ beholds everything in light. 8 Yet no perception, however holy, will last forever.

Note # 88: Perception cannot last forever because perception requires both the perceiver and the item being perceived. With the return to Knowledge, there is only a Oneness. Therefore there is nothing to perceive.

T-13.VIII.3. Perfect perception, then, has many elements in common with knowledge, making transfer to **knowledge** possible. 2 Yet the last step must be taken by God, because the last step in your redemption, which seems to be in the future, was accomplished by God in your creation. 3 The separation has not interrupted **your creation.** 4 Creation cannot be interrupted. 5 The separation is merely a faulty formulation of reality, with no effect at all. 6 The miracle, without a function in Heaven, is needful here **only in the perceived world of time and space.** 7 Aspects of reality can still be seen, and **aspects of reality** will replace aspects of unreality. 8 Aspects of reality can be seen in everything and everywhere. 9 Yet only God can gather **aspects of reality** together, by crowning them, **all the aspects of reality,** as one with the final gift of eternity.

Note # 89: Our dream that we have become separate from God holds no reality and, not being of the Mind of God, has no impact on truth. We remain a Oneness with our creator, the Father, Himself. This is truth. This is our reality.

T-13.VIII.4. Apart from the Father and the Son, the Holy Spirit has no function. 2 **The Holy Spirit** is not separate from Either, **the Father or the Son,** being in the Mind of Both, and knowing that Mind is One. 3 **The Holy Spirit** is a Thought of God, and God has given **the Holy Spirit** to you because **God** has no Thoughts **God** does not share. 4 **The Holy Spirit's** message speaks of timelessness in time, and that is why Christ's vision looks on everything with love. 5 Yet even Christ's vision is not His reality. 6 The golden aspects of reality that spring to light under **the Holy Spirit's** loving gaze are partial glimpses of the Heaven that lies beyond **time and are partial aspects of the reality of God's Thoughts.**

Note # 90: Again, we speak as if each part of the trinity is separate from each other. This is because we think in terms of duality. In reality, each "part" is holographic in nature and contains the entire whole. In reality there is only the shared Oneness since the Mind of God is all there is. Mind is One.
In time, the Holy Trinity appears to be separate parts of the One Self. In eternity, the illusion of separation and time are no more. Separation and time allowed indivisible parts to be defined with separate purposes and functions. As time's relearning function is completed, it fades away into the one and only function, which is to be Love. When there is but one shared function there is only the indivisible One extending Itself as the Thoughts of God, which are only Love.

T-13.VIII.5. This is the miracle of creation; <that **creation** is one forever.> 2 Every miracle you offer to the Son of God is but the true perception of one aspect of the whole. 3 Though every aspect <is> the whole, you cannot know this until you see that every aspect is the same, perceived in the same light and therefore one. 4 Everyone seen without the past thus brings you nearer to the end of time by bringing healed and healing sight into the darkness, and enabling the world to see. 5 For light must come into the darkened world to make Christ's vision possible even here. 6 Help **the Holy Spirit** to give **the Holy**

Spirit's gift of light**, which makes Christ's vision possible,** to all who think they wander in the darkness, and let **the Holy Spirit** gather them, **who think they wander in the darkness,** into His quiet sight that makes them, **who think they wander in the darkness**, one.

<u>Note # 91:</u> Christ's vision sees only the truth of the equality of all aspects of the oneness. The Vision of Christ is not based on any past perception since this would make the present false. Our erroneous beliefs that we normally bring from the past have been discarded or suspended. The Holy Spirit understands that past misperceptions have no impact on reality and, therefore, do not belong in the present. This understanding brings light or understanding that dissolves past misperception into the light of truth that we remain eternally changeless as God created us.

T-13.VIII.6. They, **all parts of the oneness that is creation,** are all the same; all beautiful and equal in their holiness. 2 And He, **the Christ,** will offer **all parts of the oneness that is creation** unto His Father as **all parts of the oneness that is creation** were offered unto Him, **the Sonship, which is all God created, as God created It.** 3 There is one miracle, **which is creation,** as there is one reality. 4 And every miracle you do contains them all, as every aspect of reality you see blends quietly into the one reality of God. 5 The only miracle that ever was is God's most holy Son, created in the one reality that is his Father. 6 Christ's vision is **God's** gift to you. 7 His Being is His Father's gift to Him, **God's Son**.

<u>Note # 92:</u> The miracle of creation is the process of extension. In extension, God has given Himself, which is everything, to everything, which is the Sonship. The Oneness is maintained and is shared fully. Holiness is wholeness. Cause and Effect are indivisibly intertwined thus, completing each other and are that One Self.

T-13.VIII.7. Be you content with healing, for Christ's gift **of healing** you can bestow, and your Father's gift**, your perfect wholeness,** you cannot lose. 2 Offer Christ's gift **of healing** to everyone and everywhere, for miracles, offered the Son of God through the Holy Spirit, attune you to reality. 3 The Holy Spirit knows your part in the redemption, and who are seeking you and where to find them **who seek you**. 4 Knowledge is far beyond your individual concern. 5 You who are part of it, **this perfect wholeness,** and all of it need only realize that it, **your perfect wholeness,** is of the Father, not of you. 6 Your role in the redemption leads you to it, **your perfect wholeness,** by re-establishing its oneness in your mind.

<u>Note # 93:</u> The healing power of the miracle is in its ability to correct our misperception of how we view our world of provisional reality. You see yourself and your brother as connected to the whole. This reconnects you to the holiness of the Sonship. The miracle is a change in the mind of the miracle worker. It does not take place in the mind of your brother since it sees nothing wrong with your brother's mind. The role of miracle workers is to accept the Atonement for themselves. The oneness of our brother will be realized when we see our Oneness with our Creator.

Knowledge is re-established by acceptance of your perfect wholeness in your mind. Knowledge and perfect wholeness are one and the same. You cannot have one without the other. Knowledge is cause and perfect wholeness is its effect. The Atonement process is the means by which the Sonship returns to knowledge.

T-13.VIII.8. When you have seen your brothers as yourself you will be released to knowledge, having learned to free yourself through Him, **the Christ, Who is the home of the Holy Spirit,** Who knows of freedom. 2 Unite with me under the holy banner of **the Holy Spirit's** teaching, and as we grow in strength the power of God's Son will move in us, and we will leave no one untouched and no one left alone. 3 And suddenly time will be over, and we will all unite in the eternity of God the Father. 4 The holy light you saw outside yourself, in every miracle you offered to your brothers, will be returned to you. 5 And knowing that the light is in you, your creations will be there with you, as you are in your Father.

Note # 94: To be like our Father, we need to create like our Father. Our function, with the return of knowledge, is to fulfill our role as co-creators with our Father. Thus, extension continues through the Sonship. We are the light and light extends itself. Knowledge is the returning to the Oneness. With the return to knowledge all thoughts of separation disappear.

T-13.VIII.9. As miracles in this world join you to your brothers, so do your creations establish your fatherhood in Heaven. 2 You are the witness to the Fatherhood of God, and **God, the Father,** has given you the power to create the witnesses to **your fatherhood,** which is as His. 3 Deny a brother here **in your world of provisional reality,** and you deny the witnesses to your fatherhood in Heaven. 4 The miracle that God created is perfect, as are the miracles that you established in **God's** Name. 5 They, **your brothers and your creations,** need no healing, nor do you **need healing** when you accept **your creations as part of the Oneness.**

Note # 95: In the world of perception we create our own reality. By seeing the holiness or the wholeness in all that we perceive, we accept the oneness of God. By extending oneness to our brother, we mirror what God does when God creates. Our miracles are the return to right-mindedness. These are our creations, which are saved by the Holy Spirit for us when we return to the whole-mindedness of knowledge. Your shared oneness with your brother is your creation. See your brother as perfect, whole and complete and you extend what you truly are.

T-13.VIII.10. Yet in this world **of your own perception** your perfection is unwitnessed. 2 God knows **your perfection,** but you do not **know your perfection,** and so you do not share **with God's** witness, **which is the Sonship,** to **your perfection.** 3 Nor do you witness unto **God and God's Son, the Sonship,** for reality is witnessed to as one. 4 God waits your witness to His Son and to Himself. 5 The miracles you do on earth are lifted up to Heaven and to **God.** 6 They **(the miracles you do on earth)** witness to what you do not know **(your wholeness),** and as they, **(the miracles you do on earth)** reach the gates of Heaven, God will open **the gates of Heaven.** 7 For never would **God** leave His Own beloved Son outside **the gates of Heaven,** and beyond Himself.

Note # 96: Until we reclaim our divine birthright, we cannot see ourselves as perfect, whole and complete. By rejecting the thought system of the ego, we can choose again. When we allow the Holy Spirit to reinterpret our experiences, this also reactivates the return to the Vision of Christ. With the blinders to our past misperceptions removed, we can see our brother's actions as a cry for love and then extend the healing power of forgiveness to our brother. By doing this, we extend this healing to ourselves, for by giving, do we receive. When we extend forgiveness and love to our brother, we have created a witness to our own perfection as the Christ, which is our shared Oneness with our Father. Our miracles are our creations and our witnesses to the extension of our Father, which is Love.

IX. The Cloud of Guilt

T-13.IX.1. Guilt remains the only thing that hides the Father, for guilt is the attack upon His Son. 2 The guilty always condemn, and having done so **the guilty** will still condemn. **The guilty** linking the future to the past as **this** is the ego's law, **which the guilty follow**. 3 Fidelity to this law **of linking the future to the past** lets no light in, for **this law of the ego** demands fidelity to darkness and forbids awakening. 4 The ego's laws are strict, and breaches are severely punished. 5 Therefore give no obedience to **the ego's** laws, for **the ego's laws** are laws of punishment. 6 And those who follow **the ego's laws** believe that they are guilty, and so **those who follow the ego's laws** must condemn. 7 Between the future and the past the laws of God must intervene, if you would free yourself **from the ego's laws**. 8 Atonement stands between **the ego's laws and God's laws**, like a lamp shining so brightly that the chain of darkness in which you bound yourself will disappear.

Note # 97: Since the ego's laws emphasize the use of the past in which we perceived ourselves as guilty, the guilt ridden past will continue to control our future. As long as we carry our past misperceptions to our present experiences, we will continue to make the same errors. We will remain in victim consciousness. Only by seeking the guidance of the Holy Spirit, which knows the truth of God's Laws, can we break the cycle of believing we are powerless victims.

T-13.IX.2. Release from guilt is the ego's whole undoing. 2 <Make no one fearful,> for his guilt is **your guilt**, and by obeying the ego's harsh commandments you bring **the ego's** condemnation on yourself, and you will not escape the punishment **the ego** offers those who obey **the ego**. 3 The ego rewards fidelity to **the ego's laws** with pain, for faith in **the ego** <is> pain. 4 And faith can be rewarded only in terms of the belief in which the faith was placed. 5 Faith makes the power of belief, and where **faith** is invested determines **faith's** reward. 6 For faith is always given what is treasured, and what is treasured is returned to you.

Note # 98: What we give is what we receive. This is the Law of God, which remains true even in our dream world of perception. Projection maintains the guilt within us even though projection is our attempt to transfer our guilt to something outside ourselves. Projection helps maintain our victim consciousness.

T-13.IX.3. The world can give you only what you gave **your world of perception**, for being nothing but your own projection, **your world of perception** has no meaning apart from what you found in **your world of perception** and placed your faith in. 2 Be faithful unto darkness and you will not see **with the Vision of Christ**, because your faith will be rewarded as you gave it **to the ego's laws**. 3 You <will> accept your treasure, and if you place your faith in the past, the future will be like **the past**. 4 Whatever you hold dear you think is yours. 5 The power of your valuing will make **whatever you hold dear** so.

Note # 99: Because we are the creator of the dream, whatever we wish to project will appear real to the dreamer. If we value our little "s" self, we will follow the laws of the ego. For the laws of the ego were made to confirm that we are limited ego-bodies. Believing we are limited, it is impossible for us to believe the truth about ourselves. The dreamer has mistaken the dream for reality.

T-13.IX.4. Atonement brings a re-evaluation of everything you cherish, for **Atonement** is the means by which the Holy Spirit can separate the false and the true, which you have accepted into your mind without distinction. 2 Therefore you cannot value one without the other, and guilt has become as true for you as innocence. 3 You do not believe the Son of God is guiltless because you see the past, and see him not **as he truly is, which is guiltless**. 4 When you condemn a brother you are saying, "I who was guilty choose to remain so." 5 You have denied **a brother's** freedom, and by so doing you have denied the witness unto **your freedom**. 6 You could as easily have freed **your brother** from the past, and lifted from **your brother's** mind the cloud of guilt that binds him to **guilt**. 7 And in **your brother's** freedom would have been your own **freedom**.

Note # 100: In the Atonement process, we realize that what we perceive to have happened was only a dream. Therefore, there is nothing that was real for which penance is demanded. We need only to reawaken to the reality of the truth. This is why ACIM defines forgiveness as the process in which we forgive our brother for the wrongs that we have erroneously projected upon our brother. We realize that we were the source to our experience and that our brother was only an actor in a dream play in which we wrote, directed and starred. We mistook this dream play to be our essence's actual reality. With the Atonement, we recognize the dream for what it was, and the need for fear, guilt and punishment disappear along with the dream. The problem of the separation was not the dream, but rather our association with the dream as something that is real. It was our association of our true nature with the dream that made the dream appear real to us.
We forgot it was a game; we took it seriously and replaced laughter with fear.

T-13.IX.5. Lay not your guilt upon **your brother**, for his guilt lies in **your brother's** secret thought that he has done this unto you. 2 Would you, then, teach **your brother** he is right in his delusion **of wronging you**? 3 The idea that the guiltless Son of God can attack himself and make himself guilty is insane. 4 In any form, in anyone, <*believe this not.*> **for the guiltless Son of God cannot be made guilty by self attack** 5 For sin and condemnation are the same, and the belief in **either sin or condemnation** is faith in the other **one**, calling for punishment instead of love. 6 Nothing can justify insanity, and to call for punishment upon yourself must be insane.

Note # 101: Again, God does not condemn us for some make believe dream. Even in our earthly world, we do not punish someone for something only he imaged has happened. We try to tell them the truth that nothing happened. If they insist that their dream was real, we realize that they are sick or insane and must be suffering from delusional thinking and need our help. We do not agree that they are correct in their dream and punish them for it. Dreams have no effect on reality except in the mind of the dreamer.

T-13.IX.6. See no one, then, as guilty, and you will affirm the truth of guiltlessness unto yourself. 2 In every condemnation that you offer the Son of God lies the conviction of your own guilt. 3 If you would have the Holy Spirit make you free of **our belief that you are guilty**, accept **the Holy Spirit's** offer of Atonement for all your brothers. 4 For so you learn that **the Atonement and your guiltlessness** is true for you. 5 Remember always that it is impossible to condemn the Son of God in part. 6 Those whom you see as guilty become the witnesses to guilt in you, and you will see **guilt** there, for **guilt** <*is*> there until **guilt** is undone. 7 Guilt is always in your mind, which has condemned itself. 8 Project **guilt** not, for while you do **project guilt**, **guilt** cannot be undone. 9 With everyone whom you release from guilt great is the joy in Heaven, where the witnesses to your fatherhood rejoice.

Note # 102: The Sonship is united in the Mind of God. All shattered parts of the Sonship remain as a Oneness even though in our dream we appear to have separate existences. The Sonship, which is all that God created as He created It, remains one with the Father.

T-13.IX.7. Guilt makes you blind, for while you see one spot of guilt within you, you will not see the light. 2 And by projecting **guilt** the world seems dark, and shrouded in your guilt. 3 You throw a dark veil over **the world**, and cannot see **the world** because you cannot look within. 4 You are afraid of what you would see there **within**, but **the guilt** is not there. 5 <*The thing you fear, **the guilt**, is gone.*> 6 If you would look within you would see only the Atonement, shining in quiet and in peace upon the altar to your Father.

Note # 103: The acceptance of the Atonement for yourself removes the dream of guilt you had placed upon yourself. The Atonement corrects this error in your thinking. A mistake requires only correction, not punishment.

T-13.IX.8. Do not be afraid to look within. 2 The ego tells you all is black with guilt within you, and bids you not to look **within**. 3 Instead, **the ego** bids you look upon your brothers, and see the guilt in **your brothers**. 4 Yet this **seeing of guilt in your brothers** you cannot do without remaining blind. 5 For those who see their brothers in the dark, and guilty in the dark in which they shroud **their brothers**, are too afraid to look upon the light within. 6 Within you is not what you believe is there, and what you put your faith in. **You have placed your faith in guilt and, therefore, believe that guilt is within you.** 7 Within you is the holy sign of perfect faith your Father has in you, **which is your guiltlessness**. 8 **God** does not value you as you do. 9 **God** knows Himself, and knows the truth in you. 10 **God** knows there is no difference, for **God** knows not of differences. 11 Can you see guilt where God knows there is perfect innocence? 12 You can deny **God's** knowledge, but you cannot change **God's knowledge**. 13 Look, then, upon the light **God** placed within you, and learn that what you feared was there, **your self-imposed guilt**, has been replaced with love.

Note # 104: Nothing can change in the Mind of God. God created us as perfect replicas of Himself. We share the same Mind. God's Will cannot be opposed or changed. This is where our salvation lays. Being an extension of God, Himself, we can only be as our Father, a perfect Oneness. Knowledge, which is truth, cannot be changed because someone has chosen to deny the truth. The truth remains the same regardless of how we choose to perceive it. We will always remain perfect, whole and complete because that is God's Will. Our dream world is based on sin, guilt and fear. It has no reality in the Mind of God. The Atonement process reawakens us to this fact. Our split-mind is returned to right-mindedness. The dream that we could be a little "s" self is gone.

X. Release from Guilt

T-13.X.1. You are accustomed to the notion that the mind can see the source of pain where **the source of pain** is not. 2 The doubtful service of such displacement **of the location of the real source of the pain** is to hide the real source of guilt, and keep from your awareness the full perception that **to place the source of pain where it is not** is insane. 3 Displacement always is maintained by the illusion that the source of guilt, from which attention is diverted, must be true; and must be fearful, or you would not have displaced the guilt onto what you believed to be less fearful. 4 You are therefore willing to look upon all kinds of "sources," provided **these imagined sources** are not the deeper source to which they, **these imagined sources,** bear no real relationship at all **to the true source of guilt.**.

NOTE # 105: The purpose of projection is to attempt to get rid of the source of the "guilt problem." The problem always comes from your own errors in perception and your desire to transfer the guilt generated by the problem to something outside yourself. This projection of the true source of your guilt upon something other than you, allows you to disassociate yourself as the source of the guilt. The source of the guilt can be traced back to the mind's erroneous concept of what you are. Thinking that the problem is outside you, you are now powerless to change your experience. You remain in victim consciousness and thus, maintain your belief that you are a separate little "s" self.

T-13.X.2. Insane ideas have no real relationships, for that is why **insane ideas** are insane. 2 No real relationship can rest on guilt, or even hold one spot of **guilt** to mar **a real relationship's** purity. 3 For all relationships that guilt has touched are used but to avoid the person <*and*> the guilt. 4 What strange relationships you have made for this strange purpose **of hiding the guilt from you, its true source!** 5 And you forgot that real relationships are holy, and cannot be used by you at all. 6 **Real relationships** are used only by the Holy Spirit, and it is **the use by the Holy Spirit** that makes **these real relationships** pure. 7 If you displace your guilt upon **these relationships**, the Holy Spirit cannot use **these relationships and make them pure.** 8 For, by pre-empting **these relationships** for your own ends, **which is your projection of guilt,** what you should have given **the Holy Spirit**, He, **the Holy Spirit,** cannot use **these guilt-ridden relationships** for your release. 9 No one who would unite in any way with anyone for his individual salvation will find **salvation** in that strange relationship. 10 **A pre-empted guilty relationship** is not shared, and so **a pre-empted guilty relationship** is not real.

<u>NOTE # 106:</u> Creation is extension that is shared. Projection is exclusion and cannot be shared. Relationships in our world of provisional reality must be shared with the Holy Spirit so they can be properly reinterpreted into something that can be shared, thus promoting the return to Oneness. If they are reinterpreted with the eyes of Christ, they will become a tool for forgiveness and love. This makes the relationship real because it comes from love that arises from the shared Mind of God.

T-13.X.3. In any union with a brother in which you seek to lay your guilt upon **a brother**, or share **guilt** with **a brother** or perceive **a brother's** own **guilt**, <*you*> will feel guilty. 2 Nor will you find satisfaction and peace with **a brother**, because your union with **a brother** is not real. 3 You will see guilt in that relationship **with your brother** because you put **guilt** there. 4 It is inevitable that those who suffer guilt will attempt to displace **guilt**, because they **who suffer guilt** do believe **that it is possible to project or to place their own guilt upon another thereby removing the guilt from themselves.** 5 Yet though **the people who attempt to project their own guilt upon another continue to** suffer, they will not look within and let **their own guilt** go. 6 **The person, who attempts to displace their own guilt,** cannot know they love, and cannot understand what loving is. 7 **This person's** main concern is to perceive the source of guilt outside themselves, beyond their own control.

<u>NOTE # 107:</u> This explains the use of projection and guilt in making our illusionary world of perception.

T-13.X.4. When you maintain that you are guilty but the source of your guilt lies in the past, you are not looking inward. 2 The past is not <*in*> you. 3 Your weird associations to **the past** have no meaning in the present. 4 Yet you let **your weird associations to the past** stand between you and your brothers, with whom you find no real relationships at all. 5 Can you expect to use your brothers as a means to "solve" the past, and still to see **your problems** as they really are? 6 Salvation is not found by those who use their brothers to resolve **past** problems that are not there. 7 You wanted not salvation in the past. 8 Would you impose your idle wishes on the present, and hope to find salvation now?

<u>NOTE # 108:</u> The Holy Spirit's goal is for time is to be viewed based on the present. The ego's focus with time is always with the past. This focus by the ego on past misperception helps insure the future will not change for the dreamer. If you continue to view the present from the same reference point that you judged the past with, you will obtain the same misperception that you are a limited ego-body trapped in a world of victim consciousness. In victim consciousness you can claim that you are not guilty because something outside yourself has control over you.

Your past misperceptions and the <now> are mutually exclusive.

T-13.X.5. Determine, then, to be not as you were **in the past**. 2 Use no relationship to hold you to the past, but with each one each day be born again. 3 A minute, even less, will be enough to free you from the past, and give your mind in peace over to the Atonement. 4 When everyone is welcome to you as you would have yourself be welcome to your Father, you will see no guilt in you. 5 For you will have accepted the Atonement, which shone within you all the while you dreamed of guilt. And **while you dreamed of guilt, you** would not look within and see **that the source of your guilt was imagined and not real.**

<u>NOTE# 109:</u> The Atonement releases us from the past because the Atonement is the realization that any thought of separation was not real. Thoughts of separation are not shared in the Mind of God and, therefore, are not God's Will. In the Atonement, we realize freely that our will and God's Will are shared. A dream cannot change the truth that is found in the eternal.

T-13.X.6. As long as you believe that guilt is justified in any way, in anyone, whatever **anyone** may do, you will not look within, where you would always find Atonement. 2 The end of guilt will never come as long as you believe there is a reason for **guilt**. 3 For you must learn that guilt is always totally insane, and has no reason. 4 The Holy Spirit seeks not to dispel reality. 5 If guilt were real, Atonement would not be **real**. 6 The purpose of Atonement is to dispel illusions, not to establish **illusions** as real and then forgive **the illusion**.

<u>NOTE #110:</u> If the Holy Spirit were to confirm the reality of our illusion, this would do multiple things all of which would confirm that the separation was real. It would increase our fear because the Holy Spirit would be saying that we are something other than perfect, whole and complete. This is why the Holy Spirit is gentle in helping us reawaken to our true reality. The Holy Spirit needs us to freely ask for guidance from the ego's thought system so that we rediscover our Christ center. If the Holy Spirit were to just "correct" our "problems" for us, It would be confirming that we lack within us the power to reawaken to the truth. If this were the case, again, we would be less than our Father, thus, making our Father also imperfect and not whole.

T-13.X.7. The Holy Spirit does not keep illusions in your mind to frighten you, and show **these illusions** to you fearfully to demonstrate what **the Holy Spirit** has saved you from. 2 What **the Holy Spirit** has saved you from is gone. 3 **The Holy Spirit gives** no reality to guilt, and see no reason for **guilt**. 4 The Holy Spirit does what God would have **the Holy Spirit** do, and has always done so. 5 **The Holy Spirit** has seen separation, but knows of union. 6 **The Holy Spirit** teaches healing, but **the Holy Spirit** also knows of creation. 7 **The Holy Spirit** would have you see and teach as **the Holy Spirit** does, and through **the Holy Spirit**. 8 Yet what **the Holy Spirit** knows you do not know, though it, **what the Holy Spirit knows,** is **your reality**.

<u>NOTE # 111:</u> The Holy Spirit's home is the Christ within our mind. The Christ and the Holy Spirit share the same thought system since there is a shared Oneness. This Oneness is also shared with the Father. Since we are use to thinking in terms of duality, ACIM utilizes the Holy Trinity as separate parts for discussion purposes only. The Oneness of this Trinity has never been lost. In our dream of separation, we appear to have lost the reality of what we are. This has not been lost, but merely forgotten by the dreamer who has associated himself with the dream itself. The knowledge of what we are is preserved in the Christ consciousness of our shared Mind. We can appear to imagine ourselves to be lost in time, but we remain holy, perfect and One in eternity.

T-13.X.8. <*Now*> it is given you to heal and teach, to make what will be <*now.*> 2 As yet it is not now **for you remain trapped in our past misperceptions**. 3 The Son of God believes that he is lost in guilt, alone in a dark world where pain is pressing everywhere upon him from without. 4 When **the split-minded** has looked within and seen the radiance there, **the split-minded** will remember how much his Father loves him. 5 And it will seem incredible that **the split-minded** ever thought his Father loved him not, and looked upon him, **God's Son**, as condemned. 6 The moment that you realize guilt is insane, wholly unjustified and wholly without reason, you will not fear to look upon the Atonement and accept **the Atonement** wholly.

NOTE # 112: We fear the Atonement because the ego's thought system has convinced us that we are indeed sinners and, therefore, deserve punishment and death. Because of this, the split-mind is terrified that the acceptance of the Atonement would result in its destruction by God. This belief of destruction is a part of the ego's misperception of what God is. To the ego, God is something that is the opposite of love. The god of the ego is a petty, unforgiving, revengeful god that requires sacrifice to be appeased. This is why the Holy Spirit must help us undo all that the ego has taught us so we can reawaken to our divine inheritance.

T-13.X.9. You who have been unmerciful to yourself do not remember your Father's Love. 2 And looking without mercy upon your brothers, you do not remember how much you love **God, your Father**. 3 Yet **this mutual love** is forever true. 4 In shining peace within you is the perfect purity in which you were created. 5 Fear not to look upon the lovely truth in you. 6 Look through the cloud of guilt that dims your vision, and look past darkness to the holy place where you will see the light. 7 The altar to your Father is as pure as **your Father,** Who raised **the altar** to Himself. 8 Nothing can keep from you what Christ would have you see. 9 **Christ's** Will is like His Father's, and **Christ** offers mercy to every child of God, as **Christ's Father** would have you do.

NOTE # 113: The altar to the Father is the truth of what you are. It is the Christ that we have hidden deep within our apparent split-mind. The Christ is the shared extension of what God is.

T-13.X.10. Release **your belief in your brother's guilt so that** you would be released **from your own self-imposed guilt.** 2 There is no other way to look within and see the light of love, shining as steadily and as surely as God Himself has always loved His Son. 3 <*And as His Son loves God, the Father.*> 4 There is no fear in love, for love is guiltless. 5 You who have always loved your Father can have no fear, for any reason, to look within and see your holiness. 6 You cannot be as you believed you were. 7 Your guilt is without reason because **your guilt** is not in the Mind of God, where you are. 8 And this <*is*> reason, which the Holy Spirit would restore to you. 9 **The Holy Spirit** would remove only illusions. 10 All else **the Holy Spirit** would have you see. 11 And in Christ's vision **the Holy Spirit** would show you the perfect purity that is forever within God's Son.

NOTE # 114: The Holy Spirit will restore your mind from insanity to reason and sanity by undoing your belief that you could ever be something other than God's Son, perfect, whole and complete. In order to do this, you must relearn your oneness with your brother. When you forgive your brother of the wrong that you thought he did to you, you also free yourself. This forgiveness of your brother and the automatic forgiveness of yourself which accompanies it, confirms the fact that the Law of God states that "by giving, we receive."

T-13.X.11. You cannot enter into real relationships with any of God's Sons unless you love all **parts of the Sonship** and **love them** equally. 2 Love is not special. 3 If you single out part of the Sonship for your love, you are imposing guilt on all your relationships and making **all your relationships** unreal. 4 You can love only as God loves. 5 Seek not to love unlike **God**, for there is no love apart from **God's Love**. 6 Until you recognize that this is true **that you can love only as God loves and there is no love apart from God's Love,** you will have no idea what love is like. 7 No one who condemns a brother can see himself as guiltless and in the peace of God. 8 If he is guiltless and in peace and sees it not, he is delusional, and has not looked upon himself **as he truly is.** 9 To him I say:

10 *Behold the Son of God, and look upon his purity and be still. 11 In quiet look upon* **the Son of God's** *holiness, and offer thanks unto his Father that no guilt has ever touched him.*

NOTE # 115: The Sonship is also a Oneness. As long as we perceive guilt anywhere, we are denying our divine inheritance. We can deny the truth about ourselves but we cannot change the Will of God. God created or extended Himself to His Son and His Son must share the Oneness of the Father. To be anything less than whole would be to make the Father incomplete. This is not possible for the eternal is changeless.

T-13.X.12. No illusion that you have ever held against **one of God's Sons** has touched his innocence in any way. 2 **The Son of God's** shining purity, wholly untouched by guilt and wholly loving, is bright within you. 3 Let us look upon **God's Son,** together and love him. 4 For in love of **God's Son who is your brother** is your guiltlessness. 5 But look upon yourself, and gladness and appreciation for what you see will banish guilt forever. 6 I thank You, Father, for the purity of Your most holy Son, whom You have created guiltless forever.

NOTE # 116: All of God's creations share equally in their total Oneness. There is no specialness among God's Children for they all share equally in God's love. God knows no separation, since God is all there is. There is only the extension of God's Love, which is the Sonship.

T-13.X.13. Like you, my faith and my belief are centered on what I treasure. 2 The difference is that I love <*only*> what God loves with me, and because of this I treasure you beyond the value that you set on yourself, even unto the worth that God has placed upon you. 3 I love all that **God** created, and all my faith and my belief I offer unto **all that God created**. 4 My faith in you is as strong as all the love I give my Father. 5 My trust in you is without limit, and without the fear that you will hear me not. 6 I thank the Father for your loveliness, and for the many gifts that you will let me offer to the Kingdom in honor of its wholeness that is of God.

NOTE # 117: Jesus is confirming our shared Christ consciousness with the Sonship. Jesus only has pure Love for the Father. Jesus loves us like the Father because Jesus knows we are in the Father. This is the confirmation by Jesus that we are worthy of love because we are God's Love extended. I and the Father are One.

T-13.X.14. Praise be to you who make the Father One with His Own Son. 2 Alone we are all lowly, but together we shine with brightness so intense that none of us alone can even think of **our brightness**. 3 Before the glorious radiance of the Kingdom guilt melts away, and **guilt** transformed into kindness will never more be what **guilt** was. 4 Every reaction you experience will be so purified that **every reaction you experience** is fitting as a hymn of praise unto your Father. 5 See only praise of **God** in what **God** has created, for **God** will never cease **God's** praise of you. 6 United in this praise we stand before the gates of Heaven where we will surely enter in our sinlessness. 7 God loves you. 8 Could I, then, lack faith in you and love **God** perfectly?

NOTE # 118: When we believe that we are special, we believe ourselves to be a little "s" self. When we see with the Vision of Christ, we realize that we are unlimited spirit and not a limited ego-body. When we reclaim the big "S" Self, we reaffirm our Oneness in the Mind of God. Jesus knows us as His equal. We are part of the wholeness that is the Sonship. Jesus knows that God's Will is all-powerful and, therefore, our return from the dream is both certain and our true reality.

XI. The Peace of Heaven

T-13.XI.1. Forgetfulness and sleep and even death become the ego's best advice for dealing with the perceived and harsh intrusion of guilt on peace. 2 Yet no one sees himself in conflict and ravaged by a cruel war unless he believes that both opponents in the war are real. **Peace and guilt, truth and illusion, are the opponents in this "war" upon your Big "S" Self.** 3 Believing **that both opponents in the war are real,** he must escape, for such a war would surely end his peace of mind, and so destroy him. 4 Yet if he could but realize the war is between real and unreal powers, he could look upon himself and see his freedom. 5 No one finds himself ravaged and torn in endless battles if he himself perceives **these battles to be between real and unreal powers and thus,** as wholly without meaning.

<u>NOTE #119:</u> The ego would like us to believe that we have real enemies that are "out to get us." Since our dream world of provisional reality is not real in the Mind of God, the dream itself has no power to change reality. The ego's goal for this world of perception is to get the dreamer to believe that the dream is real. Without this belief, the dream would hold no real terror to the dreamer. It would be like going to a scary movie. While watching a movie, we tend to get caught up in the movie but we always know that we are merely witnessing projected light upon a screen. The goal of the ego is that we never recover our decision-making ability, which would allow us to decide to leave the theater if we don't like the movie. The ego does not want us to rediscover that we can change the reel in the projector of our mind. This rediscovery would allow us to escape from victim consciousness.

T-13.XI.2. God would not have His Son embattled, and so His Son's imagined "enemy" is totally unreal. 2 You are but trying to escape a bitter war, **in which you played the part of a limited ego-body of the small "s" self,** from which you <have> already escaped. 3 The war is gone. **You have heard the voice for God. The Holy Spirit is calling you home.** 4 For you have heard the hymn of freedom rising unto Heaven. 5 Gladness and joy belong to God for your release, because you **did not make your release from this imagined war. God did.** 6 Yet as you made not freedom, so you made not a war that could endanger freedom. 7 Nothing destructive ever was or will be. 8 The war, the guilt, the past are gone as one into the unreality from which they, **the imagined war, the guilt and the past** came.

<u>NOTE #120:</u> Due to our belief in the separation, both guilt and the idea that we could do something other than the Will of God appeared real to the dreamer. Both of these concepts are not true. God never shared our belief and, therefore, our dream had no reality in the Mind of God. God always knew His Son to be perfect, whole and complete. God gave and placed within our mind, the Holy Spirit as our protector to safe guard God's Son during the Sonship's "voyage of rediscovery." The role of the Holy Spirit is to gently reawaken the sleeping child without increasing fear in the child. The Holy Spirit will do nothing that would make the nightmare seem real to the child. Although the child sleeps, we still have free will. It is up to the child to control his own self-generated fear and ask for the guidance of the Holy Spirit's thought system. We wanted to experience the dream of separation. The Holy Spirit will not awaken us without our permission. Because our will is God's Will, this request for our awaking must be honored and is inevitable. In the real world, which is the Mind of God, we always are perfect, whole

and complete.

T-13.XI.3. When we are all united in Heaven, you will value nothing that you value here **in the world of individual perception**. 2 For nothing that you value here **in the world of individual perception,** do you value wholly, and so you do not value **these things** at all. 3 Value is where God placed **value**, and the value of what God esteems cannot be judged, for **the value of what God esteems** has been established **by God**. 4 **What God esteems** is wholly of value. 5 **What God esteems** can merely be appreciated or not. 6 To value w**hat God esteems** partially is not to know its value. 7 In Heaven is everything God values, and nothing else. 8 Heaven is perfectly unambiguous. 9 Everything is clear and bright, and calls forth one response, **which is the love, joy and peace of the Mind of God**. 10 There is no darkness and there is no contrast. 11 There is no variation. 12 There is no interruption. 13 There is a sense of peace so deep that no dream in this world **of individual perception** has ever brought even a dim imagining of what **the peace of Heaven** is.

<u>NOTE # 121:</u> What God esteems is His Son. The Son is perfect, whole and complete, as is the Son's Father. God's Will is that His Son be happy and know the peace and joy that is the Father.

T-13.XI.4. Nothing in this world can give this peace, for nothing in this world is wholly shared. 2 Perfect perception can merely show you what is capable of being wholly shared. 3 **Perfect perception** can also show you the results of sharing, while you still remember the results of not sharing. 4 The Holy Spirit points quietly to the contrast, knowing that you will finally let **the Holy Spirit** judge the difference for you, allowing **the Holy Spirit** to demonstrate which must be true. 5 **The Holy Spirit** has perfect faith in your final judgment, because **the Holy Spirit** knows that **the Holy Spirit** will make **your final judgment** for you. 6 To doubt this would be to doubt that **the Holy Spirit's** mission will be fulfilled. 7 How is this possible, when **the Holy Spirit's** mission **of returning you to truth** is **given from** God?

<u>NOTE # 122:</u> Form cannot be shared because that would cause diminishment to the "owner" of the item. More importantly, it would be giving reality to the idea that there is something outside of you and, therefore, you would not be a Oneness. This cannot be the truth of what you are.
The home of the Holy Spirit is the Christ in you. Although for simplicities purposes, ACIM tries to explain to us this concept in a dualistic matter, in reality, there is just a Oneness even in the Holy Trinity. For ACIM purposes, the Holy Spirit is aware of both our dream and the truth. Therefore, only the Holy Spirit can judge because only the Holy Spirit knows "all the facts." The Holy Spirit's judgment comes from knowledge and correct perception. Because we believe that we are limited due to our belief in the separation, we have lost knowledge. The only judgment that we should make is that we are incapable of judging anything. Therefore, ask for the Holy Spirit's guidance. The Holy Spirit will allow the Vision of Christ to reawaken our split-mind. Only the Holy Spirit can reinterpret our perceived experience correctly based on God's Plan for the return of the Sonship to knowledge.

T-13.XI.5. You whose mind is darkened by doubt and guilt, remember this: God gave the Holy Spirit to you, and gave **the Holy Spirit** the mission to remove all doubt and every trace of guilt that **God's** dear Son has laid upon himself. 2 It is impossible that this mission **to remove all doubt and guilt could** fail. 3 Nothing can prevent what God would have accomplished from accomplishment. 4 Whatever your reactions to the Holy Spirit's Voice may be, whatever voice, **either the ego's or the Holy Spirit's, that** you choose to listen to, whatever strange thoughts may occur to you, God's Will <is> done. **Our egoic thoughts that you could do something other than God's Will has no power to change God's Will.**5 You will find the peace in which **God** has established you, because **God** does not change His Mind. 6 **God's Mind** is invariable as the peace in which you dwell, and of which the Holy Spirit reminds you **that you dwell in the Peace of God.**

NOTE # 123: God's Will is changeless for it is eternal and real. We can deny the truth, but we cannot change the truth. God's Will is truth.

T-13.XI.6. You will not remember change and shift in Heaven. 2 You have need of contrast only here **in your world of perception, which has become your provisional reality** 3 Contrast and differences are necessary teaching aids, for by **contrast and differences** you learn what to avoid and what to seek. 4 When you have learned **what to avoid and what to seek**, you will find the answer that makes the need for any differences disappear. 5 Truth comes of **truth's** own will unto **truth's** own. 6 When you have learned that you belong to truth, **truth** will flow lightly over you without a difference of any kind. 7 For you will need no contrast to help you realize that **truth** is what you want, and only **truth**. 8 Fear not the Holy Spirit will fail in what your Father has given **the Holy Spirit** to do, **which is to return you to the truth of what you are**. 9 The Will of God can fail in nothing.

NOTE # 124: God is truth. Being truth, which is changeless, the Holy Spirit's mission is to return the Sonship to the truth about itself. Being an extension of our Father, we must also be truth. We will and must return to the knowledge that we are a shared Oneness in the Mind of God.

In the world of perception, we have the idea that there is something other than a Oneness. This results in our perceiving differences. The ego utilizes these differences as witnesses that the separation must be true. The Holy Spirit utilizes these perceived differences to return you to the truth that you are a shared Oneness by teaching forgiveness. Thus, these perceived differences and contrasts are utilized by the Holy Spirit as learning devices to help you reevaluate which thought system you choose to follow. In the world of perception, all events are neutral. It is only how we choose to perceive them that colors the event as something good or bad. These contrasting viewpoints help us determine which voice we are to follow. The ego's thought system is based on the false belief in limitation. You are not the limited-ego body that you have chosen to identify yourself to be. The Holy Spirit's thought system is based on the truth that you are unlimited spirit. When we understand the truth of what we are, all thoughts of limitation will disappear

T-13.XI.7. Have faith in only this one thing, **which is the truth of the Holy Spirit**, and this **faith** will be sufficient: God wills you be in Heaven, and nothing can keep you from **being in Heaven** or **Heaven** from you. 2 Your wildest misperceptions, your weird imaginings, your blackest nightmares all mean nothing. 3 **Your misperceptions** will not prevail against the peace God wills for you. 4 The Holy Spirit will restore your sanity because insanity is not the Will of God. 5 If that suffices **the Holy Spirit**, it is enough for you. 6 You will not keep what God would have removed, because **your misperception** breaks communication with you with whom **God** would communicate. 7 **God's** Voice, **which is the Holy Spirit's** <*will*> be heard.

NOTE # 125: God's Will cannot be usurped. In the world of perception, the body is a communication device. The body, like everything in the world of perception, is neutral. The body is a learning device. It was our identifying our true unlimited spirit as being the body that birthed the thought of separation.

T-13.XI.8. The Communication Link, **which is the Holy Spirit** that God Himself placed within you, joining your mind with **God's Mind**, cannot be broken. 2 You may believe you want **the Communication Link with God's Mind** broken, and this belief does interfere with the deep peace in which the sweet and constant communication God would share with you is known. 3 Yet **God's** channels of reaching out cannot be wholly closed and separated from **the Christ in you**. 4 Peace will be yours because **God's** peace still flows to you from **God** Whose Will is peace. 5 You have **God's peace,** now. 6 The Holy Spirit will teach you how to use **God's peace,** and by extending **God's peace,** to learn that **God's peace** is in you. 7 God willed you Heaven, and will always will you nothing else **but Heaven**. 8 The Holy Spirit knows only of **God's** Will. 9 There is no chance that Heaven will not be yours, for God is sure, and what **God** wills is as sure as **God** is.

NOTE # 126: God's channel for reaching the split-minded dreamer is the Holy Spirit and the Christ consciousness. The Christ consciousness is that part of the split mind that remembers God and what you really are. The Christ part of our split-mind is the home of the Holy Spirit. While we are dreaming, we identify ourselves as being limited ego-bodies. The Christ maintains correct mindedness and provides us with perfect, correct perception when we follow the guidance of the Holy Spirit.

T-13.XI.9. You will learn salvation because you will learn how to save. 2 It will not be possible to exempt yourself from what the Holy Spirit wants to teach you. 3 Salvation is as sure as God. 4 **God's** certainty suffices. 5 Learn that even the darkest nightmare that disturbs the mind of God's sleeping Son holds no power over **God's sleeping Son**. 6 **God's sleeping Son** will learn the lesson of awaking. 7 God watches over **His sleeping Son** and light surrounds **God's sleeping Son**.

NOTE # 127: We are never outside the Grace of God. The Holy Spirit will reawaken us to reclaim our divine birthright as God's Son. Our divine inheritance can be denied but it can never be lost.

T-13.XI.10. Can God's Son lose himself in dreams, when God has placed within **God's sleeping Son** the glad Call to waken and be glad? 2 **God's sleeping Son** cannot separate himself from what is in him, **which is the call to reawaken to the remembrance of God and be the Christ.** 3 **God's sleeping Son's** sleep will not withstand the **Holy Spirit's** Call to wake. 4 The mission of redemption will be fulfilled as surely as the creation will remain unchanged throughout eternity. 5 You do not have to know that Heaven is yours to make it so. 6 **That Heaven is yours** <is> so. 7 Yet to know **that Heaven is yours**, the Will of God must be accepted as your will.

NOTE # 128: Everything is in the Mind of God. When God extended Himself, He gave everything because He is everything. Thus, our will and God's Will are the same Will. Heaven is the state of mind in which Truth reigns unopposed. When we remember God, we know the truth and reawaken in heaven, which is the holographic Mind of God, from which we never left. Knowledge has been restored to the Sonship.

T-13.XI.11. The Holy Spirit will undo for you everything you have learned **from the ego's thought system, which** teaches that what is not true must be reconciled with truth. 2 This **egoic belief that what is not true must be reconciled with truth** is the reconciliation **that** the ego would substitute for your reconciliation to sanity and to peace. 3 The Holy Spirit has a very different kind of reconciliation in **the Holy Spirit's** Mind for you, and one **the Holy Spirit** will effect as surely as the ego will not effect what **the ego** attempts. 4 Failure is of the ego, not of God. 5 From **God** you cannot wander, and there is no possibility that the plan the Holy Spirit offers <to> everyone, for the salvation <of> everyone, will not be perfectly accomplished. 6 You will be released, and you will not remember anything you made that was not created for you and by you in return. 7 For how can you remember what was never true, or not remember what has always been? 8 It is this reconciliation with truth, and only truth, in which the peace of Heaven lies. **Utilizing the Holy Spirit's guidance, we remember only the truth, which results in the disappearance of any recollection of the false. This is the only sane way to reconcile the false with the true.**

NOTE # 129: The ego would have us try to reconcile an untruth and somehow make the untruth become true. The Holy Spirit's method is simply to recognize that untruth has no reality and thus, dismiss the untruth. The Holy Spirit does not try to make an illusion into the truth. Instead, the Holy Spirit encourages the dreaming child to wake up and let the dream disappear. Only the truth remains. In the world of perception, events are only neutral learning devices. They have no life or realty of their own. When we attempt to make our dream world real, we are trying to reconcile an illusion with truth. We then fall into the ego's trap of identifying our unlimited spirit with being a limited body. Form cannot be shared. It is only the shared thoughts of forgiveness and love that have been saved in Heaven. Only the shared thoughts of forgiveness and love are our real creations. We cannot share something that we are not, since that would imply that we were something other than perfect, whole and complete. Our function in the playschool of provisional reality is to learn forgiveness. Our function in Heaven is to be co-creators with God, Who is only Love.

Chapter 14. TEACHING FOR TRUTH

Introduction

T-14.in.1. Yes, you are blessed indeed. 2 Yet in this world you do not know **that you are blessed indeed**. 3 But you have the means for learning **that you are blessed indeed** and seeing **that you are blessed indeed** quite clearly. 4 The Holy Spirit uses logic as easily and as well as does the ego, except that **the Holy Spirit's** conclusions are not insane. 5 **The Holy Spirit's conclusions** take a direction exactly opposite **the conclusions of the insane ego's thought system**, pointing as clearly to Heaven as the ego points to darkness and to death. 6 We have followed much of the ego's logic, and have seen **the ego's** logical conclusions. 7 And having seen **the ego's logical conclusions**, we have realized that **the ego's logical conclusions** cannot be seen except in illusions, for there alone **in illusions the ego's** seemingly clear **conclusions can** be clearly seen **for the insanity that they are**. 8 Let us now turn away from **the ego's insane thought system**, and follow the simple logic by which the Holy Spirit teaches the simple conclusions that speak for truth, and only truth.

Note # 1: ACIM is about to contrast the sane thought system of the Holy Spirit to the insane thought system of the ego.

I. The Conditions of Learning

T-14.I.1. If you are blessed and do not know **you are blessed**, you need to learn it must be so. 2 The knowledge **that you are blessed** is not taught, but its conditions **of you being blessed** must be acquired for it is **the conditions of you being blessed** that have been thrown away. 3 You can learn to bless, and cannot give what you have not. 4 If, then, you offer blessing, **being blessed** must have come first to yourself. 5 And you must also have accepted **being blessed** as yours, for how else could you give **blessings** away? 6 That is why miracles offer <*you*> the testimony that you are blessed. 7 If what you offer is complete forgiveness you must have let guilt go, accepting the Atonement for yourself and learning you are guiltless. 8 How could you learn what has been done for you, unknown to you, unless you do what you would have to do if **being blessed** <*had*> been done for you?

Note # 2: ACIM states that we fail to act as a Son of God because we have forgotten and denied what we truly are. Because we do not realize our true nature, we do not even attempt to test our capability of dong a given task. Like Lambert, the sheepish lion, we act like a sheep because we have allowed the ego to raise us as a sheep. We actually are unlimited spirit, but we fail to act like it. We believe that we are limited ego-bodies. We mistakenly identify ourselves as the body form, rather than as our true spiritual reality.

T-14.I.2. Indirect proof of truth is needed in a world made of denial and without direction. 2 You will perceive the need for this **indirect proof of truth** if you realize that to deny is the decision not to know. 3 The logic of the world must therefore lead to nothing, for **the** goal **of this illusionary world** is nothing. 4 If you decide to have and give and be nothing except a dream, you must direct your thoughts unto **the** oblivion **of the dream.** 5 And if you have and give and are everything, and all this, **your divine birthright of being everything,** has been denied, your thought system is closed off and wholly separated from the truth. 6 This <*is*> an insane world **of illusion,** and do not underestimate the extent of **this world of illusion's** insanity. 7 There is no area of your perception that **the belief in limitation and separation, which is the thought system of the ego,** has not touched, and your dream <*is*> sacred to you. 8 That is why God placed the Holy Spirit in you, where you placed the dream.

Note # 3: We believe that we are separate from God and that we also have a will other than God's Will. We placed this belief deep within our own split mind and it has become the egoic thought system. As soon as this belief was taken seriously by the Sonship (ACIM states "the Son forgot to laugh"), God placed that answer to this idea of the separation in our mind. The answer is within our Christ consciousness and is part of our mind. The Holy Spirit's Atonement principle is God's answer for the mind that now believes it is separate from the Mind of God. The Holy Spirit teaches us this answer and the answer is the Atonement principle. The answer was placed within our mind because the source of the problem arose within our mind. To correct the problem properly, you need to heal the cause of the problem, instead of putting a bandage over the cause's effect.

T-14.I.3. Egoic seeing is always outward. 2 Were your thoughts wholly of you, the thought system you made would be forever dark. 3 The thoughts the mind of God's Son projects or extends have all the power that **the mind of God's Son** gives to **these thoughts.** 4 The thoughts **God's Son** shares with God are beyond **God's Son's** belief, but those **thoughts** made **by the egoic little "s" self** <*are*> the egoic little **"s" self's** beliefs. 5 And it is these **self-made erroneous beliefs the egoic little "s" self** and not the truth, that **the little "s" self** has chosen to defend and love. 6 **These self-made erroneous beliefs of the egoic little "s" self** will not be taken from **the split minded.** 7 But **these self-made erroneous egoic beliefs** can be given up <*by*> **the split minded** for the Source of their undoing is in **God's Son's own split mind.** 8 There is nothing in the world to teach **God's split minded Son** that the logic of the world is totally insane and leads to nothing. 9 Yet in **the split minded** who made this insane logic there is One, **which is the Holy Spirit,** Who knows **that these self-made erroneous egoic beliefs made up this illusionary world and** lead to nothing, for **the Holy Spirit** knows everything.

Note # 4: Because we are among the trees, we cannot see the forest. Only the Holy Spirit has the proper perspective to see over the trees and know that we are in a forest of illusion. The Holy Spirit is both aware of the dream that we perceive as our provisional reality and, also, the truth about what we are, which is perfect, whole and complete. We, the dreamer, have taken our dream seriously and, therefore, believe it to be reality. Identifying ourselves with the dream, we appear to be limited by the dream. We can never find any witnesses within our own perception of the dream, which would demonstrate that we are not the dream. This is why the Holy Spirit's guidance is needed. If asked, the Holy Spirit takes the events of the dream and reinterprets them so that we can reawaken to the truth of our divine birthright. The Holy Spirit utilizes the tool of forgiveness for this purpose.

T-14.I.4. Any direction that would lead you where the Holy Spirit leads you not, goes nowhere. 2 Anything you deny that **the Holy Spirit** knows to be true you have denied yourself, and **the Holy Spirit** must therefore teach you not to deny **the truth about what you are, unlimited spirit in the Mind of God.** 3 Undoing <is> indirect, as doing is. 4 You were created only to create, neither to see nor do. 5 **To see or do** are but indirect expressions of the will to live, which has been blocked by the capricious and unholy whim of death and murder that your Father does not share with you. 6 You have set yourself the task of sharing what cannot be shared, **which is the untrue belief that you are something other than as God created you and, therefore, are limited.** 7 And while you think it possible to learn to do **something other than be as God created you and therefore limit yourself**, you will not believe all that <is> possible to learn to do.

<u>Note # 5:</u> Again, if you believe that you are limited, you will project thoughts that are based on limitation. We project or make our world based on our beliefs of separation, limitation, sin, guilt and fear. We have prejudged and now seek to verify the existence of our own projected images through the physical senses. The ego then claims that these imagined forms are the "proof" that confirms our previously determined beliefs in limitation. The ego then declares that the source of these projected images is outside us and, therefore, we did not make them and are powerless to change them. This leaves our mind in victim consciousness. We cannot find the resolution of a dream problem until we wake up to the fact that it is only a dream that has no effect on the real world. The Kingdom or the Mind of God remains unaffected by the dream of separation. When we reawaken, our dream disappears.

T-14.I.5. The Holy Spirit, therefore, must begin **the Holy Spirit's** teaching by showing you what you can never learn. 2 **The Holy Spirit's** message is not indirect, but **the Holy Spirit** must introduce the simple truth into a thought system, **which is based on the insane logic of the ego,** which has become so twisted and so complex you cannot see that **the ego's thought system** means nothing. 3 **The Holy Spirit** merely looks at **the** foundation **of the ego's thought system** and dismisses **the ego's thought system**. 4 But you who cannot undo what you have made, **which is the ego's thought system,** nor escape the heavy burden of **the** dullness **of the ego's thought system** that lies upon your mind, cannot see through **the ego's thought system**. 5 **The ego's thought system** deceives you, because you chose to deceive yourself. 6 Those who choose to be deceived will merely attack direct approaches, because **direct approaches** seem to encroach upon **the** deception **of the ego's thought system** and strike at **the ego's thought system**.

<u>Note # 6:</u> The Holy Spirit will not do anything that would increase our fear or make the dream appear to be real. If the Holy Spirit were to use a "direct approach" like slapping us across the head and telling us we are stupid, two things would happen. The first would be the confirmation that since we are "stupid,' we cannot be perfect, whole and complete. The second result would be to increase our fear. Being told by the Holy Spirit that we are stupid, we would be even more fearful than we were when the exercise first began. This is why the Holy Spirit waits patiently to be asked to help, rather than force correction upon an unwilling student. By reinterpreting the events, the Holy Spirit, can allow your Christ consciousness to recover Its ability to act as the decision-maker. You are now asked to choose again, this time allowing the choice to be based on the Vision of Christ, which is under the realm of the thought system of the Holy Spirit.

II. The Happy Learner

T-14.II.1. The Holy Spirit needs a happy learner, in whom **the Holy Spirit's** mission can be happily accomplished. 2 You who are steadfastly devoted to misery must first recognize that you are miserable and not happy. 3 The Holy Spirit cannot teach without this contrast **between misery and happiness**, for you believe that misery *<is>* happiness. 4 This **belief that misery *<is>* happiness** has so confused you that you have undertaken to learn to do what you can never do, believing that unless you learn **to do what you can never do, which is to make misery equal to happiness,** you will not be happy. 5 You do not realize that the foundation on which this most peculiar learning goal depends means absolutely nothing. 6 Yet **this goal, which is to make misery equal to happiness,** may still make sense to you. 7 Have faith in nothing and you will find the "treasure" that you seek **which is nothing**. 8 Yet you will add another burden to your already burdened mind. 9 You will believe that nothing is of value, and will value **nothing, which are your illusions**. 10 A little piece of glass, a speck of dust, a body or a war are one to you. 11 For if you value one thing made of **illusions, which are** nothing, you have believed that nothing can be precious, and that you *<can>* learn how to make the untrue true.

<u>Note # 7:</u> The goal of the ego's thought system is to create the illusion that what you perceive is real. Therefore, the ego strives to make illusions, which are not true or real, into truth. Since you have already been given everything through God's extension of Himself, the ego, which always desires specialness, must attempt to convince you that you are something other than a Oneness. Anything that is not found in the Mind of God, which is based on truth, is nothing.

T-14.II.2. The Holy Spirit, seeing where you are but knowing you are elsewhere, begins **the Holy Spirit's** lesson in simplicity with the fundamental teaching that *<truth>* is true. 2 This **fundamental teaching that <truth> is true** is the hardest lesson you will ever learn, and in the end the only one **lesson you will ever learn**. 3 Simplicity is very difficult for twisted minds. 4 Consider all the distortions you have made of nothing; all the strange forms and feelings and actions and reactions that you have woven out of it, **the illusionary world of your perception**. 5 Nothing is so alien to you as the simple truth, and nothing are you less inclined to listen to **than the simple truth that truth is true**. 6 The contrast between what is true and what is not is perfectly apparent, yet you do not see **the contrast between what is true and what is false**. 7 The simple and the obvious are not apparent to those who would make palaces and royal robes of nothing, believing they are kings with golden crowns because **they believe that their imagined dream world is real.**

<u>Note # 8:</u> If we believe that the dream is real, we have no reason to question the reality of the dream itself. This means that the Holy Spirit must correct our perception by reawakening us to the truth that we are only dreaming that we are separate from God. This reawakening process does not try to make the dream real; rather it makes the dream disappear into the nothingness from which it arose. Dreams cannot overcome the light of truth.

T-14.II.3. All this, **your belief in the realness of your illusionary world of provisional reality,** the Holy Spirit sees, and teaches, simply, that all **your belief in the reality of your illusionary world** is not true. 2 To those unhappy learners who would teach themselves nothing, and delude themselves into believing that **nothing** is not nothing, the Holy Spirit says, with steadfast quietness:

*3 The truth is true. 4 Nothing else matters, nothing else is real, and everything beside **truth** is not there.*
*5 Let Me, **the Holy Spirit,** make the one distinction for you that you cannot make, but need to learn **(that***

truth is true). *6 Your faith in nothing is deceiving you. 7 Offer your faith to Me, **the Holy Spirit,** and I will place **your faith** gently in the holy place where **your faith** belongs. 8 You will find no deception there **in the holy place where your faith belongs,** but only the simple truth. 9 And you will love **the simple truth** because you will understand **the simple truth that truth is true.***

<u>Note # 9:</u> The Holy Spirit's thought system is based on the truth that you are God's perfect Son. You are unlimited spirit. The ego's thought system is based on the idea that you are a limited ego-body in competition with other ego-bodies and live in a world of lack. As long as we believe that we are part of the ego's world of lack, we will never question the logic of the ego's thought system. Unless we realize that the ego's major premise is false, we will assume that the false idea that we are a limited ego-body is true. This is why the Holy Spirit needs only to teach the truth about our divine birthright. Truth is true, and the ego's belief system, which is based on false beliefs, must collapse.

Faith is the power behind a given belief. It is your mind's faith or lack of faith that gives a belief its "reality." The more faith you have in a particular belief, the more constantly "true" it will become for you. Without faith in a belief, the belief is powerless since it is transformed into a whimsical wish or fantasy. Your mind has failed to activate it by refusing to utilize your own mind's creative powers.

T-14.II.4. Like you, the Holy Spirit did not make truth. 2 Like God, **the Holy Spirit** knows **the truth** to be true. 3 **The Holy Spirit** brings the light of truth into the darkness, and lets **the light of truth** shine on you. 4 And as **the light of truth** shines, your brothers see **the light of truth**, and realizing that this light is not what you have made. **Your brothers** see in you more than you see. 5 **Your brothers** will be happy learners of the lesson this light brings to **your brothers**, because **the lesson that truth is true** teaches **your brothers** release from **the false illusions of** nothing and from all the works of nothing. 6 The heavy chains **of false illusions** that seem to bind **your brothers** to despair **are** not see as nothing until you bring the light, **which is the lesson that truth is true,** to **your brothers.** 7 And then **your brothers** see the chains **of these false illusions** have disappeared, and so **the chains** *<must>* have been nothing. 8 And you will see **that the chains were nothing** with **your brothers.** 9 Because you taught **your brothers** gladness and release **from the egoic illusion that the false could be made true, your brothers** will become your teachers in release and gladness.

<u>Note # 10:</u> By seeing and teaching the truth about the Oneness of the Sonship, all parts of the Sonship benefit. When there is only one, to give is to receive. By projecting forgiving and loving thoughts, these same thoughts are returned to us. By seeing and telling the truth about your brother, you learn the truth about yourself. Your faith is no longer being misplaced to make the false appear real.

T-14.II.5. When you teach anyone that truth is true, you learn **that truth is true** with him. 2 And so you learn that what seemed hardest was the easiest. 3 Learn to be a happy learner. 4 You will never learn how to make nothing everything. 5 Yet see that "**to make nothing everything**" has been your goal, and recognize how foolish it, **the ego's goal "to make nothing everything,"** has been. 6 Be glad **the ego's goal "to make nothing everything,"** is undone, for when you look at **the ego's goal "to make nothing everything,"** in simple honesty, **the ego's goal** *<is>* undone. 7 I said before, "Be not content with nothing," for you have believed that nothing could content you. 8 *<It is not so>* **that nothing could content you since you have been given everything**.

<u>Note # 11:</u> ACIM makes the point that being an extension of God, the Father, you are everything. Being everything, how can you be happy being something less than yourself? How and why would you trade the happiness of being everything, for the nothingness of an illusionary dream that brings only misery?

T-14.II.6. If you would be a happy learner, you must give everything you have learned **from the ego's**

thought system to the Holy Spirit, to be unlearned for you. 2 And then begin to learn the joyous lessons that come quickly on the firm foundation that truth is true. 3 For what is **built** there **based on the Holy Spirit's thought system** <*is*> true, and built on truth. 4 The universe of learning will open up before you in all its gracious simplicity. 5 With truth before you, you will not look back.

Note # 12: Once we realize that the thought system of the ego is based on erroneous thinking, we will abandon its falseness for truth. Once we get the major premise correct, that we are perfect, whole and complete, the rest falls into place. The return to knowledge is guaranteed to us as soon as we realize our guiltlessness as God's Son and we accept the Atonement for ourselves.

T-14.II.7. The happy learner meets the conditions of learning here **in our world of perception**, as **the happy learner** meets the conditions of knowledge in the Kingdom. 2 All this lies in the Holy Spirit's plan to free you from the past, and open up the way to freedom for you. 3 For truth <*is*> true. 4 What else could ever be, or ever was? 5 This simple lesson **that truth** <*is*> **true** holds the key to the dark door **that you invented to prevent your return to knowledge and the Kingdom. It is this door** that you believe is locked forever. 6 You made this door of nothing, and behind **this door, that you invented to prevent your return to knowledge and the Kingdom,** <*is*> nothing. 7 The key is only the light that shines away the shapes and forms and fears of nothing. 8 Accept this key to freedom from the hands of Christ, Who gives **this key to freedom** to you, that you may join **Christ** in the holy task of bringing light. 9 For, like your brothers, you do not realize the light has come and freed you from the sleep of darkness.

Note # 13: Truth dispels illusion. The only barrier to the return to the Kingdom lies within our split-mind. Correct your false belief that we can be something other than the Will of God, and all illusions disappear. The Christ consciousness will once again become the decision-maker in our mind. The Christ in us knows that we share only one mind, and that is the One Mind of God.

T-14.II.8. Behold your brothers in their freedom, and learn of **your brothers** how to be free of darkness. 2 The light in you will waken **your brothers**, and **your brothers** will not leave you asleep. 3 The vision of Christ is given the very instant that **vision of Christ** is perceived. 4 Where everything is clear, **everything** is all holy. 5 The quietness of **the lesson that truth** <*is*> **true is simple and in yet this lesson's** simplicity is so compelling that you will realize it is impossible to deny the simple truth. 6 For there is nothing else **but truth.** 7 God is everywhere, and His Son is in **God** with everything. 8 Can he sing the dirge of sorrow when this is true?

Note # 14: By reawakening to the truth about what we are, we are returned to the Oneness of God. Extension is God's Law and we have never left the Mind of God. We can deny this truth, but our denial will not make the truth become false. Truth is unchangeable and eternal. We have been, and always will be, God's beloved Child, perfect, whole and complete. This is the truth that the Holy Spirit teaches us.

III. The Decision for Guiltlessness

T-14.III.1. The happy learner cannot feel guilty about learning. 2 This is so essential to learning that **a happy learner cannot feel guilty about learning and that this** should never be forgotten. 3 The guiltless learner learns easily because his thoughts are free. 4 Yet, **that a guiltless learner learns easily because his thoughts are free** entails the recognition that guilt is interference, not salvation, and **guilt** serves no useful function at all.

Note # 15: Guilt places limits on thought and thus, impedes the free flow of thought.

T-14.III.2. Perhaps you are accustomed to using guiltlessness merely to offset the pain of guilt, and do not look upon **guiltlessness** as having value in itself. 2 You believe that guilt and guiltlessness are both of value, each representing an escape from what the other, **guilt or guiltlessness,** does not offer you. 3 You do not want either alone, for without both **guilt and guiltlessness** you do not see yourself as whole and therefore happy. 4 Yet you are whole only in your guiltlessness, and only in your guiltlessness can you be happy. 5 There is no conflict here **in your guiltlessness.** 6 To wish for guilt in any way, in any form, will lose appreciation of the value of your guiltlessness, and push **appreciation of the value of your guiltlessness** from your sight.

Note # 16: The ego has a vested interest in our belief in guilt. Guilt comes from the belief that we have usurped God's Will and are now separate from God. This usurping of God's authority, births our belief in individuality and our specialness. Unfortunately for us, the ego's belief in guilt results in pain for now we must be punished for our attack on God. Under the ego's belief system, we are constantly attempting to get rid of the pain that results from our guilt. Under the ego's thought system, we utilize projection to get rid of this guilt by claiming that we are guiltless and that we are, therefore, innocent victims. Seeing ourselves as an effect, rather than a cause, the ego maintains its control over us. We continue to believe that we lack the ability to choose again.
Truth has no opposites. If guiltlessness is true, it's opposite, which is guilt, can have no reality in the Mind of God. It is only in our world of perception that opposites appear to exist. A Oneness can know no opposites since it is everything.

T-14.III.3. There is no compromise that you can make with guilt, and escape the pain that only guiltlessness allays. 2 Learning is **the key element of** living here **in our world of individual perception**, as creating is being in Heaven. 3 Whenever the pain of guilt seems to attract you, remember that if you yield to **guilt**, you are deciding against your happiness, and will not learn how to be happy. 4 Say therefore, to yourself, gently, but with the conviction born of the Love of God and of His Son:

5 *What I experience I will make manifest.*
6 *If I am guiltless, I have nothing to fear.*
7 *I choose to testify to my acceptance of the Atonement, not to* **the Atonement's** *rejection.*
8 *I would accept my guiltlessness by making* **my guiltlessness** *manifest and sharing* **my guiltlessness***.*
9 *Let me bring peace to God's Son from his Father.*

Note # 17: Prior to the mad idea that there was a will different from the Father's Will, there was only a shared Oneness. God's Son, being an extension of the Father, created like the Father. Beingness is the nature of God and creation. Being is what is shared. Creation is sharing. With the belief in separation, knowledge was lost to the now split-minded little "s" self. The split-mind had now replaced the power of creation, with the power of decision. This power of decision arose when the belief in the Oneness had been shattered. Prior to this loss of knowledge, there was only truth and, therefore, no alternative or opposite choice existed. With the birth of perception, however, there was something to perceive and, therefore, something to decide about. Now, with a perceived something outside ourselves, there was something we could learn because we no longer believed we were perfect, whole and complete. Our private illusionary world of provisional reality now became a classroom for learning. Living is learning in our private world. Existence is what we think we are after the separation. The Holy Spirit utilizes our power of decision to reinterpret our current experiences so that we can learn to choose again and reclaim our divine birthright, which is a state of being. The ego utilizes our power of decision for the self-crucifixion of God's Son. The Atonement corrects the belief that the separation occurred and, therefore, the Atonement declares that we have always been and continue to be guiltless.

T-14.III.4. Each day, each hour and minute, even each second, you are deciding between the crucifixion and the resurrection; between the ego and the Holy Spirit. 2 The ego is the choice for guilt; the Holy Spirit the choice for guiltlessness. 3 The power of decision is all that is yours. 4 What you can decide between is fixed, because there are no alternatives except truth and illusion. 5 And there is no overlap between **truth and illusion**, because **truth and illusion** are opposites, which cannot be reconciled, and cannot both be true. 6 You are guilty or guiltless, bound or free, unhappy or happy.

Note # 18: The egoic thought system utilizes the decision for its belief in guilt as justification for crucifying ourselves. The Holy Spirit's thought system is designed so that the Christ consciousness part of our mind can regain its power of decision. Once this is done, we can choose again and reclaim, or resurrect, our divine inheritance. There can be no happiness as long as we compromise with the belief that there is guilt in the world as we perceive it. Truth is true and all illusions must be dissolved before we can reclaim our divine birthright. Only in the world of perception do opposites appear to exist. This is why ACIM states that there is no overlap between truth and illusions.

T-14.III.5. The miracle teaches you that you have chosen guiltlessness, freedom and joy. 2 **The miracle is not a cause, but the miracle is** an effect. 3 **The miracle** is the natural result of choosing right, attesting to your happiness that comes from choosing to be free of guilt. 4 Everyone you offer healing to returns **the miracle of guiltlessness to you**. 5 Everyone you attack keeps **guilt** and cherishes **guilt** by holding **guilt** against you. 6 Whether he does **hold guilt against you,** or does **not hold guilt against you,** it **will not** make **any** difference; **for** you will think he does **hold guilt against you.** 7 It is impossible to offer what you do not want without this penalty **of what you do not want being returned onto you.** 8 The cost of giving <is> receiving. 9 Either **the cost of giving** is a penalty from which you suffer, or the **cost of giving is a** happy purchase of a treasure to hold dear. **Giving is receiving.**

Note # 19: Giving is receiving because that is how projection works. Projection differs from creation since it comes from a sense of lack. Projection is exclusive, not inclusive. We try to give away or transfer our own deep-seated guilt to our brother. But by giving guilt, we receive guilt. God's Law is that what we give, we will receive. Because this is God's Law, in the world of perception, what we give, we also receive. Only by seeing our brother as guiltless is our own guiltlessness returned to us. A thought never leaves the mind of the thinker. Thoughts can be shared, but there is no such thing as an idle thought. Our thoughts become our experiences.

T-14.III.6. No penalty is ever asked of God's Son except by himself and of himself. 2 Every chance given **God's Son** to heal is another opportunity to replace darkness with light and fear with love. 3 If **God's Son** refuses **to replace darkness with light and fear with love,** he binds himself to darkness, because he did not choose to free his brother and enter light with **his brother.** 4 By giving power to nothing, **God's Son** throws away the joyous opportunity to learn that nothing has no power. 5 And by not dispelling darkness, **God's Son** became afraid of darkness and of light. 6 The joy of learning that darkness has no power over the Son of God is the happy lesson the Holy Spirit teaches, and would have you teach with Him. 7 **That darkness has no power over the Son of God** is **the Holy Spirit's** joy to teach **this lesson,** as **this lesson that darkness has no power over the Son of God** will be **your joy to also teach.**

Note # 20: Because the Atonement principle has always protected the Sonship's guiltlessness, nothing that we perceived outside the Mind of God is real. There is no punishment required by God since the Father only knows His Son as perfect, whole and complete. Only our belief in the ego's thought system makes us believe that the ego's "god of revenge" must require some sort of penance. The Holy Spirit would teach us that the ego, itself, is unreal and, therefore, nothing. The ego, being nothing, cannot have any power over the Son of God who was created perfect, whole and complete. It is only our belief in guilt that gives our ego any power over us. This apparent power of the ego comes only from our belief and decision to abdicate our divine birthright. The ego, itself, has no power over the mind. The Holy Spirit requests that we choose love over the ego's belief in fear.

T-14.III.7. The way to teach this simple lesson **that darkness has no power over the Son of God and, therefore, we must choose love over fear** is merely this: Guiltlessness is invulnerability. 2 Therefore, make your invulnerability manifest to everyone. 3 Teach him that **you are invulnerable**, whatever he may try to do to you, your perfect freedom from the belief that you can be harmed shows him that he is guiltless. 4 **Your brother** can do nothing that can hurt you, and by refusing to allow **your brother** to think he can **hurt you**, you teach **your brother** that the Atonement, which you have accepted for yourself, is also his **Atonement.** 5 There is nothing to forgive. 6 No one can hurt the Son of God. 7 **You and your brother's** guilt is wholly without cause, and being without cause, **guilt** cannot exist.

Note # 21: The Atonement acknowledges that God's Will is changeless. God created us guiltless like Himself. We will always remain perfect, whole and complete since this is God's Will. God is the only Cause and the only Source and no illusion that we have imagined can change the reality of the Mind of God.

T-14.III.8. God is the only Cause, and guilt is not of **God**. 2 Teach no one he has hurt you, for if you do **teach that someone has hurt you,** you teach yourself that what is not of God has power over you. 3 <*The causeless cannot be.*> 4 Do not attest to **the false belief that the causeless can exist in reality** and do not foster belief in **the existence of the causeless** in any mind. 5 Remember always that mind is one, and cause is one. **There is one Cause and one Mind and it is God's.** 6 You will learn communication with this oneness only when you learn to deny the causeless, and accept the Cause of God as **your cause.** 7 The power that God has given to His Son <*is*> his Son's **power**, and nothing else can His Son, **the Christ**, see or choose to look upon without imposing on himself the penalty of guilt, in place of all the happy teaching the Holy Spirit would gladly offer him, **who now suffers from split-mindedness and no longer sees himself as the Christ.**

Note # 22: The separation is referred to as the authority problem. The separation is the result of the mad idea that the child could somehow be self-created and give birth to itself. That something was created from nothing. Our denial of the Fatherhood of God is the authority problem. It claims that something other than the Mind of God is possible and that we are that something. This error resulted into our descent from knowledge into the illusionary world of perception. We became a decision maker because we denied the knowledge of our true Source and Creator. The Christ consciousness is the home of right-mindedness and the home of the Holy Spirit. The Christ in us has never lost the truth of what we are or the remembrance of the Father as our Creator. The split-minded person has abdicated his power of creation to the thought system of the ego. Believing the separation to be real, the split-mind now believes that there is lack. The split-minded have exchanged the power of creation, which is sharing and represents the power of God within us, for the limiting power of decision, which claims we are something other than as God created us. The power of decision can lead to exclusion, which can never be part of the Mind of God. When the decision-maker identifies itself with the ego's thought system, it rejects the Love of God. When God's Love has been denied by the spilt-minded child, it has been replaced by the ego's own unholy trinity of sin, guilt and fear.

The Holy Spirit teaches the split-minded to reclaim their divine birthright and to choose for the remembrances of God. God is Love. Nothing exists outside of the Mind of God. The belief in separation is unreal and causeless since the belief in separation is not part of God's Will. The Sonship, which is an extension of God, must remain guiltless, for the eternal is by definition, changeless. There is just the Oneness. We will once again remember God when we cease to deny our divine birthright inherited from our Source. Accept that the Mind of God birthed us, and we will understand that we are of the Mind of God. There is only One Mind and One Will.

T-14.III.9. Whenever you choose to make decisions for yourself you are thinking destructively, and the decision **you make by yourself** will be wrong. 2 **The decision you make by yourself** will hurt you because **this new decision is based on your erroneous** concept **that you are self-created. The belief that you are somehow self-created led to the decision that you can do something contrary to God's Will.** 3 It is not true that you can make decisions by yourself or for yourself alone. 4 No thought of God's Son can be separate or isolated in **the thought's** effects. 5 Every decision is made for the whole Sonship, directed in and out, and influencing a constellation larger than anything you ever dreamed of.

<u>Note # 23:</u> Our thoughts affect the entirety of the Sonship. In reality, there are no private thoughts. Private thoughts are not shared and, therefore, are not real. They cannot be true in the Mind of God. Private thoughts appear real to the perceiver and affect only the perceiver's perception of their illusionary world of provisional reality.

T-14.III.10. Those who accept the Atonement <are> invulnerable. 2 But those who believe they are guilty will respond to guilt, **because those who believe they are guilty** think **guilt** is salvation, and, **therefore, those who believe they are guilty** will not refuse to **see guilt** and **they will** side with guilt. **Those who believe they are guilty will also refuse to side with the Atonement and their own invulnerability. They will believe they are self-created and, therefore, can do something contrary to God's Will** 3 **Those who believe they are guilty** believe that increasing guilt is self-protection. 4 And **those who believe they are guilty** will fail to understand the simple fact that what they do not want, **which is their belief in guilt**, must hurt them. 5 All this arises because **those who believe they are guilty** do not believe that what they want is good. 6 Yet **free** will was given them because **free will** is holy, and will bring to them all that they need, coming as naturally as peace that knows no limits. **Since self-creation is impossible, having a will different from the Father's is equally impossible. Since both never happened in the Mind of God, our true will, which is found in our Christ consciousness, is the Will of God. Our free will is the shared Will of God.** 7 There is nothing their free will fails to provide that offers them anything of value. 8 Yet because they **believe they are something other than the Christ, they** do not understand their **free** will **is really the shared Will of God. The** Holy Spirit quietly understands **their free will** for them **who believe that they are guilty and have separated from God**, and gives them what they **truly** want without effort, strain, or the impossible burden of deciding what they want and need alone. **What they truly want is the return to right-mindedness. Christ consciousness is shared and is invulnerable for it is the acceptance of the Will of God.**

<u>Note # 24:</u> Because we have lost knowledge, we are incapable of knowing what we want. We have mistakenly identified our real self with the dream. We have slipped into the belief that we are something other than perfect, whole and complete. The Christ consciousness is the remembrance for God. The Christ appears to be asleep but in reality, our decision-maker is not listening to it. Our decision-maker has chosen to follow the guidance of the ego. Free will does not mean that we can establish the

curriculum for the return to the Oneness. God has already established the curriculum. Free will does mean that we can elect what parts of the course we choose to take at any given time. With the return to the thought system of the Holy Spirit, the vision of Christ will be reclaimed freely by the decision-making part of our mind. We will then freely choose God's Will as our own will. The Atonement is the remedy to the mad idea that our true identify could be something that was limited. Neither God nor His Creations can lack since They are everything. The Oneness of God is always perfect, whole and complete.

T-14.III.11. It will never happen that you must make decisions for yourself. 2 You are not bereft of help, and Help, **which is the Holy Spirit,** knows the answer. 3 Would you be content with little, which is all that you alone can offer yourself, when **the Holy Spirit,** Who gives you everything, will simply offer **everything** to you? 4 **The Holy Spirit** will never ask what you have done to make you worthy of the gift of God, **which is everything.** 5 Ask it **(the question of why you are worthy of God's Love)** not therefore of yourself. 6 Instead, accept **the Holy Spirit's** answer, for **the Holy Spirit** knows that you are worthy of everything God wills for you. 7 Do not try to escape the gift of God **that the Holy Spirit** so freely and so gladly offers you. 8 **The Holy Spirit** offers you but what God gave **the Holy Spirit** for you. 9 You need not decide whether or not you are deserving of **God's Gift of our divine birthright.** 10 God knows you are.

Note # 25: The Father knows our reality, which is eternal, changeless and true. God placed the Holy Spirit within our Christ consciousness so that we would be invulnerable to any thought of misperception. Time, which is only found in the world of form, arose out of our own misperception. In the world of time, we believe that we are limited ego-bodies. The Holy Spirit, Who is aware of both our perception and our reality, will return us to whole-mindedness. Thus, we return to the Kingdom, which in eternity has always been our home. The Atonement proves the Son's guiltlessness. The Holy Spirit teaches us to realize that the truth is always true. It teaches us that what is unreal must be always false and, therefore, nothing. Our illusions about ourselves have no power over the truth, which is the shared Mind of God.

T-14.III.12. Would you deny the truth of God's decision **that you are perfect, whole and complete,** and place your pitiful appraisal of yourself in place of **God's** calm and unswerving value of His Son, **the Big "S" Self?** 2 Nothing can shake God's conviction of the perfect purity of everything that **God** created, for **everything that God created** <is> wholly pure. 3 Do not decide against **your perfect purity**, for being of **God, your perfect purity** must be true. 4 Peace abides in every mind that quietly accepts the plan God set for its Atonement, relinquishing its own **self-made plan for its salvation, which was authored by the ego.** 5 You know not of salvation, for you do not understand **salvation.** 6 Make no decisions about what **salvation** is or where **salvation** lies, but ask the Holy Spirit everything, and leave all decisions to **the Holy Spirit's** gentle counsel.

Note # 26: Since we do not understand what we are, we are in no position to know what we truly want. Only the Holy Spirit knows that we truly seek the return to whole-mindedness. Ask the Holy Spirit who knows the truth and He will reinterpret all that the ego sees with the vision of Christ.

T-14.III.13. The **Holy Spirit is the** One Who knows the plan of God that God would have you follow. **The Holy Spirit** can teach you what **God's plan** is. 2 Only **the Holy Spirit's** wisdom is capable of guiding you to follow **God's plan of salvation.** 3 Every decision you undertake alone but signifies that you would define what salvation <is,> and what you would be saved <from.> 4 The Holy Spirit knows that all salvation is escape from guilt. 5 You have no other "enemy" **than your escape from self-inflicted guilt,** and against this strange distortion of the purity of the Son of God the Holy Spirit is your only Friend. 6 **The Holy Spirit** is the strong protector of the innocence that sets you free. 7 And it is **the Holy Spirit's** decision to undo everything that would obscure your innocence from your unclouded mind.

Note # 27: God's plan for salvation is the removal of all our self-inflicted guilt. The Atonement removes guilt because it corrects the error of our belief that the separation was real. We cannot be guilty of something that never was a part of the Mind of God. Dreams are not real and, therefore, cannot alter the truth.

T-14.III.14. Let the **Holy Spirit**, therefore, be the only Guide that you would follow to salvation. 2 **The Holy Spirit** knows the way, and leads you gladly on **the way to our recovery of our guiltlessness.** 3 With **the Holy Spirit** you will not fail to learn that what God wills for you <*is*> your will. 4 Without **the Holy Spirit's** guidance you will think you know alone, and will decide against your peace as surely as you decided that salvation lay in you alone. 5 Salvation is of **the Holy Spirit** to Whom God gave **the salvation of your guiltlessness** for you. 6 **The Holy Spirit** has not forgotten **your guiltlessness.** 7 Forget **the Holy Spirit** not and **the Holy Spirit** will make every decision for you, for your salvation and the peace of God in you.

Note # 28: Without the guidance of the Holy Spirit, we will continue to follow the thought system of the ego. Coming from lack, the ego tells us to look outside ourselves for salvation. Since the error of the belief in separation arose from our mind, the correction must be found within our mind. The Holy Spirit reawakens the Christ conscious part of our split-mind so that the decision-maker can choose again. This time, siding for the remembrance of God, which is the thought system of the Holy Spirit.

T-14.III.15. Seek not to appraise the worth of God's Son whom **God** created holy, for to do so is to evaluate his Father and judge against **His Father**. 2 And you <*will*> feel guilty for this imagined crime **of judging against God, Your Father**, which no one in this world or Heaven could possibly commit. 3 The Holy Spirit teaches only that the "sin" of self-replacement on the throne of God is not a source of guilt. 4 What cannot happen **(this imagined crime of judging against God)** can have no effects to fear. 5 Be quiet in your faith in **God** Who loves you, and would lead you out of insanity. 6 Madness may be your choice, but not your reality. 7 Never forget the Love of God, Who has remembered you. 8 For it is quite impossible that **God** could ever let His Son drop from the loving Mind wherein **His Son** was created, and where **His Son's** abode was fixed in perfect peace forever.

Note # 29: God does not punish someone He Loves. We should not try to punish ourselves because we imagined that we deny the love of God. God's love for His Son is eternal. We can deny God's Love but we cannot change it. For God's endless love of the Sonship is the Will of God. The Christ in us always abides in the Mind of God, which is our home. God's Love cannot be earned; instead, God's Love freely flows unceasingly to all of His Creation.

T-14.III.16. Say to the Holy Spirit only, "Decide for me," and it is done. 2 For **the Holy Spirit's** decisions are reflections of what God knows about you, and in this light, error of any kind becomes impossible. 3 Why would you struggle so frantically to anticipate all you cannot know, when all knowledge lies behind every decision the Holy Spirit makes for you? 4 Learn of **the Holy Spirit's** wisdom and **the Holy Spirit's** Love, and teach **the Holy Spirit's** answer to everyone who struggles in the dark. 5 For you decide for **everyone who struggles** and for yourself.

Note # 30: The decision-maker needs only to realize that lacking knowledge of what it is, the decision-maker is incapable of knowing what is in its own best interest. The decision-maker must decide to turn everything over to the Holy Spirit. Only the Holy Spirit can guide us home. Since the Sonship is part of the shared Mind of God, by making the decision to remember God, we affect the consciousness of the entire Sonship. Although we believe that we are separate from our brother, we remain connected through the Mind of God.

T-14.III.17. How gracious it is to decide all things through **the Holy Spirit's wisdom** Whose equal Love is given equally to all alike! 2 **The Holy Spirit** leaves you no one outside you. 3 And so **the Holy Spirit** gives you what is yours, because your Father would have you share **what is yours** with **your Father**. 4 In everything be led by **the Holy Spirit**, and do not reconsider. 5 Trust **the Holy Spirit** to answer quickly, surely, and with Love for everyone who will be touched in any way by the decision. 6 And everyone will be **touched by the decision**. 7 Would you take unto yourself the sole responsibility for deciding what can bring only good to everyone? 8 Would you know this?

Note # 31: Because the Sonship is actually a shared oneness, every decision made effects the collective consciousness of the whole. This is a large responsibility for anyone. Since we do not know what we are, ACIM tells us to follow someone that does know the truth. Ask the Holy Spirit and He will make the proper decision. Only the Holy Spirit is aware of the interconnectedness of the Sonship and how the parts interrelate to each other.

T-14.III.18. You taught yourself the most unnatural habit of not communicating with your Creator. 2 Yet you remain in close communication with **your Creator**, and with everything that is within **your Creator**, as it is within yourself. 3 Unlearn **the ego's belief in** isolation through **the Holy Spirit's** loving guidance, and learn of all the happy communication that you have thrown away but could not lose.

Note # 32: The Christ consciousness part of our split-mind has always remained in communication with God. Communication is sharing. Anything that we create through love and forgiveness is shared and is communicated with God. The Holy Spirit saves all our true creations for us and protects them for our return to the Kingdom where we will once again accept our function as co-creator with our Father.

T-14.III.19. Whenever you are in doubt what you should do, think of **the Holy Spirit** Presence in you, and tell yourself this, and only this:

2 *He, **the Holy Spirit**, leadeth me and knows the way, which I know not.*
3 *Yet He, **the Holy Spirit**, will never keep from me what **the Holy Spirit** would have me learn.*
4 *And so I trust **the Holy Spirit** to communicate to me all that **the Holy Spirit** knows for me.*

5 Then let **the Holy Spirit** teach you quietly how to perceive your guiltlessness, which is already there.

Note # 33: When we claim to be the little "s" self, we are powerless. When we follow the guidance of the Holy Spirit, which knows the Will of our Father, all the power of God follows through His Son. We thus, become invulnerable, as we were created.

IV. Your Function in the Atonement

T-14.IV.1. When you accept a brother's guiltlessness you will see the Atonement in **your brother. The Atonement is the acceptance of the guiltlessness of the Sonship.** 2 For by proclaiming **the guiltlessness** in **your brother** you make **guiltlessness** yours, and you will see what you sought, **which is the Atonement and your guiltlessness.** 3 You will not see the symbol of your brother's guiltlessness shining within him while you still believe **your brother's guiltlessness** is not there **within your brother.** 4 **Your brother's** guiltlessness is <your> Atonement. 5 Grant **your brother his guiltlessness** to him, and you will see the truth of what you have acknowledged **that your brother is guiltless.** 6 Yet truth **of guiltlessness** is offered first to be received, even as God gave **truth of guiltlessness** first to His Son. 7 The first in time means nothing, but the First in eternity is God the Father, Who is both First and One. 8 Beyond the First there is no other, for there is no order, no second or third, and nothing but the First.

Note # 34: God is the First and One cause of everything. What God created is eternal and real. Time is not known in eternity since the real is changeless. Time is meaningless in Heaven. Only in the dream world of perception does time serve some purpose. We make in time because what is made is not real and is subject to modification as our viewpoints change. Time allows us to relearn what we have chosen to forget and finally choose again for the certainty of truth. Time will slip into the nothingness from which it arose when we return to knowledge. There will be no change to measure since only the oneness of truth is real. Having served its purpose, time will disappear along with our dream world of perception.

The Atonement is the acceptance of the guiltlessness of God and all His Creations. The Sonship has maintained its innocence and thus, remains sinless.

T-14.IV.2. You who belong to the First Cause, created by **God** like unto Himself and part of **God,** are more than merely guiltless. 2 The state of guiltlessness is only the condition in which what is not there has been removed from the disordered mind that thought **what is not there** was **really to be found within its own disordered mind.** 3 This state **of guiltlessness**, and only this, must you attain, with God beside you. 4 For until you do **attain the state of guiltlessness**, you will still think that you are separate from **God.** 5 You can perhaps feel **God's** Presence next to you, but cannot know that you are one with **God.** 6 This **oneness with God** cannot be taught. 7 Learning applies only to the condition in which it happens of itself.

Note # 35: Guiltlessness is merely the returning to the truth about you. God knows the Sonship is guiltless. It is only God's Son that is under the insane belief that he has sinned and has separated from his Source, which is the Father.

T-14.IV.3. When you have let all that obscured the truth in your most holy mind be undone for you, and therefore stand in grace before your Father, **your Father** will give Himself to you as **your Father** has always done. 2 Giving Himself is all **your Father** knows, and so **giving Himself** is all knowledge. 3 For what **God** knows not cannot be, and therefore cannot be given. 4 Ask not to be forgiven, for this has already been accomplished. 5 Ask, rather, to learn how to forgive, and to restore what always was, **which was your guiltlessness,** to your unforgiving mind. 6 Atonement becomes real and visible to those who use **Atonement, which is the acceptance of guiltlessness.** 7 On earth **the acceptance of guiltlessness** is your only function, and you must learn that **the acceptance of guiltlessness** is all you want to learn. 8 You will feel guilty till you learn **the acceptance of guiltlessness.** 9 For in the end, whatever form **guilt** takes, your guilt arises from your failure to fulfill your function in God's Mind with

your entire mind. 10 Can you escape this guilt by failing to fulfill your function here?

Note # 36: Guilt arises from our belief in sin. Sin, like guilt is unreal. God knows that sin is impossible and is not part of the Mind of God. Since we made up sin by our belief in the separation, we must learn the unreality of sin. From our belief in sin, guilt and fear, we birthed the dream world of our provisional reality. Only in this dream can we learn how to recover our guiltlessness since it is only in this dream world that we could be "guilty." The Holy Spirit is the only teacher that has knowledge and can teach us how to undo the dream of guilt. This lesson is taught in the dream by the tool of forgiveness. The tool of forgiveness recognizes that what we thought happened was unreal and, therefore, there is nothing to forgive. Since there is nothing to forgive, there is nothing to be guilty of. Sin, guilt and fear all disappear with the acceptance of the guiltlessness of the Sonship. Time has served its purpose and we awaken from the dream. Forgiveness is our function as long as our mind is split. The acceptance of the Atonement for ourselves is what we are here to learn. The Atonement undoes the illusion within our split-mind that sin, guilt and fear have reality in the real world, which is found only in the Mind of God.

Forgiveness is accepting and sharing the guiltlessness of all. This guiltlessness must be granted and extended within our own mind to God, the Sonship and yourself. There can be no exceptions.

T-14.IV.4. You need not understand creation to do what must be done before that knowledge would be meaningful to you. 2 God breaks no barriers; neither did **God** make **barriers**. 3 When you release **barriers** they are gone. 4 God will not fail, nor ever has **failed** in anything. 5 Decide that God is right and **your perceptions and judgments** are wrong about yourself. 6 **God** created you out of Himself, but still within **Himself**. 7 **God** knows what you are. 8 Remember that there is no second to **God**. 9 **Since there is no second to God,** there cannot be anyone without **God's** Holiness, nor anyone unworthy of **God's** perfect Love. 10 Fail not in your function of loving in a loveless place made out of darkness and deceit, **which is your made-up world of individual perception,** for thus are darkness and deceit undone. 11 Fail not yourself, but instead offer to God and you, **God's** blameless Son. 12 For this small gift of appreciation for His Love, God will Himself exchange your gift for His **gift**.

Note # 37: There is nothing outside of God; God is everything. Creation by God is an extension of Himself, which is the Oneness. There are no barriers in a Oneness. We create barriers when we believe that there is something outside the Mind and Will of God. We believe that we are a second cause and that we can change what God created thus, imposing our will and changing eternity. There is only the First Cause, God. Extension can only give or share what it is. Accept your divine birthright and guilt, sin and fear must disappear because this unholy trinity is not found in God. By accepting the Atonement for ourselves, we release our mind from our belief in the reality of sin, guilt and fear. Forgive our brother and we forgive ourselves. The denial of the reality of our dream is our gift to Our Father. It is merely the acceptance of the truth about what we are. It is the acceptance of our inherited divine birthright. It is the acceptance of the Father as the First and only Cause. In exchange for this acceptance of the truth, we cease our self-denial of being the Oneness of everything that we truly are.

T-14.IV.5. Before you make any decisions for yourself, remember that you have decided against your function in Heaven, **which is extension of creation**, and then consider carefully whether you want to make decisions here **in your world of individual perception**. 2 Your function here **in your world of individual perception** is only to decide against deciding what you want, in recognition that you do not know. 3 How, then, can you decide what you should do? 4 Leave all decisions to the One, **the Holy Spirit,** Who speaks for God, and for your function as **the Holy Spirit** knows **your function, which is forgiveness.** 5 So will **the Holy Spirit** teach you to remove the awful burden you have laid upon yourself by loving not the Son of God, and trying to teach **the Son of God** guilt instead of love. 6 Give up this frantic and insane attempt **which teaches guilt to God's Son, for this attempt** cheats you of the joy of living with your God and Father, and of waking gladly to His Love and Holiness that join together as the truth in you, making you one with **God**.

Note # 38: ACIM states that since we have lost knowledge, we no longer realize our divine nature as unlimited spirit. We think that we are limited ego-bodies. We have made up an entire dream world to prove that we are limited. Since we have denied what we are, we cannot know what we really want. When we believe that the dream is real, we will cling to our claim of littleness because that is what we believe we are. Only the Holy Spirit knows the truth and, therefore, we need His help to undo what our egoic thought system has taught us. Lacking knowledge, we need to decide that we are not of sound mind to know what we want. We need to ask the Holy Spirit to guide us back to the reality of the truth, which is that we remain God's beloved Son.

T-14.IV.6. When you have learned how to decide with God, all decisions become as easy and as right as breathing. 2 There is no effort, and you will be led as gently as if you were being carried down a quiet path in summer. 3 Only your own volition seems to make deciding hard. 4 The Holy Spirit will not delay in answering your every question what to do. 5 **The Holy Spirit** knows. 6 And **the Holy Spirit** will tell you, and then do it for you. 7 You who are tired will find **allowing the Holy Spirit to decide for you,** is more restful than sleep. 8 For you can bring your guilt into sleeping, but **you cannot bring your guilt** into **allowing the Holy Spirit to decide for you**.

Note # 39: We must ask for the Holy Spirit's help, for having free will, the Holy Spirit will not "force" Himself upon an unwilling mind.

T-14.IV.7. Unless you are guiltless you cannot know God, Whose Will is that you know **God, Who is guiltless**. 2 Therefore, you <*must*> be guiltless. 3 Yet if you do not accept the necessary conditions for knowing **God**, you have **egoically** denied **God** and do not recognize **God**, though **God** is all around you. 4 **God** cannot be known without **God's Son**, whose guiltlessness is the condition for knowing **God**. 5 Accepting **God's Son** as guilty is denial of the Father so complete, that knowledge is swept away from recognition in the very mind where God Himself has placed **knowledge**. 6 If you would but listen, and learn how impossible this is! p280 7 Do not endow **God** with attributes you **egoically** understand. 8 You made **God** not, and anything you **egoically** understand is not of **God**.

Note # 40: The ego has made up a myth about what God is. The god of the ego is made in the image of the ego. As such, the mythical god of the ego is petty, revengeful, unforgiving and very judgmental and limited. Rather than the Son of God being created in the image of the God, which is a Loving Father-Mother figure, we have made the egoic God into the worst qualities that we believe ourselves to be. We believe God to be imperfect, not whole and very incomplete. This is what the ego tells us we are. The ego implies that creation or extension is similar to how God creates. So, like its petty father, the son must also be petty. The ego thus, makes up a false image of a god, and then extends this false image upon you. This means that you are self-created since the ego made the image of god. This egoic image of god then in turn made you yet you are the ego. Thus, to the ego, which claims self-creation for the son, the notion of what god must be is predicated on how the ego sees you. Therefore, the god of a limited son must also be a limited god.

ACIM states that we are created in God's loving image and, therefore, must be perfect, whole and complete. There is no guilt in the Mind of God, which is the Sonship's home.

T-14.IV.8. Your task is not to make reality. 2 **Reality** is here without your making, but **reality is** not without you. 3 You who have tried to throw yourself away and valued God so little, hear me speak for **God** and for yourself, **which is the Big "S" Self**. 4 You cannot understand how much your Father loves you, for there is no parallel in your experience of the world to help you understand **how much your Father loves you**. 5 There is nothing on earth with which **you** can compare **how much your Father loves you,** and nothing you have ever felt apart from **God** resembles **how much your Father loves you** ever so faintly. 6 You cannot even give a blessing in perfect gentleness. 7 Would you know of One, **your Father,** Who gives forever, and Who knows of nothing except giving?

<u>Note # 41:</u> God, being unconditional Love, gives everything and asks for nothing in return.

T-14.IV.9. The children of Heaven live in the light of the blessing of their Father, because **the children of Heaven** know that **the children of Heaven** are sinless. 2 The Atonement was established as the means of restoring guiltlessness to minds that have denied **their guiltlessness**, and thus denied Heaven to themselves. 3 Atonement teaches you the true condition of the Son of God. 4 **Atonement** does not teach you what you are, or what your Father is. 5 The Holy Spirit, Who remembers **what you are** for you, merely teaches you how to remove the blocks that stand between you and what you know. 6 **The Holy Spirit's** memory is **your memory**. 7 If you remember what you have **egoically** made, you are remembering nothing. 8 Remembrance of reality is in **the Holy Spirit**, and therefore in you.

<u>Note # 42:</u> Heaven resides in the Mind of God. When we believe in sin, guilt and fear, we have placed ourselves in an illusionary world outside the Mind of God. Sin, guilt and fear were never real and, therefore, the Atonement testifies to the unreality of the dream of the split-minded. The Atonement is the denial of the false, which only leaves the truth to become visible to the split minded. Reality is the return to the remembrance of God.

T-14.IV.10. The guiltless and the guilty are totally incapable of understanding one another. 2 Each perceives the other as like himself, making both unable to communicate, because each sees the other unlike the way **the other** sees himself. 3 God can communicate only to the Holy Spirit in your mind, because only **the Holy Spirit** shares the knowledge of what you are with God. 4 And only the Holy Spirit can answer God for you, for only **the Holy Spirit** knows what God is. 5 Everything else that you have placed within your **sleeping** mind cannot exist, for what is not in communication with the Mind of God has never been. 6 Communication with God is life. 7 Nothing without it, **(Life, which is communication with God),** is at all.

<u>Note # 43:</u> True communication comes from a foundation that is based on truth. Those who believe in guilt do not understand the truth about the guiltlessness of reality. They misinterpret everything because their thought system is based on the illusion of guilt. The Holy Spirit is the mediator between Level # 1 and Level # 2. Level # 2 is the dream world of individual perception. Level # 1 is the reality of Truth, which is heaven or the Kingdom. Only the Holy Spirit is aware of what we experience in Level # 2's dream world of individual perception and also is aware of the reality of the truth of Level # 1. Because of this, only the Holy Spirit can communicate, or bridge the gap between these two levels. By following the guidance of the Holy Spirit, we will cross the bridge back to the gates of heaven and God will take the final step in our return to knowledge. Forgiveness is the tool that the Holy Spirit utilizes to bridge this gap between truth and illusion, perception and knowledge.

V. The Circle of Atonement

T-14.V.1. The only part of your mind that has reality is the part that links you still with God. 2 Would you have all of **your mind** transformed into a radiant message of God's Love, to share with all the lonely ones who have denied **God and God's Love**? 3 *<God makes this possible>* **for you to transform your mind into a radiant message of God's Love** 4 Would you deny **God's** yearning to be known? 5 You yearn for **God,** as **God** for you. 6 This **mutual yearning** is forever changeless. 7 Accept, then, the immutable **that you yearn for God as God yearns for you**. 8 Leave the world of death behind, and return quietly to Heaven. 9 There is nothing of value here **in the world of death** and everything of value there **in Heaven**. 10 Listen to the Holy Spirit, and to God through **the Holy Spirit**. 11 **The Holy Spirit** speaks of you to *<you.>* 12 There is no guilt in you, for God is blessed in His Son, **the Christ,** as the Son is blessed in **God.**

Note # 44: The Christ part of our split mind has never left its source, which is the Mind of God. Tonight when you are asleep and dreaming you may visit the planet of Mars but when you awake the next morning, you will realize you never left your bed. The split-minded are like this example. The Christ-mind remains in the bed of the Mind of God. The egoic mind dreams that it is separated from the Mind of God and is actually in the dream world of death, which in this example is represented by Mars. When we awaken, we realize that our real mind, the Christ-mind, never left its home, which is Heaven or the Mind of God. You are not judged guilty for anything that you had dreamed happened while you "defended" yourself in the dream world of Mars. Dreams have no reality once you have awakened.

T-14.V.2. Everyone has a special part to play in the Atonement, but the message given to each one is always the same; *<God's Son is guiltless.>* 2 Each one teaches the message differently, and learns **the message that God's Son is guiltless** differently. 3 Yet until he teaches **the message that God's Son is guiltless** and learns **the message that God's Son is guiltless,** he will suffer the pain of dim awareness that his true function remains unfulfilled in him. **Our true function is to grant ourselves forgiveness for denying ourselves the experience of receiving God's Love. It is the restoration of our split-mind to the sanity of the Oneness.** 4 The burden of guilt is heavy, but God would not have you bound by **the burden of guilt for not fulfilling your function**. 5 **God's** plan for your awaking is as perfect as **your egoic plan** is fallible. 6 You know not what you do, but **the Holy Spirit,** Who knows is with you. 7 **The Holy Spirit's** gentleness is yours, and all the love you share with God, **the Holy Spirit** holds in trust for you. 8 **The Holy Spirit** would teach you nothing except how to be happy.

Note # 45: Our true function is to grant ourselves forgiveness for denying ourselves the experience of receiving God's Love. In the dream world of provisional reality, our function is the restoration of our split-mind to the sanity of the Oneness. After the return to whole-mindedness, our function in Heaven is to create like our Father and thus, extend the Mind of God.

God's plan for the salvation of His split –minded son is simple. Forgive and be forgiven; for as you give, you will receive. God's gift to His Son is that the truth is changeless and eternal. God's Will is that we be happy.

T-14.V.3. Blessed Son of a wholly blessing Father, joy was created for you. 2 Who can condemn whom God has blessed? 3 There is nothing in the Mind of God that does not share **God's** shining innocence. 4 Creation is the natural extension of perfect purity. 5 Your only calling here is to devote yourself, with active willingness, to the denial of guilt in all its forms. 6 To accuse is *<not to understand.>* 7 The happy learners of the Atonement become the teachers of the innocence that is the right of all that God created. 8 **Do not** deny **any part of the Sonship** what is their due, for you will not withhold **what is their due** from them alone. **You will also be denying your own guiltlessness and innocence, which is the Sonship's due or divine birthright.**

Note # 46: Being on extension of God, the Sonship must be totally guiltless, like God, its Creator. The "innocence of God" refers to that which does not exist. God is everything and has everything and knows everything. God does not know what does not exist. It is in not knowing what does not exist that God's state of innocence rests. We are like our Creator and must also be innocence. Yet, we have chosen to deny our innocence in our egoic attempt to make what does not exist, which is the false, into the real.

T-14.V.4. The inheritance of the Kingdom is the right of God's Son, given **God's Son** in his creation. 2 Do not try to steal **the divine birthright of innocence** from **God's Son**, or you will ask for guilt and will experience **guilt**. 3 Protect **God's Son's** purity from every thought that would steal **the Sonship's purity** away and keep **God's Son's purity** from his **split-minded** sight. 4 Bring innocence to light, in answer to the call of the Atonement. 5 Never allow purity to remain hidden, but **allow purity to** shine away the heavy veils of guilt within which the Son of God has hidden himself from his own sight.

Note # 47: We have cloaked the Sonship in heavy garments that are meant to hide the Christ in each part of the Sonship. These garments are made from our belief in sin, guilt and fear. The belief in sin, guilt and fear prevent us from accessing the Vision of Christ. Ask the Holy Spirit and He will remove all barriers to our ability to access the Christ in us. The acceptance of the Sonship's guiltlessness removes all these barriers.

T-14.V.5. We are all joined in the Atonement here, and nothing else can unite us in this world **but the Atonement**. 2 So will the world of separation slip away, and full communication be restored between the Father and the Son. 3 The miracle acknowledges the guiltlessness that must have been denied to produce the need of healing. 4 Do not withhold this glad acknowledgment **of guiltlessness**, for hope of happiness and release from suffering of every kind lie in **the acknowledgment of guiltlessness, which is the Atonement**. 5 Who is there but wishes to be free of pain? 6 He may not yet have learned how to exchange guilt for innocence, nor realize that only in this exchange **of guilt for innocence** can freedom from pain be his. 7 Yet those who have failed to learn need teaching, not attack. 8 To attack those who have need of teaching is to fail to learn from **those who have need of teaching**.

Note # 48: Teach the guiltlessness of God's Son to every brother and you reclaim your own guiltlessness and innocence. God's gift is simply forgive to be forgiven, for as you give, you receive. When we listen to the guidance of the Holy Spirit, we will hear this message.

T-14.V.6. Teachers of innocence, each in his own way, have joined together, taking their part in the unified curriculum of the Atonement. 2 There is no unity of learning goals apart from **the unified curriculum of the Atonement, which teaches the guiltlessness of God's Son**. 3 There is no conflict in this curriculum, which has one aim, **which is the teaching of the guiltlessness of God's Son** however **it** is taught. 4 Each effort made on **the unified curriculum of the Atonement's** behalf is offered for the single purpose of release from guilt, to the eternal glory of God and **God's** creation. 5 And every teaching that points to this points straight to Heaven, and the peace of God. 6 There is no pain, no trial, no fear that teaching **the guiltlessness of God's Son** can fail to overcome. 7 The power of God Himself supports this teaching **of the guiltlessness of God's Son** and guarantees its **teaching's** limitless results.

Note # 49: The teaching of the guiltlessness of God's Son, which is the Atonement principle, dissolves the ego's thought system, which is comprised on the unholy alliance of sin, guilt and fear.

T-14.V.7. Join your own efforts to the power that cannot fail and must result in peace, **which is the Atonement**. 2 No one can be untouched by teaching such as this, **the guiltlessness of God's Son**. 3 You will not see yourself beyond the power of God if you teach only **the guiltlessness of God's Son**. 4 You will not be exempt from the effects of this most holy lesson, which seeks but to restore what is the right of God's creation. 5 From everyone whom you accord release from guilt you will inevitably learn your innocence. 6 The circle of Atonement has no end. 7 And you will find ever-increasing confidence in your safe inclusion in the circle with everyone you bring within **the circle of Atonement's** safety and **the circle of Atonement's** perfect peace.

Note # 50: The goal of the miracle worker is to accept the Atonement for himself. By giving or teaching the Atonement, you receive the Atonement. For God's Plan is that by forgiving, you are forgiven, for as you give, you receive. By giving guiltlessness to our brother, we, in turn, receive and accept our innocence.

T-14.V.8. Peace, then, be unto everyone who becomes a teacher of peace. 2 For peace is the acknowledgment of perfect purity, from which no one is excluded. 3 Within **perfect purity's** holy circle is everyone whom God created as His Son. 4 Joy is **perfect purity's** unifying attribute, with no one left outside to suffer guilt alone. 5 The power of God draws everyone to **the circle of Atonement's** safe embrace of love and union. 6 Stand quietly within this circle, and attract all tortured minds to join with you in the safety of **the circle of Atonement's** peace and holiness. 7 Abide with me within **the circle of Atonement** as a teacher of Atonement, not **a teacher** of guilt.

Note # 51: When we attack another, which is anytime we fail to see only the face of Christ in our brother, we are teaching, or projecting guilt. Assuming our brother has not accepted the Atonement for himself; this guilt will stick to our brother and will return to us. To give is to receive. In our world of individual perception, there are only two emotions, love or fear. We cannot teach both. The teaching of guiltlessness is the voice for the remembrance of God. When we teach guiltlessness, we align ourselves with the Holy Spirit and all the Power of God is given to us. We acknowledge both our own and our brother's innocence.

T-14.V.9. Blessed are you who teach with me. 2 Our power comes not of us, but of our Father. 3 In guiltlessness we know **our Father**, as **our Father** knows us guiltless. 4 I stand within the circle **of Atonement**, calling you to peace. 5 Teach peace with me, and stand with me on holy ground. 6 Remember for everyone your Father's power that **your Father** has given **to the Sonship**. 7 Believe not that you cannot teach **your Father's** perfect peace **to every part of the Sonship**. 8 Stand not outside, but join with me within **the circle of Atonement**. 9 Fail not the only purpose to which my teaching calls you, **which is the acknowledgment of the guiltlessness of the Sonship, God's Son**. 10 Restore to God His Son as **God** created him, by teaching **the split-minded** his innocence.

Note # 52: Jesus is acknowledging that we all have an equal role to play in the God's Plan for the return of His Son to knowledge and the Kingdom. We are all joined in a common goal and purpose. The denial to any part of the Sonship of our divine birthright is to deny our inheritance to all the Sonship.

T-14.V.10. The crucifixion had no part in the Atonement. 2 Only the resurrection became my part in **the Atonement**. 3 **The resurrection** is the symbol of the release from guilt by guiltlessness. 4 Whom you perceive as guilty you would crucify. 5 Yet you restore guiltlessness to whomever you see as guiltless. 6 Crucifixion is always the ego's aim. 7 **The ego** sees everyone as guilty, and by **the ego's** condemnation **the ego** would kill. 8 The Holy Spirit sees only guiltlessness, and in **the Holy Spirit's** gentleness **the**

Holy Spirit would release **your split-mind** from fear and re-establish the reign of love. 9 The power of love is in **the Holy Spirit's** gentleness, which is of God and therefore cannot crucify nor suffer crucifixion. 10 The temple you restore becomes your altar, for **your altar** was rebuilt through you. 11 And everything you give to God is yours. 12 Thus **God** creates, and thus must you restore **the split minded to the altar of the Christ**.

Note # 53: The ego's thought system crucifies or attacks the unity of the Sonship and God. These attacks increase our belief in guilt. The Holy Spirit's thought system proclaims God's Son as innocent and guiltless. The acceptance of our guiltlessness removes the misperceptions within our mind that have been hiding the Christ within us. The Christ is the part of our mind that is the remembrance of God.

T-14.V.11. Each one you see you place within the holy circle of Atonement or leave outside **the holy circle of Atonement**, judging him fit for crucifixion or for redemption. 2 If you bring him into the circle of purity, you will rest there with him **within the circle of purity.** 3 If you leave him without, you join him there **outside the circle of purity.** 4 Judge not except in the quietness **of the Holy Spirit,** which is not of **your egoic little "s" self.** 5 Refuse to accept anyone as without the blessing of Atonement, and bring him into **the circle of Atonement** by blessing him. 6 Holiness must be shared, for therein **the sharing** lies everything that makes it holy. 7 Come gladly to the holy circle, and look out in peace on all who think they are outside. 8 Cast no one out **of the holy circle of purity**, for here is what he seeks along with you. 9 Come, let us join him in the holy place of peace which is for all of us, united as one within the Cause of peace. **This Cause is the Mind of God.**

Note # 54: We are told in sentence # 4 to "judge not except in quietness, which is not of you." This is why we are told to seek the Holy Spirit's guidance. Only the Holy Spirit has knowledge of all things and can judge properly the events that we perceive. The Atonement is the call to the return of the Sonship to the right-mindedness of the Christ. The Christ has never left the unified Mind of God. The Sonship's return to the Oneness can leave no brother behind in the darkness of the ego's thought system that demands littleness. When we quiet our egoic mind's self-talk, we will hear in the silence the voice of the Holy Spirit.

VI. The Light of Communication

T-14.VI.1. The journey that we undertake together is the exchange of dark for light, of ignorance for understanding. 2 Nothing you understand is fearful. 3 It is only in darkness and in ignorance that you perceive the frightening, and shrink away from **what you do not understand** to further darkness. 4 And yet it is only the hidden that can terrify, not for what **the hidden** is, but for its hiddenness. 5 The obscure is frightening because you do not understand **the obscure's** meaning. 6 If you did **understand the obscure's meaning**, it would be clear and you would be no longer in the dark. 7 Nothing has hidden value, for what is hidden cannot be shared, and so **the** value **of what is hidden is** unknown. 8 The hidden is kept apart, but value always lies in joint appreciation. 9 What is concealed cannot be loved, and so **what is concealed** must be feared.

Note # 55: Only what is shared is real. Creation is sharing. When we hide something, we are attempting to exclude.

T-14.VI.2. The quiet light in which the Holy Spirit dwells within you is merely perfect openness, in which nothing is hidden and therefore nothing is fearful. 2 Attack will always yield to love if **attack** is brought to love, not hidden from **love**. 3 There is no darkness that the light of love will not dispel, unless **the darkness** is concealed from love's beneficence. 4 What is kept apart from love cannot share **love's** healing power, because **what is kept apart from love** has been separated off and kept in darkness. 5 The sentinels of darkness watch over **what is kept apart from love** carefully, and you who made these guardians of illusion out of nothing are now afraid of **these guardians of illusion.**

Note # 56: These guardians of illusion protect your belief in your littleness. Sin, guilt and fear are some of the major guardians for the little "s" self.

T-14.VI.3. Would you continue to give imagined power to these strange ideas of safety? 2 **These strange ideas of safety** are neither safe nor unsafe. 3 **These strange ideas of safety** do not protect; neither do they attack. 4 **These strange ideas of safety** do nothing at all, being nothing at all. 5 As guardians of darkness and of ignorance look to them only for fear, for what **these strange ideas of safety** keep obscure <*is*> fearful. 6 But let them go, and what was fearful will be so no longer. 7 Without protection of obscurity only the light of love remains, for only **the light of love** has meaning and can live in light. 8 Everything else must disappear.

Note # 57: ACIM states that we need to bring everything into the light of love. Understanding is love. We do not understand the fearful for we have lost knowledge. We need to bring all our experiences to the light of the thought system of the Holy Spirit. The Holy Spirit will reinterpret everything we perceive with the light of love. It is our job to control our fear and remember to ask for the guidance of the Holy Spirit. Without this guidance, we will not be able to break the cycle of ignorance. We cannot bring the light of understanding by following the thought system of the ego. The thought system of the ego is the source of the sin, guilt and fear and, therefore, has a vested interest in maintaining the darkness. The ego is the home of fear and attack and knows nothing of love. Since the ego is not shared nor created by God, it is nothing and begets only nothing, for it is not real.

T-14.VI.4. Death yields to life simply because destruction is not true. 2 The light of guiltlessness shines guilt away because, when **guiltlessness and guilt** are brought together, the truth of **guiltlessness** must make the falsity of its opposite**, guilt,** perfectly clear. 3 Keep not guilt and guiltlessness apart, for your belief that you can have both **guiltlessness and guilt** is meaningless. 4 All you have done by keeping **guiltlessness and guilt** apart is lose their meaning by confusing **guiltlessness and guilt** with each other. 5 And so you do not realize that only one, **guiltlessness,** means anything. 6 The other**, guilt,** is wholly without sense of any kind.

Note # 58: Truth is true and what is false has no reality. God made us guiltless and, therefore, the idea that the Son of God could be guilty must be false. One of God's greatest gifts to His Son is that God cannot see His Son as anything other than perfect, whole and complete. This is the result of God's innocence. The Innocence of God refers to that which does not exist. Thus, God does not know the false. Our egoic belief that we could be the little "s" self is totally rejected and not part of the Mind of God. God's gift of His changeless Innocence to His Son is our protection from our self-imposed denial of the light of God's Love. If we were guilty, God, being a Oneness, would also have to be guilty. The child cannot change its creator. An effect cannot change its cause.

T-14.VI.5. You have regarded the separation as a means for breaking your communication with your Father. 2 The Holy Spirit reinterprets **the separation** as a means of re-establishing **your**

communication with your Father which was not broken, but <*has*> been made obscure. 3 All things you made have use to **the Holy Spirit**, for **the Holy Spirit's** most holy purpose. 4 **The Holy Spirit** knows you are not separate from God, but **the Holy Spirit** perceives much in your mind that lets you think you are **separate from God**. 5 All **that makes you perceive that you are separate from God** and nothing else, would **the Holy Spirit** separate from you. 6 The power of decision, which you made in place of the power of creation, **the Holy Spirit** would teach you how to use **the power of decision** on your behalf. 7 You who made **the power of decision** to crucify yourself must learn of **the Holy Spirit** how to apply **the power of decision** to the holy cause of restoration.

Note # 59: Prior to our descent into the belief in separation, there was no power of decision. There was only a oneness. So what was there to decide? There was creation but this is only the extension of the Oneness. When we decided for the mad idea of believing that we could be something other than what God created, we exchanged the power of creation for the power of the decision-maker. We decided that there could be something outside the One Self. We believed that we could do something other than share or extend love, which is the Mind of God. We believed that we could contract or exclude something from the oneness due to our desire to be special. The goal of the Holy Spirit is to reinterpret the world of individual perception to realign with the truth. The egoic world was made for the expressed purpose of keeping God's love from us. The Holy Spirit utilizes this world of illusion by reinterpreting all events into neutral learning devices, which reawaken the communication of the Christ-mind with God's Mind. The Holy Spirit reawakens and encourages the decision-maker within us to freely choose the thought system of the Holy Spirit over the ego's thought system. This is the call for the remembrance of God.

T-14.VI.6. You who speak in dark and devious symbols do not understand the language you have made. 2 **The language you have made** has no meaning, for **this language's** purpose is not communication, but rather the disruption of communication. 3 If the purpose of language is communication, how can this tongue, **which was made to disrupt communication,** mean anything? 4 Yet even this strange and twisted effort to communicate through not communicating holds enough of love to make **this twisted language** meaningful if its Interpreter is not its maker **but rather the Holy Spirit.** 5 You who made **this twisted language** are but expressing conflict, from which the Holy Spirit would release you. 6 Leave what you would communicate to **the Holy Spirit.** 7 **The Holy Spirit** will interpret **this twisted language** to you with perfect clarity, for **the Holy Spirit** knows with Whom you are in perfect communication, **which is God through the Christ part of your mind.**

Note # 60: Everything in the world of perception is a neutral learning device. It is the decision-maker that colors these events with either love or fear. This coloration of the neutral event is the choice of the decision-maker. Because of our descent down the ladder of knowledge into perception, we now find ourselves not believing that we even have any control over the events within our own dream world. We have slipped deeply into victim consciousness and forgotten that we are, in fact, the dreamer. We no longer believe we are the cause of the events, but rather, that we are an effect of everything outside ourselves. The Holy Spirit's job is first to reawaken the decision-maker within us. By succeeding in this task of reawakening the decision-maker within us, we can begin to recover our power to choose again. Our goal is not to make the decision, but rather, to realize that in our current state of confusion we do not even know what we are. Thus, it is in our best interest to hand over the task of actually making the decision to someone that knows the truth about what we truly are. The Holy Spirit is the only One Who can correctly decide on our behalf since only the Holy Spirit knows both the truth and our perceived illusion.

T-14.VI.7. You know not what you say, and so you know not what is said to you. 2 Yet your Interpreter, **the Holy Spirit,** perceives the meaning in your alien language. 3 **The Holy Spirit** will not attempt to communicate the meaningless. 4 But **the Holy Spirit** will separate out all that has meaning, dropping off the rest and offering your true communication to those who would communicate as truly with you. 5 You speak two languages at once, and this **speaking with two languages at once** must lead to unintelligibility. 6 Yet if one means nothing and the other everything, only that one is possible for purposes of communication. 7 The other **one that means nothing** but interferes with **the purposes of communication**.

Note # 61: These two languages are the language of fear and the language of love. The language of love speaks truthfully and is the language of the Father, the Holy Spirit and the Christ, the big "S" Self. The language of fear is the thought system of the ego. It is the voice for littleness and the small "s" self. It is the voice for the separation and its allies are sin, guilt and fear. It is the voice for all that is untrue and not part of the Mind of God.

T-14.VI.8.The Holy Spirit's function is entirely communication. 2 **The Holy Spirit** therefore must remove whatever interferes with communication in order to restore **communication**. 3 Therefore, keep no source of interference from **the Holy Spirit's** sight, for **the Holy Spirit** will not attack your sentinels **of guilt**. 4 But bring **your sentinels of guilt** to **the Holy Spirit** and let **the Holy Spirit's** gentleness teach you that, in the light, **your sentinels of guilt** are not fearful, and cannot serve to guard the dark doors behind which nothing at all is carefully concealed. 5 We must open all doors and let the light come streaming through. 6 There are no hidden chambers in God's temple. 7 **The** gates **of God's temple** are open wide to greet **God's** Son. 8 No one can fail to come where God has called him, if he close not the door himself upon his Father's welcome.

Note # 62: Having the power of the decision-maker does not give us the power to make what is false, into truth. Truth is unaffected by what we believe for truth is fixed and changeless in the Mind of God. The decision-maker does have the ability to choose to deny the truth. This denial of the truth does not change the truth but it allows you to choose not to recognize the truth within yourself. Only we can choose the self-imposed exile from Heaven that the denial of the truth brings to us. We can deny God's Love for us but we cannot change God's Love. Perhaps, the refusal of God to see His Son as something other than perfect, whole and complete, is God's greatest gift to His Son. This is God's innocence. Our salvation rests on this changelessness of God's Love for His Son. We do not earn God's Love. It is just given totally and freely to all. God's Plan for salvation is simple. Forgive to be forgiven, for as you give, you receive.

VII. Sharing Perception with the Holy Spirit

T-14.VII.1.What do you want? 2 Light or darkness, knowledge or ignorance are yours, but not both. 3 Opposites must be brought together, not kept apart. 4 For their separation is only in your mind, and **opposites** are reconciled by union, as you are **reconciled by union**. 5 In union, everything that is not real must disappear, for truth <*is*> union. 6 As darkness disappears in light, so ignorance fades away when knowledge dawns. 7 Perception is the medium by which ignorance is brought to knowledge. 8 Yet the perception must be without deceit, for otherwise **perception with deceit** becomes the messenger of ignorance rather than a helper in the search for truth.

Note # 63: ACIM wants us to compare the thought system of the ego, which represents darkness and ignorance, against the thought system of Holy Spirit, which represents light and comes from knowledge. If we place them side-by-side, our ability to choose for our happiness over our need to be right, even if we are wrong, becomes apparent. The decision for truth will be easily recognized.

T-14.VII.2. The search for truth is but the honest searching out of everything that interferes with truth. 2 Truth <*is.*> 3 **Truth** can neither be lost nor sought nor found. 4 **Truth** is there, wherever you are, being within you. 5 Yet **truth** can be recognized or unrecognized, real or false to you. 6 If you hide **truth**, **truth** becomes unreal to you <*because*> you hid **truth** and surrounded **truth** with fear. 7 Under each cornerstone of fear on which you have erected your insane system of belief, the truth lies hidden. 8 Yet you cannot know **that truth lies hidden under each cornerstone of fear** for by hiding truth in fear, you see no reason to believe that the more you look at fear the less you see **fear**, and the clearer **the truth that fear** conceals becomes. **What becomes clear is the truth that was hidden and concealed by your fear.**

Note # 64: By examining our fears, the truth becomes clear. We fail to examine our fear because we are afraid to look fear in the eye. ACIM states that if you can control your fear long enough to look at the source of the fear, fear will be undone by the truth. By asking for the Holy Spirit's guidance, the Holy Spirit reinterprets what we perceived wrongly, into correct perception. Our task is to control our fear and ask for guidance. The Holy Spirit cannot remove our fear, but He can shine the light of truth upon our fear and it will fade away. Fear is based on our belief that we are limited ego bodies, in competition with other ego bodies and, therefore, can be hurt. This is the thought system of the ego. The Holy Spirit speaks the truth that we are unlimited spirit that lacks nothing and cannot be hurt.

T-14.VII.3. It is not possible to convince the unknowing that they, **the unknowing**, know. 2 From **the unknowing's** point of view it is not true **that they know**. 3 Yet it is true **that they know** because God knows **all**. 4 These are clearly opposite viewpoints on what the "unknowing" are. 5 To God, unknowing is impossible. 6 **Unknowing** is therefore not a point of view at all, but merely a belief in something that does not exist. 7 **Unknowing** is only this belief that the unknowing have, and by **holding this false belief** they, **the unknowing,** are wrong about themselves. 8 **The unknowing** have **mistakenly chosen to** defined themselves as they were not created. 9 Yet, their creation by **God** was not a point of view, but rather a certainty. 10 Uncertainty brought to certainty does not retain any conviction of reality.

Note # 65: ACIM points out that we can believe any untruth about ourselves and act accordingly, but false beliefs cannot change the truth. Truth is found eternally in the Mind of God. Our limiting beliefs will impact what the believer of the limitation will attempt to do. If I believe that man was not meant to fly because he does not have wings, I will never choose to explore the possibilities for flight. My beliefs, not reality, limit what I am capable of doing. Argue for your limitations and you get to keep them.

T-14.VII.4. Our emphasis has been on bringing what is undesirable to the desirable; what you do not want to what you do **want**. 2 You will realize that salvation must come to you this way **by direct comparison between opposites**, if you consider what dissociation is. 3 Dissociation is a distorted process of thinking whereby two systems of belief which cannot coexist are both maintained. 4 If **the two systems of belief** are brought together, their joint acceptance becomes impossible. 5 But if one is kept in darkness from the other **belief system**, their separation seems to keep them both alive and equal in their reality. 6 Their joining **of the two opposing systems of beliefs** thus becomes the source of fear, for if they meet, acceptance must be withdrawn from one of them. 7 You cannot have both **belief systems**, for each denies the other. 8 **If kept** apart, this fact **that each thought system denies the other** is lost from **your** sight, for each **thought system is** in a separate place **and** can be endowed with firm belief. 9 Bring **each thought system** together, **side-by-side**, and the fact of their complete incompatibility is instantly apparent. 10 One **belief** will go, because the other **belief** is seen in the same place.

Note # 66: ACIM wants us the compare the thought system of the ego and the Holy Spirit side-by-side. If we do this, our decision-making ability will be recovered and we will freely choose for the truth of what we are. We will realize that if our goal is happiness, then our will and God's Will must be the same.

T-14.VII.5. Light cannot enter darkness when a mind believes in darkness, and will not let **darkness** go. 2 Truth does not struggle against ignorance, and love does not attack fear. 3 What needs no protection, **which is truth and love,** does not defend itself. 4 Defense is of your making. 5 God knows **defense** not. 6 The Holy Spirit uses defenses on behalf of truth only because you made **defenses** against **truth**. 7 **The Holy Spirit's** perception of **your defenses against the truth is reinterpreted** according to **the Holy Spirit's** purpose. **This reinterpretation** merely changes **your defenses against the truth** into a call for **the truth that** you have attacked with **your defenses.** 8 Defenses, like everything you made, must be gently turned to your own good, translated by the Holy Spirit from means of self-destruction to means of preservation and release. 9 **The Holy Spirit's** task is mighty, but the power of God is with **the Holy Spirit.** 10 Therefore, to **the Holy Spirit, It's task, which is the return to truth,** is so easy that **It's task of the return to truth** was accomplished the instant it was given **the Holy Spirit by God** for you. 11 Do not delay in your return to peace by wondering how **the Holy Spirit** can fulfill what God has given **the Holy Spirit** to do. 12 Leave that to **the Holy Spirit** Who knows. 13 You are not asked to do mighty tasks yourself. 14 You are merely asked to do the little that **the Holy Spirit** suggests you do, trusting **the Holy Spirit** only to the small extent of believing that, if **the Holy Spirit** asks **you to do something,** you can do it. 15 You will see how easily all that **the Holy Spirit** asks can be accomplished.

Note # 67: The small task that the Holy Spirit asks of us is to ask for His guidance and then follow it. Because we lack knowledge of what we are, we are not capable of judging what is in our best interest. We believe the dream is true. Because of this belief, we will fail to even consider the possibility that we could just awaken from our false nightmare. The Holy Spirit, if asked, will reinterpret all misperception into correct perception. We need to realize that the world of perception was made by the split-minded for the explicit purpose of making the separation appear real. The truth cannot be found in the illusion of the dream. It can only be found by bringing the illusion to the light and reawakening from the dream, itself. Only the Holy Spirit stands outside the dream yet is also aware of our delusional state for only the Holy Spirit knows the truth. The Holy Spirit will gently reawaken the sleeping son to the truth about the Son of God's divine birthright. In our innocence lies the strength of God.

T-14.VII.6. The Holy Spirit asks of you but this; bring to Him every secret you have locked away from **the Holy Spirit.** 2 Open every door to **the Holy Spirit,** and bid **the Holy Spirit** enter the darkness and lighten **the darkness** away. 3 At your request **the Holy Spirit** enters gladly. 4 **The Holy Spirit** brings the light to darkness if you make the darkness open to **the Holy Spirit.** 5 But what you hide **the Holy Spirit** cannot look upon. 6 **The Holy Spirit** sees for you, and unless you look with **the Holy Spirit, the Holy Spirit** cannot see. 7 The vision of Christ is not for **the Holy Spirit** alone, but for **the Christ within** you. 8 Bring, therefore, all your dark and secret thoughts to **the Holy Spirit,** and look upon **these dark and secret thoughts** with **the Holy Spirit.** 9 **The Holy Spirit** holds the light, and your **egoic little "s" self,** the darkness. 10 They, **light and darkness, truth and ignorance,** cannot coexist when both **the Holy Spirit and** You, **the big "S" Self,** together look on **truth and ignorance.** 11 **The Holy Spirit's** judgment must prevail, and **the Holy Spirit** will give **His judgment** to you as you join your perception to **the Holy Spirit's perception and ignorance will disappear.**

Note # 68: The Holy Spirit's home in your mind is the Christ consciousness. The Christ is what we truly are. The Holy Spirit's reinterpretation of your misperceptions, are brought before the Christ in you. If you allow yourself to see with the vision of Christ, the truth will be apparent, and the decision-maker within you will be asked to choose again. This time the decision-maker's choice will be for truth over illusion.

T-14.VII.7. Joining with **the Holy Spirit** in seeing is the way in which you learn to share with **the Holy Spirit** the interpretation of perception that leads to knowledge. 2 You cannot see alone. 3 Sharing perception with **the Holy Spirit,** Whom God has given you, teaches you how to recognize what you see. 4 **Sharing perception with the Holy Spirit** is the recognition that nothing you see means anything alone. 5 Seeing with **the Holy Spirit** will show you that all meaning, including yours, comes not from double vision, but from the gentle fusing of everything into <one> meaning, <one> emotion and <one> purpose. **This is the remembrance of God.** 6 God has one purpose which **God** shares with you. 7 The single vision which the Holy Spirit offers you will bring this oneness to your mind with clarity and brightness so intense you could not wish, for all the world, not to accept what God would have you have. 8 Behold your will, accepting **your will** as **God's Will,** with all **God's** Love as yours. 9 All honor to you through **the Holy Spirit,** and through **the Holy Spirit** unto God.

Note # 69: The Holy Spirit is the communicator between God and the split-minded son. ACIM states we need to give all our perceptions to the Holy Spirit for His correct judgment or interpretation of what they truly mean. We cannot see alone because our past erroneous viewpoints cloud or actually make our present misperceptions. The ego's thought system is always placing its emphasis on the past. By utilizing past misperception to observe the present, the ego helps insure that the future will be a duplication of the past and we will remain in victim consciousness. The Holy Spirit's emphasis is on the <now>. With the past misperceptions released, the Holy Spirit can turn the present moment into a learning lesson that will help us reawaken to the oneness that we share. God's will for His Son is to be happy. When we understand the failure of the ego's thought system to bring us happiness, we will freely reject the ego's need to be special. Our egoic specialness has cost us our happiness.

Everything in the world of perception is a neutral learning device. If we believe ourselves to be limited ego-bodies, we will always side with the ego. Since we do tend to believe that we are limited because everything in the physical universe of form points in that direction, we need to be leery of our own judgments. ACIM states clearly that we cannot hope to rediscover the truth, unless we ask for the help of someone who knows the truth. We must ask someone who is outside of our own limited and very restricted egoic point of view. The Holy Spirit is that someone. We cannot see alone. We need the Holy Spirit's guidance to reawaken the vision of Christ that lays dormant within us as long as we still remain under the influence or darkness of the ego's thought system. Once we can compare the results of these two thought systems side-by-side, we will freely make a choice for our happiness. We will realize that we can only be happy by choosing to follow the Will of God, for both our wills and God's Will are truly One.

VIII. The Holy Meeting Place

T-14.VIII.1. In the darkness you have obscured the glory God gave you, and the power **God** bestowed upon **God's** guiltless Son. 2 All this **glory and power God gave you** lies hidden in every darkened place, shrouded in guilt and in the dark denial of innocence. 3 Behind the dark doors you have closed lies nothing, because nothing can obscure the gift of God, **which is the power God gave you**. 4 It is the closing of the doors that interferes with recognition of the power of God that shines in you. 5 Banish not power from your mind, but let all that would hide your glory be brought to the judgment of the Holy Spirit, and there **what hides your glory is** undone. 6 Whom **the Holy Spirit** would save for glory <*is*> saved for **glory**. 7 **The Holy Spirit** has promised the Father that through **the Holy Spirit** you would be released from littleness to glory. 8 To what **the Holy Spirit** promised God **the Holy Spirit** is wholly faithful, for **the Holy Spirit** shares with God the promise that was given **the Holy Spirit** to share with you.

Note # 70: God established and placed the Holy Spirit within us in order to insure our return to right-mindedness and our acceptance of all the power of the Big "S" Self. The message of the Holy Spirit is shared with us and cannot fail for this mission has the power of God behind it. The Holy Spirit's message of the Atonement speaks of our innocence, guiltlessness and sinlessness.

T-14.VIII.2. The Holy Spirit shares **the promise of your glory and power** still, for you. 2 Everything that promises otherwise, great or small, however much or little valued, **the Holy Spirit** will replace with the one promise given unto **the Holy Spirit** to lay upon the altar to your Father and **God's** Son. 3 No altar stands to God without **God's** Son. 4 And nothing brought there **to the common altar to your Father and God's Son** that is not equally worthy of Both **the Father and the Son**, but will be replaced by gifts wholly acceptable to Father and to Son. 5 Can you offer guilt to God? 6 You cannot, then, offer **guilt** to **God's** Son. 7 For **the Father and the Son** are not apart, and gifts to One are offered to the Other. 8 You know not God because you know not this **shared Oneness**. 9 And yet you, **the Christ**, do know God and also this **shared Oneness**. 10 All this **shared Oneness** is safe within you, where the Holy Spirit shines. 11 **The Holy Spirit** shines not in division, but in the meeting place where God, united with His Son, speaks to **God's** Son through **the Holy Spirit**. 12 Communication between what cannot be divided cannot cease. 13 The holy meeting place of the unseparated Father and His Son lies in the Holy Spirit and in you, **the Christ**. 14 All interference in the communication that God Himself wills with His Son is quite impossible here **in the Christ**. 15 Unbroken and uninterrupted love flows constantly between the Father and the Son, as Both would have **this constant flow of love** be. 16 And so it is.

Note # 71: Even though we appear to have lost our shared Oneness with our Father, this is not our reality. The reality of the shared Oneness remains in the Christ mind. It is here, in the home of the Holy Spirit that the mutual flow of love and understanding remain constant in eternity. We can deny and choose to forget this truth in the dream of individual perception, but we cannot change the truth of its eternal reality.

T-14.VIII.3. Let your mind wander not through darkened corridors, away from light's center. 2 You and your brother may choose to lead yourselves astray, but you can be brought together only by the Guide, **the Holy Spirit,** appointed for you. 3 **The Holy Spirit** will surely lead you to where God and His Son await your recognition. 4 **God and God's Son** are joined in giving you the gift of oneness, before which all separation vanishes. 5 Unite with what you are, **God Himself**. 6 You cannot join with anything except reality. 7 God's glory and His Son's **glory** belong to you in truth. 8 **This shared glory with God has** no opposite, and nothing else can you bestow upon yourself **than this shared glory with God**.

Note # 72: Nothing can oppose God's Will. God shares all His power and glory with His creations because that is what extension or creation is. We can deny God's gifts but this does not change the Will of God for His Son. We remain like our Father; perfect, whole and complete, for this is the truth, which never can change. God's child is eternally innocent.

T-14.VIII.4. There is no substitute for truth. 2 And truth will make this plain to you as you are brought into the place where you must meet with truth. 3 And there you must be led, through gentle understanding which can lead you nowhere else **but to the place of truth**. 4 Where God is, there are you. 5 Such is the truth. 6 Nothing can change the knowledge, given you by God, into unknowingness. 7 Everything God created knows its Creator. 8 For **by** this **knowing of its Creator** is how creation is accomplished by the Creator and by His creations. 9 In the holy meeting place, **which is Heaven,** are joined the Father and His creations, and the creations of His Son with Them together. 10 There is one link that joins **the Father and His creations, and the creations of His Son** all together, holding Them in the oneness out of which creation happens.

Note # 73: God is truth. With the return of the Son to truth, the Son will reclaim the Son's rightful place in heaven. Heaven is real. Heaven is the home, or abode, of truth. Heaven is not a place, but a state of Mind. The Son's creations are what the Son extended, or created, out of the knowledge of His true nature, the Big "S" Self. Creation is shared and is inclusion. Creation is not what the little "s" self made through projection. Projection is based on exclusion and is, therefore, not real nor to be found in the Mind of God.

T-14.VIII.5. The link with which the Father joins Himself to those **the Father** gives the power to create can never be dissolved. 2 Heaven itself is union with all of creation, and with its one Creator, **the Father**. 3 And Heaven remains the Will of God for you. 4 Lay no gifts other than this **shared union of creation** upon your altars, for nothing can coexist with **the shared Oneness**. 5 Here your little offerings are brought together with the gift of God, and only what is worthy of the Father will be accepted by the Son, for whom **these offerings** is intended. 6 To whom God gives Himself, **God** <is> given. 7 Your little gifts will vanish on the altar, where **God** has placed His Own **gift upon the altar. The gift of God is all the power and glory, which is God, which God extends to His creations. It is the power of creation.** .

Note # 74: God gives Himself totally to His creations. God holds nothing back, since that would be a limitation on the Father, Himself. God is not limited. God extends everything to His Son. The Sonship has the power to create and utilizes this power when we co-create with God. The Sonship's creations must also be unlimited since that is what we truly are as the Big "S" Self. Heaven is the eternal and is the shared home of all of creation. Heaven is the truth, which is the holographic Mind of God. There is nothing outside the Mind of God. This is the Oneness and the Will of God, which is shared by all of creation. All "parts" of creation share the holographic nature of the Oneness. There is only union in the Mind of God.

Only our gifts of forgiveness and love are worthy of the Christ, God's Son. These gifts are saved by the Holy Spirit and are part of the Kingdom of Heaven. With the return to knowledge, we will rediscover our true creations. The Son has all the creative power of the Father. The only difference is that the Father is the First Cause. The Son can have "children" who themselves have "children," but the Sonship cannot birth the Father, since the Father is the First and One Source. All else is an ultimate effect of the Father. Thus, in heaven our function is to co-create with our Father. We extend the Oneness of

Everything, which is the One Self.

IX. The Reflection of Holiness

T-14.IX.1.The Atonement does not make holy. 2 You were created holy. 3 **The Atonement** merely brings unholiness to holiness; or what you made to what you are. 4 Bringing illusion to truth, or the ego to God, is the Holy Spirit's only function. 5 Keep not your making from your Father, for hiding **your making from your Father** has cost you knowledge of **your Father** and **knowledge** of yourself. 6 The knowledge **of both your Father and yourself** is safe, but where is your safety apart from **this knowledge**? 7 The making of time to take the place of timelessness lay in the decision to be not as you are. 8 Thus truth was made past, and the present was dedicated to illusion. 9 And the past, too, was changed and interposed between what always was and now. 10 The past that you remember never was, and represents only the denial of what always was.

Note # 75: Time was born with the acceptance of the mad idea by the Sonship that God's Son could be something other than perfect, whole and complete. Prior to this, there was only the Oneness. Since the idea of the separation is not part of the Mind of God, it is not real. Time was birthed with perception. Time, which measures change, had no function in eternity since there was no change to measure. When the Sonship returns to whole-mindedness, the need for time will disappear. The ego utilizes time to help maintain the illusion that you are different from the Oneness. The Holy Spirit utilizes time to correct your illusion about what you are and thus, return you to knowledge.

T-14.IX.2.Bringing the ego to God is but to bring error **of the ego,** to truth, **which is of God. This is** where **error** stands corrected because **error** is the opposite of what it meets, which **is the truth of God.** 2 **Error and the ego** are undone because the contradiction can no longer stand. 3 How long can contradiction stand when its impossible nature is clearly revealed? 4 What disappears in light is not attacked. 5 **What disappears in light** merely vanishes because **error** is not true. 6 Different realities are meaningless, for reality must be one. 7 **Reality** cannot change with time or mood or chance. 8 **Reality's** changelessness is what makes **reality** real. 9 **Reality's changelessness** cannot be undone. 10 Undoing is for unreality. 11 And this **undoing of the unreality of error is what** reality will do for you.

Note # 76: Truth will undo illusion when the thought system of the ego is compared to the Holy Spirit's thought system. God's Son is changeless and, therefore, guilty of nothing. By following the guidance of the Holy Spirit, you will inevitably accept the Atonement for yourself.

T-14.IX.3.Merely by being what **the truth** is, does truth release you from everything that **the truth** is not. 2 The Atonement is so gentle you need but whisper to **the Atonement,** and all **the Atonement's** power will rush to your assistance and support. 3 You are not frail with God beside you. 4 Yet without **God** you are nothing. 5 The Atonement offers you God. 6 The gift **of your guiltlessness** that you refused is held by **God** in you, **the Christ.** 7 The Holy Spirit holds **the gift of guiltlessness** there for you. 8 God has not left **His** altar, though **God's** worshippers placed other gods upon **the altar.** 9 The temple still is holy, for the Presence that dwells within **the temple, the Christ** <*is*> Holiness.

Note # 77: The Son of God remains holy because that is the changeless Will of God. We can deny that we are made in our Father's image. Indeed, we can even deny God's Fatherhood, but our denial does not change the truth. Perhaps the greatest gift the Father gave us is that of God's Innocence. The innocent cannot know what does not exist. Thus, our Creator has never bought into our limiting belief that His Creation, the Sonship, could be anything other than like the Father, perfect, whole and complete. Our Father's knowledge of the truth about His Son insures that we remain guiltless and that our self-imposed denial of the truth will be brief. The Holy Spirit is the Voice for God that awakes the split-minded back to the oneness of the truth of reality and the Kingdom.

T-14.IX.4. In the temple, Holiness waits quietly for the return of them **who represents our whole-minded Big "S" Self that** loves **Holiness**. 2 The Presence knows they **that are currently split-minded** will return to purity and to grace. 3 The graciousness of God will take them **that are currently split-minded** gently in, and cover all their sense of pain and loss with the immortal assurance of their Father's Love. 4 There, fear of death will be replaced with joy of life. **They that are currently split-minded will be healed.** 5 For God is life, and they **that are currently split-minded**, abide in life. 6 Life is as holy as the Holiness by which **life** was created. 7 The Presence of Holiness lives in everything that lives, for Holiness created life, and leaves not what the **Holiness of God** created holy as Itself.

Note # 78: We are the shared Oneness of God. Everything that is created is an extension of the One. All our power to create comes from the shared power of the Mind of God. The Christ remains in the Mind of God and never loses the Love of God or the Christ's love for Its Creator. God is Life. Anything outside of the Mind of God is "dead" since what could be outside everything except the illusion of nothingness. Holiness means wholeness, which is God and the everything that comprises God. The "Everything" is indivisible, changeless and eternal.

T-14.IX.5. In this world you can become a spotless mirror, in which the Holiness of your Creator shines forth from you to all around you. 2 You can reflect Heaven here. 3 Yet no reflections of the images of other gods **that would arise from the ego's thought system** must dim the mirror that would hold God's reflection in **a mirror that reflects only the truth of Heaven**. 4 Earth can reflect Heaven or hell; **Earth can reflect** God or the ego. 5 You need but leave the mirror clean and clear of all the images of hidden darkness **caused by egoic consciousness that** you have drawn upon **your mirror**. 6 God will shine upon **your mirror, which is a reflection** of **God,** Himself. 7 Only the clear reflection of Himself can be perceived upon **your mirror**.

Note # 79: When we allow all egoic thinking to disappear from the mind of the decision-maker, we reclaim our divine birthright. When error has been removed from our split-mind, the whole-mindedness of our Christ consciousness will radiate what we are, which is the perfect reflection of the Creator and First Cause.

T-14.IX.6. Reflections are seen in light. 2 In darkness **reflections** are obscure, and **reflection's** meaning seems to lie only in shifting interpretations, rather than in themselves. 3 The reflection of God needs no interpretation. 4 **The reflection of God** is clear. 5 Clean but the mirror, and the message that shines forth from what the mirror holds out for everyone to see, no one can fail to understand. 6 **The mirror's reflection of God** is the message that the Holy Spirit is holding to the mirror that is in him, **the split-minded**. 7 **The split-minded** recognizes **the message of the Holy Spirit** because he, **the split-minded**, has been taught his need for **the message of the Holy Spirit**, but knows not where to look to find **the message for the remembrance for God**. 8 Let him, **the split-minded,** then, see **the message for the remembrance for God** in you and share **the Holy Spirit's message** with you.

Note # 80: The truth of what you are will be reawakened in you through the use of the thought system of the Holy Spirit. Give all your egoic misperceptions to the Holy Spirit so that the Holy Spirit can reinterpret and correct the errors in your thinking. This will allow the decision-maker within you to choose again. For to give, is to receive. When we forgive we wipe away egoic thinking from the mirror within our mind. This mirror should reflect only the Will of God within our mind. The Christ conscious part of the split-mind knows that our will and God's will are the same. The remembrance of God is the message of the Holy Spirit. It asks us to reclaim our divine birthright and our shared inheritance with the entire Sonship.

T-14.IX.7. Could you but realize for a single instant the power of healing that the reflection of God, shining in you, can bring to all the world, you could not wait to make the mirror of your mind clean to receive the image of the holiness that heals the world. 2 The image of holiness that shines in your mind is not obscure, and will not change. 3 **The image's** meaning to those who look upon it is not obscure, for everyone perceives **the image's meaning, which is the remembrance of God,** as the same. 4 All bring their different problems to **the image's** healing light, and all their problems find but healing there **in the remembrance of God**.

Note # 81: Remember God as your Creator and all the power that is of God is given onto you. God, being perfect love, shares this with you. Healing is simply the removal of all feelings and beliefs that you could be something other than as God created you. Healing wipes away all delusions that you are a little "s" self and, therefore, removes all obstacles that were hiding the light that you are. Healing is the return to whole-mindedness. The perfectness of the Father is reflected from you because it is you. The Big "S" Self, the Christ, shines forth.

T-14.IX.8. The response of holiness to any form of error is always the same. 2 There is no contradiction in what holiness calls forth. 3 **Holiness's** one response is healing, without regard for what **error** is brought to **holiness**. 4 Those who have learned to offer only healing, because of the reflection of holiness in them, are ready at last for Heaven. 5 There **in heaven**, holiness is not a reflection, but rather the actual condition of what was but reflected to them, **who offer only healing** here **on earth**. 6 God is no image, and **God's** creations, as part of **God,** hold **God** in them in truth. 7 They, **who offer only healing here on earth,** do not merely reflect truth, for they **who offer only healing here,**<are> truth.

Note # 82: The world of perception, if given to the guidance of the Holy Spirit, becomes a temporary learning device. It becomes a tool that the Holy Spirit utilizes for the remembrance for God. If given to the thought system of the ego, the world of perception becomes a tool that the ego utilizes to bear false witness to its erroneous belief that we are limited ego-bodies in competition with other separate ego-bodies. The Holy Spirit, if asked, will correct our egoic misperceptions into correct perception. Correct perception will teach us the underlying unity of ourselves with our brothers. The Laws of God dictate that to give is to receive. This is why the Atonement's message to the split-minded son is that the son must forgive to be forgiven, for as you give you receive. Forgiveness is the "Windex" or cleaning solvent that removes all beliefs born out of guilt from the mind of the split-minded. Forgiveness removes the ego's unholy trinity of sin, guilt and fear. With the removal of sin, guilt and fear, the world of perception becomes more reflective of reality, which is the truth found in the Kingdom or Heaven.

X. The Equality of Miracles

T-14.X.1. When no perception stands between God and **God's** creations, or between **God's** children and their own **children**, the knowledge of creation must continue forever. 2 The reflections you accept into the mirror of your mind in time but bring eternity nearer or farther. 3 But eternity itself is beyond all time. 4 Reach out of time and touch **eternity**, with the help of **eternity's** reflection in you. 5 And you will turn from time to holiness, as surely as the reflection of holiness calls everyone to lay all guilt aside. 6 Reflect the peace of Heaven here **in your world of perception**, and bring this world **of individual perception** to Heaven. 7 For the reflection of truth draws everyone to truth, and as they enter into **truth** they leave all reflections behind.

Note # 83: Truth just is. Truth comes from knowledge, which is changeless. The world of individual perception is based upon the concept that separation is possible. Separation is impossible for nothing exists outside the shared Mind of God. Since we lack knowledge, the closest that we can come to experiencing heaven's reality while in the world of perception, time and space is to perceive correctly. Correct or true perception reflects the truth but the perceiver does not "know" the truth. For knowing is being. And to perceive by definition is something less than knowledge. Perception involves thinking. Knowledge just is. This is why the world of perception can only reflect the truth of heaven. For how can nothing, which is what this world of limitation is, be a symbol for the truth? An illusion, even if it represents the reality of truth, is still an illusion. An illusion can symbolize our image of the truth but it is not the truth. It is merely a learning device so that the truth can shine forth and be understood and, therefore, correctly perceived.

T-14.X.2. In Heaven, reality is shared and not reflected. 2 By sharing **the** reflection **of Heaven's reality** here **in the world of perception, Heaven's** truth becomes the only perception the Son of God accepts. 3 And thus, remembrance of his Father dawns on him, and he can no longer be satisfied with anything but his own reality. 4 You on earth have no conception of limitlessness, for the world you seem to live in is a world of limits. 5 In this world, it is not true that anything without order of difficulty can occur. 6 The miracle, **which recognizes that there is no order of difficulty within miracles**, therefore, has a unique function, and is motivated by a unique Teacher, **the Holy Spirit,** Who brings the laws of another world**, Heaven,** to this **world of perception**. 7 The miracle is the one thing you can do **on earth** that transcends order **of difficulty**, being based not on differences but on equality.

Note # 84: The miracle contracts time because the Holy Spirit does not require any time to correct error. The only time required is to determine how long you will insist on the denial of reality or truth. The miracle does not change the truth. It merely brings illusions into the light, which results in the ego's thought system dissolving into the nothingness from which it arose. The miracle is based on the truth that there is no inequality in a shared oneness. In a shared Oneness, there is nothing outside the whole. The miracle transcends time since it only removes the imagined blocks we have placed to hide the truth. It does not change the truth; it only changes misperception into correct perception.

T-14.X.3. Miracles are not in competition, and the number of **miracles** that you can do is limitless. 2 **Miracles** can be simultaneous and legion. 3 This is not difficult to understand, once you conceive of **miracles** as possible at all. 4 What is more difficult to grasp is the lack of order of difficulty that stamps the miracle as something that must come from elsewhere, not from here **in the world of form and perception, in which order of difficulty appears everywhere.** 5 From the world's viewpoint, this **lack of order of difficulty** is impossible.

Note # 85: This world of form was made to obscure the truth. Again, the thought system of the ego is the opposite of the Holy Spirit's. In the world of perception, we see that there is a difference between tasks and that some tasks are more difficult to accomplish than others. To the Holy Spirit, there is no order of difficulty because there is only the changeless truth. The Holy Spirit realizes that illusions do not change truth. Illusions can have no reality of their own. All illusions disappear when brought into the light of truth. Heaven has no order of difficulty since Heaven is the Love of God, which is the truth. The "laws of perception" have no power over the Laws of God. The Holy Spirit simply knows that, "Nothing real can be threatened. Nothing unreal exists. Herein lies the peace of God." Due to this truth, all illusions then simple melt away.

T-14.X.4. Perhaps you have been aware of lack of competition among your thoughts, which even though **your thoughts** may conflict, **your thoughts** can occur together and in great numbers. 2 You may indeed be so used to this **multiplicity of thoughts** that it causes you little surprise. 3 Yet you are also used to classifying some of your thoughts as more important, larger or better, wiser, or more productive and valuable than others **thoughts.** 4 This **varying degree of importance you place upon your numerous thoughts** is true of the thoughts that cross the mind of those who think they live apart. 5 For some are reflections of Heaven, while others are motivated by the ego, which but seems to think.

Note # 86: Since our mind is split, our thoughts come from two different thought systems. There does appear to be differences in the importance of our numerous and often conflicting thoughts. Since one is based on truth and the other on illusion, there can be no real value on illusions except in the discovery that illusions cannot change truth. Because we believe that we are a limited ego-body, the thoughts of the ego must be given to the Holy Spirit so that these ideas that bear witness to the false idea that we are separate can be brought into the light of truth. Our split-mind is too identified with form to be able to overcome the illusion of the dream of separation. Being caught up in the belief that we are limited ego-bodies, our mind accepts that there must be degrees of difficulty because the thought system is based on differences, not equality and oneness. The Christ consciousness is aware of the truth. The ego or lower mind is aware of the illusion.

T-14.X.5. The result is a weaving, changing pattern that never rests and is never still. 2 **The changing pattern** shifts unceasingly across the mirror of your mind, and the reflections of Heaven last but a moment and grow dim, as darkness blots **the reflections of Heaven** out. 3 Where there was light, darkness removes **light** in an instant, and alternating patterns of light and darkness sweep constantly across your mind. 4 The little sanity that still remains is held together by a sense of order that you establish. 5 Yet the very fact that you can do this, and bring any order into chaos shows you that you are not an ego, and that more than an ego must be in you. 6 For the ego <*is*> chaos, and if **the ego** were all of you, no order at all would be possible. 7 Yet though the order you impose upon your mind limits the ego, **the order you impose upon your mind** also limits you. 8 To order is to judge, and to arrange by judgment. 9 Therefore **the order you impose upon your mind, which is based on judgment**, is not your function, but the Holy Spirit's **function.**

Note # 87: Being split-minded and without knowledge, we are incapable of judging anything correctly. If we do not know what we are, how can we know what is in our best interest. Believing that we are a limited ego-body in competition with other ego-bodies, we fail to see the unity of creation. Believing in separation, we believe we have differing goals. Only the Holy Spirit can judge, as only the Holy Spirit knows both the truth of what we are and what we dream we are. The function of the Holy Spirit is to turn our misperception into correct perception. Only the Holy Spirit understands the "Big Picture" and the role we are to play in it. ACIM states that the only judgment that we should make is that we are incapable of judging correctly. We should let the Holy Spirit do all our judging for us until we cease identifying ourselves as being within the dream of separation

T-14.X.6. It will seem difficult for you to learn that you have no basis at all for ordering your thoughts. 2 This lesson **that you have no basis at all for ordering your thoughts**, the Holy Spirit teaches by giving you the shining examples of miracles to show you that your way of ordering is wrong, but that a better way is offered you. 3 The miracle offers exactly the same response to every call for help. 4 **The miracle** does not judge the call **for help**. 5 **The miracle** merely recognizes what **the call for help** is, and answers accordingly. 6 **The miracle** does not consider which call is louder or greater or more important. 7 You may wonder how you who are still bound to judgment can be asked to do that which requires no judgment of your own. 8 The answer is very simple. 9 The power of God, and not of you, engenders miracles. 10 The miracle itself is but the witness that you have the power of God in you. 11 That is the reason why the miracle gives equal blessing to all who share in **the miracle**, and that is also why everyone shares in **the miracle**. 12 The power of God is limitless. 13 And being always maximal, **the power of God, which is represented in the miracle,** offers everything to every call from anyone. 14 There is no order of difficulty here. 15 A call for help is given help.

Note # 88: The miracle comes from the power of God, not from us. When we ask for the guidance of the Holy Spirit, all God's power is available to us.

T-14.X.7. The only judgment involved is the Holy Spirit's one division into two categories; one of love, and the other the call for love. 2 You cannot safely make this division **into the two categories; one of love and the other the call for love,** for you are much too confused either to recognize love, or to believe that everything else is nothing but a call for love. 3 You are too bound to form, and not to content. 4 What you consider content is not content at all. 5 **What you consider content** is merely form, and nothing else. 6 For you do not respond to what a brother really offers you, but only to the particular perception of his offering by which the ego judges **the brother's offering**.

Note # 89: Believing we are limited and in competition with our brother, we cannot judge what we perceive correctly. Relying on past misperception, we reach incorrect judgments of what we currently experience. Our viewpoint comes from the ego and, therefore, we perceive everything to be an attack. These alleged attacks upon us justify our own retaliatory attack in self-defense against what the ego perceives as a threat to its existence.

T-14.X.8. The ego is incapable of understanding content, and is totally unconcerned with **content**. 2 To the ego, if the form is acceptable the content must be **acceptable**. 3 Otherwise **the ego** will attack the form. 4 If you believe you understand something of the "dynamics" of the ego, let me assure you that you understand nothing of **the "dynamics" of the ego**. 5 For of yourself you could not understand **the "dynamics" of the ego**. 6 The study of the ego is not the study of the mind. 7 In fact, the ego enjoys studying itself, and thoroughly approves the undertakings of students who would "analyze" **the ego**, thus approving **the ego's** importance. 8 Yet **the students who study the ego** but study form with meaningless content. 9 For their teacher, **which is the ego,** is senseless, though careful to conceal this fact behind impressive sounding words, but which lack any consistent sense when **the words** are put together.

Note # 90: The ego wants us to get caught up in the form of this world because form arose out of the idea that we were separate. The Holy Spirit reinterprets form into the idea that everything in the ego's world of perception must be either love or a cry for love. To the Holy Spirit, any apparent attack by a brother upon another is a cry for love and, therefore, should be responded to with love rather than attack.

To the ego this would justify a counter-attack in order to defend the ego's need to be right. All apparent form is either a demonstration of love or a cry for love. Love or a cry for love is the content that is hidden beneath all experience in the world of perception.

If we choose to study the ego, we confirm the ego's existence and its reality. This strengthens our belief that the separation is real.

T-14.X.9. This **total unconcern with content** is characteristic of the ego's judgments. 2 Separately, **the ego's judgments** seem to hold, but put **the ego's judgments** together and the system of thought that arises from joining **the ego's judgments** is incoherent and utterly chaotic. 3 For form is not enough for meaning, and the underlying lack of content makes a cohesive system impossible. 4 Separation therefore remains the ego's chosen condition. 5 For no one alone can judge the ego truly. 6 Yet when two or more join together in searching for truth, the ego can no longer defend **the ego's** lack of content. 7 The fact of union tells them that **they are joined together and that the ego's thought system** is not true.

Note # 91: The ego's thought system is based on separation, which births conflict and competition. The goal of the ego is to keep the split-minded apart so that they continue to believe that they are not connected to another and have no common purpose or goal. Love is unknown to the ego and, therefore, the ego is incapable of understanding that love or the cry for love could be the underlying content or message behind any form of experience that the ego perceives. Since God is love, we, the Sonship, must be love. The ego's thought system, which knows nothing of love, cannot make sense to the Holy Spirit Who knows us as God's loving Son. The Holy Spirit simply bypasses and ignores the insane ego and realigns our mind's thinking to the truth.

T-14.X.10. It is impossible to remember God in secret and alone. 2 For remembering **God** means you are not alone, and are willing to remember **that you are not alone.** 3 Take no thought for yourself, for no thought you hold <*is*> for yourself. 4 If you would remember your Father, let the Holy Spirit order your thoughts and give only the answer with which **the Holy Spirit** answers you. 5 Everyone seeks for love as you do, but knows **love** not unless he joins with you in seeking **love.** 6 If you undertake the search together, you bring with you a light so powerful that what you see is given meaning. 7 The lonely journey fails because **the lonely journey** has excluded what **love** would find.

Note # 92: We cannot find love by exclusion. Love is inclusive and requires more than one in the world of form. The world of form was made to exclude. We cannot find love in the world of form unless we include something to love. Love must be shared; therefore, we cannot find love alone. Since love is a shared joining, the journey for love cannot be made alone.

T-14.X.11. As God communicates to the Holy Spirit in you, so does the Holy Spirit translate **God's** communications through you, so you can understand **God's communications to you.** 2 God has no secret communications, for everything of **God** is perfectly open and freely accessible to all, being for all. 3 Nothing lives in secret, and what you would hide from the Holy Spirit is nothing. 4 Every interpretation you would lay upon a brother is senseless. 5 Let the Holy Spirit show **your brother** to you, and teach you both **your brother's** love and **your brother's** call for love. 6 Neither his mind nor **your mind** holds more than these two orders of thought. **In the world of perception there is only love or a cry for love.** .

Note # 93: God communicates with us through the constant flow of His Love to His Creations. True communication is shared with all. In the world of perception, we believe that we can have private thought. There can be no private thought that we withhold from the Holy Spirit. If we are to accept the Atonement for ourselves, we need to give all our experience over to the Holy Spirit for proper interpretation. The ego judges incorrectly since it lacks knowledge and is concerned with form and ignores content. Yet, the Holy Spirit translates everything in the world of perception as either love or a cry for love. Form is ignored and the Holy Spirit observes content. Love or a cry for love is the underlying content of all we perceive and forgiveness and love are the lessons to be remembered. These are the only thoughts that reflect the truth and are real in our mind. Attack thoughts arise from the ego's belief in lack and separation. The nothingness of egoic illusions must give way to the light of truth.

T-14.X.12. The miracle is the recognition that this is true. 2 Where there is love, your brother must give **love** to you because of what **love** is. 3 But where there is a call for love, you must give **love** because of what you are. 4 Earlier I said this course will teach you how to remember what you are, restoring to you your Identity. 5 We have already learned that this Identity is shared. 6 The miracle becomes the means of sharing **your Identity, which is love**. 7 By supplying your Identity wherever **your Identity** is not recognized, you will recognize **your Identity**. 8 And God Himself, Who wills to be with His Son forever, will bless each recognition of His Son with all the Love **God** holds for him. 9 Nor will the power of all **God's** Love be absent from any miracle you offer to **God's** Son. 10 How, then, can there be any order of difficulty among **the miracles**?

Note # 94: To remember God, Who is love, is to be loved. Love does not exclude, therefore, everything that is real is part of the Mind of God and is to be loved. We cannot deny love to a brother and not deny love to ourselves, for to give is to receive. The miracle recognizes that in the world of perception, form must not be mistaken for the underlying content. The content or message, which is actually being communicated during the experience, is either love or a cry for love. With the unity of the Sonship, all misperception can be handled the same. No illusion can stand up to the light of the truth, which holds the Power of God.

XI. The Test of Truth

T-14.XI.1. Yet the essential thing is learning that <*you do not know.*> 2 Knowledge is power, and all power is of God. 3 You who have tried to keep power for yourself have "lost" **power**. 4 You still have the power, but you have interposed so much between **power** and your awareness of **power** that you cannot use **power**. 5 Everything you have taught yourself has made your power more and more obscure to you. 6 You know not what **power** is, nor where. 7 You have made a semblance of power and a show of strength so pitiful that **what you have made of your power** must fail you. 8 For power is not a seeming strength, and truth is beyond semblance of any kind. 9 Yet all that stands between you and the power of God in you is but your learning of the false, and of your attempts to undo the true.

Note # 95: All power comes from God. When we deny what we are, which is a creation of God, we deny our inherited birthright. By denying the Fatherhood of God, we deny that we are an extension of all of the power that is of God. We deny the truth and argue for our littleness. The little "s" self lives in fear and, therefore, cannot create like God because it believes itself to be limited. Instead of creating, we utilize our mind for projection, which is a process of exclusion. Projection is based on the ego's belief in lack. We believe that we are limited ego-bodies and, therefore, sharing is impossible. When we believe we are a body, we learn from the ego's thought system that any form of sharing requires sacrifice. True love requires no sacrifice.

T-14.XI.2. Be willing, then, for all of **your learning of the false** to be undone, and be glad that you are not bound to **your false egoic learning** forever. 2 For you have taught yourself how to imprison the Son of God, a lesson so unthinkable that only the insane, in deepest sleep, could even dream of **how to imprison the Son of God**. 3 Can God learn how not to be God? 4 And can His Son, given all power by **God**, learn to be powerless? 5 What have you taught yourself that you can possibly prefer to keep, in place of what you <*have*> and what you <*are?*>

Note # 96: The egoic thought system teaches that we wish to be a little "s" self, rather than the Oneness of the Christ. To be everything is to be what we are, the Big "S" Self. If we remembered the truth, we would not choose specialness over the right to be happy. The Holy Spirit's task is to guide us through the unlearning process of everything the ego has taught us. Once the ego's thought system is brought into the light of truth, we will freely choose happiness over specialness. We will reclaim our place in the Mind of God and realize our will and the Father's Will are One.

T-14.XI.3. Atonement teaches you how to escape forever from everything that you have taught yourself in the past, by showing you only what you are <*now.*> 2 Learning has been accomplished before **learning's** effects are manifest. 3 Learning is therefore in the past, but **past learned** influence determines the present by giving **the present** whatever meaning **the past** holds for you. 4 **Yet, in fact,** <*Your*> learning gives the present no meaning at all. 5 Nothing you have ever learned can help you understand the present, or teach you how to undo the past . 6 Your past is what you have taught yourself. 7 <*Let*> **your past** all go. 8 Do not attempt to understand any event or anything or anyone in **the past's** "light," for the darkness in which you try to see can only obscure. 9 Put no confidence at all in darkness **from the past to** illuminate your understanding, for if you do you contradict the light, and thereby think you see the darkness. 10 Yet darkness cannot be seen, for **darkness** is nothing more than a condition in which seeing becomes impossible.

Note # 97: The focus of time for the ego is in the past. If the present is viewed from the reference point of past misperceptions, the ego can insure that the past "mislearnings" will generate the same misperceptions in the present and future. The Holy Spirit's emphasis is on the present or the <now>. If we do not carry past misperceptions into the present, we will be able to see the present experience as a neutral learning device and decide to choose differently.

T-14.XI.4. You who have not yet brought all of the darkness you have taught yourself into the light in you, can hardly judge the truth and value of this course. 2 Yet God did not abandon you. 3 And so you have another lesson sent from **God**, already learned for every child of light by **the Holy Spirit** to Whom God gave **the lesson**. 4 This lesson shines with God's glory, for in **this lesson** lies **God's** power, which **God** shares so gladly with His Son. 5 Learn of **God's** happiness, which is **your happiness**. 6 But to accomplish this **learning that God's happiness is your happiness**, all your dark **egoic** lessons must be brought willingly to truth, and joyously laid down by hands open to receive, not **hands** closed to take. 7 Every dark **egoic** lesson that you bring to **the Holy Spirit** Who teaches light **the Holy Spirit** will accept from you, because you do not want **the egoic lessons of darkness**. 8 And **the Holy Spirit** will gladly exchange each one for the bright lesson **the Holy Spirit** has learned for you. 9 Never believe that any lesson you have learned apart from **the Holy Spirit** means anything.

Note # 98: Give our misperception to the Holy Spirit and He will reinterpret them correctly. The Holy Spirit only teaches the truth about what you and your brother are by bringing the ego's misperception into the light of love and forgiveness. The Holy Spirit proclaims the guiltlessness of God's Son. Without the guidance of the Holy Spirit, we are unable to rediscover our guiltlessness. We believe the ego which teaches that we have sinned and so we deserve punishment. Since we believe in sin, guilt and fear, we fail to question the sanity of the ego's thought system.

T-14.XI.5. You have one test, as sure as God, by which to recognize if what you learned is true. 2 **This test is** if you are wholly free of fear of any kind, and if all those who meet or even think of you share in your perfect peace, then you can be sure that you have learned God's lesson, and not your own **egoic lesson**. 3 Unless all this is true, there are dark lessons in your mind that hurt and hinder you, and everyone around you. 4 The absence of perfect peace means but one thing: You think you do not will for God's Son what his Father wills for him. 5 Every dark lesson teaches **you that your will differs from God's Will**, in one form or another. 6 And each bright lesson with which the Holy Spirit will replace the dark ones you do not accept, teaches you that you will with the Father and His Son, **the Christ**.

Note # 99: The test is the perfect peace of God. If anyone in your world of perception, including yourself, fails to share in the peace of God, then you still harbor guilt within you. The absence of perfect peace means that you think your will for God's Son is different than what his Father wills for him. Fear cannot be undone until the Sonship's guiltlessness has been accepted unconditionally. The Holy Spirit teaches the unity of both the Sonship and the Father. Being of One Mind, They have the same shared Will. Nothing exists outside the Mind of God.

T-14.XI.6. Do not be concerned about how you can learn a lesson so completely different from everything that you have taught yourself. 2 How would you know? 3 Your part is very simple. 4 You need only recognize that everything you learned **from the thought system of the ego,** you do not want. 5 Ask to be taught **by the Holy Spirit**, and do not use your **past egoic** experiences to confirm what you have learned **from your egoic past**. 6 When your peace is threatened or disturbed in any way, say to yourself:

7 *I do not know what anything, including this, means. 8 And so I do not know how to respond to **this experience or anything**. 9 And I will not use my own past **egoic** learning as the light to guide me now.*

10 By this refusal to attempt to teach yourself what you do not know, the Guide, **the Holy Spirit,** Whom God has given you will speak to you. 11 **The Christ** will take His rightful place in your awareness the instant you abandon **the attempt to teach yourself**, and offer **this experience** to **the Holy Spirit**.

Note # 100: ACIM states that we need to realize that we do not know that we do not know. We need to realize that we operate under the egoic belief system that does not even know what we are. It is a system whose goal is to keep you ignorant to the idea that you are ignorant. If you do not know that there are other possibilities and options, you will remain in victim consciousness. We will remain at the level of learning, which would be called unconscious incompetence. There are four levels of learning.

The four levels of understanding or learning are:
1) **Unconscious Incompetence:** You don't know that you don't know. **Example:** Someone who doesn't know that he can't ride a bike.
2) **Conscious Incompetence:** You know that you don't know. **Example:** Trying to ride a bike, you fall off. Now you know, you don't know how to ride a bike
3) **Conscious Competence:** You need to be consciously aware of the task in order to perform it **Example:** When you first learn to ride a bike you need to focus your attention on the task at hand. Being attentive and careful, you succeed at riding the bike.
4) **Unconscious Competence.** You can perform the task automatically without any conscious effort.

Example: Riding a bike after you have mastered the task.

The ego's goal is to keep us unconsciously incompetent so that we remain mindless. It does this through victim consciousness. The ego does not want us to reclaim our mind's ability to act as the decision-maker. The Holy Spirit's thought system is designed to help us at least reach the level of conscious incompetence. At this level we can at least decide to choose again and quickly move up the competency ladder.

T-14.XI.7. You cannot be your guide to miracles, for it is your **egoic self** who made **miracles** necessary. 2 And because you did **make miracles necessary**, the means on which you can depend for miracles has been provided for you. 3 God's Son can make no needs his Father will not meet, if **God's split-minded Son will** but turn to **God** ever so little. 4 Yet **the Father** cannot compel His Son to turn to **the Father** and remain **God**, Himself. 5 It is impossible that God lose His Identity, for if **God** did **lose His Identity**, you would lose **your identity**. 6 And being **your identity, God** cannot change Himself, for your Identity is changeless. 7 The miracle acknowledges **God's** changelessness by seeing **God's** Son as he always was, and not as he would make himself. 8 The miracle brings the effects that only guiltlessness can bring, and thus establishes the fact that guiltlessness must be **God's Son**.

Note # 101: The Christ is the home of the Father. They are One. Perhaps the greatest gift that the Father gave to the Sonship is God's own innocence. Since God does not know what does not exist, your imagined dreams cannot affect truth's reality. Our imagined and insane dreams can do nothing to change the reality that the Sonship is an extension of the Father and always perfect, whole and complete like His Father. This is what protects the guiltlessness of the Sonship. We can pretend that we are something that we are not, but we cannot change our perfect nature as host of our Father. We have made a play school where we can pretend that we are limited and separate, but when we get tired of playing the game of specialness, we will lay down our toys and return to the real world of union with God. God has guaranteed that His Children cannot hurt themselves because their toy guns have no real bullets. We can pretend we are good or bad guys. We can pretend that we even die; yet, this pretending can never change what we are because we have always been, and always will be like our Father, changeless, perfect, whole and complete.

Projection is the egoic tool that the split-mind utilizes for image making. These projected images are what we perceive to be our provisional reality.

T-14.XI.8. How can you, so firmly bound to guilt and committed so to remain **in guilt**, establish for yourself your guiltlessness? 2 **It** is impossible for you who believe you are guilty to establish for yourself your own guiltlessness. 3 But be sure that you are willing to acknowledge that **to establish for yourself your own guiltlessness when you believe you are guilty** <*is*> impossible. 4 It is only because you think that you can run some little part, or deal with certain aspects of your life alone, that the guidance of the Holy Spirit is limited. 5 Thus would you make **the Holy Spirit's guidance** undependable, and use this fancied undependability as an excuse for keeping certain dark lessons from **the Holy Spirit**. 6 And by so limiting the guidance that you would accept **from the Holy Spirit**, you are unable to depend on miracles to answer all your problems for you.

Note # 102: As long as we fail to understand that we are totally unable to self-correct, we will insist that we can self-direct our own relearning process of what we are. We will believe that there are degrees of difficulty and that some matters can be handled by ourselves alone. We will fail to turn all of our experiences over to the Holy Spirit. Thus, we will believe that the thought system of the Holy Spirit is ineffective simply because we have failed to request the Holy Spirit's guidance of everything that matters. ACIM states that we need to control our fears and turn everything that matters over to the Holy Spirit. The Holy Spirit has been given the mission to return the split-minded to right-mindedness. The

Holy Spirit cannot fail in this mission for the power of God guarantees its success. The only thing that delays the return of the Son to the remembrance of God is the Son's claim that there is something outside the Mind of God. God's Will cannot be mocked since there is nothing outside the Will of God. When we refuse to give all our perceptions over to the Holy Spirit, it is due to our desire to maintain egoic specialness. We still place value on certain aspects of egoic specialness and we wish to continue to claim that we are the arbitrators of truth.

T-14.XI.9. Do you think that what the Holy Spirit would have you give **the Holy Spirit** would withhold from you? 2 You have no problems that **the Holy Spirit** cannot solve by offering you a miracle. 3 Miracles are for you. 4 And every fear or pain or trial you have has been undone. 5 **The Holy Spirit** has brought all of **your fear, pain or trial** to light. **The Holy Spirit** having accepted **all your fear, pain or trial on behalf of you**, **has** recognized **that your fear, pain or trial** never were **real**. 6 There are no dark lessons **the Holy Spirit** has not already lightened for you. 7 The **egoic** lessons you would teach yourself **the Holy Spirit** has corrected already. 8 **The egoic lessons you would teach yourself** do not exist in **the Holy Spirit's** Mind at all. 9 For the past binds **the Holy Spirit** not, and therefore **the past** binds not you. 10 **The Holy Spirit** does not see time as you do. 11 And each miracle **the Holy Spirit** offers you corrects your use of time, and makes **your use of time, the Holy Spirit's use of time.**

<u>Note # 103:</u> The Holy Spirit utilizes time to correct errors. Errors exist only in your mind's belief in the past. It is your belief in the past that the ego focuses upon because this guarantees that in the present you will continue to rerun your past egoic programs, thus insuring the same results. The Holy Spirit removes past misperception from your vision so that you become only aware of the <now>. Without your past baggage, the decision-maker in you can choose again.

T-14.XI.10.The Holy Spirit Who has freed you from the past would teach you are free of **your past**. 2 **The Holy Spirit** would but have you accept **the Holy Spirit's** accomplishments as **your accomplishments**, because **the Holy Spirit** did **these accomplishments** for your **behalf**. 3 And because **the Holy Spirit** did **these accomplishments on your behalf, these accomplishments** <are> **your accomplishments**. 4 **The Holy Spirit** has made you free of what you **egoically** made. 5 You can deny **the Holy Spirit**, but you cannot call on **the Holy Spirit** in vain. 6 **The Holy Spirit** always gives **the Holy Spirit's** gifts in place of **your egoic gifts, which you made to attempt to prove your belief in your own littleness.** 7 **The Holy Spirit** would establish **the Holy Spirit's** bright teaching so firmly in your mind, that no dark lesson of guilt can abide in what **the Holy Spirit** has established as holy by **the Holy Spirit's** Presence. 8 Thank God that **the Holy Spirit** is there and works through you. 9 And all **the Holy Spirit's** works are **your works**. 10 **The Holy Spirit** offers you a miracle with every **miracle** you let **the Holy Spirit** do through you.

<u>Note # 104:</u> The Holy Spirit will not fail to fulfill His function of correcting our split-minded thinking if we ask for His Guidance. Because we have free will, the Holy Spirit will wait to be asked before He can teach us the truth about our true-shared nature of the One Self. By asking for guidance, we become happy learners of the Atonement principle that the Holy Spirit teaches.

T-14.XI.11. God's Son will always be indivisible. 2 As we are held as one in God, so do we learn as one in **God**. 3 God's Teacher, **the Holy Spirit,** is as like to His Creator as is His Son, and through His Teacher, **the Holy Spirit,** does God proclaim His Oneness and His Son's **Oneness**. 4 Listen in silence, and do not raise your voice against **the Holy Spirit**. 5 For **the Holy Spirit** teaches the miracle of oneness, and before **the Holy Spirit's** lesson division disappears. 6 Teach like **the Holy Spirit** here **on earth**, and you will remember that you have always created like your Father **created**. 7 The miracle of creation has never ceased, having the holy stamp of immortality upon **the miracle of creation**. 8 This

shared Oneness is the Will of God for all creation, and all creation joins in willing this **same shared Oneness of God for all creation.**

Note # 105: The Holy Spirit does not actually teach oneness, but rather removes all the blocks we have placed to block the remembrance of the Oneness that we are. Once the blocks have been removed from our mind, we simply recall what we really are. The Holy Spirit does not have to teach us what we naturally are. It merely must gently reawaken the Son of God from what the split-minded erroneously thought we had become. We always remain perfect, whole and complete, but during the dream of specialness, we identify ourselves as actually being a body in the dream of separation. We remain the shared Oneness of the Mind of God. Created like our Father, the Son of God has been given the same power to extend the Christ to His own creations. Thus, the Father, the First Cause, "becomes" a "Grandparent" to His Son's Children. All parts share the Oneness of the Mind of God. Creation continues to extend Itself eternally and infinitely. For this is the Will of God.

T-14.XI.12. Those who remember always that they know nothing, and who have become willing to learn everything, will learn **everything**. 2 But whenever they trust themselves, **they fail to remember that they know nothing and, therefore,** they will not learn. 3 They **who fail to remember that they know nothing** have destroyed their motivation for learning by thinking they already know. 4 Think not you understand anything until you pass the test of perfect peace, for peace and understanding go together and never can be found alone. 5 **Peace and understanding** each brings the other with it, for it is the law of God **that peace and understanding** not be separate. 6 **Peace and understanding** are cause and effect, each to the other, so where one is absent the other cannot be.

Note # 106: The test to know that learning is truth is that true learning will bring you peace. If you do not recover peace from the lesson, you can be sure that you have chosen the ego's thought system as your teacher. For the ego always teaches guilt through attack. The thought system of the Holy Spirit always teaches the Peace of God. Peace and understanding are always found together. They are what the Holy Spirit teaches. The ego always teaches attack through its use of sin, guilt, and fear.

The Holy Spirit requires a happy learner who wants Its guidance. If we believe that we already know but actually are ignorant of the truth, we are at the level of unconscious incompetence. At this level of unconscious incompetence, we fail to know that we don't know and, therefore, we see no need to ask for the Holy Spirit's help. This level of understanding and learning, unconscious incompetence, is where the ego wants us to remain. The Holy Spirit needs us to be at the minimum level of conscious incompetence. At this level of conscious incompetence, we know that we do not know and, therefore, can ask for help from the Holy Spirit. We can allow the decision-maker to choose again. We are no longer trapped in victim consciousness.

Line # 6 states, "Peace and understanding are cause and effect, each to the other, so where one is absent the other cannot be." Similarly the Father is Cause and the Sonship is the Effect. We complete God. Cause and Effect are so interconnected that you cannot have one without the other. This is the inseparability of the Oneness. Only extension, not separation is possible.

T-14.XI.13. Only those who recognize they cannot know unless the effects of understanding are with them, can really learn at all. 2 For **to recognize the effects of understanding**, it must be peace they want, and nothing else. 3 Whenever you think you **egoically** know, peace will depart from you, because you have abandoned the Teacher of peace, **which is the Holy Spirit**. 4 Whenever you fully realize that you know not, peace will return, for you will have invited Him, **the Teacher of peace,** to do so by abandoning the ego on behalf of **the Holy Spirit**. 5 Call not upon the ego for anything; it is only this **abandoning of the ego on behalf of the Holy Spirit** that you need do. 6 The Holy Spirit will, of Himself, fill every mind that so makes room for **the Holy Spirit**.

Note # 107: Give all your beliefs of limitation to the Holy Spirit and those limiting beliefs will be dissolved into the nothingness. The nothingness of your limiting beliefs birthed the mad idea that your will could be different from the shared Will of the Father. The peace and understanding that is our divine birthright will not be denied us since the function of the Holy Spirit is to return us to whole-mindedness. Understanding and peace are the forerunners to the return to knowledge. God will take this final step to the return of knowledge on our behalf. Therefore, we cannot fail. Our role is merely to offer all of our perceptions to the Holy Spirit and accept the Atonement for ourselves.

T-14.XI.14. If you want peace you must abandon the teacher of attack, **which is the ego**. 2 The Teacher of peace, **the Holy Spirit,** will never abandon you. 3 You can desert **the Holy Spirit** but **the Holy Spirit** will never reciprocate, for **the Holy Spirit's** faith in you is **the Holy Spirit's** understanding. 4 **The Holy Spirit's understanding of you as the Christ** is as firm as is **the Holy Spirit's** faith in His Creator, and **the Holy Spirit** knows that faith in His Creator must encompass faith in His creation, **God's Son**. 5 In this consistency lies **God's** Holiness, which **God** cannot abandon. for it is not **God's** Will to **abandon His Holiness.** 6 With your perfection ever in **God's** sight, **God** gives the gift of peace to everyone who perceives the need for peace, and who would have **peace**. 7 Make way for peace, and it will come. 8 For understanding is in you, and from **understanding** peace must come.

Note # 108: To obtain the understanding and the peace that the Father wants for His Son, we must unlearn everything that the egoic thought system has taught us. This unlearning process is the function of the Holy Spirit. It is not our function to teach the undoing of the ego, since we lack knowledge of what we are. Believing that we are a limited-ego body, we cannot self-correct this same error. We are oblivious to even the realization that we have committed this error. Only the Holy Spirit can correct our misperception because only the Holy Spirit knows the truth about what we are and is also aware of the dream we have entrapped ourselves within. God has never abandoned His Son. The idea of the Holy Spirit came into being at the time of the separation to counteract the belief that God's Son was not guiltless. If asked, the Holy Spirit will correct the error of guilt by teaching the Atonement to the split-minded. Peace and understanding are the natural result of the lessons taught by the thought system of the Holy Spirit. Our innocence is reclaimed.

T-14.XI.15. The power of God, from which **understanding and peace** both arise, is yours as surely as **understanding and peace** is **God's**. 2 You think you know **God** not, only because, alone, it is impossible to know **God**. 3 Yet see the mighty works that **God** will do through you, and you must be convinced you did **these mighty works** through **God**. 4 It is impossible to deny the Source of effects so powerful **that these mighty works** could not be of **your egoic little "s" self**. 5 Leave room for **God**, and you will find yourself so filled with power that nothing will prevail against your peace. 6 And this will be the test by which you recognize that you have understood.

Note # 109: Of myself, my little "s" self, I can do nothing. But if I accept my divine birthright and be the Big "S" Self, God can do everything through me. This is not arrogance on my part. It is merely the acceptance of truth. The height of arrogance is when we deny God's Fatherhood and claim to make ourselves limited and little. Because we, the Sonship, are all interconnected, we cannot know God alone. Ask for the guidance of the Holy Spirit. His guidance will reunite the Sonship and reclaim our denied remembrance for God. The return of peace and understanding to our minds will demonstrate that we are following the correct Teacher, the Holy Spirit, and not the ego's thought system.

Our inner peace is the litmus test that determines with whom our decision-maker is siding. If our inner peace is lost, we have slipped into fearful egoic thinking. We need to quiet our egoic chatter and choose again. Be aware that the ego will always answer first so it is important that once we have chosen again, we recheck our feelings. If inner-peace has not been restored, we need to rerun the procedure until our peace of mind has returned.

Chapter 15. THE HOLY INSTANT

I. The Two Uses of Time

T-15.I.1.Can you imagine what it means to have no cares, no worries, no anxieties, but merely to be perfectly calm and quiet all the time? 2 Yet **to be perfectly calm all the time** is what time is for; to learn just **perfect calmness** and nothing more. 3 God's Teacher, **the Holy Spirit,** cannot be satisfied with His teaching until **His teaching** constitutes all your learning. 4 **The Holy Spirit** has not fulfilled **the Holy Spirit's** teaching function until you have become such a consistent learner that you learn only of **the Holy Spirit's thought system**. 5 When **you learn only of the Holy Spirit interpretation of what** has happened, you will no longer need a teacher or time in which to learn.

Note # 1: The goal of the Holy Spirit is to teach you Its thought system which will restore you to the Christ, which is the remembrance of God. The Holy Spirit teaches the lessons necessary for the restoration of knowledge and acceptance of your divine birthright.

T-15.I.2.One source of perceived discouragement from which you may suffer is your belief that this **perfect calmness takes time to learn** and that the results of the Holy Spirit's teaching are far in the future. 2 This is not so. 3 For the Holy Spirit uses time in **the Holy Spirit's** Own way, and is not bound by **time**. 4 Time is **the Holy Spirit's** friend in teaching. 5 **Time** does not waste **the Holy Spirit,** as **time** does **waste** you. 6 And all the waste that time seems to bring with **time** is due but to your identification with the ego, which uses time to support **the ego's** belief in destruction. 7 The ego, like the Holy Spirit, uses time to convince you of the inevitability of the goal and end of **the ego's** teaching. 8 To the ego the goal **of time** is death, which <*is*> **time's** end. 9 But to the Holy Spirit the goal **of time** is life, which <*has*> no end.

Note # 2: The ego uses time to demonstrate that you are a limited ego-body. The ultimate proof of this is your death. The Holy Spirit knows that you are unlimited spirit and that you are eternal. The Holy Spirit uses time to demonstrate that you are a shared oneness with your Creator.

T-15.I.3.The ego is an ally of time, but not a friend **of time**. 2 For **the ego** is as mistrustful of death as **the ego** is of life, and what **the ego** wants for you **the ego** cannot tolerate **for the ego, itself**. 3 The ego wants <*you*> dead, but not itself **dead**. 4 The outcome of **the ego's** strange religion must therefore be the conviction that **the ego** can pursue you beyond the grave. 5 And out of **the ego** unwillingness for you to find peace even in death, **the ego** offers you immortality in hell. 6 **The ego** speaks to you of Heaven, but assures you that Heaven is not for you. 7 How can the guilty hope for Heaven?

Note # 3: The ego associates itself with you and the body but does not wish the ultimate death of its host. If your existence were to end, the ego's existence would also be terminated. It is this termination of the ego's existence that it fears most since its specialness would end. Therefore, the ego offers you some hope that you may exist after the death of the body. Unfortunately for us, the ego's thought system has already condemned its host, our split mind, to hell. Due to our mind's acceptance of the ego's belief in sin, guilt and fear, the ego demands eternal punishment for us. Thus, we, the ego's guilty host, burn forever in Hell.

T-15.I.4. The belief in hell is inescapable to those who identify with the ego. 2 **For those who identify with the ego,** their nightmares and their fears are all associated with **hell.** 3 The ego teaches that hell is in the future, for this is what all **the ego's** teaching is directed to. 4 Hell is **the ego's** goal. 5 For although the ego aims at death and dissolution as an end, **the ego** does not believe **in death and dissolution.** 6 The goal of death, which **the ego** craves for you, leaves **the ego** unsatisfied. 7 No one who follows the ego's teaching is without the fear of death. 8 Yet if death were thought of merely as an end to pain, would **death** be feared? 9 We have seen this strange paradox in the ego's thought system before, but never so clearly as here **in the ego's teaching of death.** 10 For the ego must seem to keep fear from you to hold your allegiance. 11 Yet **the ego** must engender fear in order to maintain **the ego,** itself. 12 Again the ego tries, and all too frequently succeeds, in doing both. **The ego keeps you from fear yet also engenders fear. The ego does this** by using dissociation for holding **the ego's** contradictory aims together so that **these contradictory egoic aims of both keeping you from fear yet also engendering fear** seem to be reconciled. 13 The ego teaches thus: Death is the end as far as hope of Heaven goes. 14 Yet because you and the ego cannot be separated, and because **the ego** cannot conceive of **the ego's** own death, **the ego** will pursue you still, because guilt is eternal. 15 Such is the ego's version of immortality. 16 And it is **the ego's belief that guilt is eternal which** the ego's version of time supports.

Note # 4: The ego wants eternal life. If the ego's thought system were to result in the permanent death of the existence of its host, the ego's existence would also be terminated. In order to get around this dilemma, the ego says to its host that there is something beyond the death of the body. In the belief system of the ego, heaven or hell awaits you after death. This is because the mind is not the body and, therefore, the mind or "soul" continues after death. Unfortunately for us, sin with its accompanying guilt is also eternal. Sin demands punishment for the god of the ego is a vengeful god. The possibility of Heaven or happiness is offered to us by the ego. This egoic possibility of Heaven helps us control our fear and, therefore, our mind continues to support the ego's thought system. Yet, the law of the ego is, "Seek, but do not find." The ego tells us to look for happiness and heaven but the ego never wants us to find either. The ego's vested interest in sin, guilt and fear require that you never achieve the removal of guilt. This unholy trinity of sin, guilt and fear must always remain in our minds to insure the survival of the ego.

Hell was invented as the place where the ego can maintain its existence by keeping your mind trapped in guilt. What better place than hell to keep our mind in victim consciousness? Hell, being eternal and with no escape, insures the continuation of the ego existence. Unfortunately for us, our belief in sin, guilt and fear, dooms us to hell. Our desire for specialness and the little "s" self that specialness brings costs us our happiness. Yet, this trade-off allows us to continue to claim that we are right. We continue to claim that we are the arbitrator of truth. We have traded our divine birthright in exchange for hell so that we could say we are capable of doing something other than God's Will. We exchange the happiness of everything, which is God's Will for His Son, for the need to be special, limited, egoically "right" and unhappy. This is the logical conclusion of the ego's thought system. It is this final outcome of the ego's thought system that the ego attempts to hide from us. This is why the ego is constantly telling us that something outside ourselves will bring us happiness. The mantra of the ego is always, "I will be happy when…" Yet, when we achieve that goal and we are still unhappy, the ego tells us something else will do the trick. "Seek but do not find." is the endless goal of the ego.

T-15.I.5. The ego teaches that Heaven is here and now because the future is hell. 2 Even when **the ego** attacks so savagely that it tries to take the life of someone who thinks **the ego** is the only voice, it speaks of hell even to him. 3 For **the ego** tells him hell is here as well, and bids him leap from hell into oblivion. 4 The only time the ego allows anyone to look upon with equanimity is the past. 5 And even there, **the past's** only value is that **the past** is no more.

Note # 5: The ego's focus for time is the past. The ego knows that we were under the control of its thought system in the past. Therefore, the ego desires that we remain in the victim consciousness that our egoic past represents. We bring our egoic past judgments into the present so that we never experience the <now> and thus, our future replicates the past. Since we are never in the <now>, we fail to hear the voice of the Holy Spirit. We do not hear the call to choose again. Happiness can be in the past but it can never become our future reality. We are allowed to strive for happiness but never find it. The guilt of sin must always be maintained and sin requires eternal punishment. Under the thought system of the ego, this punishment can be temporarily put off until our body's death. At death, the wages of sin will be rewarded in the fires of hell. This is what the thought system of the ego offers us and this is why our ego does not want its host, our mind, to examine its logic.

T-15.I.6. How bleak and despairing is the ego's use of time! 2 And how terrifying! 3 For underneath **the ego's** fanatical insistence that the past and future be the same is hidden a far more insidious threat to peace. 4 The ego does not advertise its final threat, for it would have **the ego's** worshippers still believe that **the ego** can offer them escape. 5 But the belief in guilt must lead to the belief in hell, and always does. 6 The only way in which the ego allows the fear of hell to be experienced is to bring hell here, but always as a foretaste of the future. 7 For no one who considers himself deserving of hell can believe that punishment will end in peace.

Note # 6: The ego holds out the possibility that heaven may be temporarily won, but the truth of the ego's thought system is that you, its victim, must ultimately end up in hell. Moments of fleeting happiness may be temporarily won in order to keep us willing to play the egoic game of specialness. But happiness within a body can never last. Ultimately, death must be experienced. To the ego, heaven would also result in the death of ego and egoic specialness. It is only in hell that the ego's continued existence is guaranteed. Sin demands eternal punishment for the egoic god is an unmerciful, vengeful god.

T-15.I.7. The Holy Spirit teaches thus: There is no hell. 2 Hell is only what the ego has made of the present. 3 The belief in hell is what prevents you from understanding the present, because you are afraid of **the present since you believe that it results in hell**. 4 The Holy Spirit leads as steadily to Heaven as the ego drives to hell. 5 For the Holy Spirit, Who knows only the present, uses **the present** to undo the fear by which the ego would make the present useless. 6 There is no escape from fear in the ego's use of time. 7 For time, according to **the ego's** teaching, is nothing but a teaching device for compounding guilt until **guilt** becomes all-encompassing, demanding vengeance forever.

Note # 7: The Holy Spirit knows that the guiltless Son of God cannot sin. Any past guilt that you bring with you to the present has no basis in reality, for it is not found in the Mind of God. The Holy Spirit's focus on time is the present. The Holy Spirit knows that the Son's past must be sinless since sin does not exist in the Mind of God. By the removal of the past misperceptions, the Holy Spirit will reawaken the vision of Christ that appears to be asleep within your split-mind. Thus, the fear of the present will be corrected since the Holy Spirit only knows that God's Son is innocent and guiltless. The Sonship remains eternally perfect, whole and complete as the Creator intended.

Under the egoic thought system, the present is a fearful place. The present is where and when we get to experience being constantly judged, attacked and found guilty. Being under attack, we must always be enhancing our defenses. The ego tells us that the best defense is the "preemptive first strike." Yet, both attacking and defensive strategies confirm our separation. Our fear leads to additional sins which increase our guilt and in turn, compound our fear. Time becomes a vicious cycle in which we are doomed to continually repeat the failures of our past egoic misperceptions.

T-15.I.8. The Holy Spirit would undo all of this **self-imposed guilt that demands eternal vengeance** <*now.*> 2 Fear is not of the present, but **fear is** only of the past and future, which do not exist. 3 There is no fear in the present when each instant stands clear and separated from the past, without **any of fear's past** shadow reaching out into the future. 4 Each instant is a clean, untarnished birth, in which the Son of God emerges from the past into the present. 5 And the present extends forever. 6 **The Son of God** is so beautiful and so clean and free of guilt that nothing but happiness is there **in the present**. 7 No darkness is remembered, and immortality and joy are now.

Note # 8: Without the past misperception, the present can be correctly perceived. By undoing or erasing, the past misperception that we carry with us into the present, the Holy Spirit unclouds the vision of Christ. We realize through the use of the tool of forgiveness that we remain connected with our brother. God's Will is our will that we share and we are guiltless. Happiness and peace are returned to our split-mind.

When we understand that the Sonship is guiltless, the past loses the fearful grip it held upon the present. Each moment in the <now> stands alone. It is not affected by past experiences. We realize that we determine our current experiences based on our current thought patterns. This is the recovery of the creative power that resides with our decision-maker. Each moment we have the opportunity to choose again. The Holy Spirit suggests that before we decide, we should ask the Holy Spirit, "What would love have me do?" If we do this, we will follow our bliss and quickly return to the remembrance of God.

T-15.I.9. This lesson **that we are guiltless** takes no time. 2 For what is time without a past and future? 3 **The ego** has taken time to misguide you so completely, but it takes no time at all to be what you are. 4 Begin to practice the Holy Spirit's use of time as a teaching aid to happiness and peace. 5 Take this very instant, now, and think of **this very instant, the now,** as all there is of time. 6 Nothing can reach you here out of the past, and it is here, **in the now of this very instant,** that you are completely absolved, completely free and wholly without condemnation. 7 From this holy instant wherein holiness was born again you will go forth in time without fear, and with no sense of change with time.

Note # 9: Although it took the ego a long time to misguide you into your present state of victim consciousness, it requires no time for the Holy Spirit to return you to guiltlessness. For guilt never existed in reality and, therefore, there is nothing to change. The only "correction" that is needed is that the Son of God must reawaken from the dream that he could be something other than what he is. He must reawaken to his innocence. Time measures change. Once we realize the changelessness of truth, there is no change for time to measure. Time will disappear into the only reality, which is the now.

In the holy instant, all past judgments have been suspended and thus, we can experience and be in the <now>. This suspension of judgment allows us to abandon egoic "seeing" and become aware of the truth through the "eyes" of Christ.

T-15.I.10. Time is inconceivable without change, yet holiness does not change. 2 Learn from this **holy** instant more than merely that hell does not exist. 3 In this redeeming instant lies Heaven. 4 And Heaven will not change, for the birth into the holy present is salvation from change. 5 Change is an illusion, taught by those who cannot see themselves as guiltless. 6 There is no change in Heaven because there is no change in God. 7 In the holy instant, in which you see yourself as bright with freedom, you will remember God. 8 For remembering **God** <*is*> to remember freedom.

Note # 10: The consequence of the removal of all guilt within the Sonship has sweeping results. With the removal of guilt, the Sonship reawakens to the reality of what it is. The Sonship is the extension of the Mind of God. There is nothing outside the Mind of God. There is just the changeless Oneness. In the holy instant, all past judgments are suspended. This allows for the beginning of the remembrance of God. Time's ultimate function is to allow for the return of the Sonship to the remembrance of God. When this remembrance is accomplished, time has served its purpose. With the function of time fulfilled, time, which is the measurement of change, will disappear. Both the illusion of change and time disappear into the nothingness from which they arose and the changeless eternal mind of God is all that remains.

T-15.I.11. If you are tempted to be dispirited by thinking how long it would take to change your mind so completely, ask yourself, "How long is an instant?" 2 Could you not give so short a time to the Holy Spirit for your salvation? 3 **The Holy Spirit** asks no more **than an instant**, for **the Holy Spirit** has no need of more. 4 It takes far longer to teach you to be willing to give **the Holy Spirit** this **instant** than for **the Holy Spirit** to use this tiny instant to offer you the whole of Heaven. 5 In exchange for this instant **the Holy Spirit** stands ready to give you the remembrance of eternity.

Note # 11: For the Holy Spirit to return us to sanity, we must first ask for his guidance. When our need to be happy is greater than our need to be special, we will ask for the return to truth. Until that request, we will exchange our happiness for the desire to be right, even though we are wrong. We need to learn to become vigilant only for God.

T-15.I.12. You will never give this holy instant to the Holy Spirit on behalf of your release while you are unwilling to give **this holy instant** to your brothers on behalf of **your brother's release**. 2 For the instant of holiness is shared, and cannot be yours alone. 3 Remember, then, when you are tempted to attack a brother, that his instant of release is **your instant of release**. 4 Miracles are the instants of release you offer, and will receive. 5 **Miracles** attest to your willingness to <be> released, and to offer time to the Holy Spirit for **the Holy Spirit's** use of **time**.

Note # 12: To give is to receive. We cannot obtain our own freedom from guilt without giving that same freedom to our brother. We are all connected in Christ consciousness. We are One.

T-15.I.13. How long is an instant? 2 **An instant** is as short for your brother as **an instant** is for you. 3 Practice giving this blessed instant of freedom to all who are enslaved by time, and thus make time **the** friend **of all who were previously enslaved by time**. 4 The Holy Spirit gives their blessed instant to you through your giving **your blessed instant to your brothers**. 5 As you give **your blessed instant to your brothers**, He, **the Christ consciousness in your brothers,** offers **your blessed instant back** to you. 6 Be not unwilling to give what you would receive of Him, **the Christ consciousness in your brothers,** for you join with Him, **the Christ consciousness in your brothers,** in giving. 7 In the crystal cleanness of the release you give is your instantaneous escape from guilt. 8 You must be holy if you offer holiness **to your brother.**

Note # 13: Holiness is wholeness. When we see ourselves as whole, we see our brother as whole. In the reality of our holiness and wholeness, we rediscover our shared Oneness. By granting our brother his guiltlessness, we receive and reclaim our own.

T-15.I.14. How long is an instant? 2 As long as it takes to re-establish perfect sanity, perfect peace and perfect love for everyone, for God and for yourself. 3 **An instant is** as long as it takes to remember immortality, and your immortal creations who share **your immortality** with you. 4 **An instant is** as long as it takes to exchange hell for Heaven. 5 **An instant is** long enough to transcend all of the ego's making, and ascend unto your Father.

Note # 14: All that is needed for the return to knowledge is the willingness to accept only the truth. Truth never changes but we can deny the truth. ACIM asks how long we will cling to our desire to be special when the price is our happiness? Happiness can only be found in truth. Only the insane believe that they are the arbitrators of the truth. Our little willingness is our request for the Holy Spirit to guide us home.

T-15.I.15.Time is your friend, if you leave **time** to the Holy Spirit to use **on your behalf**. 2 **The Holy Spirit** needs but very little **time** to restore God's whole power to you. 3 **The Holy Spirit,** Who transcends time for you, understands what time is for. 4 Holiness lies not in time, but **holiness lies** in eternity. 5 There never was an instant in which God's Son could lose his purity. 6 **The Son of God's purity is the Son's** changeless state, **which** is beyond time, for his purity remains forever beyond attack and without variability. 7 Time stands still in his holiness, and **time** changes not. 8 And so **time, which measures change,** is no longer time at all. 9 For caught in the single instant of the eternal sanctity of God's creation, **time** is transformed into forever. 10 Give the eternal instant, that eternity may be remembered for you, in that shining instant of perfect release. 11 Offer the miracle of the holy instant through the Holy Spirit, and leave **the Holy Spirit's** giving **this perfect release** to you to Him.

Note # 15: When all guilt has been removed from the mind of the Sonship, the need for time will be no more. Time came into our awareness to allow for the correction of the belief that we could be separate from our Father. With the acceptance of the Atonement, we reawaken to the fact that we are and always will be guiltless. Sin is impossible. With the acceptance of the Atonement for ourselves, we give the Atonement's guiltlessness to all our brothers since we are all connected within the Mind of God. Time no longer has a purpose since the Mind of God is changeless. Therefore, there is no change to measure. Sanity is the return to whole-mindedness and the end of the mad idea that God could be limited. The release from littleness that arose from the desire to be special has been obtained.

II. The End of Doubt

T-15.II.1.The Atonement is <*in*> time, but **the Atonement is** not <*for*> time. 2 Being in you, **the Atonement** is eternal. 3 What holds remembrance of God, **the Atonement,** cannot be bound by time. 4 **With the Atonement** no more are you **bound by time**. 5 For unless God is bound, you cannot be **bound**. 6 An instant offered to the Holy Spirit is offered to God on your behalf, and in that instant you will awaken gently in **God**. 7 In the blessed instant you will let go all your past learning, and the Holy Spirit will quickly offer you the whole lesson of peace, **which is the truth that God's Son is guiltless**. 8 What can take time, when all the obstacles to learning **the whole lesson of peace, which is the truth that God's Son is guiltless** have been removed? 9 Truth is so far beyond time that all of **truth** happens at once. 10 For as **truth** was created one, so **truth's** oneness depends not on time at all.

Note # 16: Truth is constant. The Atonement removes the obstacles that we place in front of truth. Our belief in guilt hides the truth of what we are. Remove the guilt and only truth remains. There is no lesson to learn about truth since truth is all there is. We need only wake up from the illusionary world that we perceive of as sin, guilt and fear.

T-15.II.2. Do not be concerned with time, and fear not the instant of holiness that will remove all fear. 2 For the instant of peace is eternal <*because*> **peace** is without fear. 3 **Peace** will come, being the lesson God gives you, through the Teacher, **the Holy Spirit, which God** has appointed to translate time into eternity. 4 Blessed is God's Teacher, **the Holy Spirit,** Whose joy it is to teach God's holy Son his holiness. 5 **The Holy Spirit's** joy is not contained in time. 6 **The Holy Spirit's** teaching is for you because **the Holy Spirit's** joy is **your joy**. 7 Through **the Holy Spirit** you stand before God's altar, where **the Holy Spirit** gently translates hell into Heaven. 8 For it is only in Heaven that God would have you be.

Note # 17: The function of the Holy Spirit is to teach you the truth of your Holiness, which is your wholeness with God and all His creations. This is taught by removing the obstacle to truth, which is your belief in guilt. By the removal of guilt, all that is left is the truth of what you truly are, unlimited spirit, which is perfect, whole and complete.

T-15.II.3. How long can it take to be **in Heaven** where God would have you? 2 For you are **in Heaven** where you have forever been and will forever be. 3 All that you have, you have forever. 4 The blessed instant reaches out to encompass time, as God extends Himself to encompass you. 5 You who have spent days, hours and even years in chaining your brothers to your ego in an attempt to support **the ego** and uphold **the ego's** weakness, do not perceive the Source of strength, **which is the power of God**. 6 In this holy instant you will unchain all your brothers, and refuse to support either their weakness or your own **weakness.**

Note # 18: A decision for the ego is a choice for littleness. When we deny our divine birthright, the price of specialness comes at the cost of everything. For God created us, as an extension of Himself. The Creator gave everything to us. When we deny God his Fatherhood, we deny that we have been created holy and have all the power of God at our disposal. We believe ourselves to be limited, which is the denial of truth.

T-15.II.4. You do not realize how much you have misused your brothers by seeing **your brothers** as sources of ego support. 2 As a result, **your brothers** witness to the ego in your perception, and seem to provide reasons for not letting **your perceptions** go. 3 Yet **your brothers** are far stronger and much more compelling witnesses for the Holy Spirit. 4 And **your brothers** support **the Holy Spirit's** strength. 5 It is, therefore, your choice whether **your brothers** support the ego or the Holy Spirit in you. 6 And you will recognize which you have chosen by < *your brother's* > reactions. 7 A Son of God who has been released through the Holy Spirit in a brother is always recognized **as a Son of God.** 8 **A Son of God who has been released through the Holy Spirit** cannot be denied. 9 If you remain uncertain, it is only because you have not given complete release **to your brothers.** 10 And because **you have not given complete release to your brothers**, you have not given a single instant completely to the Holy Spirit. 11 For when you have **given a single instant completely to the Holy Spirit,** you will be sure you have **been released from your misperceptions**. 12 You will be sure because the witness to **the Holy Spirit** will speak so clearly of **the Holy Spirit** that you will hear and understand **that your brothers are witness for the Holy Spirit**. 13 You will doubt **that your brother can be a compelling witness for the Holy Spirit** until you hear **a brother as** one witness whom you have wholly released through the Holy Spirit. 14 And then you will doubt no more.

Note # 19: All that we perceive are actually neutral experiences or events. Yet, these perceptions can be utilized as witnesses for either the true or the false. The Holy Spirit has the ability to remove past egoic misperceptions so that current events can be perceived correctly. The ego relies on past misperception to maintain its control over the decision-maker, and thus, keep you playing the role of victim. Our brother is a witness for the ego when we perceive him to be like the little "s" self we claim to be. We perceive our brother as only a limited ego-body. Perceiving ourselves to be separate, limited and sinful, we project these same imagined traits upon our brother. If we see ourselves under the thought system of the Holy Spirit and the vision of Christ, we perceive a brother as deserving of love. The Holy Spirit correctly interprets any perception as a neutral event deserving of only love. The proper interpretation is that an event is either a cry for love or is love. The proper response to any event is, therefore, only love.

T-15.II.5. The holy instant has not yet happened to you. 2 Yet **the holy instant** will, and you will recognize **the holy instant** with perfect certainty. 3 No gift of God is recognized in any other way **except with perfect certainty**. 4 You can practice the mechanics of the holy instant, and will learn much from doing so. 5 Yet **the holy instant's** shining and glittering brilliance, which will literally blind you to this world by its own vision, you cannot supply. 6 And here **the recognition of the gift of God** is, all in this **holy** instant, complete, accomplished and given wholly.

Note # 20: The purpose of the Holy Instant is to suspend judgment entirely. This suspension of judgment removes all barriers that prevent the Holy Spirit from teaching the meaning of love. God is Love. The Holy Instant allows for the reclaiming and reawakening of the Christ, which is the Big "S" Self. The Sonship shares with God as God shares His Self with Christ. All brothers are joined in the Christ. This is the recognition that there is but One Self that is the extension of the shared Oneness of the Mind of God. The Holy Instant is the realization that we are not separate and that the separation has never occurred. Both God and His Child's innocence is reclaimed. We, like our Father do not know what does not exist and this is the innocence of God. All that remains is the truth. Thus as ACIM states, "Nothing real can be threatened. Nothing unreal exists. Herein lies the peace of God."

T-15.II.6. Start now to practice your little part in separating out the holy instant. 2 You will receive very specific instructions as you go along. 3 To learn to separate out this single second, and to experience **this single second** as timeless, is to begin to experience yourself as not separate. 4 Fear not that you will not be given help in this **rediscovery that you are not separate**. 5 God's Teacher, **the Holy Spirit,** and **the Holy Spirit's** lesson will support your strength. 6 It is only your weakness that will depart from you in this practice **of rediscovery that you are not separate**, for it is the practice of the power of God in you. 7 Use **the power of God in you** but for one instant, and you will never deny **the power of God in you** again. 8 Who can deny the Presence of what the universe bows to, in appreciation and gladness? 9 Before the recognition of the universe that witnesses to **God's power** your doubts **of the power of God within you** must disappear.

Note # 21: ACIM implores us to start today to practice experiencing the end of our belief in separation. We do this by dropping our egoic judgments and following our inner guide, the Holy Spirit. By following this guidance, we will be provided with experiences supporting our rediscovery that we are not separate from the power of God within us.

III. Littleness versus Magnitude

T-15.III.1. Be not content with littleness. 2 But be sure you understand what littleness is, and why you could never be content with **littleness**. 3 Littleness is the offering you **egoically** give yourself. 4 You offer **littleness** in place of magnitude, and you accept **littleness**. 5 Everything in this world is little because **this world** is a world made out of littleness, in the strange belief that littleness can content you. 6 When you strive for anything in this world in the belief that **anything in this world** will bring you peace, you are belittling yourself and blinding yourself to glory. 7 Littleness and glory are the choices open to your striving and your vigilance. 8 You will always choose **either littleness or the glory of magnitude** at the expense of the other.

Note # 22: This world was born out of the desire to be separate from God. It is the attempt of the ego to keep out God's Love for His Son. It was born out of the desire for specialness, which is to be something less than "the everything" that the Sonship was created to be. The egoic little "s" self wanted to be the arbitrator of truth and thus, usurp God's authority. Specialness is the desire to get, which flows from the belief that you no longer are everything. The Christ is the Home of "the everything" that we are. The Christ is the big "S" Self. The ego's thought system is the origin for our belief in "littleness."

T-15.III.2. Yet what you do not realize, each time you choose, is that your choice is your evaluation of yourself. 2 Choose littleness and you will not have peace, for you will have judged yourself unworthy of **peace**. 3 And whatever you offer as a substitute **for peace** is much too poor a gift to satisfy you. 4 It is essential that you accept the fact, and accept it gladly, that there is no form of littleness that can ever content you. 5 You are free to try as many **forms of littleness** as you wish, but all you will be doing is to delay your homecoming **to the glory of your own magnitude**. 6 For you will be content only in magnitude, which is your home.

Note # 23: Being everything, we cannot be happy with less than what we are

T-15.III.3. There is a deep responsibility you owe yourself, and **this responsibility that you owe yourself**, you must learn to remember all the time. 2 The lesson **of responsibility that you owe yourself** may seem hard at first, but you will learn to love **the lesson** when you realize that **the lesson** is true and **the lesson** is but a tribute to your power. 3 You who have sought and found littleness, remember this: Every decision you make stems from what you think you are, and **every decision you make** represents the value that you put upon yourself. 4 Believe the little can content you, and by limiting yourself you will not be satisfied. 5 For your function is not little, and it is only by finding your function and fulfilling **your function** that you can escape from littleness.

Note # 24: Our responsibility is to be as the Father created us. We are seekers and our single purpose is to reach the truth. Nothing "sources" or causes my perceived experience but my own thinking in each moment. Nothing has an effect on me since everything in the world of perception is neutral. Every decision I make is a decision of love or fear. Nothing can have any effect on me unless I chose to allow it to affect me. This understanding that I am responsible for my own viewpoint is critical for my ability to recover my decision-making abilities. Until I claim self-responsibility of my private world, I remain in the ego's world of victim consciousness. Once I realize I am not a victim, I can ask for guidance of the Holy Spirit and choose again. We are seekers and our single purpose is to reach the truth. With the Holy Spirit as our guide, our rediscovery of the truth is inevitable.
While we perceive ourselves to be in time and space, our function is forgiveness. In eternity, our function is co-creation. Our destiny is the peace of God. Love is our reality and truth.

T-15.III.4. There is no doubt about what your function is, for the Holy Spirit knows what **your function** is. 2 There is no doubt about **your function's** magnitude, for **your function's magnitude** reaches you through **the Holy Spirit** <*from*> Magnitude. 3 You do not have to strive for **your function's**

magnitude, because you have **your function's magnitude**. 4 All your striving must be directed against littleness, for **littleness** does require vigilance to protect your magnitude in this world. 5 To hold your magnitude in perfect awareness in a world of littleness is a task the little cannot undertake. 6 Yet **the task of holding your magnitude in perfect awareness in a world of littleness** is asked of you, in tribute to your magnitude and not your littleness. 7 Nor is **the task of holding your magnitude in perfect awareness in a world of littleness** asked of you alone. 8 The power of God will support every effort you make on behalf of His dear Son. 9 Search for the little, and you deny yourself **God's** power. 10 God is not willing that His Son be content with less than everything. 11 For **God** is not content without His Son, and His Son cannot be content with less than **the everything that** his Father has given him.

Note # 25: In the world of perception, we are asked to freely choose for the Will of our Father. We are asked to choose between the oneness of everything versus the specialness of limitation. Although the choice would appear obvious to the sane person, we need to realize that the split-minded are not sane. The split-minded have sided with the ego to experience littleness. Littleness is separate individuality. Littleness is specialness. When you look at the planet earth, you see that the desire for separate autonomy is great. We, as a society highly value individuality. We value it so much that according to ACIM, we sacrifice our happiness for the wish to be right, even if we are wrong. Ask yourself this question. Would I rather be happy or would I rather be right? We are seekers and our single purpose is to reach the truth. Truth cannot be found if we are not willing to look at our beliefs and question whether they serve our search for truth. It is important to realize that if you believe that an illusion is true, you will never be able to question the validity of the illusion because you will never think to question it. We are suffering from a form of unconscious incompetence. We don't know that we don't know. ACIM ask that we question what we believe and not simply accept it because we were indoctrinated into a particular belief system.

T-15.III.5.I asked you earlier, "Would you be hostage to the ego or host to God?" 2 Let this question, **"Would you be hostage to the ego or host to God?"** be asked you by the Holy Spirit every time you make a decision. 3 For every decision you make does answer this **question of "Would you be hostage to the ego or host to God?"** and invites sorrow or joy accordingly. 4 When God gave Himself to you in your creation, **God** established you as host to **God** forever. 5 **God** has not left you, and you have not left **God**. 6 All your attempts to deny **God's** magnitude, and make **God's** Son hostage to the ego, cannot make little whom God has joined with **Himself**. 7 Every decision you make is for Heaven or for hell, and brings you the awareness of what you decided for.

Note # 26: There are only two choices, truth or the falsity of illusion. Every decision we make is a choice between following the ego's thought system of littleness or the thought system for magnitude or truth, which is the thought system of the Holy Spirit. The Holy Spirit's thought system leads us back to the truth that we are a Big "S" Self. We are perfect, whole and complete. We are part of the shared Will of God. The Mind of God is changeless and this is our home. We can deny the truth about ourselves, but we cannot change the truth. Truth is the great gift that we received when God extended Himself to His Son. Our magnitude is simply the truth about what we are.

T-15.III.6. The Holy Spirit can hold your magnitude, clean of all littleness, clearly and in perfect safety in your mind, untouched by every little gift the world of littleness would offer you. 2 But for this, **the magnitude of your Christ consciousness,** you cannot side against **God** in what **God** wills for you. 3 Decide for God **through the use of your Christ consciousness. For the Christ is the home of** the **Holy Spirit in your apparent split-mind.** 4 For littleness, and the belief that you can be content with littleness, are decisions you make about yourself **when you follow the thought system of the ego.** 5

The power and the glory that lie in you from God are for all who, like you, perceive themselves as little, and believe that littleness can be blown up into a sense of magnitude that can content them. **The power and the glory that lie in you from God reside in your Christ conscious part of your split-mind.** 6 Neither give littleness, nor accept **littleness**. 7 All honor is due the host of God, **the Christ**. 8 Your littleness deceives you, but your magnitude is of **God,** Who dwells in you, and in Whom you dwell. 9 Touch no one, then, with littleness in the Name of Christ, eternal Host unto **God,** His Father.

<u>Note # 27:</u> The Christ is the part of the mind that always remembers God. For discussion purposes, ACIM speaks in terms of the Holy Trinity as if each part was separate and distinct from the other parts. This is done because we are use to dualistic thinking. We do not perceive the true oneness of the whole, which is the Mind of God. In reality, the Father, Sonship and Holy Spirit are different aspects of the whole. There is only the Oneness but since we have lost the use of knowledge, we must speak in terms of symbols. The Father, the Sonship and the Holy Spirit abide in each other for They are only the One Self, a Oneness of Everything, which is the Mind of God, eternal, changeless, perfect, whole and complete.

T-15.III.7. In this season (Christmas) which celebrates the birth of holiness into this world, join with me**, Jesus,** who decided for holiness for you. 2 It is our task together to restore the awareness of magnitude to the host, **the Christ**, whom God appointed for Himself. 3 It is beyond all your littleness to give the gift of God, but not beyond **your magnitude to give the gift of God.** 4 For God would give Himself <*through*> you, **the Christ, the Big "S" Self.** 5 **God** reaches from you to everyone and beyond everyone to the Son of God's creations, but without leaving you, **the Christ.** 6 Far beyond your little world but still in you, **God** extends forever. 7 Yet **God** brings all **God's** extensions to you, as host to **God.**

<u>Note # 28:</u> This speaks of the shared Oneness. Everything extends from the Mind of God and is the Mind of God. There can never be separation in a Oneness comprised of everything. Only the extension of the Oneness is possible.

T-15.III.8. Is it a sacrifice to leave littleness behind, and wander not in vain? 2 It is not **a** sacrifice to wake to glory. 3 But it is **a** sacrifice to accept anything less than glory. 4 Learn that you must be worthy of the Prince of Peace, **the Christ,** born in you in honor of **God** Whose host you are. 5 You know not what love means because you have sought to purchase **love** with little gifts, thus valuing **love** too little to understand **love's** magnitude. 6 Love is not little and love dwells in you, for you are host to **God.** 7 Before the greatness that lives in you, your poor appreciation of yourself and all the little offerings you give slip into nothingness.

<u>Note # 29:</u> Illusions must give way to the truth. The glory of God, which resides in us, cannot be limited by our denial of the truth. The little "s" self arose because of our belief in the separation. It has never been shared in the Mind of God and, therefore, being nothing, is nothing. Nothingness can have no impact on everything. When we remove all the veils of guilt that attempt to hide the truth from our split-minds, all that remains is the truth that we are the Christ. The Christ is the expression of the love of God. The truth is that there is only Love. We are the Love of God and the Love of God is "Us", the Big "S" Self.

T-15.III.9. Holy child of God, when will you learn that only holiness can content you and give you peace? 2 Remember that you learn not for yourself alone, no more than I, **Jesus,** did. 3 It is because I learned for you that you can learn of me. 4 I would but teach you what is yours, so that together we can replace the shabby littleness that binds the host of God to guilt and weakness with the glad awareness of the glory that is in him. 5 My birth in you is your awakening to grandeur. 6 Welcome me not into a manger, but into the altar to holiness, where holiness abides in perfect peace. 7 My Kingdom is not of this world because **My Kingdom** is in you. 8 And you are of your Father. 9 Let us join in honoring you, who must remain forever beyond littleness.

Note # 30: Jesus expresses the fact that we are all interconnected. Each part is a hologram of God, Himself. God abides in you and me, as we abide in God. God is like the ocean and we are like a wave. But in reality, we are only "ocean" for the ocean is all that is. We can dream or appear for a split second to be a wave but in the end we dissolve back into the ocean.

T-15.III.10. Decide with me, **a symbol for the Christ and the thought system of the Holy Spirit,** who has decided to abide with you. 2 I will as my Father wills, knowing **our Father's** Will is constant and at peace forever with itself. 3 You will be content with nothing but **God's** Will. 4 Accept no less **than God's Will,** remembering that everything I learned is yours. 5 What my Father loves I love as **God** does, and I can no more accept **God's Will** as what it is not, than **God** can **accept what is not His Will.** 6 And no more can you **accept what is not God's Will.** 7 When you have learned to accept what you are, you will make no more **egoic** gifts to offer to yourself, for you will know you are complete, in need of nothing, and unable to accept anything for yourself. 8 But you will gladly give, having received. 9 The host of God**, you, the Christ,** needs not seek to find anything **for you are everything**.

Note # 31: There is no will but God's Will. Because of what we are, which is an extension of God, we are everything. The idea that we are everything is difficult for us to comprehend because we associate ourselves so strongly as "the body." We need to constantly remind ourselves that we are not a limited ego-body in competition with other ego-bodies, but rather unlimited spirit. God is not form. God is Unlimited Spirit, Mind, an Idea, a Thought. We are not a body. We are unlimited spirit, mind, an idea and a thought. Thoughts can be shared. When thoughts are shared, they are strengthened. There is not loss; there is just the extension of the thought. No sacrifice is required. Having received a thought, we in turn give the thought to another. There is no diminishment. The thought of God is Love. This is what we are, for Love is everything. Love is the Truth about God. Love is the Truth about us. And the truth will set us free. As ACIM proclaims, "I am not a body. I am free, for I am exactly as God created Me."

T-15.III.11. If you are wholly willing to leave salvation to the plan of God and unwilling to attempt to grasp for peace yourself, salvation will be given you. 2 Yet think not you can substitute your **egoic** plan for **God's Plan for salvation.** 3 Rather, join with me in **God's Plan for salvation,** that we may release all those who would be bound, proclaiming together that the Son of God is host to **God.** 4 Thus will we let no one forget what you would remember. 5 And thus will you remember **you are host to God.**

Note # 32: Being an extension of God, we must be guiltless as our Father, who is us. God's Plan for Salvation is the Atonement. The acceptance of the Atonement is the acceptance of truth and the denial and abandonment of all that is false. It is the acceptance that God's Son is guiltless and that sin is impossible. By accepting the Atonement for ourselves, we allow for the awakening of the Christ consciousness within us. We thus, have the return of the remembrance of God.

T-15.III.12. Call forth in everyone only the remembrance of God, and of the Heaven that is in him**, the Christ**. 2 For where you would have your brother be, there will you think you are. 3 Hear not **your brother's** appeal to hell and littleness, but **hear** only **your brother's** call for Heaven and greatness. 4 Forget not that **your brother's** call is **your call,** and answer **your brother** with me. 5 God's power is forever on the side of **God's** host, **the Christ,** for **God's power** protects only the peace in which **God** dwells. 6 Lay not littleness before **God's** holy altar, which rises above the stars and reaches even to

Heaven, because of what is given **God's holy altar**. **God's holy altar is everything, because it is the Power of God.**

Note # 33: We are God's altar and the only thing worthy to be place on God's altar is the truth. When we attempt to place the egoic gift of littleness upon God's altar, it cannot be accepted. For the false has no place on the altar of Truth. Instead of the gift of magnitude upon God's altar, we place the gifts of limitation on the altar to the false gods of the ego. The gift of littleness comes from the ego's thought system. It comes from the belief that we have some power outside the power of God. By myself, I can do nothing. But if I act as an instrument of my Father, God can do everything through me for I am the recipient of the Power of God.

IV. Practicing the Holy Instant

T-15.IV.1. This course is not beyond immediate learning, unless you believe that what God wills takes time. 2 And this **course is not beyond immediate learning; it** means only that you would rather delay the recognition that **God's** Will is so. 3 The holy instant is this instant and every instant. 4 **The Holy Instant is when** you want it to be **the Holy Instant** is. 5 The one **instant** you would not have **the Holy Instant** be is lost to you. 6 You must decide when **the Holy Instant** is. 7 Delay **the Holy Instant** not. 8 For beyond the past and future, where you will not find **the Holy Instant, the Holy Instant** stands in shimmering readiness for your acceptance. 9 Yet you cannot bring **the Holy Instant** into glad awareness while you do not want **the Holy Instant**, for **the Holy Instant** holds the whole release from littleness.

Note # 34: When the Holy Instant is recognized by us, it is under our control. The Holy Instant will appear in our consciousness the moment we recognize there is no will but God's Will. We share God's Will because we are the host of God. A Oneness knows no separation. The Holy Instant will be when we choose again for the truth. Ideas never leave their source. Thoughts we hold are mighty and illusions are as strong in their effect upon the thinker as the truth would be. It is our refusal to reject all thoughts of separation that keep us trapped in the unreal world of erroneous thoughts. Change our thoughts and our world of provisional reality changes. We need to change from egoic thinking to the thought system of the Holy Spirit. We need to reawaken to the fact that the separation is not real and has never occurred and thus, suspend all past judgments. God's Son is holy, sinless and innocent. When we freely and wholly choose against the littleness of the ego, the Holy Instant will arrive.

T-15.IV.2. Your practice must therefore rest upon your willingness to let all littleness go. 2 The instant in which magnitude dawns upon you is but as far away as your desire for **magnitude, which is the choice to be your Big "S" Self.** 3 As long as you **do not** desire **magnitude** and cherish littleness instead, by so much is **the Holy Instant** far from you. 4 By so much as you want **magnitude; due to your desire for magnitude** will you bring **the Holy Instant** nearer. 5 Think not that you can find salvation in your own way and have **littleness**. 6 Give over every **egoic** plan you have made for your salvation in exchange for God's **plan for salvation**. 7 **God's plan for salvation** will content you, and nothing else can bring you peace. 8 For peace is of God, and no one beside **God**.

Note # 35: God's Plan for salvation rests upon you reclaiming your Big "S" Self. The ego's plan for salvation is based on your desire for the specialness that comes from littleness. Our claim for our littleness is the demand for specialness and individuality that comes from inequality. The acceptance of the Atonement is the rejection of littleness and the guilt that arose from our mad idea that we could be something other than as we were created.

T-15.IV.3. Be humble before **God**, and yet great *<in>* **God**. 2 And value no plan of the ego before the plan of God. 3 For you leave empty your place in **God's** plan, which you must fill if you would join with me, by your decision to join in any plan but **God's plan**. 4 I call you to fulfill your holy part in the plan that **God** has given to the world for **your** release from littleness. 5 God would have His host, **which is you, the Christ,** abide in perfect freedom. 6 Every allegiance to a plan of salvation apart from **God's plan** diminishes the value of **God's** Will for you in your own mind. 7 And yet it is your mind that is the host to **God**.

Note # 36: Be humble before God, and yet great *<in>* God, calls for the recognition that by myself I can do nothing, but through me, God can do everything. We are the host of God. If we choose not to be arrogant, we will accept our role as the Big "S" Self. We are an extension of the Mind of God. The Mind of God is limitless. It cannot be made little because we imagine something about ourselves that is not true. The acceptance of the Atonement is the removal of any thoughts of guilt that prevent us from reclaiming our magnitude, our Big "S" Self, the Christ, which is the Host for God.

T-15.IV.4. Would you learn how perfect and immaculate is the holy altar on which your Father has placed Himself? 2 This **holy altar** you will recognize in the holy instant, in which you willingly and gladly give over every plan but **God's plan for salvation**. 3 For **in the acceptances of God's plan for salvation,** there lies peace, perfectly clear because you have been willing to meet **peace's** conditions, **which is the abandonment of egoic thinking**. 4 You can claim the holy instant any time and anywhere you want **the Holy Instant**. 5 In your practice, try to give over every **egoic** plan you have accepted for finding magnitude in littleness. 6 *<Salvation from littleness is not there **in any egoic plan for salvation**.>* 7 Use the holy instant only to recognize that you alone cannot know where **salvation** is, and can only deceive yourself **with egoic planning.**

Note # 37: Because our ego does not remember what we are, we cannot expect to find the truth about ourselves from something like the ego, which does not know truth. The ego is the representative for untruth and littleness. The ego knows nothing because it is nothing. The ego is not real. Only the Holy Spirit is the proper guide for God's plan since only the Holy Spirit can bridge the gap between your illusion about yourself and the truth. Only the Holy Spirit knows the truth about what you are and is aware of your self-imposed belief in littleness.

T-15.IV.5.I stand within the holy instant, as clear as you would have me. 2 And the extent to which you learn to accept me is the measure of the time in which the holy instant will be **your Holy Instant**. 3 I call to you to make the holy instant **your Holy Instant** at once, for the release from littleness in the mind of the host of God depends on **the host of God's** willingness **to be released from his belief in littleness**, and not on time.

Note # 38: Time "exists" only to serve as a measure for change during our journey home from perception to truth. Time measures change and change exists only in the world of perception. The world of perception was born only in the split-mind of one who believed in specialness, which is the call for the littleness of separation. Since ideas never leave their source, the belief that we are separate must be changed within our own minds. This is why ACIM asks us to choose again. This time siding for the truth that is the magnitude of the Christ.

T-15.IV.6. The reason this course is simple is that truth is simple. 2 Complexity is of the ego, and **complexity** is nothing more than the ego's attempt to obscure the obvious, **which is the truth**. 3 You could live forever in the holy instant, beginning now and reaching to eternity, but for a very simple reason. 4 Do not obscure the simplicity of this reason, for if you do **obscure the truth**, it will be only because you prefer not to recognize **the truth** and not to let go **of the ego's attempt to obscure the obvious, which is truth**. 5 The simple reason **that you are not living forever in the holy instant currently is**, simply stated, this: The holy instant is a time in which you receive and give perfect communication. 6 This means, however, that **the holy instant** is a time in which your mind is open, both to receive and give **communication**. 7 **The holy instant** is the recognition that all minds are in communication. 8 **The holy instant** therefore seeks to change nothing, but merely to accept everything.

Note # 39: The Holy Instant cannot change truth, since truth is the changeless eternal. The holy instant seeks the acceptance of truth, which is everything that is real and, therefore, everything that is real is also eternally changeless. The egoic thought system places clouds over the truth, but cannot change the truth. The Holy Spirit teaches how to remove the ego's barriers to truth, which all arise from sin, guilt and fear. As long as we place value in egoic thinking, we are unable to be a clear channel for the thought system of the Holy Spirit. Lacking this commitment to only receive and give communication for truth, we postpone the realization of the holy instant within our own mind. An attempt to communicate the false is an attempt to communicate nothing, for the false is nothing.

T-15.IV.7. How can you do this, **communicate with an open mind that both gives and receives proper communication**, when you would prefer to have private thoughts and keep **private thoughts**? 2 The only way you could **keep private thoughts** would be to deny the perfect communication that makes the holy instant what **the holy instant** is. 3 You believe you can harbor thoughts you would not share, and that salvation lies in keeping thoughts to yourself alone. 4 For in private thoughts, known only to yourself, you think you find a way to keep what you would have alone, **which are your private thoughts**, and share what <*you*> would share, **which are your non-private or shared, thoughts**. 5 And then you wonder why it is that you are not in full communication with those around you, and with God Who surrounds all of you together.

Note # 40: Perfect communication is open to all. It is both given and received by all. This is why reality is a shared Oneness. Nothing is unknown from the whole. Private thoughts are not shared with all and, therefore, are meant to exclude, rather than include. The Holy Instant is inclusive; nothing is left outside the communication process of the whole. The whole is the Mind of God.

Our world of egoic perception is predicted on projection. In projection, we take a fear-based thought we do not want, like guilt, and project it out of our mind upon another. Our senses then "observe" this same thought as being outside ourselves. This "observation" is merely a confirmation of our prejudged belief that we have projected from our mind. Thus, our egoic senses are not objective, but rather predetermined thought confirmation devices. They witness only for our private thoughts. We then deny that we are the source for these projected, private thoughts and misperceive and judge our world. This is not sharing or communication. It is delusional and exclusive.

T-15.IV.8. Every thought you would keep hidden shuts communication off, because you would have **the private, hidden thoughts not shared with the whole**. 2 It is impossible to recognize perfect communication while breaking communication holds value to you. 3 Ask yourself honestly, "Would I want to have perfect communication, and am I wholly willing to let everything that interferes with **perfect communication** go forever?" 4 If the answer is no, then the Holy Spirit's readiness to give **perfect communication** to you is not enough to make **perfect communication** yours, for you are not ready to share **perfect communication** with **the Holy Spirit**. 5 And **perfect communication** cannot come into a mind that has decided to oppose **perfect communication**. 6 For the holy instant is given and received with equal willingness, being the acceptance of the single Will that governs all thought.

Note # 41: In order to want perfect communication, we must give all our perceptions to the Holy Spirit for reinterpretation into correct perception. Correct perception will only see love or a cry for love and, therefore, respond appropriately. The appropriate response to a cry for love is love. We cannot have perfect communication with the Holy Spirit if we are unwilling to turn over all our perceptions. If we still choose to value certain aspects of the ego's thought system, we will be unwilling to turn these private thoughts over to the Holy Spirit for correction. We cannot pick and choose. The Holy Instant is an all or nothing decision. For the Holy Instant to arrive in our mind, we must surrender all of our perceptions over to the thought system of the Holy Spirit so that we can "be" the Christ that we are.

T-15.IV.9. The necessary condition for the holy instant does not require that you have no thoughts that are not pure. 2 But **the holy instant** does require that you have **no egoic thoughts** that you would keep **private.** 3 Innocence is not of your making. 4 **Innocence** is given you the instant you would have **innocence.** 5 Atonement would not be if there were no need for **Atonement.** 6 You will not be able to accept perfect communication as long as you would hide **perfect communication** from yourself. 7 For what you would hide <*is*> hidden from you. 8 In your practice, then, try only to be vigilant against deception, and seek not to protect the **private** thoughts **of the ego, which** you would keep to yourself. 9 Let the Holy Spirit's purity shine **your egoic thoughts** away, and bring all your awareness to the readiness for purity **the Holy Spirit** offers you. 10 Thus will **the Holy Spirit** make you ready to acknowledge that you are host to God, and hostage to no one and to nothing.

Note # 42: We believe we are the host of the ego; not the host to God. The Holy Spirit's thought system is the means for the return of God's Son to right-mindedness. The supposed split mind is comprised of two parts, the ego and the Christ consciousness. For the decision-maker to reclaim his divine birthright, he must freely choose to follow the guidance of the Holy Spirit. Following this guidance leads to the return to the whole-mindedness of the Christ. God's Son will reawaken to the perfect communication, which continues to always flow between the Christ and His Father even during the apparent dream of separation. We will reclaim our magnitude, the Big "S" Self, which is the shared Mind of God. The Father shares Himself as His Son shares His Big "S" Self. Perfect communication is reestablished throughout the Oneness. We drop the desire for private thought, which we would not share. All identification with egoic thoughts disappears into the nothingness from which they arose.

V. The Holy Instant and Special Relationships

T-15.V.1. The holy instant is the Holy Spirit's most useful learning device for teaching you love's meaning. 2 For **the holy instant's** purpose is to suspend judgment entirely. 3 Judgment always rests on the past, for past experience is the basis on which you judge. 4 Judgment becomes impossible without the past, for without **the past** you do not understand anything. 5 You would make no attempt to judge, because **without the past,** it would be quite apparent to you that you do not understand what anything means. 6 You are afraid of this **suspension of the past and its related reference points for judgment** because you believe that without the ego, all would be chaos. 7 Yet I assure you that without the ego, all would be love.

Note # 43: The thought system of the Holy Spirit is based on truth. God is love and, therefore, truth is love. The thought system of the ego is based on limitation. The unholy trinity of sin, guilt and fear, teach that we are limited ego-bodies, in competition with other ego- bodies. This belief system breeds competition and conflict since everything becomes a "zero sum game". For me to win, someone else must lose. There is no such thing as a "win-win solution." For unlike the world of thought and ideas, form cannot be shared. Sharing form would result in diminishment to the one that originally possessed the object. Sacrifice would, therefore, be required of the giver.

T-15.V.2. The past is the ego's chief learning device, for it is in the past that you learned to define your own needs and acquired methods for meeting **your own needs** on your own **egoic** terms. 2 We have said that to limit love to part of the Sonship is to bring guilt into your relationships, and thus make **your relationships** unreal. 3 If you seek to separate out certain aspects of the totality and look to **certain aspects of the totality** to meet your imagined needs, you are attempting to use separation to save you. 4 How, then, **since you are introducing the belief in separation,** could guilt not enter? 5 For separation is the source of guilt, and to appeal to **separation** for salvation is to believe you are alone. 6 To be alone <*is*> to be guilty. 7 For to experience yourself as alone is to deny the Oneness of the Father and His Son, and thus to attack reality.

Note # 44: When we believe that we are separate, we believe that we come from lack. Lacking the belief in our own oneness, we believe that we are incomplete. We then look outside ourselves for what we perceive we lack. Being not everything, we are lonely for we no longer know ourselves to be perfect, whole and compete. We usurp the authority of the Creator and claim that we are something other than as He created us. We claim that our ego mind is the arbitrator of truth. This rejection of both our Father's Will and His Love for us leaves us with a belief that we have sinned. Sin spawns guilt and the fear that we must be punished for our supposed "sins." The Atonement is the reestablishing of the guiltlessness of God's Son. Yet, before the guiltlessness is returned to our consciousness, all judgment must be suspended. Without the suspension of judgment, which is the purpose of the holy instant, we would never be willing to turn the misperceived events of the day to the Holy Spirit for His correction. By correcting our misperception, the Holy Spirit reawakens our Christ consciousness so that the Christ can once again assume its role as advisor to the decision-maker of our mind. We can once again make the choice for love, which is the choice for Christ, our Big "S" Self, which is also the host of God. The Oneness of the Father and His Son has been returned.

T-15.V.3. You cannot love parts of reality and understand what love means. **You must love the whole.** 2 If you would love unlike to God, Who knows no special love, how can you understand **love**? 3 To believe that <*special*> relationships, with <*special*> love, can offer you salvation is the belief that separation is salvation. 4 For it is the complete equality of the Atonement in which salvation lies. 5 How can you decide that special aspects of the Sonship can give you more than other **aspects of the Sonship**? 6 The past **judgment on behalf of separation** has taught you **those <*special*> relationships, with <*special*> love, can offer you salvation.** 7 Yet the holy instant teaches you it is not so **that <*special*> relationships, with <*special*> love, can offer you salvation.**

Note # 45: The holy instant's purpose is to teach the suspension of all judgments. Judgment is based on your misperception from the past in which you misperceived yourself to be a limited ego-body that could be hurt and made to suffer. Believing that we are guilty, we attempt to project our guilt upon the imagined outside world. Since ideas never leave their source, we maintain both our guilt and our imagined outside world. Both these ideas appear to have reality only within the split-mind of the dreamer. Believing that we are not a Oneness but rather a little "s" self, we look for something outside ourselves to complete us. A special relationship is the egoic quest to get something that you believe you lack from someone you believe has what you want. Unfortunately, since we perceive a world of limitation and lack, we now must take or steal from another what we believe we are lacking. The egoic thought system states that what you have, you have taken. This egoic belief places us on the slippery slope of sin, guilt and fear. We are caught within the victim consciousness of the ego's thought system. Rather than correct the mistake in our original thinking, we remain trapped in this perpetual cycle of egoic victim consciousness. This all arose from our belief that the separation was real. Anytime we relive the present through the eyes of past egoic judgments, we get to keep these same past results. We never become aware of the now. The future constantly reconfirms these false witnesses from our past. To break the cycle of victim consciousness, we need to suspend all judgments, which are always based on our past misperceptions. The holy instant is the suspension of all these judgments.

T-15.V.4. Because of guilt, all special relationships have elements of fear in **the special relationship**. 2 This is why **special relationships** shift and change so frequently. 3 **Special relationships** are not based on changeless love alone. 4 And love, where fear has entered, cannot be depended on because **love, where fear has entered,** is not perfect **love**. 5 In **the Holy Spirit's** function as Interpreter of what you made, the Holy Spirit uses special relationships, which you have chosen to support the ego, as learning experiences that point to truth. 6 Under **the Holy Spirit's** teaching, every relationship becomes a lesson in love.

Note # 46: The Holy Spirit does not take your special relationships from you. The Holy Spirit utilizes these relationships to teach the lessons of forgiveness and love. To the Holy Spirit, the events surrounding these relationships are either love or a cry for love. The Holy Spirit will reinterpret these relationships so that we relearn the interdependence of giving and receiving. What we give, we receive. We must learn to control our fear and turn all perceived events over to the guidance of the Holy Spirit. The event, as in all things in the world of perception, is simply a neutral learning device and only our response to the experience colors the event as "good, bad or neutral". The ego teaches fear and attack. The Holy Spirit teaches forgiveness and love. We, as decision maker, must choose what thought system we will support.

T-15.V.5. The Holy Spirit knows no one is special. 2 Yet **the Holy Spirit** also perceives that you have made special relationships, which **the Holy Spirit** would purify and not let you destroy. 3 However unholy the reason you made **a special relationship** may be, **the Holy Spirit** can translate **these special relationships** into holiness by removing as much fear as you will let **the Holy Spirit remove**. 4 You can place any relationship under **the Holy Spirit's** care and be sure that **placing any relationship under the Holy Spirit's care** will not result in pain, if you offer **to the Holy Spirit** your willingness to have **the relationship** serve no need but **the Holy Spirit's need, which is to teach love and never fear**. 5 All the guilt in **these special relationships** arises from your use of **guilt**. 6 All the love **in these special relationships arises** from **the Holy Spirit's use of love**. 7 Do not, then, be afraid to let go your imagined **egoic** needs, which would destroy the relationship. 8 Your only need is **the Holy Spirit's need**.

Note # 47: The Holy Spirit takes our special relationships and utilizes them to teach love and the truth of our interconnectedness within the Mind of God. The Holy Spirit keeps the shared parts of the relationship, our love and forgiveness, which are real, and removes or reinterprets the false perceptions of the relationship, which are based on our belief in lack, sin, guilt and fear. We must be willing to control the fear that arose from our belief in littleness. When we control our fear, we are able to turn our misperceived events over to the guidance of the Holy Spirit's thought system.

T-15.V.6. Any relationship you would substitute for another **relationship** has not been offered to the Holy Spirit for **the Holy Spirit's** use. 2 There <*is*> no substitute for love. 3 If you would attempt to substitute one aspect of love for another **aspect of love**, you have placed less value on one **aspect of love** and more on the other **aspect of love**. 4 You have not only separated **each relationship into separate aspects of love,** but you have also judged against both **relationships as lacking love.** 5 Yet you had judged against yourself **as lacking love** first, or you would never have imagined that you needed your brothers, as they were not, **which is the belief that your brothers also lack love and are incomplete.** 6 Unless you had seen yourself as without love, you could not have judged **your brothers as** so like you in lack **of love.**

Note # 48: Seeing ourselves as limited, imperfect and not complete, we cannot see our brother as perfect, whole and complete. Coming from the ego's thought system, we view everything as a zero-sum game. We lack and, therefore, we must take what we need. "Love" becomes conditional love at best. Conditional love says to another, "I will love you if you do this and that for me." Pure love is unconditional. It asks for nothing. God gives everything to everything. God's love has no conditions. It is not earned. It is given freely and without any sacrifice on the part of the giver. This is the love that the Holy Spirit would teach us. In reality, the Holy Spirit does not teach us how to love, for love is what we are. Rather the Holy Spirit teaches us how to remove all the barriers we have placed before love. We never lacked love; we just forgot that we had hidden it from ourselves.

T-15.V.7. The ego's use of relationships is so fragmented that **the ego** frequently goes even farther; one part of one aspect suits **the ego's** purposes, while **the ego** prefers different parts of another aspect. 2 Thus does **the ego** assemble reality to **the ego's** own capricious liking, offering for your seeking a picture whose likeness does not exist. 3 For there is nothing in Heaven or earth that resembles **this egoic picture whose likeness does not exist,** and so, however much you seek for **the ego's** reality, you cannot find **the ego's reality** because **a picture of limited and separate aspects of the indivisible whole does not exist and** is not real.

Note # 49: The ego's motto is, "seek and never find." The ego is very good at telling us, "We will be happy when…" Of course, when we achieve the when or what that we had been told to seek, we discover that it does not bring us happiness. At best, it appears to bring us temporary happiness but this happiness is fleeting and quickly dissipates. The ego guarantees that even if we were to somehow find "happiness" here on earth, death will inevitably take away what we value. The ego tells us to constantly look outside ourselves to be happy. Believing in lack, we fail to look within for the truth about ourselves. Being an extension of God, Who is love, we have always had everything within our mind that we sought outside of it. The ego's search for happiness is endless, because the ego does not know that we are unlimited spirit. We are not what the ego teaches. We are not limited ego-bodies that are in competition with other ego-bodies. We are unlimited spirit or mind. How can the ego correctly advise us on our happiness when the ego denies the reality of what we are? The ego attempts to fragment the indivisible whole into parts. It then judges these imagined separate aspects of the whole as not perfect, whole and complete. This is a self-fulfilling prophecy. The ego's purpose of separation determines its warped perception.

T-15.V.8. Everyone on earth has formed special relationships, and although this is not so in Heaven, the Holy Spirit knows how to bring a touch of Heaven to **the special relationships that we have formed on earth.** 2 In the holy instant no one is special, for your personal needs intrude on no one to make your brothers seem different. 3 Without the values from the past, you would see **your brothers** all the same and like yourself, **perfect, whole and complete.** 4 Nor would you see any separation between yourself and **your brothers**. 5 In the holy instant, you see in each relationship what **each relationship** will be when you perceive only the present.

Note # 50: We judge our present perceptions based on past egoic viewpoints and beliefs. The holy instant removes the guilt and judgments we associate with the past experiences. Seeing each event without previous judgments, we have no reference points to judge the current event. We are being present in the <now> of the moment. Since everything in the world of perception is neutral, we can learn the lesson of the day with an open mind. We can choose again if we so desire.

T-15.V.9. God knows you <*now.*> 2 He remembers nothing, having always known you exactly as **God** knows you now. 3 The holy instant reflects **God's** knowing by bringing all perception out of the past, thus removing the **past** frame of reference you have built by which to judge your brothers. 4 Once **the past frame of reference you have built by which to judge your brothers is gone**, the Holy Spirit substitutes His frame of reference for **your past frame of reference**. 5 **The Holy Spirit's** frame of reference is simply God. 6 The Holy Spirit's timelessness lies only here, **in the now**. 7 For in the holy instant, free of the past, you see that love is in you, and you have no need to look without and snatch love guiltily from where you thought it was, **which was outside of you**.

Note # 51: For the Holy Spirit, the important aspect of our notion of time is the present. Unlike the ego's thought system, the past is not the focus. In eternity, which is beyond time, there is only the changeless <now>. In the world of perception, the present time frame is the closest thing that resembles the eternal <now>. By the removal of the past, the Holy Spirit removes the reference point for judgment. This allows us the opportunity for the decision-maker within us to choose again.

T-15.V.10. All your relationships are blessed in the holy instant, because the blessing is not limited. 2 In the holy instant the Sonship gains as one, and united in your blessing **the Sonship** becomes one to you. 3 The meaning of love is the meaning God gave to **love**. 4 Give to **love** any meaning apart from **God's meaning**, and it is impossible to understand **love**. 5 God loves every brother as **God** loves you; neither less nor more. 6 **God** needs them all equally, and so do you **need them all equally**. 7 In time, you have been told to offer miracles as I direct, and let the Holy Spirit bring to you those who are seeking you. 8 Yet in the holy instant you unite directly with God, and all your brothers join in Christ. 9 Those who are joined in Christ are in no way separate. 10 For Christ is the Self the Sonship shares, as God shares His Self with Christ.

Note # 52: We are all part of the Mind of God and, therefore, interconnected as a united oneness. All parts benefit equally since there is no separation.
Note: Christ is defined as the Big "S" Self that the Sonship shares with the God, the Creator. God also shares Himself completely with the Christ, our Big "S" Self. The "Christ" is the home of the Father, the Holy Spirit and our Big "S" Self. When the mad idea of the separation occurred, the unified Sonship appeared to shatter into innumerous pieces. Each one of us perceives ourselves as one of these separate pieces. This is an illusion within our mind. We have chosen through the use of projection, to deny knowledge and project part of our thoughts outside the whole. We claim that we do not know what we are. The whole mind now appears to be split in two. Instead of the state of knowing and certainty, we enter into a state of "What Am I?" Uncertainty has arisen and perception has been substituted for knowledge. The shattering of the Sonship is not real, but is how we perceive ourselves to be. In the real world, the Kingdom, the unity of the Oneness remains perfect, whole and complete.

T-15.V.11. Think you that you can judge the Self of God? 2 God has created **the Self of God** beyond judgment, out of **God's** need to extend His Love. 3 With love in you, you have no need except to extend **love**. 4 In the holy instant there is no conflict of needs, for there is only one **need, which is the**

extension of love. We are co-creators with God. 5 For the holy instant reaches to eternity, and to the Mind of God. 6 And it is only there, **in the Mind of God, that** love has meaning, and only there **in the Mind of God** can **love** be understood.

Note # 53: Love does not judge. Love only accepts. We are an expression of God's Love. In reality there is nothing outside the Mind of God since there is only the Mind of God. This Mind is eternal and changeless. The Sonship is the extension of this Mind. We are co-creators with God. While on earth, our function is forgiveness and our purpose is love. While in Heaven, our function is co-creation. We extend the Mind of our Creator.

VI. The Holy Instant and the Laws of God

T-15.VI.1. It is impossible to use one relationship at the expense of another **relationship** and not to suffer guilt. 2 And it is equally impossible to condemn part of a relationship and find peace within **the relationship**. 3 Under the Holy Spirit's teaching all relationships are seen as total commitments, yet **all relationships** do not conflict with one another in any way. 4 Perfect faith in each **relationship, for the relationship's** ability to satisfy you completely, arises only from perfect faith in yourself. 5 And **perfect faith in yourself,** you cannot have while guilt remains. 6 And there will be guilt as long as you accept the possibility, and cherish **the possibility,** that you can make a brother into what he is not, **which is a limited ego-body,** because you would have **a brother be** so **limited**.

Note # 54: We must make a choice as to what we believe. If we believe that we are a body, as opposed to unlimited spirit, we will see ourselves as being vulnerable. If we are vulnerable, we must be a body, which is something that can be hurt and has needs. We will also view our brother as someone we are competing against in this frightening world of limited resources. We will always be attempting to get our perceived needs met by entering into a special relationship in which we can steal from another that which we believe we lack. To have needs implies that we lack something and that our brother has it. Sacrifice and bartering are required in this type of relationship. Seeing ourselves as something other than perfect, whole and complete, we perceive ourselves as something less than the everything God created us to be. We need perfect faith in what we are, our Big "S" Self. If we see ourselves as the Big "S" Self, which is everything, we can communicate like our Father. Extension is possible because we have accepted our true reality as unlimited spirit. "I am not a body. I am free, for I am still as God created me." Believe our brother is limited and we place the same chain of limitation on ourselves. For an idea never leaves its source.

T-15.VI.2. You have so little faith in yourself because you are unwilling to accept the fact that perfect love is in you. 2 And so you seek without for what you cannot find without, **which is perfect love**. 3 I offer you my perfect faith in you, in place of all your doubts. 4 But forget not that my faith must be as perfect in all your brothers as **my faith** is in you, or **my faith** would be a limited gift to you. 5 In the holy instant we share our faith in God's Son because we recognize, together, that **our brother** is wholly worthy of **our faith,** and in our appreciation of his worth we cannot doubt **our brother's** holiness. 6 And so we love **our brother**.

Note # 55: Jesus, like the Holy Spirit, knows what we are. He sees us perfect, whole and complete; a united oneness with our brother. Being a Oneness, nothing can be viewed as limited or imperfect, for to do so would limit the Oneness. Our split-mind is unwilling to accept the fact that we must be perfect love since we are an extension of the Father. Holiness is the recognition that we are as God created us, whole, perfect and complete.

T-15.VI.3. All separation vanishes as holiness is shared. 2 For holiness is power, and by sharing **holiness, holiness** gains in strength. 3 If you seek for satisfaction in gratifying your needs as you perceive **your needs,** you must believe that strength comes from another, and what you gain he loses. 4 Someone must always lose if you perceive yourself as weak. 5 Yet there is another interpretation of relationships that transcends the concept of loss of power completely.

<u>Note # 56:</u> When we follow the ego's thought system, we believe that we are involved in a zero-sum game. To win, someone else must lose.

T-15.VI.4. You do not find it difficult to believe that when another calls on God for love, your call **still** remains as strong. 2 Nor do you think that when God answers him, your hope of **God answering your call** is diminished. 3 On the contrary, you are more inclined to regard his success as witness to the possibility **that your call will be successfully answered by God.** 4 That is because you recognize, however dimly, that God is an idea, and so your faith in **God** is strengthened by sharing **the idea of God.** 5 What you find difficult to accept is the fact that, like your Father, <you> are an idea. 6 And like **your Father,** you can give yourself completely, wholly without loss and only with gain. 7 Herein **the belief that you are an idea and, therefore, can share yourself without diminishment** lies peace, for here **being an idea** there <is> no conflict.

<u>Note # 57:</u> Ideas can be shared and by sharing an idea, the idea is strengthened. Form cannot be shared because to share form would result in diminishment to the giver. If a giver had two dollars and gave you one of his dollars, together you would still have two dollars. The giver would have lost one of his dollars to you. The world of form is a zero-sum game. If we believe that we are a bodily form, we cannot share that form without diminishment and sacrifice. The ego's thought system tells us that we are limited ego-bodies. The thought system of the Holy Spirit, states that we are unlimited spirit, an idea or thought of God. Ideas can be shared. Thus, the two thought systems are constantly arriving at opposite conclusions because their underlying major premises are contradictions of each other. Accept the major premise of either thought system and the rest follows logically. ACIM asks us to question what appears to be the unthinkable. What if everything we see within our world of form, which appears so solid, is merely a dream or thought that we made up in our imagination? Because we have identified ourselves so heavily with the dream, the dreamer no longer is aware that he, the dreamer, is the cause of the dream he "sees." ACIM states that if the dreamer chose to awaken, the dream of the limited ego-body would disappear. We are an unlimited idea in the Mind of God and thus, everything is possible. Ideas can be extended without diminishment By giving an idea, we reinforce or receive the idea. To give, therefore, is to receive. Conflict, which is birthed out of belief in the limitation caused by form, has disappeared.

This paragraph is clear that the terms such as spirit, mind, God and ourselves are not physical but rather thoughts or ideas. Form is but perceived images that arise from our thoughts and ideas. If they are shared with love, they create. If they are fear-based, they are not shared and result in making by projection. Thus, heaven and hell are not places but states of mind.

T-15.VI.5. In the world of scarcity, love has no meaning and peace is impossible. 2 For gain and loss are both accepted **in a world of scarcity,** and so no one is aware that perfect love is in him. 3 In the holy instant you recognize the idea of love in you, and unite this idea **of love in you** with the Mind that thought it and could not relinquish **that idea of love in you.** 4 By holding **perfect love** within itself, there <is> no loss. 5 The holy instant thus becomes a lesson in how to hold all of your brothers in your mind, experiencing not loss but completion. 6 From this **lesson in how to hold all of your brothers in your mind and experiencing not loss but completion,** it follows you can only give. 7 And this **ability to only give** <is> love, for this alone, **the giving of love,** is natural under the laws of God. 8 In the holy instant the laws of God prevail, and only **the laws of God** have meaning. 9 **In the holy instant** the laws of this world cease to hold any meaning at all. 10 When the Son of God accepts the laws of God as what he gladly wills, it is impossible that he be bound, or limited in any way. 11 In that instant **when the Son of God accepts the laws of God as what he gladly wills,** he, **God's Son,** is as free as God would have him be. 12 For the instant he, **God's Son,** refuses to be bound, he is not bound.

Note # 58: Because we are an extension of God, we have free will. We have the right to believe anything we would like to believe. If we choose to believe something in our dream world of provisional reality, the belief will appear to be true to us. We would act as if we are bound by what we imaged to be true. By denying the reality of the truth, our false beliefs become binding upon us within our dream. Due to the creative power of the mind, even our beliefs in limitation appear and act real within the dream. Only someone who is aware of both the truth and the dream can reawaken the dreamer safely to the truth of his real Big "S" Self. The Holy Spirit is this guide. The holy instant is the dropping of our judgments of the past, which form the basis for our belief in sin, guilt and fear. See your brother as guiltless and he is free. Since to give is to receive, his freedom becomes our own road to salvation.

T-15.VI.6. In the holy instant nothing happens that has not always been. 2 Only the veil that has been drawn across reality is lifted. 3 Nothing has changed. 4 Yet the awareness of changelessness comes swiftly as the veil of time is pushed aside. 5 No one who has not yet experienced the lifting of the veil **of time**, and felt himself drawn irresistibly into the light behind **the veil of time**, can have faith in love without fear. 6 Yet the Holy Spirit gives you this faith **in love without fear**, because **the Holy Spirit** offered **this faith in love without fear** to me and I accepted **this faith in love without fear**. 7 Fear not the holy instant will be denied you, for I **did not deny the holy instant**. 8 And through me the Holy Spirit gives **the holy instant** unto you, as you will give **the holy instant onto another**. 9 Let no need you perceive obscure your need of this **faith in love without fear**. 10 For in the holy instant you will recognize the only need the Sons of God share equally, and by this recognition you will join with me in offering what is needed, **which is faith in love without fear.**

Note # 59: Faith in love without fear is the result of the holy instant. The Holy Spirit shares with you His faith in love and knows not fear. The purpose of the holy instant is to suspend all judgment entirely. This teaches love. When we suspend judgment, we remove the source of guilt. To the ego, to judge is to make guilty. The holy instant restores perfect communication because we are now able to both give and receive complete communication. Guilt never comes alone. Guilt is always associated with sin and fear. Because the world of form arose out of the belief in sin, guilt and fear, we must see the Son of God as guiltless in order to allow perfect love into this world of fear. Within the world of fear, we believe that even if we were to somehow find love, we would quickly lose it again. Since we believe that love is outside us, we fear that love can always be taken away. Love cannot last in the unstable world of dreams.

T-15.VI.7. It is through <us> that peace will come. 2 Join me in the idea of peace, for in ideas minds can communicate. 3 If you would give yourself as your Father gives His Self, you will learn to understand Selfhood, **the Big "S" Self**. 4 And therein **in total giving of yourself** is love's meaning understood. 5 But remember that understanding is of the mind, and only of the mind. 6 Knowledge is therefore of the mind, and **knowledge's** conditions are in the mind with **understanding**. 7 If you were not an idea, and nothing but an idea, you could not be in full communication with all that ever was. 8 Yet as long as you prefer to be something else, **like a bodily form, rather than an idea,** or would attempt to be nothing else and something else together, you will not remember the language of communication, which you know perfectly.

Note # 60: The language of communication is love. Love communicates through ideas, not form. When you realize your oneness with all, you will be at peace. The understanding of what you are will transform you from the world of perception in which you saw yourself as form, back to the world of knowledge, which we never left. We are a thought in the mind of God. Time will fade away as communication with God returns the remembrance of God to our mind. The split-minded will be made whole and we will understand that we are part of the Mind of God and are limitless thought.

T-15.VI.8. In the holy instant God is remembered, and the language of communication with all your brothers is remembered with **God.** 2 For communication is remembered together, as is truth. 3 There is no exclusion in the holy instant because the past is gone, and with **the past** goes the whole basis for exclusion. 4 Without **exclusion's** source, **which is the belief in separation that arose in the past, all** exclusion vanishes. 5 And this permits your Source and the **Source** of all your brothers, **which is God, your Father,** to replace **the belief in separation from** your awareness. 6 God and the power of God will take Their **(the Father and the Christ)** rightful place in you, and you will experience the full communication of ideas with ideas. 7 Through your ability to **experience the full communication of ideas with ideas,** you will learn what you must be, for you will begin to understand what your Creator is, and what His creation, **the Christ,** is along with **His Creator.**

Note # 61: Perfect communication is the return to knowledge and the Oneness. This requires the removal of any egoic thoughts, which support the belief that the separation was real. It requires complete faith that you remain exactly as you were created, perfect, whole and complete. The Sonship is all God created, as He created it. We, the Christ, have been given all the power of God. When we create from the idea of perfect love, which is what God is, we are given all the power of God. The creative power of the Christ is the demonstration of the power of God, for the Christ is the power of God. What we must be is a creator like our Father. We will extend the idea of God, which is love, to our own creations, which like ourselves, are an idea, not a form. Perfect communication is creation.

VII. The Needless Sacrifice

T-15.VII.1. Beyond the poor attraction of the special love relationship, and always obscured by **the poor attraction of the special egoic love relationship,** is the powerful attraction of the Father for His Son. 2 There is no other love that can satisfy you, because there <is> no other love **than the Father's love for His Son.** 3 This **love of God** is the only love that is fully given and fully returned. 4 Being complete, **the love of God** asks nothing. 5 Being wholly pure, everyone joined in **the love of God** has everything. 6 **The love of God** is not the basis for any relationship in which the ego enters. 7 For every relationship on which the ego embarks <is> **a** special **relationship.**

Note # 62: The Christ and the Father share Themselves in perfect love. The ego sees itself as not whole and does not share. Being incomplete the ego believes that it must take something from outside itself to become whole. The ego looks to the special relationship for something it feels it lacks and, therefore, believes it must steal from the other party.

T-15.VII.2. The ego establishes relationships only to get something. 2 And **the ego** would keep the giver bound to itself through guilt. 3 It is impossible for the ego to enter into any relationship without anger, for the ego believes that anger makes friends. 4 This, **the ego's idea that anger makes friends**, is not **the ego's** statement, but it <*is*> **the ego's** purpose. 5 For the ego really believes that **the ego** can get and keep <*by making guilty.*> 6 **The ego's idea that you can get and keep** <*by making guilty*>, is the ego's one attraction; an attraction so weak that **the ego** would have no hold **on you** at all, except that no one recognizes **the ego's purpose is to make everything appear guilty**. 7 For the ego always seems to attract through love, and **the ego** has no attraction at all to anyone who perceives that **the ego** attracts through guilt.

<u>Note # 63:</u> The ego is the master of guilt projection. Sin, guilt and fear go hand in hand and "prove" that you are not perfect, whole or complete.

T-15.VII.3. The sick attraction of guilt must be recognized for what **the sick attraction of guilt** is. 2 For **since guilt has** been made real to you, it is essential to look at **guilt** clearly, and by withdrawing your investment in **guilt**, to learn to let **guilt** go. 3 No one would choose to let go what he believes has value. 4 Yet the attraction of guilt has value to you only because you have not looked at what **the attraction of guilt** is, and have judged **the attraction of guilt** completely in the dark. 5 As we bring **the sick attraction of guilt** to light, your only question will be why it was you ever wanted **to be attracted to guilt and therefore made guilty**. 6 You have nothing to lose by looking open-eyed **at your attraction to guilt**, for ugliness such as this **sick attraction of guilt** belongs not in your holy mind. 7 This host of God, **your holy mind,** can have no real investment here **in guilt**.

<u>Note #64:</u> Guilt's attraction is that guilt confirms that you are special. The ego claims that you are the arbitrator for truth. When we claim to be separate, we also claim that we have either self-created ourselves or successfully opposed our Creator's Will. In either case, instead of being the unlimited everything, we have made ourselves into a limited something else. The price for this sin of usurping God's authority is guilt and fear. The ego demands that the egoic god of revenge administer the required punishment of eternal damnation as the price for our sin. Guilt and fear is the reward for the ego's specialness since you know that God must punish you. It is this desire to be special that birthed the wish to be guilty of something. Guilt in a sick way "proves" that we are special.

T-15.VII.4. We said before that the ego attempts to maintain and increase guilt, but in such a way that you do not recognize what **guilt** would do to you. 2 For it is the ego's fundamental doctrine that what you do to others you have escaped **from having been done onto you**. 3 The ego wishes no one well. 4 Yet **the ego's** survival depends on your belief that you are exempt from **the ego's** evil intentions. 5 **The ego's** counsels, therefore, that if you are host to **the ego, the ego** will enable you to direct **the ego's** anger outward **upon something else**, thus protecting you **from the ego's anger**. 6 And thus, **the ego** embarks on an endless, unrewarding chain of special relationships, forged out of anger and dedicated to but one insane belief; that the more anger you invest outside yourself, the safer you become **from your own ego's anger**.

<u>Note # 65:</u> The ego must be careful with guilt and anger. The ego must provide some promise to you that if you learn to cope with your guilt, anger and pain in a certain way, the egoic thought system will eventually be able to return you to happiness. If happiness cannot be obtained, a reduction in misery is offered by the ego as a reward for your loyalty to its belief system. For otherwise, you would realize that the ego's thought system is a dead-end that can never lead to peace and happiness. If you did realize the

ego's insanity, you would wake up and quickly choose again. This time, your decision-maker would side with the thought system of the Holy Spirit. This is why projection is the tool of the ego. In projection, we take an idea that our mind fostered and project that same idea outside our split-mind in a vain attempt to get rid of the thought. We attempt to project our sin and guilt out of our mind, which was the source of the problem, onto a guiltless world that appears to be outside our mind. This is what the ego uses special relationships for. Special relationships become the "guilt catchers" of our sins.

T-15.VII.5. It is this chain **of special relationships** that binds the Son of God to guilt, and it is this chain **of special relationships** the Holy Spirit would remove from his holy mind. 2 For the chain of savagery belongs not around **you,** the chosen host of God, who cannot make himself host to the ego. 3 In the name of **the split-minded's** release, and in the Name of **the Holy Spirit,** Who would release the **split-minded,** let us look more closely at the relationships the ego contrives, and let the Holy Spirit judge **these special relationships** truly. 4 For it is certain that if you will look at **these special relationships,** you will offer them gladly to **the Holy Spirit.** 5 What **the Holy Spirit** can make of **these special relationships** you do not know, but you will become willing to find out **what the Holy Spirit can make of these special relationships**, if you are willing first to perceive what you have made of **these egoic special relationships**.

Note # 66: Because of our belief in the ego's thought system, we are incapable of judging truly what the ego's special relationship does to us and how it keeps us always searching for love and salvation where love cannot be found   The motto of the ego is "Seek and do not find." In egoic special relationships, we continue this pattern of endless searching. The egoic special relationship confirms that we lack wholeness. If we understood that any form of specialness sends us away from the goal of rediscovering our divine birthright of the Oneness of everything, we would choose a different path. Guilt cannot be removed by projection since an idea never leaves its source.

T-15.VII.6. In one way or another, every relationship the ego makes is based on the idea that by sacrificing itself, **the ego** becomes bigger. 2 The "sacrifice," which **the ego** regards as purification, is actually the root of **the ego's** bitter resentment. 3 For **the ego** would prefer to attack directly, and avoid delaying what **the ego** really wants **which is to keep your split-mind in victim consciousness.** 4 Yet the ego acknowledges "reality" as **the ego** sees **reality,** and recognizes that no one could interpret direct attack as love. 5 Yet to make guilty <is> a direct attack, although **to make someone guilty** does not seem to be **a direct attack.** 6 For the guilty expect attack, and having asked for **attack, the guilty** are attracted to **attack.**

Note # 67: The ego first convinces us that we have sinned and, therefore, are guilty. Being guilty, we learn to expect to be attacked. Any attack is proof that we have succeeded in our quest to be separate and special. ACIM describes the ego as a separate entity for the purpose of ease in understanding. In reality, the ego is the part of your split-mind that believes it has separated itself from God and God's Love. The ego is the desire to be special or different. It seeks to be something other than an extension of our Father, which is only love. The ego is the part of your mind that claims it does not know what it is. It has abandoned knowledge and now seeks to recreate itself as something other than God's Effect.

T-15.VII.7. In such insane relationships, the attraction of what you do not want seems to be much stronger than the attraction of what you do want. 2 For each one thinks that he has sacrificed something to the other, and hates **the other for the sacrifice he believes he has made.** 3 Yet this **self-sacrifice that results in hate for the other** is what he thinks he wants. 4 He is not in love with the other at all. 5 He merely believes he is in love with sacrifice. 6 And for this sacrifice, which he demands of himself, he demands that the other accept the guilt and sacrifice himself as well. 7 Forgiveness becomes impossible, for the ego believes that to forgive another is to lose him. 8 It is only by attack without forgiveness that the ego can ensure the guilt that holds all its **egoic special** relationships together.

Note # 68: The ego does not understand what love is. God's love is unconditional. God being all, gives all, and asks nothing in return. The ego teaches that giving is not receiving and that since you are a limited ego-body, you must take what you lack from another. The ego gives only to get. From the egoic point of view, both "good and bad" relations are special in that they confirm that we are separate from the whole. For the sake of discussion, however, I will focus on the typical person's understanding of a special friendly or "loving" relationship on planet earth.

In our typical friendly special relationship, we agree to do something in exchange for the other party doing something for us. This agreement is not unconditional love but rather a form of bartering. We negotiate the best deal we can extract from the other side. If we demand too much, the other party will perceive that they are getting less than what we are getting and, therefore, decide not to make the "deal." In order to keep them around, we must sacrifice something that we possess to keep them wanting to play the game of "Let's Make a Deal" with us. By making some self-sacrifice to appease the other party, we leverage this self-sacrifice as the means to get what we want. We tell them that they must scratch our back because we scratch theirs. This sacrificial offering is really designed to be a guilt-throwing device that chains them to us. It is their guilt that keeps them beholden to us. Special "friendly" relationships are, therefore, utilized to throw and catch guilt. Our idea of love is "I will love you if you do this…" We call this "love" but in reality it is just a form of bartering or high stakes poker. It is not given freely because we belief that to give requires sacrifice. We believe that when we give, we do not receive. We view our "sacrifice" as a debt to be repaid. We want love, yet, what we get is the sense of being betrayed by the object of our "love." Even in the "perfect" relationship that meets all of our supposed desires, we are ultimately denied our reward by the death of one party. Because we perceive or identify ourselves to be a body, we can never find lasting happiness and peace in the world of form. Form cannot be shared. For sharing of form requires some sacrifice on the part of the giver. The giver always has less of the item than when he started. Only ideas or thoughts can be shared. By sharing thoughts, there is no diminishment to the person that originally shared the idea. Instead, the idea may actually be strengthened. In the world of the ego, special relationships, although cloaked in the words of love and friendship, are devices for self-sacrifice and guilt and result in resentment, guilt and fear for both parties. Once again we find that the ego has failed to keep its promise of, "I will be happy when…" and all we end up with is pain and sacrifice.

T-15.VII.8. Yet **special relationships** only <*seem*> to be together. 2 For relationships, to the ego, mean only that bodies are together. 3 It is always this **bringing together of bodies** that the ego demands **in its relationships**, and **the ego** does not object where the mind goes or what **the mind** thinks, **for what the mind thinks** seems unimportant **to the ego.** 4 As long as the body is there to receive its sacrifice, **the ego** is content. 5 To the ego the mind is private, and only the body can be shared. 6 Ideas are basically of no concern **to the ego**, except as **something that** brings the body of another closer or farther. 7 And it is in these terms **of whether an idea brings the body of another closer or farther apart** that **the ego utilizes to evaluate** ideas as good or bad. 8 What makes another guilty and holds him through guilt is "good." 9 What releases **another** from guilt is "bad," because he would no longer believe that bodies communicate, and so **the other** would be "gone."

Note # 69: The ego is the symbol or idea for the separation. The body is the symbol for the ego. The ego wants us to believe that we are a body. If we are a body, we are form and, therefore, cannot be an unlimited idea or spirit. The ego's goal is to maintain control over the mind by keeping the decision-making ability of the mind in victim consciousness. Sacrifice comes from the idea that we are form, and as form, we must be diminished when we share our form with another. Sacrifice always is accompanied by guilt. Only the guilty are required to make sacrifice and we make sacrifice because we are guilty. It is guilt and sacrifice that hold the special egoic relationship together. To the ego, we communicate to another by transmitting our guilt and sacrifice to the other party. Guilt and our ability to make the other party feel guilty bind the egoic relationship together. If the other party attempts to leave against your will, we lay a "guilt trip" upon the other party claiming that they still owe us loyalty for all the sacrifices we have made on their behalf. We claim that we are the innocent victims of their treachery. The ego believes that if we release the other party from guilt, they must leave us since only guilt holds egoic relationships and bodies together. This is why guilt is so highly valued by the egoic thought system. The ego does not know what love is and thus, to the ego, love has no power of attraction.

T-15.VII.9. Suffering and sacrifice are the gifts with which the ego would "bless" all unions. 2 And those who are united at **the ego's** altar accept suffering and sacrifice as the price of union. 3 In their angry alliances, born of the fear of loneliness and yet dedicated to the continuance of loneliness, each seeks relief from guilt by increasing **guilt** in the other. 4 For each believes that **by increasing guilt in the other,** this decreases guilt in **himself.** 5 The other seems always to be attacking and wounding him, perhaps in little ways, perhaps "unconsciously," yet never without demand of sacrifice. 6 The fury of those joined at the ego's altar far exceeds your awareness of **the fury and anger.** 7 For what the ego really wants you do not realize, **which is the suffering, sacrifice and anger that results from your continuing belief in separation and loneliness.**

<u>Note # 70:</u> The sacrifice and guilt that result from a special relationship will lead to anger. The anger will arise from your sense of betrayal because our "needs" were not meet by the party. The source of our anger is our belief that someone or something outside ourselves did not behave the way we required them to and, therefore, they failed to meet our needs.

T-15.VII.10. Whenever you are angry, you can be sure that you have formed a special relationship, which the ego has "blessed," for anger <is> **the ego's** blessing. 2 Anger takes many forms, but **anger** cannot long deceive those who will learn that love brings no guilt at all, and what brings guilt cannot be love and <must> be anger. 3 All anger is nothing more than an attempt to make someone feel guilty, and this attempt **to make someone feel guilty** is the only basis the ego accepts for special relationships. 4 Guilt is the only need the ego has, and as long as you identify with **the ego,** guilt will remain attractive to you. 5 Yet remember this; to be with a body is not communication. 6 And if you think **to be with a body is communication,** you will feel guilty about communication and will be afraid to hear the Holy Spirit, recognizing in **the Holy Spirit's** Voice your own need to communicate.

<u>Note # 71:</u> Anger arises when you perceive that your needs are not being met by the other party in the special relationship. Needs are the ego's confirmation that you are not perfect, whole and complete. Needs confirm that you believe that the separation is real and that you are a limited ego-body and can be made to suffer and die. Mind communicates through ideas. Although the body is recognized by the Holy Spirit to be a neutral communication device, the ego perceives this same body as a means or tool to prove that the separation was real. The ego does not communicate for communications would require both giving and receiving, which the ego has no desire to do. If you identify yourself as a body with a brain, you cannot communicate. Communication requires mind and sharing. The ego will not share and the body cannot share.

T-15.VII.11. The Holy Spirit cannot teach through fear. 2 And how can **the Holy Spirit** communicate with you, while you believe that to communicate is to make yourself alone? 3 It is clearly insane to believe that by communicating you will be abandoned. 4 And yet many do believe **that by communicating you will be abandoned.** 5 For they think their minds must be kept private or they will lose **their minds**, but **they think** if their bodies are together their minds remain their own. 6 The union of bodies thus becomes the way in which they **who believe that by communicating you will lose your mind** would keep minds apart **and therefore private**. 7 For bodies cannot forgive. 8 **Bodies** can only do as the mind directs.

Note # 72: The ego teaches that you are a body and that the brain is just a body part. The Holy Spirit teaches that we are mind and not the body. Mind can communicate because ideas can be shared. The ego would have you believe that you can maintain the privacy of the mind because if your mind is located within the brain, which is a body part, you must be separate. Private thoughts are the thoughts of judgment, which must foster guilt. We do not wish to share our private thoughts because we value these unloving thoughts that prove our specialness. We refuse to give them over to the Holy Spirit's guidance. The Holy Spirit knows that the mind is shared and interconnected with the Mind of God. All thoughts of judgment must be stopped in order for communication to be restored.

T-15.VII.12. The illusion of the autonomy of the body and its ability to overcome loneliness is but the working of the ego's plan to establish its own **egoic** autonomy. 2 As long as you believe that to be with a body is companionship, you will be compelled to attempt to keep your brother in his body, held there by guilt. 3 And you will see safety in guilt and danger in communication. 4 For the ego will always teach that loneliness is solved by guilt, and that communication is the cause of loneliness. 5 And despite the evident insanity of this lesson **that loneliness is solved by guilt, and that communication is the cause of loneliness,** many have learned **this lesson**.

Note # 73: The ego teaches that our brother, like ourselves, is a body. In the world of form, to have is to hold. By keeping our brother close to us, we maintain both mutual guilt and sacrifice. It is our private thoughts, unshared with our brother that we continually utilize to judge and declare our brother's guilt. These private thoughts corrupt the special relationship with our brother by making it into an unholy relationship based on lack and fear. Guilt is the powerful tool used by the ego to keep the special relationship together.

T-15.VII.13. Forgiveness lies in communication as surely as damnation lies in guilt. 2 It is the Holy Spirit's teaching function to instruct those who believe communication to be damnation that communication is salvation. 3 And **the Holy Spirit** will **teach that communication is salvation** for the power of God in **the Holy Spirit** and **in** you is joined in a real relationship so holy and so strong, that **the power of God** can overcome even **the egoic belief that communication is damnation** without fear.

Note # 74: Through the teaching of forgiveness, the Holy Spirit shows us that the Son of God is guiltless. The teaching of forgiveness restores the unity of what appears to be separate minds. Communication is being restored. The guilty refuse to communicate since they believe it will result in their damnation. The guilty have already condemned themselves and thus, are afraid to listen to their final sentencing to hell by the "Hanging Judge," which is the egoic god of revenge. Those who see themselves as guilty have forgotten the truth that the final judgment from the God of Love must be that His Son is innocent, sinless and guiltless like Himself.

T-15.VII.14. It is through the holy instant that what seems impossible is accomplished making it evident that it is not impossible. **What seemed impossible was the accomplishment of the suspension of all judgment, which fostered guilt.** 2 In the holy instant guilt holds no attraction, since communication has been restored. 3 And guilt, whose only purpose is to disrupt communication, has no function here **in the holy instant**. 4 Here, **in the holy instant,** there is no concealment, and no private thoughts. 5 The willingness to communicate attracts communication to it, and overcomes loneliness completely. 6 There is complete forgiveness here **in the holy instant,** for there is no desire to exclude anyone from your completion, in sudden recognition of the value of his part in **the holy instant and communication**. 7 In the protection of your wholeness, all are invited and made welcome. 8 And you understand that your completion is God's **completion** Whose only need is to have you be complete. 9 For your completion makes you **God's completion** in your awareness. 10 And here **in the holy instant, which is your completion, is** it that you experience yourself as you were created, and as you are.

<u>Note # 75:</u> With the removal of all guilt, the Sonship is once again reawakened to its divine birthright. Realizing our innocence, we freely choose to come home and be what we are, the shared Oneness of the Mind of God. When God created the Sonship, He extended Himself. By co-creation with God, we complete God.

VIII. The Only Real Relationship

T-15.VIII.1. The holy instant does not replace the need for learning, for the Holy Spirit must not leave you as your Teacher until the holy instant has extended far beyond time. 2 For a teaching assignment such as His, **the Holy Spirit** must use everything in this world for your release. 3 **The Holy Spirit** must side with every sign or token of your willingness to learn **from the Holy Spirit** what the truth must be. 4 **The Holy Spirit** is swift to utilize whatever you offer **the Holy Spirit** on behalf of this **learning of what the truth must be.** 5 **The Holy Spirit's** concern and care for you are limitless. 6 In the face of your fear of forgiveness, which **the Holy Spirit** perceives as clearly as **the Holy Spirit** knows forgiveness is release, **the Holy Spirit** will teach you to remember that forgiveness is not loss, but **that forgiveness is** your salvation. 7 And that in complete forgiveness, in which you recognize that there is nothing to forgive, you are absolved completely.

<u>Note # 76:</u> In the holy instant, all judgment is suspended. There still remains the requirement that the split-minded decision-maker must choose again. This time the decision-maker must freely choose the thought system of the Holy Spirit. Forgiveness is the bridge that the Holy Spirit utilizes to teach the lessons that bring us to the realization of the truth about ourselves. With forgiveness, we cross over the chasm that separates illusion from truth. The Holy Spirit is the bridge-keeper. He carries or guides us from the world of illusion to the real world, which is the Kingdom or Heaven. The world of illusion is our world of provisional reality that we individually perceive. Our illusionary world of perception is a world based on fear, the laws of chaos, time and space. The Kingdom or Heaven is the eternal world of changeless truth and love. Forgiveness is the tool that brings illusion into the light of the truth. When we bring illusions into the light of truth, forgiveness teaches us that the illusion has no reality. The thought of the illusion fades from our memory. Only the truth about your brother and yourself remain. Forgiveness is the tool that the Holy Spirit utilizes to teach us the truth about our joint divine inheritance that we share with all the Sonship.

T-15.VIII.2. Hear **the Holy Spirit** gladly, and learn **from the Holy Spirit** that you have need of no special relationships at all. 2 You but seek in **special relationships** what you have thrown away, **which is the truth of the love of God.** 3 And through **special relationships** you will never learn the value of what you have cast aside, **the love of God,** but still desire with all your heart. 4 Let us join together in making the holy instant all that there is, by desiring that **the holy instant** <be> all that there is. 5 God's

Son has such great need of your willingness to strive for **making the holy instant all that there is** that you cannot conceive of need so great **as making the holy instant all that there is**. 6 Behold the only need that God and His Son share, and will to meet together. 7 You are not alone in this **need to meet together with God**. 8 The will of your creations calls to you, to share your will with **your creations**. 9 Turn, then, in peace from guilt to God and **to your creations**.

Note # 77: The ego utilizes the special relationship as a device to teach sacrifice and guilt, which are the opposite of love. By giving your special relationship over to the Holy Spirit, He can utilize them as lessons of forgiveness and love.

T-15.VIII.3. Relate only with what will never leave you, and what you can never leave, **which is the truth of the love of God.** 2 The loneliness of God's Son is the loneliness of his Father. 3 Refuse not the awareness of your completion, and seek not to restore **your completion from** yourself. 4 Fear not to give redemption over to your Redeemer's Love. 5 **The Christ** will not fail you, for **the Christ** comes from **God, the Father, the** One, Who cannot fail. 6 Accept your sense of failure as nothing more than a mistake in who you are. 7 For the holy host of God, **the Christ** is beyond failure, and nothing that he wills can be denied. 8 You are forever in a relationship so holy that **this relationship with the Father** calls to everyone to escape from loneliness, and join you in your love. 9 And where you are must everyone seek, and find you there, **in this, your loving relationship with God**.

Note 78: Although we perceive ourselves as outside the love of God, this too is but an illusion. The Christ, which is what we truly are, has never lost the remembrance of God or that we are God's Son, perfect, whole and complete. We may dream that we are an individual, a separate little "s" self, but we remain a Oneness. Our illusion of separation must be treated only as a mistake that needs correction, rather than a sin that requires punishment. The Christ is and always will be, One with the Father for the Christ is the extension of the Mind of God and the home of the Father.

T-15.VIII.4. Think but an instant on this: God gave the Sonship to you, to ensure your perfect creation. 2 **The Sonship** was **God's** gift, for as **God, the Father,** withheld Himself not from you, **God, the Father,** withheld not His creation, **the Sonship, from you**. 3 Nothing that ever was created but is yours. 4 Your relationships are with the universe. 5 And this universe, being of God, is far beyond the petty sum of all the separate bodies you perceive. 6 For all **the Sonship's** parts are joined in God through Christ, where **all the Sonship's parts** become like to **God,** their Father. 7 Christ knows of no separation from His Father, Who is **Christ's** one relationship, in which **Christ** gives as His Father gives to **the Christ**.

Note # 79: There is only One relationship that is real. This is the shared relationship of God and the Sonship, which is the Christ and the Christ's own creations. This is why ACIM ask us to be vigilant for God. Our relationship with God is the only thing that matters. If we know what we are, we will know the peace of God. We are not an individual, we are a Oneness. This Oneness is our sharing of the Mind of God. There is nothing else.

T-15.VIII.5. The Holy Spirit is God's attempt to free you of what **God, the Father,** does not understand. 2 And because of the Source of the attempt **is from God, the attempt to free you** will succeed. 3 The Holy Spirit asks you to respond as God does, for **the Holy Spirit** would teach you what you do not understand. 4 God would respond to every need, whatever form **the need** takes. 5 And so **the Holy Spirit** keeps this channel open to receive **God's** communication to you, and **your communication** to God. 6 God does not understand your problem in communication, for **God, the Father,** does not share **your problem of communication** with you. 7 It is only you who believe that **your problem of communication** is understandable. 8 The Holy Spirit knows that **your problem of communication** is not understandable, and yet **the Holy Spirit** understands **your problem of communication** because you made **your problem of communication between yourself to God**.

Note # 80: God, the Father, only knows the changeless reality of truth. Because of this, the Father does not share in any illusions that the split-minded have made in their egoic attempts to replace reality with the false. God is innocence and, therefore, does not know what does not exist. Truth cannot be altered in any way. The split-minded operate under the false illusions of the egoic thought system. Truth is true and illusion cannot change the truth. God would free you of your belief that what does not exist is real by sharing His Innocence with you. Your imagined illusions of separation do not exist. Only the Holy Spirit is aware of both the truth of what you are and the illusions of what you believe yourself to be. Your beliefs are based on your "private thoughts" of separation. Therefore, the Holy Spirit is the only one Who can bridge the gap between your illusions of provisional reality and the real world of Heaven, which is the home for the truth

T-15.VIII.6. In the Holy Spirit alone lies the awareness of what God, **the Father,** cannot know, and what you do not understand. 2 It is **the Holy Spirit's** holy function to accept them both, **(what God cannot know, and what you do not understand)**, and by removing every element of disagreement, to join **what God cannot know, and what you do not understand** into one. 3 **The Holy Spirit** will do this **by removing every element of disagreement between the two,** because it is **the Holy Spirit's** function **to bridge this gap in communication**. 4 Leave, then, what seems to you to be impossible, to **the Holy Spirit,** Who knows **this bridging of this communication gap** must be possible because it is the Will of God. 5 And let **the Holy Spirit,** Whose teaching is only of God, teach you the only meaning of relationships, **which is love**. 6 For God created the only relationship that has meaning, and that is **God's** relationship with you.

Note # 81: God, being love, is love. Everything that is real must be love. Our ultimate purpose is to be only love. We are the extension of God and, therefore, we must create like our Father. The Holy Spirit teaches that the world of the ego, which is the world based on the mad idea that we could be separate from the Mind and Will of God, is an illusion. The Holy Spirit also teaches that everything is, and always will be, the changeless, eternal love of God. The Holy Spirit utilizes the tool of forgiveness to teach our split-mind the reality of the Oneness of the loving Mind of God. To be love, we must teach only love. Although ACIM does not teach us how to love, ACIM does teach us how to remove all the obstacles that we have placed to block love's presence.

We bridge this gap in communication between the Son and the Father when the Sonship accepts and relearns about his shared innocence with his Creator. What God cannot know and what you do not understand is that, "Nothing real can be threatened. Nothing unreal exists." This is the lesson the Holy Spirit would teach the split-minded who believe that illusions are real and can threaten the truth. God cannot know the false since the false cannot be understood. The false merely does not exist.

IX. The Holy Instant and the Attraction of God

T-15.IX.1. As the ego would limit your perception of your brothers to the body, so would the Holy Spirit release your vision and let you see the Great Rays shining from **your brother**, so unlimited **are the Great Rays shining from your brother** that they reach to God. 2 It is this shift to **Christ** vision **from**

egoic sight that is accomplished in the holy instant. 3 Yet it is needful for you to learn just what this shift entails, so you will become willing to make **this shift to the vision of Christ** permanent. 4 Given this willingness **the vision of Christ** will not leave you, for **the vision** <*is*> permanent. 5 Once you have accepted **the vision of Christ** as the only perception you want, **the vision of Christ** is translated into knowledge by the part that God Himself plays in the Atonement, for the **return to knowledge** is the only step in **the Atonement**, God, the Father, understands. 6 Therefore, in this **return to knowledge of the Sonship by the Father,** there will be no delay when you are ready for **the return to knowledge by your willingness to accept and utilize only Christ's vision.** 7 God is ready now, but you are not **ready for the return to knowledge**.

Note # 82: The Father has not stopped communicating with the Christ. The split minded, however, are under the illusion that communication with God has been broken. Since the split-minded believe that they have lost communication with God, their One Source, the split-minded have also lost knowledge. The split-minded live in their own private world of perception. The Holy Spirit uses the tool of forgiveness to reestablish correct perception within the split-minded. For this to happen, we must request the Holy Spirit's guidance. When we have suspended all judgment and reclaim both our brother's and our own guiltlessness, God, the Father, will take the final step and return us to knowledge, which is truth or Heaven. Both the suspension of judgment and the return to the belief in the guiltlessness of our brother and ourselves is accomplished in the holy instant. In the holy instant, we accept and receive our joint innocence for all.

T-15.IX.2. Our task is but to continue, as fast as possible, the necessary process of looking straight at all the interference and seeing **all the interference** exactly as it is, **which is an obstacle to our return to knowledge**. 2 For it is impossible to recognize as wholly without gratification what you think you want. 3 The body is the symbol of the ego, as the ego is the symbol of the separation. 4 And both **the body and the ego** are nothing more than attempts to limit communication, and thereby to make **communication** impossible. 5 For communication must be unlimited in order to have meaning, and deprived of meaning, **communication** will not satisfy you completely. 6 Yet **communication** remains the only means by which you can establish real relationships, which have no limits, having been established by God.

Note # 83: Communication's purpose is to experience the oneness of the whole; to share the truth. We cannot communicate when we are attempting to exclude. The belief that we have private thoughts is a block to communication. Private thoughts are based on the idea of separation; that we can communicate with one part yet withhold that communication from the whole. Communication requires both the giving and the reception of communication. We believe that we are a body-form and do not see ourselves to be unlimited mind or spirit. Believing ourselves as separate, autonomous, individualized parts, we fail to see the oneness of our being. Since we do not know truth, we cannot communicate the truth. By believing an illusion about ourselves, it prevents us from communicating with anyone. For in a dream, only the dreamer believes in the dream. Any information that he attempts to share means nothing since the "potential recipient" would have no knowledge about the dreamer's dream. The recipient would reject the communication as the ravings of a mad man. Illusion cannot communicate truth. Coming from the false belief in separation and limitation, "egoic communication" is designed to confuse the false for the true. The idea of egoic communication, like all the beliefs of the ego, can only be an illusion.

T-15.IX.3. In the holy instant, where the Great Rays replace the body in awareness, the recognition of relationships without limits is given you. 2 But in order to see **the Great Rays that led to recognition of relationships without limits**, it is necessary to give up every use the ego has for the body, and to accept the fact that the ego has no purpose you would share with **the ego**. 3 For the ego would limit everyone to a body for **the ego's** own purposes, and while you think **the ego** has a purpose, you will choose to utilize **the body, which is** the means by which **the ego** tries to turn **the ego's** purpose into accomplishment. 4 **The egoic purpose of making the illusion of separation real** will never be accomplished. 5 Yet you have surely recognized that the ego, whose goals are altogether unattainable, will strive for **the attainment of its own egoic goals** with all **the ego's** might, and will **strive to** do so with the strength that you have given **the ego**.

Note # 84: The ego has no power of its own. The ego is that part of your mind which believes in the separation. The only power the ego has is limited to the power you as the decision-maker have chosen to give to it. It is our mind's belief in the idea of the separation that gives the ego all its power. Correct the belief in the separation and the ego, like any other illusion, will disappear. All that will be left is truth. Truth sets us free to be the Oneness that we share. Pure and perfect communication will be restored. In the hands of the Holy Spirit, the body becomes a neutral communication device, not an egoic tool for attack.

T-15.IX.4. It is impossible to divide your strength between Heaven and hell, God and the ego, and release your power to creation, which is the only purpose for which **your power to create** was given you. 2 Love would *<always>* give increase. 3 Limits are demanded by the ego, and represent **the ego's** demands to make little and ineffectual. 4 Limit your sight of a brother to his body, which you will do as long as you would not release him from **his bodily form**, and you have denied his gift **of love** to you. 5 His body cannot give **love**. 6 And seek **love** not through **your body**. 7 Yet your minds are already continuous, and their **mind's** union need only be accepted and the loneliness in Heaven is gone.

Note # 85: We are mind, not a body. Spirit is everything and any aspect of spirit contains the oneness of everything. Spirit cannot be separate and always remains whole and communicates perfectly. The body appears to separate us from the shared mind of God. The body is an illusion and is not real. While time exists, the body is a neutral communication device that can be utilized as a tool to teach union or separation. What we choose to teach will depend on which thought system our decision-maker will choose to follow. The body cannot serve two masters. Our decision maker must choose between the ego and the Holy Spirit

T-15.IX.5. If you would but let the Holy Spirit tell you of the Love of God for you, and the need your creations have to be with you forever, you would experience the attraction of the eternal. 2 No one can hear **the Holy Spirit** speak of this **Love of God for you** and long remain willing to linger here **in the illusionary world of perception**. 3 For it is your will to be in Heaven, where you are complete and quiet, in such sure and loving relationships that any limit is impossible. 4 Would you not exchange your little relationships for this **sure and loving relationship in Heaven**? 5 For the body *<is>* little and limited, and only those whom you would see without the limits the ego would impose on them can offer you the gift of freedom.

Note # 86: By seeing your brother as a limited ego-body, you limit yourself to the same thing. For what you give you receive and perceiving your brother as limited you get to keep that same limitation. Your perception of your brother is your salvation or condemnation, for ideas do not leave their source. Grant your brother his freedom from your perceived chains of limitation and in his escape from limitation, you also receive your own. Any belief that we are a body is the belief in egoic limitation.

T-15.IX.6. You have no conception of the limits you have placed on your perception, and no idea of all the loveliness that you could see. 2 But this you must remember; the attraction of guilt opposes the attraction of God. 3 **God's** attraction for you remains unlimited, but because your power, being **God's**

power, is as great as **God's power**, you can turn away from love. 4 What you invest in guilt you withdraw from God. 5 And your sight grows weak and dim and limited, for you have attempted to separate the Father from the Son, and limit **the Father and Son's** communication. 6 Seek not Atonement in further separation. 7 And limit not your vision of God's Son to what interferes with **the Son of God's** release, and what the Holy Spirit must undo to set **the Son of God** free. 8 For **the Son of God's** belief in limits <*has*> imprisoned **God's Son**.

Note # 87: As long as we believe that we exist within the dream of separation, there can be no escape from the dream. Illusion cannot be removed by placing another illusion over the first one for the dreamer will still be dreaming. Only by awakening the dreamer can the illusion be removed from the mind of the dreamer. The Holy Spirit, if asked, will gently awaken God's sleeping Sons and guide us back to the truth about what we are.

T-15.IX.7. When the body ceases to attract you, and when you place no value on **the body** as a means of getting anything, then there will be no interference in communication and your thoughts will be as free as God's **thoughts**. 2 As you let the Holy Spirit teach you how to use the body only for purposes of communication, and renounce **the body's** use for separation and attack which the ego sees in **the body**, you will learn you have no need of a body at all. 3 In the holy instant there are no bodies, and **in the holy instant** you experience only the attraction of God. 4 Accepting **only the experience and communication of the attraction of God** as undivided, you join **God** wholly, in an instant, for you would place no limits on your union with **God**. 5 The reality of this relationship **of your union with God** becomes the only truth that you could ever want. 6 All truth <*is*> here **in your union with God**.

Note # 88: When you cease to be attached to the body, all thoughts of the mind's identification with being the body will also disappear. The mad idea that you could be happy by being limited or special is gone. It was the desire to experience ourselves as special that resulted in the separation. Our belief that we could be happy by being something other than what we are resulted in our quest for specialness. Being an extension of God, we can only be happy within the wholeness that is the Mind of God. With our total rejection of the egoic illusion that we are the body-form, the body can become a communication device for forgiveness and love. The Oneness that is pure and perfect communication is restored. For being all, what else is there to be?

X. The Time of Rebirth

T-15.X.1. It is in your power, in time, to delay the perfect union of the Father and the Son. 2 For in this world **of perception**, the attraction of guilt does stand between **the perfect union of the Father and the Son**. 3 Neither time nor season means anything in eternity. 4 But here **in this world of time and perception,** it is the Holy Spirit's function to use both **the perception of time and seasons**, though not as the ego uses **time and seasons**. 5 This is the season when you would celebrate my birth into the world. 6 Yet you know not how to **celebrate my birth into the world**. 7 Let the Holy Spirit teach you, and let me celebrate <*your*> birth through **the Holy Spirit**. 8 The only gift I can accept of you is the gift I gave to you, **which was release from this world of time**. 9 Release me as I choose your own release. 10 The time of Christ we celebrate together, for **the time of Christ** has no meaning if we are apart.

Note # 89: The world of perception is the world of time and space. Prior to the loss of knowledge, there was only the oneness with no illusion of separation. With the birth of separateness, the concept of change arose. We perceived ourselves guilty of the sin of usurping God's authority. Within our split-mind, something had changed. We had lost the certainty that we were a Oneness of everything. We discarded knowledge and claimed that we did not know ourselves and so the world of illusion was born. Our state of consciousness moved from the "I AM" to the "WHAT AM I?" state.

The "WHAT AM I?" state is full of illusion and thus, both unstable and unreal.

Change was possible in the "WHAT AM I?" state of consciousness. Certainty that arose from knowledge has also been lost. Time, the measure of change, now becomes very relevant. The "I AM" state more closely resembles Heaven. In the real world of Heaven there is only the changeless eternal. It is the <now> and we, the Christ, remain in perfect union with Our Father. In Heaven, time serves no function and is meaningless. Only in the "WHAT AM I?" state can the dream of the separation be mistaken for reality. In the "WHAT AM I?" state, our own mind's beliefs and desires control what we perceive as reality. We become the arbitrators of truth within the dream of our insane mind. What we claim to be "the facts" are only the results of our own mind's previously determined judgments and goals. What we "see" coming at us is what we wanted to experience in our field of awareness. This is projection. We predetermine what we wish to believe and our senses seek out positive confirmation to "prove" we were "right." As long as we choose to judge a brother as sinful, we will perceive ourselves guilty and separate from God. Our release requires "seeing" with the vision of Christ. In Christ vision, we see the guiltlessness of all our brothers; by giving forgiveness, we receive forgiveness.

T-15.X.2. The holy instant is truly the time of Christ. 2 For in this liberating **holy** instant no guilt is laid upon the Son of God, and his unlimited power is thus restored to the Son of God. 3 What other gift can you offer me, when only **the restoration of God's guiltless Son to the unlimited power of his Father was the gift** I choose to offer you? 4 And to see me **as the Christ, God's guiltless Son** is to see me in everyone, and offer everyone the gift **of guiltlessness** you offer me. 5 I am as incapable of receiving sacrifice as God is **incapable of receiving sacrifice**, and every sacrifice you ask of yourself you ask of me. 6 Learn now that sacrifice of any kind is nothing but a limitation imposed on giving. 7 And by this limitation **on giving** you have limited acceptance of the gift I offer you.

Note # 90: The holy instant is the release of all judgments and, therefore, is a release from the past. All judgment comes from past misperception based on the ego's thought system. Because the Law of God states that to give is to receive, Jesus, who saw only the perfection of God in his brother, received this same perfection of God in himself. Jesus became the Christ incarnate. Offer your brother his guiltlessness and you recover your own. The Christ is always in the now, for Christ is eternal and is not limited by time.

T-15.X.3. We who are one cannot give separately. 2 When you are willing to accept our relationship **that we are one and cannot give separately** as real, guilt will hold no attraction for you. 3 For in our union you will accept all of our brothers. 4 The gift of union is the only gift that I was born to give. 5 Give **the gift of union** to me, that you may have **the gift of union**. 6 The time of Christ is the time appointed for the gift of freedom, offered to everyone. 7 And by your acceptance of **the gift of union and freedom**, you offer **the gift of union and freedom** to everyone.

Note # 91: We are all interconnected in the Mind of God. It is through the gift of union from which the Oneness arose that our freedom is obtained and guaranteed. God birthed the gift of union when She chose to extend Herself in the creative process. The total freedom that results from being the shared Oneness of everything is real and extends to the entire Sonship. Private thoughts, which arise from fear and limitation, are not real because they are made to exclude and not share. Although we are one in reality, we believe that the separation is real. Because of this, we also believe our private thoughts are real even though they cannot be shared and are not part of the Mind of God. It is this belief that gives our private thoughts apparent reality in our world of perception. They become the "reality" that governs our illusionary world of egoic consciousness.

T-15.X.4. It is in your power to make this season holy, for it is in your power to make the time of Christ be now. 2 It is possible to do **this making of the time of Christ be now** all at once because there is but one shift in perception that is necessary **to make the time of Christ be now** for you made but one mistake. 3 It seems like many **mistakes**, but it is all the same **mistake**. 4 For though the ego takes many forms, the **mistake** is always the same idea. 5 **The error is that you fail to realize that** what is not love is always fear, and nothing else but fear.

Note # 92: The Holy Spirit teaches us that there are only two ways to correctly perceive any experience in the field of our awareness. These two are love and the cry for love. The proper response to a cry for love is always to respond with love. The thought system of the ego claims that the world was born of sin, guilt and fear. This unholy trinity rules the egoic world. The ego teaches that the proper response to guilt and fear is to attack. Defense is just another form of attack. Any defense is the admittance that you are vulnerable to attack, are limited and can be hurt. In the time of Christ, we will see the equality of the Sonship in the guiltlessness of God's Son. By giving up all judgments, we become guiltless. This can be done in one holy instant. It is for our decision-maker to decide when we will finally release ourselves from this self-imposed guilt and accept our innocence. The Christ lives in the eternal <now>. God, the Holy Spirit and the Christ all know that we are perfect, whole and complete. In truth, we always are a Oneness but while time lasts, fear blocks this realization from our split-mind.

T-15.X.5. It is not necessary to follow fear through all the circuitous routes by which **fear** burrows underground and hides in darkness, to emerge in forms **that appear** quite different from what **fear** is. 2 Yet it <is> necessary to examine each one **of the forms of fear** as long as you would retain the principle that governs all of **the forms of fear**. 3 When you are willing to regard **all of the forms of fear**, not as separate, but as different manifestations of the same idea, and one **fearful idea** you do not want, **all of the forms of fear** go together **and become one**. 4 The idea is simply this: You believe it is possible to be host to the ego or hostage to God. 5 This is the choice you think you have, and the decision you believe that you must make. **You believe you must be either host to the ego or hostage to God**. 6 You see no other alternatives **than you must be either host to the ego or hostage to God**, for you cannot accept the fact that sacrifice gets nothing. 7 Sacrifice is so essential to your thought system that salvation apart from sacrifice means nothing to you. 8 Your confusion of sacrifice and love is so profound that you cannot conceive of love without sacrifice. 9 And it is this **confusion of sacrifice with love that** you must look upon; sacrifice is attack, not love. 10 If you would accept but this one idea, **that sacrifice is attack and not love,** your fear of love would vanish. 11 Guilt cannot last when the idea of sacrifice has been removed. 12 For if there is sacrifice, someone must pay and someone must get. 13 And the only question that remains is how much is the price **of sacrifice**, and for getting what.

Note # 93: Under the ego's thought system, God is something to be feared. Because the ego teaches that we have usurped or stolen the authority of God, we have sinned against our Father. The god of the ego now requires that we must be punished for our sin. We must sacrifice something to appease this revengeful god of egoic thought. This egoic god is always holding us hostage and at any time and without any other "sin" on our part may decide to behead us. The god of the ego is not somebody you would like to meet in a dark alley! This god of revenge is arbitrary and fickle. There is no telling what he might do if he gets his hands on us. Appearing concerned for our safety, the ego tells us that we must seek shelter from the god of revenge by allowing the ego to protect us. We freely choose to invite the ego to rule and control our mind. We side with the ego and turn our decision-making abilities over to its thought system. The ego demands that we, its host, make sacrifices for the gifts the ego offers us. This world was made by the ego to hide supposed sinners from the ego's god of revenge and thus, prove that the separation was real.

Because we are convinced that we are guilty sinners and that God demands our damnation, we freely chose to come under the influence and protection of the egoic thought system. This is a fear-based thought system. Egoic thinking requires that someone must pay the price for our sin but it doesn't care who. The ego also tells us that we can transfer our sin, guilt and even our punishment to someone other than ourselves. Projection is the egoic tool that allows us to escape the punishment this god requires for our sins. Something must be sacrificed, but it does not have to cost us everything. The ego tells us that even the Son of God can be killed on behalf of our sins. This egoic god does not care who or what is sacrificed, but at least temporarily, it must be appeased. The ego, therefore, associates sacrifice with its warped sense of love and links the two together. To the ego, which is incapable of understanding what love is, sacrifice is the price that love demands. To the guilt-throwing ego, sacrifice must be required because we have sinned. The ego's unholy trinity of sin, guilt and fear requires that sacrifice be made in the name of love.

T-15.X.6. As host to the ego, you believe that you can give all your guilt away whenever you want, and thereby purchase peace. 2 And the payment **for the purchase of peace** does not seem to be **your payment**. 3 While it is obvious that the ego does demand payment **the ego** never seems to be demanding **payment** of you. 4 You are unwilling to recognize that the ego, which you invited, is treacherous only to those who think they are **the ego's** host. 5 The ego will never let you perceive this **treachery that the ego bears to its host**, since this recognition would make **the ego** homeless. 6 For when the recognition dawns clearly **that the ego actually requires direct payment from its host,** you will not be deceived by any form the ego takes to protect itself from your sight. 7 Each form **the ego takes** will be recognized as but a cover for the one idea that hides behind them all; that love demands sacrifice, and **love** is therefore inseparable from attack and fear. 8 And that guilt is the price of love, which must be paid by fear.

Note # 94: In projection we attempt to get rid of something we don't want. We project our guilt outside ourselves upon another. It thus, appears that we have removed the guilt from our mind by assigning our guilt to an outside "victim.' Unfortunately, projection gains us nothing since thoughts never leave their source. Our mind, being the source of the thought, gets to keep its self-imposed guilt. Guilt is the price for our belief in sin. Sin is defined as a belief in the lack of love and we are sure that we have lost God's love. Under the laws of chaos, which govern the egoic world, there is a substitute for God's love. This substitute for God's love takes many forms, but always rests on the underlying belief that we are unholy, guilty, incomplete and full of fear. The ego's substitute for God's love is the egoic special relationship.

T-15.X.7. How fearful, then, has God become to you, and how great a sacrifice do you believe **God's** Love demands! 2 For total love would demand total sacrifice. 3 And so the ego seems to demand less of you than God, and of the two, **the ego** is judged as the lesser of two evils. One, **the ego, is** to be feared a little, perhaps, but the other, **God requires that you** be destroyed. 4 For you see love as destructive, and your only question is who is to be destroyed, you or another? 5 You seek to answer this question in your special relationships, in which you seem to be both destroyer and destroyed in part, but able to be neither completely. 5 And this, **the ego's special relationships,** you think saves you from God, Whose total Love would completely destroy you.

Note # 95: Because we follow the ego's thought system, we do not understand that God's Love requires nothing from us. God's love gives everything and demands nothing. No sacrifice is required and God's love is freely given. God's love cannot be earned. Because we lack knowledge of what love is, we allow the ego to redefine what love is. To the ego, love must require sacrifice and thus, love and sacrifice are always linked together. The more we sacrifice, the stronger our love.

The ego's special relationship demonstrates its warped concept of love. This unholy relationship always comes with strings attached. The string's ability to bind is derived from the sacrifices that we perceive we have made on behalf of another. We can make the other party feel guilty if they don't fulfill their part of the bartering agreement that the ego calls "love." The special relationship does not require that you sacrifice everything since it only gives to get. It does, however, require some pain, suffering and sacrifice on your part. Yet, if you made a "good trade," you will be able to extract more sacrifice from the other side than you gave. In a special relationship, we always begin by believing that we are making a "good trade." This is because what we "give up" is not valued as much as what we hope to gain from the other party. When the other party does not fulfill our predetermined needs, we feel justified in our anger. We blame the other party as the cause of our unhappiness. We become a combination of innocent victims, sinners, guilt throwers and guilt catchers. Because sin is unforgivable, the egoic version of love concludes that our total damnation would be the price that God would demand for the forgiveness of our sin of usurping His authority.

T-15.X.8. You think that everyone outside yourself demands your sacrifice, but you do not see that only you demand sacrifice, and only **sacrifice** of yourself. 2 Yet the demand of sacrifice is so savage and so fearful that you cannot accept **the demand of sacrifice** where it is, **which is in you**. 3 The real price of not accepting this **fact that only you are demanding sacrifice** has been so great that you have given God away rather than look at **your own demand for self-imposed sacrifice**. 4 For if God would demand total sacrifice of you, it seems safer to project **God** outward and away from you, and not be host to **God**. 5 To **God** you ascribed the ego's treachery, inviting **the ego** to take **God's** place **so that the ego can** protect you from **God**. 6 And you do not recognize that it is what you invited in, **which is the ego,** that would destroy you, and **that the ego** does demand total sacrifice of you. 7 No partial sacrifice will appease this savage guest, **the ego,** for **the ego** is an invader who but seems to offer kindness, but always to make the sacrifice complete.

<u>Note # 96:</u> Egoic thought attempts to make the false true and the truth, false. Because of this, the ego ascribes the attributes of the ego to God. Being trapped in egoic thinking, we cannot escape the ego's logic within the illusionary dream that bares false witness against the truth. The belief system of the ego follows logically once you accept the erroneous idea that you are a limited ego-body. If you identify yourself as the body, everything the ego teaches appears to be correct. This is why ACIM states that you must question the major premise of the ego's thought system. The Holy Spirit states you are not a body, but rather, you are unlimited spirit. Being unlimited extensions of the Mind of God, we have nothing to fear. We are actually host to God. Being one with God, God requires no sacrifice. What can a Oneness sacrifice and to whom? The only sacrifice would be self-sacrifice but to whom? We can pretend that we are required to make sacrifices, but to do so we must also pretend that we are not a Oneness. By pretending we are not a Oneness, we make the separation appear real. Our fantasies, however, will never change the truth. For truth is the changeless and just is.

T-15.X.9. You will not succeed in being partial hostage to the ego, for **the ego** keeps no bargains and would leave you nothing. 2 Nor can you be partial host to **the ego**. 3 You must choose between total freedom and total bondage **to the ego**, for there are no alternatives but these. 4 You have tried many compromises in the attempt to avoid recognizing the one decision you must make. 5 And yet it is the recognition of the **one** decision, <*just as it is,*> that makes the decision so easy. 6 Salvation is simple, being of God, and therefore very easy to understand. 7 Do not try to project **salvation** from you and see **salvation** outside yourself. 8 In you are both the question and the answer. **In you are both** the demand for sacrifice and the peace of God.

Note # 97: The only limits or sacrifices that we make are self-imposed. God has given us everything and demands nothing. Salvation only requires our complete acceptance of the truth of what we are. There can be no compromise with truth. The only decision we need to realize is that the truth is true and the false cannot change the truth. This is what the Holy Spirit teaches us. We cannot serve two masters. Reject the ego's thought system and accept the Holy Spirit's and the return to knowledge will be upon us. We will remember God for we will be remembering the truth.

XI. Christmas as the End of Sacrifice

T-15.XI.1. Fear not to recognize the whole idea of sacrifice as solely of your making, **for sacrifice is not of God's making**. 2 And seek not safety by attempting to protect yourself from where **fear** is not. 3 Your brothers and your Father have become very fearful to you. 4 And you would bargain with **your brothers and your Father** for a few special relationships, in which you think you see some scraps of safety. 5 Do not try longer to keep apart your **egoic** thoughts **of separation and limitation** and the Thought **from the Holy Spirit** that has been given you. 6 When **the thoughts of the two thought systems** are brought together and perceived where they are, the choice between **the two thought systems** is nothing more than a gentle awakening, and as simple as opening your eyes to daylight when you have no more need of sleep.

Note # 98: ACIM states that if we can compare each thought clearly, the choice for the Holy Spirit's thought system will become obvious. The ego's thought system, which is based on limitation, always requires sacrifice. The Holy Spirit's is based on abundance and, therefore, demands nothing. The ego's thought system attempts to make what is the false, true. The Holy Spirit brings the false before the light of truth and what is false simply disappears leaving only truth to be recognized.

T-15.XI.2. The sign of Christmas is a star, a light in darkness. 2 See **the light** not outside yourself, but shining in the Heaven within **your mind**, and accept **the light within you** as the sign the time of Christ has come. 3 **Christ** comes demanding nothing. 4 No sacrifice of any kind, of anyone, is asked by **Christ**. 5 In **Christ's** Presence the whole idea of sacrifice loses all meaning. 6 For **Christ** is Host to God. 7 And you need but invite **Christ** in Who is there already, by recognizing that **God's** Host, **Christ**, is One, and no thought alien to **God's** Oneness can abide with **Christ** there. 8 Love must be total to give **Christ and God** welcome, for the Presence of Holiness creates the holiness that surrounds it. 9 No fear can touch the Host, **Christ,** Who cradles God in the time of Christ, for the Host, **Christ,** is as holy as the perfect Innocence which **God** protects, and **God,** Whose power protects **Christ**.

Note # 99: The Christ, which is what we truly are, is the host to God. Being of one Mind, God and the Christ are intertwined and inseparable. God is the Cause and the Christ is God's Effect. The power of God protects the holiness and innocence of the Christ, because both are shared equally with the Christ. For the split-minded to recognize the Christ within themselves, it is necessary that there must be the removal of guilt and the acceptance of love. This requires no sacrifice. The only requirement is the acceptance of truth and the recognition that what is false can never be true.
Christmas is the time for the birth of Jesus, who represents Christ consciousness. Christmas time is the

symbol for the reawakening of the Christ within our split-mind.

T-15.XI.3. This Christmas give the Holy Spirit everything that would hurt you. 2 Let yourself be healed completely that you may join with **the Holy Spirit** in healing, and let us celebrate our release together by releasing everyone with us. 3 Leave nothing behind, for release is total, and when you have accepted **release** with me you will give **release** with me. 4 **When you have accepted release,** all pain and sacrifice and littleness will disappear in our relationship, which is as innocent as our relationship with our Father, and as powerful **as our relationship with our Father**. 5 Pain will be brought to us and disappear in our presence, and without pain there can be no sacrifice. 6 And without sacrifice there love <*must*> be.

<u>Note # 100:</u> By accepting the Atonement for ourselves we are released from all illusion. With this release, we accept the truth of our divine birthright and reject the illusion of pain and sacrifice. The pain and sacrifice, which we had been projecting from our mind, will disappear leaving only the truth. Only the love that we really are will remain.

T-15.XI.4. You who believe that sacrifice is love must learn that sacrifice is separation from love. 2 For sacrifice brings guilt as surely as love brings peace. 3 Guilt is the condition of sacrifice, as peace is the condition for the awareness of your relationship with God. 4 Through guilt you exclude your Father and your brothers from yourself. 5 Through peace you invite **your Father and your brothers** back, realizing that they are where your invitation bids **your Father and your brothers to** be. 6 What you exclude from yourself seems fearful, for you endow **what you would attempt to exclude from yourself** with fear and try to cast it out, though **what you attempt to exclude from yourself remains** part of you. 7 Who can perceive part of himself as loathsome, and live within himself in peace? 8 And who can try to resolve the "conflict" of Heaven and hell in him by casting Heaven out and giving **Heaven** the attributes of hell, without experiencing himself as incomplete and lonely?

<u>Note # 101:</u> Sacrifice brings guilt because it is attack. Attack cannot be love. Love is all-inclusive. Sin, guilt, fear all demand sacrifice. They are all designed to exclude and to make the false seem real. For the ego, the purpose of time is to make the false, true. The denial of the truth is the making of hell. Hell is the effect of the denial of your divine birthright. Heaven is the effect of the acceptance of truth. To deny the truth is to deny that the Mind of God is all-inclusive. There is nothing outside the Mind of God for God is Truth. To exclude a brother from the union of the Oneness is to cast yourself into the separation that makes hell. Everything is the perfect extension of God. In the Mind of God, there is no difference between any part and the whole. In the Mind of God, the part is the whole, and the whole is the part. There is only the One. This is the truth of Heaven. There can be no conflict in Heaven since only truth exists.

T-15.XI.5. As long as you perceive the body as your reality, so long will you perceive yourself as lonely and deprived. 2 And so long **as you perceive yourself as lonely and deprived** will you also perceive yourself as a victim of sacrifice, justified in sacrificing others. 3 For who could thrust Heaven and its Creator aside without a sense of sacrifice and loss? 4 And who could suffer sacrifice and loss without attempting to restore himself **to his previous state of wholeness prior to the loss?** 5 Yet how could you accomplish **the return to your previous state of wholeness** yourself, when the basis of your attempts **for return to wholeness** is the belief in the reality of the deprivation, **which is your belief that you are the body?** 6 Deprivation breeds attack, being the belief that attack is justified. 7 And as long as you would retain the deprivation, attack becomes salvation and sacrifice becomes love.

<u>Note # 102:</u> Once you identify yourself as a body, you have become trapped in the logic of the egoic

thought system. We are caught in an endless cycle of victim consciousness. We can never escape this cycle of sin, guilt and fear that leads to sacrifice. Sacrifice, in turn, only leads to more sin, guilt and fear that demand greater sacrifice. Only by asking for the guidance of the Holy Spirit can we escape this belief that we are a sinful body.

T-15.XI.6. So is it that, in all your seeking for love, you seek for sacrifice and find **sacrifice**. 2 Yet you find not love. 3 It is impossible to deny what love is and still recognize **love**. 4 The meaning of love lies in what you have cast outside yourself, and **what you have cast outside yourself** has no meaning apart from you. 5 It is what you prefer to keep**, the guilt that requires sacrifice** that has no meaning, while all **the love** that you would keep away holds all the meaning of the universe, and holds the universe together in **love's** meaning. 6 Unless the universe were joined in you **the universe** would be apart from God, and to be without **God** <*is*> to be without meaning.

Note # 103: God is love and God is truth. Truth, therefore, must be love and love, truth. They are all inseparable. There is nothing outside of God. To dream that we can cast ourselves outside of God is the denial of truth. The false has no reality and, therefore, is meaningless. We can pretend and believe that we are outside the Mind of God, but all our denial cannot make what is false, true. We will always remain as God created us, a changeless, perfect whole.

T-15.XI.7. In the holy instant the condition of love is met, for minds are joined without the body's interference, and where there is communication there is peace. 2 The Prince of Peace, **Jesus,** was born to re-establish the condition of love by teaching that communication remains unbroken even if the body is destroyed, provided that you see not the body as the necessary means of communication. 3 And if you understand this lesson **that the body is not necessary for communication**, you will realize that to sacrifice the body is to sacrifice nothing, and communication, which must be of the mind, cannot be sacrificed. 4 Where, then, <*is*> sacrifice **if the body is nothing**? 5 The lesson I was born to teach, and still would teach to all my brothers, is that sacrifice is nowhere and love is everywhere. 6 For communication embraces everything, and in the peace **communication is** re-establishes **and** love comes of itself.

Note # 104: Jesus has stated previously that his resurrection was the most important part of his life. The resurrection proved that we are not a body and that the abandonment of the body has no effect on our unlimited spirit. A body is not required for communication, for the body is not life. When we stop identifying ourselves as a limited ego-body, we realize that we are the Big "S" Self of Christ. Communication, the remembrance of God, is restored.

T-15.XI.8. Let no despair darken the joy of Christmas, for the time of Christ is meaningless apart from joy. 2 Let us join in celebrating peace by demanding no sacrifice of anyone, for so you offer me the love I offer you. 3 What can be more joyous than to perceive we are deprived of nothing? 4 Such is the message of the time of Christ, which I give you that you may give **the same message that we are deprived of nothing** and return **the same message** to the Father, Who gave **the same message that we are deprived of nothing** to me. 5 For in the time of Christ communication is restored, and **God** joins us in the celebration of His Son's creation.

Note # 105: Christ is God's Effect. Christ is as God created us. Being everything, God gave everything to His Creation. When the Sonship creates, the Christ, which is everything, also extends everything to the Sonship's own creations. We are co-creators with the Father. Being a Oneness of everything, perfect communication is restored within all parts of the Mind of God. Cause and Effect communicate as One Self.

T-15.XI.9. God offers thanks to the holy host, **Christ,** who would receive **God,** and lets **God** enter and abide where **God** would be. 2 And by your welcome does **God** welcome you into Himself, for what is contained in you who welcome **God** is returned to **Christ**. 3 And we but celebrate **God's** Wholeness as we welcome **Christ** into ourselves. 4 Those who receive the Father are one with **Christ,** being host to **God, the Father** Who created them. 5 And by allowing **Christ** to enter, the remembrance of the Father enters with **Christ**, and with **God** they remember the only relationship they ever had, and ever want to have.

Note # 106: This shows the interrelationship of God, the Father, the Son, the Sonship, the Christ and the Holy Ghost. The Christ is the Host to God. The Father created the Sonship, Which is God's Son. The Holy Ghost is the communication or bridge between the Father and the Son. This demonstrates why the Laws of God state that a part is equal to the whole, and the whole is equal to a part. Because of our dualistic thinking, ACIM discusses these concepts as separate ideas or "entities with different and distinct functions" yet they are inseparable in reality. There is only the One, which is the "everything" that comprises the Mind of God.

T-15.XI.10. This is the time in which a new year will soon be born from the time of Christ. 2 I have perfect faith in you to do all that you would accomplish. 3 Nothing will be lacking, and you will make complete and not destroy. 4 Say, then, to your brother:

5 *I give you to the Holy Spirit as part of myself.*
6 *I know that you will be released, unless I want to use you to imprison myself.*
7 *In the name of my freedom I choose your release, because I recognize that we will be released together.*

8 So will the year begin in joy and freedom. 9 There is much to do, and we have been long delayed. 10 Accept the holy instant as this year is born, and take your place, so long left unfulfilled, in the Great Awakening. 11 Make this year different by making **this year** all the same. 12 And let all your relationships be made holy for you. 13 This is our will. 14 Amen.

Note # 107: Jesus ends this chapter with a request that we accept the truth about our brother and ourselves. Unless we see our brother as guiltless, we cannot be free. By giving all our private thoughts to the Holy Spirit, all our past judgments are removed. This is the beginning of the acceptance of the Atonement for ourselves. The Atonement process will lead to the truth and the denial of the false. The return to Heaven is the return to Truth.

Becoming a Practical Modern Day Mystic

Knowledge is experiential, not just a lot of words. Words at best are symbols of ideas. They are a poor substitute for being or knowing. Thinking and being are not the same. No matter what your source, always ask for inner guidance. We challenge you to become a modern day mystic. All mystical traditions advise the student to go within and discover their own personal pathway home. Ask and go within to find your own perfect path.

Revelation is a personal matter between you and God. You should not settle for less. A Course in Miracles states that the world as we perceive it is but an illusion. Yet, since we all have decided to experience the world of perception, time and space, it behooves us to maximize our learning experiences while playing in this medium for the illusion of separation. When we give our thoughts over to the guidance of the Holy Spirit, this playschool can be an effective tool for relearning the Truth.

It is our intent to provide additional material that will allow the individual the ability to be in this world but not of this world. We want ACIM to be a practical guide to living, rather than an intellectual exercise in the esoteric. One might hear the comment that someone is "so spiritual" that they are of no use to anyone, including themselves. Again, our goal is that we become practical mystics. Each day, we may still chop wood and gather water, but we will do it with a different purpose, a different spiritual paradigm.

Your current path is contingent on where you perceive yourself to be. It may first be necessary to move from victim consciousness to become a deliberate creator. Next, we may move from a deliberate creator into allowance and honoring each person's own path. Ultimately, we will surrender our egoic thought system and join with the One Self. We always remain an extension of the Mind of God. It matters not the particular path we take for the outcome of our return to knowledge is guaranteed. We remain free to experience whatever we choose but we always remain as God created us, perfect, whole and complete.

In the world of perception, we have been given all the time we need to "get it right." We can take time to stop and smell the roses. We can always choose again. Eventually, we will discover that the return to the truth is our only real choice. In time, our purpose is forgiveness, our function is love and our destiny is the peace of God. Our Creator guarantees our successful return home.

About the Website:

acourseinmiraclesfordummies.com

The purpose of our website, **acourseinmiraclesfordummies.com,** is to provide a central reference point that can become the primary resource tool for the serious ACIM student. We are directly linked to web pages from other sites that we believe are helpful to the independent minded students. It is our belief that each student will find his or her own perfect path by going within and asking for guidance from the Holy Spirit. All material and advice needs to be questioned by the seeker. Just because the information comes from an "expert," it does not mean it is right for you. It is easy to find someone else's "word lesson" in a book or lecture. Yet, another person's "word lesson" falls short of the personal "world lessons" that we each need to experience in order to rediscover the truth about ourselves. True learning only takes place when it results in a change in your behavior.

This is why we encourage reading source material instead of relying upon some person's opinion that is many times removed from the source. If possible, always go to the source. If you cannot directly understand the source material by yourself, go to the next closest material that you can understand. As your understanding grows, you may discover that you have "graduated" up the ladder toward the source materials. Ultimately, all learning must give way to personal revelation. Always be wary of the teacher that claims to know the truth for you and demands that you surrender your inner guidance in favor of the teacher's truth. Seek the guidance of the Holy Spirit. The Holy Spirit will not fail you.

Other Books by Tom Wakechild

A Course In Miracles for Dummies

Book Description: The text of <u>A Course in Miracles</u> (ACIM) is difficult and mystifying for most readers. Both teachers and students struggle for many years with little success in unlocking the secrets to understanding this Course. They often abandon their studies and end up confused and discouraged. This ACIM for Dummies series cuts through the mystery of the Course's esoteric text and makes Jesus' message understandable to the ordinary reader. ACIM uses a unique terminology that references two different levels of being that are dominated by two opposing thought systems. This book demystifies the text by replacing the pronouns and unclear references with their meanings and clarifies the appropriate level associated with each passage. All antecedent references made to ACIM's second edition are clearly noted in bold print for easy reference to the original text. Each text paragraph is then followed by an explanatory note to assist the reader in their own interpretation of the paragraph. These notes are designed to foster discussion and clarity, not to limit ideas and prevent individual interpretation. As such, <u>ACIM for Dummies</u> can be utilized as either a primary or secondary text for independent or group study. <u>ACIM for Dummies</u> is an excellent reference tool for those who seek a deeper level of understanding of the Course teachings. The complete digital edition of <u>A Course in Miracles for Dummies</u> covers the entire ACIM text which consists of 31 chapters. Due to its length and printing restrictions, it is published and must be sold as two separate paperback volumes. Volume I covers Chapters #1-15 of ACIM's text. Volume II covers Chapters #16-31 of ACIM's text.

Note: <u>A Course In Miracles Workbook for Dummies</u> is a companion in this series and covers the 365 daily lessons found in the ACIM Workbook for Students

A Course in Miracles Workbook for Dummies

Book Description: This book is part of the ACIM For Dummies series and covers the ACIM Workbook for Students. All of the 365 daily workbook lessons from <u>A Course in Miracles</u> are covered in detail by this book. Each lesson utilizes the "Dummies format" that replaces unclear references and pronouns with their proper antecedents. Any substitutions are clearly shown in bold print for easy reference to the original workbook. Each lesson is then followed by an explanatory note to aid in your understanding and implementation of the exercise. In this modified format, these lessons become the vehicle for ending the blame, shame and guilt games that once dominated your life. The richness of these lessons now becomes apparent, understandable but more importantly, practical. You now have the tools you need to be the agent for change in your life. You no longer have any excuse not to complete these exercises and gain the insight that they provide. This book's focus is on you. Therefore, it provides the numerous tools you need to help uncover the blocks that are preventing the flow of love into your daily life. By completing the workbook lessons, your heart will be open through an experiential learning process. This knowing will allow you to automatically begin implementing the principles of ACIM into your daily life.

Note: <u>A Course In Miracles for Dummies, Vol 1 and Vol. 2</u> is a companion in this series and covers the entire ACIM Text of 31 chapters.

Decoding and Living a Course in Miracles: A 12 Session Workbook

Book Description: If your spirituality cannot bring joy, peace and happiness into your life today, what good is it? Learn how to handle life's events without sacrificing your spiritual values or losing your inner peace. Life does not have to be a struggle. This book unlocks the secrets of <u>A Course in Miracles</u> so you can live your life in internal integrity and escape the blame, shame and guilt game that dominates our world. This twelve session program provides a comprehensive study guide that familiarizes the reader with the main principles, terms and concepts that are encountered in <u>A Course In Miracles</u>. These materials instruct and teach the core ACIM principles in a systematic, logical, and easy to follow order without your deciphering the ACIM Text. Both newcomers and long time students agree that this book builds a solid foundation for both the practical implementation of the principles and any ongoing study of the ACIM Text.

These materials are appropriate for both individual and group studies of <u>A Course in Miracles</u>. No previous knowledge of ACIM is required. This book can be used as a stand-alone program. Additional support materials for this course can be found at the following link: Decoding and Living ACIM: 12 Week Online Class

Uncovering Your Default Programming: How to Regain Control Over Your Life

Book Description: What is actually running your life? Why do you keep repeating the same mistakes over and over again? What makes change seem so impossible? This book helps you uncover your personal default operating belief system that is secretly running the show. With that discovery, you will probe into those previously hidden beliefs. You will finally comprehend their devastating impact on your happiness and well-being. Until you understand the limitations of your current internal belief system, your future will be a replay of your past. Once uncovered, however, you can objectively look upon each belief and modify them as needed. Each chapter will discuss one or more of the fundamental concepts that form the bedrock of your personal operating belief system. We will question both the validity and the natural consequence of your current belief system. Alternative beliefs will be provided that can generate alternate realities. Only when you realize that your current beliefs no longer serve you, will you finally decide to change them. Thoughts, raised to the level of beliefs, become things. They are the forerunners of your tomorrows. Your beliefs are the governing factors of your life. Your beliefs determine your perception. Your perception determines your experiences. Rather than change your world, you will learn how to change how you view your world. When you change how you view your world, your world will automatically realign to your new viewpoint. Learn how to reclaim your power as the decision-maker in your own life. Stop arguing for your limitations. Instead, choose differently. Become the agent for the change that you seek in your life.

Printed in Great Britain
by Amazon